The ...
by trav...

Visit TripAdviso...
Find the best place...

MAR 2012

NOV 2

APR 2

D0717481

Top-Rated Hotels

1 Cocos Beach Bungalows ⊕⊕⊕⊕⊕
Broome
"A lovely oasis for a family vacation"

2 Windmills Break ⊕⊕⊕⊕⊕
Yallingup
"Unpretentious quality and service"

3 The Richardson Hotel & Spa ⊕⊕⊕⊕⊕
Perth
"A+ inside and out, super friendly and relaxed"

Popular Restaurants

1 Opus Restaurant ⊕⊕⊕⊕⊕
Perth
"Somewhat of a secret gem"

2 Restaurant Amuse ⊕⊕⊕⊕⊕
Perth
"Reasonably priced for a degustation menu"

3 Voyager Estate ⊕⊕⊕⊕⊕
Margaret River
"The most gorgeous place to have lunch"

Amazing Things to Do

1 Kings Park & Botanic Garden ⊕⊕⊕⊕⊕
Perth
"The best viewpoint to photograph the city from"

2 Pinnacles Desert ⊕⊕⊕⊕⊕
Cervantes
"Amazing scenery - a photographer's heaven"

3 Caversham Wildlife Park ⊕⊕⊕⊕⊕
Perth
"I loved hanging out with the kangaroos"

tripadvisor.co.uk | tripadvisor.it | tripadvisor.es | tripadvisor.de | tripadvisor.fr | tripadvisor.se | nl.tripadvisor.com
tripadvisor.dk | tripadvisor.ie | tripadvisor.no | pl.tripadvisor.com | tripadvisor.ru

Ratings were accurate as of April 2011 and may change over time. Visit tripadvisor.co.uk online for current ratings.

Footprint story

It was 1921

Ireland had just been partitioned, the British miners were striking for more pay and the federation of British industry had an idea. Exports were booming in South America – how about a handbook for businessmen trading in that far away continent? The Anglo-South American Handbook was born that year, written by W Koebel, the most prolific writer on Latin America of his day.

1924

Two editions later the book was 'privatized' and in 1924, in the hands of Royal Mail, the steamship company for South America, it became The South American Handbook, subtitled 'South America in a nutshell'. This annual publication became the 'bible' for generations of travellers to South America and remains so to this day. In the early days travel was by sea and the Handbook gave all the details needed for the long voyage from Europe. What to wear for dinner; how to arrange a cricket match with the Cable & Wireless staff on the Cape Verde Islands and a full account of the journey from Liverpool up the Amazon to Manaus: 5898 miles without changing cabin!

1939

As the continent opened up, the South American Handbook reported the new Pan Am flying boat services, and the fortnightly airship service from Rio to Europe on the Graf Zeppelin. For reasons still unclear but with extraordinary determination, the annual editions continued through the Second World War.

1970s

Many more people discovered South America and the backpacking trail started to develop. All the while the Handbook was gathering fans, including literary vagabonds such as Paul Theroux and Graham Greene (who once sent some updates addressed to "The publishers of the best travel guide in the world, Bath, England").

1990s

During the 1990s the company set about developing a new travel guide series using this legendary title as the flagship. By 1997 there were over a dozen guides in the series and the Footprint imprint was launched.

2000s

The series grew quickly and there were soon Footprint travel guides covering more than 150 countries. In 2004, Footprint launched its first thematic guide: Surfing Europe, packed with colour photographs, maps and charts. This was followed by further thematic guides such as Diving the World, Snowboarding the World, Body and Soul escapes, Travel with Kids and European City Breaks.

2011

Today we continue the traditions of the last 90 years that have served legions of travellers so well. We believe that these help to make Footprint guides different. Our policy is to use authors who are genuine experts who write for independent travellers; people possessing a spirit of adventure, looking to get off the beaten track.

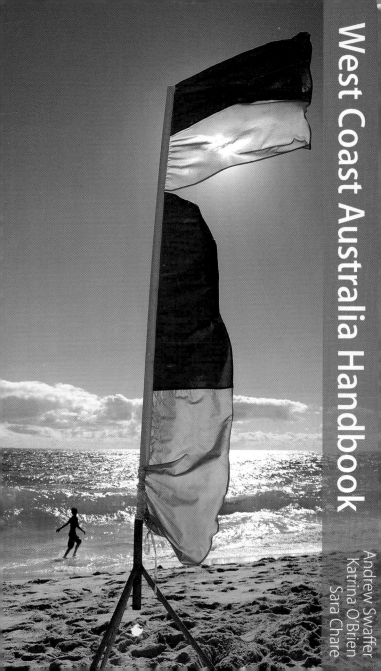

West Coast Australia Handbook

Andrew Swaffer
Katrina O'Brien
Sara Chare

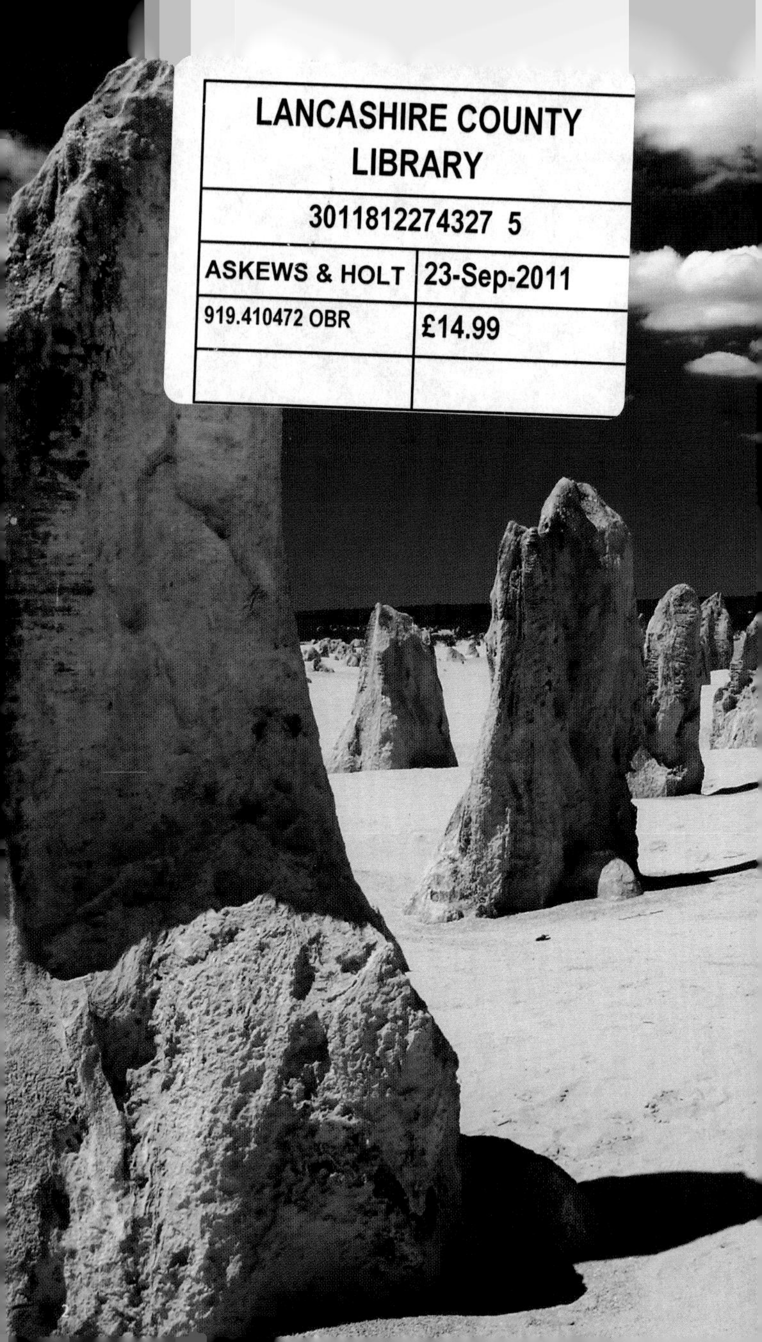

The people of Australia's west coast cling to the land's edge – and for good reason. At their back lies an ocean of desert. Like so many western coastlines across the globe, Australia's can be a wild place. It is hot and dry country with little fresh water and few safe harbours. Much of the state is, in fact, virtually uninhabitable. Its tiny population, vast size and isolation, mean that the west coast is wonderfully unspoiled. There is hardly a high-rise to be found along its entire length and its inhabitants are determined to keep it that way. Solitude is always just around the corner and close encounters of the animal kind are commonplace in a state where the natural world is not outnumbered or overpowered by people.

The obvious thing to be said about Western Australia is that it's big – very big – covering a third of the Australian continent. It's three times larger than Texas and about the same size as Western Europe, yet only two million people, or 10% of Australians, occupy all this land and three quarters of them live in the state capital Perth. Few visitors ever make it the 4000 km across the Nullarbor to the west coast – most are enticed by the rock, the reef and Sydney harbour – and even most Australians are unaware of the wonders of the west.

Amid the dazzling light of the west coast and the clean air of its constant sea breeze, life seems pared back, easy and uncomplicated, and while you have all the comforts you need, civilization is far, far away. Off the beaten track, the west coast offers an unhyped and unhurried experience – it's a part of the country in which you can still find some secret places and penetrate the heart of the space, sunshine and adventure that Australia has to offer.

This page Natural limestone formations, known as the Pinnacles, Nambung National Park.
Previous page Lifesaver flags identify safe swimming areas on Cottesloe Beach, Perth.

Indian Ocean

❿ Derby

❾ Broome

Port
Hedland

Karratha Cossack

Fortescue
Roadhouse   Millstream-   Marble Bar
                 Chichester
Onslow   ♦ National Park

                 Mt Stevenson   Auski
                 (1172m)   ❽ ○ Roadhouse
Cape Range   Tom Price
National Park ♦ Mt Tom Price
                 (1072m)   Mt Bruce   ○ Newman
Nanutarra   (1235m)
Roadhouse

Coral Bay ○   Little Sandy
        ❼   Desert
Lake   Minilya
Macleod   Roadhouse   Kumarina
Quobba ○   Roadhouse

Carnarvon ○   Gascoyne   WESTERN AUSTRALIA
              Junction
        ❻
Monkey Mia ○ ○ Gladstone   Meekatharra ○   Wiluna ○

Hamelin ○   ○ Overlander   Leinster
            Roadhouse

        ❺   Kalbarri   Mount
Kalbarri ○   ♦ National Park   Magnet   Leonora

Lynton ○
Abrolhos   Geraldton   Menzies
Islands
        Dongara ○   ○ Morawa   Kalgoorlie-
                                              Boulder
            ○ Eneabba
Green Head ○   Koorda   Southern
Cervantes ○   Cross   Kambalda
         Yanchep
Lancelin ○ National
           Park   ○ Merredin

              ❶ Perth

Rottnest Island ○   ○ Hyden
Rockingham ○ Serpentine
Lane-Poole   National Park
Reserve ♦   ♦ Dryandra
            Woodland
Bunbury ○   Esperance
Dunsborough ○ Warren   Jerramungup ○
               National   ❹   ○ Hopetoun
Margaret River ○ Park

N   Pemberton ○ Denmark ○ Albany
                                ❸ ♦ Torndirrup
200 km   Walpole ○   National Park
200 miles

4

Highlights

See colour maps at the end of book

1 Rottnest
Perth's 'holiday isle': cute quokkas, great beaches and the best snorkelling around the capital.
▸▸ page 106

2 Cape-to-Cape region
Coastal walks, wonderful wine, awesome caves and serious surf.
▸▸ page 161

3 Walpole and Denmark
Soaring forests meet granite coasts and snowy beaches.
▸▸ pages 206 and 208

4 Stirling Ranges
Bush-cloaked ranges provide superb hill walking and views.
▸▸ page 227

5 Kalbarri
WA's prettiest seaside town, surrounded by massive coastal cliffs and spectacular inland gorges.
▸▸ page 249

6 Shark Bay
Brilliant Blue vistas hide a vast sea-grass plain, home to dolphins, dugongs, sharks and turtles.
▸▸ page 264

7 Ningaloo Reef Marine Park
Snorkel over the reef from pristine beaches and swim with whale sharks.
▸▸ page 275

8 Karijini National Park
Incredibly deep, tight gorges meet expansive view of red and gold ranges.
▸▸ page 302

9 Broome
Quasi-Asian architecture, Cable Beach and the laid back 'Broometime'.
▸▸ page 310

10 Lombadina
Pristine coast and a warm Aboriginal welcome.
▸▸ page 324

ysdale River
ational Park ♦
Wyndham ○

Kimberley

Warmun ○

○ Fitzroy
Crossing

*t Sandy
esert*

*Lake
Mackay*

*Gibson
Desert*

○ Tjukayirla
Roadhouse

Cocklebibby
○
○
Calguna

e Arid

*Southern
Ocean*

Whale sharks congregate off the Ningaloo Marine Park between March and June

The barren outback is transformed into a carpet of wildflowers each spring.

BROOME & AROUND
PILBARRA
GASGOYNE
MIDWEST
AROUND PERTH
PERTH
SOUTHWEST COAST
TIMBER TOWNS
SOUTH COAST

Contents

Footprint features

Essentials

Planning your trip

Where to go

Western Australia is the world's single biggest political unit that isn't actually a country. It constitutes a third of an island so big that it isn't even accorded the status of the world's biggest (usually given to Greenland), but rather its smallest continent. Western Australia is not far off the size of India. If you only have a couple of weeks for a visit, don't try to see too much. Where you choose to visit will primarily be determined by the time of year. Broadly speaking, the far north is extremely hot, humid and monsoonal from October to April. Some enthusiasts extol the delights of the north in the 'Wet', but most visitors will want to enjoy the glorious summer weather in the southern regions at this time and avoid the humidity up north. A visit during May to September opens up the north, but also allows an itinerary to range almost anywhere in the state, though it can be a bit wet and cold down south.

One-week trip

If you've only got a few days on your way through, then **Perth** or **Fremantle** make excellent bases and you'll probably have time for an overnight trip down to the **Cape-to-Cape region** to explore the wineries, caves and beaches, or over to **Rottnest Island** to see the quokkas. Interesting day trips from Perth include a quick tour east into the **Perth Hills** to see **Mundaring Weir** and **York**, a circuit north to see **New Norcia** and **Lancelin**, and the short journey south to **Rockingham** to see the penguins and swim with dolphins.

Two-week trip

In addition to the itinerary above, a two-week visit can allow a longer tour around the south including a trip along the southern coast to **Albany** before heading back up to Perth. A fortnight is also long enough for a return trip up the coast to **Kalbarri**, or even **Shark Bay**. The more energetic might consider walking parts of the **Cape-to-Cape Track** or **Bibbulmun Track**, or learning to dive, sail or surf off the beautiful beaches around the capital.

Three- to four-week trip

In three weeks you can begin to consider exploring the coast both south and immediately north of Perth, or even the great West Coast trip from Perth to Broome or vice-versa, flying the reverse direction. The latter journey would even allow for a serious side-trip, for instance into **Millstream-Chichester National Park** or **Karijini National Park**. At least a month is required to see a good spread of most of the highlights detailed in this guide, and to journey the full length of the West Coast between Albany and Broome.

When to go

Climate

As this state is the only one that stretches from the bottom of the country to the top, you can visit WA at any time of year. Generally the state has a superb climate and is sunny much of the time. The northern region is mildly tropical and has a build-up of humidity from October to December and occasional monsoonal downpours in January to April, known as the 'Wet' (a period characterized by high humidity, heat, tremendous

Packing for Australia

If you forget an essential item you should be able to find it in the major cities.

Special respect must be paid to the Australian sun. A decent wide-brimmed hat and factor 30+ suncream (cheap in Australian supermarkets) are essential. Light, long-sleeved tops and trousers cut down the necessity for quite as much suncream, help keep out the mosquitoes and keep you warm in the early evening when the temperature can drop markedly. Even in the north it can get cold in winter so a few warm clothes are a good idea.

If you're planning on doing some walking or trekking, come as prepared as you would do for wetter climes, including packing some decent boots. The weather can change rapidly, particularly in the south in winter, and trails can get boggy. It is quite easy to get lost on longer treks, so pack a compass and map (see page 27).

A sleeping bag is useful in hostels and caravan parks, as linen is not always supplied. In summer a sheet sleeping bag and pillowcase will usually suffice.

Other useful items include: day bag, waterproof sandals, penknife (with bottle and can opener), padlock and length of light chain for security, head torch, water bottle (such as the Platypus), plastic lunchbox and a travel alarm clock.

Having said that, other than boots, most walking and camping equipment can usually be hired in the larger cities.

monsoonal rainfall and occasional, powerful cyclones). Many roads and tourist facilities close at this time but if you can stand the heat you might enjoy the drama of it. The 'Dry' (May to September) is the best time to visit the Gascoyne and Pilbara as temperatures hover around a delightful 25-30°C (whale sharks swim over the Ningaloo Reef near Exmouth from April to June). As a general rule, the further north you travel, and the further in time from July, the hotter it gets. And hot means very hot: days over 40°C regularly occur in summer in the arid regions, and even Perth averages over 30°C. The central or Midwest region is warm and dry for most of the year with little rain, although spring is the ideal time to visit for the wildflower season. The south, including Perth and the southwest, is sunny throughout spring, summer and autumn and these are the ideal seasons to visit. Perth gets an average of 7½ hours of sunshine a day. The southern winter lasts from June to August and this is when this region receives most of its rainfall and gets fairly cold (5-17°C). If you want to see whales though, it will have to be winter or spring when they migrate past the southwest coasts (June to November).

Australia is the driest inhabited continent, and virtually nowhere further than 250 km inland gets more than an average of 600 mm of rain a year. About half the continent, in a band across the south and west, gets less than 300 mm and much of it is desert. The only area in WA that gets significant rainfall spread over more than 160 days a year is the southwest tip.

Weather forecasts: T1900 955366, www.bom.gov.au. **Cyclone information**: T1300 659210, www.bom.gov.au/weather/cyclone. Also useful is www.fesa.wa.gov.au.

Holidays and events

Areas such as Rottnest, the Margaret River region, Kalbarri, Monkey Mia and Broome get completely booked out during school holidays. The main holidays start in mid-December and carry on through to the end of January. Schools also close for the two weeks after Easter, for two weeks in mid-July, and for another two weeks in early October. Backpackers don't need to be too concerned about visiting at these times as accommodation and tours aimed at that market are less affected.

WA's major festival, the **Perth Festival**, is held annually in January and February, and the start more or less coincides with state's biggest international sporting event, Tennis' **Hopman Cup**. ⟫ *For public holidays and other important dates, see Festivals and events, page 36.*

What to do

In Australia, sport takes on a religious significance for many. Even the smallest towns will have a footy pitch or cricket pitch and golf course, and they don't have to be much of a size to have tennis and netball courts, a swimming pool, and a horse-racing track. In most cases there is easy public access at reasonable rates, so if you feel you won't be able to go without a round or a set then bring the minimum of gear and expect to be able to get a game almost anywhere. If you're a real adrenaline junkie then WA can offer a range of heart-stopping activities, most of them involving moving quickly over water, slowly but precariously over or under rock, or with gut-wrenching inevitability through nothing but fresh air. Many of the best are offered by specialist tour and hire operators, and if you have some specific goals it is essential to check out your options carefully in advance as the time of year and availability of spaces can make a big difference to what is possible. *Wild Magazine* has a good website, www.wild.com.au, and publishes walking and adventure guides.

Climbing and abseiling

Although much of Australia is flat as a tack there are a few fabulous climbing spots. To find out more get hold of *Climbing Australia: The Essential Guide* by Greg Pritchard or see www.climbing.com.au.

Head for: **Cape-to-Cape region**, page 161; **Albany**, page 212; **Kalbarri**, page 250; or **Karijini National Park**, page 302.

Cycling and mountain biking

Bicycles are commonly available for hire in cities and major towns, but facilities are scarce otherwise. If you plan to do most of your touring on a bike you will need to either bring your own or buy in Perth, as long-term hire facilities are virtually non-existent. One alternative is to join a cycle-based tour, such as those organized by **Remote Outback Cycles**, www.cycletours.com.au.

Diving and snorkelling

Australia is famous for the Great Barrier Reef, and for decades backpackers have made a beeline there to earn their diving spurs. However, increasingly, travellers are also heading for the west coast to learn to dive on the lesser-known Ningaloo Reef, off Coral Bay and Exmouth. However, this is by no means the only good diving area around this immense coast, which boasts a diversity of options from kelp forests and encrusted jetties to wrecks old and new. The seas around Albany, Dunsborough, Busselton, Rottnest Island and the Abrolhos Islands are very popular spots and local operators offer dive trips, tuition and gear hire. If you're content to simply snorkel then the best destinations are Busselton, Rottnest Island, the Abrolhos Islands, Coral Bay and Exmouth.

The websites **www.diveoz.com.au** and **www.scubaaustralia.com.au**, have useful information on sites, dive centres and charter boats. **www.divedirectory.net** has details of several multi-day diving trips.

Head for: **Rottnest Island**, page 106; **Abrolhos Islands**, page 244; or **Ningaloo Reef**, Coral Bay, page 275.

Fishing

Fishing is in some areas the only recreational activity available to locals and is pursued with an almost religious obsession. As you head north surfboards begin to disappear from vehicle roof racks only to be replaced by 'tinnies', short aluminium boats that allow the fishing family to go where they please. Excellent offshore sport fishing is widely available as a day tour, usually for around $200-250. There are several excellent websites on recreational fishing in Australia, with location reports and details of tour operators and retailers, including www.fishnet.com.au, www.fishing australia.com.au and local site www.fishingwa.com. See www.fish.wa. gov.au for rules on recreational fishing.

Head for: **Coral Bay**, page 275; **Mandurah**, page 134; or **Pemberton**, page 191.

Golf

Almost every town in Australia has at least 1 golf course, even in the outback, though the feel of the greens may not be too familiar, and most welcome visitors. See www.ausgolf.com.au.

Head for: **Perth**, page 85; or **Mandurah**, page 134.

Skydiving and bungee jumping

Many of the several dozen skydiving clubs in WA offer short, usually 1-day courses in parachuting (also known as 'skydiving'), including a jump or 2, and some cut out much of the training by organizing tandem jumps.

If a quick thrill is all you're after then the latter is the better option as it usually involves 30-60 seconds of freefall and costs around $250-300. A list of skydiving clubs affiliated to the **Australian Parachute Federation**, T02-6281 6830, can be found at www.apf.asn.au. If you fancy jumping out into thin air without a parachute then bungee jumping is just about the safest option going.

Head for: **Northbridge**, Perth, page 85.

Spectator sports

It's enough to make an Englishman spit. Any sport Australia takes seriously, it does very well at. Their cricketers seem to score more runs, their rugby players launch themselves for more tries, their swimmers outperform respectably fast fish, their netballers shoot more goals, their top tennis players regularly beat even the Americans, and they have recently had world champions in everything from darts to squash. This awful challenge for their opponents converts to a glorious opportunity for visitors to Australia. If you choose to be a spectator at a sport the Aussies really get into, then you're in for a treat: world-class competition at relatively low prices. And you'll usually be in the company of thousands of exuberant locals yelling their lungs out.

Australian rules football (AFL)
This is the classic Down Under game, to the casual observer a free-for-all that defies the gods in causing as few broken necks as it does. A derivative of the rough football that was being played in Britain and Ireland in the late 1700s it shares an affinity with Gaelic Football; indeed Ireland and Australia meet to contest an 'international rules' cup.

As with rugby and soccer, it's a winter game, with most leagues playing between Mar and Sep. The game is contested on a huge oval pitch, up to 200 m long, between 2 teams of 18 players each. At each end of

Ten West Coast adventures

- Canoe or abseil in Kalbarri National Park.
- Explore the plunging gorges of the Karijini.
- Gain an understanding of Aboriginal people and their culture by staying with them at places like Lombadina near Broome.
- Head for the Ningaloo Reef to snorkel amongst teeming fish, swim with whale sharks and dive with manta rays.
- Hike a section or two of the Bibbulmun Track along the south coast between Pemberton and Albany, or the Cape-to-Cape Track between Yallingup and Augusta.
- Sample the caves, wines, and arts of the Cape-to-Cape region, and leave some time to sit by the sea, particularly when the whales are around.
- Sleep outside in a comfy swag with only the stars and a billy on the fire for company.
- Stay on an outback station.
- Swim with dolphins from one of the towns just south of Perth.
- Take a sailing trip from Dunsborough, Fremantle, Monkey Mia or Broome.

the pitch 4 high posts denote the goal mouth, and it is through these that the teams attempt to get the oval-shaped ball. If the ball goes directly between the central 2 posts a goal is scored and 6 points awarded. If it goes between 1 of the central posts and an outer post, or is touched by the defending team on the way, then a 'behind' is scored and a single point awarded. Players may kick or hand pass the ball in any direction, but not throw it. To hand pass is to punch the ball from the palm of 1 hand with the clenched fist of the other. If the ball is kicked over 10 m and cleanly caught then the catcher can call a mark. He can't be tackled and has time to kick the ball toward goal or a teammate unmolested. The game is split into 4 quarters, each lasting 25 mins. Scoring is usually regular, and winning teams with an excess of 100 points are not unusual. The national league, the AFL, is followed most closely, in fact obsessively, though there are enthusiastic state and local amateur leagues throughout the country. Most of the AFL clubs are in and around Melbourne, where the game was invented, but the national league also has 2 top-flight teams from Perth: the *Fremantle Dockers* and the *West Coast Eagles*.

Cricket

Once the footy seasons ends in around Sep a large number of Australian minds switch, almost like clockwork, to cricket, just another major international team sport at which Australians just happen to be, more or less, better than anyone else. The national side is involved in Test series against England (for the Ashes) and other major cricketing countries and in limited-overs internationals; some of these games are staged at the WACA ground in Perth. There are 2 interstate competitions, both Oct-Feb, and involving WA's *Western Warriors* (who play at the WACA). The Ford Ranger Cup is the 1-day competition, and the Sheffield Shield decides who has the best 4-day team. For round-ups on Australian and international news see www.cricket.com.au.

Horse racing

There are horse racing or pacing (horse and trap) tracks all over the country, in all but the tiniest towns, and there are usually a dozen or so meetings every day, and dozens of races to satisfy the most dedicated of punters. Most of the country's betting is via the state TABs, a pooling system similar to the UK's Tote. There are some high-street TABs, but most can be found in the public bars of the nation's pubs. Take a look at www.nvo.com/racing.

Rugby union

Rugby union traditionally had much less of a grass roots following until the national side, the *Wallabies*, won the Rugby World Cup in 1991. Since that victory they can claim to have always rated in the world's top 5 teams, and frequently vie with arch rivals, the New Zealand All Blacks, for status as world's best. Aside from the World Cup (which they won again in 1999) and regular international tours, the Wallabies compete in an annual 3-way competition (the 'Tri Nations') against South Africa and New Zealand. The winners of the Aussie vs Kiwi games gain possession of the much-prized Bledisloe Cup, which has been contested by the 2 countries since 1931. Every Apr to Sep the 10 top WA clubs (mostly based in and around Perth) contest the KWIK Premier Grade Trophy. Take a look at www.rugby.com.au.

Swimming

Australia is rightly known as a cradle of outstanding swimmers and has produced a number of world champions. There was much excitement over the announcement that 5-time Olympic champion Ian Thorpe (the 'Thorpedo', size 16 feet) will compete in the London Olympics in 2012 ending several years of retirement. The women's team is also very strong with world record breaking stars such as Libby Trickett and Leisel Jones. Another legend, Grant Hackett, retired in 2008, is known as one of the greatest distance swimmers in history.

The Australian National Championships are the best domestic competition in the world to go and see. They're held in Mar, see www.swimming.org.au, for details.

Tennis

Unlike their swimmers Australia has for a long time had to depend on just 1 or 2 brilliant players to keep the male flag flying, and the women's game has until recently been surprisingly weak. Australia hosts one of the world's 4 Grand Slam competitions, the Australian Open, www.ausopen.org, in

Melbourne in Jan. Perth hosts the Hopman Cup, www.hopmancup.com.au, every Jan at Burswood Dome, where international teams of one man and woman compete against each other. For round-ups on tennis news see www.tennis.com.au.

Surfing, windsurfing and kitesurfing

If an Aussie lives near the beach there's a fair bet they'll be a surfer; if they're inland and anywhere near water then waterskiing will probably be their thing. This makes for a great many local clubs, tuition and equipment hire. Surfing is generally best in the southern half of the state with famous, and often jealously guarded spots. Windsurfing and kitesurfing are also widespread as the west coast is one of the contenders for the best coast in the world for the sports. Websites include www.surfinfo.com.au, which links to a great many surf retail and travel businesses, and www.realsurf.com, which has condition reports from all the major spots around the country. There's also information to be found at www.windsurfing.org.

Head for: **Fremantle**, page 94; **Lancelin**, page 124; **Margaret River**, page 170; **Geraldton**, page 241; or **Kalbarri**, page 250.

Walking and trekking

A certain amount of walking is necessary to see many of the west coast's great natural sights, but WA can also boast a great range of short, day and overnight walks, mostly in the many national parks, and even a few excellent multi-day treks. Bushwalking clubs are a good source of local advice and often welcome visitors. See www.bushwalking.org.au.

Starting in Kalamunda, the long-distance Bibbulmun Track winds its way south through Dwellingup, Balingup, Pemberton and Walpole before finally ending up, 963 km later, in Albany. As well as passing

Where in the west ...

Many of the following creatures, though widespread, are not always easy to see. With patience sightings are likely, if not guaranteed, at the following places (tours and entry fees sometimes apply). Note that koalas, platypus and wombats are not native to Western Australia.

Blue (fairy) wrens Cape-to-Cape region.
Corals Busselton, Rottnest Island, Abrolhos Islands, Coral Bay and Exmouth.
Crocodiles Broome and the Dampier Peninsula.
Dolphins Bunbury, Mandurah, Monkey Mia and Rockingham.
Dugongs Monkey Mia and Port Hedland.
Eagles and kites Northern WA.
Echidnas Common but elusive: try Avon Valley National Park, near Perth.
Emus Common, 'tame' in Donnelly.
Fairy penguins Penguin Island.
Kangaroos Almost anywhere around dawn and dusk.
Manta rays Coral Bay.
Parrots Southwest and south coast.
Quokkas Rottnest Island.
Seals and sea lions Jurien Bay, Leeman and Rockingham.
Stingrays Augusta, Hamelin Bay, Coral Bay and Exmouth.
Turtles Monkey Mia, Coral Bay, Exmouth and Port Hedland.
Whales Albany, Augusta, Dunsborough, Perth, Kalbarri, Coral Bay, Exmouth and Port Hedland.
Whale sharks Coral Bay and Exmouth.

through these picturesque towns the track also winds through reserves and parks, much of the southern forests and some of the spectacular south coast. There are nearly 50 bush campsites en route, each with a simple 3-sided timber bunk shelter, picnic tables, water tank and pit toilets. There are no cooking facilities, water needs to be boiled or treated, and there is no toilet paper. The whole walk takes about 6-8 weeks, but few tackle it in a single go and DEC have suggestions for various short day sections. The track is at its best in autumn and spring. Consider carefully before tackling any of it in high summer or in the winter. There is a 2-volume guide to the track and a series of 8 maps also dedicated to it, all available at the Perth Map Centre among other outlets. For more information see www.naturebase.net or contact the **Friends of the Bibbulmun Track**, T08-9481 0551, www.bibbulmuntrack.org.au.

The 140-km Cape-to-Cape Walk Track follows the coast from Cape Naturaliste to Cape Leeuwin via Yallingup and Prevelly, and takes about a week. Campsites are provided where there are no commercial facilities, but there may be long stretches where no water is available. DEC publish annotated maps that cover the entire route ($8), and you can also get advice from **Friends of the Cape-to-Cape**, www.capetocapetrack.com.au.

Head for: **Bibbulmun Track**, pages 119, 189, 194, 206 and 211; or **Cape-to-Cape Walk Track**, page 164.

Wildlife spotting

The unique Australian wildlife experience is one that goes far beyond meeting friendly kangaroos and coming face-to-face with turtles on the Ningaloo. Almost everywhere you go wildlife surrounds you and can be observed; from parrots in Perth's Kings Park to occasional dolphins off almost any beach on the coast. The concept that almost all of it, beyond the humble roo, is out to clamp its jaws, fangs or stinging tentacles in to you is greatly over exaggerated. True there are many venomous and potentially dangerous creatures out there, but nothing a bit of common sense and respect won't protect you from. On the other hand, you can easily harm the wildlife. Drive sensibly and you will largely avoid hitting small mammals, birds and reptiles; don't disturb the natural environment (including collecting firewood) as this is their home; and don't feed wildlife as animals that get used to being hand fed can become sick, aggressive and dependent. In summary, provided you retain an open mind, patience and keep your eyes open, you will return home with an armoury of interesting memories, stories and photographs that will confirm the fact that Australia is one of the best places to encounter wildlife on the planet.

Taking a tour

There are a number of specialist tour operators, see page 47 for a comprehensive list. The state government tourism body is **Tourism Western Australia** ① *Forrest Pl, Perth, T08-9483 1111, T1300 361351, www.westernaustralia.com*, which provides brochures and information. There is an **office in the UK** ① *6th floor, Australia Centre, The Strand, London, WC2B 4LG, T020-7438 4647*. The state government's site, **www.wa.gov.au**, has some useful links. Backpackers might find Perth's **Traveller's Club** ① *T08-9226 0660*, a helpful source of information. **Conservation Volunteers** ① *T08-9227 5711, www.conservation volunteers.com.au*, is also useful. **Tourism Australia** ① *T02-9360 1111, www.australia. com*, can be of great help, and there is also a wealth of all sorts of information to be found on the federal and government websites, **www.fed.gov.au**. For details of many Aboriginal cultural centres and tours check out **www.aboriginaltouroperators.com.au**. Be aware though that the history of the indigenous Aboriginal people, though prodigious in terms of tenure, is sometimes conspicuous by its absence. The preservation and display of the 'European' history of Australia is, as to be expected, much more extensive.

National parks and reserves generally constitute natural areas of ecological, cultural and/or simply aesthetic importance, and can claim to encompass almost all of Western Australia's most jaw-dropping and sublime natural attractions. The **Department of Environment and Conservation (DEC)** ① *T08-6467 5000, www.naturebase.net*, can give further information, including details of visiting and staying in them. Park entry fees are usually $11 a car, but for most visitors it is better value to buy a Holiday Pass ($40) allowing entry into all WA parks for four weeks. If you plan a longer stay it's worth considering the Annual Pass ($80), valid for 12 months from date of purchase. Passes can be bought at many parks and VICs or from the **Perth Visitor Centre** in Forrest Place (see page 55).

Getting there

Air

As Australia is an island nation, and a considerable distance from anywhere except Indonesia and Papua New Guinea, the vast majority of international visitors arrive by air. There are international flights direct to Perth from many cities around the world as well as interstate ones from most other Australian state capitals, see Getting around, page 23. However, it is usually possible to book internal Australian flights when booking your international ticket, at lower prices than on arrival. Some do not even require a stated departure and arrival point. If you have any plans to fly within Australia check this out with your travel agent prior to booking.

There are now enormous numbers of high street, phone and internet outlets for buying your plane ticket. This can make life confusing but the competition does mean that dogged work can be rewarded in a very good deal. Fares will depend on the season, with prices much higher during December-January unless booked well in advance. Mid-year tends to see the cheapest fares. **Qantas** and **Virgin Blue** are Australia's main international airlines and fly from a considerable number of international capitals and major cities. Most other major airlines have flights to Australia from their home countries or Europe.

One-way flight tickets are not necessarily a lot more expensive than half a return fare. If you are contemplating a lengthy trip and are undecided about further plans, or like the idea of being unconstrained, then a single fare could be for you. Australian immigration officials can get very suspicious of visitors arriving on one-way tickets, however, especially on short-term visas. Anyone without long-term residency on a one-way ticket will need to show proof of substantial funds enough for a stay and onward flight. Discuss your circumstances with your local travel agent or directly with the Australian embassy or high commission in your country before committing to a one-way ticket.

Round-the-World (RTW) tickets can be a real bargain if you stick to the most popular routes, sometimes working out even cheaper than a return fare. RTWs start at around £950 (€1200 or US$1500), depending on the season. Perth is easy to include on a RTW itinerary. When trying to find the best deal, make sure you check the route, journey duration, stopovers, departure and arrival times, restrictions and cancellation penalties. Many cheap flights are sold by small agencies, most honest and reliable, but there may be some risks involved with buying tickets at rock-bottom prices. Avoid paying too much money in advance and check with the airline directly to ensure you have a reservation.

From Europe The main route, and the cheapest, is via Asia, though fares will also be quoted via North America or Africa. The Asia route usually takes 20-24 hours including stops. There are as yet no non-stop routes (though Boeing's 787 could in theory do London to Perth in one hop), so it's worth checking out what stopovers are on offer: this might be your only chance to see Kuala Lumpur. Stopovers of a few nights do not usually increase the cost of the ticket appreciably. The cheapest return flights, off-season, will be around £700 (€900), with stand-by prices rising to at least £1400 (€1800) around Christmas. Flights to Perth are usually marginally cheaper than to the other state capitals.

Airlines from Europe: **Air New Zealand**, www.airnz.co.uk; **British Airways**, www.british airways.com; **Cathay Pacific**, www.cathaypacific.com; **Emirates**, www.emirates.com;

Malaysia Airlines, www.malaysiaairlines.com; Qantas, www.qantas.co.uk; Singapore Airlines, www.singaporeair.com; Virgin Atlantic, www.virgin-atlantic.com.

From New Zealand There are direct Qantas flights from Auckland, Christchurch and Wellington to Brisbane, Melbourne and Sydney. Air New Zealand, www.airnz.co.nz, and Virgin Blue, www.virginblue.com.au, are the other two main carriers, both offering routes that Qantas do not. Expect to pay a minimum of NZ$1000 for a return flight to Perth.

From North and South America There are direct Qantas flights from Los Angeles to Brisbane, Melbourne and Sydney, and from Vancouver and New York to Sydney. The cost of a standard return in the high season starts from around US$1500 from Vancouver, New York, and Los Angeles. There are also direct flights from Buenos Aires to Sydney.

Airlines from the Americas: Air Canada, www.aircanada.com; Air New Zealand, www.air newzealand.com; Qantas, www.qantas.com.au; Singapore Airlines, www.singapore air.com; United, www.united.com; Virgin Atlantic, www.virgin-atlantic.com.

From South Africa There are direct Qantas flights from Johannesburg to Perth. South African Airways, www.flysaa.com, also flies direct in around 11 hours.

Airport information
Perth Airport, 10 km east of the city centre, has two terminals – domestic and international. With no direct link between the two, transfers are via the perimeter highways. The domestic terminal, Brearley Avenue, has a wide range of services including ATMs, Travelex foreign exchange, luggage lockers, cafés and all the major car hire firms. The international terminal, Horrie Miller Drive, is slightly further out. Facilities are just as comprehensive, the Thomas Cook foreign exchange counters remaining open before and after all flights. ▸▸ See also Perth Ins and outs, page 54.

Rail

Great Southern Rail ① T132147 or T08-8213 4592 (outside Australia), www.gsr.com.au, operates The Indian Pacific service to Perth from Sydney and Adelaide with connections from Darwin, Alice Springs and Melbourne. An unbroken trip from Sydney takes three days and nights. The Ghan connects Darwin and Alice Springs to Adelaide (46 hours). The Overland connects Melbourne to Adelaide (10 hours). Unless coming from Sydney an overnight stopover in Adelaide may be required. Vehicles can be brought along and sometimes special deals can make this well worth considering.

There are three ticket levels on The Indian Pacific and The Ghan. The 'Gold Kangaroo' passenger gets a small sleeping cabin, all meals in the 'Gold' dining car, and a lounge. 'Red Kangaroo' passengers have separate lounge and dining car (meals not included), and either a cabin or day/nighter seat (an ordeal for some). The seat-only prices are roughly equivalent with interstate buses, with the red cabins about 2½ times the cost and gold cabins 3½ times. Concessions are good value, particularly for the long-distance, 'red' seats (Sydney to Perth for as little as $315). The Great Southern Rail Explorer Pass ($590) allows unlimited travel in a 'red' day/nighter seat on The Ghan, The Indian Pacific and The Overland for six months. Pass holders must be members of a recognized backpacker organization (eg YHA). Upgrades to sleeping berths are allowed, but surcharges apply.

Road

Bus

McCaffertys/Greyhound ⓘ *T1300 473 946, www.greyhound.com.au*, have services throughout Australia and it's possible to get a long ride (via the 'top end' only) from most of the mainland state capitals to Perth, Broome and most of the coastal towns in between. See Getting around, page 24, for details of travel passes.

Car

Driving to Western Australia involves a trip of at least 1500 km from anywhere else in the country and conceivably up to about 5000 km. Before deciding and setting out on a self-drive road trip to WA first ensure that the vehicle driver(s) and passengers are all able, willing, well prepared and aware of what the journey involves! Whether coming across the north from NT to the Kimberley and Pilbara, or from the south across the Nullarbor, and especially via the unsealed Outback Highway from Yulara, the journey will involve at least one to two days' driving across very hot, arid and sparsely populated regions. See Getting around, page 25, for further information on preparation and driving in Australia. Details of the route from WA out east are given on pages 143 and 230.

Getting around

Public transport in and around Perth, based on bus and train networks, is generally good and efficient, and often easier than driving. Many of the larger cities also have modest bus services, but these are often not aimed at tourists and many important outlying attractions are missed off the bus routes completely. Some cities are compact enough for this to be a minor irritation, others are so spread out that the visitor must invest in an expensive tourist bus service or taxis to get around. In such places staying at a hostel or B&B with free or low-cost bicycle hire can save a lot of money.

By far the best way of seeing the west coast is under your own steam, or with a tour operator with an in-depth itinerary. The further from Perth you go, the more patchy and irregular public transport becomes. If short on time and long on funds, flying can save a lot of time and effort. In some cases it is the only real option.

Air

As the biggest state, and one with much profitable mining industry, air travel is common within WA. Though not usually very cheap, a couple of judicious flights can save days of travel if you're short of time. **Skywest** ⓘ *T1300 660088 or T08-9477 8301 (outside Australia), www.skywest.com.au*, is the principal state airline with flights from Perth to all the major towns. NT's **Air North** ⓘ *T1800 627 474, www.airnorth.com.au*, has connections between Broome, Kununurra and Darwin. **Qantas** ⓘ *T131313, www.qantas.com.au*, provides direct flights between Perth and the main northern towns. If the latter does operate a route they are likely to offer the cheapest fare, usually $100-500 one-way. You could also try **Virgin Blue** ⓘ *T136789 or T07-3295 2296, www.virginblue.com.au*.

Flight agencies worth checking out include: **Flight Centre** ⓘ *T133133, www.flight centre.com.au*; **Harvey World Travel** ⓘ *T1300 855492, www.harveyworld.com.au*; **JetSet** ⓘ *T136383, www.jetset.com.au*; and **STA** ⓘ *T134782, www.statravel.com.au*.

Rail

There are limited local lines operated by **TransWA** ① *T1300 662205, www.transwa. wa.gov.au*, and integrated into their general schedules. Some journeys alternate between bus and train. Tickets are available at coach and bus stations, and by telephone. See Bus, below, for contact details.

Road

Bus

If travelling by bus around the west coast, always check the journey duration and time of arrival. Some routes can literally take days, each with 24 hours of travel with just a handful of short meal stops. Many coaches are equipped with videos, but you may want a book to hand. It's also a good idea to take warm clothing, socks, a pillow, toothbrush and ear plugs. There's a good chance you will arrive in the late evening or the early hours of the morning. If this is the case, book accommodation ahead and, if possible, arrange your transfer in advance. At least ensure you know how to get to your accommodation, and try to avoid walking around alone late at night. Also double-check times of connections: many travel arrangements have been disrupted by the discovery that a bus was on a different day than assumed.

TransWA ① *T1300 662205, www.transwa.wa.gov.au*, runs the main train and bus services around the state though their network only extends as far as Kalbarri to the north. If they do operate a route they are likely to be the cheapest option. **Integrity** ① *T08-9574 6707, www.integritycoachlines.com.au*, heads north on the inland route to Port Hedland, while **South West Coachlines** ① *T08-9261 7600, www.veoliatransportwa.com.au*, has the most comprehensive around the southwest. The national coach carrier **Greyhound** ① *T1300 473 946, www.greyhound.com.au*, plugs some of the gaps with coastal services from Perth to Broome and beyond. As well as scheduled routes and fares they offer a variety of jump-on, jump-off passes. The **Western Explorer Pass** will take you from Perth to Darwin over 183 days (5300 km, $874), while the slightly pricier **Kilometre Pass** allows travel anywhere on the network over the course of a year. A 2000-km pass is $382, with each extra 1000 km costing around $150.

Backpacker and tour buses There are now several operators which make the assumption that the most important part of your trip is the journey. Over a dozen Western Australian companies offer one- to 10-day trips around the WA coast and venturing inland and most can be used as a way of getting from A to B. They are well worth considering, especially if you are travelling alone. In terms of style, price (around $150-200 per day) and what is included they vary greatly, and it is important to clarify this prior to booking. Some offer transport and commentary only, others include accommodation and some meals, a few specialize in 4WD and bush camping. The latter are not for everyone, but for many will provide an unforgettable experience. Make sure you ask around and chat to some of the operators before committing yourself. Ask about the average age and size of the tour group, the activity level, and details of the itinerary so you can be sure you will see and experience what you want to in a way that suits your ability and comfort level. One of the principal differences between the operators is in the sleeping arrangements they offer. For details of these tour operators, see page 47.

Distances and bus journey times
Accumulated journey times are likely to be longer due to rest stops.

Perth to Bunbury	180 km	2¼ hours
Bunbury to Busselton	53 km	¾ hour
Busselton to Margaret River	62 km	1¼ hours
Margaret River to Pemberton	140 km	2½ hours
Bunbury to Pemberton	160 km	2¼ hours
Pemberton to Walpole	120 km	1¾ hours
Walpole to Albany	117 km	1¾ hours
Perth to Albany	410 km	6 hours
Perth to Cervantes	255 km	4 hours
Cervantes to Geraldton	205 km	3¼ hours
Geraldton to Kalbarri	155 km	2¼ hours
Geraldton to Overlander	280 km	3½ hours
Kalbarri to Overlander	245 km	3¼ hours
Overlander to Monkey Mia	155 km	2¼ hours
Overlander to Carnarvon	205 km	3 hours
Carnarvon to Coral Bay	245 km	3¼ hours
Coral Bay to Exmouth	150 km	2 hours
Carnarvon to Karratha	630 km	9 hours
Karratha to Port Hedland	235 km	3½ hours
Port Hedland to Broome	605 km	7½ hours

Car, motorbike and bicycle

There is no substitute in Western Australia for having your own transport. As a general rule of thumb consider buying a car if you are travelling for more than three months. If hiring or buying a car, consider a campervan as an alternative. Long-term bicycle hire is rarely available, and touring cyclists should plan to bring their own bike or buy one in Perth.

Traffic congestion is rarely an issue, even Perth has nothing like the traffic of most cities, so driving itineraries can be based on covering a planned distance each day. Up to, say, 100 km for each solid hour's driving. The key factor in planning transport is distance. Driving or cycling outside of the main cities is pretty stress-free, but the distances can be huge. Drivers can quickly get very bored and very sleepy. There are a lot of single-vehicle accidents in Australia, and many are a result of driver fatigue.

Watch out for large animals in the country. Kangaroos and emus can appear seemingly out of nowhere, particularly at dawn and dusk, and sheep and cattle frequently stray onto unfenced roads. Collisions with animals are a major cause of single-vehicle accidents and can be serious: hitting a kangaroo, emu or sheep may write off the vehicle and cause injury. Hitting cattle or a camel is considerably worse. Drive only in full daylight if possible.

On country roads you will also meet road trains. These trucks can be over 50 m long including up to four separate trailers strung along behind the main cab. Overtaking them entails great care; wait for a good long stretch before committing. If you are on a single track bitumen road or an unsealed road pull right over and slow considerably when one comes the other way. Not only can dust cause zero visibility, but you will also minimize the possibility of stones pinging up and damaging your windows.

The other major factor when planning is the type of roads you may need to use. All the main highways are 'sealed', but many country roads and outback 'tracks' are unsealed, usually meaning a stony or sand surface. When recently graded (levelled and compacted) they can be almost as pleasant to drive on as sealed roads, but even then there are reduced levels of handling. After grading, unsealed roads deteriorate over time. Potholes form, they can become impassable when wet, and corrugations usually develop. These are regular ripples in the road surface, perpendicular to the road direction, and can go on for tens of kilometres. Small ones simply cause an irritating judder, large ones can reduce tolerable driving speeds to 10-20 kph. Generally, the bigger the wheel size and the longer the wheel-base, the more comfortable journeys over corrugations will be. Many unsealed roads can be negotiated with a two wheel-drive (2WD), low-clearance vehicle, but the ride will be a lot more comfortable, and safer in a four wheel-drive (4WD) high-clearance one. Most 2WD hire cars are uninsured if driven on unsealed roads. Some unsealed roads are designated as 4WD-only or tracks, though individual definitions of some differ according to the map or authority you consult. In dry weather and after recent grading some can be driven in well-prepared 2WD cars. At other times they cannot without serious risk of accident, vehicle or tyre damage or getting bogged. If in any doubt whatsoever, stick to the roads you are certain are safe for your vehicle, and you are sufficiently prepared for. Always check with the hire company where you can and cannot take your 4WD vehicle (some will not allow them off graded roads), and also what your liability will be in the case of an accident. Of particular note are the roads in the Pilbara. Although generally passable for 2WD, they are notoriously good at causing punctures on all types of vehicles. Experiencing two or three punctures here on a single trip is not uncommon.

Prepare carefully before driving to remote areas. Even if there are regular roadhouses, try to carry essential spares and tools such as fan belts, hoses, gaffer tape, a tyre repair kit, extra car jack, extra spare wheel and tyre, spade, decent tool kit, oil and coolant, and a fuel can. Membership of the RAC is recommended, as is informing someone of your intended itinerary. Above all carry plenty of spare water, at least 10 litres per person, 20 if possible.

The **RAC** ① *T131703, www.rac.com.au*, breakdown service and motoring organization is affiliated to the **Australian Automobile Association** (**AAA**), www.aaa.asn.au, which your home country organization may have a reciprocal link with. All other Australian states motoring organizations also have reciprocal links. Note that you will normally only be covered for about 100 km (depending on scheme) of towing distance.

Rules and regulations To drive in WA you must have a current driving licence. Foreign nationals may need an international driver's licence, available from your national motoring organization. In Australia you drive on the left. Speed limits vary between town and country, with maximum urban limits of 50-60 kph and maximum country limits of 100-110 kph. Speeding penalties include a fine, and police allow little leeway. Seatbelts are compulsory for drivers and passengers. Driving under the influence of **alcohol** is illegal over certain (very small) limits and penalties are severe. To check road conditions contact **Main Roads Western Australia** ① *T1800 013314, www.mainroads.wa.gov.au*, or the RAC.

Fuel Fuel costs are approximately half that in Britain and nearly twice that in the USA, fluctuating between $1.30 a litre in and around Perth and at least 10% higher in the country. Anyone driving long distances in WA will soon find that fuel expenses exceed those of food and rival those of accommodation. Budget at least $20 for every estimated 100 km.

Vehicle hire Car rental costs vary according to where you hire from (it's cheaper in Perth, though small local companies have good deals), what you hire and the mileage/insurance terms. You may be better off making arrangements in your own country for a fly-drive deal. Watch out for kilometre caps: some can be as low as 100 km per day. The minimum you'll pay is around $200 a week for a small car. Drivers need to be over 21. At peak times it can be impossible to hire at short notice, and some companies may dispose of a booked car within as little as half an hour of you not showing up for an agreed pick-up time. If you've booked a car but are going to be late ensure that you let them know. Some companies will offer one-way hire on certain models and under certain conditions.

Buying a vehicle Buying a vehicle in WA is a relatively simple process provided you have somewhere you can give as an address. Cars and vans that go the distance can be picked up from $2500, or $6000 for a 4WD. Paying more increases peace of mind, but obviously increases possible losses when you sell it. If you're dealing with a second-hand **car dealer** you may be able to agree a 'buy-back' price. Another factor in favour of dealers is that they usually offer some sort of warranty. The alternatives are fellow travellers, hostel notice boards and classifieds advertisements. The principal advantage to buying privately is cost – vehicles sold by travellers in a hurry can be bargains. The **RAC** offers vehicle checks for around $100. An older vehicle may need a little TLC so the availability of **spares** should be a consideration. Availability is best for Fords and Holdens, but Toyota parts are also common.

You will need to formally complete the transfer of registration with the transport department, presenting them with the papers and a receipt (there is a stamp duty tax of about 5%). Registration must be renewed, in the state the vehicle was last sold, every six or 12 months. Third-party personal injury **insurance** is included in the registration, but you are advised to invest at least in third-party vehicle-and-property insurance, even in comprehensive cover if you cannot afford to lose the value of your vehicle.

Hitchhiking
Hitchhiking, while not strictly illegal, is not advisable. There will always be the odd twisted soul around who will assault or abduct. This is not to say that hitching is more dangerous in WA than elsewhere else, but simply that bad things happen.

Maps
Touring maps and street maps for touring can be viewed and printed from **www.maps.google.com.au**. *Streetsmart* is a series of regional touring maps produced by the government; these are probably the best maps available for drivers as they are very detailed and note points of interest. These can be bought online at **www.landonline.com.au**, from bookshops, VICs or from **Landgate** ① *T08-9273 7373, 1 Midland Sq, Midland*. The **Chart and Map Shop** ① *14 Collie St, Fremantle, T08-9335 8665, www.chartandmapshop.com.au*, and **Perth Map Centre** ① *900 Hay St, Perth, T08-9322 5733, www.mapworld.net.au*, both stock a range of national, state and regional maps, bike maps, Bibbulmun and Cape-to-Cape track maps. The **RAC** ① *832 Wellington St, West Perth, T08-9436 4999, www.rac.com.au*, sells handy fold-out maps (only $3 for members). The *UBD Country Towns and Street Directory: Western Australia* has good information on towns (excluding Perth) and includes a road atlas for the whole state. The best street directories available for Perth are also published by UBD.

Hotel price codes

LL	$360 and over for a double or twin	**D**	$60-89 for a double or twin,
L	$270-359 for a double or twin		$35-50 for a single or dorm
A	$195-269 for a double or twin	**E**	$45-59 for a double or twin,
B	$135-194 for a double or twin		$25-34 for a single or dorm
C	$90-134 for a double or twin	**F**	$24 and under for a single or dorm

Prices refer to a double or twin room (unless otherwise stated) for one night, in the high season. Where rooms or units sleep more than two people a nominal extra charge will sometimes be levied for a third and fourth person.

Sleeping

There is a diverse and attractive range of accommodation options, from cheap national park campsites alive with wildlife to exclusive and luxurious retreats. Given the weather and the environment, travelling on a budget does not in any way detract from the enjoyment of a trip. On the contrary, this is a place where nights under canvas in national parks, or preparing your porridge on a campfire under the gaze of a possum is an absolute delight.

If we haven't provided the sleeping option to match your ideal, local VICs can supply full accommodation listings. Booking in advance is highly recommended, especially in peak seasons. Useful websites include: **www.globalstore.com.au**, **www.jasons.com.au**, **www.travel.com.au** and **www.babs.com.au**. Single rooms are relatively scarce outside of pubs, hostels and roadhouses. Air conditioning is common, but check when booking, and if they don't have it ask how they keep their rooms cool. There are plenty of rooms without air conditioning in Australia that are impossible to sleep in during hot weather.

Hotels, motels and resorts

At the top end of the scale are some impressive international-standard hotels and resorts, with luxurious surroundings and facilities, attentive service and often outstanding locations. Rooms will typically start in our **L** range. In the main cities are a few less expensive hotels in the **A-B** range. Most 'hotels' outside the major towns are pubs with upstairs or external accommodation. If the room is upstairs it is likely to have access to shared bathroom facilities, while external rooms are usually standard en suite motel units. The quality of pub-hotel accommodation varies considerably, but is usually a budget option (**C-D**). Linen is almost always supplied.

Motels in Australia are usually anonymous, but dependably clean and safe, and usually offer the cheapest en suite rooms. Most have dining facilities and free, secure parking. Some budget motels will fall into our **D** range, most will be **B-C**. Linen is always supplied.

B&Bs and self-catering

Bed and Breakfast (B&B) is in some ways quite different from the British model. Not expensive, but rarely a budget option, most fall into our **B-C** ranges. They offer very comfortable accommodation in upmarket houses. Rooms are usually en suite or have access to a private bathroom. Bathrooms shared by more than two rooms are rare. Hosts are usually friendly and informative. Some B&Bs are actually a semi or fully self-contained cottage or cabin with breakfast provisions supplied. Larger ones may have full kitchens. As well as private houses, self-contained, self-catering options are provided by caravan parks and hostels, and some resorts and motels with apartment-style units. Check whether linen is supplied in self-catering accommodation.

National parks, farms and stations
Some national parks and rural cattle and sheep stations have old settlers or workers' homes that have been converted into accommodation, usually self-contained. They are often magical places to stay and include many old lighthouse keepers' cottages and shearers' quarters. Stations may also invite guests to see or even get involved in the day's activities. Transport to them can be difficult if you don't have your own. Linen is often not supplied in this sort of accommodation. See www.tacawa.com.au for information.

Hostels
Western Australia has a large network of good-value hostels (D-F). They are popular centres for backpackers and provide a great opportunity for meeting fellow travellers. Most will have at least one double room and possibly singles, sometimes with linen. Almost all hostels have kitchen and common room facilities. A few, particularly in cities, will offer freebies including breakfast and pick-ups. Standards vary considerably, and it's well worth asking other travellers about the hostels at your next ports of call. Most are effectively independent and the best tend to be those that are owner-managed. International visitors can obtain a Hostelling International Card (HIC) from any YHA hostel or travel centre. For this you get a handbook to YHA hostels nationwide and around $3-4 off every night's YHA accommodation. The hostel associations **NOMADS** ① T02-9280 4110, www.nomads world.com, no membership fee, and **YHA** ① www.yha.com.au, seem to ensure the best consistency of quality. **YMCA** ① T08-9473 8400, www.ymca.org.au, and **YWCA** ① T02-6230 5150, www.ywca.org.au, hostels are usually a clean and quiet choice in the major cities.

Caravan and tourist parks
Almost every town will have at least one caravan park with unpowered and powered sites, varying from $10-25 for campers, caravans and campervans, a wash block and usually a camp kitchen or BBQs. Some will have permanently sited caravans (on-site vans) and cabins. On-site vans are usually the cheapest option (E-F) for families or small groups wanting to self-cater. Cabins are more expensive (C-D). Some will have televisions, en suite bathrooms, separate bedrooms with linen and well-equipped kitchens. Power is rated at the domestic level (240/250v AC), which is convenient for budget travellers. Joining a park association will get you a discount in all parks that are association

Ten great hostels

Bay Lodge YHA, Denham, page 268.
Bayview YHA, Albany, page 219.
Beaches of Broome, Broome, page 316.
The Emperor's Crown, Perth, page 68.
Kalbarri Backpackers YHA (Pelican's Nest), Kalbarri, page 254.

Kimberley Klub YHA, Broome, page 315.
Kookaburra Dream, York, page 130.
Lancelin Lodge YHA, Lancelin, page 125.
Sundancer, Fremantle, page 99.
Underground, Perth, page 69.

members. Associations include: **Big 4** ⓘ *T03-9811 9300, www.big4.com.au;* **Family Parks of Australia** ⓘ *T1300 855 707, www.familyparks.com.au;* and **Top Tourist Parks** ⓘ *T08-8363 1901, www.toptourist.contact.com.au.*

Roadhouses

Where roads connect towns more than about 100 km apart there will usually be roadhouses on the way. They vary from simple fuel stops and small stores to mini-resorts with accommodation, small supermarkets, post offices, daytime cafés, evening restaurants and bars. They will often have simple single and double rooms in what look for all the world like converted shipping containers (they often are), known as **dongas**. These usually fall into the **B-C** range.

Camping in national parks

Some national parks allow camping, mostly in designated areas only, with a few allowing limited bush camping. Facilities are usually minimal, with basic toilets, fireplaces and perhaps tank water; a few have BBQs and shower blocks. Enjoyable camping necessitates being well prepared. Payment is often by self-registration (around $10 per person), and BBQs often require $0.20, $0.50 or $1 coins, so have small notes and change ready. In many parks you will need a gas stove. If there are fireplaces you must bring your own wood. Collecting wood within parks is prohibited, as logs and twigs are an important habitat for native animals. No fires may be lit, even stoves, during a **Total Fire Ban**. Even if water is supposedly available it is not guaranteed so take a supply, as well as your own toilet paper. **Bush camping** in national parks is strongly regulated. The key rules are to be particularly careful with fire, camp at least 20 m from any waterhole or course, and to disturb the environment as little as possible. Nothing must be left behind, and nothing removed, even rocks. Toilet waste should be carefully buried, at least 100 m from any waterhole or course. To find parks with camping options, check www.dec.wa.gov.au.

Bush and roadside camping

There are many spots outside parks where camping is also expressly allowed. On rare occasions there may be basic toilets, water and fireplaces. Out of courtesy and regard for the environment, act as if you were in a national park. Some parking bays allow caravans or campervans to stop overnight. Even if not allowed, stop for a sleep if the choice is between that or driving while very tired. Publications describing free roadside and bush-camping spots are widely available.

Campervans

A popular choice for many visitors is to hire or buy a vehicle that can be slept in, combining the costs of accommodation and transport (although you will still need to book into caravan parks for electricity and washing). Ranging from the popular VW Kombi to enormous vans with integral bathrooms, they can be hired from as little as $60 per day to as much as $1000. A van for two people at around $120 per day compares well with hiring a car and staying in hostels, and allows greater freedom. High-clearance 4WD campervans are also available, and increase travel possibilities yet further. Kombis can usually be bought from about $2500. A cheaper though less comfortable alternative is to buy a van or station wagon (estate car) that is big enough to sleep in.

Campervan companies **Apollo** ① *266 Great Eastern Highway, Belmont, T1800 777 779, www.apollocamper.com.au*; **Backpacker** ① *471 Great Eastern Highway, Redcliffe, T08-9479 5208, www.backpackercampervans.com*; **Britz** ① *471 Great Eastern Highway, Redcliffe, T08-9479 5208, www.britz.com*; **Getabout** ① *T02-9528 8015, www.getaboutoz.com*; **Maui** ① *471 Great Eastern Highway, Redcliffe, T08-9479 5208, www.maui-rentals.com*; **Discover West** ① *T08-6263 6475, www.discoverwest.com.au*; **Wicked** ① *T1800 246 869, www.wicked campers.com.au*. The latter are proving immensely popular with the backpacker set. However, they may not suit everyone (you'll see what we mean).

Swags

Swags are large lined pieces of canvas that enclose a thin mattress and sleeping bag, for outdoor use, placed directly on the ground. They are very much a part of Australian folklore and are still widely used in the country. There's nothing quite like lying in bed and watching the sun rise in the morning as the cockatoos screech overhead. The main disadvantages to swags are their weight and the space they take up, and also that they are open to the elements and insects.

Eating and drinking

Food

The quintessential image of Australian cooking may be of throwing some meat on the barbie but Australia actually has a dynamic and vibrant cuisine all its own. Freed from the bland English 'meat and two veg' straitjacket in the 1980s by the skills and cuisines of Chinese, Thai, Vietnamese, Italian, Greek, Lebanese and other immigrants, Australia has developed a fusion cuisine that takes elements from their cultures and mixes them into something new and original. Asian ingredients are easily found in major cities because of the country's high Asian population and might include coriander, lemongrass, chilli, and Thai basil. Australia makes its own dairy products so cheese or cream may come from Tasmania's King Island or Margaret River. Of course there is also plenty of seafood, including some creatures that will be unfamiliar to most travellers like the delicious crustaceans: bugs, yabbies, and crayfish (lobster). Mussels, oysters and abalone are all also harvested locally. Fish is a treat too; try the firm white flesh of snapper, dhufish, coral trout and red emperor. WA's isolation and clean environment also ensures that all these ingredients taste as good as possible.

Restaurant price codes

🍴🍴🍴 $45 and over   🍴🍴 $35-44   🍴 $34 and under

Prices refer to a two-course meal (starter plus main course) excluding drinks and service charges.

Freshness is the other striking quality of this cuisine, dubbed **Modern Australian**. This is achieved by using produce from the local area, and cooking it in a way that preserves the food's intrinsic flavour. The food shines for itself without being smothered in heavy or dominating sauces. Native animals are sometimes used, such as kangaroo, emu and crocodile, and native plants that Aboriginal people have been eating for thousands of years such as quandong, wattle seed or lemon myrtle leaf.

While you're licking your lips with anticipation: a word of warning. This gourmet experience is mostly restricted to Perth and the largest towns. There are pockets of foodie heaven in the southwest, but these are usually associated with wine regions and are the exception rather than the rule.

There are a few special foods that Australians produce and treasure and that can be found pretty much throughout WA. The **meat pie** is the favourite Australian fast food, about the size of your palm and filled with mince or steak and gravy. Quality can vary from soggy cardboard to something a French pastry chef wouldn't be ashamed of. If tempted, your best bet is a fresh one from a bakery rather than a mass-produced one (sealed in a little plastic bag) that sits in a shop's warming oven all day. **Fish and chips** are also popular and these are often good in Australia because the fish is fresh and only light vegetable oils are used for frying.

Vegemite spread is a dark and sticky yeast extract that looks a bit like axle grease. It's the Aussie equivalent of British Marmite, though fans of one usually detest the other. **Tim Tams** are a thick chocolate biscuit, very similar to the Brits' Penguin and reputedly the country's best-selling snack. What Brits call crisps, Aussies call chips ('hot chips' are fried chips), with **Twisties** a very Australian favourite.

Damper is bread made of flour, salt and water, best baked out bush in the ashes of a campfire. Nothing beats warm damper slathered with jam and butter. Another Aussie baking favourite is the **lamington**: a block of sponge that has been dipped in chocolate and rolled in coconut. The **pavlova** is a classic Australian dessert, created for the visit of Russian ballerina, Anna Pavlova. The 'pav' is like a cake-sized meringue, served topped with whipped cream and fresh fruit. It is rarely consumed without an argument about whether it was actually invented in Australia or New Zealand. One great icon associated with the outback campfire is **Billy Tea**. It is the fiendishly simple concept of putting a few eucalyptus leaves in with the brew to add that distinctive Aussie flavour. To mix the flavour of the tea leaf with the eucalypt the 'billy can' is held in the hand and swung a couple of times from the shoulders. This is quite a delicate art and can, for the uninitiated, result in considerable drama when the handle breaks.

The Aussie barbie

"Throw another shrimp on the barbie." The image is very familiar to travellers well before they arrive, and for once this is no myth. Aussies love a BBQ, and many households will have a couple a week as a matter of course. Public BBQs are common, often found in town and national parks, and beach foreshores. Unless free, a $0.20, $0.50 or $1 coin will get you 15-30 minutes of heat. You'll need to bring your own utensils. At private BBQs, bringing your own meat and alcohol is the norm, with hosts usually providing salads, bread and a few extra snags (sausages).

Drink

Australian **wine** is now imported in huge quantities into Europe and the USA. The industry has a creditable history in such a young country, with several wineries boasting a tradition of a century or more, but it is only in the last 25 years that Australia has become one of the major players on the international scene. The price of wine is unexpectedly high given the relatively low cost of food and beer. Even those from Britain will find Australian wines hardly any cheaper at the very cellar door than back home in the supermarket. The joy of Australian wine, however, is in its variety and quality. There are no restrictions, as there are in parts of Europe, on what grape varieties are grown where, when they are harvested and how they are blended. The 'Mediterranean' climate of much of the south of the country is very favourable for grape-growing, and the soil is sufficient to produce a high-standard grape.

Wineries range in size from vast concerns to one-person operations producing a few hundred bottles a year. Cellars range from modern marble and glass temples to venerable, century-old former barns of stone and wood. Some will open for a Saturday afternoon, others every day. In some you'll be lucky to get half a dry cracker to go with a taste, others boast some of the best restaurants in the country. A few are in small town high streets, others are set in hectares of exquisitely designed and maintained gardens. The wonderful thing is that this tremendous mix of styles is found within most of the regions, making a day or two's tasting expedition a scenic and cultural as well as an Epicurean delight. WA has a handful of wine regions, one as far north as Geraldton and several along the south coast. The biggest are the **Swan Valley**, just outside Perth, and **Margaret River**, which is spread over much of the northern half of the Cape-to-Cape region. The latter is one of the most pleasant wine regions in the country. ▶▶ See page 47 for details of operators offering wine-tasting tours.

The big two **beer** brands of WA are **Swan** and **Emu**, both are middle-of-the-road beers available in full and mid-strengths. The state also has a number of small independent brewers, one or two of which are becoming well known even outside the state. These include long-established **Matilda Bay**, producers of the popular **Redback**, and **Little Creatures** who are a little more creative than most of their peers and have a wonderful brewery/bar/restaurant/gallery in Fremantle. Pubs producing their own exceptionally good beers include the **Rose & Crown** in Guildford (see page 116), and **Matso's** in Broome (see page 316). Beer is usually served in a 7 oz 'middy', though you can also ask for a 10 oz 'pot' or in some pubs a regular British-style pint. Beer tends to be around 4-5% alcohol, with the popular and surprisingly pleasant tasting 'mid' varieties about 3.5%, and 'light' beers about 2-2.5%. Drink-driving laws are strict, and the best bet is to not drink alcohol at all if you are driving. As well as being available on draught in pubs, beer is also available from bottleshops (or 'bottle-os') in cases (or 'slabs') of 24-36 cans ('tinnies' or 'tubes') or bottles ('stubbies') of 375 ml each. This is by *far* the cheapest way of buying beer (often under $1.50 per can or bottle).

Eating out

Restaurants are common even in smaller towns. It is a general, but by no means concrete rule of thumb that the smaller the town the lower the quality, though not usually the price. Chinese and Thai restaurants are very common, with most other cuisines appearing only in the larger towns and cities. In Perth and Fremantle you will find everything from Mexican to Mongolian, Jamaican to Japanese. Corporate hotels and motels almost all have attached restaurants as do traditional pubs which also serve counter meals. Some may have a more imaginative menu or better-quality fare than the local restaurants. Most restaurants are licensed for the consumption of alcohol. Some are BYO only, in which case you bring wine or beer and the restaurant provides glasses. Despite the corkage fee this still makes for a better deal than drinking alcohol in fully licensed premises. European-style cafés are only rarely found in the country, and as in many Western countries the distinction between cafés, bistros and restaurants is blurred.

If you can't do without your burgers or southern-fried chicken or fish and chips then fear not. Australians have taken to fast food as enthusiastically as anywhere else in the world. Alongside these are food courts, found in the shopping malls of cities and larger towns. These have several takeaway options, usually including various Asian cuisines, surrounding a central space equipped with tables and chairs. Also in the budget bracket are the delis and milk bars, also serving hot takeaways, together with sandwiches, cakes and snacks. These make up a fair proportion of the country's cafés, with a few seats inside and often out on the pavement.

If you cook for yourself you'll find just about everything in an Aussie supermarket that you would find in Europe or the USA, and at very reasonable prices. An excellent meal for two can easily be put together for under $25.

Ten great bars and pubs

Bush Shack Brewery, Dunsborough, page 166.
Clancy's Fish Pub, Fremantle, page 101.
Cowaramup Brewing Company, Cowaraup, page 168.
Divers Tavern, Broome, page 317.
The Garden, Leederville, page 79.

Hula Bula Bar, Perth, page 77.
Little Creatures, Fremantle, page 101.
Matso's Broome Brewery, Broome, page 316.
The White Star, Albany, page 222.
Whim Creek Hotel, Whim Creek, page 293.

Entertainment

As in most Western nations, much of the country's entertainment is provided by its **pubs** and **bars**. Not only are they a social meeting point but many put on regular live music, DJs, karaoke and quiz nights. The typical Aussie pub is a solid brick and wood affair with wide first-floor verandas extending across the front, and sometimes down the sides as well. These usually have separate public and lounge bars, a bottleshop (off-licence) off to the side, and increasingly a separate 'bar' full of pokies (slot machines or one-armed bandits). The public bar often doubles as a TAB betting shop. Pubs and bars vary as much in style as anywhere in the western world. Some pubs are rough as guts and a stranger venturing in is guaranteed a hard stare. Others go out of their way to make a visitor feel welcome. Some haven't seen a paintbrush since the day they were built, others have been beautifully renovated in styles ranging from modern to authentic outback, saloon to the gimmicky Irish. In some medium-sized towns they also operate a club or discotheque. True **nightclubs** will only be found in the cities and larger towns, and then usually only open a few nights of the week. They do generally charge an entrance fee, usually around $10-20, though entry will commonly be free on some mid-week nights or before a certain time.

The **cinema** is popular in Australia and some will have outdoor screens with either deckchair seating or drive-in slots. Expect to pay $15-20 for an adult ticket, but look out for early week or pre-1800 specials. Every big city in the country has its major **casino**. Most are open 24 hours a day and, as well as offering gaming tables and rank upon rank of pokies, also have live music venues and good-value food halls and restaurants.

Other indoor pursuits found in most large towns and cities include ten-pin bowling, bingo, karting, snooker and pool halls, and large recreational centres offering everything from swimming to squash, basketball to badminton.

Festivals and events

Most major events and festivals are held in and around Perth, where nearly three quarters of Western Australians live. The year kicks off with the **Hopman Cup**, www.hopmancup. com.au, an international tennis championship that attracts some big tennis names with its unusual format: teams of one male and one female player representing eight nations competing in a 'round robin' format. It is held at Perth's Burswood Dome over New Year. The arts year starts in January-February with the biggest and the best: **Perth International Arts Festival**, www.perthfestival.com.au. This includes local and international theatre, opera, dance, visual arts, film and music. Down in Margaret River the main event of the summer is the **Leeuwin Estate Concert**, www.leeuwinestate.com.au, held over a weekend in February, when sees musical performances given in the lovely grounds of this premium winery. Attracting quite a different crowd, the **Margaret River Salomon Masters** international surfing competition is held at Prevelly over a week in mid-April. Waves are also the focus of the **Avon Descent** in early August, a 133-km whitewater competition on the Avon River from Northam to Perth. Up north, Broome celebrates the Festival of the Pearl, **Shinju Matsuri**, for a week in late August or early September. Events include parades, dragon boat racing and the Shinju Ball. In spring, wildflowers are out all over the state but if you are short of time you can see many varieties at the **Kings Park Festival**, held in September. In the southwest, the **Bridgetown Blues Festival** is held in late November. See www.westernaustralia.com, for exact dates of forthcoming events.

Public holidays

New Year's Day 1 Jan; **Australia Day** 26 Jan 2011, 26 Jan 2012, 28 Jan 2013; **Labour Day,** 7 Mar 2011, 5 Mar 2012, 4 Mar 2013; **Good Friday**, 22 Apr 2011, 6 Apr 2012;

Easter Monday, 25 Apr 2011, 9 Apr 2012; **Anzac Day**, 25 and 26 Apr 2011, 25 Apr 2012; **Foundation Day**, 6 Jun 2011, 4 Jun 2012; **Queen's Birthday**, 3 Oct 2011, 1 Oct 2012; **Christmas Day** 25 Dec; **Boxing Day** 26 Dec.

Shopping

Tourist shops exploit the cute and cuddly factor of Australian native mammals, so most tourist merchandise seems to consist of soft toy kangaroos and koalas and brightly coloured clothing featuring the same creatures. Other typical items perpetuate the corny Australian stereotypes. Beware of hats strung with corks; not only will you be slapped every five seconds and look foolish but no Australian has ever been spotted wearing one. Corkless **hats**, however, are a popular and practical souvenir, particularly the distinctively Australian *akubras*, made from felt in muddy colours. Along the same lines, stockman's **clothing** made by **RM Williams** is also popular and very good quality. Two of the company's bestsellers are elastic-sided boots and moleskins (soft brushed-cotton trousers cut like jeans). The **Driza-bone** long oilskin raincoat is also an Aussie classic. Australian surfwear is sought after worldwide and is a good buy while in the country. Look for labels such as **Ripcurl, Quiksilver, Mambo** and **Billabong**.

Australia is a good place to shop for **jewellery**, and WA is one of the world's greatest producers of gold, pearls and diamonds. There are many talented craftspeople making exquisite metal and beadwork. The widest range will be available in the cities but, as in most countries, products are often cheapest at the source and a wonderful memento of place. Look for **pearls** in Broome or champagne-coloured Argyle **diamonds** from the Kimberley.

In the tourist shops Aboriginal art designs are as ubiquitous as cuddly toys and printed on everything from T-shirts to tea-towels. Some of these designs can be beautiful but be aware that many articles have no link to Aboriginal people and do not benefit them directly check the label. **Desert Designs** is a successful label printing the stunning designs of the late, great Sandy Desert artist Jimmy Pike on silk scarves and sarongs. It is possible to buy genuine Aboriginal art and craft but it is more commonly available in country areas close to Aboriginal communities or from Aboriginal-owned or operated enterprises. This applies more to craft items such as **didgeridoos** and **scorched carvings** than paintings and of course there are reputable vendors everywhere but if in doubt ask for more information. Art and crafts bought from reputable sources ensures that the money ends up in the artist's pocket and supports Aboriginal culture, skills and self-reliance.

Many people are keen to buy an **Aboriginal dot painting**, usually acrylic on canvas. Also note that there are different styles of Aboriginal art, often depending on the region the artist comes from. For example, the x-ray paintings on bark only come from Arnhem Land. The best Aboriginal paintings sell for many thousands but there are also many thousands of average paintings sold for a few hundred dollars. A good painting will cost at least $800-1500. Simple works on canvas can be as little as $100 and make good souvenirs. Visit public and private galleries where you can see work of the highest quality – you may not be able to afford it but you'll learn something of what makes a good piece of Aboriginal art. Some of the qualities to look for are fine application, skilful use of colour and a striking design. The major cities all have commercial galleries selling Aboriginal art.

Responsible travel

One of Australia's main attractions is the natural environment and its wildlife, and there are many opportunities for eco-tourism.

Fire is a critical issue in Western Australia's hot, dry environments where only a spark is needed to create a fire that can get out of control and destroy an area the size of a small country, perhaps threatening lives and property. For this reason, in some areas, there are total fire bans. In extreme circumstances a national park, scenic attraction or walking trail may be closed because the risk of fire is so high. Fire bans or restrictions usually apply in summer (November-March) in the south and during the late dry season in the north (July-November). Check restrictions before travel with the nearest parks, shire, police or VIC as they may affect your preparations.

It is also good practice to keep your walking or camping gear clean between different environments, particularly in the southern forest areas affected by **dieback** (*Phytophthora cinnamomi*), a fungus that attacks the roots of plants. It is spread when soil or roots are moved, possibly via your boots, car or tent. Dieback areas are usually closed to the public but boot-cleaning stations are provided for high-risk walking areas and tracks.

Travellers in Western Australia will also come across '**sacred sites**', areas of religious importance to indigenous people, and naturally it is important to respect any restrictions that may apply to these areas. Permission is usually required to enter an Aboriginal community and you may be asked to comply with restrictions, such as a ban on alcohol. If you visit a community, or travel through Aboriginal land, respect the privacy of Aboriginal people and never take photographs without asking first.

How big is your footprint?

- Follow the minimal impact bushwalking code for walking and camping. Details can be obtained from any park office. Also see **Leave No Trace Australia**, www.lnt.org.au.
- Choose a responsible operator. **Ecotourism Association of Australia**, T07-3252 1530, www.ecotourism. org.au, promotes ecologically sustainable and responsible
- products and tourism.
- Try not to drive at dawn, dusk or at night, both to avoid killing native animals and for your own safety.
- Water is a precious resource in Australia – don't waste it or pollute it. In dry conditions camp away from waterholes so that animals are not afraid to approach the water.
- Carrying sufficient water, food and fuel and appropriate clothing or equipment may save your life and avoid danger, expense and inconvenience for those who might otherwise have to rescue you.
- If you have to pass through gates in national parks or on private property the rule is 'leave them as you find them'.
- There are many opportunities for recycling glass, plastic, paper, etc. Look out for recycling bins in supermarket car parks.
- Don't feed wild animals.

For more about environmental issues contact the **Australian Conservation Foundation** ① T1300 473 946, www.acfonline.org.au or **The Wilderness Society** ① *T08-9420 7255, www.wilderness.org.au.* The quarterly wilderness magazine *Wild* is also a good source of information and is available at newsagents.

Local customs and laws

Anyone travelling from Western Europe or the USA will find Australia's laws and customs very similar to their own, with few unusual prohibitions. In particular laws against recreational drugs are severe and are closely policed. European visitors may find traffic penalties being more harshly enforced; there is very little leeway given on speeding and none on alcohol consumption, and parking attendants are ever alert (watch out for 'rear to kerb only' parking spots). Smoking is now illegal where food is publicly available and on public transport.

Many towns have banned the consumption of alcohol on selected beaches, in parks and in other public spaces; if this is the case signs will be conspicuous. There are several sensible guidelines for behaviour within national parks, forests and on Aboriginal land and many of these are backed by the force of law. In particular are prohibitions against fires during 'fire bans'; again look for signs. Tipping is not the norm in Australia, but a discretionary 5-10% tip for particularly good service will be appreciated.

Essentials A-Z

Accident and emergency

Dial 000 for the emergency services.
The 3 main professional emergency services are supported by several others, including the **State Emergency Service** (SES), **Country Fire Service** (CFS), **Surf Life Saving Australia** (SLSA), **Sea-search and Rescue**, and **St John's Ambulance**. The SES is prominent in co-ordinating search-and-rescue operations. The CFS provides invaluable support in fighting and controlling bush fires. These services, though professionally trained, are mostly provided by volunteers. Seasonal fire bans are managed by local shires. Contact the shire directly or the nearest VIC for advice.

Children

Australia is a wonderful place to take children. Don't be put off by far-fetched stories of child-eating snakes or man-eating sharks. If children are aware and supervised, Australia will provide a memorable holiday experience for all the right reasons.

If you are concerned about the threat of the rumoured nasty native wildlife a trip to Perth Zoo, or indeed any of the numerous wildlife parks around the state, will soon put your mind at rest that prevalent as it might be it's unlikely to feast on your kids. Wildlife in Australia, whether captive or not, offers one of the greatest natural history educational platforms for children on the planet and encounters can become any foreign child's fondest memory.

As far as accommodation is concerned the vast majority of establishments, beyond the usual exclusive retreats for couples, welcome kids and offer reasonable financial concessions. Tourist-based attractions and activities too, many of which are directed at the children's market, usually offer reduced rates for children and family concessions. When it comes to eating out, like most developed countries, some eateries welcome children, while others don't. In general you are advised to stick to eateries that are obviously child-friendly or ask before making a booking.

In summary there are a multitude of excellent venues to take children or to keep them happily entertained.

Customs and duty free

The limits for duty-free goods brought into the country include: 2.25 litres of any alcoholic drink (beer, wine or spirits), and 250 cigarettes, or 250 g of cigars or tobacco. There are various import restrictions, mainly there to help protect Australia's already heavily hit ecology. These primarily involve live plants and animals, plant and animal materials (including all items made from wood) and foodstuffs. If in doubt, confine wooden and plant goods to well-worked items and bring processed food only (even this may be confiscated, though Marmite is accepted with a knowing smile). Muddy walking boots may also attract attention. Declare any such items for inspection on arrival if you are unsure. See www.customs.gov.au for more details.

Disabled travellers

Disabled travellers to Western Australia will find that although there is a good range of facilities meeting their needs, they can be spread quite thinly, especially outside the major cities. Although all public buildings have to meet certain government standards, the standards actually in place can vary. High-profile sights and attractions, and even parks, have good access. The key to successful travel is planning, and there are several organizations who can help.

As with many major airlines Qantas, T1800 652660, has considerable experience with disabled passengers. If you have to be accompanied by a support person on any internal flight, they offer the passenger and the nominated carer a 50% discount off the full-economy or business-class fare. A Carer Concession Photo ID is required. Contact NICAN (see below) for further details. Guide dogs may be brought into Australia without being subject to a quarantine period if the dog has the correct certification. Contact the Australian Quarantine & Inspection Service, T02-6272 3933, www.daff.gov.au/aqis, for further details. The interstate railways generally have facilities for the disabled but public transport in many states is not always well designed unless you have assistance. The major interstate bus operators are pleased to accommodate disabled travellers but prefer notice, though few coaches are equipped with lifts or lowered floors. The major hire car companies have adapted vehicles available. Disabled overseas and interstate parking permits are valid in WA.

All Transperth train carriages are accessible to passengers with disabilities, however, not all the train stations are. Perth Central Area Transit System (CATS) buses all have low-floor access, and some have extendable ramps. There are 2 wheelchair spaces on each bus. See the Transperth website, www.transperth.wa.gov.au or call T136213, for a list of bus routes outside the CAT area that are serviced by accessible buses.

The (unfortunately ageing and hard-to-find) guidebook *Easy Access Australia: A Travel Guide to Australia* by Bruce Cameron (ISBN 095775101X), is useful. The following organizations are helpful: NDS, 1/59 Walters Drive, Osborne Park, WA 6017, T08 9242 5544, www.nds.org.au, is the national industry association for disability services. NICAN, Unit 5, 48 Brookes St, Mitchell ACT 2911, T02 6241 1220, www.nican.com.au, provides information

on recreation, tourism, sport and the arts. People with Disabilities, T08-9485 8900, www.pwdwa.org, is a consumer lobby group, which also provides information for travellers, including accessible accommodation and transport. Many organizations are equipped for handling TTY calls. For information contact: Australian Communication Exchange (ACE), T07-3815 7600 or T07-3815 7602 (TTY), www.ace info.net.au, a free service for TTY users, relaying messages between TTY and hearing phone users. Telstra Disability Services, T1800 068424, T1800 808981 (TTYs), www.telstra.com.au/disability.

Electricity

The current in Australia is 240/250v AC. Plugs have 2- or 3-blade pins and adaptors are widely available.

Embassies and commissions

For a list of Australian embassies and high commissions worldwide, see www.embassy.gov.au.

Gay and lesbian travellers

Gay & Lesbian Community Services, T08-9486 9855, www.glcs.org.au, can help with general travel and accommodation advice. Perth's Pride Parade, inaugurated in 1990 and held the last 2 weeks of every Oct, has in excess of 5000 participants and over 75,000 spectators. Followed by a popular dance party, Pride also includes theatre, exhibitions and a Fair Day. Perth's dedicated gay and lesbian publication is *Shout*, a free newspaper available from city music or book shops. International Gay & Lesbian Travel Association (IGLTA), www.iglta.com, is also a good place to go for travel advice. There are several national magazines keeping lesbians and gay men in touch with what's going on, including *Lesbians on the Loose* and *DNA*. Check www.qbeds.com, for lesbian and gay-friendly accommodation. See also www.gayaustraliaguide.com.

Health

Australia is known as the 'lucky country' and in health terms it is. There are few nasty diseases and the healthcare facilities are of a high standard. The national, government-funded healthcare scheme is called **Medicare**. Australia has a reciprocal arrangement with a handful of countries that allows citizens of those countries to receive free 'immediately necessary medical treatment' under the Medicare scheme. The arrangements with New Zealand and the Republic of Ireland provide visitors to Australia with free care as a public patient in public hospitals and subsidized medicines under the Pharmaceutical Benefits Scheme. In addition to these benefits, visitors from Finland, Italy, Malta, the Netherlands, Sweden and the UK also enjoy subsidized out-of-hospital treatment (ie visiting a doctor). All visitors to Australia are, however, strongly advised to get medical insurance.

See your doctor or travel clinic at least 6 weeks before your departure for advice on health risks. Make sure you have travel insurance, get a dental check (especially if you are going to be away for more than a month), know your own blood group and if you suffer a long-term condition such as diabetes or epilepsy, make sure someone knows or that you have a **Medic Alert** bracelet/necklace.

Health risks

Dengue fever can be contracted throughout Australia. In travellers this can cause a severe flu-like illness, which includes symptoms of fever, lethargy, enlarged lymph glands and muscle pains. It starts suddenly, lasts for 2-3 days, seems to get better for 2-3 days and then kicks in again for another 2-3 days. It is usually all over in an unpleasant week. The local children are prone to the much nastier haemorrhagic form of the disease, which causes them to bleed from internal organs, mucous membranes and often leading to death. The traveller's version of the disease is self-limiting and forces rest and recuperation on the sufferer. The mosquitoes that carry the dengue virus bite during the day unlike the malaria mosquitoes. Repellent application and covered limbs are a 24-hr issue.

Hepatitis means inflammation of the liver. Viral causes of the disease can be acquired anywhere in Australia. The most obvious symptom is a yellowing of your skin or the whites of your eyes. However, prior to this all that you may notice is itching and tiredness. Early on, depending on the type of hepatitis, a vaccine or immunoglobulin may reduce the duration of the illness. Hepatitis A is transmitted through food or water contaminated by faeces; a pre-travel vaccine is the best prevention. Hepatitis B (for which there is also a vaccine) is spread through blood and unprotected sexual intercourse, both of these can be avoided. Unfortunately there is no vaccine for Hepatitis C or the increasing alphabetical list of other Hepatitis viruses.

Snakes and other poisonous things are always a risk in Australia. A bite itself does not mean that anything has been injected in to you. However, a commonsense approach is to clean the area of the bite (never have it sutured early on) and get someone to take you to a medical facility as soon as possible. Keep calm and still: the more energy you expend the faster poisons spread. Do not try to catch the snake or spider but it is helpful if you can described what it looks like. For some snake bites a knowledgeable first aider can provide appropriate bandaging. Specialist anti-venoms will be administered by an experienced doctor.

In terms of **sexual health**, unprotected sex can obviously spread HIV, Hepatitis B and C, gonorrhea (green discharge), chlamydia (nothing to see but may cause painful

Keeping safe in the water

On the beach there is little to trouble holidaymakers who stick to the shore and swim between the patrolled flags, but you must be aware of hidden dangers. The main one is the rip – a strong, offshore undertow that can sweep even waders off their feet, submerge them and drown them astonishingly quickly. Always look out for signs indicating common rip areas, and ask locals if you are at all unsure. See the **Surf Life Saving Australia** website at www.slsa.asn.au, for more information.

Much publicized, but out of all proportion, is the danger from sharks. There are a handful of shark attacks in Australia each year, and usually one or two are fatal, but this must be balanced against the number of times someone goes for a swim or surf each year – hundreds of millions. Several other sea creatures are far more likely to do you harm, biggest of these are the estuarine crocodiles ('salties') of the far north. If given the opportunity they will ambush and eat any animal or person careless enough to stray near or into their river or estuary. Always check whether a waterhole or river is likely to be a crocodilian home, and if in doubt assume it is. Australian coastal waters are also home to a host of fish, jellyfish, octopuses, urchins, coral and even molluscs that can inflict extremely painful, sometimes lethal stings and bites.

Take precautions. Park rangers and the police are good sources of information. If you have the time learn about the various local poisonous marine creatures, their tell-tale wound-marks and symptoms, and the correct procedure for treatment. See page 41. Tell someone on-shore you are going for a swim. Avoid swimming alone, and keep swimming partners in sight. While snorkelling or diving, do not touch either creatures or coral. Even minor coral scratches can lead to infections, and it doesn't do the coral any good either. Wear a wetsuit or T-shirt and shorts even if the water is warm. This will lessen the effect of any sting and help protect against the sun. Wear waterproof sunscreen, and reapply frequently. If wading around in shallow water, particularly near reefs, wear a pair of old trainers or waterproof sandals. A large number of the little beasties that can do you serious harm do so when you tread on them (they don't enjoy the experience much either). If you are bitten or stung, get out of the water, carefully remove and keep any spine or tissue, seek advice as to appropriate immediate treatment and apply it, and quickly seek medical help. When jumping off rocks into water, always first check that the depth is sufficient.

urination and later female infertility), painful recurrent herpes, syphilis and warts, just to name a few. You can cut down the risk by using condoms, a femidom or avoiding sex altogether. Commercial sex workers in Australia have high levels of HIV. If you do have sex, consider getting a sexual health check on your return home.

Take care with **sun protection**. Sunburn is painful and followed by flaking of skin. Aloe vera gel is a good pain reliever. Long-term sun damage leads to a loss of elasticity of skin and the development of pre-cancerous lesions. Many years later a mild or a very malignant form of cancer may develop. The milder basal cell carcinoma, if detected early, can be treated by cutting it out or freezing it. The much nastier malignant melanoma may have already spread to bone and brain at the time that it is first noticed. SPF stands for Sun Protection Factor. The higher the SPF the greater the

Keeping safe on land

There are numerous creatures with very poisonous bites on land. Most will only bite, however, if trodden on, cornered or harassed. The most common poisonous spider is the tiny, shy redback, which has a shiny black body with distinct red markings. It regularly sets up shop under rocks or in garden sheds and garages. Outside toilets are also a favourite. There are dozens of venomous snake species. Few are actively aggressive and even those only during certain key times of year, such as mating season, but all are easily provoked and for many an untreated bite can be fatal.

The main dangers while bushwalking are dehydration from a lack of water, heatstroke, and getting lost. Before setting out seek advice about how to access the start and finish of the track, the terrain you are planning to traverse, how long it will take given your party's minimum fitness level and the likely weather conditions, and prepare accordingly. Park rangers and the police are good sources of information. Learn about the various local poisonous snakes, their seasonal habits, tell-tale wound-marks and symptoms, and the correct procedure for treatment.

Plan, if possible, to walk in the early morning or late afternoon when a gorgeous golden glow often takes hold just before sunset. These are also the best times for viewing wildlife. Take a decent map of the area, a compass, and a first-aid kit. Take full precautions for the sun, but also be prepared for wet or cold weather. Take plenty of water, in hot weather at least one litre for every hour you plan to walk (a frozen plastic bottle will ensure cold water for hours). On long-distance walks take something to purify stream and standing water as giardia is present in some areas. Wear stout walking shoes and socks. Tell someone where you are going and when you plan to get back. Avoid striding through long grass and try to keep to tracks. If the path is obscured, make plenty of noise as you walk. If you do see a snake, give it a wide berth.

If you need to squat to go to the toilet, or are collecting firewood, bash the undergrowth around your position. If you do get bitten by either a spider or snake stay calm and still, apply pressure to the bite area and wind a compression bandage around it (except for redback bites). Remain as still as possible and keep the limb immobile. Seek urgent medical attention. A description of the creature, and residual venom on the victim's skin, will help with swift identification and so treatment. Anti-venom is available for most spider and snake bites. Avoid walking alone, and always keep walking partners in sight. Keep to paths and avoid cliff edges.

protection. However, do not use higher factors just to stay out in the sun longer. 'Flash frying' (desperate bursts of excessive exposure) is known to increase the risks of skin cancer. Follow the Australians' with their Slip, Slap, Slop campaign.

Australia has the 4th lowest level in the world for **tuberculosis** and is well protected by health screens before people can settle there. Symptoms include a cough, tiredness, fever and lethargy. Have a BCG vaccination before you go and see a doctor early if you cough blood or have a persistent cough, fever or unexplained weight loss.

Underwater health if you go diving make sure that you are fit do so. **British Scuba Association** (BSAC) in the UK (T01513-506200, www.bsac.com) can put you in touch with doctors who do medical examinations. Check that any dive company you use know what they are doing, have appropriate certification from BSAC or PADI, (www.padi.com), and that the equipment is well maintained. Protect your feet from cuts, beach dog parasites (larva migrans) and sea urchins. The latter are almost impossible to remove but can be dissolved with lime or vinegar. Keep an eye out for secondary infection. See the boxes on pages 42 and 43 for further details about keeping safe on land and in the sea.

Medical services

Medical services are listed in the Directory section of the relevant areas in this guide. There are numerous hospitals, pharmacies and medical centres across the west coast.

Useful websites

www.btha.org British Travel Health Association (UK). The official website of an organization of travel health professionals. **www.cdc.gov** US Government site that gives excellent advice on travel health and details of disease outbreaks. **www.fitfortravel.scot.nhs.uk** A-Z of vaccine/health advice for each country. **www.who.int** The WHO Blue Book lists the diseases of the world.

Insurance

It's a very good idea to take out some form of travel insurance, wherever you're travelling from. This should cover you for theft or loss of possessions and money, the cost of medical and dental treatment, cancellation of flights, delays in travel arrangements, accidents, missed departures, lost baggage, lost passport and personal liability and legal expenses. Also check on inclusion of 'dangerous activities' such as climbing, diving, skiing, horse riding, even trekking, if you plan on doing any.

You should always read the small print carefully. Not all policies cover ambulance, helicopter rescue or emergency flights

home. Find out if your policy pays medical expenses direct to the hospital or doctor, or if you have to pay and then claim the money back later. If the latter applies, make sure you keep all records. There are a variety of policies to choose from, so it's best to shop around. Your travel agent can advise on the best deals.

If you are unfortunate enough to have something stolen, make sure you get a copy of the police report, as you will need this to substantiate your claim.

Companies include: **Access America**, T1800 284 8300, www.accessamerica.com. (In USA). **Age Concern**, T0800 009966, www.ageconcern.org.uk. (For older travellers in UK). **Columbus**, T0870 033 9988, www.columbusdirect.com. (In UK). **Direct Travel Insurance**, T0845 605 2700, www.direct-travel.co.uk. (In UK). **Flexicover Group**, T0845 223 4520, www.flexicover.co.uk. (In UK). **STA**, T800 7814040, www.statravel.com. (In USA). **Travel Insurance Services**, T800 9371387, www.travelinsure.com. (In USA).

Internet

Internet access, and thus email, is widely available in hostels, hotels and cafés. Expect to pay $2-5 for 30 mins.

Media

The *West Australian* is published daily except Sun, general entertainment listings published daily in *Today* section. *The Australian* is the only national paper.

Foreign newspapers and magazines are widely available in the main urban centres. It is also possible to buy special weekly editions of British papers such as the *Daily Mail* and *The Guardian*. There are Asian editions of *Time* and *The Economist*.

There are 5 main television channels in Western Australia; the publicly funded

ABC and SBS, and the independent, commercial stations, **Channel 7** (called **GWN** in country regions), **Channel 9** (**WIN** in country regions) and **Channel 10**. The ABC aims for Australian high-quality content including many **BBC** programmes. The SBS focuses on multinational culture, current affairs, sport and film. The SBS has the best world news, shown daily at 1830.

The ABC broadcasts several national radio channels: **Radio National** features news, current affairs, culture and music; **Classic FM** is self-explanatory; and **Triple J** is aimed at a young, 'alternative' audience. There are also many local commercial radio stations that feature a mix of news, talk-back, and music.

Money

Exchange rates (May 2011):
1 Aus$ = US$1.05, £0.65, €0.75.
All dollars quoted in this guide are Australian unless specified otherwise.
The Australian dollar ($) is divided into 100 cents (c). Coins come in denominations of 5c, 10c, 20c, 50c, $1 and $2. Banknotes come in denominations of $5, $10, $20, $50 and $100.

Banks

The 4 major banks, **Westpac**, **Commonwealth**, **NAB** and **ANZ**, are usually the best places to change money (and traveller's cheques), though bureaux de change tend to have slightly longer opening hours and often open at weekends. Typical bank opening hours are Mon-Fri 0930-1630.

Cost of living/travelling

Accommodation, particularly outside Perth, is good value, though prices can rise uncomfortably in peak seasons. Eating out can be indecently cheap. Around $175 is enough to cover dinner for 2 at the very best restaurants in Perth and the bill at many still excellent establishments can be half that. Transport varies considerably in price and can

be a major factor in your travelling budget. Beer is about $5-8 a throw in pubs and bars, as is a neat spirit or glass of wine. Wine will generally be around 1½ times to double the price in restaurants as it would be from a bottleshop. The general cost of living in Australia is reckoned to be equivalent to the USA and slightly cheaper than the UK.

The minimum budget required, if staying in hostels or campsites, cooking for yourself, not drinking much and travelling relatively slowly is about $90 per person per day, but this isn't going to be a lot of fun. Going on the odd tour, travelling faster and eating out occasionally will raise this to a more realistic $110-140. Those staying in modest B&Bs, hotels and motels as couples, eating out most nights and taking a few tours will need to reckon on about $200-300 per person per day. Non-hostelling single travellers should budget on spending around 60-70% of what a couple would spend.

Debit and credit cards

You can withdraw cash from **ATMs** (cashpoints) with a debit or credit card issued by most international banks. Most hotels, shops, tourist operators and restaurants in Australia accept the major credit cards, though some places may charge for using them. When booking always check if an operator accepts them.

If you need money urgently, the quickest way to have it sent is to have it wired to the nearest bank via **Western Union**, T1800 173833, www.westernunion.com. Charges apply but on a sliding scale. Complete online services are available with **Travelex**, www.travelex.com.au. Money can also be wired by **Amex** or **Thomas Cook**, though this may take a day or 2, or transferred direct from bank to bank, but this can take several days. Within Australia money orders can be used to send money, www.auspost.com.au.

Discounts

Many forms of transport and most tourist sites and tours will give discounts to all or some of the following: students, backpackers, the unemployed, the aged (all grouped as 'concessions' in this guide) and children. Proof will be required, a passport is usually sufficient for children or the aged.

Traveller's cheques

The safest way to carry money is in traveller's cheques, though travellers' dependence on them is fast becoming superseded by the prevalence of ATMs. **American Express**, **Thomas Cook** and **Visa** are the cheques most commonly accepted. Remember to keep a record of the cheque numbers and the cheques you've cashed separate from the cheques themselves. Traveller's cheques are accepted for exchange in banks, large hotels, post offices and large gift shops. Some insist that at least a portion of the amount is in exchange for goods or services. Commission when cashing traveller's cheques is usually 1% or a flat rate. Hotel rates are often poor.

Opening hours

Office and shop hours are typically Mon-Fri 0830-1700. Many convenience stores and supermarkets are open daily. Late-night shopping is generally Thu or Fri. See also under Banks and Post offices.

Post

Most post offices are open Mon-Fri 0900-1700, and Sat 0900-1230. Sending a postcard, greeting card or 'small' letter (less than 130 x 240 mm, 5 mm thick and 250 g) anywhere in Australia is $0.60 and should arrive within 3 days. Airmail for postcards and greetings cards is $1.45 anywhere in the world, small letters (under 50 g) from $1.50 (USA/UK: $2.20). Parcels can be sent by sea or air. Most of the principal or main offices in major towns and cities offer **Post Restante** for those peripatetic and quixotic travellers with no fixed address who still receive physical post.

Safety

In Perth and the other major cities, as in almost any city in the world, there is always the possibility of muggings, alcohol-induced harassment or worse. The usual simple precautions apply, like keeping a careful eye and hand on belongings, not venturing out alone at night and avoiding dark, lonely areas. Footprint is a partner in the Foreign and Commonwealth Office's 'Know before you go' campaign, www.fco.gov.uk/travel.

Student travellers

If you're a student make sure you have identification as it will be a ticket to much in the way of discounted accommodation, tours and more. There are various official youth/ student ID cards available, including the widely recognized **International Student ID Card (ISIC)** and **International Youth Travel Card (IYTC)**, both available from www.isic.org. Also the **Euro 26 Card**, www.euro26.org, and **Go-25 Card**. Each conveys benefits from simply getting discounts, to emergency medical coverage and 24-hr hotlines. The cards are issued by student travel agencies and hostelling organizations. Backpackers will find a YHA or VIP membership card just as useful.

Tax

There are currently a number of **departure taxes** levied by individual airports (such as noise tax) and the government. All departure taxes are included in the cost of a ticket, but may not be included in a quote when you first enquire about the cost of a ticket. Almost all goods in Australia are subject to a **Goods and Services Tax (GST)** of 10%. Visitors from outside Australia will find certain shops can deduct the GST if you have a departure ticket.

Telephone

→ *Country code: +61. Western Australia*
code: 08, followed by an 8-digit number.
Most public payphones are operated by
Telstra, www.telstra.com.au. Some take
phonecards, available from newsagents and
post offices, and credit cards. A payphone call
within Australia requires $0.50. If you are
calling locally (within approximately 50 km)
this lasts indefinitely. **STD** calls outside this
area will use up your 50c in less than a minute
and cost about 1c a second thereafter.

There are no area phone codes, but you
will need to use a **state code** for numbers in:
ACT/NSW (02); VIC/TAS (03); QLD (07).

To call **Western Australia** from overseas,
dial the international prefix followed by 618,
then the 8-digit number. To call WA from
ACT/NSW/VIC/TAS/QLD, dial 08 followed by
the 8-digit number. You can access the
national database of telephone numbers
and their accompanying addresses at
www.whitepages.com.au. The *Yellow
Pages* is at www.yellowpages.com.au.

To call **overseas from Australia** dial 0011
followed by the country code. Country
codes include: **Republic of Ireland** 353; **New
Zealand** 64; **South Africa** 27; the **USA** and
Canada 1; the **UK** 44. By far the cheapest
way of calling overseas is to use an
international pre-paid phonecard (cannot
be used from a mobile phone, or some of
the blue and orange public phones), unless
you can find somewhere offering Skype.

Worth considering if you are in Australia
for any length of time is a **pre-paid mobile
phone**. Telstra and **Vodaphone** give the best
coverage and widely available for less than
$100. Calls are more expensive, of course.

Time

Western Standard Time: GMT+8 hrs. 1½ hrs
behind SA and the NT, 2 hrs behind the
eastern states. Daylight Saving from Apr-Oct
is GMT + 9 hrs.

Tour operators

In Australia
AAT Kings, www.aatkings.com, and APT,
www.aptouring.com.au, are the main
2 national, coach-based operators, both
offering comparable options.
Adventure Tours Australia, T08-8132 8230
or freecall T1800 068886, www.adventure
tours.com.au. Offers a variety of camping
and 4WD trips all around coastal WA;
expect to pay around $150-200 per day.
Australian Adventure Travel, T08-9248
2355 or freecall T1800 621625,
www.safaris.net.au. A WA-based company
that runs 4-9 day tours up the west coast
(Perth to Monkey Mia 4 days from $535,
Perth to Broome including Kalbarri, Ningaloo
Reef and Karijini, 9 days $1410), Exmouth
to Broome including Karijini (4 days $715)
and 5-14 day Kimberley trips, staying in
farm stays, cabins or camping.
DEC together with the **UWA**, see
www.naturebase.net (under Community/
Landscope) or contact T08-6488 2433,
extension@uwa.edu.au, organizes a number
of eco expeditions/Landscope research
expeditions each year where small numbers
of the general public are invited to join them.
Trips last 6-10 days, cost $300-500 per day,
and conditions are usually pretty basic.
Locations are, however, incredible and
activities usually revolve around turtle-
tagging or the identification of many
other animal or plant species.
Pinnacle Tours, T08-9417 5555 or freecall
T1800 046819, www.pinnacletours.com.au.
The most luxurious large local coach operator,
with several 1-day options to southwest
destinations (around $170), 2- to 5-day tours
around the southwest ($200 per day, 2-day
Margaret River daily, other tours depart
Sun-Tue), and an extensive range of longer
tours throughout WA ($150-200 per day).
Planet Perth, T08-8132 8294 or freecall
T1800 099533, www.planettours.com.au.
Operates fun and friendly tours for
backpackers and travellers, including the

southwest for 3 days (Thu, $375), the west coast (4 days, Sat, $490) and Perth–Karijini return (Sat, 9 days $1495).
ROC Tours, T1300 948911, www.cycle tours.com.au. Runs a number of 4- to 11-day mostly outback tours that let you cycle the best bits.
STA Travel, T134782, www.statravel. com.au, and **Travellers Contact Point**, 92 Barrack St, Perth, T02-9221 8744, www.travellers.com.au. Specializes in putting together itineraries incorporating bus, plane and train, with a high degree of flexibility.
Venture Winetours Australia, www.venturewinetours.com.au. Offers a wine-tasting tour of the Swan Valley.
Western Travel Bug, T08-9486 4222, www.travelbug.com.au. Makes use of budget hotels and motels on their 2- to 6-day southwest tours (around $160-200 per day). Also Midwest and Karijini tours plus local day tours.

In UK and Ireland
Australia Travel Centre, 43-45 Middle Abbey St, Dublin, Ireland, T3531-8047100, www.australia.ie. Good source of general advice for those travelling from Ireland.
Contiki, UK: T1300 266845, www.contiki.com. One of the world's largest travel companies catering primarily for the 18-35s market with affordable Australian options.
Travelbag, UK: T0871 703 4698, www.travelbag.co.uk. Reputable UK-based firm offering a good range of general and tailor-made trips to Australia at reasonable prices.
Wildlife Worldwide, UK: T0845 130 6982, www.wildlifeworldwide.com. One of the best wildlife-oriented global operators offering tailor-made, mainly small-group trips to Australia.

In USA
Abercrombie and Kent, 1520 Kensington Rd, Suite 212, Oak Brook, Illinois, T60523-2156, T800 554 7016, www.abercrombie kent.com. Well-established US company

offering a diverse range of luxury, locally guided global trips to Australia.
Earthwatch Research and Exploration, PO Box 75, Maynard, MA 01754, USA, T978 461 0081, www.earthwatch.org. Runs excellent eco-tourism trips to Australia in combination with conservation research on Australian wildlife.

Tourist information

Tourist offices, or **Visitor Information Centres** (VICs), can be found in all but the smallest Western Australian towns. Their locations, phone numbers, website or email addresses, and opening hours are listed in the relevant sections of this guide. In most larger towns they have to have met certain criteria to be officially *accredited*. This usually means that they have some paid staff and will almost certainly mean they are open daily 0900-1700 (except, usually, Christmas Day). Smaller offices may close at weekends, but given that many are run entirely by volunteers something to bear in mind when someone struggles to find an obscure piece of information the level of commitment to the visitor is impressive. All offices will provide information on accommodation, and local sights, attractions, and tours. Many will also have information on eating, local history and the environment, and sell souvenirs, guides and maps. Most will provide a free town map.

Weights and measures

All metric.

Women travellers

In Australia the concept of chauvinism and the archetypal Bruce and Sheila (the classic beer-drinking male and do-as-you-are-told spouse) is fast becoming an old-fashioned myth. Generally speaking women are given all due respect in all but the most backward of outback settlements.

For lone women travellers all the usual common-sense recommendations apply. Australia is a big place and given so much space it seems logical you may find yourself alone and 'out there' some of the time. Indeed, the occasional abduction and murder of male and female tourists, especially in the outback, does occur. So try to avoid getting yourself in that situation and always let people know about your intentions. Hitchhiking alone is not recommended for anybody, but especially women. Other than that, keep your wits and good company about you, especially at night.

Working in Western Australia

To work in Western Australia you will need an appropriate visa (or be a citizen of Australia or New Zealand). These are not easy to come by and your local Australian High Commission can advise on your likely eligibility. Under 30s may, however, be eligible for a temporary working holiday visa. You need a return air ticket or sufficient funds, plus sufficient funds for the first part of your holiday. What this actually means in cash terms depends on where you are travelling from your local Australian embassy can advise. The easiest work to get, though not to do, is generally fruit harvesting or packing. The pay isn't sensational, though hard workers can do alright, but it's sociable and can be fun. The majority of jobs available are fruit picking and tree planting, although there are also some professional, blue collar and service jobs. For information and advice on working in the state see **Workstay WA**, www.workstay.com.au, set up to help travellers on a working holiday visa. The website has a current job vacancies list. Alternatively try employment agency, **The Job Shop** with offices in Perth and Kununurra, T08-9228 1457, www.thejobshop.com.au.

Other outdoor work can also be found at farms and stations. In the cities work opportunities are usually tipped firmly in favour of women. The hospitality industry (hotels, pubs and bars) is the biggest employer of casual workers. Those with the right qualifications will find medical employment quite easy to come by. Jobs are advertised in local newspapers and on the internet, though the best place to start are the noticeboards of backpacker hostels, or contacting them in advance. If working is going to form a major part of your travels, or you are thinking of emigrating to Australia, then consider a publication such as *Live and Work in Australia* (ISBN 9781854584182). The following organizations are helpful: **Conservation Volunteers**, T1800 032501, www.conservationvolunteers.com.au, organizes volunteer conservation projects. Overnight costs are around $40 per day, including accommodation, food and travel. **National Harvest Labour Information Service,** T1800 062332, www.job search.gov.au/harvesttrail, provides info and opportunities for harvest work. **Visitoz**, T07-4168 6185, www.visitoz.org, puts you in touch with outback stations looking for workers. **Willing Workers on Organic Farms**, T03-5155 0218, www.wwoof.com.au, specializes in matching travellers with their 1400 affiliated farms and stations. The $55 membership gets you a guidebook on the scheme, friendly advice and insurance against accidental injury.

Visas and immigration

Visas are subject to change, so check first with your local Australian Embassy or High Commission. All travellers to Australia, except New Zealand citizens, must have a valid visa to enter Australia. These must be arranged prior to travel (allow 2 months) and cannot be organized at Australian airports. **Tourist visas** are free and are available from your local Australian Embassy or High Commission, or in some countries, in electronic format (an Electronic Travel Authority or ETA) from their websites, and from selected travel agents and airlines. Passport holders eligible to apply for an ETA include those from Austria, Belgium, Canada, Denmark, Finland, France, Germany, Greece, Hong Kong, the Irish Republic, Italy, Japan, Netherlands, Norway, Spain, Sweden, Switzerland, the UK and the USA. Tourist visas allow visits of up to 3 months within the year after the visa is issued. 6-month, multiple-entry tourist visas are also available to visitors from certain countries. Tourist visas do not allow the holder to work in Australia. See also www.immi.gov.au.

The **working holiday visa**, which must also be arranged prior to departure, is available to people aged 18 to 30 from certain countries that have reciprocal arrangements with Australia, including Canada, Denmark, France, Germany, Irish Republic, Italy, Japan, Korea, Netherlands, Norway, Sweden, Taiwan and the UK. The working holiday visa allows multiple entries for 1 year from first arrival. It is granted on the condition that the holder works for no more than 3 months for a single employer. Your local Australian Embassy or High Commission issues the visa, for which there is a charge. Application forms can be downloaded from www.immi.gov.au.

Contents

Perth

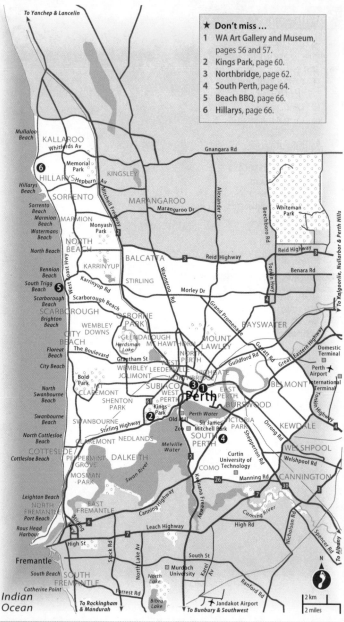

★ Don't miss ...
1 WA Art Gallery and Museum, pages 56 and 57.
2 Kings Park, page 60.
3 Northbridge, page 62.
4 South Perth, page 64.
5 Beach BBQ, page 66.
6 Hillarys, page 66.

One of the most isolated cities in the world, Perth is a green, clean and spacious city on the banks of the wide, blue Swan River. The city is about three times the size of Greater London (with an eighth of the population), contained by coastline to the west and the low Perth Hills of the Darling Range to the east. Although it is about the same age as Adelaide, there is little evidence of its past. It's a sparkling, modern place, reminiscent of American cities with its freeway, flyovers and dependence on the car.

Perth's best asset is an incredible climate. The sun simply never stops shining and each perfect sunny day is taken for granted. The endless expanse of blue sky and sea is a constant reflection in both the city's skyscrapers and residents' sunglasses. This makes for a city lived in the outdoors where the beaches, ocean, river and parks are the favourite haunts of the friendly, laid-back people of Perth.

History and culture are not major preoccupations of the 'sandgropers', although the city hosts an excellent international arts festival. The city centre is often criticized for being soulless by day and empty by night and it is true that it suffers from a lack of inner-city residents. The action in Perth is to be found out in the central and coastal suburbs, where you can watch the sun set into the Indian Ocean, see a film outdoors, go sailing on the river or stroll the café strips.

Getting there

Perth Airport, www.perthairport.net.au, a little over 10 km east of the city centre, has two terminals: domestic and international. With no direct link between the two, transfers are via the perimeter highways (shuttle $8, transfer vouchers for passengers flying with Qantas or OneWorld available at Qantas ticketing counter, T9365 9777). The **domestic terminal**, Brearley Avenue, has a wide range of services including ATMs, **Travelex** foreign exchange, luggage lockers, cafés and all the major car hire firms. There are several transport options into Perth: a taxi costs around $30; the **Connect Airport Shuttle**, T1300 666 806, www.perthairportconnect.com.au, meets all flights ($15 one way, $25 return); the **Transperth** bus No 37 (bus stop opposite Qantas terminal, $3.70, 35 minutes) runs to the Esplanade Busport. Buses leave at least every 30 minutes (hourly after 1840) Monday-Friday 0600-2240; every 30-60 minutes on Saturday 0650-2240; and hourly on Sunday 0820-1820. The **international terminal**, Horrie Miller Drive, is slightly further out. Facilities are just as comprehensive and the **Thomas Cook** foreign exchange counters remain open before and after all flights. There is, however, no public bus route from this terminal, so it's either the shuttle ($18 one way, $30 return, details as above) or a taxi (about $35). There are also shuttles to Fremantle, T9457 7150, www.fremantleairport shuttle.com.au, and Scarborough, T0427 082652 (pre-booking required, $30-60).

Wellington Street Bus Station is the main terminal for interstate coaches and some independent state services. **Greyhound** ① *East Perth Terminal, T1300 473946, www.grey hound.com.au*, runs the interstate services to Adelaide, Darwin and beyond. **TransWA** ① *T1300 662205 and T9326 2600, www.transwa.wa.gov.au*, operates most coach and train services within the state from the East Perth Terminal. The **Railway Station** on Wellington Street services the five suburban lines, while most metropolitan buses terminate at the **Esplanade Busport.** ›› *See Transport, page 86, for further details.*

Getting around

Both Perth and Fremantle have free city centre buses known as CATs (Central Area Transit), T136213, circulating the city on three different routes every seven to five minutes during the day and less regularly at night. **Transperth** ① *T136213, www.transperth.wa. gov.au, Mon-Thu 0500-2430, Fri-Sat 0500-0200, Sun 0500-2400*, operates the city's buses, trains and ferries and has several information centres where you can pick up timetables and ask for help. These are located at the Esplanade Busport, the main Railway Station and Wellington Street Bus Station. Urban bus routes tend to radiate out from the city centre, and travelling between peripheral areas, though usually possible, can be a tortuous affair. It is far simpler to take the train, services run regularly.

City sightseeing ① *T9203 8882, www.citysightseeingperth.com.au, $27.50, children $10, concessions $22.50,* buses leave regularly throughout the day from major tourist sights in central Perth and operate a hop-on hop-off system. There is also the **City Explorer** ① *T9322 2006, www.perthtram.com.au, $30, children $12, concessions $25, sectional trips available for $8, children $4,* which offers a hop-on hop-off service by tram and open-top double-decker bus. The ticket is valid for two days and takes in Perth's major and historic attractions including Hay Street, Barrack Street Jetty, Kings Park, the Perth Mint and also stops at some of the major hotels.

As it's a fairly flat city Perth is ideal for cycling, see bike hire under Transport. Ferries sail from Barrack Street Jetty over to South Perth. ▶▶ *See Transport, page 86.*

Orientation

The core of the city lines the banks of the Swan River from its mouth at Fremantle to the central business district (CBD), 19 km upstream, just north of an open basin known as Perth Water. Perth is contained by the coast to the west and the low 'Perth hills' of the Darling Ranges to the east, a corridor about 40 km wide. In the last 10 years the city has expanded rapidly along the sand dunes of the north coast to Joondalup and to the south almost as far as Rockingham. The northern suburbs, which are serviced by the freeway and the Joondalup train line, are a sea of new brick bungalows and modern shopping malls.

The oldest suburbs are those close to the river, particularly on the northern side such as Dalkeith and Peppermint Grove; these have always been the most wealthy and desirable places to live. The beach suburbs close to the city centre such as Cottesloe and City Beach are also affluent. Inner-city suburbs like Subiaco, Leederville and North Perth have become increasingly gentrified and sought after for their location and attractive old architecture.

The city centre is a small grid, just north of the river, of about 2 km by 1 km. The river is bordered by a strip of green lawn throughout the entire city area, and there is a walking trail alongside the river on both north and south banks. However, although the CBD faces the river, it is cut off from it by busy roads and freeways so the foreshore is not quite the asset it could be. South Perth is an attractive area with a wide grassy foreshore heavily used by joggers and picnickers. This is a fashionable suburb with many apartment blocks, making the most of views of the city skyline. Further south lies a large area of well-established middle-class suburbs around the Canning River and inland from Fremantle.

Tourist information

The **Perth Visitor Centre** ① *Forrest Pl, T9483 1111 and T1300 361 351, www.western australia.net, Mon-Thu 0830-1800, Fri 0830-1900, Sat 0930-1630, Sun 1200-1630,* is the main VIC for the state. You can pick up free maps and brochures for Perth and Fremantle, and booklets on each state region. It acts as a travel agent and sells national park passes. There is an **information kiosk** at the junction of Forrest Place and the Murray Street Mall; it's run by volunteers and not aimed specifically at tourists but it's a good place to ask for directions or advice. Free walking tours of the city leave from the kiosk Monday-Saturday at 1100 and Sunday at 1200. The **Traveller's Club** ① *92-94 Barrack St, T9226 0660, www.travellersclub.com.au, Mon-Sat 0900-2000, Sun 1000-2000,* is a very useful contact point for backpackers. It offers help and information, has travellers' noticeboards, cheap internet and acts as a tour booking centre. Aside from the VIC, information on national parks can be obtained from the **Department of Environment and Conservation** (DEC) ① *T9334 0333.* DEC produces a small brochure on each park and excellent publications on walking, fauna and flora. It is also possible to visit the **DEC information centre** ① *17 Dick Perry Av, Kensington, Mon-Fri 0800-1700,* to collect brochures, but this is out of the way.

Sights

Perth is primarily an outdoor city. A place to soak up the perfect sunny climate by going to the beach, sailing on the Swan River or walking in Kings Park. The city has few grand public institutions and much of its early colonial architecture has been demolished to create a glossy modern city. The most impressive cultural sights are gathered together in the plaza called the Cultural Centre, just north of the railway line in Northbridge. The Art Gallery and the Western Australian Museum are both excellent and give a fine insight into the history and culture of the state. Kings Park, just west of the city centre, is the largest green space close to any state capital and is the city's most popular attraction. The park is regularly used by the locals for its views, peaceful walks and picnic spots, café and outdoor cinema. Swan Bells tower also has good city views, and can easily be combined with a visit to Perth Zoo, which is an unexpected oasis of bush and jungle set back from the river shore of South Perth. ▸▸ *For listings, see pages 67-89.*

Central Perth and Northbridge

The city centre is laid out in a grid just north of the river. Four main streets run east–west within this grid. St George's Terrace is the commercial district, full of skyscrapers and offices. Hay and Murray streets are the shopping and eating streets, while Wellington borders the railway line and is slightly seedier. Just north of the railway line is Northbridge. This is reached by a walkway from Forrest Place, over Wellington Street and the Perth train station to the Cultural Centre. Northbridge lies just to the west of the plaza, bordered by William Street. This whole area is undergoing regeneration, with a lot of building work and land-scaping taking place around the Cultural Centre. The main shopping district is contained within the Hay and Murray Street Malls and the arcades running between the malls.

Art Gallery of Western Australia

ⓘ *Perth Cultural Centre, T9492 6600 and T9492 6644 (for bookings), www.artgallery.wa. gov.au, Wed-Mon 1000-1700, free; guided tours run most days, Blue CAT route, stop 7, walkway to Perth train station, car parking within the Perth Cultural Centre precinct.*

The gallery forms the southern point of the **Cultural Centre** triangle of public institutions. The main gallery was built in 1979 to house the **State Art Collection** and the clean lines of its featureless exterior walls conceal cool white hexagonal spaces inside. The ground floor is used for temporary exhibitions and this is where the state's most prestigious visiting exhibitions are shown. The central spiral staircase leads to the Aboriginal Art and Contemporary Art collections on the first floor. The gallery's collection of **Aboriginal Art** is one of the most extensive and impressive in Australia, encompassing bark paintings from Arnhem Land, dot paintings by Central Desert artists and works by WA artists such as Jimmy Pike and Sally Morgan. This collection is enhanced by detailed explanations of each painting and biography of the artist. The **Contemporary Art** collection also includes the best of craft and design in ceramics, glass, furniture and metalwork. More traditional work can be seen in the **Centenary Galleries** in the elegant former Police Court building (1905). The emphasis is on Western Australian art from colonial times to the present but also includes painters such as John Glover, Eugene Von Guérard, and Frederick McCubbin's iconic *Down on His Luck*, 1887. The gallery has an excellent shop stocking fine craft work and a huge range of art books. The spacious, relaxed café opposite does good casual Mediterranean-style food (Monday-Friday 0800-1700, Saturday-Sunday 0900-1700).

Perth Institute of Contemporary Arts (PICA)

ⓘ *Perth Cultural Centre, T9228 6300, www.pica.org.au, Tue-Sun 1100-1800, free entry, Blue CAT route, stop 7.*

Just down the steps from the Art Gallery is PICA, which showcases Australian and international visual, performance and cross-disciplinary art. The exhibitions change regularly and there are performances of contemporary dance and theatre to be enjoyed. PICA prides itself on nurturing new talent and challenging its visitors. The artwork may not be to everyone's tastes, but visit the website to see what's on or just head down and take a look.

State Library of Western Australia

ⓘ *Perth Cultural Centre, T9427 3111, www.slwa.wa.gov.au, Mon-Thu 0900- 2000, Fri 0900-1730, Sat-Sun 1000-1730, book to use internet (1 hr) or queue for an express computer (20 mins usage), Blue CAT route, stop 7.*

Opposite the Art Gallery is the complementary modern architecture of the state reference library. The **JS Battye Library**, on the third level, is a comprehensive collection of WA history titles and archives. Recent national and international newspapers and magazines can be read on the ground floor, where there is also free internet access. The **State Film and Video Archive** is on the second level and visitors can choose a film from the catalogue and use the viewing facilities on request. Other facilities include a café, lockers and a discard bookshop selling ex-library books. The library shop stocks the city's best range of books on WA.

Western Australian Museum

ⓘ *Perth Cultural Centre, T9212 3700, www.museum.wa.gov.au, 0930-1700, free, Blue CAT route, stop 7.*

The natural science collection of the Western Australian Museum came together during the gold boom of the 1890s when the new settlers had the money to think up fine public facilities. The site held the combined functions of the state library, museum and art gallery until 1955 and sprawls over a large area containing many different architectural styles. The main entrance on James Street joins the Jubilee Building and Hackett Hall. The Jubilee Building was built in 1899 in Victorian Byzantine style, from Rottnest and Cottesloe sandstone. It houses the **Mammal Gallery**, which still displays specimens in their cedar and glass cases from 1903 and bird, butterfly and marine galleries. Visitors will also find the **Diamonds to Dinosaurs Gallery** here, where they will be taken on a journey through time from the origins of the universe to the evolution of life on Earth. Some of the fossils on display are incredible. The beautiful Hackett Hall was built to house the library in 1903 and still retains the original fittings, now a backdrop to the museum's best exhibition, *WA Land and People*. This is a contemporary look at Western Australia from its ancient geological beginnings to Aboriginal life, European invasion and the ways in which the land has both shaped and been shaped by its residents. The fascinating **Aboriginal Gallery** is in the Beaufort Street Gallery, the former art gallery. This is called Katta Djinoong, meaning 'see us and understand us' and goes a long way towards its aim. The exhibition examines the past and present of WA's different indigenous groups, and contemporary issues such as the 'stolen generation'. Displays on the European history of WA are shown in the Old Gaol, which was built by convicts as a gaol and courthouse and used until 1899 when the prisoners were transferred to Fremantle gaol. Beyond the gaol is the Megamouth shark display. The **museum shop** ⓘ *Mon-Fri 1000-1645, Sat-Sun 1100-1645,* has a good range of books, as well as gifts and museum souvenirs. There is also a **café** ⓘ *Mon-Fri 0930-1600, Sat-Sun 1100-1600,* for light snacks and drinks.

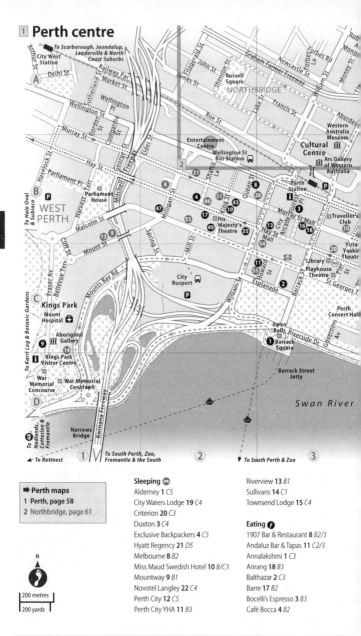

1 Perth centre

To Scarborough, Joondalup,
Leederville & North Coast Suburbs

City West
Station

Arthur St

Delhi St

Railway Par

Market St

Sutherland St

Wellington Pl

Wellington St

Wellington St

Murray St

Gordon St

Coolgardie St

Havelock St

Parliament Pl

Hay St

George St

Elder St

Shenton St

Mitchell Freeway

Fitzgerald St

John St

James St

Shenton St

Roe St

Russell
Square

NORTHBRIDGE

Graham Farmer Freeway

Newcastle St

Forbes Rd

Francis St

Lake St

William St

Aberdeen St

Western
Australia
Museum

Cultural
Centre

Art Gallery
of Western
Australia

WEST
PERTH

To Hale Oval
& Subiaco

Parliament
House

Harvest Terr

Malcolm St

Milligan St

Spring St

Mill St

Entertainment
Centre

Wellington St
Bus Station

Queen St

His
Majesty's
Theatre

Perth
Station

Murray St Mall

City
Arcade

Hay St
Mall

Traveller's
Club

Yirra
Yaakin
Theatr

To Karri Log & Botanic Gardens

Cliff St

Fraser Av

Bellevue Terr

Mount St

Mounts Bay Rd

City
Busport

William St

Barrack St

Howard St

Esplanade

Library
Playhouse
Theatre

St Georges T

Perth
Concert Hall

Kings Park

Mount
Hospital

Aboriginal
Gallery

Kings Park
Visitor Centre

War
Memorial
Concourse

War Memorial
Cenotaph

Swan
Bells

Riverside Dr

Barrack
Square

Governors Av

Barrack Street
Jetty

Swan River

To Nedlands,
Cottesloe &
Fremantle

Narrows
Bridge

Kwinana Freeway

To Rottnest

To South Perth, Zoo,
Fremantle & the South

To South Perth & Zoo

N

200 metres
200 yards

E Cucina **35** *B2*

Fraser's **9** *C1*

Han Palace **37** *C5*

Hans **10** *B2*

Jaws **13** *B3*

Jaws Mint **45** *C4*

Mai's **44** *C5*

Matsuri **47** *B2*

Merchant Tea &
  Coffee Company **16** *B3*

Old Swan Brewery **48** *D1*

Tiger Tiger Coffee Bar **43** *B2*

Velvet Espresso **49** *B2*

Bars & clubs ⬤

Belgian Beer Café Westende **51** *B2*

Durty Nelly's Irish Pub **46** *B2*

George **53** *B2*

Greenhouse **54** *B/C3*

Grosvenor Hotel **26** *C4*

Helvetica **55** *C2/3*

Hula Bula **27** *C4*

Moon & Sixpence **28** B2/3

Tiger Lil's **31** *B2*

Red Cat route ·◄·

Blue Cat route ·◄ ·

Perth Mint

ⓘ *310 Hay St, T9421 7223, www.perthmint.com.au/visit, Mon-Fri 0900-1700, Sat-Sun 0900-1300, tours every hour Mon-Fri0930-1530, Sat-Sun 0930-1130, gold pours on the hour, entry and tours $15, children $5, concessions $13, Red CAT route, stop 11.*

During the 19th century London's Royal Mint established three branches in Australia. The last to be opened, just two years before Federation, was in Perth as a direct result of the gold-rushes that were then gripping the colony and stripping it of ready currency. Built of Rottnest limestone the buildings have endured and the work of the mint has continued to the present day. Although it no longer produces day-to-day currency, it is still the major refiner of WA gold and buys and sells it at market prices. They also mint a wide range of commemorative medals and coins. Several display rooms are open to the public. Some have windows through to the production area, others contain some of WA's most historic and largest nuggets, and one contains a solid 400 oz gold bar. It's half as big as a house brick but about 10 times as hard to pick up, and you're allowed to have a try. There are regular guided tours and some culminate in a live 'gold pour', quite a spectacular sight.

Swan Bells

ⓘ *Barrack Sq, T6210 0444, www.ringmybells.com.au, daily from 1000 (closing times vary seasonally), $11, children and concessions $8, the bells are rung Sat-Tue and Thu 1200-1300 and visitors can have a go Wed and Fri 1130-1230, Blue CAT route, stop 19.*

It is little known in England that the church bells of St Martin-in-the-Fields, the ones that ring in the new year at Trafalgar Square, are almost brand new and made from Western Australian metals. The original bells, cast in the 1700s from bell metal that was possibly first poured a thousand years ago and used to celebrate Captain Cook's home-coming, were found to be stressing the church tower, and it was decided to gift them to WA to commemorate Australia's bicentenary in 1988. Exerting a force of over 40 tonnes, the bells needed a substantial bell-tower to house them. Perth not only provided just that, but made the tower the centrepiece of Old Perth Port, a striking, sweeping construction soaring 80 m with twin, copper-clad sails. The bell-chamber is easily accessed and walled with almost sound-proof doubled-glazed windows. These are now the only church bells in the world you can watch without being deafened.

Kings Park

ⓘ *T9480 3659, www.bgpa.wa.gov.au, 0930-1600, free, No 33 bus from St Georges Terr to Fraser Av or Blue CAT bus to stop 21 and walk up Jacob's Ladder.*

This huge playground for the city and central suburbs is just about everything you could want a park to be. A large area of natural bush, threaded through with unsigned bush walks, is bordered to the south and east by broad bands of carefully manicured lawns and gardens, these in turn encompassing the excellent **Botanic Gardens**. From many of these are tremendous views across to the city centre and Barrack Street jetty, particularly beautiful at sunset, and very popular with picnickers. The main visitor area is at the end of Fraser Avenue, opposite the **State War Memorial**, one of many memorials in the park as well as one of the best city-viewing spots. There's a **kiosk** ⓘ *daily 0900-1700*, some superb tea-rooms and restaurants, the visitor centre and public toilets. Here you can pick up a map of the park, self-guided walking maps, and details of the various events and activities.

There are free guided walks from the old Karri log near the centre every day at 1000 and 1400 (bookings not necessary), usually focusing on either the Botanic Gardens or the history of the park, but with variations in winter and spring looking at the local wildflowers and bushland. Walks usually take about 1½ hours, bushland walks about 2½ hours. Also close by the War Memorial is a lookout, and underneath this the **Aboriginal Gallery** ⓘ *T9481 7082, www.aboriginalgallery.com.au, Mon-Fri 1030-1630, Sat-Sun 1100-1600*, a workshop and gallery for local artists.

Away from the views is a large area devoted to families with young children. **Hale Oval** has an extensive, imaginative playground, several free electric BBQs with covered seating (though strangely no tables), plus a kiosk-café, **Stickybeaks** ⓘ *T9481 4990, 0830-1700,*

② Northbridge

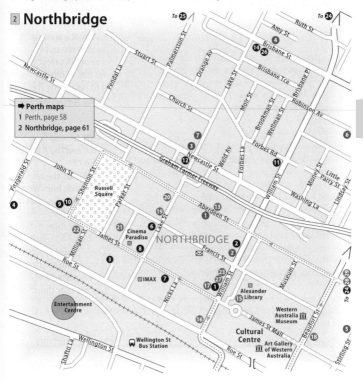

100 metres
100 yards

Sleeping 🛌
Bambu Backpackers **1**
Britannia on William **2**
Coolibah Lodge **4**
Emperor's Crown **5**
Governor Robinson **6**

Northbridge **7**
Underground **3**

Eating 🍴
Brass Grill Restaurant **1**
Chef Hans Café **2**
Chimney **3**
Dizzy Witch Café **14**
Dusit Thai **4**
Jackson's **24**
Le Papillon **25**
Maya Masala **6**
Old Shanghai Foodcourt **7**

Rochelle Adonis **26**
Sorrento **8**
Sri Melaka **9**
Tansawa Tei **10**
Viet Hoa **11**
Zebba **12**

Bars & clubs 🍸
Aberdeen **13**
Bar Open **15**
Bird **16**
Brass Monkey **17**
Court **18**

Elephant &
 Wheelbarrow **19**
Grapeskin Wine Bar **27**
Library **20**
Luxe **28**
Must Winebar **29**
Rocket Room **21**
Rosie O'Grady's **22**
Universal Wine Bar **23**

Blue Cat route ---◄---

The Old Swan Brewery

The Old Swan Brewery occupies a very desirable site on the river between the university and the city. Local Aboriginal people protested for many years against the re-development of the old brewery as the site was an important camping place, initiation site for men and connected with the Waugyl, a creator figure, embodied as a snake, who made the southwest rivers and Mount Eliza in Kings Park. Despite many years of wrangling, the Old Swan Brewery is now a luxurious complex of million dollar apartments, offices and two restaurants.

with a good range of snack meals and takeaways. There are also events held at the playground, contact the café for details. Other BBQ areas are located at the Pines, off Fraser Avenue, Saw Avenue and Lakeside. The latter two picnic areas are at the west end of the park. Some BBQs, including those in the Pines, are wood-fired with wood provided free, and may be out of bounds in summer.

Northbridge and around

Across the railway line from Perth CBD, and in the same area as the Cultural Centre, visitors will find Northbridge. Best known for its restaurants, bars and clubs, it is also home to a good cinema and some interesting small specialty boutiques. Perth's **Chinatown** can be found here and there are an astonishing variety of Asian restaurants and grocers, excellent for those who are self-catering.

Northbridge has undergone urban regeneration in the last few years to make it a safer place to visit and to promote Perth as a 24-hour city. The **Northbridge Piazza**, at the corner of Lake Street and James Street, is a new community space where there is free Wi-Fi access, outdoor furniture and a big screen. Since its unveiling in 2009 the Piazza has played host to Perth's New Year celebrations, the **Summer Film Festival**, and has become a popular place for screening live sports.

Separated from the main Northbridge strip by the Cultural Centre is **Beaufort Street**, home to more nightlife and the local police station. North along here are the areas of **Highgate** and **Mount Lawley**, which are quieter but offer some good restaurants and cafés.

Central suburbs

The suburbs north of the river and west of the city centre are some of the most attractive in the city. These suburbs all have their own character and most have eating and shopping strips that are more lively than the city centre.

Subiaco and around

Subiaco is a stylish eating destination, although it is more expensive than Northbridge and too trendy for some. It now has a large, busy suburban commercial strip but it had spiritual beginnings far from its current celebration of materialism. It was founded as a monastery, New Subiaco, by two homesick Italian monks who also founded the more famous monastery at New Norcia. There are two small museums here, both worth a look if you have the time. The **WA Medical Museum** ① *Harvey House, Barker St, T9340 1506, Wed 1030-1600, Sun 1400-1600, $4, children $1,* is an exhibition of the history of medicine in WA housed in Perth's first maternity hospital. The **Subiaco Museum** ① *Rokeby Rd, T9237 9227, Tue-Sun 1400-1700, gold coin donation*, displays local artefacts and memorabilia charting the history of Subi from one-time Benedictine monastery to the buzzing suburb that it is today.

Between Subiaco and the city centre, **West Perth** is mostly a professional suburb where architects, accountants and dentists have their offices. There are also lots of apartments and it makes a very convenient base close to Kings Park, Subiaco restaurants, the city and the freeway.

Just north of Subiaco, **Leederville** is an alternative and funky suburb with some great cafés, a lively pub and an arthouse cinema with indoor and outdoor screens. The shops are all independent establishments selling books, clothing, homewares and music.

East Perth

East Perth is developing into a centre for accommodation and eating but is still fairly quiet and businesslike. It is also a convenient base, although parking can be difficult. As for sights, it is home to **WACA** ① *Nelson Crescent, off Murray St, T9265 7318, www.waca. com.au, museum Mon-Fri 1000-1500 except match days, $5, children $3, ground tours Mon-Thu 1000 and 1300 except match days, $12.50, children $5, concessions $10, Red CAT route, stop 6*, (pronounced simply 'wacker'), WA's premier sporting stadium. It is now used almost exclusively for cricket and there are regular tours of the ground and a small but

Subiaco

N

200 metres
200 yards

Sleeping 🛏
Eight Nicholson 1
Richardson Hotel & Spa 2

Eating 🍴
Alaturka 11

Brew-Ha 3
Buddhabar 4
Chutney Mary's 12
Rialto's 1
Walk Café 8
Witch's Cauldron 9

Zen 10

Bars & clubs 🍸
Subiaco Hotel 12

fascinating museum, mostly filled with a 100 years' worth of cricketing memorabilia and including a Bradman room. Head to gate two for both tours and museum.

Opposite the WACA, the **Queen's Gardens** are a picturesque set of lawns and palm trees set around a series of lily ponds, a surprisingly quiet spot. In the other direction **Gloucester Park** ① *T9323 3555, www.gloucesterpark.com.au, $10, children (under 18) free, concessions $5*, is a trotting circuit that holds horse races every Monday afternoon from 1300 and Friday evenings from 1800 (gates open from 1700).

Nedlands and Claremont

Heading southwest, the Stirling Highway is an arterial route between the river and coast from the city to Fremantle, and links the leafy, establishment suburbs of Nedlands, Claremont and Cottesloe. **Nedlands** abuts the western border of the University of Western Australia (UWA), the state's oldest university with a beautiful garden campus and an excellent art gallery. **Claremont** has some great shopping and is the haunt of 'ladies who lunch'.

South Perth

Just across Perth Water, South Perth has the best city views and a lovely foreshore. This is a great place for sailing or waterskiing and there are hire outlets here during the summer. Several cafés and restaurants are located right on the riverbank and although you might pay a little more for the view, it is a pleasant place to spend a few hours. Alternatively, just head for the eastern end of the foreshore where there are also plenty of good places to picnic, BBQ and walk by the river. In South Perth, the incongruous **Old Mill** ① *T9367 5788, Tue-Fri 1000-1600, Sat-Sun 1300-1600, gold coin donation, by Narrows Bridge, catch a ferry to Mends St jetty, then walk towards the bridge (10 mins) or take bus No 108 or 109 from the Busport*, tucked under the freeway, is an unusual survivor from the early days of the Swan River Settlement in the 1830s. Although the windmill looks quaint, it is technically an industrial site and one of the oldest in the state. It was built in 1835 by William Shenton to grind wheat that fed the young colony. On a windy day the mill averaged 680 kg of flour a day and its location by the river meant that the flour could easily be transported to the city. Incredibly the mill was almost lost when the freeway and Narrows bridge were built in 1955. The government planned to demolish the site to make way for the freeway but there was such public protest that the building was saved and it is now managed by the National Trust. An exhibition in the whitewashed miller's cottage explains the history of the mill.

Also in South Perth, is **Perth Zoo** ① *20 Labouchere Rd, T9474 0444, www.perthzoo.wa. gov.au, 0900-1700, $20, children under 15 $10, concessions $16-17, Transperth ferry from Barrack St jetty to Mends St jetty, then 5-min walk or catch bus No 30 or 31 from the Esplanade Bus Station*. The zoo covers just 19 ha in a block between the river and the freeway but manages to squeeze in 1300 animals in attractive natural settings. The three main habitats are the Australian Bushwalk, Asian Rainforest and African Savannah. The zoo participates in a native species breeding program, Western Shield, that aims to save the many local WA species close to extinction, releasing zoo-bred animals in to the wild. The results of this programme can be seen in the Australian Bushwalk, housing creatures such as the tiny Western Swamp Tortoise, one of the world's rarest tortoise species, and the unusual termite-eating Numbat. A highlight of the wetlands area is the horrifyingly large saltwater crocodile. This 50-year-old from Darwin is 550 kg of power and his enclosure allows visitors to see him whether he is in the water or basking in the sun. The Asian rainforest is home to elephants, monkeys and orang-utans but the most compelling creatures are the Sumatran tigers, clearly visible through a glass wall. The displays highlight their endangered status.

More big cats as well as giraffes, zebra and rhinos can be seen in the African Savannah. The zoo café and shop are located near the entrance. The café menu is limited to junk food but there is also a grassy picnic and BBQ area. On a hot day remember to take a drink or change for the drink machines en route as it can be quite a walk back to the café.

Coastal suburbs

The coastal suburbs are where you'll see Perth locals at their most relaxed. Surfwear is the customary attire and although you may not want to become familiar with a surfer's feet, you will because bare feet on the street or in shops are entirely unremarkable. These suburbs are mostly residential but most have at least one great café or restaurant on the beach. Swimming is fine at all of the beaches, although there is often a steep shore break. As always in Australia, watch out for rips. If you want the reassurance of lifeguards, swim between the flags at Cottesloe, or Scarborough beaches. City Beach, Floreat and Trigg also often have lifeguards on duty at weekends in summer. Swanbourne is a nudist beach and Trigg is mostly for surfers but the rest are used by all. All west coast beaches are most pleasant in the morning before the sea breeze, known locally as the Fremantle Doctor for the relief it brings, kicks in from the south in the afternoon. Early evening is also lovely at the beach, when the sun melts into the Indian Ocean and there are often magnificent sunsets.

Cottesloe → *Colour map 1, B1. 11 km from city centre, 7 km from Fremantle.*
Perth's most attractive and lively beach suburb, Cottesloe, is the kind of place to make anyone envy the local lifestyle, or persuade them to immigrate here as soon as possible. The blindingly white beaches of Cottesloe and North Cottesloe slope into the clear, warm water of the Indian Ocean and there is usually a bit of a swell for bodysurfing. The beaches attract a hardy band of local swimmers early in the morning who are replaced later in the day by the city's best bodies and bikinis. There are always teenage boys showing off on the pylon and walkers striding along the ocean-side path. The cafés overlooking the ocean are busy from sunrise to sunset, when the sun dips into the sea as if curtsying to Cottesloe alone. It's not glitzy though and owes its contented, laid-back atmosphere to its happy locals who far outnumber visitors. Just inland is the shopping area of Napoleon Street, just off Stirling Highway, full of classy homeware shops catering to the residents of the surrounding suburbs.

Eating 🍴
Amberjacks Fish Café 5
Barista 7
Beaches 2
Blue Duck 3
Blue Waters 6
Indiana 4
Ogdens Bar & Grill
  at Albion Hotel 1
VanS 8

Sleeping 🛏
Cottesloe Beach 1
Cottesloe Beach Chalets 2
Ocean Beach 3
Ocean Beach Backpackers 4

Cottesloe to Scarborough
→ *Distance 12 km.*
One long, sweeping beach extends all the way from Cottesloe to Scarborough, incorporating a nudist section near the military base at **Swanbourne**. This whole

stretch of coast is a favourite of surfers and windsurfers alike and swimming can be hazardous. Stick to the patrolled areas. Mid-way are two small developed enclaves, and these make two of the best spots on the Perth coast if you want to get away from the serious crowds. **City Beach** has an extensive grassy foreshore hard up against a very broad section of beautiful white-sand beach. Facilities include BBQs, picnic tables and toilets and a small complex with a kiosk, café and the best restaurant in Perth that actually hangs over a beach. See Eating, page 76, for details of the great eatery, **Oceanus**.

Just a few hundred metres north, **Floreat Beach** is much more modest in scale, but with a superb children's playground, BBQs and some unexpectedly stylish, covered picnic tables. There are also two beach volleyball courts; free, collect a ball and net from the kiosk. There is a laid-back, friendly terrace café (see Eating, page 76).

Scarborough → *Colour map 1, B1. 14 km from city centre, 9 km from Hillarys.*
Where Cottesloe is an almost accidentally popular beach suburb, laid-back and effortless, Scarborough's attractions are more carefully designed. The suburb is dominated by the **Rendezvous Observation Tower**, a multi-storeyed icon built by Alan Bond that somehow slipped through council planning regulations in the 1980s. It is the only skyscraper on the entire city coastline. In front of it a small café strip has developed, separated from the wide beach by a road, narrow grassy foreshore and a thin line of remnant dunes. Facilities are good and family-friendly including toilets, BBQs, picnic tables, takeaway kiosks and a small cabin hiring out a variety of games, skates and bikes. Around the main junction of the West Coast Highway and Scarborough Beach Road is a cluster of shops and services, including a Coles supermarket. Beyond these are a large number of three- to four-storey holiday apartment complexes. **Scarborough Beach Markets**, held every weekend, pale besides those in the city and Fremantle, but are worth a visit for a well- stocked second-hand book stall.

Scarborough to Sorrento
A kilometre or so north of Scarborough the long sweep of beach that has extended practically all the way from Port Beach finally starts to break into a series of smaller bays and coves. The sand at this breakpoint is called **Trigg Beach**, and it is one of the city's best surfing spots. The beach backs onto large, grassy **Clarko Reserve**, where there are BBQs, covered picnic areas, toilets and changing rooms, and a children's playground. Just to the south, almost on the beach, is the **Trigg Island Café** (see Eating, page 76).

A little further north **Mettam's Pool** is one of the few beaches on the Perth coast that favours swimmers and snorkellers over surfers, due to an off-shore reef, close to the surface, that has created a sheltered 'pool'. There are toilets and changing rooms available, and a few picnic tables. Continuing north you will pass the quite average **Waterman's Beach**. Not at all average is the small, funky terrace café across the road, the BYO **Wild Fig** (see Eating, page 76).

Hillarys and Sorrento → *Colour map 1, A1. 25 km from centre, 27 km from Swan Valley.*
The beach suburbs of Hillarys and Sorrento have put themselves well and truly on the map, particularly for families, by building **Hillarys Boat Harbour**. Primarily containing private moorings the harbour does have a few commercial operations, but has become better known for the shops, restaurants and activities on and around the mall-like **Sorrento Quay**, a pier which almost bisects the harbour and ensures a very well-protected beach. Two major family attractions means the harbour and quay really hum on a weekend and during school holidays, particularly as the harbour also protects a sandy beach.

AQWA ① *Southside Dr, T9447 7500, www.aqwa.com.au, daily 1000-1700, $28, children $16, concessions $20,* WA's premier aquarium, is an impressive showcase for the sealife that inhabits the coastal waters around the state. The centrepiece is a large walk-through tank with a good variety of fish, sharks and rays, but the many side tanks are just as fascinating with several devoted to corals and jellyfish. You'll want the Moon jellyfish tank back home in your living room. There are also discovery pools, crocodiles, a theatre showing almost continuous undersea documentaries and a large outdoor seal pool with an adjacent underground viewing room. Regular feeding and educational sessions can easily turn this into a half-day visit. A cheap café serves healthy sandwiches, cheap hot lunches, cakes and drinks.

The Great Escape ① *T9448 0800, www.thegreatescape.com.au, slides Feb-Dec 1000-1700, Dec-Jan 0900-2100, high ropes course daily 1000-1800, complex Mar-Sep 1000-1700, Oct-Feb 1000-2000,* serving as the backdrop to the harbour beach, is a no-nonsense children's attraction with several diversions clustered around the all-important water slides. These are open for three fixed three-hour sessions, so best to arrive just after the start of one of them. Unfortunately everything is priced separately so it can rack up a bit if the kids insist on trying everything. A kiosk supplies drinks and snacks.

◉ Perth listings

For Sleeping and Eating price codes and other relevant information, see pages 28-34.

◉ Sleeping

Central Perth p56, map p58

St George's and Adelaide Terraces are home to many of the big modern, glitzy hotels in Perth, all with superb balcony rooms overlooking the riverside parks and the river itself. All offer cheaper 'getaway' specials so it might be worth asking what's going.
LL-L The Duxton, 1 St George's Terr, T9261 8000, www.duxton.com. The closest to the city centre and its rooms and services are, by a whisker, the benchmark for the rest. Facilities include Wi-Fi. The main restaurant is also good.
LL-A Hyatt Regency, 99 Adelaide Terr, T9225 1234, www.perth.hyatt.com. The last of the clutch of international standard hotels strung out along this street. It is arranged around an impressive atrium foyer and has recently been refurbished. Wi-Fi and underground parking facilities available. Self-parking $20, valet parking $30.
L-A The Melbourne, corner of Hay and Milligan Sts, T9320 3333, www.melbourne hotel.com.au. Boutique hotel with 33 rooms in an ornate, restored 1890s pub building.

Rooms have TV, en suite, some with veranda. Bar, café and restaurant. 24-hr reception.
A-B Miss Maud Swedish Hotel, 97 Murray St, T9325 3900, www.missmaud.com.au. A very central hotel within easy reach of the main shopping streets and train station. The 52 rooms are standard and some of the Scandinavian decor may not be to guest's taste but it's clean and the Smörgåsbord breakfast is included in the rate (you may not have to eat again for the rest of the day). There is a restaurant but no parking.
A-B Sullivans, 166 Mounts Bay Rd, T9321 8022, www.sullivans.com.au. Just below Kings Park, this comfortable, modern hotel has 68 rooms (some with balcony and river views) and 2 apartments. Also pool, free bikes, free internet, parking, restaurant, café and 24-hr reception. Convenient location, free city bus (Blue CAT) at door.
A-C Criterion Hotel, 560 Hay St, T9325 5155, www.criterion-hotel-perth.com.au. A glorious art deco façade does not prepare you for the interior. The hotel has been refurbished to provide 69 comfortable but bland modern rooms, all a/c with minibar. Convenient location in heart of city, also a good brasserie and pub on site. Wi-Fi but no parking.

C-E Perth City YHA, 300 Wellington St, T9287 3333. One of the few hostels in Perth CBD, the rooms are nothing to write home about but the facilities are good. The communal spaces and bathrooms are large and clean, and there is even a gym on site. The bar serves up cheap meals and there's car parking from $10-11.50. It is however, next to the train line so it's noisy.

D Townsend Lodge, 240 Adelaide Terr, T9325 4143, www.townsend.wa.edu.au. Mostly used for student accommodation, the friendly Townsend has 60 clean single rooms and 2 doubles on separate male and female floors. Lots of facilities including pool table, TV room, DVD hire, internet access, laundry and courtyard BBQ. Price drops by 30% for stays of 2 nights or more. Helpful staff. Reception hours 0900-1900, Sat-Sun 0900-1700.

Self-contained

A-B Riverview on Mount Street, 42 Mount St, T9321 8963, www.riverviewperth.com.au. Stylish, well-equipped studio apartments, all with balconies or patio gardens. Quality with value for couples, friendly and helpful staff. There is a restaurant next door for those who don't want to cook, it's open daily for breakfast and lunch and Tue-Sat for dinner.

B-C Mountway, 36 Mount St, T9321 8307, www.mountwayunits.com.au. A far less glamorous high-rise block overlooking the freeway and the city. Kitchens are basic and the traffic noise can be considerable, but these self-contained units are fairly spacious. All have balconies; linen, blankets and towels are provided. Facilities include internet and laundry. Limited off-street parking available.

C City Waters Lodge, 118 Terrace Rd, T9325 1566, www.citywaters.com.au. Clean and comfortable studio units (58) and 2-bed apartments (3) overlooking Langley Park. Each unit has a kitchen, bathroom, TV, a/c and Wi-Fi, serviced daily. German-speaking staff, continental breakfast available. Good value.

Northbridge and around *p62, maps p58 and p61*

L-D Northbridge Hotel, corner of Lake and Brisbane Sts, T9328 5254, www.hotelnorth bridge.com.au. Renovated old corner hotel with veranda. Luxurious hotel rooms (50) with spa and full facilities, bar and mid-range restaurant. Budget rooms in the old part of the hotel with shared facilities, TV, fridge.

C-E The Emperor's Crown, 85 Stirling St, T9227 1400, www.emperorscrown.com.au. Friendly hostel with dorms (maximum 5-bed), twins, triples and en suite doubles (these have fridge, kettle and tea and coffee). Away from the main hubbub of Northbridge but just around the corner from the CAT bus stop. Pricey for a hostel and there's no breakfast included, but the rooms are clean, the communal spaces are large and bright and there is a café just next door. Luggage storage is also available. Recommended.

D-E Bambu Backpackers, 75-77 Aberdeen St, T9328 1211, www.bambu.net.au. Asian-style boutique backpackers with large kitchen, internet access, Wi-Fi, free breakfast, pool table and outdoor BYO lounge. Very friendly staff. Special weekly rates and a lot of guests are long-stayers. There's a party every Fri night.

D-E Coolibah Lodge, 194 Brisbane St, T9328 9958, www.coolibahlodge.com.au. Hostel with 4- and 6-bed dorms in restored colonial house. Good doubles with fridge, kettle and sink in newer extension. All rooms a/c. Small but pleasant courtyard BBQ areas and good communal areas. Other facilities include licensed bar, laundry and Wi-Fi. 24-hr reception and check-in. For those who want a quieter time, head to the sister hostel **12:01 East**, which is on Hay St in East Perth.

D-E Governor Robinson, 7 Robinson Av, T9328 3200, www.govrobinsons.com.au. This boutique hostel occupies a couple of 100-year-old cottages and a sympathetic extension in a very quiet street, 10-min walk from the centre. Small, but the central room and kitchen have the look and feel of a private home, not a hostel. Fresh, light rooms and linen, backpack-sized lockers, jarrah floorboards and classy bathrooms. Doubles, some with en suite, are of hotel standard. No pick-up, street parking.

D-E Underground, 268 Newcastle St, T9228 3755. Massive central hostel with swimming pool, bar, well-equipped kitchen and spacious internet and guest area. Breakfast available. 4- to 10-bed dorms, all the same price. No BYO, fully licensed, free drink on arrival. 24-hr reception. Parking and internet available. Recommended.

D-F Britannia on William, 253 William St, T9227 6000, www.perthbritannia.com. A large, clean, comfortable hostel with 160 beds, good kitchen and dining facilities. Facilities include bike and DVD hire, darts, book exchange, laundry and internet access. 24-hr reception. No parking available.

Subiaco and around *p62, map p63*
LL The Richardson Hotel & Spa, 32 Richardson St, West Perth, T9217 8888, www.therichardson.com.au. A luxury boutique hotel with 74 rooms and suites, most with balconies. Facilities include internet access, valet parking and access to the Spa. The **Opus Restaurant** is open for dinner and there is a cocktail bar.

L-A Eight Nicholson, 8 Nicholson Rd, Subiaco, T9382 1881, www.8nicholson.com.au. Boutique luxury B&B in an historic Subiaco house. The beds are huge and the decor contemporary. Guests (there are 4 rooms) have their own entrance and breakfast can be enjoyed in the sunshine.

East Perth *p63, map p58*
L-B Novotel Langley, 221 Adelaide Terr, T9221 1200, www.novotelperthlangley. com.au. Opposite the **Sheraton**, does a commendable job at offering a similar experience at a slightly cheaper price. Parking.

C Perth City, 200 Hay St, T9220 7000, www.comforthotelperthcity.com.au. Staff are friendly, furnishings bright and cheerful. Wheelchair access, internet, 24-hr reception.

E Exclusive Backpackers, 156 Adelaide Terr, T9221 9991, www.exclusivebackpackers. com. 25 good-quality rooms, particularly the doubles. Quiet communal areas are homely and characterful, kitchen basic. Internet and laundry facilities, reception closes at 2230.

Self-contained
B The Alderney, 193 Hay St, T9225 6600, www.alderney.com.au. Has 80 very comfortably furnished, fully self-contained apartments. Indoor pool and gym and undercover parking are included. Reception hours Mon-Fri 0800-1900, Sat-Sun 0900-1500.

Nedlands *p64*
B Caesia House, 32 Thomas St, T9389 8174, www.caesiahouse.com. B&B in comfortable modern house. Excellent breakfast and very knowledgeable hosts, particularly on nearby Kings Park and its flora. Also offers a self-contained apartment. Non-smoking, unsuitable for children.

Cottesloe *p65, map p65*
A-C Ocean Beach Hotel, corner of Marine Parade and Eric St, T9384 2555, www.obh.com.au. Elegant rooms, some with ocean views, in a high rise opposite the beach and next to OBH bars and restaurant.

B Cottesloe Beach Hotel, 104 Marine Terr, T9383 1100, www.cottesloebeach hotel.com.au. Comfortable art deco hotel with 13 small rooms and standard facilities. The best rooms (6) face the ocean and have a small balcony. Note that rooms are above a very popular and noisy pub. The price includes breakfast in the café. Reception opens 0800-1700.

D-E Ocean Beach Backpackers, 1 Eric St, T9384 5111, www.oceanbeachbackpackers. com.au. This hostel is all about location, North Cott beach lies just over the road. There are dorms, twins and doubles on offer and all are en suite. Facilities include bike hire free surfboard and bodyboard hire, an in-house café, internet access, TV lounges and an XBox.

Self-contained

A Cottesloe Beach Chalets, 6 John St, T9383 5000, www.cottesloebeachchalets.com.au. A complex of 30 modern self-contained flats close to the beach that sleep 5. Full kitchen, bathroom, and 2 bedrooms on mezzanine level. The complex also has a pool and BBQs. Off-street parking. Price covers 1-5 people.

Scarborough *p66*

LL-A Hotel Rendezvous, 33 The Esplanade, Scarborough, T9340 5555, www.rendezvous hotels.com. The majority part of the Rendezvous Observation Tower, is Perth's premier non-city centre hotel. It has striking views up and down the coast and facilities include 2 restaurants, café, heated outdoor pool with spa, gym, Wi-Fi, tennis courts, 24-hr reception and room service. Parking.
L-B Sunmoon, 200 West Coast Highway, T9245 8000, www.sunmoon.com.au. Striking resort-style complex, with a faintly Asian feel and a wide range of hotel rooms and self-contained apartments. Hotel rates include a cooked breakfast. Wi-Fi and on-site parking available.
D-E Perth Beach YHA, 256 West Coast Highway, T9245 3388, www.indigonet. com.au. A 5-min walk from the Esplanade, this unpretentious hostel has 60 beds in a variety of singles, doubles, 4- and 6-bed dorms. The reception area doubles as an expensive internet café and they also offer bike and board hire. Other facilities include a garden area with BBQ.

Self-contained

L-A Sandcastles and **Seashells**, 170-178 The Esplanade, T9341 6644, www.seashells.com.au. 2 large resort complexes with 2-3 bedroom self-contained apartments and some motel-style rooms. Most rooms have balcony views though there is a lot of car park between the resorts and the beach. All rooms have fully equipped kitchen and laundry facilities, TV, internet access and a/c. General facilities include BBQ area and 2 outdoor swimming pools.

Hillarys and Sorrento *p66*

L-A Hillarys Harbour Resort Apartments, 68 Southside Dr, Hillarys, T9262 7888, www.hillarysresort.com.au. Well furnished, comfortable and modern 1- to 3-bedroom fully self-contained apartments. Most have private balconies or courtyards overlooking either the harbour or the courtyard pool. Facilities include BBQ area, heated spa and sauna. Underground parking available.

Caravan and tourist parks

B-D Kingsway Tourist Park, corner of Kingsway and Wanneroo Rd, T9409 9267, www.acclaimparks.com.au. Tourist park with chalets, smaller cabins and powered sites.
C-E Cherokee Village, 10 Hocking Rd, T9409 9039, www.istnet.net.au/~cherokee. Self-contained cabins, some en suite. Free gas BBQ and pool. No pets allowed.

Airport

B-E Perth International, T9453 6677, www.perthinternational.com.au. A Big4 caravan park with self-contained chalets and cabins. These are well-equipped and comfortable, some with spas, others with the budget conscious in mind. The grounds are immaculate, the facilities excellent, and nothing is too much trouble for the staff. Recommended.

● Eating

Eating in Perth is characterized by location rather than cuisine; it is overwhelmingly an outdoor scene that makes the most of a stable, sunny climate. Many restaurants have very little indoor space and every eating area is crammed with pavement tables or open terraces. Despite Perth's isolation, the food is fresh and varied as it is mostly grown or harvested within the state. Seafood is very good and Asian or Italian food introduced by migrants is very popular. As in the other Australian states most fine restaurants make the best of both produce and flavour with a typically Modern Australian fusion of Eastern and Western cuisine.

Central Perth p56, map p58

There are several food courts in the city that are cheap but can be dim, messy and crowded. There is a good one upstairs in the City Arcade with an outdoor terrace overlooking Murray St Mall. Also try the Carillion Arcade.

ꭧꭧꭧ 1907 Bar & Restaurant, 26 Queens St, T9436 0233, www.1907.com.au. Lunch Tue-Fri 1200-1500, dinner Tue-Sat 1800-2100. Bar Wed-Thu 1700-2400, Fri-Sat 1700-0100. Housed in a 100-year-old factory in Perth's former fashion district, this is a romantic, atmospheric place serving excellent food. Opulent in its decor, the dishes are classics and for those who can't decide what to choose there's a tasting menu (Prestige). If finances can't stretch to dinner, there's a bar downstairs offering delicious cocktails.

ꭧꭧꭧ Balthazar, 6 The Esplanade, T9421 1206. Mon-Fri 1200-1500, Mon-Sat 1800-2200. Indulgent wine bar and restaurant that cleverly combines the traditional crisp lines of folded white table linen with the even crisper lines of the metal and wood architecture. Mediterranean-influenced food is matched by the music and supported by an extensive wine list. There's a cheap bar menu for those with shallower pockets and they dig into the cellars to hold wine-tastings every 4-6 weeks.

ꭧꭧꭧ Fraser's, Fraser Av, T9481 7100, www.frasersrestaurant.com.au. Breakfast on Sun from 0800, lunch daily from 1200, dinner daily from 1800. Has for years been one of the city's best in terms of both food, location and ambience. The view of the city is slightly obscured by trees, but it's still pretty impressive and there are a few terrace tables to make the most of it. Cuisine is Modern Australian, predominantly seafood, with a few grills, and it's supported by an extensive, quality wine list. The attached **Botanical Café** (T9482 0122) is open daily 0700-2200, and offers slightly cheaper, good-quality food.

ꭧꭧꭧ Old Swan Brewery, 173 Mounts Bay Rd, T9211 8999, www.theoldbrewery.com.au. Daily 0730-2200. Contemporary space with lots of black furniture and a warehouse feel, with a wide terrace on the river. Modern Australian food with an emphasis on grills, including native meats.

ꭧꭧꭧ Andaluz Bar & Tapas, Basement, 21 Howard St, T9481 0092, www.andaluzbar. com.au. Mon-Thu 1200-2400, Fri 1200-0100, Sat 1800-0100. A bar serving good Spanish tapas. It has a very extensive cocktail menu to complement the wines and the digestifs. Visit in the week when it's not too busy.

ꭧꭧ Barre, 825 Hay St, next door to His Majesty's Theatre, T9226 1006. Lunch only Mon-Fri, dinner when performances are running next door. A refined and elegant café with dark wood fittings. The menu is less formal, with glammed-up burgers, pizzas, salads and pasta.

ꭧꭧ Café Bocca, Shafto Lane, 872 Hay St, T9226 4030. Mon-Thu 0730-1530, Fri 0730-2200. Stylish, contemporary Italian in a lovely shady courtyard by a tranquil fountain. Most tables are outdoors.

ꭧ Annalakshmi, Jetty 4, Barrack St, T9221 3003, www.annalakshmi.com.au. Tue-Sun 1200-1400, Tue-Sun 1830-2100, closed Sat for lunch. Friendly Indian vegetarian buffet where all profits go to food and arts charities. There is no set price – you simply pay what you feel you can afford. They also put on monthly displays of Indian dancing, usually on the Sat closest to the full moon. No alcohol allowed. Booking advised.

ꭧ Arirang, 91 Barrack St, T9225 4855, www.arirang.com.au. Daily 1130-1500, Sun-Thu 1730-2130, Fri-Sat 1730-2200. Unusual Korean BBQ restaurant with a stylish, contemporary interior. Charcoals are brought to the table for you to cook your own meat in a central well to combine with rice and sauces. Good fun with a focus on the best fresh food and Korean culture. Dinner is in the mid-range price bracket.

Hans, 24 Forrest Chase, T9228 8151. Daily 1100-2100. Chain of casual restaurants, always packed for their good value Thai, Japanese and Chinese dishes. Licensed.

Jaws, Hay St Mall. Mon-Thu 1130-1900, Fri-Sat 1130-2100, Sun 1130-1800. A true sushi bar with seats in a horseshoe facing the very cheap dishes whizzing past on the conveyor belt. Always a busy lunch spot for office workers.

Jaws Mint, corner of Hay St and Hill St, T9225 4573. Mon-Fri 1100-1500, 1800-2130. Principally a Japanese takeaway but has eat-in tables.

Matsuri, 250 St Georges Terr, T9322 7737, www.matsuri.com.au. Mon-Fri 1200-1430, Mon-Sat 1800-2200. Sushi takeaway bar on the QV1 Plaza. Good-value set menus.

Cafés

Many cafés stay open later on Fri night.
Bocelli's Espresso, a large bustling outdoor café in the heart of Forrest Pl. Daily until 1800 (until 2100 on Fri). A good place for a casual bite while watching the crowds. Gourmet sandwiches, cakes, drinks, also breakfasts.
E Cucina, 777 Hay St, next to City Park. Smart Italian food and, around the corner, a straight- up espresso bar for city workers on the run.

Merchant Tea and Coffee Company, 183 Murray St Mall (and others). Mon-Sat 0700-1900, Sun 0900-1900. An elegant respite from the mall, lined with dark wood and with cool high ceilings. Sandwiches, cakes and coffee ordered at the counter. Also pavement tables.

Tiger Tiger Coffee Bar, 4/329 Murray St, T9322 8055, www.tigertigercoffeebar.com. Mon-Wed 0700-2000, Thu-Sat 0700-2200. Good range of coffee and all-day food and breakfast. Free Wi-Fi available.
Velvet Espresso, 5/172 St Georges Terr, T9322 5209. Mon-Fri 0630-1600. A stylish but relaxed little café with 5 Senses coffee and fresh friand pastries baked by the owner.

Northbridge and around *p62, maps p58 and p61*

The **Old Shanghai** foodcourt on James St has a good range of Asian stalls. Mon-Thu 1100-2200, Fri-Sun 1100-2300.

Jackson's, 483 Beaufort St, Highgate, T9328 1177, www.jacksonsrestaurant.com.au. Mon-Sat 1900-late. One of Perth's finest, enjoy Neal Jackson's international menu in this award-winning restaurant. Treat yourself with a 9-course tasting ('The Dego') and a glass of wine from the impressive wine list.

Brass Grill Restaurant, corner of William and James Sts, T9227 9596, www.the brassmonkey.com.au. Tue-Sat 1800-late Fri for lunch 1200-1430. This brasserie on the balcony is one of the most pleasant places to dine in Northbridge. The Modern Australian menu changes regularly to reflect the use of fresh seasonal produce. Recommended.

The Chimney, 171 James St, opposite Cinema Paradiso, T9328 6870. A friendly, stylish restaurant serving modern Australia and Italian meals. There is also a good wine list. Outdoor seating is available in the courtyard. Recommended.

Dusit Thai, 249 James St, T9328 7647, www.dusitthai.com.au. Tue-Sun 1800-2200. Award-winning, elegant and ornate Thai serving consistently fresh and creative food. Licensed and BYO. Takeaway also available. Runs cooking classes.

Sorrento Restaurant, 158 James St, T9328 7461, www.sorrentorestaurant.com.au. This popular Italian serves good-value pizzas and a decent range of Mediterranean dishes. Fully licensed, BYO Mon-Thu.

Tansawa Tei, 1 Shenton St, T9228 0258. Tue-Sat 1130-1430, 1800-2230. Elegant and contemporary Japanese overlooking the park. Set menus are good value for the whole culinary experience but lunch or a light meal can be had for under $20.

Chef Han's Café, 245 William St, T93228 8122 and T9328 8119, www.hanscafe.com.au. Daily 1100-2200.

Very busy large noodle bar with most dishes around $10-12. Flavour makes up for very bland surroundings.

♀ Maya Masala, corner of Lake St and Francis St, T9328 5655. Daily 1130-late. Wonderful Indian food in groovy, contemporary style. Specialities are dosa, thali, curries and tandoori but also particularly perfect Indian sweets. Prices are almost too good to be true. Licensed and BYO. Recommended.

♀ Sri Melaka, 220 James St, T228 2882 and T9328 6404, www.yongcorp.com.au. Tue-Sun 1130-1530, 1730-2130. Buffet or à la carte veggie versions of Chinese, Indian and Malaysian favourites. Also a good range of salads, tasty desserts and non-alcoholic drinks. The surroundings are fairly simple but it's good-value food with friendly service. Vegetarian market next door.

♀ Viet Hoa, 349 William St, T9328 2127. Daily 1000-2200. Vietnamese and Chinese food served in this large, businesslike restaurant. Always very busy and great value. Most dishes are under $15. Not licensed, BYO. Takeaway available.

Cafés

The Dizzy Witch Café, 197 Brisbane St, T9228 1501, www.thedizzywitchcafe.com.au. Tue-Sun 0700-1600. Offers a good and varied breakfast menu, as well as hearty lunch options. Cakes and coffees, and free Wi-Fi.

Le Papillon, 274 Bulwer St, Highgate, T9227 6664. Mon-Fri 0700-1600, Sat-Sun 0700-1700. A little out of the way but the coffee and patisseries are worth the trip. A good place for breakfast, lunch or just a cup of tea and a cake, it has a nice French vibe to it. The outside tables are next to a busy road.

Rochelle Adonis, 193 Brisbane St, T9227 0007, www.rochelleadonis.com.au. Tue-Sat 1000-1600. Cakes and confections, think delicate cupcakes and strawberry tarts.

Zebba, 101 Lake St, T9228 4029. Mon-Fri 0700-1700 and Sat 0800-1400. A hole-in-the-wall café serving good coffee and simple but filling food.

Subiaco and around *p62, map p63*

Subiaco is fast becoming central Perth's social hub. Rokeby Rd, between Bagot and Roberts Sts, is the main strip, with several good options along Hay St.

♀♀♀ Rialto's, 424 Hay St, T9382 3292, www.rialtos.com.au. Wed-Fri 1200-late, Tue and Sat 1800-late. Large dining room suited to the serious business of eating award-winning top-quality cuisine. The menu is tight on choice, but supported by a considerable wine list.

♀♀♀ Witch's Cauldron, 89 Rokeby Rd, T9381 2508, www.witchs.com.au. Daily 0730-1100, 1200-2130, weekends until 2230. Formal restaurant with a traditional feel only slightly off-set by pictures of pointy-hatted ladies. Cuisine is Modern Australian and dependably good. Mostly seafood, chicken and steak grills with a few veggie options.

♀♀♀-♀ Alaturka, 420 Hay St, T9388 9029, www.alaturka.com.au. Daily 0930-2200. A friendly Turkish restaurant in modern surrounds. Staff are very helpful and are happy to offer suggestions if guests are new to Turkish cuisine. Licensed and BYO. Takeaway available.

♀♀ Buddhabar, 88 Rokeby Rd, T9382 2941, www.buddhabar.com.au. Fri-Sat 1200-1430, Tue-Sun 1800-late. Hip Indian that puts as much creativity into its music and surrounds as its curries. Relaxed and friendly, their late night 'supper clubs' give a whole new cultured meaning to a late-night curry. Licensed, live music Tue-Sat.

♀♀-♀ Chutney Mary's, corner of Hay St and Rokeby St, T9381 2099, www.chutney marys.com.au. Open Mon-Sat for lunch and daily for dinner from 1730. A popular Indian restaurant, book ahead if coming on Fri or Sat night when it can be very noisy. The menu has a wide variety of options and the lunch specials are good value. Fully licensed.

♀ Zen, 1 Seddon St, T9381 4931, www.zen-perth.com. Tue-Fri 1200-1400, Tue-Sat 1800-2200, Sun 1800-2100. Traditional, licensed Japanese with seriously cheap takeaway lunch specials. BYO.

Cafés

There are several good cafés in Subiaco and they can all be relied upon for a decent coffee. The 2 below are located on pedestrian walk-throughs, and so have the appeal of larger outdoor areas that are away from road traffic.

Brew-Ha, 162 Rokeby Rd, T9388 7272, www.brew-ha.com.au. Open 0630-1800. Fresh coffee and tea, by the packet or the cup. Comfy chairs and laid-back style make this a good spot to enjoy the morning paper.

Walk Café, Forrest Walk. Open 0730-1530. Cool, contemporary and relaxed with plenty of outside tables. Light lunches come in big servings.

Leederville *p63*

This inner-city suburb has developed an alternative vibe and small café scene around the junction of Oxford and Newcastle Sts. At its heart is the arthouse **Luna Cinema**. The Leederville pub is also a big draw for the area.

↑↑↑-↑↑ Kailis Bros Fish Café, 101 Oxford St, T9443 6300, www.kailisbrosleederville. com.au. Daily 0830-2130. An unusual but elegant seafood restaurant that shares an open space with a fresh fish market. You can even select seafood to be cooked for you. Every kind of fish and seafood, Greek mezze plates, dips and wonderful seafood platters. Also takeaways and breakfast.

↑↑ Giardini, 135 Oxford St, T9242 2602, www.giardini.com.au. Daily 0730-late. Sophisticated Italian with good service and a modern twist to the cooking. Large, relaxing space has cane chairs and lots of greenery.

↑ Banzai, 741 Newcastle St, T9227 7990. Mon-Sat 1800-2130. A slick modern sushi and noodle bar. Also has internet access. Licensed and BYO.

↑ Hawkers Hut, 150 Oxford, T9444 6662. Open daily for lunch and dinner. Asian food under $10,

Cafés

Greens & Co, 123 Oxford St, T9444 4093. 0630-2400. The doors open out onto the street and invite patrons in for a cup of coffee and a huge slab of cake. Rolls are available for lunch. Paper lanterns hang from the ceilings and the walls are covered in posters. The clientele is a nice mix of families, students and tourists all relaxing on the comfy sofas.

East Perth *p63, map p58*

↑↑ Han Palace, 73 Bennett St, T9325 8883. Tue-Thu 1200-1500, 1800-2200, Fri 1200-1500, 1800-2200, Sat 1800-2300, Sun 1800-2130. A traditional Chinese with a very regal dining room. The food is very good and you can eat cheaply. Fully licensed.

↑ Mai's, 51 Bennett St, T9325 6206. Mon, Wed-Fri 1130-1430 and 1730-2230, Sat-Sun 1700-2200. A decidedly unsexy, traditional Vietnamese with a much more attractive cheap menu. BYO.

Cafés

Epic Espresso, 5/1297 Hay St (entrance on Outram St), T9485 1818, www.epicespresso. com.au. Mon-Fri 0630-1600. Serves seriously good gourmet coffees plus heavenly Belgian and French hot chocolates for non-coffee drinkers. It also offers barista workshops.

Claremont *p64*

Most of the eating options in Claremont can be found in a small area around Bay View Terr and Stirling Highway.

↑↑↑ On the Terrace, 37 Bay View Terr, T9284 5400, www.ontheterrace.com.au. Mon-Sat 0800-late, Sun 0800-1600. The outdoor terrace is the place to be seen in this very sophisticated, fashionable restaurant and bar. Pizzas, salads, pasta and an inventive tapas menu. The bar serves a good range of cocktails at night. DJs on Thu until 0200, live jazz on Fri and Sat evenings. Champagne breakfast on Sun.

↑↑ Pronto, 16 Bay View Terr, T9284 6090. Tue-Sat 0730-2230. Always buzzing for its clever combination of effusive, charming service, colourful smart room and good-value pizzas and pasta.

Rudy's, 3 Bay View Terr, T9385 5282. Mon-Sat 1000-2200. Another Italian eatery serving good pizzas, pastas and salads, Takeaway available.

Nedlands p64

Nedlands is more spread out but there are some good places only a short distance from public transport.

Jojo's Café, Broadway Jetty, T9386 8757, www.jojosrestaurant.com. Tue-Sat 1130-late, Sun to 1600, closed for breakfast during Nov-Jan. Fine water-view restaurants with boardwalk tables and a good range of light and seafood dishes.

Pata Negra, 26 Stirling Highway, T9389 5517, www.patanegra.com.au. Fri 1200-1500, Tue-Sat 1700-late. A tapas bar, combining Spanish and Middle Eastern influences. Good range of beers and wines. It can, however, be noisy when it gets busy.

Hot Box, 38 Broadway, T9386 6600. For takeaways, fresh noodles, rice, curries, pasta $10-15.

Cafés

Barrett's Bread, 19A Broadway, T9389 6404. Mon-Fri 0630-1730, Sat and Sun 0630-1530. Bakery café with an awesome selection of French and Italian breads and pastries. Great place for a quick coffee and cake or picnic supplies.

South Perth p64

With a million-dollar view over Perth Water to the city, you'd expect a host of restaurants and cafés to enjoy it from, but there are only a handful. **Boatshed's** view is the best, and the **Bookcaffe** doesn't have one.

Boatshed Café, Coode St Jetty, T9474 1314, www.boatshedrestaurant.com. Mon-Fri 0730-2200, Sat and Fri 0800-2200. On the river foreshore facing the city skyline, this airy, open restaurant is smart but unfussy. Modern Australian food that steals flavours from every major world cuisine. Fully licensed. Also has a cheap kiosk (open 0700-2000) on one side selling drinks, fish and chips, scones and

muffins, with outdoor tables so the impecunious can also enjoy the view.

Coco's, corner of South Perth Esplanade and Mends St, T9474 3030, www.westvalley.com.au. Daily 0800-late. One of Perth's swankiest establishments, specializing in seafood and grills. Frequently changing menus. Specials depend on what's looking best at the markets.

Bellhouse, Mends St Jetty, T9367 1699. Daily 0700-2300. Warm upmarket food café with lots of golden wood fittings, perched at the end of the jetty. The menu is mostly seafood, with a few snack options, also breakfast at the weekends.

Cafés

Mill Point Caffé Bookshop, 254 Mill Point Rd, T9367 4567. Daily 0830-1730. Sells a good range of new books that you can purchase then read to your heart's content over a coffee or a light meal.

Cottesloe p65, map p65

Most of the mid-range restaurants are cheap for lunch.

Indiana, 99 Marine Parade, T9385 5005, www.indiana.com.au. Daily 1200-1530, 1800-late. This mansion above the surf club and Cottesloe Beach is a colonial-style restaurant with echoes of the Raj in its cane armchairs and fine linen. The food, mostly seafood, is very good and the ocean views magnificent but this is one of the most expensive restaurants in the city. Very pleasant for afternoon tea.

Blue Duck, 151 Marine Parade, T9385 2499, www.blueduck.com.au. Daily 0630-2100. A long-standing Cottesloe favourite, the café hangs above the beach with mesmerizing views. Particularly good for breakfast, light lunches include wood-fired pizzas and pasta, more emphasis on fish and seafood for dinner. Takeaway fish and chips available 1200-2100. Recommended.

VanS, 1 Napoleon St, T9384 0696. Daily 0700-late. A classy but casual café with sophisticated sandwiches, salads and platters to share. Simple pasta and seafood dishes that let the quality of the ingredients shine.

₩₩-₩ Blue Waters, 110 Marine Parade, T9385 3130, www.blue-waters.com.au. Mon-Sat 0800-late and Sun 0800-1500. Open for breakfast, lunch and dinner and offering a wide range of interesting options using fresh and often local ingredients.

₩ Ogdens Bar and Grill, Albion Hotel, T9383 0021. Daily 1200-1430, Mon-Wed, Sun 1800-2100, Thu-Sat 1800-2200. A smart 'cook your own' grill with a good selection of salads and other accompaniments. A small section of the dining room is inside an old tram, which also provides part of the outer wall.

₩₩-₩ Barista, 38 Napoleon St, T9383 3545. Daily 0600-1700. Funky café offering burgers, sandwiches and cakes. Licensed.

₩ Amberjacks Fish Café, corner of Marine and John St, T9385 0977. Daily 1100-2000. Head here for fish and chips on the beach.

₩ Beaches, 122 Marine Parade, T9384 4412. Daily 0630-1600. Always busy, most of this café's seating is arranged under a shaded terrace next to a Norfolk pine. Breakfast menu served all day.

Cottesloe to Scarborough p65

₩₩-₩ Oceanus, 195 Challenger Parade, City Beach, T9385 7555, www.oceanus.com.au. Tue-Sat 1200-1500, 1800-late, Sun 0800-1700. Has a large wood-beamed dining room with floor-to-ceiling windows overlooking the ocean. Most seating is indoor with a few tables on a small balcony to the side. The expensive fusion cuisine is excellent and the service friendly and attentive. The upper floor houses a showcase gallery for WA artists. Mezze, snacks and coffee available in the Oceanus Café daily 0800-1600.

₩ Costa Azzurra, Floreat Av, Floreat Beach, T9285 0048. Serves a good range of light Mediterranean meals daily from 0700-2200 in summer, 0900-2100 in winter. The café is beachside with tables overlooking the ocean. BYO.

Scarborough p66

₩₩-₩ Zanders, 1 Scarborough Beach Rd, T9245 2001, www.zanders.com.au. Daily 0700- late. This corner restaurant serves excellent European cuisine, has friendly service and is a prime spot to watch Scarborough's busy Esplanade. Also takeaways.

₩ Jimmy Dean's, 2nd floor, Esplanade, corner of Manning St, T9205 1271, www.jimmydeansdiner.com. Daily 1200-late. Friendly American diner with a range of quality grills and cheap burgers, some good-value mid-week lunch specials. Some balcony tables have good ocean views.

₩ Peters by the Sea, 128 Esplanade, T9341 1738. Open from 0900 to past midnight. A takeaway and the automatic choice for locals. They serve up excellent fish and chips, kebabs and souvlaki, and even provide covered terrace tables.

Scarborough to Sorrento p66

₩₩-₩ Wild Fig Café, 33 West Coast Dr, Waterman's Beach, T9246 9222, www.wildfig.com.au. Daily 0630-late. Relaxed, people- and eco-friendly and the staff donate all tips and corkage to charity. It serves lots of tasty snacks and salads, juices and smoothies, and has live music Tue-Fri and Sun nights. Tue is curry and Wed vego night. Licensed and BYO. Also takeaway and free Wi-Fi. Recommended.

₩ Trigg Island Café, 360 West Coast Dr, Trigg Beach, T9447 0077, www.triggisland cafe.com.au. Daily from 0830, main meals from 1200 and dinner from 1800, weekend breakfast 0800-1030. A large, sunny and very popular place with a beachside terrace. Dependably good, light mid-range meals include pastas, salads, seafood and grills.

Hillarys and Sorrento p66

₩ Portofinos, Hillarys Boat Harbour, Southside Dr, T9246 4700, www.porto finos.com.au. Mon-Sat 1100-2100, Sun from 0800. Stylish Italian restaurant with a Romanesque interior and large covered terrace. Extensive menu includes pasta, oysters, salads and wood-fired pizzas, plus breakfast on Sun.

Jetty's, Sorrento Quay, T9448 9066, www.jettys.com.au. Open 0700-1030, 1200-1530, 1730-2200. Large smorgasbord affair with good food at reasonable prices. Seafood is always on a menu that changes its theme each month. Café area open all day.

Spinnakers, 95 Northside Dr, T9203 5266, www.spinnakerscafe.com.au. Sun-Tue 0800-1700, Wed-Sat 0800-2300. Ploughs its lone furrow on the 'opposite' side of the harbour to all the rest. Its great position is enhanced by friendly service, fresh simple meals and a bright decor. The few covered tables on the outside decking are the ones to go for. BYO only. It serves delicious banana pancakes and more for breakfast, coffee and terrific cakes until 1730. Recommended.

Bars and clubs

Central Perth p56, map p58
See the website www.teknoscape.com.au, for details of club nights and events.

Belgian Beer Café Westende, corner of Murray and King Sts, T9321 4094, www.belgianbeer.com.au. Meals Sun-Thu 1200-2130, Fri-Sat 1200-2200. Mon-Tue 1100-2300, Wed-Sat 1100-2400 and Sun 1100-2200. As you'd expect, Belgian beer on tap and good selection in the fridge. Serves pub food and bar snacks, also does specials such as Oyster Hour. Spacious wooden interior and pavement tables. Sat and Thu live music, burlesque dancing first Fri of the month.

Durty Nelly's Irish Pub, Shafto Lane, T9226 0233, www.durtynellys.com.au. Irish pub with a dark, cosy interior enriched by a large outdoor terrace on the lane. Irish dishes and Australian pub food Mon-Sat 1130-2100, Sun 1200-2000. Lunch specials available. Live music on Fri and Sat night, and Sun during the day.

The George, 216 St George's Terr, T6161 6662, www.thegeorgeperth.com.au. Mon-Fri 0700-2400, Sat 1700-2400. A tavern that offers restaurant standard food. Breakfast, nibbles and hearty mains, the dishes vary from pub favourites to more sophisticated fare. The cocktails are very good and the wine list comprehensive. It gets busy at weekends, so if coming for food arrive early.

Greenhouse, 100 St Georges Terr, T9481 8333, www.greenhouseperth.com. Mon-Sat 0700- late. Visitors can't miss this establishment with its outside walls covered in terracotta potted strawberry plants. Inside, the insulation is straw, the furniture is recycled timber and booze bottles are artistically hung from ropes above the bar. There is a restaurant and bar downstairs serving seasonal fare, and a separate bar upstairs surrounded by a garden growing ingredients for the kitchen. Live music on Sat nights. Good cocktails.

Grosvenor Hotel, corner of Hay and Hill Sts, near the Perth Mint, T9325 3799, www.thegrosvenorperth.com.au. Mon-Sat 1100-2400, Sun 1100-2200. Has a large outdoor terrace, well shaded and with lots of tables. A contemporary, stylish feel has been grafted into this old pub, but the menu combines traditional counter meals with a few spicy snacks available Mon-Fri 1200-1500 and 1600-2100, Sat-Sun 1200-2100.

Helvetica, near 101 St George's Terr (laneway off Howard St), T9321 4422, www.helvetica bar.com. Tue-Thu 1500-1200, Fri 1200-1200, Sat 1800-1200. A stylish place hidden amongst the tower blocks. See the blackboard behind the bar the newest drinks, or lose yourself in the whisk(e)y menu. There are cocktails, beers and a good wine list as well as tasty bar snacks. Free Wi-Fi.

Hula Bula Bar, 12 Victoria Av, T9225 4457, www.hulabulabar.com. Wed-Fri 1600-late, Sat 1800-late. This funky Tiki cocktail bar serves inventive drinks in creative mugs. Groovy 1950s-1970s music, relaxed atmosphere. Recommended.

Moon and Sixpence, 300 Murray St. Very British, popular with those wanting a drink in the sun. More than 15 beers on tap.
Tiger Lil's, 437 Murray St, T9322 7377, www.tigerlils.com.au. Tue-Sat from 1200. This Asian pub offers a mix of authentic shared dishes, creative cocktails, international beers and DJ music in an oriental setting.

Northbridge and around *p62, maps p58 and p61*

Aberdeen, 84 Aberdeen St, T9227 9361, www.thedeen.com. Mon and Sat 1800-0200, Thu-Fri 1700-0200. A huge venue popular with students and backpackers, especially on Mon night when there are drink specials and DJs. Thu is Latin Beats.
Bar Open, 232-234 William St, T9227 0106. Wed-Thu 2000-0300, Fri-Sat 2000-0600. One of Perth's hidden secrets, this club can only be reached via a back alley. It is small but popular among those in the know. DJ music.
The Bird, 181 William St, www.william streetbird.com. This music venue hosts a range of live bands and has an alternative vibe. It's small so arrive early or you'll n ever get to the bar. Check the website to find out what's on.
The Brass Monkey, 209 William St, T9227 9596, www.thebrassmonkey.com.au. Mon-Tue 1100-2400, Wed-Thu 1100-0100, Fri-Sat 1100-0200, Sun 1100-2200. Northbridge's distinctive landmark, built in 1897. Mellow old front bar, quiet courtyard seats and the Tap Room for serious beer drinkers and sports watchers. Excellent brasserie upstairs (see Eating, page 72), sophisticated wine bar next door.
The Court, 50 Beaufort St, T9328 5292, www.thecourt.com.au. Gay venue with DJs, drag shows and live bands. Also pool tables, bar snacks and a beer garden.
Elephant and Wheelbarrow, 53 Lake St, T9228 4433, www.elephantandwheelbarrow. com.au. Mon-Thu 1100-2400, Fri-Sat 1200-0300, Sun 1200-2400. British-style pub popular with backpackers. British and Irish beers on tap and in bottles, live covers

and retro music Wed-Sun, cheap pub grub and pleasant shady terrace.
Grapeskin Wine Bar, 209 William St, T9227 9596. Bar Mon-Tue 1200-2400, Wed-Thu 1200-0100, Fri-Sat 1200-0200, Sun 1200-2200. Stylish, contemporary bar and bottleshop attracts a sophisticated crowd of beautiful people. Also has good menu of grazing and sharing food available 1200-2200. Shares food specials with The Brass Monkey next door.
Library, 69 Lake St, T9328 1065, www.librarynightclub.com.au. Open 2000-late. DJs entertain clubbers in the 4 bars set out over 3 levels. The decor is opulent with crystal chandeliers, marble columns and velvet furnishings. Funk and House.
Luxe Bar, 446 Beaufort St, Highgate, T9228 9680. Wed-Sun 2000-late. Enjoy a cocktail and the luxurious atmosphere in one of the 3 highly fashionable lounges.
Must Winebar, 519 Beaufort St, Highgate, T9328 8255, www.must.com.au. Open 1200-2400. A heaven for wine lovers that also serves superb French-style food.
Rocket Room, 174 James St (downstairs), T9328 9633. Fri-Sat 0800-0400. The place to come for live performances of rock and metal bands, including a number of album launches and local talent. It can be heavy stuff though, so consider your ear plugs if you're heading down.
Rosie O'Grady's, corner of James and Milligan Sts, T9328 1488. Typical 'Irish' pub, dark and green cosiness and a good range of British and Irish beers. Backpacker night with drink specials Tue and Sun from 1800. Live music Wed-Sun.
Universal Wine Bar, 221 William St, T9227 6771, www.universalbar.com.au. Wed-Sun. Wed-Thu, Sun 1700-2400, Fri-Sat 1700-0200. Hip without being slick, the Universal's long room opens to the street but becomes dim and jazzy at the back. Good snack menu Wed-Sun from 1700. Live blues and jazz every night.

Subiaco and around *p62, map p63*
Subiaco Hotel, corner of Rokeby Rd and Hay St, T9381 3069. Large historic hotel refurbished in smart, contemporary style, and now the social hub of Subi. 3 main areas: edgy public bar serving up cheap counter meals, 1200-2300 with live music Thu, Sat, DJs Fri and **Subiaco Café**, the hotel's upmarket, mid-range terrace restaurant, jazz band on Wed and Sat nights. Café meals 0700-late.

Leederville *p63*
The Garden, 742 Newcastle St, T9202 8282, www.thegarden.net.au. A bar/pub attracting a slightly older crowd than the Leederville next door. Patrons can sit in the spacious beer garden and sip wine or draught beer, there is a good selection of both, and tuck in to the good quality food. There are small plates for sharing such as the cheese selection, the smoky almonds or the Fremantle octopus, or larger meals such as steak or salads. A lovely place to kick back and relax.
Hip-E Club, corner of Newcastle and Oxford Sts (rear of Leederville Village), T9227 8899, www.hipeclub.com.au. Tue-Wed and Fri from 2200, Sat from 2100. 70s, 80s and early 90s psychedelia and backpacker specials (Tue from 2000).
The Manor, Newcastle St, T9272 9893, located behind the **Hip-E Club**. French-style bar with a relaxed atmosphere in the lounge upstairs and DJ music downstairs with the 'Grand Piano' DJ desk as an eye catcher. Fri-Sat 2100-0500.
Niche, off Oxford St, T9227 1007, www.niche bar.com.au. Wed 1900-0200, Thu 2100-0200, Fri-Sat 1900-0300. Popular, fashionable bar.

Claremont *p64*
The Claremont, 1 Bay View Terr, T9286 0123, www.theclaremont.com.au. Corner pub with large terrace and lots of standing space. Inside is leather and wood, and there's a pool table. Live music or DJs Thu-Sun. Tue is quiz night, Wed there are salsa classes upstairs and on Sat all cocktails are $10.

Nedlands *p64*
Captain Stirling, 80 Stirling Highway, T9386 2200, www.captainstirlinghotel.com.au. Stylish old pub renovated in colonial style and located in the **Captain Stirling Hotel**, popular with an older crowd. Excellent food daily 1200-2200.

Cottesloe *p65, map p65*
Cottesloe is renowned for its Sun sessions. Sun afternoons in the extensive beer gardens of the 'Cott' or the 'OBH' attract thousands of svelte and tanned beach boys and girls. Shades, attitude and surf attire are all essential.
Cottesloe Beach Hotel, see Sleeping. The mustard-coloured art deco Cott has an ocean-facing balcony (although the view is not quite as good as the **OBH**) and a contemporary stylish bar. The Sun session is most popular here and the pub has live music from Wed-Sat. The pub also has an ATM and a pleasant colourful café, open daily for lunch, dinner Tue-Sun and breakfast on weekends.
Ocean Beach Hotel, see Sleeping. The long back bar has pool tables but the front bar is the one to head for at sunset. Picture windows overlook the ocean in a large wood-lined room.

⦿ Entertainment

The main agency is **Ticketmaster**, infoline T1900 933666, bookings T136100, www.ticketmaster.com.au. Ask for the nearest retail outlet. Theatre tickets are usually handled by **BOCS Ticketing**, T9484 1133, www.bocs ticketing.com.au. BOCS ticket outlets: Perth Concert Hall, His Majesty's Theatre, Playhouse Theatre and Subiaco Arts Centre.

Cinema
Indoor Screening details are published daily in the *West Australian* newspaper.
Ace Cinema, 500 Hay St, Subiaco, T9388 6500, www.moviemasters.com.au. Mainstream movies, parking available.

Cinema Paradiso, 164 James St, Northbridge, T9227 1771. Arthouse and mainstream features. Has a good bar and is fully licensed so patrons can enjoy a drink with their film.

Luna, 155 Oxford St, Leederville, T9444 4056, www.lunapalace.com.au. Mainstream and alternative movies. Themed double features on Mon evenings.

Windsor, 98 Stirling Highway, Nedlands, T9386 3554, www.lunapalace.com.au. Old-fashioned, small cinema, where the first subtitled film was shown in Perth. Now screens a combination of mainstream and indie flicks.

Outdoor One of the best things to do in Perth is to see a film at an outdoor cinema. You can usually take a picnic and nothing beats having a drink while you recline in a deck chair and gaze at the stars during the slow bits. Season limited to summer only (Dec-Apr).

Camelot, 16 Lochee St, Mosman Park, T9385 4793, www.lunapalace.com.au. Recent releases in a fairly classy setting, also home to the Flickerfest short film festival in Mar. Licensed venue, bar profits support the Mosman Park Arts Foundation. Wood-fired pizzas available. No BYO.

Luna Outdoor, 155 Oxfords St, Leederville, T9444 4056, www.lunapalace.com.au. Aims to screen films that can't be seen elsewhere such as Japanese horror or cult skate flicks. Picnics OK but venue is licensed so no BYO.

Moonlight Cinema, www.moonlight. com.au. Synergy Parkland in King's Park, screens popular favourites and cult classics (Jan-Mar). Limited number of bean beds available ($6). Tickets on the website or at the box office near the entrance from 1800.

Somerville Auditorium at UWA, T9380 1732, and **Joondalup Picture Garden**, T6304 5888, at Edith Cowan University in Joondalup both screen arthouse and foreign films from the Perth International Arts Festival (Feb-Mar). Tickets at the door or from the website www.perthfestival.com.au. Arrive by 1800 for a good seat at the picturesque Somerville.

Theatre

Contact **BOCS** for theatre tickets and current performances.

Belvoir Amphitheatre, T9296 3033, www.belvoir.net.au, and **Quarry Amphitheatre**, T9385 9263, www.quarryamphitheatre.com.au, both lovely stone amphitheatres in classical Greek style. Look out for events.

His Majesty's, 825 Hay St, T9265 0900, www.hismajestystheatre.com.au. A beautiful Edwardian theatre and the state's main venue. Also home of the WA Ballet and WA Opera companies. There is a Museum of Performing Arts here as well, Mon-Fri 1000-1600, gold coin donation entry.

Perth Concert Hall, 5 St Georges Terr, T9231 9900, www.perthconcerthall.com.au. The main venue for classical performances, particularly from the West Australian Symphony Orchestra.

Playhouse, 3 Pier St, T9323 3400, www.playhousetheatre.com.au. Modern proscenium arch theatre and home of the Perth Theatre Company, producing contemporary and classic works with local and national performers.

Regal, 474 Hay St, Subiaco, T132 849, www.regaltheatre.com.au. Puts on a wide range of local and touring shows and performers. Bookings BOCS.

Subiaco Arts Centre, 180 Hammersley Rd, Subiaco, T9380 3000, www.subiacoarts centre.com.au. A major venue set in lovely gardens near the top of Rokeby Rd. A 300-seat auditorium and smaller studio performance space. Home to the **Barking Gecko Theatre Company**, www.barkinggecko.com.au.

Yirra Yaakin Noongar Theatre, 65 Murray St, T9202 1966, www.yirra yaakin.asn.au. A Noongar company that produces Aboriginal theatre using Aboriginal writers, directors, designers and production staff.

⊛ Festivals and events

Perth has just one major festival and lacks major sporting events due to its isolation and small population. Most events are held during spring and summer.

Jan Hopman Cup, www.hopmancup. com. A tennis championship held at Burswood Dome running for a week. International teams of 1 man and woman from each country, compete against each other. Attracts some big tennis names but there are fears Perth may lose the event to another state in the next few years.

26 Jan Skyworks, held every Australia Day, is a fireworks show set to music broadcast on a local radio station. It is Perth's most popular event, attracting 400,000 people who picnic in Kings Park and along the Swan River foreshore to watch the fireworks. Get a position many hours before the show starts.

Feb Rottnest Channel Swim, www.rottnest channelswim.com.au, about 1200 people race from Cottesloe Beach to Rottnest (20 km). It's all over pretty quickly but fun to watch the start and finish.

Feb-Mar Perth International Arts Festival, the main event of the year, including hundreds of events all over the city. This includes the best local and international theatre, opera, dance, visual arts and music. The cultural centre acts as a focus point, alive with activity from 1730-0300. A film festival is also part of the programme, held outdoors from Dec-Apr at the Somerville at UWA and Joondalup Pines at Edith Cowan University. Programs are widely available from Dec, all festival tickets from BOCS or the festival website. For more info T6488 2000, www.perthfestival.com.au.

Early Aug Avon Descent, www.avon descent.com.au, a 133-km whitewater competition on the Avon River from Northam to Perth. It's always an exciting event, involving some portage, but gets hairy when water levels are low and kayaks or rafts get stuck on rocks.

Sep Kings Park Wildflower Festival, is a huge indoor and outdoor display of native plants and flowers. This is a good way to see the state's incredible variety of wildflowers if you're not able to get to the wildflower country (mid-west region) during the Sep-Oct wildflower season. Held for about one month. Information can be found at www.bgpa.wa.gov.au.

Oct Pride Festival is a celebration of gay and lesbian arts, culture and entertainment. Ends with a fantastic parade through the streets of Northbridge and a dance party. For more info T9427 0828, www.pridewa.asn.au.

Nov-Dec Artrage Festival, T9227 6288, www.artrage.com.au. Alternative arts festival including theatre, dance, music, street performers, comedy and visual arts. Perth and Fremantle.

○ Shopping

Shopping hours are Mon-Thu 0830-1730 with late-night shopping until 2100 in the city and Fremantle on Fri, and in the suburbs on Thu. Sat hours are 0830-1700. On Sun, city hours are 1100-1700, Fremantle 1000-1800.

Central Perth *p56, map p58*
Perth's compact shopping area consists of the parallel Hay St and Murray St Malls and the arcades connecting them. The shopping also continues west along Hay St as far as King St, which is a trendy pocket of high-end fashion and homewares shopping, galleries and cafes. The city has 2 major department stores, **Myers** in Forrest Pl, and **David Jones** occupying a block between the Malls. These both sell almost everything and David Jones has an excellent food hall.

Arts and crafts
Aspects of Kings Park, Fraser Av, Kings Park, T9480 3900, www.aspectsofkings park.com.au, daily 0900-1700. Top quality gallery and gift shop, owned by the Botanic Gardens and Parks Authority and featuring

works by local artists that reflect on the natural environment. There is also a good selection of natural history titles.

Creative Native, 58 Forrest Chase, Forrest Pl, T9221 5800, www.creativenative.com.au. Open 0900-1700. Large commercial Aboriginal art gallery and shop. Also good books on Aboriginal art.

Form Contemporary Art and Design, 357 Murray St, T9226 2799, www.form.net.au. Mon-Thu 0900-1730, Fri 0900-1800, Sat 0900-1700. A shop featuring the very best of contemporary Australian design, including ceramics, glass work, jewellery, textiles, sculpture and woodwork.

Books and maps

The main chains are **Dymocks**, **Borders**, both in Hay St Mall, and **Angus and Robertson**, in the Murray St Mall, diagonally across from the entrance to Myers. These chains can also be found in suburban shopping centres.

All Foreign Language Bookshop, 572 Hay St, T9485 1246. Mon-Sat 0930-1700, Fri 0930-1900, Sat 1030-1600. Dictionaries, some foreign language titles and language learning tools such as tapes and books. The usual French and Spanish, but also Laotian, Swahili and books on Macedonian poetry.

Boffins, 806 Hay St, T9321 5755, www.boffinsbookshop.com.au. Mon-Thu 0900-1730, Fri 0900-2000, Sat 0900-1700, Sun 1200-1700. An independent selling practical, technical and special interest books. It has a travel section on the ground floor.

Elizabeth's Second-hand Bookshop, 820 Hay St, T9481 8848. Perth's best second-hand range. Also suburban branches including 375 Roberts Rd, Subiaco, T9381 5886 and a number in Fremantle.

Fantasy Planet, 8 Shafto Lane, T9481 8393. Sci-fi and fantasy. Mon-Thu 1000-1800, Fri 1000-2100, Sat 0930-1730.

The Perth Map Centre, 900 Hay St, T9322 5733, www.mapworld.com.au. Mon-Fri 0900-1730, Sat 1000-1500. Maps and guidebooks for every state and country. Full range of topographic maps, also Munda Biddi maps, Bibbulmun and Cape-to-Cape track maps. See also **Art Gallery of WA** (page 56), **WA Museum** (page 57) and **Alexander Library** (page 57).

Clothes

Outback Red, Plaza Arcade. Bushwear such as boots, hats and moleskins.

R M Williams, upstairs in the Carillion Arcade. Sell rugged countrywear such as boots, hats and moleskins.

Surf & Skate, 328 Murray St. Good surfwear and wide range of flip flops.

Underground Surf Sports, corner Plaza Arcade and Hay St Mall. Good for surf and swimwear.

Wheels & Dollbaby, 26 King St, T9481 8488, www.wheelsanddollbaby.com.au. Mon-Thu and Sat 1000-1800, Fri 1000-2100, Sun 1100-1700. Vintage and rockabilly inspired fashion, popular with celebrities and with a price tag to match.

Jewellery

The city centre is awash with jewellery shops. For cheaper imported jewellery try the Fremantle markets.

Antika, Shop 39 London Court, T9325 3352. There's nowhere better for silver jewellery.

Rosendorff's, 673 Hay St Mall, T9321 4015, www.rosendorffs.com. One of the best, for Arygle diamonds, Broome pearls and Australian opal in a classy environment.

Markets

The king of Perth markets is actually to be found in Fremantle. These markets are fairly permanent, well-established affairs.

Canning Vale Markets, 280 Bannister Rd, Canning Vale, T9455 1389, www.canningvale markets.com, just east of Jandakot airport. Huge flea market with hundreds of stalls. Sun 0700-1530. During the week this is WA's biggest undercover wholesale market for meat, fish, flowers and fruit and veg. Clearance sale on Sat.

Wanneroo Market, 33 Prindiville Dr, Wanneroo, 22 km north of city centre, T9409

8397. Fri, Sat and Sun 0900-1700. A huge a/c indoor market selling everything and anything. Also has a food court.

Music

78 Records, 914 Hay St, T9322 6384, www.78records.com.au. Mon-Thu 0900-1730, Fri 0900-1900, Sat 0900-1700, Sun 1200-1700. Huge selection, also ticket outlet for gigs and sells music mags.
Beat Route, 37 Barrack St, T9218 9981, www.beatrouterecords.com.au. New and second-hand vinyl, as well as CDs and books.
Wesley Classics, 800 Hay St, opposite Wesley Arcade, T9321 1978, www.wesleyclassics. com.au. Mon-Fri 0900-1730, Sat 0900-1700. Classical CDs.

Outdoor

The outdoor shops are all clustered together on Hay Street, a number sell maps for the Bibbulmun and Cape-to-Cape tracks, as well as the Munda Biddi Trail.
Kathmandu, 895 Hay St, www.kathmandu.com.au.
Mainpeak, 858 Hay St, T9322 9044, www.mainpeak.com.au. Mon-Thu 0900-1800, Fri 0900-2100, Sat 0900-1700, Sun 1200-1700. Well-stocked store, strong on local knowledge. Trekking slide shows year-round, also hire of almost all gear except boots. There are 2 other stores at 31 and 35 Jarrad St, Cottesloe, T9385 2552, which also hire out sea kayaks.
Mountain Designs, 862 Hay St, T9322 4774, www.mountaindesigns.com.
Paddy Pallin, 884 Hay St, T9321 2666, www.paddypallin.com.au.

Northbridge and around *p62, map p61*
There are number of interesting small boutiques in Northbridge, and most can be found on William St. The many Asian supermarkets are on William St between Newcastle and Brisbane.
Fi & Co, 289 William St, T9328 6007, www.fiandco.com.au. Beautiful new and vintage clothes (for men and women), as well as colourful shoes and accessories.

Kakulas Brothers, 183 William St, T9328 5744, www.kakulasbros.com.au. Fantastic shop, with towers of spices and self-serve vats of pulses, nuts and dried fruit. Also offers delicatessen food such as cheese and meats. Stocks imported goods; English jam and squash, Swiss chocolate and Greek tea. Reasonably priced and offers takeaway, freshly ground coffee.

Subiaco and around *p62, map p63*
Rokeby Rd is a good spot for clothes shopping.
Chokeby Rd, 175 Rokeby Rd, Subiaco, T9481 1144. Chocolate specialists, bursting with both hand-crafted and European goodies.
Earth Market, 14/375 Subiaco Mews, Hay St, Subiaco, T9382 2266, www.earthmarket. com.au. Mon-Fri 0900-1800, Sat 0900-1700. Organic food store and café.
Kailis Fish Market, 101 Oxford St, Leederville, T9443 6300, www.kailisbrosleederville. com.au. Daily 0700-1800. Every kind of fresh fish and seafood available relatively close to the city centre.
Linney's, 37 Rokeby Rd, Subiaco. Mon, Wed, Fri 0930-1700, Tue 1000-1700, Thu 0930-2000, Sat 0930-1600. Specializes in WA pearls, diamonds and gold.
Mr Sparrow, 223 Bagot Rd, Subiaco, T9381 6362, www.mrsparrow.com.au. Mon-Fri 0930-1730, Sat 1000-1700. A boutique selling interesting jewellery, homewares and gardening gifts.
Oxford St Books, 119 Oxford St, Leederville, T9443 9844. Open until 2230 every night. A good range of books and helpful staff.
Rockeby Records, 16A Rokeby Rd, Subiaco, T9381 5126. Has a big mainstream range.
Subiaco Bookshop, 113 Rockeby Rd, T9382 1945. An independent with a interesting selection of titles. The tables are bound to yield some treasures.
Tea for Me, corner of Rokeby Rd and Church St, Subiaco, T9380 9377, www.teaforme. com.au. Mon-Fri 0930-1700, Sat until 1600. Nearly 100 different flavoured Ceylon teas, available in leaf or as teabags. Also sells exquisite ceramic tea sets.

Nedlands and Claremont p64

The best clothes shopping is found in Subiaco and Claremont. Bay View and St Quentins Terraces in Claremont are full of fashion boutiques, and it is shoe heaven with a number of good shoe shops.

Claremont Fresh, 333 Stirling Highway, Claremont, T9383 3066. Daily 0700-1900. A fruit and veg market, also selling seafood, bread and some groceries.

Fresh Provisions, 303 Stirling Highway, Bayview Shopping Centre, Claremont, T9383 3308, www.provisions.com.au. A small supermarket open 0900-2200.

The Lane Bookshop, 52C Old Theatre Lane, Claremont, T9384 4423, www.lanebook. com.au. Mon-Wed and Fri 0900-1730, Thu 0900-2100, Sat 0900-1700, Sun 1030-1330. Fine range of literary, arts and travel titles and knowledgeable, helpful staff.

Peter's Choice Butchery, 3 St Quentin Av, Claremont, T9383 3637. Sells takeaway pastas and curries by weight.

Zenith Music, 309 Stirling Highway, Bayview Shopping Centre, Claremont, T9383 1422, www.zenithmusic.com. One of Perth's most comprehensive selections of CDs, also instruments and sheet music.

Zomp, 2 Bayview Terr, Claremont, T9384 6250, www.zomp.com.au. A wide range of good-quality women's shoes, from sky-high heels to biker boots. There's another branch on King St in Perth CBD.

South Perth p64

Mill Point Caffé Bookshop 254 Mill Point Rd, South Perth, T9367 4567. Daily 0830-1730. Knowledgeable staff and a pleasant café.

▲ Activities and tours

AFL (Australian rules)

West Coast Eagles and the *Fremantle Dockers* both play at the Subiaco Oval. Each have home games, once a fortnight on either a Sat or Sun, from the end of Mar to Aug. See www.afl.com.au for fixtures. Tickets from Ticketmaster, T1300 136100. Tickets go on sale 2 weeks before a match and often sell out, so it's best to book.

Backpacker buses

Easyrider, T1300 308477, www.easyrider tours.com.au. Offers hop-on hop-off transport up to Exmouth, Broome and the southwest.

Nullarbor Traveller, T8687 0457 and T1800 816858, www.the-traveller.com.au. Runs excellent 9-day adventure trips to Adelaide ($1350, concessions $1295) that include swimming with tuna, departing most Sun at 0700 from Welling St coach rank. There is also a 6-day camping trip from Perth to Esperance ($770, concessions $740).

Boat cruises

For maximum time at Rottnest, take an early trip from Fremantle. Several companies operate cruises on the Swan River from the Barrack St Jetty.

Captain Cook Cruises, Pier 3, Barrack St, T9325 3341, www.captaincookcruises. com.au. Cruises range from short runs to Fremantle, lunch and dinner cruises (around $64-99), to gourmet wine-tasting trips upriver to Swan Valley ($146).

Mills Charters, T9246 5334, www.mills charters.com.au. Heads out from Hillarys Boat Harbour (see page 66) for deep-sea fishing most days of the week (depending on demand) at 0630 ($185 weekdays, $210 weekends). Also offers 3-hr whale-watching trips ($80, concessions $65, children $55) departing Tue, Thu, Sat and Sun at 0900. Night-fishing trips run Fri and Sat 1730-0200.

Rottnest Express, Pier 2, Barrack St Jetty, T1300 467688, www.rottnestexpress.com.au. Day returns to Rottnest for $79.50, Also offers accommodation packages, and bike and snorkel gear hire.

Rottnest Fast Ferries, Hillarys Boat Harbour (see page 66), T9246 1039, www.rottnest fastferries.com.au. Day returns to Rottnest for $82. Offers accommodation packages, bike hire, snorkel hire and also options that combine a cruise around Rottnest with surf lessons or entry to the aquarium. Whale-watching tours run Sep-Dec (2 hrs) and cost $62, children $36, concessions $51. Pick-ups available from Perth.

Cricket
WACA, T9265 7222, www.waca.com.au. The state side *Western Warriors* play during summer. The ground also occasionally hosts international matches.

Cycling tours
Remote Outback Cycle Tours, T03445 4927, T1800 157830, www.cycletours.com.au. Offers superb 4WD and cycle combination tours, including from Perth to Uluru, $4420, 24 days.

Diving
Aqwa, Hillarys Boat Harbour (see page 66), T9447 7500. You can arrange to scuba dive or snorkel with the sharks. Daily 1300 and 1500, $175-199.
Australian Diving Academy, T9356 9677, www.ausdiving.com.au. Runs PADI courses and dive trips to Rottnest.

Golf
Perth has excellent courses that welcome visitors and have relatively low fees.
Burswood Park, Roger Mackay Dr, Burswood, T9470 2992, www.burswoodparkgolfcourse. com. Great city views. Equipment hire.
Vines Resort, Verdelho Dr, Swan Valley, T9297 3000, www.vines.com.au. A 36-hole championship course along banks of Ellen Brook, good facilities nearby at the resort.
Wembley, The Boulevard, Floreat, T9484 2500, www.wembleygolf.com.au. Two 18-hole layouts, also driving range, pro shop and bar.

Kayaking and rafting
Rivergods, 3/10 Whyalla St, Willetton, T9259 0749, www.rivergods.com.au. Heads out daily Sep-Jun to Penguin Island off Rockingham to see the penguins and seals ($139, concessions $125, children $95). Trips

further afield and personalized canoeing/rafting trips available.

Kitesurfing
This fast-growing sport of surfing harnessed to a parachute offers awesome power and speed, and is generally practised off the beaches between Cottesloe and Fremantle.
Choice Kitesurfing, 4/54 Rockingham Rd, Hamilton Hill, T9336 7884, www.choice kitesurfing.com.au. Lessons, beginners $160 for 2 hrs. Unlimited free lessons if purchasing a kite and board package.

Parasailing
South Perth Parasailing, Mill Point Rd, T0408 382 595, www.southperthpara sailing.com.au. Daily in summer (weather permitting). Single $80, tandem $140.

Sailing
Funcats, Coode St Jetty, South Perth, T0408 926003, www.funcats.com.au. Daily 0930-1830, Oct-Apr. Surfcat hire for $30 per hr, free tuition (1-3 people).
Wind Dancer, Hillarys Boat Harbour, T9448 2496. Available for charter for a wide range of sailing excursions ($650 per day, max 12 passengers) and also heads out for half-day cruises about once a week depending on demand ($35 per person).

Scenic flights
Rottnest Air Taxi, T9292 5027 and T1800 500006, www.rottnest.de. Offers a range of flights from Jandakot Airport. A 35-min flight over Perth, and Rottnest is $100, minimum 2 people.

Skydiving
WA Skydiving Academy, 48 William St, Northbridge, T9227 6066 and T1300 137855, www.waskydiving.com.au. Accelerated freefall $550. Perth City tandem jumps Mon-Thu $450-530. Pinjarra tandem jumps $240-400.

Surfing and bodyboarding

There is an artificial reef called Cables, south of Cottesloe Beach, ensuring consistent breaks all year round. **Whalebone Classic** is a Malibu competition attracting about 5000 people over a weekend in mid-Jul.

Fun's Back Surf, 120 Marine Parade, T9284 7873. A good point of ontact for information. Surfboard hire is $35, snorkel gear $25.
Vision Surf, Esplanade, T9245 3227. Hires out surfboards for $30/2 hrs, bodyboards for $25 for 2 hrs and wetsuits for $10 a day.

Tour operators

Out & About, T9377 3376, www.outandabouttoursocm.au. Takes small groups to visit wineries plus the chocolate and cheese factories. All tours include lunch/dinner, free pick-up and drop-off in Perth. Prices between $95-135.
Planet Perth, T9225 6622, www.planet tours.com.au. Tours to the Pinnacles, Monkey Mia and the Southwest.
Swan Valley Tours, T9274 1199, www.svtours.com.au. Swan Valley tours, wine tasting, cheese tastings, a visit to a microbrewery, the nougat factory, the chocolate factory and Guildford. Also offers cruise options. $65-130 including lunch.
Two Feet and a Heartbeat, www.twofeet.com.au. Evening walking tours of Perth. The main tour is one of the CBD where the guide tells stories and provides information on the history and architecture, 2 hrs, $40 (only $20 on Tue). The tour starts at 1730 and ends with a drink in **Rosie O'Grady's** in Northbridge. Another option is a tour of Perth's small bars (3 hrs) for $40, including tapas and drinks tasting. Shopping tours run on the last Sat of the month ($89) and include lunch and a chat with a stylist.
Urban Aboriginal Tours, T0403 529473, www.urbanindigenoustours.com. An opportunity to indulge in contemporary Aboriginal Australia by visiting suburban art studios, meeting with local Aboriginal artists, sampling contemporary bush foods and stopping for lunch at a local Indigenous café.

The day ends with a didgeridoo workshop. $125, concessions $110.
Western Xposure, T9371 3695 and T1800 621200, www.westernxposure.com.au. For direct 4WD trips to Alice Springs. It also heads down to the southwest and up around the coast as far as Darwin.

Waterskiing

Extreme Ski WA, Narrows Bridge, South Perth, T0417 792118, www.extremeskiwa. com. Oct-Apr Tue-Sun, May-Sep Sun. Water-skiing and wakeboarding is $35 for 15 mins (free coaching), tubing $20 for 15 mins.

⊖ Transport

Air

Skywest flies daily to **Albany**, **Broome**, **Carnarvon** (Tue, Thu, Fri, Sat and Sun), **Esperance** (Sun-Fri), **Exmouth** (Sun-Fri), **Geraldton**, **Kalgoorlie** (Sun-Fri), and **Port Hedland** (Wed-Sat). Qantas provides daily flights to **Broome**, **Kalgoorlie**, **Karratha** and **Port Hedland**. It also has daily flights to most state capitals (except Hobart) and **Alice Springs**. Virgin Blue flies daily to **Adelaide**, **Broome**, **Melbourne** and **Sydney**.

Airlines Air New Zealand, 178 St George's Terr, T9442 6077. British Airways, 77 St Georges Terr, T9425 5333. Garuda Indonesia, 40 The Esplanade, T9321 5100. Malaysia Airlines, 56 William St, T9263 7007. Qantas, 55 William St, T131313. Royal Brunei, 216 St George's Terr, T9321 8757 or 131223. Singapore Airlines, 178 St George's Terr, T9479 8166 or 131011 Skywest, Perth Domestic Airport, T9477 8301 or 1300 660088. South African Airways, Perth International Airport, T9477 1314. Virgin Blue, T136789.

Bicycle

Perth is ideal for cycling and there a number of bike shops that will hire out gear for good prices. Pick up detailed maps of cycle routes: *Bikewest Perth Bike Map Series* is good.

Ticket to ride

Transperth routes extend beyond Hillarys to the north, out to the Swan Valley and Perth Hills, and south as far as Mandurah. Fares are worked out according to how many zones you cross. The central suburbs are encompassed by zone 1, and zone 2 extends to include Fremantle, Cottesloe, Scarborough and Midland. Tickets are valid for two to three hours, and cost $2.50 for travel within one zone, $3.70 for two zones. A multi-zone *DayRider* ticket is available for $9 after 0900 and is valid all day. *FamilyRider* ticket is a real bargain: two adults, plus up to five children, travel anywhere and back for $9. It's available all day weekends, after 0900 school holiday weekdays, after 1800 Monday-Thursday, and 1500 Friday. Standard tickets, *DayRiders* and *FamilyRiders* can be purchased on board buses and ferries, and at train stations. If travellers are going to be in Perth for a month or more it is worth investing in a *SmartRider*, an electronic ticket to which value is added. Don't forget to tag on and tag off if using it. For more information take a look at www.transperth.wa.gov.au or call the infoline on T136213.

About Bike Hire, Causeway car park, corner Plain St and Riverside Drive, East Perth, T9221 2665, www.aboutbikehire.com.au. Apr-Nov daily 0900-1700 and Dec-Mar 0900-1800. $36 for 24-hr rental. Prices drop if hiring for more than 1 day.

Cycle Centre, 282 Hay St, opposite Perth Mint, T9325 1176. Mon-Fri 0900-1730, Sat 0900-1500, Sun 1300-1600. Hires bikes for $25 a day.

Bus

Local The free city centre buses, CATs, T136213 take 3 circuits. **Blue Cat** travels around Northbridge, through city centre, and around Riverside Drive and Mounts Bay Rd. Buses every 7 mins Mon-Fri 0650-1820, and every 15 mins on Fri 1820-0100, Sat 0830-0100, and Sun 1000-1700. **Red Cat** heads to East Perth just short of the WACA, and to West Perth as far as Outram St. The service runs much of the length of Hay St in a westerly direction, and Murray St the other way. Buses every 5 mins Mon-Fri 0650-1820, and every 25 mins Sat-Sun 1000-1815. The **Yellow Cat** operates in a loop from East Perth to West Perth, from Claisebrook train station along Wellington St to the Princess Margaret Hospital. Buses every 10 mins Mon-Fri 0650-1820, and every 30 mins Sat-Sun 1000-1815. All 3 services run within 200 m of the Wellington St Station, the Blue Cat stops at both the Esplanade Busport and Barrack Sq (for the Barrack St Jetty). No CAT services on public holidays.

Selected bus services from Wellington St Bus Station: **Airport** (domestic terminal), 37; **Fremantle** (Queen St and/or Railway Station) via **East Perth**, 103, 106, 160; **Kalamunda**, 283, 296, 299; **Kings Park Rd, Nedlands, Claremont**, 102, 103.

Long distance The majority of services are run by the state-owned company TransWA, Perth Business Centre and main stations, T1300 662205, www.transwa.wa.gov.au, whose routes extend right around the southwest, east as far as Norseman, and north as far as Kalbarri and Meekatharra. There are a handful of other operators that may prove more convenient. **South West Coachlines**, 3 Mounts Bay Rd, T9324 2333, www.southwestcoachlines.com.au, has a couple of southern routes, including one terminating at **Dunsborough**, and another to **Manjimup**. Integrity, 554 Wellington St, T1800 226339 and T9226 1339, www.integritycoachlines.com.au, runs a route up the **Great Northern Highway** via **Meekatharra** and **Newman** to **Port Hedland** (departing Perth Wed 0900, arriving in Port Hedland Thu 1900). Given the sparsity of land transport in some parts of the state, **Greyhound**, East Perth Terminal, T1300 473946, www.greyhound.com.au, usually considered an interstate operator only, provides a few further, very useful options. Their main northbound service leaves Perth (East Perth bus station) at 0730, travels up the Great Northern Highway through **Geraldton**, stops at **Port Hedland** on the way up to **Broome**. This continues on via **Kununurra** and **Katherine** to Darwin (60 hrs). **Selected services** TransWA routes from Perth Railway Station or East Perth Terminal: **Albany** via **Mount Barker**, daily, GS1, GS2; **Albany** via **Timber towns**, daily, GS3; **Bunbury**, **Cape-to-Cape** towns, Sun-Fri, SW1; **Geraldton** via **Dongara**, Sun-Fri, N1; **Geraldton** via **Kalbarri**, Sun-Fri, N1; **Northam**, **York**, Sun-Wed, Fri, GS2; **Pemberton** via **Cape-to-Cape towns**, Sun-Thu, SW1; **Pemberton** via **Bunbury**, Mon, Wed, Sun, SW2.

Car
Perth is a fairly easy place to get around by car and there are no special restrictions or toll fees. The freeways are the arterial routes and entry and exit points are marked by large green signs. Kwinana Freeway services the southern suburbs, the Mitchell Freeway services the northern suburbs. The Graham Farmer Freeway is a short stretch just north of the city centre that connects the Mitchell Freeway to the Great Eastern Highway (and airports). The speed limit in built-up areas is 50 kph, unless signposted otherwise.
Car hire Bayswater, 160 Adelaide Terr, T9325 1000, www.bayswatercarrental. com.au, is one of the best value of many operators in the city, though they do not have a depot at either airport terminal.
Car parking Council car parks in Roe St, behind train station. Restricted meters in the city centre, several car parks off Riverside Drive and better value ones by the WACA. For more information on the car park, see www.perth.wa.gov.au/parking.

Car servicing Ultra Tune, 25 Newcastle St, Northbridge, T9227 5356, www.ultratune. com.au, has many other branches in the city.

Ferry
See also Boat cruises, above.
Transperth operates ferries from Barrack Street Jetty over to South Perth. Those to Mends St are the best for the zoo and main restaurants and leave every 20-30 mins daily from 0750-1924, and also to 2115 on Fri-Sat in Sep-Apr. Last return ferry is at 1930 (2130 Fri-Sat during Sep-Apr).

Taxi
There are dozens of taxi ranks around the city. A few are: outside Perth Station on Wellington St, southwest corner of junction of Adelaide Terr and Hill St, opposite the Melbourne on south side of Hay St. Also **Black & White**, T131008, www.blackandwhitetaxis.com.au. **Swan**, T131330, www.swantaxis.com.au.

Train
Local There are 5 suburban lines radiating like spokes from Perth station. All run regular services from early morning to past midnight. To the north the Joondalup line stops at **Leederville** and **Stirling** (change for Scarborough Beach) on the way, while the Fremantle line calls at **Subiaco**, **Claremont** and **Cottesloe** (with a 15-min walk to the beach). The Midland line has stops at **East Perth** (for TransWA services) and **Guildford** (the Swan Valley), and trains to **Armadale** call at **Burswood**. The Mandurah line runs via **Murdoch**, **Cockburn** and **Rockingham**. Fares are as per the bus services.
Long distance TransWA, Perth Business Centre and main stations, T1300 662205 or T9326 2600, www.transwa.wa.gov.au, most useful rail services are the *Prospector* line to **Toodyay**, **Northam** and **Kalgoorlie**, the *Australind* line to **Bunbury** and the *AvonLink* to **Avon Valley**. *The Indian Pacific*, T132147, www.gsr.com.au, heads to **Adelaide** (43 hrs) and **Sydney** (70 hrs) at 1155 on Wed and Sun.

❶ Directory

Banks The major banks have ATMs on Hay St Mall and Murray St Mall. They are also liberally located in all the central suburbs. Foreign exchange: American Express, 645 Hay St, T9221 0693. Mon-Fri 0900-1700, Sat 0900- 1200. **Embassies and consulates** Canada, 267 St George's Terr, T9322 7930. Germany, 8th floor, St George's Court, 16 St George's Terr, T9325 8851. Irish Republic, 10 Lilika Rd, City Beach, T9385 8247. Italy, 1292 Hay St, T9322 4500. Japan, Level 21, The Forrest Centre, 221 St George's Terr, T9480 1800. Netherlands, 1/88 Thomas St, T9486 1579. Spain, 23 Barrack St, T9225 5222. Sweden, Courier Australia, 23 Walters Dr, Herdsman, T9204 0900. UK, Level 26, Allendale Sq, 77 St George's Terr, T9224 4700. USA, 13th floor, St George's Court, 16 St George's Terr, Perth, T9202 1224.

Internet Free at Alexander Library, 1 hr only, booking required, T9427 3104, or 20 mins on the express terminals. Free Wi-Fi available at the Perth Cultural Centre and in Northbridge Piazza. **Medical services** 24-hr chemists: Beaufort Street Chemist, 647 Beaufort St, Mt Lawley, T9328 7775. Dentists: Lifecare Dental, 419 Wellington St, T9221 2777. Daily 0800- 2000. Medicare, T132011. For claims or to register visit city office 81 St George's Terr. Hospitals: Royal Perth, Wellington St, City, T9224 2244. Sir Charles Gairdner, Hospital Av, Nedlands, T9346 3333. Medical centres: Perth Medical Centre, 713 Hay St, T9481 4342, bulk bills. Mon-Thu 0800-1800, Fri 0800-1700, Sat 1000-1400. **Police** 1 Hay St, East Perth, T9222 1432. **Post** Forrest Pl, Mon-Fri 0830-1730, Sat 0900-1230. Poste Restante (take photo ID) 66 St George's Terr, Mon-Fri 0800-1700.

Contents

Footprint features

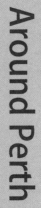

Around Perth

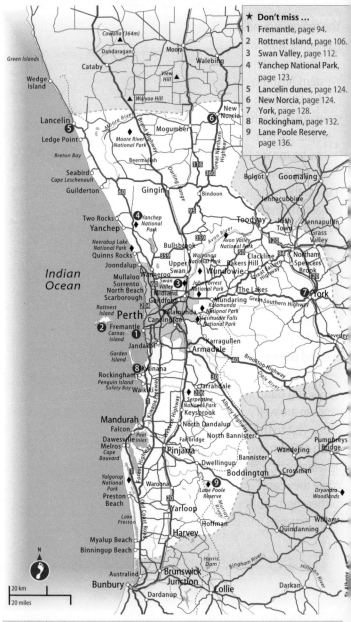

Green Islands

Cowalla (364m)

Dandaragan

Moora

Walebing

Wedge Island

View Hill

Cataby

Walyoo Hill

New Norcia ⑥

Mogumber

Lancelin ⑤

Ledge Point

Moore River National Park

Great Northern Highway

Breton Bay

Beermullah

Bolgot

Goomaling

Seabird
Cape Leschenault

Guilderton

Gingin

Bindoon

Jennacubbine

Indian Ocean

Two Rocks

Yanchep ④ National Park

Yanchep

Bullsbrook

Avon River
Avon Valley National Park

Toodyay

Irish Town

Jennapullin

Grass Valley

Neerabup Lake National Park

Quinns Rocks

Joondalup

Upper Swan

Walyunga National Park

Bakers Hill

Clackline

Northam

Spencers Brook

Great Eastern Highway

Mullaloo

Wanneroo

John Forrest National Park

Wundowie

The Lakes

Sorrento

North Beach

Scarborough

Swan ③ Valley

Midland

Guildford

Mundaring

Great Southern Highway

York ⑦

Rottnest Island

Perth

Kalamunda National Park

Beverley

Fremantle ①

② Carnac Island

Cannington

Kalamunda

Lesmurdie Falls National Park

Jandakot

Karragullen

Garden Island

Armadale

Brookton Highway

Dale River

Rockingham ⑧

Kwinana

Jarrahdale

Penguin Island

Safety Bay

Waikiki

Serpentine National Park

Albany Highway

Kwinana Freeway

Keysbrook

Mandurah

Forrest Highway

North Dandalup

Falcon

Peel Inlet

Dawesville

Fairbridge

North Bannister

Pumphreys Bridge

Melros

Cape Bouvard

Pinjarra

Bannister

Wandering

Crossman

Dwellingup

Boddington

Yalgorup National Park

Waroona

Lane Poole ⑨ Reserve

Murray River

Dryandra Woodlands

Preston Beach

Lake Preston

Yarloop

Hoffman

Williams

Quindanning

Myalup Beach

Binningup Beach

Harris Dam

Bingham River

Hillman River

Old Coast Road

Australind

Brunswick Junction

Bunbury

Dardanup

Collie

Darkan

N

20 km
20 miles

The region around Perth presents a microcosm of the southern half of the state with some exceptional beaches, wildlife encounters, extensive bushland, a wine region and some of Western Australia's oldest European heritage. Much can be seen on day trips from Perth, or included on longer itineraries to the southern or northern parts of the state.

Fremantle is Perth's port and effectively a suburb of the city. It is by no means eclipsed, however, and a visit to Perth is incomplete without time spent in this small historic outpost. It's also the principal jumping-off point for Rottnest Island, the penal settlement turned holiday playground. The Swan Valley is Perth's very own wine region and a pleasant place for lunch in a vine-covered courtyard on a sunny day.

Running parallel to the coast, about 30 km inland, the Perth Hills provide an extensive network of walking, mountain biking, and horse-riding tracks. It's from here that the Bibbulmun Track starts its winding 963-km route to Albany in the south. To the east lies the fertile Avon Valley where the Avon River flows through low, bare hills and pockets of woodland. Some of the state's oldest colonial settlements are found here, such as the charming town of York.

Heading north into a more arid region, the sand dunes of Lancelin are well worth seeing at sunset and can be combined with a visit to the monastical settlement of New Norcia. To the south of Perth stretches an almost unbroken line of coastal development, including the towns of Rockingham and Mandurah. While they cant compete with the really spectacular attractions further south, both towns are worth a look for their relaxed pace, water activities and dolphins.

Fremantle

→ *Colour map 1, C1. Population: 25,600.*

Ports are not usually known for their charm but Fremantle is a fine exception. Founded at the same time as Perth, Fremantle has kept the 19th-century buildings that Perth has lost and retained its character and spirit. A strong community of immigrants and artists contribute to the port city's alternative soul. Freo, as the locals call it, is full of street performers, markets, galleries, pubs and restaurants as well as fishing boats and container ships. Many Southern Europeans have settled here and their simple Italian cafés have merged into the busy cappuccino strip of the olive-tree-lined South Terrace. Fishing Boat Harbour has become an alternative hub of eating and entertainment activity, and manages to mix some seriously good restaurants in with some of the country's biggest fish and chip shops. Fremantle's lively atmosphere draws people from all over Perth, particularly at weekends, and it makes an interesting base for travellers. ►► *For listings, see pages 99-105.*

Ins and outs → *20 km from Perth centre, 7 km from Cottesloe.*

Getting there
The private **Fremantle Airport Shuttle** ① *T9457 7150, www.fremantleairportshuttle. com.au*, runs between Perth airport and Fremantle and offers a door-to-door service from terminal to hotel if booked in advance. Fares are $30 single, $40 for two, add $10 for each additional passenger for groups of up to four. They will soon be running a timetable service and this will cost $15 per person. A cheaper ($3.70, concessions $1.50) but much longer option from the domestic terminal is to take the No 37 bus to the Esplanade Busport (see page 54) and change. A taxi will cost around $55. The main service between the Esplanade Busport and Fremantle is the 106, which runs every 30 minutes daily 0845-2100, then 2115, 2215 and 2315; the journey takes about 45 minutes (single tickets $3.70, concessions $1.50). The train runs from Perth to Fremantle regularly throughout the day and the journey takes about half an hour ($3.70, concessions $1.50). ►► *See Transport, page 105.*

Getting around
Fremantle is a good city to wander around on foot, however if you want to try something a bit different hire a scooter (see page 105). Alternatively, the free Fremantle CAT circles around the town in a figure of eight that stretches from the railway station to the Arts Centre, and from Victoria Quay to south of the hospital. Buses leave every 10 minutes or so Monday-Friday 0730-1830 and Saturday-Sunday 1000-1830.

Tourist information
The Travel Lounge ① *16 Market St, T9335 1614, www.thetravellounge.com.au, Mon-Fri 0800- 2000, Sat-Sun 1000-1800*, acts as a general booking agent and net café and is also happy to provide information and advice to all travellers. The **VIC** ① *Kings Sq, T9431 7878, www.fremantle.com.au, Mon-Fri 0900-1700, Sat 1000-1500, Sun 1130-1430*, is located in the town hall and is also runs a tours and accommodation booking service. Also try www.visitfremantle.com.au.

Sights

There are some interesting historic sights in Freo but it is also well worth having a walk around the well-preserved port precinct of the west end. Phillimore Street and Cliff Street, and the surrounding streets, contain some lovely Victorian buildings, such as the Customs House. If exploring Freo's sights on foot, there are plenty of refuelling café-stops.

The Round House

ⓘ *Between High St and Bathers Bay, T9336 6897, 1030-1530, gold coin donation, volunteer guides available if visitors want to know more.*

As convicts did not reach the Swan River colony until 1850, Western Australia's oldest building need not necessarily be a gaol, but the fact remains that it is. Not actually round, the 12-sided 1831 building was built on the commanding promontory of Arthur Head, and the precinct still affords good views over the boat harbour and across to offshore islands. Built as a prison for immigrant and native wrong-doers, it was too small to house the large number of British convicts and slowly became redundant, last being used as a lock-up in 1900. For a while it was used as police living quarters, but fell into disuse when the headland became a favoured site for defensive gun batteries. The precinct has also been the site of lighthouses and, from 1900-1937, a Time Ball, looked to by mariners and locals alike to accurately fix their timepieces. A mock-up of the apparatus has been erected and is activated, complete with the accompanying cannon-fire, every day at 1300.

Port Authority Building

ⓘ *1 Cliff St, T9430 3555, www.fremantleports.com.au.*

Fremantle's docks are just north of the Roundhouse and from Victoria Quay you can often see massive ships loaded with sheep for live export negotiating the narrow passage. Presiding over all shipping movements is the modern Port Authority; its tower is far higher than any other structure in Freo.

Western Australian Maritime Museum

ⓘ *Victoria Quay Rd, T9431 8444, www.museum.wa.gov.au/maritime, main museum Thu-Tue 0930-1700, $10, children $3, concessions $5; submarine tours Thu-Tue every 30 mins, 1000-1600 (1 hr), $8, children $3, concessions $5 (buy ticket at museum first, joint tickets available for $15, children $5, concessions $8); Shipwreck Galleries, Cliff St, 0930-1700, gold coin donation.*

The striking Western Australian Maritime Museum sits on the quay looking out towards the western horizon. The six themed galleries look at WA's past and future as a community on the edge of the Indian Ocean. With significant historic objects and boats that highlight the state's sporting and adventure heritage (such as *Australia II*, the yacht that wrestled the America's cup from the USA in 1983), the exhibitions tell many fascinating stories of human endeavour. Part of the new museum, the *Oberon* class submarine **HMAS Ovens**, was commissioned in 1969 and saw active service for over 25 years. It is 90 m long and had a crew of over 60. Today it is in dry-dock and part of the WA Maritime Museum. The submarine is in very much the state it was when decommissioned in 1995, giving a rare glimpse into the strange lives of the submariners who crewed it. The fascinating and entertaining tours are conducted by volunteers, many of whom are former or serving submariners.

Housed in a complex of old dock buildings the original Maritime Museum is now called the **Shipwreck Galleries** and is primarily dedicated to the preservation and display of artefacts from the principal WA shipwrecks, mostly of the Dutch East India Company. Intermingled with the recoveries are numerous charts, logs and journals from the period

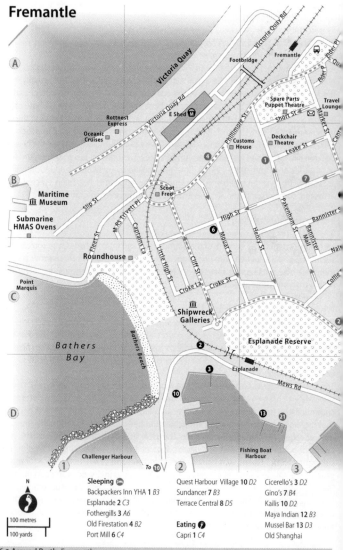

Fremantle

Sleeping 🛏️
Backpackers Inn YHA **1** B3
Esplanade **2** C3
Fothergills **3** A6
Old Firestation **4** B2
Port Mill **6** C4

Quest Harbour Village **10** D2
Sundancer **7** B3
Terrace Central **8** D5

Eating 🍴
Capri **1** C4

Cicerello's **3** D2
Gino's **7** B4
Kailis **10** D2
Maya Indian **12** B3
Mussel Bar **13** D3
Old Shanghai

and the combination presents an interesting historical overview of European exploration of Australia's west coast. There is everything from cannon to candelabra recovered from wrecks such as the *Zuytdorp* and the *Zeewijk*, but the most fascinating gallery has to be the one dedicated to the *Batavia*. A large part of the ship's hull is on display, plus a replica

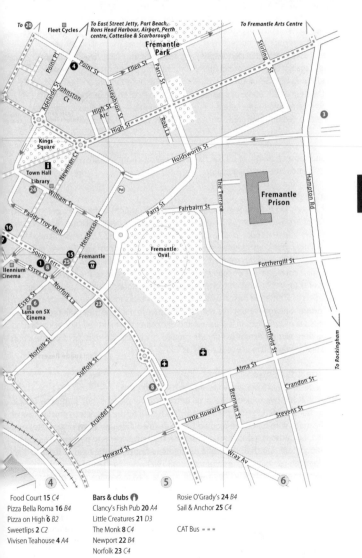

Food Court **15** *C4*	**Bars & clubs** 🍸	Rosie O'Grady's **24** *B4*
Pizza Bella Roma **16** *B4*	Clancy's Fish Pub **20** *A4*	Sail & Anchor **25** *C4*
Pizza on High **6** *B2*	Little Creatures **21** *D3*	
Sweetlips **2** *C2*	The Monk **8** *C4*	CAT Bus = = =
Vivisen Teahouse **4** *A4*	Newport **22** *B4*	
	Norfolk **23** *C4*	

Oh islands in the sun

Garden Island is connected by bridge to Rockingham but the public have no access by road. It's about 3 km long and 500 m wide and has been both a holiday resort and a naval base over the last century. It was once the home of the secret Z-Force involved in clandestine missions against the Japanese in the Second World War. Since 1978 it has been the permanent home of a naval support facility with public access restricted to certain small areas in daylight hours, via private boat only. **Carnac Island**, just to the north, is a fraction of its size. The whole island is a nature reserve, home to populations of Australian sea lions, fairy penguins and shearwaters. Snorkelling in the clear surrounding waters over the fish and coral is a popular activity. Carnac Island can be visited by private boat or on a commercial cruise but no overnight camping is allowed. See Activities and tours, page 104, for details.

cabin, and most chillingly of all the hacked skeleton of one of those murdered on the Abrolhos Islands (see box, page 235).

Fremantle Prison

① *1 The Terrace, T9336 9200, www.fremantleprison.com.au. Entry by tour only, every 30 mins 1000-1700 (1 hr), $18, children $9.50, concessions $15 (choose between Doing Time Tour and Great Escapes Tour or do both for $24, children $15.50, concessions $21). Torchlight tours Wed and Fri evening, bookings required, $24, children $14, concessions $20. Tunnels tours run regularly from 0900, bookings required, $59, children $39, concessions $49.*

With the first consignment of convicts in 1850 it became clear to the governors of the Swan River colony that a much bigger prison than the Roundhouse would be required. The building of Fremantle Prison was one of the first tasks to be undertaken by the first convict groups and took about five years to construct. In this time they built themselves a prodigious set of buildings in a huge walled enclosure, the main cell block dominating and brooding over an expansive parade ground. Such was the solidity of construction that the prison was still in use as recently as 1991.

Fremantle Arts Centre

① *1 Finnerty St, T9432 9555, www.fac.org.au, 1000-1700, free.*

Set on a low hill overlooking the main town is an impressive but imposing Gothic limestone building dating back to the 1860s. It was built by the convicts to house those of their colleagues who had gone mad and were deemed a danger to fellow inmates and their jailers, but although still a part of the convict system it seems to have been built with considerably more flair than the stolid penitentiary just down the road. It remained an asylum, for both convicts and immigrants, until 1909 when the last of the patients were transferred to new premises in Claremont. It was planned to be allowed to run down, but at the last moment was deemed suitable as a shelter for elderly women. The US Navy took it over as their HQ during the Second World War, after which the buildings existence hung in the balance, sometimes in the shadow of imminent demolition, always gradually deteriorating. The building was finally converted to a museum and arts centre between 1965 and 1972, the museum closed in 2009. The magnificent wooden staircases and floors and spacious high-ceilinged rooms are ideal for its current purpose as an arts centre. The centre is run by a dynamic arts organization and is well worth a visit. It holds regular exhibitions of contemporary visual arts and crafts, runs arts courses and literary events, acts as a small but respected publisher and hosts free music in the courtyard every Sunday 1400-1600 (January-April). The music ranges from jazz and folk to funk and classical and, played under several large shady trees, is an excellent escape from the summer heat. Pick up a program of events at the VIC or at the centre itself. There is also a great craft shop selling the best of local work at good prices and a small bookshop. The leafy courtyard café serves cakes, coffee and light, healthy lunches (daily 1000-1600; shorter hours in winter).

Beaches

There's a beach just to the north of the harbour, but it's not the area's best. Head north of the river to **Port** and **Leighton** beaches or head south. Port Beach is a safe swimming beach, although like all west coast beaches, best in the morning before the afternoon sea breeze gets going. That same breeze is heaven for windsurfers and Leighton is a good spot for it. It's worth coming here on a windy day to watch the rainbow-coloured sails skimming across the sea.

⊙ Freemantle listings

For Sleeping and Eating price codes and other relevant information, see pages 28-34.

⊜ Sleeping

Fremantle *p94, map p96*
See Bars and clubs for pub accommodation.
LL-L Esplanade, corner of Marine Terr and Essex St, T9432 4000 and T1800 998201, www.esplanadehotelfremantle.com.au. Freo's flagship, an elegant Federation hotel that has been the automatic choice for many visitors for over a century. Facilities include 3 courtyard pools with spa, sauna, smorgasbord, à la carte and buffet restaurants, fitness centre and bike hire. Many of the 300 rooms have access to the balconies. Internet available and free parking if you book directly online.
D-E Old Firestation, 18 Phillimore St, T9430 5454, www.old-firestation.net. Has a laid-back atmosphere and lots of freebies, including off-street parking and internet. Dorms can be large, ranging from 4-15 people. It has an alcohol licence and well-equipped kitchen. It is also good at tracking down employment and has cheap curries for residents downstairs at **Bengal**. 24-hr reception, late check-in can be arranged by phone.

D-F Backpackers Inn YHA, 11 Packenham St, T9431 7065. Has 41 rooms and good facilities including internet access and large, well-equipped kitchen. En suite doubles and dorms (single sex or mixed).
D-F Sundancer, 80 High St, T9336 6080, www.sundancerbackpackers.com. The best of the big hostels and very well positioned. Rooms and communal facilities are bright and clean, the big kitchen is well-equipped and there is a sunny rear courtyard with pool. Free internet, a licensed bar and bike hire. 24-hr reception and check-in. Parking. Recommended.

B&Bs

If you're looking for a heritage B&B you're going to be spoilt for choice and the following are just a selection. All have friendly hosts who serve up excellent breakfasts. Most, however, do not have parking facilities.
L-B Terrace Central, 79-85 South Terr, T9335 6600, www.terracecentral.com.au. Bright and breezily decorated 1890s cottage (with extension) offering apartments, spacious doubles, twin and executive rooms. All have a/c, TVs and are en suite. Free Wi-Fi and off-street parking available. Continental

breakfast included with the B&B rooms.
Some rooms come with a 2-night
minimum stay.

A-B Fothergills, 20 Ord St, T9335 6784,
www.babs.com.au/fothergills. Large, stately
colonial house with 6 spacious en suite
rooms, subdued but luxurious, and a very
pleasant upstairs balcony. Breakfast in a
sunny conservatory. Some parking. Wi-Fi
access available.

A-B Port Mill, 17 Essex St, T9433 3832,
www.babs.com.au/portmill. The whitewashed rough stone walls and tight cottagey
staircase make it hard to believe this new
building isn't just as old as the 1863 flour
mill opposite. 3 bright en suite rooms with
balconies; the front 2 have great views.
Continental breakfast to be enjoyed in
the room included in the tariff.

Self-contained

L Quest Harbour Village, Mews Rd,
Challenger Harbour, T9430 3888, www.quest
harbourvillage.com.au. Modern, luxury
apartments perched in a great spot between
Challenger and Fishing Boat harbours.
Parking and internet access available.

A-B Westerley, 1A Tuckfield St, T9430 4458,
www.westerley.com.au. A number of
comfortable and centrally located properties
including studios, converted warehouse,
town houses and harbourside apartments.
Free Wi-Fi available at most properties.

Caravan parks

B-D Coogee Beach, Cockburn Rd, 4 km
south of town, T9418 1810 and T1800
817016. With direct beach access, BBQ, camp
kitchens, motel and en suite cabins, tent sites.

B-E Fremantle Village, 25 Cockburn Rd,
3 km south of the city centre on the coast road,
T9430 4866, www.fremantlevillage.com.au.
Village facilities include camp kitchens, Wi-Fi
and broadband internet, laundry facilities and
free gas BBQs. Motel units, cabins and chalets
as well as en suite caravan sites and normal
tent sites. No pets allowed.

❷ Eating

Fremantle *p94, map p96*
The choice in Fremantle is staggering and
it's a favourite eating destination for those
who live in Perth. With its sunny climate,
almost every restaurant and café has outdoor
or pavement tables and many have been
built to open onto the street so that they
barely seem to have walls at all. The city's
large Italian population has helped to build a
very continental culture of coffee drinking,
posing and long, leisurely hours of eating.
Italian food and seafood predominate, but
there are few Asian flavours here, too. The
main eating areas are South Terr and around
the Boat Harbour. It is said that it's hard to find
a bad meal in Freo, and the following does not
even begin to exhaust the possibilities.

¶¶¶ Mussel Bar, 42 Mews Rd, T9433 1800,
www.musselbar.com.au. Mon 1800-2200,
Tue-Sun 1200-2200. Large, contemporary
dining room with sloping glass windows
looking out over the harbour, giving it the
feel of a ship's wheelhouse. Excellent mussels,
but also a range of seafood and grills.

¶¶¶ Red Herring, 26 Riverside Rd, East
Fremantle, T9339 1611, www.redherring.
com.au. Daily 1200-1500 and 1700-2300,
Sun also for breakfast 0800-1100. Considered
one of the best seafood restaurants in Perth
and running out of wall space for its awards,
this contemporary restaurant sits on pylons
over the river. Central sushi and oyster bar
makes for a terrific appetizer. Save room for
the fine dessert and cheese menu. Excellent
wine list and wine-matching suggestions.
Best to book in advance.

¶¶¶-¶ Capri, 21 South Terr, T9335 1399.
Open 1200-1400, 1700-2130. This is the real
thing: classic old-fashioned Italian cooking in
a simple wood-panelled room. No fuss, no
frills but wonderful flavours. Many seafood
dishes. Unlicensed. BYO.

¶¶¶-¶ Left Bank, 15 Riverside Rd, East
Fremantle, T9319 1315, www.leftbank.com.au.
Café daily from 0700, restaurant Mon-Sat from
1200. A large, open pub on the river that

concentrates on its food. Café-style menu downstairs with burgers and salads and very popular breakfasts, go early at the weekend. Classy mid-range restaurant upstairs with some romantic balcony tables. One of the more popular spots for the traditional Perth Sun session.

†↑-† Maya Indian, 75-77 Market St, T9335 2796, www.mayarestaurant.com.au. Dinner Tue-Sun 1800-2200. Fri lunch 1200-1430. The authentic Indian food has won many awards and it's always busy. A short, traditional menu, fully licensed. Also offers regional tasting menus for parties of 4-people or more. Takeaway available.

†↑-† Pizza Bella Roma, 14 South Terr, T9335 1554. Tue-Thu 1700-late, Fri-Sun 1200-late. The best pizza and chilli mussels in an unpretentious setting. Licensed and BYO.

† Cicerellos, 44 Mews Rd, on the harbour itself, T9335 1911, www.cicerellos.com.au. Open 1000-late. A dominating boatshed-style building that serves up portions of fish and chips to hundreds of tourists every day.

† Kailis, 46 Mews Rd, T9335 7755, www.kailis.com. Massive boatshed-style building, similar to **Cicerellos**, also serving fish and chips.

† Old Shanghai Food Court, 4 Henderon St, next to the **Sail & Anchor**. Wed-Thu 0930-2100, Fri-Sun 1000-2130. Good food from Japanese to juices and lots of pavement tables in the mall. Dead cheap.

† Pizza On High 33 High St, T9335 4234. Lunch Mon-Fri 1100-1500, Dinner Wed-Sat 1730-late. Offering an all-you-can-eat 4 nights of the week, and BYO. The lunch specials are good value and takeaway is available.

† Sweetlips, 47 Mews Rd, T9430 6902, www.sweetlips.com.au. Mon-Thu 1000-2030, Fri-Sun 1000-2100. A little further away from the harbour, behind **McDonalds**. Away from the crowds, offers good range of fish and chips. Café enclosed.

† Vivisen Teahouse, 15 Point St, T9336 6699, www.vivisenteahouse.com. Daily 1100-1500, 1700-2200. Chinese restaurant offering a wide range of options, including home-made Dim Sum. Visitors should try the house special, Goji tea. BYO.

Cafés

There are dozens of cafés in and around Fremantle, and most can be relied upon for great coffee and service.

Fremantle Arts Centre, see Sights, page 98. A peaceful café, great for coffee or lunch.

Ginos, 1 South Terr, T9336 1464, www.ginoscafe.com.au. Daily 0700-2230. One of the original Italian cafés, **Ginos** has stuck to its simple formula of fast, honest Italian food, great coffee and friendly service. Order at the counter.

⊙ Bars and clubs

Fremantle *p94, map p96*
Note that dress codes and restrictions may apply at most venues, especially at night.

Clancy's Fish Pub, 51 Cantonment St, T9335 1351, www.clancysfishpub.com.au. Mon-Sat 1200-2400, Sun 1200-2200. A bit out of the way but one of the most relaxed pubs in Freo, Clancy's has a funky, alternative feel and great food available all day (Sun-Thu 1200-2100, Fri-Sat 1200-2130). The menu concentrates on fish and seafood but pasta, noodles and cakes are also on offer. The veranda is a fine place for a quiet drink. Entertainment and live music almost every day. Always packed for the Sun session. Recommended.

Little Creatures, 40 Mews Rd, T9430 5555, www.littlecreatures.com.au. Brewery Mon-Fri 1000-2400, Sat-Sun 0900-2400. A former boatshed and crocodile farm, now a cool, cavernous brewery and bar with a spacious veranda and boccia pitch. Excellent, inventive cheap food, including wood-fired pizzas, mussels and tapas, available all day. Laid-back atmosphere and friendly service. Quiz on Thu nights. **Creatures Loft** upstairs plays host to live bands and the occasional film night and is open Thu-Sun.

The Monk, 33 South Terr, T9336 3100, www.madmonk.com.au. Open 1100-2300. A microbrewery offering up porter, pale ale and bitter, amongst others, and tips on which will best complement your food. Wine and the occasional cider are available for the non-beer drinkers. A wide range of tapas dishes as well as pizzas and more hearty dishes. The terrace area is good for people watching.

Newport, 2 South Terr, T9335 2428, www.thenewport.com. Mon-Thu 1200-2400, Fri-Sat 1200-0100, Sun 1200-2200. A lively, relaxed pub smartened up with polished floors and aluminium chairs. Pool tables, atrium courtyard, dedicated room DJs who play every night. Backpacker and student night is Wed.

Norfolk, corner of Norfolk St and South Terr, T9335 5405, www.norfolkhotel.com.au. A social pub with a great enclosed stone courtyard, huge on Sun afternoons. Live music Thu-Sat in the Basement Lounge. Bar food available 1200-2100. The 9 rooms are some of the towns best pub options (**B-C**), those with shared facilities are cheaper.

Rosie O'Gradys, 23 William St, T9335 1645, www.rosieogradys.com.au. Pleasant, airy and spacious Irish theme pub (a chain). The walls and slate floors are green, of course, but the heritage building has been cleverly converted to Australian-style drinking rather than dark and cosy Irish-style. Cheap and hearty food (daily 1100-1500 and 1700-2100) and 17 bland but comfortable hotel rooms (**B-C**). Live music and entertainment every night.

Sail & Anchor, 64 South Terr, T9431 1666, www.sailandanchor.com.au. The pub that started the boutique beer and good food revolution in Freo around the time of the Americas Cup. The pub has a microbrewery producing many of the beers sold on site. The bistro does wood-fired pizzas, steaks and light meals. There is a lounge bar upstairs open at weekends. Also a good bottle shop. Brewery tours by appointment.

Clubs

Although Fremantle is not the automatic choice for clubbers there are a couple of options. Try **Kulcha**, www.kulcha.com.au, 13 South Terr, or **Metropolis**, www.metropolis fremantle.com.au, 58 South Terr.

⦿ Entertainment

Fremantle *p94, map p96*
Cinema
Luna on SX, 13 Essex St, T9430 5999, www.lunapalace.com.au. Fremantle's grooviest cinema, with discounts for students and YHA members.

Theatre
Deckchair Theatre, Victoria Hall, 179 High St, T9430 4771, www.deckchairtheatre.com.au. Puts on contemporary, home-grown productions, often with a Fremantle or multicultural theme.
Spare Parts Puppet Theatre, 1 Short St, T9335 5044, www.sppt.asn.au. Produces inventive children's entertainment.

⦿ Festivals and events

Fremantle *p94, map p96*
For more detailed information on festivals in Fremantle, visit www.fremantlefestivals.com.
Mar/Apr The Street Arts Festival, held every Easter, is Australia's biggest street performance festival and features artists from all over the world.
Mid-Nov The Fremantle Festival is held annually at various venues around the city. Over 120,000 people flock to the city to see and participate in dozens of events featuring local and world music, dance, acrobatics and art. Contact the City of Fremantle T9432 9888.

O Shopping

Fremantle p94, map p96

There's some excellent shopping in the port city. Although the major chains are here, in or around High St Mall, there are also many quirky and interesting shops that help to give Fremantle its character. Fremantle shopping hours are generally 0900-1700 with the exception of late-night shopping on Fri until 2100. Most shops are also open at the weekend. The **Fremantle Markets** are the best in WA, still held in the original Victorian market hall. The markets have a fresh fruit and vegetable section and sell clothes, jewellery, art and a whole host other items. The Henderson Mall entrance leads to shops selling wonderful fresh food such as bread, cheese and fish, so it's a good place to stock up for a picnic. Open Fri 1000-2000, Sat-Sun and public holiday Mon 1000-1800. The **E Shed Markets**, T9430 6393, www.eshed markets.com.au, do not match up to this high standard, but still have a few jewellery, clothes and craft shops that are worth a look if you're waiting for a ferry. Open Fri-Sun 0900-1730, food court and cafés to 2000.

Arts and crafts

Bead Post, 3/13 Market St, T9335 3936, www.thebeadpost.com.au. Beads and beading accessories. Offers jewellery repair services, as well as classes and workshops.
Creative Native, 65 High St. Mon-Fri 0900-1700, Sat 1000-1700 and Sun 1100-1700. One of several indigenous art shops on this strip. Aimed more at the casual tourist than the serious art buyer.
Didgeridoo Breath, 6 Market St, T9430 6009, www.didgeridoobreath.com. A good range of didgeridoos and they will teach you to play for free. There's also the option of shipping your purchase home.
Fremantle Arts Centre, 1 Finnerty St, T9432 9569. Excellent-quality craft work (ceramics, wood, textiles, jewellery) by WA artists at very reasonable prices.

Japingka, 47 High St, T9335 8265, www.japingka.com.au. Authentic high-quality Aboriginal art, sculpture and craftwork.

Bookshops

Chart and Map Shop, 14 Collie St, T9335 8665, www.chartandmapshop.com.au. Mon-Fri 0900-1700, Sat 00900-1600 and Sun 1000-1600. For maps and guides check out their excellent range.
Elizabeth's Second-hand Bookshop, there are a number of branches of this excellent second-hand shop in Fremantle, including Street Mall, T9430 6700, and 8 South Terr, T9433 1310.
New Edition, 82 High St, T9335 2383. Sun-Thu 0900-1930 and Fri-Sat 0900-2130. One of Freo's best-loved shops in the heart of the cappuccino strip. Fantastic range of literature, art, travel and design books and an atmosphere conducive to hours of browsing. Fi & co also have a small boutique at the back selling clothes and accessories.

Clothing and jewellery

There are a few cutting-edge fashion boutiques in Market St.
Jalfreezi, South Terr Piazza, T9433 3340. A good range of attractive and cheap Indian clothing. Also visit the Fremantle Markets for this kind of clothing.
Zingara, Fremantle Markets (opposite the Market Bar). High-quality silver jewellery.

Food

The first stop has to be the markets, but failing that these are good options.
The Fremantle Bakehouse, 52 South Terr, T9430 9592, www.fremantlebakehouse. com.au. Stop at this busy café and bakery to sample some tasty fresh breads and pastries.
Kakulas Sister, 29-31 Market St, T9430 4445, www.kakulassister.com.au. Sells delicatessen foods and Italian groceries.
Woolstore Shopping Centre, 28 Cantonment St. Mon-Fri 0800-2100, Sat 0800-1700 and Sun 1200-1700. For general needs; houses a Coles, a pharmacy, etc.

Music
Record Finder, 87 High St. Daily Mon-Sat 1000-1700, Sun 1100-1700. A large affair with a huge stock of vinyl.

Outdoor equipment
Mountain Designs, Shop 3 Queensgate Centre, William St, T9335 1431, www.mountaindesigns.com. Head to this well-known and helpful chain store for all your outdoor needs.

▲ Activities and tours

Fremantle *p94, map p96*
Boat cruises
See also Sailing, below.
Captain Cook Cruises, T9325 3341, www.captaincookcruises.com.au. Runs several cruises from East St Jetty. These include daily cruises to Perth (90 mins), Swan River scenic cruises (4 hrs), lunch cruises (3 hrs) and dinner cruises (4 hrs).
Rottnest Express, T1300 467688, www.rottnestexpress.com.au. Offers daily (in summer) Swan River Cruises that include morning tea and a full commentary. Whale-watching tours in season (Sep-Nov) cost about $50.

Diving
Australian Diving Academy, T9356 9577, www.ausdiving.com.au. Runs PADI courses and dive trips to Rottnest for $210. Meals are included on trips.
Dolphin Dive, 1 Cantonment St, T9336 6286, www.dolphindiveshop.com. Organizes several boat dives, including wreck and night dives, and has hire facilities. PADI courses are also offered. A Rottnest double dive with equipment costs $185.

Golf
Fremantle Public Golf Course, Montreal St, T9336 3933. Daily 0530-1900. Green fees are: $15 for 9 holes, $22 for 18 holes. Equipment hire available and there's also a driving range.

Parasailing
Westcoast Parasail, Mews Rd, Fishing Boat Harbour, T0417 188502, www.westcoast parasail.com.au. $75 for a single, $120 for a tandem jump.

Sailing
Leeuwin Ocean Adventure Foundation, B Berth, Victoria Quay, T9430 4105, www.sailleeuwin.com. Fremantle's resident tall ship, a magnificent 3-masted vessel that dominates Victoria Quay when it is moored there. It sails out on a variety of trips depending on the season. In summer it is based in the port and there are plenty of opportunities to get aboard for a day sail, mostly at weekends. Most trips last around 3 hrs and cost $95, children $60. Longer sailing trips are also available.

Tour operators
Fremantle Tram Tours, T9433 6674, www.fremantletrams.com.au. Trundle around Fremantle on their buses-dressed-as-trams on a hop-on hop-off service. The tour takes in Victoria Quay, Fremantle Prison, Arts Centre, Fishing Boat Harbour, Esplanade Hotel, Town Hall ($22, children $5, concessions $18). Longer tours also on offer. On Fri nights at 1845 there is a Ghostly Tram Tour, which includes torchlight tours of the Prison, Arts Centre and The Round House. Fish and chip dinner is included in the price ($60, children $45).

⊖ Transport

Fremantle p94, map p96
See also Activities and tours for transport around Fremantle. For more information , T136213 or www.transperth.wa.gov.au.

Air
Light aircraft from Jandakot Airport, east of Fremantle, take passengers to **Rottnest Island**, see page 106.

Bicycle/scooter
Fleet Cycles, 66 Adelaide St, T9430 5414, www.fleetcycles.com.au. Mon-Fri 0900-1730, Sat 1000-1700, Sun 1100-1700. Hires out bicycles.
Scoot Freo, 2 Phillimore St, T9336 5933, www.scootfreo.com.au. Mon-Fri 1000-1600, Sat-Sun 0900-1700. Hires out scooters and 3-wheel, 2-person scootcars. Closed if wet.

Bus
The main bus terminal is in front of the railway station.
Selected bus services from Fremantle: **Booragoon**, **City Busport**, **East Perth**, 105; **City Busport**, **East Perth** (from Queen St), 106, 111; **Cottesloe**, **Stirling Highway**, **Kings Park**, **St Georges Terr**, 103, 104; **Cottesloe**, **Claremont**, 70; **Port Beach**, **Cottesloe Beach**, **Scarborough**, 381 (weekdays); **Port Beach**, **Cottesloe Beach**, **Scarborough**, **Hillarys**, 582 (weekends only during Oct-Apr); **Rockingham Bus Station**, 126 (weekdays only), 920.

Car hire
Ace, T9472 4222, www.acerent.com.au. **M2000**, T9438 2828, www.m2000car.com.au.

Ferry
Fremantle presents the cheapest options for getting to **Rottnest**. Oceanic Cruises, T9335 2666, www.oceaniccruises.com.au, and

Rottnest Express, T9335 6406, www.rottnestexpress.com.au, both offer services daily from C-Shed, near the railway station ($59.50 day return). The latter also has several ferry/hotel packages worth looking at and both can arrange bike hire packages. For those who want to reach Rottnest that bit quicker, Rottnest Express also runs the *Mega Blast*, Sep-May Thu-Mon 0925, returns 1645, It's the same price as the ferry and is great fun, there are splash jackets available and you may want one if you're sitting at the front.

Taxi
There is a supervised taxi rank on South Terr, near Fremantle Markets, Fri-Sat 2300-0500. Swan, T131330, **Black & White**, T131008, www.blackandwhitecabs.com.au. From Perth a journey costs $40-45.

Train
The Fremantle Line runs between Perth and Fremantle via **Subiaco**, **Claremont** and **Cottesloe**. Services are every 10-15 mins 0530-1930 and every 30-60 mins 1900-0230. Sat services are at similar times running 0600-0230 and Sun 0730-2330. The journey takes about 30 mins in total.

⊙ Directory

Fremantle p94, map p96
Banks ATMs for major banks on Adelaide St between Point and Queen Sts. **Interforex**, next to VIC, 0800-1930. **Internet** Travel Lounge, 16 Market St, Mon-Fri 0800-2000, Sat-Sun 1000-1800. **Library** 8 William St, T9432 9766. Mon and Fri 0930-1730, 0930-1720, Tue-Thu 0930-2000, Sat 0930-1700. **Medical services** Fremantle Hospital, corner of Alma St and South Terr, T9431 3333. **Police** 45 Henderson St, T9430 1222. **Post** 13 Market St, T9239 7600, Mon-Fri 0900-1700.

Rottnest Island

→ *Colour map 2, B1.*

Rotto, as the locals call it, once a penal settlement, is now Perth's holiday playground. Just 20 km west of the city, it feels a long way from the metropolitan commotion. Generations of Perth families have come to frolic here every summer and it's a traditional place to celebrate the end of school, university or parental control. The entire coast is one long cordon of quite magical sandy bays and clear aquamarine water and so, understandably, come summer, many beaches get very busy. However, even at this time, you'll find almost deserted stretches towards the western and southern parts of the island. The offshore reefs are full of brightly coloured fish, exotic corals and limestone caves, and littered with wrecks. The island itself is 11 km long and 4 km wide and covered in low bushy scrub with some patches of eucalypt woodland. Much of this provides cover for the island's famous small wallaby, the quokka, after which the island was dubiously named. There are few permanent human residents as the island is carefully managed to preserve the environment and scarce water resources. The number of overnight visitors is kept to a sustainable level and cars are not allowed. ▶ *For listings, see pages 109-111.*

Ins and outs

Getting there There are two ways of getting to Rotto: by air (from Jandakot Airport) and ferry. The cheapest way is to take public transport to Fremantle and take a ferry from there. ▶ *See Transport, page 57, and under the relevant departure point.*

Getting around As only essential service vehicles and buses are allowed on the island, there are just two principal choices if you want to see more of the island than Thomson Bay Settlement: bikes and buses. There is a free shuttle bus that operates between the main accommodation areas on the island. It leaves from the main bus stop in Thomson Bay, travels to Geordie Bay Store for Geordie, Fay's and Longreach Bays, then returns to the main bus stop before heading to the airport and Kingstown Barracks. The **Bayseeker** bus travels clockwise right around the coast road, but doesn't get out to the West End. It operates a jump-on, jump-off system with 18 stops on the circuit and goes every 30-60 minutes. A day fare is $12, children $5.50, concessions $10. Services run 0830-1630. There is also a train service going to and from the south end of the Settlement and Oliver Hill lookout; fares

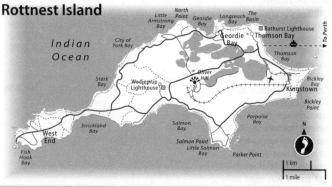

Rottnest Island

Quokka spotting

When the Dutch explorer Willem Vlamingh encountered Rottnest Island he encumbered it with a name that suggests the opposite of its natural beauty. In Dutch Rottnest means 'rat nest'. Europeans simply had no language to describe the unique Australian fauna. The 'rats' Vlamingh saw were the small wallabies (*Setonix bracyurus*), which still populate the island. Now commonly known as the quokka, from the Noongar word, these appealing wallabies are about 30 cm high. Although most closely identified with the island, the habitat of quokkas actually spreads along the southwestern coastal region. However, on the mainland they have become endangered due to predation by foxes and habitat loss. There are a few left in Dwellingup, the Stirling Ranges and on Bald Island, but Rottnest is the last bastion of a sizeable population, with about 8000-10,000. Even so, they suffer in summer because freshwater supplies are much lower than they were before settlement. Constant interaction with people, to their detriment, has also made some of them quite tame so you have a very good chance of seeing them. Visitors are now asked not to touch or feed them. If you're not venturing beyond the settlements you should always be able to find them hanging around the shop at Geordie Bay, alongside the Garden Lake boardwalk behind the Lodge, and at the short boardwalk opposite the turn-off to Kingstown Barracks.

includes a tour at Oliver Hill, except for the last ride of the day. Two-hour round trips hourly 1030-1430 in summer, 1230-1430 in winter. Tickets $25, children $15, concessions $20, available from the VIC.

Tourist information VIC ① *Thomson Bay Settlement, T9372 9732, Sat-Thu 0730-1700, Fri 0730-1930.* Also in Thomson Bay is a small shopping mall with a post office, ATM, takeaways, general store, bakery and clothes/gift shops. The general store stocks books and has a bottle shop. It also offers a free delivery service to the island's accommodation from 0800-1800. There is a similarly stocked store at Geordie Bay, where there's also a café serving light meals in peak season. Both open daily. There is a **Wellness Centre** near the mall, which offers beauty treatments as well as being home to the island's pharmacy. The island has a nursing post, T9292 5030, police station, T131 444, and ranger's office, T9372 9788. See also www.rottnestisland.com.

Background

Until 7000 years ago Rottnest was a peninsula, attached to the mainland. Since the connecting bridge drowned, a result of the ending of the last ice age, the island was abandoned by any Aboriginals who may have been living there and the new island christened *Wadjemup* by the mainland local peoples. In 1696 the island was first visited by Europeans in a Dutch vessel commanded by Willem de Vlamingh. Seeing the island swarming with the small wallabies, the Dutch considered the island a rat's nest and named it accordingly. As well as the quokkas, as they are known to the Noongar, the island is home to a variety of animals and flora marooned when the island was cut off. The fact that it was an island close to a European colony doomed it to become a penal settlement, but this time with a difference. A few convicts were shipped over, but for the most part it was used to imprison Aboriginal criminals who incurred the authority's displeasure on the mainland. Many of the buildings constructed for this purpose still remain in and around the island's only village, known simply as the Settlement. For the last 80 or so years the island has served a dual purpose as holiday destination and military encampment, with the latter moving out in the 1980s.

Sights

While **Thomson Bay Settlement** has the ferry terminal, is the main settlement and has most of the island's services, it is also something of an open-air museum, and the general layout is claimed to be Australia's oldest intact streetscape. Most interesting is the part of the Lodge known as the **Quod**, and the heritage precinct in front of it. Once one of the most feared places on the island, it was built in 1838 to house dozens of Aboriginal criminals in horrendous conditions. There were still prisoners on the island when it was converted into a tourist hostel in 1911. Most of the current double rooms were once two cells holding about 10 men. The **museum and library** ① *museum daily 1045-1530, gold coin donation; library 1400-1545, free*, just behind the general store in the mall, are the main repositories of the islands history. Museum displays include the early days as a prison for Aboriginal men, island shipwrecks, military use and its development as Perth's holiday isle.

Also in Thomson Bay the original **Salt Store** has a small gallery where artists exhibit their work, and an exhibition that focuses on the island's early colonial history. This is also where the Rottnest Volunteer Guides can be found, and where a number of free guided tours depart from. Further afield there is an interesting walk south through the dunes at Kingstown Barracks to the **Bickley Battery**. The 45-minute stroll takes you past several ruined buildings that were once gun emplacements, built in the 1930s to defend Perth against any interlopers. Almost in the centre of the island is **Oliver Hill** ① *tours on the hour 1000-1400, Apr-Jun, $7, children $3, concessions $5, or included in cost of the train from Thomson Bay, 1 hr to walk, 30 mins to cycle*, used during the Second World War as another gun emplacement. Underground is a small maze of tunnels. The nearby **Wadjemup Lighthouse** ① *T9372 9732, $7, children $3, concessions $5*, built in 1896, is accessible to visitors and tours run every 30 minutes 1100-1430. The 360-degree views over Rottnest Island are outstanding. The island's second lighthouse, **Bathurst**, is nearer to Thomson Bay and was built in 1900 to support Wadjemup following the City of York shipping disaster in 1899. It is not open to the public, although the Volunteer Guides do run a free walk up to the lighthouse during which they tell of the exploits of the pilots (experienced sailors who guided ships around the dangerous reefs) and crew on Rottnest.

Beaches are what Rottnest is all about for most visitors. There are over a dozen picture-postcard bays with white-sand beaches and usually clear, intensely blue water. Reefs lie just offshore from some beaches and many are enclosed by dramatic limestone headlands. The most sheltered are along the north shore and these also get the busiest, especially the **Basin**, the most picturesque bay on the island. The Basin has covered picnic tables and toilets, adding to its popularity. Other small bays a bit further from Thomson Bay include **Little Armstrong** on the north shore and **Little Salmon** on the south. The water can get choppy in the afternoons at the latter. **Longreach** and **Geordie** are long sweeping bays overlooked by accommodation and often crowded with boats. **Salmon Bay** in the south is of a similar scale, clear of boats and can be good for boogie boarding, though there are no facilities.

Diving and **snorkelling** is excellent off Rottnest, with a large variety of wrecks, fish, corals and limestone caves. Particularly good snorkelling spots can be found off Parker Point, where there is a marked out trail, Little Salmon Bay, parts of Salmon Bay and the Basin. **Surfing** is best at Strickland, Salmon and Stark Bays.

◉ Rottnest Island listings

For Sleeping and Eating price codes and other relevant information, see pages 28-34.

● Sleeping

Rottnest Island p106, map p106

Most of the accommodation on the island is in self-contained cottages, villas or cabins. There is also a youth hostel, which operates out of Kingstown Barracks, and camping. All need to be booked through the **Accommodation Office**, T1800 111111 or T9432 9111, reservations@rottnestisland.com, Mon-Sat 0830-1700.

Thomson Bay has the most self-catering accommodation and accordingly has a resort feel about it. There are also options at the former military Kingstown Barracks, and also at Geordie Bay on the north coast. During the Dec-Jan summer period it is virtually impossible to find a room, cabin or space to pitch your tent unless you've booked it months in advance. Even outside of this period weekends commonly see the island booked almost full, so either book well ahead or plan for a mid-week visit. During peak WA school holidays a ballot system is used to allow visitors equal chances of reserving accommodation. You need to enter the ballot if you wish to book accommodation for these specific periods. See www.rottnestisland.com for more information. Some of the ferry companies offer ferry/accommodation/bike packages that may shave a few dollars off the cost.

LL-A Rottnest Lodge, Kitson St, Thomson Bay, T9292 5161, www.rottnestlodge.com.au. The island's premier establishment, which incorporates many of the early colonial prison buildings, including the Quod. Rooms are furnished in contemporary style and most face onto a courtyard, the pool or the Quod. A few face a lake, but this can smell a little in high summer. All rooms en suite and continental breakfast is included. Other facilities include a licensed restaurant, pub and a cocktail bar.

L Hotel Rottnest, Bedford Av, Thomson Bay, T9292 5011, www.hotelrottnest.com.au. Converted from a former residence for the Western Australian governor, it has a dozen fully serviced motel-style rooms with private bathrooms, mostly around an adjacent courtyard, but some overlooking the bay (these are more expensive). The rooms are pricey for what they are, and there's no breakfast included, but the hotel is very near the restaurants and the jetty. There is a bar and restaurant, with a wide selection of wines and beers.

Self-contained

There is a wide choice of accommodation on the island, almost all around the eastern bays, ranging from beautifully renovated colonial cottages to small huts. Each is reasonably well equipped, and you just need to bring sheets and pillowcases. In size most range from 4 to 8 beds, though there are a few larger ones around Kingstown Barracks (up to 18 beds). Of the hundreds available the following represent a few of the best options. Prices drop considerably if you're staying more than 1 night. At certain times of year, however, principally school holidays, the demand for accommodation is such that it is allocated by ballot about 6 months beforehand. Ballot application forms can be found on the Rottnest website. Kingstown is, strictly speaking, an alcohol-free area. Bookings for all these are through the Accommodation Office up to a year in advance.

L Commander's House, more isolated than most in an inland position, but with fine views down across the ocean.

L Lighthouse Keeper's Cottages (villas 547 and 548), www.lighthouse.net.au, are in a wonderful shore-side spot next to Bathurst Lighthouse, with front verandas looking across to Perth. Slightly cheaper than **Commander's House**. Linen provided, book well in advance. Recommended.

A-B Geordie Bay, modern, villas all have good views across the bay and immediate access to the beach.
C-D Caroline Thomson, the best budget option, 1 room cabins with kitchenette and bathroom in Thomson Bay.

Camping

There is a small area set aside for camping in Thomson Bay it is not allowed over the rest of the island. Adults $10 per night. The **Allison Camping Area** has fresh water and gas BBQ facilities but it is unpowered. Booking sites in peak times is as necessary as booking cabins and villas, and can be done through the Accommodation Office. The camping area is an alcohol-free zone.

❶ Eating

Rottnest Island *p106, map p106*
ⓘⓘ-ⓘ Aristos, just along from **Dtme**, the long boardwalk also looks out over the harbour, T9292 5171, www.aristosrottnest.com.au. Mon-Fri 1000-2000, Sat-Sun 1000-2030 (coffee and cakes from 1000, lunch from 11.30 every day). A chain eatery offering fish and chips, oysters, chilli mussels, lobster, chowder and seafood platters. All served up with great views of the ocean. Coffee and cake is served all day and there are bacon and egg rolls on the breakfast menu.
ⓘⓘ-ⓘ Hotel Rottnest, see Sleeping. Offers old favourites such as burgers, seafood dishes, pizzas, salads and steak. Food from 1100-2030. There is a large ocean-front bar and seating area, and live music on Sat nights.
ⓘⓘ-ⓘ Rottnest Lodge, see Sleeping. **Marlins Restaurant** is surprisingly reasonably priced given its decidedly upmarket feel. The evening à la carte menu (1800-2100) is slightly pricier than lunch, but the food is the best on the island. The **Governor's Bar** serves pub grub.
ⓘ Dtme, central to Thomson's Bay with terrace views over the harbour, T9292 5286, Open 0700-2100. Part of the gallic-style chain.

Simple meals from Thai chicken curries to steak and Guinness pies. The place gets very busy but there are no bookings.

▲▲ Activities and tours

Rottnest Island *p106, map p106*
Boat and kayak tours
Rottnest Adventure Centre, Henderson Av, T9292 5292. Rents out kayaks (double for $50, single $30 for 2 hrs), fishing and snorkelling gear, and bikes. Can also supply weight belts and tanks for those who are diving.
Rottnest Express, T1300 467688, www.rottnestexpress.com.au. Sep-Jun from Mon-Thu at 1100. Offers eco-adventure tours around the island, with commentary on the island's unique wildlife and geography. $50, children $25, concessions $45.
Underwater Explorer, T9292 5292. A large glass-bottomed boat that heads out several times a day on a variety of short cruises including a 45-min wreck and reef tour ($29, children $15, concessions $27), and longer snorkelling trips (1 hr, $39, children and concessions $35), equipment hire $15.

Cinema

The latest releases are shown at the **Rottnest Island Picture Hall**. Session times are posted outside or are available from the VIC. Make sure to check the **Transfer Bus** timetables, as some films finish after the last service. $10, children $8. Open all year.

Diving

As a rule of thumb the wind comes from the east in the morning and the southwest in the afternoon. Precisely where it is best to jump into the water around the island depends on the weather and prevalent wind direction. In general it is best to be in the lee of the wind, but before deciding where to head for have a chat with the VIC. There are plans to open a Dive Centre behind **Dtme**, where it will be possible to hire equipment and re-fill tanks.

Dive operators in Perth (see page 85), Fremantle (see page 104) and even as far away as Rockingham (see page 140) and Busselton (see page 159) offer dive trips to Rottnest.

Golf and bowls
Golf and Country Club, Sommerville Dr, T9292 5105. Tue-Sat 0830-1100, 1400-1900 in summer, daily 0900-1630 in the main winter season. Has a 9-hole course and a bowling green. Club hire available.

Surfing
There are a few good breaks around the island, notably at Stark Bay, Strickland Bay, North Point and Salmon Point. Take note, these are all reef breaks and are not suitable for beginners.

Tennis
There are free tennis courts at Bathurst Point, Geordie Bay and Kingstown Barracks. Racket hire is available from **Rottnest Island Bike Hire** in Thomson Bay.

Tour operators
Discovery Tour, is a 1-hr coach tour which sets off around the island from Thomson Bay at 1120, 1340 and 1350, with full commentary on the human and natural history of the island. The tour includes visits to Wadjemup Lighthouse and the West End. Adults $32, children $15, concessions $25. Tickets can be bought at the VIC.
Rottnest Island Joyflights, T9292 5027 or T1800 500006, www.rottnest.de. Scenic flights operating from the airport. Minimum 2 passengers, operates on demand 1030-1530, $35 per person for 10 mins over the island, $85 per person for 35-min flights over Perth and $100 per person for a combination of the 2.
Rottnest Voluntary Guides, T9372 9777. Conduct guided walks daily around Thomson Bay, mostly focusing on the islands penitential and military history. In summer the programme is extended to include evening walks that include star-gazing and ghost stories. Gold coin donation appreciated, see VIC for current programme.

⊖ Transport

Rottnest Island *p106, map p106*
Air
Rottnest Air Taxi, T9292 5027 and T1800 500006, www.rottnest.de. Offers return trips from Jandakot Airport, east of Fremantle, anytime during daylight hours. Fares from $80 per person, depending on numbers ($150 return if there are just 2 of you). Once on the island they also offer quick scenic flights (see **Rottnest Island Joyflights**, above).

Bicycle
Bikes can be brought over on the ferries, and the ferry companies also offer bike hire packages. Hire on the island is from **Rottnest Bike Hire**, behind Rottnest Hotel, T9292 5105, which has a wide range to suit all ages including some tandems ($20-27, children $13.50-21, tandem $45 per day) and free electric beach wheelchairs. Open 0830-1700. It also offers a recovery service in case you suffer a flat tyre and need to be rescued. Beware, however, that the coast road around the island undulates over the dunes like a roller-coaster. The slopes may be short, but they are often quite steep and cycling is a tiring business, so avoid single speed bikes. Also note that there is no fresh water west of either Geordie Bay or Kingstown Barracks and you should take plenty to drink in summer.

Ferry
Ferries run to Barrack Street Jetty in **Perth**, the C-Shed in **Fremantle** and Hillarys. See the Transport sections at the departure point for details.

Swan Valley

→ *Colour map 1, B3.*

The Swan Valley is Perth's wine region, just a 45-minute drive from the city. In truth it's half a valley, bordered to the east by the Darling Range, but running flat to the west all the way to the northern Perth suburbs. It was settled early in Perth's history and vines were being grown by 1836 at what is now Houghtons, the valley's best-known winery. All sorts of other fruit and vegetables are also grown here, and it seems that almost every other house has a sign outside advertising table grapes and rock melons. At the southern end of the valley is Guildford, an inland port established in 1829, but falling out of favour early in its history, which helped preserve many early Victorian buildings.
▶▶ *For listings, see pages 116-117.*

Ins and outs

Getting there and around Trains leave from East Perth station to Guildford and Midland, but this isn't the ideal way to tour the valley. Ideally you need your own transport, or to take a tour. A taxi to or from Perth airport costs $30, double that from Perth.

Tourist information The main **VIC** ① *on the corner of Meadow and Swan Sts, T9379 9400, www.swanvalley.com.au, 0900-1600,* for the region is in Guildford. The helpful staff will advise visitors on a route depending on what they'd like to taste (ie only sparkling wines).

Sights

Wineries

There are some 40 wineries in the region, ranging from one of the largest producers in the state to several one-person operations. Most offer wines in the $15-30 range. Cellar door hours vary widely, and Monday to Tuesday is probably the worst time to visit as some of the smaller wineries keep these as their days off. Many have cafés or restaurants, most of which have outdoor vine-covered courtyards. ▶▶ *See Eating, page 116.*

The following is only a small selection of the wineries operating in the Swan Valley, the route outlined below takes visitors on a circuit starting and finishing at the VIC. Travel north along West Swan Road to find **Sandalford** ① *3210 West Swan Rd, T9374 9374, www.sandalford.com, cellar door 1000-1700,* one of the two heavyweights in the valley offering an extensive range of wines. The 2005 Prendiville Reserve Cabernet Sauvignon is the specialty. Winery tours run from 1100-1500 and are rounded off with a full appreciation and tasting session ($22), and every Saturday (at 1100) you can become a winemaker for a day on a tour that includes an exclusive blending session and a set lunch ($125). Wines cost $14-90.

Little River ① *2 Forest Rd, T9296 4462, www.littleriverwinery.com, daily 1000-1700,* is signposted further up West Swan Road. Wines include the rare Viognier Marsanne and are priced $14-144. **Edgecombe Brothers** ① *Gnangara and West Swan Rds, T9296 4307, www.edgecombebrothers.com.au, daily 1000-1700,* is family-run and one of the most laid-back and welcoming wineries in the valley. Wines cost $18.50-68. The unpretentious shop sells an excellent range of home-produced jams, sauces and produce. The café serves breakfast, a simple light lunch using seasonal ingredients or cream tea. Try the famous Muscat ice cream.

Swan Valley

To Walyunga NP, Nen
Norcia, Brand Hwy,
Pinnacles Coast &
Geraldton

Millhouse Rd

To Northern Perth Suburbs

Brookleigh

Cathedral Av

All Saints   Mann

Edgecombe

Memorial Av

Haddrill Rd

Lamonts

Campersic Rd

Gnangara
Rd

Upper
Reach

Swanbrook

Moore Rd

Henley St

Great Northern Hwy

Maalinup

William St

Park St

Lefroy Av

Murray
Rd

Little River

Sittela

George St

Woollcott
St

Barret St

To Battistessa

Harrow St

Oakover Rd

Yukich Cl

Taylor Studios

To Toodyay

To Whiteman Park

Margaret
River
Chocolate
Company

West Swan Rd

Dale Rd

Houghton

Jane Brook

To Scarborough

Arthur
St

Middle Swan Rd

Sandalford

Toodjay Rd

To John Forrest NP Mundaring,
Northam, York & Kalgoorlie

Benara Rd

Caversham Av

Midland

Hamersley Rd

Great Eastern Hwy

Guildford

James St

Great Eastern Hwy Bypass

To ⑥ &
Southwest

To Airport & Perth

N

1 km
1 mile

As the West Swan Road merges with the Great Northern Highway head south again and turn off onto Memorial Avenue. Here visitors will find **Mann** ① *105 Memorial Av, T9296 4348, Aug-Dec Wed-Sun 1000-1700*, a one-man operation continuing three generations of expertise in producing a smooth, dry Mithode Champenoise. A bargain at $20. Jack Mann has also produced an entirely new variety of grape, the Cygneblanc, though the wine is a little pricier at $30. Also on Memorial Avenue is **Upper Reach** ① *Memorial Av, T9296 0078, www.upperreach.com.au, daily 1100-1700*, a friendly winery that produces some of the valley's finest wines, particularly their Shiraz and Chardonnay. Wines cost $15-30. They also rent out a fully self- contained 2-bedroom cottage with indoor spa and views of the vineyard (**LL-A**). Note Saturday night is only available as part of a two-night booking.

Lamonts ① *85 Bisdee Rd, T9296 4485, www.lamonts.com.au, Fri-Mon 1000-1700*, is a large family-run winery with well-respected wines costing $15-65. Light snacks can be enjoyed while wine tasting. From here re-join the Great Northern Highway until Barrett Street. **Sittella** ① *100 Barrett St, T9296 2600, www.sittella.com.au, Tue-Sun 1100-1600*, claims one of the valleys best views from its large covered wooden deck. The sparkling Chenin is a specialty. Wines cost $14-38. Winery tours by arrangement.

Houghton ① *Dale Rd, T9274 9540, www.houghton-wines.com.au, daily Sep-May 1000-1700, Jun-Aug 1000-1600*, is the valley's expansive elder statesman and produces some of the most popular wines in Australia. Wines cost $15-70. Its cheaper ranges, such as Houghton Stripe, are consistently good. It has a small museum, gallery, children's playground and simple café but the big draw is its long lawn dotted with tall jacaranda trees. Picnickers are welcome, though platters, ploughmans and pizzas are available daily for lunch.

Jane Brook ① *229 Toodyay Rd, T9274 1432, www.janebrook.com.au, daily 1000-1700*, is slightly set apart from the rest of the action. A family-run winery it has a large covered decking area devoted to serving up substantial gourmet platters. The Plain Jane range is good value at $15, while more traditional vintages go for $20-35.

Around the valley

The Swan Valley is not just a haven for wine buffs. If you're interested in early Perth history this is also a good place to trace some of the earliest developments in the colony. WA's oldest church, **All Saints**, was built on the furthest spot Captain Stirling reached in his exploration of 1827. The simple red-brick building, over 160 years old, is still in use today and is usually open to visitors.

The arts scene has been growing for some time and there are now a number of seriously exciting artists in the valley. Antonio Battistessa, the Wizard of Fire, has been creating ornate iron sculptures and furniture for years and his work can be found all over Perth. His studio, **Battistessa** ① *corner of Campersic and Neuman Rds, T9296 4121, 0900-1600*, is continuously growing. **Maalinup** ① *West Swan Rd, T9296 0711, www.maalimia.com.au, 1000-1700*, is an Aboriginal-owned and operated cultural centre with workshops and two galleries. The premier room exhibits a few fine original artworks, woodcarvings and didgeridoos, the other houses the more run-of-the-mill works found in many gift shops. Jude Taylor, the proprietor of **Jude Taylor Studio** ① *510 Great Northern Highway, T9250 8838, www.taylorstudio.com.au, opening hours vary so call ahead*, can seemingly turn her hand to almost anything and the studio houses a brilliant collection of art, sculpture and furniture. There is also a nice little café where you can enjoy food and drinks indoors or on beautiful wooden furniture outdoors. **Lamonts winery** (see above) has a gallery featuring many local and WA artists.

The **Margaret River Chocolate Company** ① *5123 West Swan Rd, T9250 1588, www.chocolatefactory.com.au, daily 0900-1700*, offers some sweet relief from wine and galleries. Housed in a smart building, it has a long counter in front of a huge wall of chocolate, within which is a window onto the chocolate-making activities beyond. The wide range of delicious chocs can be bought individually or by the bag, and there's a café (open 0900-1630).

Guildford → *Colour map 1, B3.*

Guildford, 20 km from Perth, 16 km from Mundaring, retains many old buildings from its early founding as the agricultural base to supply the Swan River Colony, but as yet makes very little of them other than as accommodation. The **courthouse** and **gaol complex** ① *corner of Swan and Meadow Sts, 0900-1600, $2*, dates back to 1841 and, as a museum, now has a collection of colonial memorabilia. Entry to these also includes a peek inside one of the original settlers' cottages, constructed around 1880. Next door is **Guildford Village Potters** ① *22 Meadow St, T9279 9859, www.guildfordpotters.webs.com, Mon-Fri 0930-1500, Sat-Sun 1000-1630*, a commercial operation that displays work from over 20 local potters. On show is a wide range, mostly a mix of practical, rustic ceramics with some fairly esoteric decorative pieces.

Walyunga National Park → *Colour map 2, B2.*

① *$11 per car.*

Some 15 km north of central Swan Valley, this 18-sq-km block sits on the western escarpment of the Darling Range at the point at which the Avon River winds its way through to the plains to the west. It's a river that draws many visitors, particularly during the **Avon Descent**, www.avondescent.com.au, in the first weekend in August when competitors brave the length of Syds Rapids in their race downstream. Permanent water and a good supply of native tucker also made this a fine spot for the areas first inhabitants and one of the park's shorter trails describes some of the local Aboriginal stories. There are two parking areas, both with toilets and wood-fired BBQs. The further of the two, adjacent to **Boongarup Pool**, tends to be the quieter and is closer to the rapids. Three longer circular bush walks head off from the car parks: the shortest is the **Kangaroo Trail**, taking about one hour; the longest, the **Echidna Trail**, takes about four hours. The latter reaches the highest point in the park (260 m) and you'll get views across the Avon Valley.

Whiteman Park → *Colour map 1, A3.*

① *T9209 6000, www.whitemanpark.com, Mon-Fri 0830-1800, Sat-Sun 0830-1900, entry via Lord St, where the No 336 Morley-Ellenbrook bus drops off, use the courtesy phone at the entrance building to arrange a pick-up.*

Covering more than 3000 ha of natural and regenerated bush, Whiteman Park, 20 km from Perth, is the most family-orientated of Perth's peripheral parks, focusing on children's activities, picnic facilities and visitor attractions rather than extensive bushwalking. The park hosts equestrian and shooting centres but the main visitor area is at the **Village**, with extensive picnic facilities (and associated car parks) around nearby **Mussel Pool**, a small lake and area of wetland. The picnic facilities are impressive: dozens of gas-fired and wood-fired BBQs with firewood provided free. There are vast lawned areas and quite a few covered tables, some of which can be booked ahead. **Mussel Pool West** is home to the **Birds of Prey Flying Displays** ① *T0438 388383, Sat-Sun 1100 and 1430, weather permitting, $9, children $5, concessions $7,* operated by the WA Birds of Prey Centre.

In the village are the **visitor centre** ① *Mon-Fri 0830-1700, Sat-Sun 1000-1600,* café, a few craft shops, children's playground and pool, and the **Motor Museum of WA** ① *T9249 9457, 1000-1600, $8, children and concessions $5,* which has the largest collection of vintage vehicles in the state. Adjacent is a separate **Tractor Museum** ① *T9209 3480, Wed, Sat and Sun 1000-1400, gold coin donation.* Theres also a **Transport Heritage Centre** ① *trams/trains operate Tue, Thu, Fri, Sat and Sun 1100-1400, $5-8, children $2.50-4,* where tourist trains and vintage trams snake through the bush and connect the village with Mussel Pool. Another attraction in the park is **Caversham Wildlife Park** ① *T9248 1984, www.cavershamwildlife.com.au, 0900-1730 (last entry 1630), $22, children $8.* This park holds the largest collection of animals in the state. They have over 200 species of birds, mammals and reptiles from all over the country, and a few from overseas. Highlights include the wombats, some of which can be met and cuddled.

The **Whiteman Explorer** ① *T9209 6000, Mon 1100 and 1300, free,* offers 45-minute guided tours of Whiteman Park in a restored vintage bus.

As well as the static attractions, Whiteman Park plays host to a series of regular child- and adult-orientated events, including concerts and funfairs.

⊙ Swan Valley listings

For Sleeping and Eating price codes and other relevant information, see pages 28-34.

⊜ Sleeping

Swan Valley *p112, map p113*
L Swan Valley Oasis Resort, West Swan Rd, T9296 5500, www.swanvalleyoasis.com. Luxurious resort with 28 rooms, all have king-sized beds and there is also a self-contained 1-bedroom apartment with spa and balcony. The on-site restaurant is open for breakfast, lunch and dinner every day and home-brewed beer is served in the adjacent **Mash Brewery**, T9296 5588, www.mashbrewing. com.au. There is also a swimming pool and a golf course nearby.
A Chapel Farm Getaways, 231 Toodyay Rd, T9250 4755, www.chapelfarmgetaways. com.au. 6 unusual en suite a/c rooms. Cooked breakfast included. Also outdoor pool, spa and licensed restaurant, Thu lunch, Fri-Sun lunch and dinner. It also does Mongolian BBQs on Fri and Sun. Recommended.
A Settlers Rest Farmstay, George St, T/F9250 4540, www.settlersrest.com.au. Historic, beautifully furnished 3-bedroom weatherboard cottage in a quiet, central spot. Open fires, a/c and traditional verandas. Minimum 2-night stay at weekends.

Caravan parks
B-D Swan Valley Tourist Park, West Swan Rd, T9274 2828. Small, homely campground with swimming pool, on-site vans and en suite cabins. In the middle of the wine region.
C-D Banksia Tourist Park, 219 Midland Rd, T9250 2398, www.banksiatourist.com.au. Self-contained units and en suite chalets. The excellent facilities include a swimming pool, a covered playground, a deli/café and internet access.

Guildford *p114, map p113*
L-B Rose & Crown, 105 Swan St, T9279 8444, www.rosecrown.com.au. This grand old coaching inn is officially the oldest pub in WA, and does indeed ooze its early colonial character. The 4 rooms upstairs are sumptuous, unashamedly old-worldy, but scale dramatically in price. Modern motel rooms also available. All rooms are en suite. Meals available include substantial breakfasts 0700-0900, simple cheap light lunches 1200-1500 and mid-range dinners from Mon-Sat 1800-2100.
B The Hollies, 5 Water St, T9279 3641, www.thehollies.com.au. Separated from the main house, guests stay in the self-contained **Summer House**. Continental breakfast is included.

❼ Eating

Swan Valley *p112, map p113*
Wineries and breweries
♯♯♯ **Sandalford**, 3210 West Swan Rd, T9374 9374, www.sandalford.com. Daily 1200-1500. Delicious and filling food in a great location. The cuisine is Modern Australian with a strong Italian influence, and uses a lot of fresh, simple flavours. The cheese selection will make any foodie happy.
♯♯♯-♯ **Elmar's In the Valley**, 3781 West Swan Rd, T9296 6354, www.elmars.com.au. Wed-Thu 1000-1700, Fri-Sun 1000-2200. A German microbrewery and restaurant. Schwarzbier and Pilsner are served up with hearty meals such as bratwurst, schnitzel and pork shank. There are also tasting plates, snacks and salads.
♯♯ **Little River**, 6 Forest Rd, T9296 4462. Fri-Wed 1030-1630. A little bit of rustic France in the Swan, both food and wine being strongly gallic influenced. Casual menu, cream teas, home-made desserts and ice creams. The duck confit is especially good.

¶¶ Sittella, 100 Barrett St, T9296 2600,
www.sittella.com.au. Tue-Sun 1100-1600.
Eat on the covered deck or inside the large,
contemporary but earthy dining room.
A la carte or set menus for lunch, with an
emphasis on seafood. Recommended.

¶¶-¶ Upper Reach, Memorial Av, T9296 0078,
www.upperreach.com.au. Daily 1100-1700.
This winery is in a very picturesque location
and has a pleasant café that serves up a
good snack and chat range, as well as more
substantial dishes. It offers platters, good
coffee and teas, but the real highlight is
the extensive breakfast menu on Sun
(0830-1000).

¶ Jane Brook, 229 Toodyay Rd, T9274 1432,
www.janebrook.com.au. Open 1000-1700.
Famous for its summer gourmet platters, in
winter it serves up very tasty home-made
pies. There are other small snacks,
cheeseboards and a dessert of the day.
Afternoon teas are also served.

Around the valley
Taylors Art and Coffee House,
510 Great Northern Highway, T9250 8838,
www.taylorstudio.com.au. Open for breakfast
and lunch Wed-Sun 0900-1700. This pleasant
café adjacent to the **Taylor Studio**, serves
up excellent food. Friendly service and a
beautifully designed setting make it the
perfect place to relax. Takeaway available.
Recommended.

Guildford p114, map p113
¶¶ Padburys Café Restaurant,
114 Terrace Rd, T9378 4484, www.padburys
restaurant.com.au. Sat-Sun for breakfast
0830-1100 and Tue-Sun for lunch 1100-1500
and dinner 1700-late. Award-winning
restaurant with a Modern Australian menu.
Alfresco dining, fully licensed.

▲ Activities and tours

Swan Valley p112, map p113
Beer Nuts Brewery Tours, T9295 0605,
www.beernuts.com.au. Tours around
the Swan Valley's microbreweries for beer
lovers. Visits include Elmar's in the Valley,
Mash Brewing, Ironbark Brewery, The Feral
Brewing Company, Duckstein Brewery and
The Kimberley Rum Company from Thu-Sun.
Tours range from those where you bring your
own lunch ($70 per person for 3-8 people),
to those where lunch, snacks and drinks
tastings are included ($140 for 1-8 people).
Pick-ups available.

Out and About Wine Tours, T9377 3376,
www.outandabouttours.com.au. Relaxed
but informative winery tours in the region.
Half-day, full-day and twilight tours/cruises.

Swan Valley Shuttle Service, T9274 6569.
Offers a good hop-on hop-off service that
leaves from the VIC Wed-Sun every hour
0930-1630, $60). Can be booked through
the VIC.

Swan Valley Tours and Cruises, T9274 1199,
www.svtours.com.au. Offers various wine and
gourmet tours and cruises with pick-ups from
central Perth or Guildford.

Wagon Winery Trails, T0412 917496,
www.swanvalleywa.com. Take the decidedly
slow option in horse-drawn pioneer wagons.
Lots of different packages, but none go
very far from their starting point in Upper
Swan. Transfers available from Guildford
train station.

⊖ Transport

Swan Valley p112, map p113
Train There are frequent train services
between **Midland**, **Guildford** and **Perth**.
Last trains leave Midland Mon-Fri 2400,
Sun (ie Sat night) 0130 and Sun 2330.

Perth Hills

The sharp, 400-m-high western escarpment of the Darling Ranges runs parallel to the coast about 30 km inland, forming a natural eastern border to the rapidly expanding Perth suburbs, and a western border to WA's huge and ancient inland plateau. Large areas of the scarp have been set aside as reserves and parks, preserving the characteristic gum woodlands and providing city dwellers and visitors with an extensive network of bush walking, mountain biking and horse-riding tracks. Some of the valleys that snake inland have been cultivated by European settlers to produce fruit, vegetables and grapes. Although not as well known as the more extensive producers on the coastal plain in Swan Valley, several wineries have been established, and some can claim the prettiest settings near Perth. ▶▶ *For listings, see pages 121-122.*

Ins and outs

There are some buses from Perth and Midland. An excellent way of getting a flavour of the hills forests is by bike, and there are a number of circular trails. ▶▶ *See Activities and tours and Transport, page 122, for details.*

The main VICs are in **Kalamunda** ① *Library building, Railway Parade, next to History Village, T9293 4872, daily 1000-1600*; and **Mundaring** ① *7225 Great Eastern Highway, T9295 0202, 1000-1600*. **Perth Hills National Park Centre** ① *Allen Rd, off Mundaring Weir Rd, T9295 2244, Mon-Fri 1000-1630*, has brochures and maps for the Bibbulmun Track and Munda Biddi Track, and will advise on current trail accessibility.

Kalamunda → *Colour map 2, B2. 25 km from Perth, 25 km from Mundaring.*

Kalamunda is a good-sized modern town, seemingly built around a central shopping centre and shoving its history to the fringes. Its main claim to fame is as the northern terminus of the prodigious **Bibbulmun Track**, but the **Kalamunda History Village** ① *Railway Rd, T9293 1371, Mon-Thu 1000-1500, Sat 1000-1200 and Sun 1330-1630, $5, children $2, concessions $4*, is well worth a stroll around. Although a small example of an assembled village, all the dozen or so buildings and their copious contents are authentic and well laid out around the towns original railway station.

Gooseberry Hill and the Zig Zag → *15-km loop driving circuit.*

From Kalamunda it is worth driving out on Williams Street to Gooseberry Hill, where the road winds one-way down to close to the base of the scarp. At almost every point along the series of switchbacks there are sweeping views of the coastal plains and Perth city centre. No entry fees apply. The road comes out on Ridge Hill Road. Turn right, left into Helena Valley Road, right again into Scott Street for the Great Eastern Highway. Turn left, then left again for Kalamunda Road and the Roe Highway.

Bickley Valley → *Colour map 2, B2.*

Reached by taking Mundaring Weir Road from Kalamunda and then turning right into Aldersyde Road, Bickley Valley is one of the most picturesque of several small valleys that have been partially cultivated for fruit and wine. Fairly steep-sided, it is a patchwork of native forest, pasture and groves of fruit trees, always with a green, lush feel even in the heat of summer. There are a handful of small wineries dotted along and just off Aldersyde Road and Walnut Road, but they are only open for tastings at weekends. At

Bibbulmun Track

Started in the 1970s the long-distance Bibbulmun walking trail was last upgraded in 1998 and is now well marked along its entire route. Starting in Kalamunda it winds its way south through North Bannister, Dwellingup, Balingup, Pemberton and Walpole before finally ending up, 963 km later, in Albany. As well as passing through these picturesque towns the track also winds through several reserves and parks, much of the southern forests and some of the spectacular south coast. There are nearly 50 bush campsites en route, each with a simple three-sided timber bunk shelter, picnic tables, water tank and pit toilets. Note that there are no cooking facilities, water needs to be boiled or treated, and there is no toilet paper. None of the shelters are accessible by private vehicle, a great idea on the part of designers. There are also a few B&Bs that offer pick-ups and drop-offs to sections of the track. The whole walk generally takes around six to eight weeks, but few choose to tackle it in a single go. DEC have suggestions for various short-day sections. The track is by far at its best in winter and spring, think twice, and then again before tackling any of it in high summer. There is a two-volume guide to the track and a series of eight maps also dedicated to it, all available at the **Perth Map Centre** (see page 82) amongst other outlets.

For more information see www.bibbulmuntrack.org.au or www.naturebase.net, or contact the **Friends of the Bibbulmun Track** by calling T9481 0551.

the far end of the valley is the **Perth Observatory** ① *337 Walnut Rd, T9293 8255, www.perthobservatory.wa.gov.au; day tours 1st Sun in Jun, Jul, Aug and Sep at 1400 (1 hr), other days as per demand, $7, children and concessions $5; viewing nights $20, children and concessions $12, 2 sessions each evening, the last of which sometimes stretches beyond the usual 1 hr,* which regularly holds viewing nights throughout the year. Each month they generally have a week of 'night sky evenings', when the moon is fuller and visible, and a week of 'deep sky nights', when the moon's absence allows even more to be seen, including other galaxies. Parties of 12 usually get to see six objects through three separate telescopes. These evenings are some of the best value of their kind, and bookings are essential. Also available are day tours, more appropriate for children, which include a slide show and sometimes sunspot viewing.

Mundaring → *Colour map 2, B2. 40 km from Perth, 55 km from Northam.*

Straddling the Great Eastern Highway with its thunderous, constant traffic, Mundaring is a modern town of pale-coloured brick with glimpses of an earlier history peeping through the cracks. Its chief attractions lie outside the town itself, west along the highway at John Forrest National Park, and south at Mundaring Weir. The **VIC** ① *The Old School, 7225 Great Eastern Highway, T9295 0202, www.mundaringtourism.com.au* is able to provide useful information and advice on nearby sights.

John Forrest National Park → *Colour map 2, B2. 30 km from Perth, 10 km from Mundaring.*

① *$11 per vehicle, T9298 8344. Access is via looping Park Rd, off the highway, a side road taking you into the visitor area where a fee applies.* At the visitor area are a few facilities including bush BBQs, picnic tables and a ranger station.

The first formal reserve in WA, declared in 1900, John Forrest is still one of the biggest parks dedicated to preserving the original wildlife and gum woodlands of the scarp, extending about 4 km along the side of the Great Eastern Highway and 5 km north.

The main draw of the park is its walking trails, best undertaken in winter or spring when the brooks are flowing. It is absolutely riddled with tracks, but many are unmarked so take care to stick to the signposted trails. For a short easy stroll, the **Glenn Brook Trail** takes about 45 minutes from the visitor area and winds its way around the Glen Brook Dam that you will have seen on your right while driving in. The trail is relatively flat, has views across the dam and passes a large number of wildflowers in spring. Considerably more challenging is the **Eagles View Walk Trail**, a six- to seven-hour loop that takes in much of the park's area and scenery. Taking the clockwise option the walk begins with an uphill section to a lookout, with views over the coast plain to Perth, then along a pretty valley that is also thick with wildflowers in spring. The return section undulates over a couple of rocky ridges, once again affording views of Perth, but this time also over much of the park in the foreground.

Mundaring Weir → *Colour map 2, B2. 8 km from Mundaring, 16 km from Kalamunda.*

In 1895, with the Kalgoorlie goldrushes in full swing, WA's Engineer-in-Chief CY O'Connor, was given the task of supplying water to the new goldfields. Over 500 km inland, in one of Australia's driest areas, the task seemed to many impossible but it simply had to be done to sustain the new cash cow and O'Connor was the man for the job. His solution was simple, but challenged the technology of the day. He proposed building a massive reservoir in the Perth Hills near Mundaring and from there a pipeline all the way to Kalgoorlie. The scheme was widely derided as unworkable, but O'Connor got his green light. The dam, enlarged to 40 m high in the 1950s and still performing its intended purpose, is a testament to his vision and capability, but sadly he didn't live to see it in operation. He killed himself weeks before the initial trials in 1902, a result of the intense pressure and harassment the scheme brought him.

Today a small huddle of buildings sits in the forest to the north of the main dam wall, among them the excellent pub built to cater for the original workers and engineers, and a YHA hostel. Theres also an art and craft gallery that is open on weekends and public holidays. A little beyond the village the **No 1 Pump Station** ① *T9295 2455, Mar-Jan Wed-Sun and public holidays 1000-1600, $5, children and concessions $3, National Trust operated,* utilizes the original pumphouse and carefully details the development of the goldrushes and the building of both dam and pipeline. In the other direction the **Perth Hills National Parks Centre** ① *Allen Rd, T9295 2244, www.dec.wa.gov.au/n2n,* is the place to visit for advice on walking or driving through the Perth Hills. There is also camping here for $9 per person and the Bibbulmun Track passes nearby. The **Kookaburra Cinema** ① *T9295 6190, nightly Nov-Apr, current releases,* has an outdoor screen and seating. In summer, the **Mundaring Weir Hotel** (see Sleeping, page 121) hosts the **Mundaring Weir Summer Festival**, a series of concerts in the hotels outdoor amphitheatre. They are very popular and accommodation rises in price at these times.

There are a few walking trails in and around the weir. The **Weir Walk**, following yellow-collared posts, takes a little less than an hour and winds around the area between the pub and the weir, over the weir (gates close at 1800), around the picnic areas to the south and through the pumping station complex. It formally starts outside the museum but can be started outside the pub. The **O'Connor Trail**, following the green-collared posts, starts opposite the pub at the craft centre, and follows a loop through the forest, past the discovery centre and cinema. Allow about two hours.

For Sleeping and Eating price codes and other relevant information, see pages 28-34.

● Sleeping

Kalamunda *p118*

D Kalamunda Hotel, 43 Railway Terr, T9257 1084, www.kalamundahotel.com.au. Built in 1902, has 3 simple upstairs doubles, all en suite with a/c. Downstairs, the traditional bars have been smartly refurbished and the dining room serves a good range of Mediterranean-style meals. Continental breakfast is included in the price. Meals Mon-Sat 1200-1500, 1800-2100, Sun 1000-2100. Cheaper counter meals are available daily 1200-2100 from the bar.

Bickley Valley *p118*

A Brookside Vineyard, 5 Loaring Rd, T9291 8705, www.brooksidevineyard.com.au. Has a charming garden cottage, built and furnished in the style of the adjacent Federation homestead. Open-plan with combined living and bedroom, pot belly stove, en suite bathroom, and veranda. Substantial, full cooked breakfast and evening meals by arrangement. Cheese platter and wine on arrival.

Mundaring *p119*

LL LooseBox, 6825 Great Eastern Highway, 2 km west of Mundaring, T9295 1787, www.loosebox.com. Everything about this place exudes quality and indulgence. In the garden are 6 luxury chalets, available as part of a lunch or dinner package Wed-Sun, B&B packages are available every day. See Eating for information on the restaurant.

Mundaring Weir *p120*

B-C Mundaring Weir Hotel, T9295 1106, www.mundaringweirhotel.com.au. A grand old pub hotel perched on the hill above the weir pump stations, and a favourite Sun

destination when a lamb spit-roast is prepared for lunch. The main bars capture a feel for the pubs century of history, but you'll be likely to head for the garden tables. Fresh, inventive meals are mostly cheap, available Mon-Sat 1200-1430, Fri-Sat 1800-2000, Sun 1200-1800. Accommodation is in 9 external motel-style units, each with an open fireplace, grouped alongside the pubs pool. Room/dinner packages only Sun-Thu. Every Sun there a live bush band plays in the beer garden and a spit roast lamb is for sale from 1500 until sold out.

D-E Perth Hills Forest Lodge YHA, Mundaring Weir Rd, T9295 1809. A small, relaxed hostel with 36 beds in dorms, twins and singles. General facilities aren't extensive, but clean and comfortable and include a wood-burning stove and well-equipped kitchen. Popular with groups so make sure you ring ahead.

F Perth Hills National Parks Centre, Allen Rd, T9295 2244. A handful of camping sites, with toilets and hot showers. There's also a camp kitchen. Book before you arrive.

● Eating

Kalamunda *p118*

♔-♔ Le Paris-Brest, Haynes St, T9293 2752. Tue-Sun 0700-1730 and public holidays. Something of a cultural oasis in Kalamunda, a small, cheerful Gallic corner providing a patisserie and café, ongoing art exhibitions, and monthly live jazz on their wraparound terrace. Everything is home-made, including all the cakes and ice cream.

♔-♔ Thai on the Hill, on the corner of Haynes Rd and Railway Rd, T9293 4312. Tue-Sun 1800-2200. Has a pleasant rich-red formal dining room and serves Thai food with an extensive range of cheaper veggie options. Licensed.

Gooseberry Hill *p118*

Le Croissant du Moulin, 169 Railway Rd, T9293 4345. Wed-Sun 0730-1700. Tucked away but what a find. This patisserie, boulangerie and café offers authentic French baking. Breads, pastries, quiches and good coffee. Come for breakfast and tuck in to a croissant or a bowl of hot chocolate.

Bickley Valley *p118*

Packing Shed, 101 Loaring Rd, T9291 8425, almost next door to **Brookside**. Open for lunches and teas, Fri-Sun 1000-1400 and public holidays. The restaurant, the **Lawnbrook Estate**, now much better known for its food than its wine. Essentially a barn with a large brick terrace, the excellent food is country Mediterranean style, spiced with the odd curry.

Mundaring *p119*

Loose Box, 6825 Great Eastern Highway, 2 km west of Mundaring, T9295 1787, www.loosebox.com. Wed-Sat 1900-2200, Sun 1200-1400. This restaurant, a winner of a constant stream of state and national awards since it opened in 1980, is a century-old weatherboard house, now opened up into several formal dining areas. The seriously expensive cuisine is classical French, with Australian influences, using local produce. Bookings recommended. Recommended.

Little Caesars Pizzeria, 7125 Great Eastern Highway, T9295 6611, www.littlecaesars pizzeria.com.au. Wed-Mon 1600-late. World-famous pizzeria with a vast menu, including many seafood and meat options. Vegans, and vegetarians are also well catered for. Visitors have to try one of the dessert pizzas, such as New York pecan pie.

▲ Activities and tours

Walking
The principal 40-km loop trail heads out from Midland, up the scarp and through John Forrest National Park, steers well clear of the highway and drops around to Mundaring. Much of the return to Midland is along the route of the Old Eastern Railway. From Mundaring a connecting 15-km loop heads south through the state forest to Mundaring Weir.

⊖ Transport

Bus
Metropolitan buses for **Mundaring** leave from the train station at **Midland**. Buses to **Kalamunda** leave Perth City Busport several times a day. There are direct TransWA coaches from **East Perth** that call at **Mundaring**, leaving at Mon 0715, Tue, Thu and Sun 0800, Thu 0930, and Fri 0900.

North of Perth

The coastal road north of Perth runs as far as Lancelin at present but work is currently underway to seal the sandy 4WD track between Lancelin and Cervantes, and the extension should be open by mid-2011. This will create a coastal route all the way from Perth to Geraldton and will bring much change to the string of sleepy fishing and holiday towns between the two cities. Yanchep National Park makes a fine day trip from Perth, with its tranquil lakes and birdlife, but it is worth continuing north for a night in Lancelin. It is windsurfing heaven but if you are weedy of arm then come for the dunes. Lancelin has a long expanse of silky dunes that are magical at sunset and only a short walk from the town centre. Inland, the appealing town of Gingin lies on the Brand Highway and can make an interesting stop on the way to or from Geraldton. Further east, the curious settlement of New Norcia straddles the Great Northern Highway. New Norcia is a small community of Benedictine monks living a contemplative life in their grand edifices, as road trains thunder past. ►► For listings, see pages 125-126.

Yanchep National Park → *Colour map 2, B2. 50 km from Perth, 80 km from Lancelin.*
ⓘ *$11 per car. Crystal Cave Tours (45 mins) 1030, 1130, 1300, 1400, 1500. Aboriginal Experience (45 mins) Sat hourly 1300-1500, Sun hourly 1400-1600. $10, children $5.*
Perched just inland, 15 km away from Perth's northernmost suburbs, lies one of the region's best parks. Encompassing two lakes, **Loch McNess** and the larger **North Lake**, the area was ear-marked as a nature reserve in 1905, but the park has developed slowly since then and has also seen military use. Yanchep has a wide range of attractions for the visitor. Its bush-covered dunes, teeming with Western Grey kangaroos, overlay a large network of limestone caves (see below). There are many walking trails, threading their way through and around heathland, gum woods and wetland, and there are opportunities for overnight hikes, with camping at the far end of North Lake. As well as the wild 'roos there are two animal enclosures, one for kangaroos and emus, and a large koala enclosure where they actually get to live up trees. A few are brought down occasionally during the day to a smaller area where visitors can have their photograph taken with them. The park is also home to dozens of bird species. Simply sitting by the lakes in summer you are likely to see flocks of galahs and black cockatoos, not to mention the inquisitive ducks. There are several picnic areas with BBQs and some covered tables.

The park puts on a constant programme of activities, especially in summer; some free, some not (contact the visitor centre for a current programme). Most take place in the area between the visitor centre, Loch McNess and the **Yanchep Inn**. Aboriginal performances of dancing, didgeridoo playing and weapon throwing take place regularly throughout the day. There are also cultural talks and demonstrations about the area's traditional Aboriginal lifestyle. Rowing boats on Loch McNess can be hired at the visitor centre. There's public access to two caves. There are regular tours of the **Crystal Cave**, a still active and therefore quite damp cave, or you can book to explore **Yonderup Cave**, now dry. Occasional adventure caving trips are also organized for Yonderup. The park has its own nine-hole golf course. Several short walks of around 2 km (one hour) head around Loch McNess and the caves area, all described on the free map you will receive on entering the park. For details of the longer and overnight walks contact the visitor centre.

The **VIC** ⓘ *T9561 1004*, is close to the park entrance, next to a kiosk and tearooms.

Lancelin → *Colour map 2, A1. Population: 900. 130 km from Perth, 75 km from Gingin.*

At the current end of the coastal highway, Lancelin is a small, spread out fishing town that has become a firm favourite of windsurfers and kitesurfers during the main October-May season. The strong dependable off-shore winds are also responsible for the naked dunes that run for a couple of kilometres just inland of the town. They make an excellent venue for sandboarding, and are also used by local trailbikers, four-wheel drivers and tour operators, but they are at their most striking when devoid of traffic and lit up by a strong sunset when they fleetingly turn blush pink. The dunes start about 1 km north of town, and you should arrive about 25 minutes before sunset to get the full effect. The town beaches are not the coast's best but a few decent surf breaks, snorkelling and diving spots help make this a popular destination. The town has all the basic services, including an ATM in the **Gull** service station. There is no public transport to or from Lancelin. The **VIC** ① *T9655 1100, daily 0900-1800 (shorter hours in winter),* is located on the main road.

Gingin → *Colour map 2, A2. Population: 600. 80 km from Perth, 225 km from Dongara.*

A tiny, picturesque rural town, Gingin sits inside a loop of Gingin Brook and is the centre of a thriving agricultural community. Beef cattle are traditionally farmed here but, increasingly, olive tree plantations are dominating the area. The town has a fine grassy park by the brook and a few lovely old stone buildings, such as **St Lukes Church** (1860) and **Dewars House** (1880), an unusual two-storey private residence. There are a few basic services on Brockman Street, including a post office and general store, and a good pub on Jones Street between the brook and railway line. To the west of Gingin, Gingin Brook Road (32 km) runs between the Brand Highway and the main coast road to Guilderton and Lancelin. Near here is where the **Gravity Discovery Centre** ① *Military Rd, T9575 7577, www.gdc.asn.au, Tue-Sun 0930-1700, $15, children $10, concessions $12,* can be found. The interactive nature of the exhibits makes this a great option for those with kids. There is the Leaning Tower of Gingin where visitors can climb 222 steps and drop water balloons through special shoots re-enacting Galileos experiment in Pisa, The Cosmology Gallery houses works of art relating to science and evolution, and there is information on black holes, gravity, the Big Bank and so forth. There is a café, as well as an observatory for star gazing.

New Norcia → *Colour map 2, A2. Population: 50. 130 km from Perth, 80 km from Gingin.*

New Norcia is one of the most unusual settlements in Australia. A small community of Benedictine monks live a traditional Benedictine life of work and prayer within an astonishingly grand setting on the hot and dry Victoria Plains. The first Bishop of Perth, Dr John Brady, was concerned for the welfare of Western Australia's indigenous people and thought the blessing of civilization and religion would save them. He persuaded two Spanish monks to come to Australia to establish a mission and they set off from Perth on foot for the Victoria Plains in 1846 to do so. Dom Rosendo Salvado, the first Abbot, aimed to encourage local Aboriginal people to become farmers and to educate Aboriginal children within a self-sufficient religious community. It is hard to say how successful he was but the second Abbot, Torres, pursued markedly different aims. New Norcia became less of a bush mission and more of a monastic community and centre for education. Torres was also an architect and during his short stint from 1901 to 1914 most of the enormous, elaborate buildings were constructed or simple existing buildings, such as the Abbey Church, were given a face-lift. These days there are only seven monks but they employ a workforce of about 60 to keep the place running. Much of the place is off-limits but there is an interesting **museum and art gallery** ① *T9654 8056, www.newnorcia.wa.edu.au, 0900-1630, $10,* *children under 12 free, concessions $6, daily tours of the town 1100, 1330. $14.50, children under 12 free, concessions $9 (2 hrs), combined tickets are available for $23, children under 12 free, concessions $14-20*, that focuses on the history of the mission and displays some of New Norcia's rare and valuable artwork and treasures. There is also the opportunity to 'Meet a Monk' on weekdays at 1030 and ask questions about monastic life. A shop sells high-quality pottery, souvenirs and items made by the monks, including olive oil and the renowned preservative-free New Norcia bread, baked daily in a wood-fired oven and served in many Perth restaurants. For more information contact the **VIC** ① *T9654 8056, www.newnorcia.wa.edu.au*, at the museum.

⦿ North of Perth listings

For Sleeping and Eating price codes and other relevant information, see pages 28-34.

⬤ Sleeping

Yanchep National Park *p123*
B-D Yanchep Inn, 200 m north of visitor centre, T9561 1001, www.yanchepinn.com.au. Has 14 luxurious motel units, some with spa, and cheaper hotel-style accommodation with communal facilities. The restaurant serves mid-range meals and has an extensive wine list.
C Yanchep Holiday Village, 56 St Andrews Dr, 10 km from the park near the small coastal settlement of Yanchep, T9561 2244, www.yanchepholidays.com. A small number of self-contained apartments around a central pool area, surrounded by bush. Facilities include BBQs, open fireplaces and laundry.

Lancelin *p124*
C Lancelin Beach Hotel, north end of town, T9655 1005, www.lancelinbeachhotel. com.au. Has motel-style en suite rooms and self-contained units. The licensed, mid-range restaurant overlooks the shore. There is also a bar and an outdoor pool with spa.
C-D Lancelin Holiday Accommodation, T9655 1100. Has a few self-contained, 1- to 2-bedroom units. They can also organize a variety of houses for short stays in the town. No linen provided. Book through VIC.
D-E Lancelin Lodge YHA, south end of town, 10 Hopkins St, T9655 2020,

www.lancelinlodge.com.au. Has just about everything you look for in a hostel. Great rooms and communal facilities, friendly, pool, volleyball court, lots of freebies including bikes, and excellent local knowledge. They will even pick up from Perth (cost involved). Weekly discounts available. Recommended.

Camping
There are 2 caravan parks, both with on-site vans and both close to the shore. The one at the north end, T9655 1115, is also close to the dunes.

Gingin *p124*
C Gingin Hotel, 5 Jones St, T9575 2214, www.ginginhotel.com.au. A country hotel with imaginative rustic decor and a lovely outdoor terrace. There are 6 hotel rooms with share facilities and 6 en suite motel units. Pub food and internet available.
C-D The Runners Rest, 182 Cockram Rd, T9575 1414, B&B on a working farm, with self-catering breakfast provided.
C-E Liberty Roadhouse, corner of Brand Highway and Dewar Rd, T9575 2258. Runs the caravan park next door, sites and cabins.
E Willowbrook Farm, 1679 Gingin Brook Rd, T9575 7566, Powered and unpowered sites for tents and caravans. Enjoy the complimentary freshly baked scones, home-made jam and cream on Sun morning; just bring a cup of tea or coffee to wash them down.

New Norcia *p124*

C New Norcia Hotel, T9654 8034. Built for parents visiting their children in the colleges next door. The exterior is fit for a king, indeed Abbot Torres hoped the King of Spain would visit, but inside it is a pretty simple country pub with 15 tired double and single rooms with shared facilities. A continental breakfast is included in the price. General facilities include tennis and basketball courts, swimming pool and 9-hole golf course (in winter).

D Monastery Guesthouse, T9654 8002. 8 comfortable twin en suite rooms around a courtyard within the monastery. The price (a recommended donation) includes 3 meals of the same fare as the monks, although the dining room is separate. Male guests may be asked to eat with the monks. Book in advance, especially at weekends.

Camping

Caravan and Camping, T9854 8097. Self-contained caravan stopover is possible. There are also a 8 powered tent/caravan sites with basic amenities near the roadhouse.

Eating

Lancelin *p124*

Lancelin Bay Restaurant, Miragliotta Rd, T9655 2686. Tue-Sun 0900-2100. Serves up breakfast, seafood dishes, coffee and cake. In the evenings the meals become more sophisticated. The outdoor terrace is a mere stones throw from the beach. Licensed and BYO.

Endeavour Tavern, T9655 1052. Daily 1200-1400 and 1800-2000. Characterful, modern but rustic, with lots of rough timbers and bare antique brick. The pub garden overlooks the shore and ocean. DJs and live music every weekend.

New Norcia *p124*

New Norcia Hotel, see Sleeping. Lunch Mon-Fri 1200-1400, Sat-Sun 1230-1430, and dinner Mon-Fri and Sun 1800-2000, Sat 1800-2030. Serves good food, such as grills, seafood and pizzas. At the bar visitors can try the New Norcia Abbey Ale or the Abbey Wine.

There is also a roadhouse where you can get fast food and sandwiches to eat in or take away, open daily 0900-1700.

▲ Activities and tours

Lancelin *p124*

Surf-cam and weather updates at www.stormsurf.com.

Desert Storm Adventures, T9655 2550, www.desertstorm.com.au. Runs a jacked-up yellow bus with enormous tyres, claiming to be above and beyond all other 4WDs. Tours into the dunes for a roller-coaster drive and a spot of sandboarding (45 mins $55, children $35; 1 hr, $70, children $50).

Lancelin Surfsports, T9655 1441, www.lancelinsurfsports.com. Sandboard and surfboard hire.

Werners Hot Spot, T0407 426469, www.windsurfwa.com/werner/werner.html. Hire (from $25 per hr) and lessons. Packages including airport transfer available.

Transport

Bus Some TransWA buses (N1) pass through **Gingin** on their way north, departing **East Perth** Mon-Sat 0830, Fri 1630 and Sun 0930. Other services (N2) head to **Geraldton** via **New Norcia**, leaving Tue, Thu and Sat 0930, Sun 1145. **Integrity**, Wellington St Bus Station, Perth, T1800 226339, T9574 6707, www.integritycoachlines.com.au, also operate a service up the west coast, stopping at **New Norcia** and running on Wed.

Avon Valley

The area just to the east of the Darling Range is threaded through by the Avon River (pronounced as in 'have', not 'grave'), and is a picturesque country of rolling hills, pasture and woodland. Early European settlers soon found it to be one of the most fertile regions around Perth, and substantial urban and agricultural progress was already being made when the gold rushes began in the 1890s. This saw the area's importance increase yet more as a goods marshalling point and the last place to collect water. Some of the oldest towns in WA can be found here, including York, one of the most attractive towns in the state. ▶▶ *For listings, see pages 129-131.*

Avon Valley National Park → *Colour map 2, B2. 65 km from Perth, 35 km from Toodyay.*
ⓘ *$11 car, camping $7 per person, both payable at self-registration stations.*

Avon Valley is a pretty and peaceful small park around a section of the Avon River. The steep-sided valley is covered in woodland and granite outcrops. The park has an interesting mix of flora and fauna as it includes the northern limit of jarrah and the wandoo woodland found in drier country to the east. Marri and grass trees are also common in the park. Euros, western grey kangaroos and more than 90 species of bird live in the park. In the 1860s this area was one of the most inaccessible in the Darling Ranges and was used as a hide-out by bushranger Moondyne Joe. More law-abiding types still use it as a hide-out from the city; there are a handful of tranquil camping spots, each with wood BBQs, picnic tables and pit toilets. **Valley Campsite** is the most popular, often used for launching canoes although the river retreats to a series of pools in summer and autumn. The campsites are about 10 km along steep unsealed roads. There are great views over the valley from Bald Hill.

Toodyay → *Colour map 2, B3. Population: 800. 85 km from Perth, 27 km from Northam.*

Like York, its more famous southern neighbour, Toodyay (pronounced Two-jay), has retained a fine collection of Victorian buildings, and also sits alongside the Avon. At this point the river is frequently dry, though its setting is one of prettiest in the area, with several low hills surrounding the small town centre. Toodyay is now closely associated with **Moondyne Joe**, the complex bushranger who for some time in his chequered career camped in the hills around the town (see box, page 128).

A visit to the informative **Newcastle Gaol** ⓘ *follow main Stirling Terr west under the railway bridge, turn left and follow to Clinton St, approximately 1 km, Mon-Fri 1000-1500, Sat-Sun 1000-1530, $3,* illustrates Moondyne Joe's story, and gives another grisly reminder about the shocking treatment the early colonial authorities meted out to the local Aboriginals. In the main street is **Connors Mill** ⓘ *Stirling Terr, 0900-1600, $3, entry via the VIC,* a building that had careers both as a flour mill and a mini power station. It has been restored, with authentic machinery, to a semblance of how it probably looked in its flour-grinding days. The **Cola Café** on Stirling Terrace, is well worth a visit to see the extensive collection of Coca-Cola memorabilia on show (see Eating, page 130). The **VIC** ⓘ *T9574 2435, www.toodyay.com, daily 0900-1700,* is adjacent to the mill and also houses a sweet shop.

Northam → *Colour map 2, B3. Population: 7000. 95 km from Perth, 500 km from Kalgoorlie-Boulder.*

Chosen early in the 20th century as the main rail junction for the region, Northam is still the Avon Valley's principal service town. Although there is little hard grist for the tourist

Moondyne Joe

Englishman Joseph Johns, convicted of stealing food in 1848, was transported to the Swan Valley colony in 1853. A non-violent and slightly eccentric man, his career as a criminal was chequered with many visits to Toodyay and Fremantle prisons (the latter even built him a special 'escape-proof' cell) and as many escapes. As a felon-at-large and bushranger he frequently took to the area near Toodyay, known to the local Aborigines as 'Moondyne' and now the Avon Valley National Park, so gaining his nickname by a sympathetic public. Then, and now, seen as a somewhat comic figure, his final years were actually extremely sad, his mind succumbing to dementia. He was incarcerated in an asylum, but could never be convinced it wasn't prison and still repeatedly escaped until his quiet death in 1900.

mill, a stroll around town will reveal many Victorian buildings, several good pubs and the surprisingly wide **Avon River**, bridged for pedestrians by the longest suspension span of its kind in Australia. This pleasant stretch of water also has another claim to fame, the country's only breeding population of introduced white swans, a novel sight to Perth weekenders, more familiar to many international visitors. During the first weekend in August, the town is packed for the **Avon Descent** race, www.avondescent.com.au. The river can get very white in places on its 133-km way downstream, but the start here is noted more for the screams of spectators than participants.

The town has the usual services, mostly along Fitzgerald Street or in the adjacent shopping centre, including a cinema. The **VIC** ① *2 Grey St, T9622 2100, www.visit northamwa.com.au, Mon-Fri 0900-1700, Sat-Sun 0900-1600*, which houses an exhibition on post-war immigration to the area, is by the river and suspension bridge.

York → Colour map 2, B3. Population: 3200. 95 km from Perth, 35 km from Northam.

In 1830 European settlers from the Swan River Colony explored the country east of the Darling Range and were delighted to find the Avon Valley. It seemed so fertile that Governor Stirling felt that success of his new colony was assured and one of his companions suggested the area be called Yorkshire as the rolling green hills reminded him of home. Land was grabbed eagerly and the district has been a successful agricultural region ever since. Situated by the Avon River, York experienced a short boom in the 1890s when gold was discovered in the east of the state. At the time York was the easternmost rail terminus and the last source of fresh water but was soon passed by when both water and rail reached Kalgoorlie. Northam was chosen as the major rail junction to the goldfields and became the regional centre, leaving York with a magnificent collection of 19th-century buildings to be left in peace for another century. The town is now an appealing, friendly place with museums, cafés, antique shops and bookshops along the main street that draw lots of visitors from Perth at weekends. York is also known for its festivals; vintage cars in July and jazz in October, www.yorkjazz.com.au.

The chief attraction of York is its remarkable 19th-century streetscape, mostly built between 1880 and 1910. It is well worth a stroll up and down the main street, Avon Terrace, and some of the back streets (local guide and architecture expert Adelphe King can be booked for personalized tours, T9641 1799). The most impressive building is the **Town Hall**, an opulent Edwardian hall. Visitors are welcome to explore the building, which is home to the **VIC** ① *81 Avon Terr, T9641 1301, www.yorkwa.org, 0900-1700*. Also prominent are the post office and courthouse, both designed by architect George Temple-Poole in the 1890s and built of brick and Toodyay stone.

The **Old Gaol and Courthouse** ① *132 Avon Terr, T9641 2072, Mar-Jan 1000-1600, $5, children and concessions $3*, are managed by the National Trust. An influx of land-grabbing Europeans naturally dismayed the Aboriginal people of the area who began to attack the new settlers in the mid-1830s. Soldiers were sent to York to protect the settlers so the town had a strong military and later police presence from its earliest days. The complex began as mud-brick in the 1840s and grew into the grand formal buildings of the courthouse in the 1890s. Visitors can stroll through the courthouses, cell block, stables and a troopers cottage dressed in the furnishings of 1867.

Next door is the **York Motor Museum** ① *116 Avon Terr, T9641 1288, 0930-1500, $8.50, children $3.50, concessions $6.50*, a $20 million private collection of classic cars and sports cars whose highlight is its grand prix racers. The cars range from an 1886 Benz to a 1979 Williams FW07 Cosworth. About 50 of them are kept in working order and are driven around the town in age order during the **Festival of the Cars** in July.

In the oldest part of York, the eastern side, is the **Residency Museum** ① *Brook St, T9641 1751, Tue-Thu 1300-1500, Sat-Sun and public holidays 1100-1530, $4, children $1, concessions $3*. The building housing the museum was originally part of York's Convict Hiring Depot and was then the official residency of the towns early magistrates. It now houses a collection of photographs, clothes and household items.

The **Mill Gallery** ① *13 Broome St, T9641 2900, www.theyorkmill.com.au, Mon-Fri 1000-1600, Sat-Sun 1000-1700*, is a large space showcasing paintings, furniture, woodwork and jewellery. There are also some small craft boutiques on the premises and good views from the upper floors of the old mill. There is a shop and a popular café.

⊚ Avon Valley listings

For Sleeping and Eating price codes and other relevant information, see pages 28-34.

⊜ Sleeping

Toodyay *p127*
There are a couple of standard hotels in the centre of Toodyay, whilst the majority of B&Bs are some distance away. The VIC has a full list of accommodation.
B-E Toodyay Caravan Park, Railway Rd, T9574 2612, www.toodyaycaravan parks.com.au. The closest caravan park, it has on-site vans, a strawbale chalet, self-contained cabins, BBQs, a playground and a saltwater swimming pool. There is a path by the river that leads into town.
C Pecan Hill B&B, 59 Beaufort St, T9574 2636, www.pecanhill.com.au. A charming B&B with swimming pool and guest lounge

with log fire. All rooms are en suite and have access to the veranda. Evening meals can be arranged.

Northam *p127*
A Brackson House, 7 Katrine Rd, T9622 5262, www.bracksonhouse.com.au. A luxurious B&B with spacious, stylish en suite rooms. The guest lounge is furnished with plush sofas, has a library, log fire and internet access. There is also an outdoor spa and a beautiful courtyard.
A-B Shamrock Hotel, 112 Fitzgerald St, T9622 1092, www.shamrockhotel northam.com.au. Has been splendidly renovated in keeping with its Victorian heritage. The 13 rooms are luxurious without being fussy and types vary from simple en suites to luxury spa with champagne and chocolates included. All have a/c, TV and

fridge. Continental breakfast is included. The main bar is uncluttered and comfortable and the food is consistently good. The restaurant is mostly mid-range, open Mon-Sat 1800-2100.

E-F Northam Guest House, 51 Wellington St, T9622 2301. The most budget-conscious will head here, 30 basic rooms, mostly doubles, twins and singles and use of a kitchen. It ain't pretty but it is clean and secure. Seriously cheap special rates for long-term stays apply.

D-E Northam Caravan Park, 150 Yilgarn Av, T9622 1620. On-site cabins and vans, powered tent sites, laundry facilities and BBQ.

York p128

Unsurprisingly there are a good number of heritage and heritage-style B&Bs in the area, mostly in the **A-B** price range, though bargains can be had off-season (Dec-Mar) when Perth weekenders find it too hot.

L-A The York, 145 Avon Terr, T9641 2188, www.theyork.com.au. An imposing grey structure, with 8 luxury suites in the restored main building and 15 modern en suite terrace rooms. Dinner packages are available, and there's a good restaurant on the ground floor. This is a modern take on period renovation so don't expect to be transported back in time.

B York Cottages, 2 Morris Edwards Dr, T9641 2125, www.yorkwa.com.au/yorkcottages. Modern and fully self-contained more luxurious than their ancient counterparts. Both have open fires, BBQs and can sleep 6-8. There is also an outdoor spa, children's playground and a tennis court.

C Settlers House, 125 Avon Terr, T9641 1096, www.settlershouse.com.au. An English bar with comfy red couches in a refurbished 1845 house. The 18 period rooms with en suite and a/c are situated around the courtyard. Continental breakfast included. Good value. The hotel also contains a swimming pool and a restaurant serving mid-range meals every day.

D-E Kookaburra Dream, 152 Avon Terr, T9641 2936, www.kookaburradream.com.au.

A very pleasant, friendly hostel in a suitably old building with dorms and twins. Good facilities and extras make this the best budget option.

D-F York Caravan Park, 2 km north of town on Eighth Rd, T9641 1421. In a peaceful spot, this site has well-equipped on-site vans and helpful management. Theres a camp kitchen and BBQs are available for use.

🍴 Eating

Toodyay p127

†††-† **Cola Café**, 128 Stirling Terr, T9574 4407, www.colacafe.com.au. Mon-Fri 0900-1630, Sat-Sun 0800-1700. The town's best café, a shrine to that great god of commerce. Styled as an American diner, specialities are burgers and omelettes, shakes, juices and, of course, the great drink itself.

Northam p127

†††-† **Mon Petit**, 100 Fitzgerald St, T9622 8805. Daily 0700-2200. Offers tapas and light meals. BYO.

† **Café Yasou**, 175 Fitzgerald St, T9622 3128, www.cafeyasou.com.au. Mon-Fri 0800-1600, Sat 0800-1200. A stylish organic café that serves tasty Greek and Cypriot dishes.

† **Riversedge Café**, in the VIC building. Tue-Thu 0800-1500 and Fri-Sun 0730-1500. The veranda here is a pleasant place for a light lunch or coffee. It hangs over the riverbank.

† **Two Stories Book Café**, 80 Fitzgerald St, T9622 2282. Wed-Sun 1000-1700. A second-hand bookshop with tables and sofas dotted around and a counter serving coffee, tea and home-made cakes and snacks.

York p128

†††-††† **The York** 145 Avon Terr, T9641 2188, www.theyork.com.au. Wed-Fri 1100-1430 and 1800-2130, Sat 0800-1430 and 1800-2130, Sun 0800-1430. Sophisticated seasonal dishes are served in the dining room overlooking the main street. Early evening tapas and mezze Wed-Sat. Also offers luxury accommodation (**L-A**) in recently refurbished rooms.

†† Greenhills Inn, 8 Greenhill Rd, 22 km from York along the road to Quairading, T9641 4095. Wed-Thu 1700-2100, Fri-Sun 1200-1400 and 1700-2100. If time and transport allow try to get out to this pub. It's got loads of character, is full of antiques and there are plenty of interesting locals. The restaurant serves excellent Modern Australian meals.

††-† Café Bugatti, 104 Avon Terr, T9641 1583. Wed-Mon 0730-1630. A long-established favourite for great coffee and a good range of traditional Italian dishes such as *osso buco* and veal *parmigiana*, and cheap pasta. Warm timber dining room lined with motoring memorabilia.

† The York Mill Café & Restaurant, The York Mill Gallery, 13 Broome St, T9641 2447. Mon, Tue, Thu 0900-1600, Fri 0900-2100, Sat 0800-2100, Sun 0800-1700. Warm little café within the mill complex making casual food such as burgers and salads.

† Jules Café, 121 Avon Terr, T9641 1832. Mon-Fri 0800-1630, Sat 0830-1500. A good spot for a bite of lunch with a few tables on the pavement. Wholesome food including falafel, kebabs, veggie sandwiches, home-made pastries, biscuits and muffins. Recommended.

† Yorky's Coffee Carriage, South St, T9641 1554. Nov-Mar Thu-Sun 1700-2100, Apr-Oct Thu 1000-1530, Fri-Sun 1000-2100. Novel café in a railway carriage parked by the riverbank. Basic outdoor seating and a simple cheap menu of light afternoon meals, burgers, fish and chips, quiche and lasagne.

▲ Activities and tours

Northam *p127*

Northam has become a very popular ballooning destination and there are a couple of companies who arrange flights from Apr-Nov. $270 per person weekdays and $370 per person at weekends, prices include breakfast after the flight.
Avon Valley Ballooning, 100 Fitzgerald St, T9622 8805, www.avb.net.au.
Windward Balloon Adventures, T9621 2000, www.ballooning.com.au.

⊖ Transport

Avon Valley *p127*

TransWA Prospector train service leaves **East Perth** for **Toodyay** and **Northam** (1 hr) 1-2 times a day, continuing on to **Kalgoorlie**. Their GS2 bus service to **Albany** calls at both **Northam** and **York** (2 hrs), departing Mon and Fri at 0900, Tue 1700, Wed 0945, Fri 1800, and Sun 1300.

South of Perth

The coast immediately south of Fremantle is not the state's prettiest and the region sometimes gets dismissed as a serious destination. From Rockingham the scenery improves, however, and both Rockingham and Mandurah do have their charms, not least the dolphins that live in the waters off both cities. There are tours to see or even swim with dolphins, and the experience here or in Bunbury is usually considerably richer than up at Monkey Mia. Inland, the Darling Range continues south and harbours several forested parks and reserves, which reward the time and effort required to visit them. ▸▸ *For listings, see pages 137-142.*

The coast to Rockingham

There may be a lot of coast between Fremantle and Rockingham, but it's not the sort of coast that need detain you. The area does seem to attract recreational and theme parks, however, and these may be worth a look if time allows.

Araluen Botanic Park ① *362 Croyden Rd off Brookton Highway, T9496 1171, www.araluenbotanicpark.com.au, 0900-1800. $10, children $5, concessions $8*, is thought by many to be the best of its kind around Perth. Set among the waterfalls, rock pools and tall woodland of the hills, the park features exotic species such as magnolias, rhododendrons and camellias and is known for wonderful flower displays. Facilities include BBQs, picnic areas, a restaurant and kiosk. Electric scooters and free wheelchairs available for visitors with impaired mobility and during peak season the *Araluen Train* runs. It's best to visit in spring, especially when the tulips are out.

Aviation Heritage Museum ① *on the corner of Kwinana and Leach Highways, T9311 4470, www.raafawa.org.au, 1000-1600, $10, children $5, concessions $7.50, Bull Creek station is on the Northern Suburbs to Mandurah railway line and from there it's a 10-min walk*, is one of the country's best military aircraft museums, with over 30 planes. There's a selection from the Second World War, including a Lancaster bomber, and several Australian aircraft. A separate wing documents the development of flight and space travel.

Adventure World ① *179 Progress Dr, Bibra Lake, T9417 9666, www.adventure world.net.au, Sep-Apr 0900-1700 (closed Tue-Wed school days), $47, children and concessions $39*, is a theme park incorporating a wildlife park and over 30 fairground rides and attractions. On the same road is **Bungee West** ① *T9417 2500*, offering bungee jumps and abseils down their purpose-built tower.

Rockingham → *Colour map 2, B2. Population: 90,000. 30 km from Fremantle and Mandurah.*

The coast south of Fremantle extends along three long bays, each overlooked by suburbs, naval establishments and industry. **Mangles Bay**, the furthest south, is sheltered to the west by **Garden Island** and forms the northern shore of a roughly square peninsula now occupied for the most part by the city of Rockingham and its suburbs. A thin line of dunes or grassy foreshore just separates these developments from the many excellent beaches that slope gently into relatively calm seas. The combination of usually flat water plus afternoon breezes can make southern **Safety Bay** a popular spot for windsurfers. Its foreshore is virtually undeveloped, with just a few beach facilities, including BBQs, toilets and picnic tables around the junction of Safety Bay Road and Malibu Road. **Rockingham Beach**, on the north shore, does have a few cafés and a couple of hotels. The roads leading away from this beach also mark the original commercial centre of the city, though there are larger and more modern shops and services along Read Street in the centre of the

Fairy penguins

Also known as Little Penguins, these tiny birds, the world's smallest penguins, have colonies right around Australia's southern coasts. The Penguin Island colony is the largest in WA with about 600 breeding pairs. They like to nest in small natural caverns, under thick vegetation or in sand burrows.

They spend most of the day out at sea feeding, normally only coming in at dusk or even remaining out at sea for several days. Activity on land increases around March when they start to get frisky. Egg laying happens from May to October with incubation taking about 35 days.

peninsula. The waters around the peninsula teem with wildlife and have been declared a marine park, see Penguin Island, below. The **VIC** ① *19 Kent St, T9592 3464, www.rockinghamvisitorcentre.com.au, Mon-Fri 0900-1700, Sat-Sun 0900-1600*, close to Rockingham Beach, acts as an agent for much of the city's holiday homes.

Penguin Island
① *T9591 1333, www.penguinisland.com.au, island ferry $17.50 return, children $14.50, concessions $16.50 (hourly 0900-1500), island cruises $34.50, prices include Discovery Centre entrance. Note the island is closed to visitors from Jun to mid-Sep.*

Just off the southwest corner of the Rockingham Peninsula, opposite the third main beach area off Arcadia Drive, is tiny Penguin Island, known locally as Pengos. Just 1 km long it has the feel of a miniature Rottnest, a similar landscape of scrub overlying undulating dunes on a limestone base. There are no quokkas here, but there are birds by the thousand, including seagulls, shearwaters, terns and a substantial colony of fairy penguins. Because of this riot of birdlife, and also a few visiting sea lions, the island is a sanctuary and is mostly off-limits. You can access many of its beaches, plus the **Island Discovery Centre**, an information kiosk with a small, enclosed amphitheatre behind. At the centre of several rows of seating is a large glass tank, freely accessible to wild penguins, many of which know they'll get a modest feed daily at 1030, 1230 and 1430 (weather permitting). This is well worth a look even though you are likely to see penguins while walking around the island. Another key attraction of the island is the wealth of snorkelling to be done just off its beaches, particularly the eastern ones where there is a small wreck. While on the island you may see sea lions on the beach, and they or dolphins may come and check you out while snorkelling. There are surf breaks on the western side of the island. There are also several cruises around the island to see and swim with the local sea lions.

Serpentine National Park → *Colour map 2, B2. 55 km from Perth, 30 km from Rockingham.*
This park is named after the river that flows through it and is dammed at two locations. The **Serpentine Falls** are the main attraction and are accessible by an easy 15-minute walk from a picnic site. The falls are not high; the river flows over smooth and gently sloping granite into a pool and is only really impressive after good rains. There is a popular campground on the northeastern side, accessible from the small town of **Jarrahdale**, a timber town for workers cutting jarrah in the area. The park was originally set aside as a flora and fauna reserve in the 1890s when local naturalists realized all their timber would soon be gone. Unfortunately, the reserve only lasted for a couple of decades until the

government permitted it to be cleared for orchards but the falls area was preserved. It is a pleasant place for a picnic or walk and just off the main South Western Highway. There are good views of the plain from **Baldwins Bluff**, a walking trail through woodland to the granite bluff above (6 km, two hours).

Mandurah → *Colour map 2, C2. Population: 61,000. 110 km from Bunbury, 20 km from Pinjarra.*

Mandurah straddles the Mandurah Estuary, a narrow channel that flows into **Peel Inlet**, an enormous body of water just to the south of the town. Naturally, water activities dominate, and the place is in the process of transforming itself from a sleepy seaside town into an expensive and desirable place to live. During the late 1980s and the 1990s new suburbs were created on the south side of the estuary by digging canals, now full of flashy homes with boats tied at the door. The town has traditionally had a large retiree population and is also popular with WA families during school holidays for boating, fishing and swimming. Mandurah is closely identified with crabs, which can be picked up in the estuary and are celebrated in an annual **crab festival** in March. Dolphins are often seen in the estuary and are the focus for regular boat cruises. Two of the best beaches are **Blue Bay** and **Silver Sands**, both calm swimming beaches.

Mandurah was settled by Thomas Peel in 1830. The name is a corruption of the Noongar word *mandja* meaning meeting 'place'. Peel and others were settlers from the Swan River colony who chose land grants in this area to develop for agriculture. Many surviving buildings such as **Christ's Church** and those of **Café Pronto** date from the 1870-1890s when the town developed, thanks to sawmilling nearby and the arrival of the railway. There are few recognizably old buildings left but the oldest part of town is the land around the junction of Mandurah Terrace, Pinjarra Road and the old bridge. There is a small museum here, **Mandurah Community Museum** ① *3 Pinjarra Rd, Tue-Fri 1000-1600, www.mandurahcommunitymuseum.org, Sat and Sun 1100-1500, by donation*, in school buildings dating from 1900, which has some interesting exhibits and information on local history. The old bridge spans the estuary at the southern end of Mandjar Bay, and the struts underneath are a popular fishing spot. Cross the bridge to see one of Mandurah's oldest buildings, **Halls Cottage** ① *T9535 8970, Sun 1300-1600*. Built in 1832 by farmer Henry Edward Hall, it has been restored and heritage listed. To see more pick up a brochure for the heritage artwalk trail from the VIC. Back on the eastern bank is another old house that once belonged to a local named Tuckey, who had a fish cannery next door. Tuckey's house is now used for a commercial gallery, Emz Art. Another gallery worth a look is the one in the **Mandurah Performing Arts Centre** ① *T9550 3900, www.manpac.com.au, Mon-Fri 0900-1630, Sat 1000-1600, Sun when performance is scheduled, free*, the glass-fronted building that dominates the boardwalk precinct. The **VIC** ① *75 Mandurah Terr, T9550 3999, www.visitmandurah.com, daily 0900-1700*, sits behind the boardwalk at the northern end of Mandjar Bay. Nearby is the **Australian Sailing Museum** ① *22 Ormsby Terr, T9534 7256, www.australiansailingmuseum.com.au, daily 0900-1700, $10, children and concessions $5*, which is really only for the enthusiast. It contains memorabilia and artwork, and has a café.

Down the coast to Bunbury

The 100-odd km south to Bunbury can be covered by heading inland to Pinjarra, with perhaps a diversion to Dwellingup then south on the South Western Highway. Slightly slower is the Old Coast Road. After staying close to the coast for about 10 km, this road cuts slightly inland, the long **Yalgorup National Park** separating it from the sea. The park

The 'Battle' of Pinjarra

Pinjarra, named for the local Bindjareb tribe, was settled early in the colony's history. As such, it swiftly became a flashpoint of antagonism between the indigenous people and the settlers, both sides wanting control of the relatively fertile land. A series of incidents finally led the Bindjareb to seek blood retribution on the invaders and a young man called Hugh Nesbit was speared to death in an ambush. This prompted Captain Stirling to take action. In an act of punitive revenge, he and about 25 other well-armed men ambushed the Bindjareb at a site just south of the town on 28 October 1934. Accounts vary as to the immediate effects on the people, Stirling estimated about 15 killed, all men. Bindjareb oral histories put the figure well above this, possibly over 100, and most of these women and children. The long-term effect on the Bindjareb was dire. The survivors did not dare take on the settlers again and had to simply retreat in the face of their expansion. One of their own customs forbade the eating of certain totemic animals after an older custodian had died. This, coupled with the loss of available resources, almost certainly led to hardship and starvation.

preserves a large area of coastal vegetation, particularly tuart and peppermint woodlands, and also encompasses several lakes. The largest of these, **Clifton Lake**, is the very rare home of a colony of **thrombolites** small, dome-like structures built up by the photosynthetic process of billions of microbes. The process involves drawing in water rich in calcium carbonate and this slowly accumulates in layers as the microbes die. (This is a different process to that which forms the stromatolites in Cervantes and Shark Bay, which are basically layers of sediment trapped in slime.) The thrombolites line the wide white shore of Lake Clifton as far as the eye can see and make an arresting site on a fine day. A boardwalk has been built a short way out over the water, ensuring a close-up view of a scene that would have been a lot more common 600 million years ago. To get to the boardwalk follow the sign for the **Cape Bouvard Winery** about 27 km south of Mandurah. The winery, open daily and about 3 km off the highway, is 100 m from the boardwalk and has a large lawn and picnic tables for customers and tasters. A second access point to the park is off Preston Beach Road, about 10 km south of the thrombolites.

Shortly before Bunbury, about 6 km after the turn-off to Binninup Beach, take the right-hand Cathedral Road. The adjacent partly sealed Buffalo Road heads into **Leschenault Peninsula Conservation Park**, another area of preserved coastal vegetation, also with a campground. Cathedral Road is the scenic route into Bunbury, hugging the shore of picturesque Leschenault Inlet and passing early on by a couple of spots where you're likely to see kangaroos. At the end turn right back onto the Old Coast Road then right again after the bridge into Estuary Drive. This brings you out onto Koombana Drive, turn right to head into the centre of Bunbury.

Pinjarra → *Colour map 2, C2. Population: 4000. 85 km from Perth, 24 km from Dwellingup.*
A medium-sized service town, Pinjarra straddles both the Murray River and South Western Highway about 20 km inland from Mandurah. There is a long riverside park on the western bank with a few picnic tables and a BBQ next to the pedestrian suspension bridge. Opposite this, and also near the road bridge, is the **Edenvale Complex**. This small group of buildings dates back to the 1880s and includes the impressive house built by a

local parliamentarian, Edward McLarty. One of his sons, Duncan Ross, became Premier of WA in 1947 and the house has a long association with state politics. The rear part of the house is a tearoom and much of the rest of the complex is now used for art and craft shops, studios and a small machinery museum. The town's **VIC** ① *Fimmel Lane, T9531 1438, www.pinjarravisitorcentre.com.au, Mon-Fri 0930-1600, Sat-Sun 1000-1500*, is by the railway station where visitors can catch the train to Dwellingup (See page 141 for details of the Hotham Valley Railway). This is also where the **Discover Alcoa Tours** ① *T9530 2400, www.alcoa.com.au, mid-Jan to mid-Dec daily at 0930 and 1st Fri of the month at 1000, bookings essential,* leave from. These free tours take in the bauxite mine, the alumina refinery and the rehabilitation area.

Nearby is **Peel Zoo** ① *Sanctuary Dr, T9531 4322, www.peelzoo.com, Mon-Fri 1000-1600, Sat-Sun 0900-1700*, which is 2 km west of Pinjarra and home to koalas, emus, Tasmanian Devils and kangaroos.

Dwellingup → *Colour map 2, C2. Population: 450. 24 km from Pinjarra.*

Still a timber milling town, Dwellingup is a sleepy settlement in the hills surrounded by extensive jarrah forests. Although it has a long history in the timber felling and milling industry there is little of this heritage left to speak of as most of the town was razed to the ground by a fierce bushfire that swept through in 1961. The focus of the town is now switching more and more to providing activities that best show off the extensive natural attractions around the town, primarily the forest and the Murray River. It is also a stop on the **Munda Biddi Cycle Trail**. Facilities are modest, including a pub, store, post office and an expensive petrol station. See page 141 for details of the Etmilyn Forest Tramway.

North of town the **Forest Heritage Centre** ① *Acacia Rd, T9538 1395, www.forest heritagecentre.com.au, 0900-1600, $5.50, children $2.20, concessions $4.40, 1-hr guided tour $6.60 (minimum 10 people), signposted 1 km from the VIC*, is a leaf-shaped set of buildings showcasing the process of carpentry from forest to furniture. Outside are several bushwalks, from five to 20 minutes long, each focusing on a different aspect of the forest: from canopy viewing, identifying tree species and their Aboriginal use, to wildflowers. Inside are a forest interpretative centre, carpentry workshops and finally a gallery and shop selling exquisite handmade wooden furniture and turned items. West of town the **Marrinup Reserve** is the site of an old Second World War internment camp, now a pleasant picnic and bushwalking spot.

The **VIC** ① *Marrinup St, opposite the pub, T9538 1108, www.murray.wa.gov.au, Mon-Fri 0900-1500, Sat-Sun 1000-1500*, and has a good range of local maps and guides. The local **DEC office** ① *Banksiadale Rd, T9538 1078, 0800-1630*, is close by.

Lane Poole Reserve → *Colour map 2, C2.*

① *T9538 1078, camping $7, children $2, concessions $5, maximum 14 days' camping during school holidays, detailed map and guide available at the VIC, the best time to visit the forests around Dwellingup is spring and autumn.*

South of Dwellingup, 7 km down Nanga Road, is the northern boundary of Lane Poole Reserve, an extensive area of pretty jarrah and marri forest through which the Murray River runs for several dozen kilometres. There are a number of bush and riverside campsites, most with fireplaces, picnic tables and toilets. The Bibbulmun Track (see box, page 119) passes through the reserve and the river, though long and flat in parts, has some stretches of white water. There are also other walking and mountain-biking trails, and lots of swimming spots. The roads within the reserve are unsealed.

Dryandra Woodlands → *Colour map 3, A4. 160 km from Perth, 140 km from Dwellingup.*

Dryandra is within the wheatbelt region and is a vital remnant of the kind of vegetation that used to cover the area before it was cleared for farming. The reserve is formed from 17 blocks of bush and is a major focus of conservation in the state. Species of mammals that were nearly extinct have been saved by Western Shield, a DEC programme of wildlife conservation, involving fox control and breeding enclosures. The park is best known for the numbat, an ant- and termite-eating marsupial that feeds in daylight hours but is difficult to see because of its keen senses of hearing and smell. This striped creature looks a bit like a large squirrel and can stand on its hind legs. You'll need to stay upwind or it will scamper off as soon as it gets a whiff of you. Other rare animals of the Dryandra are the woylie and tammar wallaby. The reserve is also a haven for birds and birdspotters have counted about 130 species here. The woodland is open, consisting mostly of wandoo, powderbark and brown mallet, with many walking trails. It is a special place where you may see some of WA's rarest animals if you are patient. Probably your best chance of seeing some of Dryandra's shy nocturnal creatures, such as the bilby, western barred bandicoot, hare-wallaby and burrowing bettong, is to join a guided night tour from the **Barna Mia Centre** ① *T9881 9200 or T9881 2064, tours begin after sunset on Mon, Wed, Fri and Sat, $13, children $7, families $35, book before 1600.* The nearest town to pick up supplies is Narrogin, a large farming community 27 km east, and you can get DEC brochures on Dryandra from the Narrogin **VIC** ① *corner of Fairway and Park Sts, T9881 2064, Mon-Fri 0900-1700, Sat 1000-1600, Sun 1100-1500.*

◉ South of Perth listings

For Sleeping and Eating price codes and other relevant information, see pages 28-34.

● Sleeping

Rockingham *p132*

Self-contained apartments, units and holiday homes are the big thing in Rockingham. Many apartments and homes can only be rented by the week, contact the VIC for options. There are a number of B&Bs in town, all priced around **B-C**.

L-B Beachside Apartment Hotel, 58 Kent St, T9529 3777, www.beachsideapartment. com.au. At the top end of the market with several smart modern 1- to 3-bedroom apartments overlooking the Rockingham foreshore and beach. The enclosed **Y2K Café Restaurant** offers various meals, BYO possible.

B Manuel Towers, 32A Arcadia Dr, Shoalwater, T9592 2698, www.manueltowers. com.au. A little way out of town with views over the ocean, the Penguin room overlooks Penguin Island. Forget Fawlty Towers and

think courtyard garden, relaxing atmosphere and a killer breakfast.

D CWA Apartments, 108 Parkin St, T9527 9560, 200 m back from northern Palm Beach. At the budget end of the market.

Mandurah *p134*

Most accommodation in town is holiday units and houses. Contact the VIC for more options as it acts as a booking service. Thanks to Mandurah's proximity to Perth, occupancy and prices rise at weekends and on public and school holidays. Book ahead at these times.

LL-B Dolphin Houseboats, Ocean Marina, T9535 9898, www.dolphinhouseboats.com. Attractive and comfortable 4-, 6-, 8- or 10-berth houseboats. Most with bunks, kitchen, bathroom and eating area. Price applies to boat so good value for 4-8 people. Prices rise steeply for weekends and public holidays.

L-A Quest Apartments, 20 Apollo Pl, T9535 9599, www.questmandurah.com.au. Elegant serviced apartment complex on the southern shore. Apartments have 1-3 bedrooms and full kitchen, complex also has BBQs, pool, spa and boat pens.

L-C Atrium, 65 Ormsby Terr, T9535 6633, www.atriumhotel.com.au. Multi-storey hotel with 117 smart a/c rooms around a central atrium furnished with plants and an indoor pool. There are also self-catering apartments here and a restaurant, outdoor pool, BBQs, tennis courts, saunas. 24-hr reception.

B-E Mandurah Caravan & Tourist Park, 522 Pinjarra Rd, T9535 1171, www.mandurah caravanpark.com.au. A large park with chalets and cabins, pools, kiosk, BBQ areas, Wi-Fi and playground. There's even a crab cooker.

C-D Foreshore Motel, 2 Gibson St, T9535 5577, www.mandurahwa.com.au/ foreshoremotel. Good location a few steps from the foreshore café strip, a/c rooms with TV, phone, fridge, tea/coffee.

D Belvedere Caravan Park, 153 Mandurah Terr, T9535 1213. Small, quiet caravan park close to town centre with on-site vans and cabins. BBQ areas available, dogs are allowed by prior arrangement only.

Pinjarra p135

L Lazy River B&B, 9 Wilson Rd, T9531 4550, www.lazyriver.com.au. Enjoy the peace and quiet, kayak on the river, fish or just read the paper. The 4 rooms are well-appointed and some have 4-posted beds. Complimentary champagne and canapés are provided in the evening, and a breakfast hamper is included in the price. A 3-course evening meal is available on request for $60 per person, handy if you don't want to drive anywhere.

B-C Pinjarra Motel, South Western Highway, T9531 1811, www.pinjarramotel.com.au. Standard and deluxe motel rooms, a swimming pool and a fully licensed restaurant.

D-E Fairbridge Village, 10 km up the highway, T9531 1177, www.fairbridge.asn.au. A large activity and education centre, the renovated timber cottages once housed English orphans. Now catering mainly for large groups, they have a few self-contained cottages (sleeping 2-56) that are good for families and small groups. Facilities include a snack shop, free sports (swimming, tennis, and adventure playground), bushwalks and BBQs. No linen provided.

D-F Pinjarra Cabins and Caravan Park, 1716 Pinjarra Rd, T9531 1374, www.pinjarracaravanpark.com.au. A short distance out of town. Tent sites, cottages and cabins. There's also a pool and a nearby golf course.

Dwellingup p136

There are a handful of B&Bs in the forest surrounding the town.

B Milltree Cottage, T9447 5686, www.dwellingupaccommodation.com.au. A self-contained cottage with 3 bedrooms surrounded by jarrah trees, sleeping up to 8. Facilities include BBQ, TV and a/c. Minimum stay of 2 nights.

C-D Dwellingup Community Hotel/Motel, Marrinup St, T9538 1056. A large, friendly open-plan pub with cheap counter meals, bands during the Sun afternoon sesh, cheap hotel rooms, including singles, and a few external motel rooms. Meals daily 1200-1400, Mon-Sat 1800-2000.

Lane Poole Reserve p136

C-E Nanga Bush Camp, T1800 801807, www.nangabush.com. Just by the entrance to the reserve (follow the main road around to the right across one-lane bridge), and right by the river. Primarily catering for large school groups, they have a few self-contained bush cabins, expensive for 1-2 people, good value for 6-10.

Dryandra Woodlands p137

There are good campsites at Congelin Dam.

E Dryandra Woodland Village, T9884 5231, www.dryandravillage.org.au. Comfortable self-contained accommodation within the reserve in the settlement. Simple but charming timber workers cottages are equipped with a full kitchen and BBQ but own linen required. The smaller cottages sleep 2, 4, 10 and 12 and there is a complex that caters for large groups up to 56.

⊘ Eating

Rockingham p132

With so much ocean it's a shame not to eat within sight of it.

₦₦₦ Emmas on the Boardwalk, The Boardwalk, 1 Railway Terr, T9592 8881, www.emmasontheboardwalk.com.au. Wed-Sun 1200-1400 and 1800-2100. A Modern Australian restaurant serving quality food. The service is impeccable and the views over the ocean an added bonus.

₦₦-₦ Bettyblue Bistro, The Boardwalk, just along from Emmas, T9528 4228. Tue-Sun 0900-late. Good views over the water and a popular choice for breakfast, lunch or dinner, specializes in seafood. Weekdays there is a $25 dinner special in low season.

₦₦-₦ Winstons, T9527 1163, on the main Rockingham Rd cappuccino strip. Daily 0800-2030. Snacks and coffee outside of main mealtimes. Pavement tables.

₦ La Gelateria, corner Rockingham Beach Rd and Railway Terr. A mid-range café with an excellent range of ice cream. It also serves good coffee and a variety of sweet treats.

₦ Pengos, 153 Arcadia Dr, Shoalwater Bay, at the ferry terminal opposite Penguin Island, T9592 6100. Sun-Thu 0700-1700, Fri-Sat 0700-1900. A simple café serving seafood and burgers. Also offers a range of salad options, and is good stop for breakfast or a coffee and cake.

Mandurah p134

Picnic tables and free BBQs on the foreshore.

₦₦ Café Pronto, on the corner of Mandurah Terr and Pinjarra Rd, T9535 1004, www.cafepronto.com.au. Daily 0700-2100. One of the best places to eat in town, this relaxed brasserie takes up 2 historic old houses on a busy corner. Food is a good mix

of seafood, steak and Asian dishes like curries, stir-fries and warm salads. Also more snacky light meals (cheap), wood-fired pizzas and extensive all-day breakfast menu.

₦₦ M on the Point, 1 Marco Polo Dr, T9534 9899, www.m-onthepoint.com.au. Daily 0700-late. A popular restaurant and bar with a spacious terrace overlooking the water. There is a choice of casual food, such as hot pork rolls or pizza, or more filling pasta dishes, burgers or seafood. Cocktails, early evening specials and live music at weekends. More of pub atmosphere than a restaurant. Half-price Wed (casual menu only) attracts a lot of people.

₦ Cicerellos, 73 Mandurah Terr, T9535 9777, www.cicerellos.com.au. Daily 1030-2030. A branch of the famous Fremantle restaurant, this place offers upmarket fish and chips and is licensed but has no table service. Pleasant balcony tables upstairs, overlooking the bay. Also takeaway.

₦ Foreshore Takeaway, 25 Mandurah Terr. Fish and chips to eat on the grass opposite.

₦ Penang House, 45 Mandurah Terr, T9535 8891. Daily 1645-2000. One of the towns most popular restaurants. Good Chinese and Malaysian dishes under $20. BYO.

₦ Ruffinos, Scotts Plaza, 52 Mandurah Terr, T9534 9906, www.mymandurah.com/ ruffinos. Tue-Thu 1700-late, Fri-Sun 1100-late. Italian family restaurant with 18 types of pizza and 30 varieties of pasta. Italian mains are mid-range. Leave room for the gelato. Fully licensed, BYO wine only.

₦ Taku Japanese Kitchen, Scotts Plaza, 52 Mandurah Terr, T9582 7308. Tue-Sun 1130-1430, Tue-Sat 1700-2100, Sun 1700-2030. Small dining room and cheap sushi, sashimi, noodles and teriyaki meats. Also takeaway.

Cafés

The Merchant Tea & Coffee Co, 9 Mandurah Terr, T9535 2634. Daily 0730-2100. A franchise café but one of Mandurah's most popular, with a terrace overlooking the water. Good coffee and cakes, and light meals (cheap).

Simmo's Icecream, Boardwalk, T9582 7177, www.simmos.com.au. Mon-Fri 1000-1700, Sat 1000-1800, Sun 1000-1730. Ice creams, plus waffles, coffee and drinks in an attractive room overlooking the bay.

Pinjarra *p135*
Ť Edenvale Tea Rooms, in the Edenvale complex, T9531 2223. Open daily around 1000-1600 for lunch and afternoon teas.

Dwellingup *p136*
ŤŤ Millhouse, McLarty St, T9538 1122. Mon-Thu and Sun 0830-1600, Fri-Sat 0830-2000. The towns little touch of class, a chic restaurant, café and chocolate-maker.

▲ Activities and tours

Rockingham *p132*
Diving and snorkelling
Pick up a copy of the *Diving & snorkelling* guide from the VIC, as it details all the nearby sites. The diving shops in town offer PADI courses and boat dives. Alternatively, there is the self-guided **Rockingham Wreck Trail** (you need a buddy to dive this).
Subanautics Diving, 33 Dixon Rd, T9524 4447, www.scubanautics.com.au. Boat dives out to the marine park. Also runs courses and hires out equipment.

Dolphin cruises
The bays around Rockingham are home to about 130 dolphins, many of whom have been become friendly to people.
Rockingham Wild Encounters, T9591 1333, www.rockinghamwildencounters.com.au. Runs 2 excellent tours to see them, both operating daily between mid-Sep and May. Dolphin Watch Eco-Adventure ($65, children $50-60) leaves the Yacht Club jetty, the Esplanade, Rockingham, at 0830, returning about 1100. Swim with Dolphins Tour ($205 including snorkelling gear, wetsuits and lunch) leaves the jetty at 0730, returning around 1100-1500. There are Perth bus

pick-ups for both tours from the Wellington St Bus Station (costs a bit more). Booking essential. Wild Encounters also offers tours to Penguin and Seal Island.

Kayak tours
Capricorn Kayak Tours, T6267 8059, www.capricornseakayaking.com.au. Takes small groups out sea kayaking around some of Penguin and Seal islands best offshore spots, past colonies of sea lions, pelicans and Fairy Penguins. Also includes a guided walk of Penguin Island. Equipment, morning tea and lunch. Pick-ups are available from Perth and Fremantle, or meet near Pengos. Full-day tours from Nov-Mar, $149.

Mandurah *p134*
Boat hire/cruises
A free *Mandurah Boating Guide* is available at the VIC, with a map of local waters and details of boating regulations.
Blue Manna Boat Hire, Mandurah Ocean Marina, T9535 5399, www.bluemanna boathire.com.au. Has 8-seater runabouts for hire ($45 for 1 hr). Standard pontoons are $65 for 1 hr, deluxe $85.
Mandurah Boat Hire, Mandurah Terr, T9535 5877. Sep-May 0800-sunset, Jun-Aug 0900-sunset. Has runabouts and punts for hire, plus bicycles. Pontoons $50 per hr, dinghies $80 per hr (4 people), bicycles $10 per hr.
Mandurah Ferry Cruises, 73 Mandurah Terr, opposite the VIC, T9535 3324, www.mandurahferrycruises.com. Sep-May Tue-Sun 1030-1530. Good-value half-day cruise up the Murray River, past canals, dolphins and the Peel Inlet, 3-course lunch at a restaurant en route included and a trip aboard the historic the *Peel Princess*. $72, children $47, concessions $66. Tickets on board or at office opposite the VIC.

Diving
Noted for wreck dives. Ask at the VIC and dive shops for locations and advice.

David Budd Diving Academy, The Plaza Shopping Centre, corner of Mandurah Terr and Tuckey St, T9535 1520, www.davidbudd diving.com.au. Offers hire, lessons and great friendly advice. A Rottnest double dive with full gear and lunch is $198.

Family

On the other side of the river there is a summer theme park with crazy golf, ferris wheel, and all the usual entertainment. A special runs on Fri night with a happy hour from 1900-2200 where a $16 ticket will give unlimited ride access.
Just4Fun Aqua Park, Western Foreshore, T0422 439008, www.just4funaquapark.com. Open Nov-April. Water activities and paddle boats for the whole family, day passes $40.

Fishing/crabbing

Blue Manna crabs can be caught in the Peel Inlet and Mandurah Estuary in summer and autumn. The Fisheries Department of WA sets rules on methods, size and quantity, check with the VIC. Equipment can be hired from the boat-hire businesses.
Aqualib Marine Charters, T9586 9778, www.aqualib.com.au. Game fishing, deep-sea fishing and 3-day Rottnest Excursion available. Prices include lunch, tackle and bait. Call ahead to check if trips are running as minimum numbers are needed.

Golf

There are 2 major golfing resorts, both north of Mandurah.
Meadow Springs Golf & Country Club, Meadow Springs Dr, T9581 6002, www.msgcc.com.au. Bushland golf course.
Secret Harbour Golf Links, Secret Harbour Blvd, T9524 7133, www.secretharbourgolf links.com.au. Links course.

Pinjarra *p135*

Hotham Valley Railway, T9221 4444 (Perth office), www.hothamvalleyrailway.com.au. From the railway station over the river the *Steam Ranger* heads up to Dwellingup Wed and Sun at 1030. After a 2-hr stopover visitors hop back on and return to Pinjarra for 1600 ($40, children $20). The *Dwellingup Forest Train* departs Dwellingup station Sat-Sun and public holidays at 1100 and 1400 (weekdays by prior arrangement) to Etmilyn Siding ($18, children $9). Theres also an evening train on Sat at 1945, this journey includes a 5-course meal in the vintage dining car ($75). Bookings in advance recommended for all journeys and essential for the evening ride.

Dwellingup *p136*

Dwellingup Adventures, corner Marrinup and Newton Sts, T9538 1127, www.dwellingupadventures.com.au. Organizes a variety of self-guided rafting and canoeing tours along the Murray. They range from half-day excursions (from $97 for a 2-person canoe), to overnight canoe adventures (from $192 for a 2-people canoe). Guided rafting trips along the Murray River depart every Sun ($130 per person, including hot soup), Hires camping gear, mountain bikes and kayaks.
School of Wood, based in the Forest Heritage Centre, T9538 1395, www.forestheritagecentre.com.au. The school runs introductory courses (160 hrs for $215) alongside their 2-year diplomas. Participants come away with their own self-made box, chair or even mandolin, constructed from the finest WA or Tasmanian timbers, and for around half the cost you'd see it in a shop. It also offers a variety of other creative workshops, prices start from about $165 per course. Contact the centre for a programme.

⊖ Transport

Rockingham *p132*

Bus Rockingham lies under the umbrella of Perth's metropolitan bus network. There are frequent services daily: north to **Perth**, south to **Mandurah**, and also various routes around the peninsula. The main bus station is in the centre of the peninsula on the corner of Council Av and Clifton St. Aside from the metropolitan services, Rockingham lies on both TransWAs and South West Coachlines (T9324 2333, www.southwest coachlines.com.au) main southbound routes. Some TransWA services, which leave from the central Read St shopping centre, head for **Bunbury**, **Busselton**, and the Cape-to-Cape towns. Other buses call at Bunbury before heading through the Timber Towns to **Pemberton**. South West Coachlines have similar though shorter services, daily to **Dunsborough**, Mon-Fri to **Manjimup**.

Penguin Island *p133*

Ferry A ferry leaves for the island from the Mersey Point Jetty, Shoalwater Bay, every hour, daily 0900-1500, last return 1600. Return tickets cost $12 or $17.50 and include Discovery Centre entry, children $16.50. The ferry does not operate Jun-Sep as the island is closed to visitors.

Serpentine National Park *p133*

Train TransWA's *Australind* train line stops at **Serpentine** on its way to **Bunbury**. Services leave Perth daily.

Mandurah *p134*

Bus TransWA bus services leave from the corner of Sutton and Davey Sts for **Bunbury**, **Busselton**, and the Cape-to-Cape towns, while others call at Bunbury before heading through the Timber Towns to **Pemberton**. South West Coachlines have similar, shorter services, **Dunsborough** and **Manjimup**. There are services from Dower St to **Rockingham** (connections to **Fremantle** Mon-Fri only) and **Perth**.

Train Trains on the Mandurah line leave regularly every day to/from the underground terminal of **Perth** train station (50 mins).

Pinjarra *p135*

Train TransWAs *Australind* train line stops at **Pinjarra** on its way to **Bunbury**. Services leave Perth daily.

⊕ Directory

Mandurah *p134*

Banks Major banks have branches and ATMs on Pinjarra Rd. **Internet** Lasar, 264 Pinjarra Rd, T9535 3947, Mon-Fri 0900-1730, Sat 0900-1300, internet access, printing and scanning. **Medical services** Peel Health Campus, 110 Lakes Rd, T9531 8000. **Police** 333 Pinjarra Rd, T9581 0222. **Post** 30 Pinjarra Rd.

Routes east

The most direct route east is to take the highway out through Midland and Northam (see page 127) and continue on through the Goldfields towns of Coolgardie, and possibly Kalgoorlie-Boulder, to the Eyre Highway. This crosses the infamous Nullarbor Plain to Ceduna, the first major town in South Australia. The adventurous might wish to consider the unsealed Great Central Road (The Outback Highway), that runs from Laverton, north of Kalgoorlie, through the isolated settlement of Warburton and then on to Yulara, the tourist resort for visitors to Uluru (Ayers Rock).

Northam to Kalgoorlie-Boulder → *Kalgoorlie 500 km from Northam, 185 km from Norseman, 360 km from Laverton.*

The Great Eastern Highway passes through a handful of wheatbelt towns before striking out across the scrub to the original WA goldfield town of **Coolgardie**. It is possible to stay here, and then continue directly to Norseman, or to **Kalgoorlie-Boulder**, www.kalgoorlie tourism.com, makes a much more interesting stopover and involves a detour of about 60 km. The pubs, the **Super Pit**, Langtrees brothel and the **Mining Hall of Fame** are the principal attractions. **Norseman**, also has a still-operating goldmine, but is a much smaller town. Theres little to see but this is the last opportunity to grab groceries and reasonably priced fuel before Ceduna, and the accommodation options are all very welcoming.

Great Central Road (The Outback Highway) → *Laverton to Yulara is 1000 km.*

Laverton has the last decent supermarket and cheapest fuel before hitting the dirt road to the 'red centre'. It also has a post office, car hire, the **Desert Inn pub and Motel** ① *T9031 1188*, and the **Desert Pea Caravan Park** ① *T9031 1072*. **The Great Beyond Explorers Hall of Fame** ① *T9031 1361, Mon-Fri 0900-1630, Sat-Sun 0900-1300, $10, children $5, concessions $8*, and the **VIC** are in the same building on Augusta Street. Here visitors can learn more about what it was like to live and work on the goldfields during the pioneer days.

Though it is sometimes successfully tackled in a 2WD, the Outback Highway is generally considered a 4WD-only route, and even then it is recommended to travel in a well-prepared and self-sufficient convoy. From Laverton, it's 315 km to the **Tjukayirla Roadhouse** ① *T9037 1108, fuel and meals Mon-Fri 0800-1800, Sat-Sun 0900-1800, plus accommodation*. From here it's a further 255 km to the small town of **Warburton**, where there is a **roadhouse** ① *T8956 7656, Mon-Fri 0800-1700, Sat-Sun 0900-1500*. If you do get out this way, don't miss a visit to the **Tjulyuru Cultural Centre** ① *T8956 7966, www.tjulyuru.com, Mon-Fri 0830-1600, by donation*, part of a grand scheme to bridge the gap between the local Ngaanyatjarra and non-Aboriginal people. Further fuel and food are available at the **Warakurna Roadhouse** ① *Giles, 230 km from Warburton, T8956 7344, Mon-Fri 0830-1700, Sat-Sun 0900-1500, phone ahead for opening times on public holidays (Central Standard Time)*. From Giles it's about 200 km to the tourist village of Yulara.

For current road conditions contact T1800 013314 (WA section) and T1800 246199 (NT section). Separate permits are required for traversing Aboriginal lands in both WA and NT. Contact the **Department of Indigenous Affairs** ① *8 Victoria Av, Perth, T9325 8000*, for WA, and the **Central Land Council** ① *27 Stuart Highway, Alice Springs, T8951 6211*, for NT. For more information on the highway visit www.outbackway.org.au, which has information on road conditions, distances, safety tips and maps. Alternatively, see the appropriate *Westprint* map.

The Eyre Highway → *Eucla 725 km from Norseman, 505 km from Ceduna.*

In a country with a lot of long, straight and quiet roads the **Nullarbor** is a legendary drive that takes on almost mythic qualities to both those who have and haven't driven it. What is really striking is how flat the entire landscape is. It is pretty likely your backside will take on the same contours after two to three days of driving but fortunately there are a few interesting stops to break the journey, such as caves and blowholes around **Cocklebiddy**, the sand dunes and beach around the telegraph station at **Eucla**, and whale watching and spectacular cliffs at the **Head of Bight**. Before setting off pick up a copy of *The Nullarbor* map, which details sites along the way and accommodation options and rest stops.

The first roadhouse, 195 km from Norseman, is **Balladonia** ① *T9039 3453,* (**C-E**). It has an interesting **heritage museum** and a range of accommodation, from deluxe to backpacker and campsites. Petrol and food available in summer 0600-2100 and winter 0800-2030.

The unmarked turn-off to **Cocklebiddy Cave** is at the rear of a small parking bay, 245 km from Balladonia, 54 km from Caiguna, and 10 km short of the **Cocklebiddy Roadhouse**. One of many huge caves under the plain, this is the most accessible and a rewarding excursion. The track, rough but fine for 2WD when dry, passes a sign for Nuytsland Nature Reserve after 100 m then interweaves its way for 10 km to the cave. Wear sturdy shoes for the steep and rocky climb down and take a good torch each. If you've any plans to stay in the area, check out the **Eyre Bird Observatory** ① *T9039 3450, www.eyrebirds.org*, occupying an old telegraph station 40 km off the highway from the roadhouse and right on the coast. Day visitors are welcome ($10 per vehicle) but will only make it to the car park and lookout unless driving a 4WD. Staff will collect you if you're staying overnight ($90 per person, all-inclusive except for linen, advance bookings essential) and are in a 2WD vehicle; arrange this prior to arrival. Recommended. The highway drops down through the **Madura Pass**, 95 km after Cocklebiddy, to the **Madura Pass Oasis** ① *T9039 3464, 0630-2000,* (**D-E**), a large resort-style roadhouse at the base of the escarpment.

Eucla makes a good stop just before the South Australian border. It was home to one of Australia's busiest telegraph stations in the 1880s, sending more than 11,000 messages a year, but the ruins of the station and the old settlement are disappearing fast under sand dunes. There is a motel (T9039 3468, 0600-2200, **C-E**), budget rooms and camping. A large fibreglass whale and a disconcerting snake collection distinguish the **Nullarbor Roadhouse** ① *T8625 6271, 0700-2300,* (**C-E**), 190 km from Eucla, which has motel units and camping. **Whale-watching flights** (June-September) can be taken from here, contact **Chinta Air** ① *T0488 994988, chintahob@bigpond.com*. The turn for the Head of Bight, a cliff-top whale-watching platform, is another 15 km, and the large town of **Ceduna** a further 285 km.

Contents

Footprint features

Southwest Coast

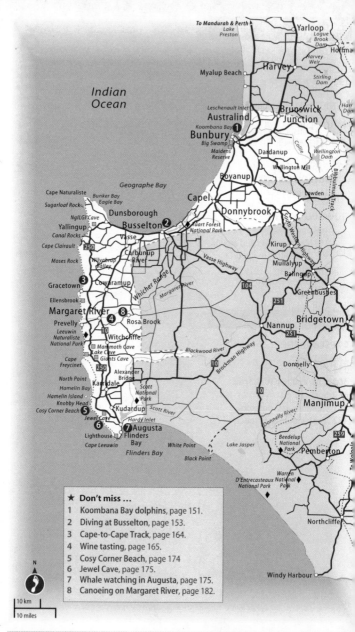

Indian
Ocean

To Mandurah & Perth
Lake Preston
Yarloop
Logue Brook Dam
Hoffma
Harvey
Harvey Weir
Stirling Dam
Myalup Beach
Brunswick Junction
Harr Dam
Leschenault Inlet
Australind
Koombana Bay **1**
Bunbury
Big Swamp
Maidens Reserve
Collie
Wellington Dam
Dardanup
Wellington Mill
Bibbulmun Track
Boyanup
Cape Naturaliste
Bunker Bay
Eagle Bay
Geographe Bay
Capel
Lowden
Donnybrook
Sugarloaf Rocks
NgILGI Cave
Dunsborough
Busselton **2**
Hart Forest National Park
Yallingup
Canal Rocks
Cape Clairault
Vasse
Carbunup River
Vasse Highway
Kirup
South Western Highway
Moses Rock
Wilyabrup Valley
Whicher Range
Mullalyup
Balingup
104
Gracetown **3**
Cowaramup
Margaret River
Greenbushes
251
Ellensbrook
Margaret River
8
4 Rosa Brook
Nannup
251
Bridgetown
Prevelly
10
Witchcliffe
Blackwood River
Brockman Highway
Donnelly
Leeuwin Naturaliste National Park
Mammoth Cave
Lake Cave
Giants Cave
Cape Freycinet
Alexander Bridge
10
North Point
Hamelin Bay
Hamelin Island
Knobby Head
Cosy Corner Beach **5**
Kaardale
Scott National Park
Scott River
Donnelly River
Manjimup
Jewel Cave **6**
Kudardup
Hardy Inlet
Augusta **7**
Flinders Bay
Beedelup National Park
259
Lighthouse
Cape Leeuwin
Flinders Bay
White Point
Lake Jasper
Pemberton
Black Point
D'Entrecasteaux National Park
Warren National Park
Northcliffe

★ **Don't miss ...**
1 Koombana Bay dolphins, page 151.
2 Diving at Busselton, page 153.
3 Cape-to-Cape Track, page 164.
4 Wine tasting, page 165.
5 Cosy Corner Beach, page 174
6 Jewel Cave, page 175.
7 Whale watching in Augusta, page 175.
8 Canoeing on Margaret River, page 182.

N

10 km
10 miles

Windy Harbour

Some of the most beautiful and varied country in Western Australia is packed into the southwest, and particularly into the neat rectangular notch of the Capes region. Within 100 km or so lie flawless beaches, a classy wine region, sophisticated restaurants and galleries and acres of tall forests. From Cape Naturaliste to Cape Leeuwin you can go caving in limestone caves, reef and wreck diving, surf some of Australia's best waves, walk some of its best coastal trails, watch whales in winter, and swim with dolphins further north in the region's main town of Bunbury. What are few and far between are high-rise blocks, traffic jams and crowded beaches. It's the kind of place that people come to for a day and stay for a week, with plenty to keep you occupied for double that time.

Naturally this abundance of natural beauty is no secret. It is Western Australia's favourite corner for a holiday and this means it is still relatively the busiest and most developed area outside Perth. For all that, this region simply cannot be missed. If you want to escape there are still plenty of wild and quiet places to be found in the southwest, from cool remnants of woodland like that around Wellington Dam, to beaches, such as Cosy Corner and Indijup, which stay miraculously free of the main crowd.

Ins and outs

Getting there and around

The ideal way to explore this region is to drive yourself as there is so much to see and no great distances to endure. There are three main routes south from Perth to Bunbury: the newly completed Freeway; the coastal route via the Kwinana Freeway and Old Coast Road; or the inland route, the South Western Highway. From Bunbury, the inland route veers southeast, reaching the coast at Walpole. To reach the southwest coast, take the Bussell Highway southwest to Busselton. Once in the Capes region there are two main routes to Augusta. The Bussell Highway is the faster and most direct inland route, passing through Cowaramup and Margaret River. Caves Road runs parallel to the highway but is closer to the coast. This is a narrow and windy route but definitely the more scenic, providing access to the caves and beaches of the region.

For those relying on public transport, **TransWA** coaches leave the East Perth Terminal to Bunbury (three hours), Busselton (four hours), Dunsborough (4½ hours), Yallingup, Margaret River (5½ hours), and Augusta (six hours) from Sunday to Thursday at 0830 and 1220, and on Friday at 0830 and 1630. **South West Coachlines**, T9324 2333, buses leave from the City Bus Port, Mounts Bay Road, daily at 0845, 1315 and 1745 for Bunbury and Busselton, with connections for Dunsborough. There are no train services except for the **TransWA** *Australind* line between Perth Railway Station and Bunbury, which has two services daily (2¼ hours). ▸▸ *See individual transport sections for more details.*

Best time to visit

The region has a mild climate but is at its best in summer, although spring and autumn are also very pleasant. Winter (June-August) is often cold (15-18°C) and wet, although excellent for whale watching around Augusta. The southwest coast is an extremely popular holiday destination for the people of Perth so all weekends, public holidays and school holidays are busy but the whole region gets booked out well in advance over summer (Christmas to end of January) and prices rise accordingly.

Geographe Bay

The long sweep of Geographe Bay from Bunbury to Cape Naturaliste provides some of this region's calmest and warmest beaches, particularly the further west you travel, culminating in crescents of serene perfection close to the tip of the Cape. Of the three towns on this bay, Bunbury is the second largest city in the state but still has wild dolphins swimming into a city beach most days. Busselton and Dunsborough are sleepier holiday towns offering superb water activities such as reef and wreck diving, whale watching and looking at the marine life under Busselton jetty as it hangs in the current like party streamers. ▸▸ *For listings, see pages 155-160.*

Bunbury ▸▸ *For listings see pages 155-160. Colour map 3, A2.*

→ *Population: 31,800. 180 km from Perth, 100 km from Margaret River, 160 km from Pemberton.*

Sitting on Koombana Bay, at the northern end of the beautiful sweep of Geographe Bay, is Bunbury, the major port for the southwest. It is far from a natural harbour though, as the original shape of the coastline has been dramatically altered by cutting a channel through the **Leschenault Peninsula** to the sea and by the construction of boating and shipping harbours. Major exports include mineral sands, alumina and woodchips and, until recently, industry has come first in Bunbury and has been allowed to dominate the coastline. However, in the last few years grain silos have been demolished and train yards moved to create a far more attractive foreshore. The city's greatest natural attraction is its resident population of dolphins who live in Koombana Bay and swim in to the beach regularly. Bunbury also has a sophisticated 'cappuccino strip' along Victoria Street, good shopping and beautiful ocean beaches on Geographe Bay. It's an appealing and relaxed place with the services of a large city and the slow, sunny pace of a small seaside town.

Ins and outs

Getting there and around There are regular bus services down the coast from Perth taking about three hours. Despite its sprawling and rapidly increasing size, the town centre is very compact and almost everything of interest can easily be reached on foot. ▸▸ *See Transport, page 160.*

Tourist information **VIC** ① *Carmody Place, T9792 7205, www.visitbunbury.com.au, Mon-Fri 0900-1700, Sat 0930-1630, Sun 1000-1400,* is housed in the former railway station in the centre of town.

Sights

A good way to take in the sights of the town is by foot. This walk starts at the VIC in the century-old railway station. Walk beside the inlet towards the roundabout. This area is known as **Bicentennial Square** and was formerly an ugly area of railyards. Head straight across to the tall, white **grain silos**. Several were demolished but these remaining ones have been heritage listed and have been turned into a hotel complex, there are cafés, restaurants and clubs on the foreshore. The **old timber jetty** ahead, dating from 1864, was used for all shipping until the 1970s. Just to the left of the jetty is **Jetty Baths Beach**, where you once would have seen neck-to-knee bathing costumes. Head west along Wollaston Street to reach Marlston Drive and the **Marlston Hill Lookout**. The hill was used for whale watching when that was a less innocent pastime. Follow the road around to reach Ocean

Bunbury

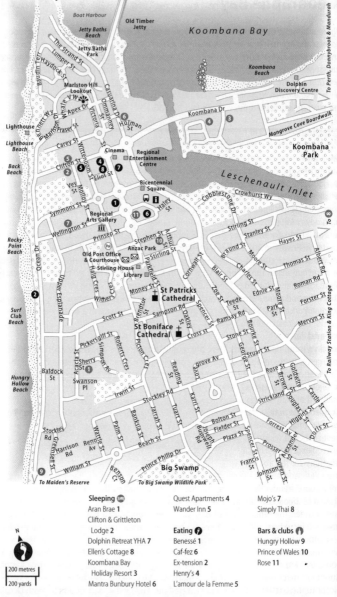

Sleeping		
Aran Brae 1	Quest Apartments 4	Mojo's 7
Clifton & Grittleton	Wander Inn 5	Simply Thai 8
Lodge 2		
Dolphin Retreat YHA 7	Eating 🍴	Bars & clubs 🍸
Ellen's Cottage 8	Benessé 1	Hungry Hollow 9
Koombana Bay	Caf-fez 6	Prince of Wales 10
Holiday Resort 3	Ex-tension 2	Rose 11
Mantra Bunbury Hotel 6	Henry's 4	
	L'amour de la Femme 5	

200 metres
200 yards

Drive and walk past the black-and-white **lighthouse** to Ocean Beach. This is a good spot for a swim. The rocks here are basalt, rare in Australia, formed from lava flow 150 million years ago. Head back towards the town centre along Clifton Street and turn right into Victoria Street. The **Bunbury Tower** dominates the street. It was built to resemble the prow of a ship and is full of private and government offices. Stroll past the shops and cafés and the **Rose Hotel**, built in 1898, then turn right up Prinsep Street to Wittenoom. The pale pink building on the corner dates from 1883 and is a former convent and chapel. The convent is now used as the **Regional Art Gallery** ① *64 Wittenoom St, T9721 8226, www.brag.org.au, 1000-1600, free and holds regular exhibitions of work by artists and craftspeople of the southwest*. With your back to the tower continue along Wittenoom Street to the next corner to see one of Bunbury's oldest buildings, the **Old Post Office** and **Courthouse** (1855). Continue around the corner into Stirling Street. On the right by Anzac Park is **Stirling House**, built as a home for the town clerk in the 1880s. Pass the park and turn right into Parkfield Street. About 100 m down this street are the city's cathedrals. **St Patrick's** on the right, was built in 1921. Its steeple was lost in a shipwreck so it went without until 1967. The pews are made of local jarrah. The more modern **St Boniface**, on the left side, has lovely stained-glass windows and native blackbutt floors and ceiling. Retrace your steps to Stirling Street, cross the road and continue along Victoria Street, then turn right down Wellington Street to return to the VIC.

Bottlenose dolphins have been visiting the beach in front of the Dolphin Discovery Centre for many years and it is estimated that about 100 live in Koombana Bay. To encounter these curious locals you can simply wade in off the beach, take a short cruise into the bay, kayak through their territory or go on an outstanding swimming tour. See page 158 for details of the tours. The **Dolphin Discovery Centre** ① *Koombana Dr, T9791 3088, www.dolphindiscovery.com.au, Nov-May 0800-1600, Jun-Sep 0900-1400, $10, children/concessions $5, 1.5 km from town centre*, manages dolphin beach encounters and conducts research into the Koombana Bay pods. It is a non-profit community organization run mostly by volunteers on donations and sponsorship. The centre has a small museum that explains the biology and behaviour of dolphins and other local marine creatures and shows excellent short videos about the Koombana Bay dolphins. The main attraction is the interactive zone, an area of shallow water that's been roped off to allow encounters between dolphins and people. Volunteer guides are on hand to ensure that visitors behave correctly but you are allowed to stand waist deep in the water or even float with a mask and snorkel as the dolphins approach you. The crowds are usually small, especially if you arrive early (0800-0900) which is also when you have the best chance of seeing the dolphins. The focus is on keeping the dolphins wild so they are not fed except for a few individuals who have become used to feeding in the past. These dolphins are fed about 500 g of local fish (1-2% of their daily intake) but this happens irregularly and not usually in front of tourists. The dolphins generally visit the interactive zone more frequently in summer. Cruises and swim tours leave from the beach and should be booked at the centre. There's a café, shop and showers, but bring your own snorkel gear. The centre welcomes travellers into its volunteer programme if they can be involved for at least six weeks.

Bunbury has two **mangrove colonies** that are remarkable for their southerly position. The nearest mangroves in the state are found on the Abrolhos Islands, off Geraldton, some 600 km further north, and become more common in the far northern regions. Bunbury's mangroves are believed to date from 10,000 years ago and were once much closer to the coastline. In the years since European settlement the coastline has moved

200 m further west. There are short boardwalks through the colonies and these are a great place to see water birds. **Mangrove Cove** walk is opposite the Dolphin Discovery Centre on Koombana Drive and focuses on shipwrecks that have occurred in the bay with a series of shelters and lookouts. The **Big Swamp** is a wetland just to the south of the city, close to the coast, and attracts water birds such as herons and swans. Long-necked turtles can also be seen there. There is a 100-m boardwalk which connects to a 2-km circuit of the swamp and a bird hide.

Adjacent to the Big Swamp is the **Big Swamp Wildlife Park** ① *Price Philip Dr, T9721 8380, daily 1000-1700, $6, children $4, concessions $5.* Its main ticket office also houses a swamp interpretative centre, well worth a look if you're about to walk around the swamp and boardwalks, entry to this is free. The wildlife park has a few kangaroos, some emus, a wombat and a large aviary, but there's nothing here to really get excited about. On the other side of Bunbury Plaza shopping centre, is **King Cottage** ① *77 Forrest Av, T9721 7546, 1400-1600, $5, children $1.50, concessions $3,* the home of the King family from 1880 to 1920 and furnished as it would have been around 1900.

Around Bunbury

Leschenault Peninsula Conservation Park

This is a long, thin peninsula of sand dunes and peppermint woodland that divides the ocean from the Leschenault inlet, just north of Australind. The park can be accessed at the northern end from the Old Coast Road. Unsealed roads lead to **Buffalo** and **Belvidere Beach**, both popular for fishing and with no facilities. From the highway it is 7 km around the shore of the inlet to a lovely camping area among shady peppermint and Tuart trees. In Australind, a **Discovery Centre** on the foreshore provides information on the park; it is currently closed for refurbishment.

Collie River Valley → *Colour map 3, A2. 50 km from Bunbury.*

Set amidst extensive peppermint and jarrah forests, **Wellington Dam** is one of Perth's principal reservoirs. There is a viewing area over the dam, and a small café (0830-1630). The Collie River flows downstream from the dam to Leschenault Inlet and there are a few bush camps on the way, including a campground ($7 per person) at picturesque **Honeymoon Pool**, a popular swimming spot. Facilities here include fireplace BBQs (firewood supplied April to November), picnic tables, toilets and tank water. The viewing platform provides good access to the river for swimmers. Access to the dam, and a lakeside campground, is via the sealed Wellington Weir Road, which heads south from the main Coalfields Road between Bunbury and Collie. Honeymoon Pool is accessed via an unsealed road off this. Close to Honeymoon Pool are two other campsites, **Stones Brook** and **Gelcoat** ($7, small tents only). The **VIC** ① *156 Throssell St, Collie, T9734 2051, www.collierivervalley.org.au, Mon-Fri 0900-1630, Sat-Sun 1000-1500,* is located in the Old Post Office.

A number of the roads south of the dam and pool are unsealed, and meet up and continue south to the sealed road that threads back through the **Ferguson Valley**, a fledgling wine area, to Bunbury. Alternatively another unsealed road heads in the opposite direction through the forests to the old milling area of **Wellington Mill**. A sealed road from here heads to the tiny community of **Lowden** and the main road back to Bunbury via **Donnybrook**. The whole area is interlaced with unsealed and 4WD tracks and there are a number of isolated sleeping options.

Donnybrook → *Colour map 3, A2. 35 km from Bunbury, 30 km from Balingup.*

A small, well-kept town, Donnybrook serves as the focus for a thriving apple orchard area. The best product of the area has to be the **Old Goldfields Orchard and Cider Factory** ① *T9731 0311, www.oldgoldfields.com.au, Wed-Sun 0930-1630, daily in school holidays, tours $4, includes tasting, signposted off Capel Rd.* This enterprising orchard, centred around the towering poppet-head of a now-defunct goldmine, has a restaurant, picnic garden, small goldfields interpretative shed and also produces wine. The ciders are strong but smooth and include an unusual, zesty ginger brew. Backpackers seeking casual work will find plenty of picking November-June by contacting the **harvest office** ① *T1800 062332, www.harvesttrail.gov.au.* The town has a great hostel set up specifically to cater for working backpackers, though you certainly don't have to be picking to stay there. The Munda Biddi Trail (see page 188) also passes through here.

Busselton ⇢ *For listings see pages 155-160. Colour map 3, B1.*

→ *Population: 18,000. 55 km from Bunbury, 45 km from Margaret River.*

Busselton is a laid-back town, originally one of the main export ports for WA's timber, now simply a relaxed family holiday town with a large number of tourist parks and motels strung out along the Bussell Highway.

The town has a wonderful piece of heritage from its days as a port, **Busselton Jetty** ① *T9754 0900, www.busselton jetty.com.au, $2.50, children under 15 free, trains daily unless windy, on the hour, 1000-1600,* a very pleasant walk that conceals beneath its timbers a riot of marine life including some amazingly colourful soft corals. The jetty has recently undergone a long refurbishment and there is public access 24 hours a day (small charge for walkers). It takes about 25 minutes to walk the 1600 m to the 'cut', but if your legs don't fancy it a small tourist train heads out there too. The **Interpretative Centre** at the base of the jetty (free entry) has many superb photographs of life under the jetty's tip. By donning a mask and snorkel and getting into the water by the weather station just before the cut you will be able to see much of the coral and fish life living on the piles. You're still 8 m from the bottom, however, and to really appreciate this wonderful artificial reef up close a scuba dive is necessary, at night if possible. If you don't want to get wet, the **Under Water Observatory** ① *T9754 0900, 1000-1600,*

Busselton

Kookaburra Caravan Park 5
Paradise Motor Inn 6
Phat Sam's Busselton
  Backpackers 1

Sleeping 🛏
Baudins 3
Esplanade 2
Jacaranda 4

Eating 🍴
Cod Rocks 1
Equinox 2
Goose 3
More Café 4

Jetty tales

The **Busselton Jetty** is the longest in the southern hemisphere at 1841 m. Originally constructed out of jarrah in 1865, the jetty was built to allow swifter and easier loading of timber from the shore to awaiting ships. By the early 1900s sand build-up, partly caused by the jetty itself, had extended the shoreline out some 70 m, and had decreased the depth further out. The far part of the jetty was extended in 1911 and a spur added that could carry a railway, so increasing the efficiency of loading. Shipping use continued until 1972 and in 1978 much of the original part of the jetty was destroyed by Cyclone Alby, though the railway spur and extension survived, leaving the boomerang-shaped structure you see today. In 1999 a fire created a huge hole in the structure and effectively cut off the last 200 m. In this case it meant fishermen could no longer reach the end of the pier and this has been very beneficial. It has allowed the already vigorous growth of soft corals and sponges to continue unhampered, and for marine life to proliferate. Species brought down by the offshore Leeuwin Current, normally only found much further north, have found a home alongside more local inhabitants and the marine life under the jetty, which adheres to the massive piles, is spectacularly colourful and a wonderful sight.

$28, children $14 (40-min guided tour, all day jetty access and return train ride, offers the next best thing – an opportunity to catch a lift down into an underwater glass-walled room located near the end of the pier.

Stretching away on either side of the jetty the beach is a beauty, with white sand sloping gently into the clear water. The grassy foreshore around the jetty has plenty of shade and there are toilets by the café. The **Old Courthouse Complex** ① *T9751 4651, www.artgeo.com.au, daily 1000-1600,* at the end of Queen Street, now houses exhibitions and local art and crafts instead of criminals. There is a tearoom in the adjacent Old Post Office. The **VIC** ① *38 Peel Terr, T9752 1288, www.downsouth.com.au, Mon-Fri 0900-1700, Sat 0900-1600, Sun 1000-1600,* is also the **TransWA** bus terminal. **South West Coachlines** stop around the corner on Albert Street.

Dunsborough ›› *For listings, see pages 155-160. Colour map 3, B1.*

→ *Population: 4000. 24 km from Busselton, 45 km from Margaret River.*

Sharing the same long north-facing beach as Busselton, Dunsborough is as much a holiday town as its neighbour, in fact more so for its proximity to **Cape Naturaliste** and the region's main wine area. The beach remains shallow way out to sea and there are extensive grassed and bush foreshore areas that separate it from the town. Other than heading for the beach there is not a great deal to do in the town itself, and most visitors use it as a base to explore the northern part of the Capes region, dive the *HMAS Swan* (see page 159) and head out on the various tours.

The helpful **VIC** ① *T9755 3299, www.downsouth.com.au, Mon-Fri 0900-1700, Sat-Sun 0900-1600,* is in the **Dunsborough Park Shopping Centre**, and can supply details of the many private holiday homes and units available for let in the town.

For Sleeping and Eating price codes and other relevant information, see pages 28-34.

● Sleeping

Bunbury *p149, map p150*

L-C The Clifton & Grittleton Lodge, corner of Clifton and Molloy Sts, T9792 6200, www.the clifton.com.au. Part of the Best Western chain, in a restored Victorian building. Well placed for both the centre and back beach.

A-B Mantra Bunbury Hotel, 1 Holman St, attached to the Silo development, T9721 0100, www.mantra.com.au. Studio as well as 2- and 3-bed apartments. A short walk to town, facilities include spa, pool, tennis courts and art gallery. Well placed for the jetty restaurants and bars.

A-B Quest Apartments, corner of Koombana and Lyons Drive, T9722 0777, www.questapartments.com.au. 52 smart, contemporary apartments in a complex a few mins' walk from the town centre. 1- and 2-bed apartments have full kitchen and laundry, studio apartments have a kitchenette. Tennis court, pool and BBQs.

B Ellen's Cottage, 41 King Rd, T9721 4082. Historic self-contained farmers cottage built by a convict in 1878. Handmade beams and glass, open fires, cottage garden, and claw foot bath. Modern kitchen and laundry. Breakfast basket supplied.

B-D Koombana Bay Holiday Resort, Koombana Dr, T9791 3900. Well-maintained Big4 caravan park opposite the Dolphin Discovery Centre with 3-bedroom chalets, en suite cabins and en suite sites. The complex has a pool, campers' kitchen, shop, café and tennis courts, and is the closest to town.

C Aran Brae, 5 Sherry St, T9721 2177, www.aranbrae.com.au. B&B with an en suite garden apartment, private courtyard and BBQ, and a very warm, Irish welcome. Continental breakfast supplied.

D-E Wander Inn, 16 Clifton St, T9721 3242 and T1800 039 032, www.bunbury

backpackers.com.au. Excellent, friendly and clean backpackers in a great location by the cafés and the beach. Singles, twins and doubles make up many of the 54 beds. Lovely, shady back garden and BBQ area, and all the usual facilities. Free daily breakfast, cake and coffee. Also bike hire and internet available. Recommended.

E Dolphin Retreat YHA, 14 Wellington St, T9792 4690, www.dolphinretreatbunbury. com.au. A smaller option with internet access and lots of freebies including pool tables, air hockey, bike and boogie board hire.

Donnybrook *p153*

E Brook Lodge Backpackers, 3 Bridge St, T9731 1520, www.brooklodge.com.au. Has over 80 beds, mostly in 3-bed dorms. 4 doubles have their own share kitchen and bathroom. On the edge of town, the hostel is set in large grounds and the excellent facilities include lots of outdoor areas, and 5-a-side soccer pitch. There's even a café and licensed bar. Recommended.

Busselton *p153, map p153*

B Baudins, 87 Bussell Highway, T9751 5576, www.baudins.com.au. Central B&B, a short distance from the beach and town. Internet access is available and a full English breakfast is served in the morning (there are 'healthier' options available too).

B-C Esplanade Hotel (the 'Nard'), Marine Terr, T9752 1078, www.thenard.com. Pleasant dining rooms serving cheap counter meals, front terrace tables and a range of rooms from the simple to luxurious. Meals daily 1200-1400, Sun-Wed 1800-2000, Thu-Sat 1800-2030.

C Jacaranda, 30 West St, T9751 4973, www.jacarandaguesthouse.com. Friendly B&B with 7 rooms, continental breakfast and gardens. Parking.

C-E Kookaburra Caravan Park, 66 Marine Terr, T9752 1516. Of a number of caravan parks along the highway, this one is the closest to the centre. It has a good campers' kitchen and is near a phone box and a supermarket. Some en suite accommodation available.

D-E Paradise Motor Inn , 6 Pries Av, T9752 1200, www.paradisemotorinn.com.au. The closest motel to town and one of the cheapest. Standard motel doubles with swimming pool plus a 'lodge' with a few good-value singles, a television room and kitchenette. Internet access, meals available on request. Reception open daily 0600-2200, late check-in can be arranged by phone.

D-E Phat Sams Busselton Backpackers, 14 Peel Terr, T9754 2763, www.phatsams.com.au. A relaxed hostel with dorms, doubles and the usual facilities. It's looking a little tired but it's clean and spacious, has a large covered BBQ courtyard and, like the town, is a good place to unwind. The friendly owner helps to find jobs for his guests.

Dunsborough *p154*

Most of the really luxurious accommodation is out of town toward the cape or the wine district. There are a few budget choices, the last hostels before Margaret River.

LL-A Waterfront, 4 Lecaille Court, T9756 8924, www.waterfrontdunsborough.com. A range of single and double storey houses near the ocean. The majority come with TV/DVD player, terrace and well-equipped kitchen. Linen is supplied.

A-E Dunsborough Inn, 50 Dunn Bay Rd, T9756 7277. A modern brick complex with pretty open-plan self-contained units and a separate budget section with singles, doubles, twins, triples and quads. Clean and comprehensive hostel-style communal facilities include a games room and garden BBQ area. The friendly owners often take guests out on snorkelling trips when they have time.

B-D Dunsborough Lakes Holiday Resort, Commonage Rd, T9756 8300. The town's only caravan park, it is more functional than picturesque. Keep $1 coins handy if you want to use the kitchen facilities.

B-D Whalers' Cove Villas, 3 Lecaille Court, T9755 3699, www.whalerscove.net. Spacious beachfront villas with BBQs, verandas and communal gardens. A short walk to town and an even shorter walk to the beach.

D-E Dunsborough Beachouse YHA, 201 Geographe Bay Rd, T9755 3107, www.dunsboroughbeachouse.com.au. The homeliest and liveliest with 70 beds in small dorms and a few pretty doubles and twins. Fantastic beachside position with a huge rear garden overlooking the ocean, excellent facilities including bike hire, internet access, free DVD library, TV, pool table, free coffee and tea, free boogie boards and snorkelling gear hire. The obvious big drawback is the 40-min walk to town, but there is a shuttle bus and pick-ups are usually possible if pre-arranged.

Eating

Bunbury *p149, map p150*

There are a number of eateries on the redeveloped jetty, including **Vat 2** for a treat or **Aristos** for fish and chips and a beer. All have great views. See also Bars and clubs, below, for pub fare.

TTT L'amour de la Femme, corner Wittenoom and Clifton Sts, T9791 5504, www.lamourrestaurant.com.au. Wed-Sat 1800-late, Sat-Sun for lunch 1130-1430. The seasonal menu and smart wine list in this beautiful, contemporary setting makes it one of Bunbury's finest. Fully licensed. Also runs a 1-bedroom chalet nestled next to the restaurant with its own private courtyard and Wi-Fi access (**B**), T0408 948962. Booking in advance advised.

TTT-TT Mojo's, Victoria St, T9792 5900. Daily 0800-2200. Sleek and stylish place offering all-day breakfast and cheap café menu that varies from classy versions of nachos, burgers and fish and chips to pastas, salads and nibbles plate. Evening meals change to mid-range Modern Australian.

¶ **Bunbury Noodle House**, Victoria St, next door to **Mojo's**, T9791 7638. Cheap and cheerful. Most dishes under $10, takeaway available. Fri-Sun 1100-1430, 1600-late.
¶ **Simply Thai**, 33 Victoria St, T9791 9901. Thai cooking with a good range curries. BYO. Thu-Fri 1200-1400 and daily 1730-late. Also does takeaways.

Cafés

Caf-fez, 18 Prinsep St, T9721 3699. Mon-Sat 0700-1700 and Sun 0800-1600. A comfortable café serving all day breakfast and light lunches. Offers a great selection of cakes and serves up Yahava coffee. Free Wi-Fi.
Ex-tension, Ocean Dr, T9791 2141. Mon-Wed 0800-1500, Thu-Sat 0800-late, Sun 0800-1600. Hanging over the beach the café is a good spot to catch a sunset, though the decor is a little ordinary. Mid-range grills and seafood, cheaper options and also a kiosk. At weekends there is a buffet breakfast from 0800-1100.
Henry's, corner of Victoria and Clifton Sts, T9792 4060. Open daily until late. Genteel style with raffia chairs and pavement tables. Mostly cheap meals.

Busselton *p153, map p153*

¶¶¶-¶¶ **The Goose**, Geographe Bay Rd, on the foreshore near the jetty, T9754 7700, www.thegoose.com.au. Daily 0700-late. A large stylish restaurant, close to the water. Serves breakfast, light lunches and evening meals. Tapas dishes and cake and coffee are available all day. Good food and the best view.
¶¶¶-¶ **Equinox**, jetty end of Queen St, T9752 4641, www.theequinox.com.au. Daily 0830-1100, 1130-1500, 1730-late, closed Sun for dinner. A large, friendly café. All tables are inside, but there are large panoramic windows overlooking the beach and jetty. Breakfast, light lunches and evening meals include snacks and platters. Separate takeaway kiosk (daily 0800-1800, later in peak summer) has a few tables underneath the huge adjacent Moreton Bay fig trees.
¶ **Cod Rocks**, 27 Queen St, T9754 1881. Tue-Sun 1200-1400 and 1700-1930. One of several takeaways, this fish and chip shop, open daily until 2000, also sells burgers (lunch only), and fresh and frozen seafood.
¶ **More Café**, 65 Kent St, T9752 3676, www.morecafe.com.au. Mon-Fri 0730-1600, Sat-Sun 0730-1500. A popular café serving up hearty breakfasts, as well as a good choice of lunch options.

Dunsborough *p154*

¶¶¶ **Food Farmacy**, 9 Dunsborough Park Shopping Centre, T9759 1877, www.food farmacy.com.au. Daily 0800-2200. Modern and innovative cuisine in interesting surrounds, with condiments in test tubes on the table. The menu makes good use of seasonal produce and for dessert try the chocolate tapas.
¶ **Squid Lips**, Dunsborough Centrepoint Shopping Centre, T9759 1799, www.squid lips.com.au. Wed-Sun 1200-1500, 1700-2000. Specializes in squid and chips, but also offers a selection of fresh fish (and chips), Tempura prawns, scallops, Thai fish cakes and some tasty salads including pear and rocket.

Cafés/delicatessens

Artézen, 234 Naturaliste Terr, T9755 3325, www.artezen.com.au. Daily 0700-1700. Offering the best value in town, this chic but earthy café serves an interesting range of light meals and a seasonal menu It is a good spot to chill out.
Dunsborough Bakery, 243 Naturaliste Terr, T9755 3137. Daily 0630-1700. Renowned for quality bread and pastries.
Tealicious House, 237 Naturaliste Terr, T9755 3308. Daily 0800-1700. Serves up a wide range of tea, coffee and deli food. Also offers high tea if booked in advance.

♦ Bars and clubs

Bunbury *p149, map p150*

Hungry Hollow, 316 Ocean Dr, T9791 5577. The only pub with views over the ocean, this cheerily decorated brasserie does breakfast at weekends and meals daily.

Prince of Wales, 41 Stephen St, T9721 2016.
Open 1000-late. Popular with the 18-35
crowd, and the place to be for live music at
weekends. Meals 1130-1400 and 1800-2000.
Rose, Victoria St, T9721 4533, www.rosehotel.
com.au. This 100-year-old pub with iron lace
verandas is an elegant place for a drink, and is
often where the evening starts for Bunbury
locals. Large range of imported beers and
40 wines by the glass. Cheap bar meals and
snacks 1200-1400, 1800-2000. Also has 25
en suite motel rooms and 10 hotel rooms with
shared facilities (**C-D**). Breakfast available.

Dunsborough *p154*
Dunsborough Tavern, 536 Naturaliste Terr,
T9755 3657. The only pub, it has a large
open-plan bar serving cheap counter meals
daily 1200-1500, 1800-2000, poker night on
Thu, live music Fri-Sat.
Malt Market, 26 Dunn Bay Rd, T9759 1720,
www.maltmarket.com.au. Daily 1600-late.
Offers a wide choice of local and international
beers, and is a good place to spend some
time. There's wine and cider for the non-beer
drinkers, and tapas, pizzas bistro food and
snacks. DJs and live music at the weekends,
check the website for what's on. Also offers
booze to take away. Recommended.

☻ Entertainment

Bunbury *p149, map p150*
Grand Cinema, corner of Victoria and
Clifton Sts, T9791 4455.
Regional Entertainment Centre, Blair St,
T9791 1133, T1300 661 272. Regular
performances of music, dance, theatre
and film. Box office open Mon-Fri
0900-1730 and 45 mins prior to shows.

Busselton *p153, map p153*
ACE Cinema, 27 Albert St, T9752 3655.
Single screen showing a thoughtful range
of current releases. They also advise on what's
on at the drive-in screen further down the
highway, www.bussletondrive-in.com.au.

Nautical Lady, T9752 3473, www.nautical
lady.com. Daily summer 0930-1700, winter
0930-1630, weather permitting. A centre with
a range of activities for children including
mini-golf, water slides, in-line skate area and
flying fox, each costing from $4-12 for a go or
session. The lookout tower is a good place to
get a photo of the jetty, $4.

O Shopping

Bunbury *p149, map p150*
Bunbury Book Exchange, Victoria St.
Mon-Tue 0900-1600, Wed 0900-1700,
Thu-Fri 0900-1640, Sat 0900-1300, Sun
1000-1400. Sells second-hand books.
Rose and Leo's Book Exchange,
42 Wellington St. Mon-Fri 0900-1600,
Sat 0900-1300. Second-hand books.
South African Shop, 12 Prinsep St, T9721
1998. Mon-Fri 0930-1700 and Sat 0900-1300.
For those who can't be without their biltong
or grape flavoured Fanta.

Busselton *p153, map p153*
There are a number of interesting boutiques
in the **Fig Tree Lane Arcade**.
Busselton Books, 26 Queen St, T9754 2044.
Sells second-hand books.
Caravan Doctor, Strelly St, T9752 3100.
Repairs, hires and sells caravans. It also has a
good range of spare parts and accessories.
Geographe Camping & Outdoors,
5 Bussell Highway, T9754 2909. This outdoor
shop sells a good range of camping, fishing
and sports gear.

▲ Activities and tours

Bunbury *p149, map p150*
Aspenz Cookery School, 42 Wellington St,
T9791 9455. A kitchenware shop, with a
kitchen at the back. Chefs from Margaret River
wineries and restaurants in Perth come by of
an evening to give cookery demonstrations.
Ring up to see who's doing what next.

Diving in the bay

The bay north of Busselton and Dunsborough is a huge sea-grass plain, known as a good place to spot the beautiful common sea dragon. As well as the amazing 'reef' under Busselton Jetty, there are two other artificial reefs in the bay, plus the limestone contour called **Four Mile Reef**, which runs east–west across it. The contour is about 18 m deep, covered in many types of corals and sponges, and attracts whales. The first artificial reef is a collection of constructions made from old car tyres, covering about 1 ha under about 21 m of water, and now harbouring a large array of marine life. However, the star attraction in the bay is undoubtedly the *HMAS Swan*. This warship was sunk in 1997 off Eagle Bay, near Dunsborough, and the collection of sea life it has grown since then makes it an absolutely unforgettable dive.

Skydive Adventure, 116 Blair St, T9791 7311, www.skydiveadventure.com.au. Offers solo and tandem parachute jumps.
South West Yacht Charters, T9721 7664, www.swyachtcharters.com.au. A variety of yachts for hire, and sailing courses.

Dolphin watching and swimming

Taking a boat cruise into the bay allows you to see the dolphins in their own environment engaging in natural behaviour such as catching fish or raising calves. There are several pods living in the bay and the tour operators usually know where the dolphins can be found. They love riding the bow wave of the boat and the guides swear they line up to take turns at it. During the summer, the swim tours take a similar route by boat but stop at places where the dolphins are known to play. Swimmers don wetsuits and snorkelling gear and jump in for about 15 mins at a time. To see the dolphins underwater, hear them clicking and whistling and have them swim around you is an unforgettable experience. Do keep in mind that while sightings are likely, they are not guaranteed.
Dolphin Discovery Centre, T9791 3088, www.dolphindiscovery.com.au. 'Dolphin Eco Cruise' Oct and May daily 1100 and 1300, Nov-Apr 1100 and 1500. $53, children $35, concessions $45. 'Swim tour' Oct and May 0800, Nov-Apr 0800 and 1200. $185.

Busselton *p153, map p153*
Cycling

Cycling is a popular pastime in Busselton, and the **Geographe Path** takes riders from one end of Geographe Bay to the other. See Transport, page 160, for bicycle hire.

Diving

Dive operators offer regular boat dives to the jetty and the *Swan*, and hire out equipment. Expect to pay from $205 for a 2-dive trip including gear, and $100 for a single jetty dive.
The Dive Shed, 21A Queen St, T9754 1615, www.diveshed.com.au. Daily 0900-1700, closed Sun and Mon in winter. In addition to the dives mentioned above, it also offers an introductory dive at the jetty for $145. It won't count towards a qualification, but this is a terrific place to get a taster. Call to check what's running.

Dunsborough *p154*
Dunsborough School of Natural Horsemanship, Abbeys Farm Rd off Wildwood Rd, T0433 477372. A variety of horse rides and lessons.
Naturaliste Charters, T9725 8511, www.whales-australia.com. Runs deep-sea fishing trips Dec-May ($200 per day, share line $100, 0700-1500), dolphin tours ($53, children $35, concessions $45) and whale-watching trips ($75, children $35, concessions $65) daily in season.

Taste the South, T0438 210373, www.tastethesouth.com.au. Wine-tasting tour includes lunch, chocolate and cheese factory (1100-1730), $75, brewery tour $95 (see also Margaret River Activities and tours, page 183).

Diving

The main dive season is Nov-Apr; not much happens Jul-Aug. You'll pay about $195 for a 2-dive trip to the *Swan*, including gear hire, and about $115 for a single dive.
Cape Dive, 222 Naturaliste Terr, T9756 8778, www.capediveexperience.com. Offers dozens of dive combinations, mostly focusing on the *Swan*. Also offers jetty dives, reef dives and runs PADI dive courses.

⊖ Transport

Bunbury *p149, map p150*
Bus
Local A metropolitan bus service, T9791 1955, www.bct.com.au, serves some of the more outlying suburbs and the railway station. Buses depart from the bus station next to the VIC, with most fares $2.40-3.60 (children and concessions $0.90-1.40). No Sun services, frequency of buses on other days varies considerably. Buses from the railway station to town leave every 20-40 mins, Mon-Fri 0730-1800, Sat 0740-1415.
Long distance TransWA services to Perth depart daily from the VIC. Services to the **timber towns** (**Pemberton** 2½ hrs) leave the VIC every day except Sat, **South West Coachlines** services leave from Bicentennial Sq 3 times daily. The **Busselton** services go at least twice a day.

Car hire

Avis, 76 Blair St, T9721 7873. **Go West**, 24 Denning Rd, T9791 4143, www.gowesttours.com.au, rents out cars and buses.

Taxi

Call T131008.

Train

The *Australind* goes to **Pinjarra**, **Serpentine** and **Perth** daily at 0600 and 1445.

Busselton *p153, map p153*
Bicycle hire
Busselton Bike Hire, T0413 017871. Bikes can be delivered to your accommodation. $35 for a day, children $20. If hiring for more than 1 day the price drops to $20, children $10. Rates include helmet and lock; child seats and baskets cost an extra $5-10.

Bus

TransWA bus services leave from the VIC for **Perth** every day. Services to the **Capes** also daily. **South West Coachlines** also operate daily north and south services.

Car servicing

Gull, corner of Albert and West Sts, T9752 1274.

⊕ Directory

Bunbury *p149, map p150*
Banks Major banks have branches and ATMs on southern end of Victoria St, except **Commonwealth** on Stephen St. **Internet** Internet Planet, 79 Victoria St, T9791 2200. Mon-Fri 0930-1800, Sat 1000-1600. **Medical services** Bunbury Regional Hospital, Bussell Highway, corner of Robertson Drive, T9722 1000. **Police** Prinsep St, T131 444. **Post** Corner of Victoria and Stirling Sts.

Busselton *p153, map p153*
Banks Major banks have branches and ATMs on Queen St. **Medical services** Chemists: Amcal, Boulevard Shopping Centre, Prince St, T9752 4200. Mon-Wed and Fri 0830-1800, Thu 0830-1900, Sat 0830-1700, Sun 1100-1700. Hospital: Mill Rd, T9752 1122. DEC, 12 Queen St, Mon-Fri 0800-1700. **Police** Duchess St, T9754 1222. **Post** Prince St.

Cape to Cape

It is no exaggeration to say that this tiny section of the west coast from Cape Naturaliste to Cape Leeuwin is one of the most gorgeous regions in Australia. West Australians will tell you that it's busy and over-developed but it's a quiet backwater compared to many of the beauty spots of the east coast and local residents are trying hard to preserve its low-key and non-elitist nature. Fortunately, much of the coast is protected by the Leeuwin-Naturaliste National Park, accessible by road at a few points but best seen on a section of the wonderful Cape-to-Cape Walk Track. Just inland is a network of limestone caves and patches of thick karri forest to explore. Margaret River is at the centre of the region and is the focus for a top-end wine and gourmet food industry as well as the arts and crafts produced by the region's thriving artistic community. Tiny Augusta, at the southern end of the region, is a great spot for whale watching in winter and a reminder of what the west coast towns used to be like: simple, slow and unsophisticated. ►► For listings, see pages 176-184.

Cape Naturaliste ►► *For listings, see pages 176-184. Colour map 3, A1.*

The cape is a wild triangle of hardly developed land where you can find a perfect beach and peaceful isolation less than 30 minutes' drive from Dunsborough and Busselton. Dunsborough sits at its eastern corner on Geographe Bay and a string of spectacular quiet bay beaches stretch to the tip where there is a lighthouse. These beaches all have dazzling fine white sand, turquoise water and shallow safe swimming. Tall trees and vegetation can grow right down to the shore on this northeastern coast as they are protected from the strong salty breeze on the other side. The western coast takes the full force of the prevailing southwesterly breeze and is a wilder surf coast that is mostly inaccessible until you reach Yallingup at the western base of the cape.

Cape Naturaliste Road

Cape Naturaliste Road leads out to the cape and there are small settlements on the calm eastern side of this road. Take a detour along the **Eagle Bay Meelup loop** to see something of the coastline. **Castle Rock Beach** is a small sandy cove that was once the site of a whaling station. There are shady picnic tables, BBQs and toilets. Further along is **Meelup Beach**, the most popular on the cape. The beach was named by the Noongars of the Wardandi people who lived in the coastal region from Busselton to Augusta. The name means 'place of the moon' because the moon rises from the sea at certain times of the year. Meelup is a long sandy beach with scrub almost to the shore so you can sit on the grass under a tree to escape the sun for a while. There are also picnic tables and toilets here. The next beach is **Eagle Bay**, although there are small beaches all the way along the coast from Meelup and plenty of places to stop. Head for one of these if you want the beach to yourself. Eagle Bay has a settlement of holiday homes. The coastal road terminates here and you need to take Eagle Bay Road uphill to re-join the main road to the cape, passing **Wise** winery on the way.

Sugarloaf Rock

A further 4 km northwest on the main road is the turn-off to Sugarloaf Rock. This is the only point to access the western coast of the cape and the 3-km sealed road leads to the striking formation named for a cone of sugar (sugar was once sold wrapped in a twist of paper). The pale slabbed rocks lean at 45 degrees and create small sheltered pools. The rock is home to a small colony of rare red-tailed tropic birds in summer. It's an idyllic swimming spot in calm weather, dramatic in wild weather and a fine place to take a bottle of wine and watch the sun set into the ocean.

Bunker Bay and Cape Naturaliste Lighthouse

Back on the main road, turn right after 1 km to reach **Bunker Bay**. This is the most beautiful sandy beach on the eastern side but there are no facilities here so it is less frequented that the others. At the western end of the beach is a pretty cove with granite boulders and sheltered pools and the appropriately named **Shelley Beach**. From here you can walk to the lighthouse. **Cape Naturalise Lighthouse** ① *T9755 3955, www.geographebay.com, $11.50, children $6, daily 0930-1600, school holidays 0930-1700, tours every 30 mins, discount entry tickets available for the lighthouse and Ngilgi Cave $27, children $13.50,* is just 2 km further along the main road, set back from the coast by a few kilometres. The 23-m lighthouse was built in 1903 from limestone quarried at Bunker Bay and is still in use today. The light is operated automatically now and on electricity rather than the oil and kerosene that was used in the past. Guided tours allow access to the lens and balcony, and all visitors can access a small maritime museum in a lighthouse keeper's cottage.

There is a walking track along the coast from **Dunsborough to Eagle Bay** (6 km) that starts from Forrest Street on the far western edge of Dunsborough. Ask at the Dunsborough VIC for a map or directions. The long-distance **Cape-to-Cape Walk Track** (see map, page 163) starts from the Cape Naturaliste Lighthouse car park and traverses the western coastline of the cape. There are also several short walking tracks from the lighthouse to the coast and this is an excellent spot for **whale watching**, September to November. There is a detailed walking trail map at the entrance to the lighthouse complex. The **Whale Lookout Track** is the shortest to the coast and leads to watching platforms (40 minutes return). The **Cape Naturaliste Track** leads to the far western end of the cape and an area called the Pinnacles for some rock formations, while the Bunker Bay track leads around the coast to the bay.

Cape-to-Cape Walk Track (1)

The first section of the track follows a fairly flat path along 50-m cliff tops most of the way to **Yallingup** (14 km). There are no facilities along the way. You could also consider walking as far as Yallingup, staying overnight in the caravan park and walking back. The first walk from the Cape to **Sugarloaf Rock** (3.5 km) makes a pleasant introduction to the track and a good short walk. You could have a swim at Sugarloaf and return to the cape car park (7 km return). The southern part traverses some really interesting scenery and some of the track's best short sections. From the southern end of **Smiths Beach** it is only 2 km to **Canal Rocks**, passing through coastal heath and tea-tree on its way across the granite headland. A further 2 km from Canal Rocks to **Wyardup** provides magnificent views of the rock formations and south to **Cape Clairault**. From Cape Clairault you can walk a loop by heading south across the cape and then dropping down to the beach and following the rocks and beaches north, back around to **Indijup Beach** (7 km). It is 20 km from Cape Naturaliste to Wyardup.

1 Cape to Cape

Indian Ocean

Cape Naturaliste Lighthouse — Bunker Bay — Rocky Point — Eagle Bay — Geographe Bay

Sugarloaf Rock

Wise — Meelup Beach — Castle Rock Beach

NgILGI Cave — Dunsborough

Yallingup — Smiths Beach — Gunyulgup Galleries — Palmer Wines — Happs — Goanna — Gallery Café — Carbunup — Rivendell — Wild Wood Rd

Canal Rocks — Yallingup Galleries

Indijup Beach — Wyadrup Rocks — Cape Clairault

Driftwood — Clairault — Knee Deep Wines

Moses Rock

Leeuwin-Naturaliste National Park — Wilyabrup Valley Wineries — Cowaramup

Gracetown

Ellensbrook

Cape Mentelle — Margaret River — Rosa Brook

Prevelly & Gnarabup — Xanadu — Eagles Heritage Centre — Yahava Koffeeworks — Swallows Welcome — Minot — Voyager — Leeuwin — Redgate

Redgate Beach — Witchcliffe — Mammoth Cave — Giants Cave — Boranup Gallery

Cave Works & Lake Cave — Conto Beach — Cape Freycinet

Leeuwin-Naturaliste National Park — North Point — Boranup Forest

Hamelin Bay — Hamelin Island — Karridale

Knobby Head — Cosy Corner Beach — Cape Hamelin — Kudardup — Jewel Cave

Augusta — Skippy Rock — Flinders Bay — Cape Leeuwin Lighthouse — Seal Island

To Busselton, Bunbury and Perth
To Nannup
To Nannup, Pemberton & The South
Blackwood River
Caves Rd
Bussell Highway
Cape to Cape Track

Cape to Cape maps
1 Cape to Cape, page 163
2 Wilyabrup Valley wineries, page 167

4 km / 4 miles

Sleeping
Cape Lodge 1
Empire Retreat 3
Erravilla 4
Wildwood Valley B&B 5
Windmills Break 2

Yallingup and around ⟫ For listings, see pages 176-184. Colour map 3, B1.

Yallingup → Population: 300. 10 km from Dunsborough, 20 km from Willyabrup wineries.

This tiny beach settlement spreads down a hill to a long beach and reef-protected lagoon. To the north and south are isolated and pristine surfing beaches. The main attractions are swimming, surfing, and the NgILGI Cave, although Yallingup also makes a mellow base close to the wineries and galleries just inland. At the top of the hill is the venerable Caves House, a caravan park, and a shop. **Yallingup Surf Shop** ① T9755 2036, 0900-1700, is also here hiring out surfboards. Surfing lessons are available from **Yallingup Surf School** ① T9755 2755, www.yallingupsurfschool.com, private lesson for about $110; group lessons from $50 per person. Follow the road downhill to reach the beach and the main area of holiday homes. By the beach there is a grassy foreshore with playground and BBQs, a café and gallery. There are several walking trails around Yallingup, such as the **Wardanup Hill loop** (5 km, 2½ hours), from the beach car park. This heads uphill past NgILGI Cave and a lookout and circles back to the coast. You can access the Cape-to-Cape track from the foreshore.

NgILGI Cave

① Caves Rd, about 1 km east of Yallingup, T9755 2152, www.geographebay.com, daily 0930-1630 (last entry 1530), $18.50, concessions $16.50, children $9.50 (cash only); 15-min semi-guided tour and a self-guided 1-hr tour.

This cave was the first to be opened to the public in 1901 and launched tourism in the area. It is a beautifully deep and decorated limestone cave, with magnificent shawls, stalagmites, stalactites and helictites. NgILGI cave (pronounced nil-gee) is thought to be about 500,000 years old and gets its name from an Aboriginal creation myth. NgILGI was a good warrior spirit who

Cape-to-Cape Walk Track

The spectacular **Cape-to-Cape Walk Track**, or part of it at least, is a must if you are staying in the area for any length of time. This track follows the coastline from Cape Naturaliste to Cape Leeuwin (140 km) and is a superb way to see coastal and forest scenery in the region, much of it inaccessible by car. The walk, rated as one of the best coastal walks in the country, is mostly within the **Leeuwin-Naturaliste National Park**, a narrow strip less than 10 km wide in places, along a limestone ridge. Unusually for a long Australian track it is accessible year-round, rarely either too hot or cold, though it's not at its best on wet wintry days or scorching summer ones. There are regular road access points so it is easy to walk short sections or day trips and these are suggested at appropriate points in the text. Unfortunately the nature of the track allows for hardly any loop trails, and so most short or day walks will involve returning along the same path unless you can arrange a pick-up. Basic campsites reserved for walkers can be used along the way. Tents, water and fuel stoves must all be carried and waste carried out. The track is administered by **DEC** who produce an excellent pack ($8) containing walk maps and notes in five sections covering the whole route. There are no charges or permits. For more information contact **DEC** in Busselton, T9752 1677, **DEC** in Margaret River T9757 2322, or see www.naturebase.net. A few companies organize guided walks along the track. **Environmental Encounters**, T9330 2060, www.environmentalencounters.com.au, periodically run eight-day fully supported trips that cover the entire track, for around $2125.

lived by the sea. Wolgine, an evil spirit, lived in the cave and had been drying out local waterholes and tempting children into the cave. NgILGI whipped up a storm, cutting the cave off from the sea and driving Wolgine deep into the cave and out through the present entrance. It then became his own *nurilem* (cave). Entry to the cave is only by semi-guided tour. A guide takes you down into the cave and another remains in the main chamber but once inside you are free to wander about at your own pace. Most people take about an hour to look around. There are also adventure tours that involve wriggling though some tight spaces, climbing and crawling around areas not normally seen by the public. Wear enclosed boots and clothes that you don't mind getting grubby.

Beaches around Yallingup

Much of the Cape-to-Cape coast is actually inaccessible to anyone but walkers, but Yallingup is at the end of one of three sealed roads in quick succession that lead to a series of rocky headlands and almost impossibly perfect beaches.

Some 5 km south of Yallingup, Canal Rocks Road leads both to Canal Rocks and Smiths Beach. **Smiths Beach**, one of the most popular in the area thanks to the adjacent caravan parks, stretches all the way from Yallingup, a long, broad stretch of white sand sloping gently into the sea. The sea itself is often not so gentle, but when it's calm and the sun is shining the iridescent blues and greens of the water make an arresting sight. **Canal Rocks** is a bare rocky headland with a maze of fissures worn so deep and wide as to create a series of islands, separated by canal-like channels and pools. Snorkelling and swimming can be a lot of fun here, but do beware the very strong currents and swells created by the narrow channels – they can make such pursuits extremely hazardous. A narrow bridge connects the mainland to the first island. The small adjacent bay is a popular boat-launching site and there are public toilets in the car park.

About 10 km south via Wyardup Road, but just a magnificent 2-km cliff-top walk via the Cape-to-Cape track, are **Wyardup Rocks** and **Indijup Beach** stretching to **Cape Clairault**. The rocks, similar to though not quite as broken up as Canal Rocks, are immediately adjacent to the beach, which is easily a match for Smiths. The main difference between the two spots is that the latter rocks and beach have no facilities, except some toilets at the south end of the beach, and consequently far fewer people.

Wardan Aboriginal Cultural Centre

① *55 Injidup Springs Rd, T9756 6566, www.wardan.com.au, Sep-Mar daily 1000-1600, Apr-Jun and Aug Wed-Fri, Sun-Mon 1000-1600, 1-hr tours available $15, children $8.*
On the way out to the beach look out for the Wardan Aboriginal Cultural Centre. Inside the rammed-earth walls, the centre aims to give visitors insight into the Bibelmen Mia culture through an art gallery, interpretive centre and amongst other activities a 1-km bushwalking trail demonstrating traditional plant uses.

Yallingup Shearing Shed

① *1442 Wildwood Rd, T9755 2309, daily 1000-1600, shearing demonstrations at 1100, except Fri, $10, children $5.*
This is an unusual diversion in the area, 6 km from Yallingup on the Wildwood Road. Principally a sheep farm, part of the woolshed is now a fairly uninspiring knitwear shop. Most of it, however, is still very much a shearing shed and the owners ensure that there are sheep to be shorn all year round. Lively demonstrations happen every day except Friday (when shearers go to the chiropractor), and spectators get to take part in much of the process save the actual clipping.

Northern Margaret River wine area ▶▶ *For listings, see pages 176-184.*

The area between Dunsborough and Yallingup, the northern of three principal areas that together have become famous as the Margaret River Wine Region, is covered in a maze of picturesque, mostly sealed lanes, with a gallery or winery seemingly around every corner.

Willyabrup Valley wine area, to the south, is the core of the Margaret River Wine Region. It is a few kilometres north of Gracetown and Cowaramup with most of the wineries packed along Caves Road and slightly inland between Metricup and Harmons South roads. Mildly hilly, many of the wineries have large, scenic dams with cafés and restaurants taking full advantage of them. As a rule most wineries, particularly the smaller, cellar-door-only ones, do not charge for tastings and are open daily. As well as wine there are also opportunities to taste cheese, chocolate, coffee and beer. ▶▶ *See maps on pages 163 and 167, for the location of wineries and galleries.*

Dunsborough and around → *Colour map 3, B1.*

Goanna Gallery Café ① *278 Hayes Rd, T9759 1477, www.goannagallery.com.au, Wed-Fri 0900-1600, Sat-Sun 0830-1600,* houses local art and craft work in a small-scale bush setting. The gallery has a café serving cheap good food, home-made cakes, jams and preserves and an outdoor terrace. It's a lovely little place that also has a sculpture walk. Recommended.
Gunyulgup Galleries ① *Gunyulgup Valley Dr, T9755 2177, www.gunyulgupgalleries.com.au,*

1000-1700, is the finest in the southwest, set in a grand formal space overhanging a lake and surrounded by bush. High-quality paintings, sculpture, jewellery, glass and ceramics. **Happs** ① *Commonage Rd, T9755 3300, www.happs.com.au, 1000-1700*, is a welcoming winery and pottery. There is an extensive and unusual range of wines, such as Viognier, but the most popular is Fuchsia, a light pink made from 19 red varieties. There are also a few preservative-free wines. The pottery is attractive domestic ware. Wines cost $16-55. **Bush Shack Brewery** ① *3 Hemsley Rd, T9755 2848, www.bushshackbrewery.com.au, Sun-Thu 1000-1700, Fri-Sat 1000-1800*, is a small brewery making speciality beers such as chilli, chocolate, ginger and passionfruit. Visitors can taste six for $12. There's a bar, beer garden, pool tables and arcade games. Snacks are served 1100- 1600, rugs are provided for those who want to sit on the grass and there are BBQs for use. Visitors who don't like beer are also catered for. **Yallingup Galleries** ① *corner Caves Rd and Gunyulgup Valley Rd, T9755 2372, www.yallingupgalleries.com.au, 1000-1700*, is surrounded by bush with a focus on paintings and furniture and a good range of prices. During busy holiday periods special exhibitions are held at the **Garden Art Studio**.

The main small cluster of wineries in this northern end of the region is on, or just off Wildwood Road. **Rivendell** ① *T9755 2090, www.rivendellwines.com.au, Thu-Mon 1100-1600*, complement their wines with rambling gardens, a tearoom and a restaurant serving good mid-range lunches and cream teas from Thursday to Monday 1000-1600. Saturday nights for dinner from 1800. Wines cost $17-28. It's also possible to stay overnight (see Sleeping, page 177). On the way out of town towards Busselton is **Palmer Wines** ① *1271 Caves Rd, T9756 7034, www.palmerwines.net.au, wine tasting daily 1000-1700, restaurant Thu-Mon 1000-1700, Sat 1000-late; booking essential for dinner*, which has a popular restaurant and a cellar door. Wines cost $20-28.

South of the main area, on Caves Road is **Driftwood** ① *T9755 6338, www.driftwoodwines.com.au, 1000-1700*, which offers consistently good Modern Australian cuisine and is open for dinner on Saturday. Wines cost $15-55. **Clairault** ① *off Pusey Rd, T9755 6655, www.clairaultwines.com.au, 1000-1700, restaurant daily 1200-1530*, is around the block from Driftwood. This is the largest family owned and run winery in the region, and has one of the most stylish tasting and dining rooms, a smooth assemblage of polished timber, contemporary furniture and rich tones. Attention to culinary detail is just as close, with excellent expensive international cuisine available. Wines cost $20-45. Turn off Caves Road onto Johnson Road to find **Knee Deep** ① *T9755 6776, www.kneedeepwines.com.au, daily 1000-1700*, a small, friendly cellar door and excellent restaurant. The Shiraz and Chardonnay are well regarded and the Knee Deep Sweet is very tasty. Wines cost $22-45.

Willyabrup Valley wine area → *Colour map 3, B1. 30 km from Busselton, 20 km from Margaret River.*
The short stretch of Caves Road that passes through this area is the epicentre of the Margaret River wine region with over a dozen wineries along 5 km of bitumen.

Moss Brothers ① *T9755 6270, www.mossbrothers.com.au, 1000-1700*, is the most northerly winery with a warm welcome. Its premium range includes an excellent Shiraz. Wines $16-35. It usually has a good stock of museum wines.

Pierro ① *T9755 6220, www.pierro.com.au, 1000-1700*, has a rustic, unpretentious and friendly rammed-earth and jarrah cellar door that hints little at the superb quality of their $24-70 wines. The smooth top-of-the-range Chardonnay is considered one of the very best wines in the region and both their Pierro and Fire Gully ranges are highly sought after. All their wines are available for tasting if they haven't sold out.

Cullen ① T9755 5277, www.cullenwines.com.au, 1000-1630, a large solid-looking building, much of it a large restaurant (T9755 5656), which serves fresh biodynamic and organic produce from the local area and the winery's own garden. The home-made cakes are excellent and can be eaten with a coffee out on the deck. Wines cost $19-220.

Vasse Felix ① T9756 5055, www.vassefelix.com.au, 1000-1700, restaurant Mon-Fri 1000-1530, Sat-Sun 1000-1600, at the end of its own tree-lined driveway, is still making some of the region's best wines and is particularly well known for its flagship Heytesbury Chardonnay. Now owned by the influential Holmes à Court family, the winery has a separate café and excellent first-floor restaurant. A large exhibition and performance space is becoming a key WA arts venue. Wines cost $15-80.

After **Pierro** (see above) there are a few more wineries along Metricup Road that are well worth the visit. **The Grove** ① T9755 7458, www.thegrovevineyard.com.au, 0900-1700, is a stylish fusion of companies and ideas sharing the same buildings and the objective of offering the visitor something a bit different. Premium wines are complemented by innovative liquors ($2 for three tastings plus a cocktail) and spirits served on the balcony overhanging the large lily-covered dam. There is also a restaurant at the back, which serves light breakfast, lunch, coffees and cakes. Cooked breakfasts are available at the weekend. **Woody Nook** ① 506 Merricup Rd, T9755 7547, www.woodynook.com.au, 1000-1630, is about as laid-back and rustic as it gets around here. It's not relaxed about the winemaking, however, and the Cabernet Sauvignon and Sauvignon Blanc are consistently good. Its ports are very fine too. The unpretentious café (T9755 7030) serves light meals using seasonal produce, 1000-1600, reservations recommended. Wines cost $19-65.

2 Wilyabrup Valley wineries

➡ Cape to Cape maps
1 Cape to Cape, page 163
2 Wilyabrup Valley wineries, page 167

Sleeping 🛏
Taunton Farm Caravan Park 1

Wineries 🍷
Clairault 13
Cullen 1
Grove 4

Hay Shed Hill 5
Moss Brothers 6
Palandri 7
Pierro 8
Treeton 9
Vasse Felix 10
Willespie 11
Woody Nook 12

Off Metricup Road, Harmons Mill Road heads down to the Bussell Highway. Along it are a couple more small wineries quietly producing superb wines, and the **Margaret River Chocolate Factory** ① Harmons Mill Rd, T9755 6555, www.chocolatefactory. com.au, 0900-1700, which boasts about 20 different varieties of chocolates based on the milk, white and plain favourites. These bases are available for tasting as small buttons and there are also home-made jams, sauces and pickles for sale. There is a factory viewing window and a café serving up mainly chocolate-based treats as well as paninis and coffees. Follow the internal road and you will reach **Providore Farm Shop** ① T9755 6366, www.providore. com.au, 0900-1700, café 0900-1630, where there is wine, olive oil and chutney tasting, and a café.

Hay Shed Hill ① 511 Harmans Mill Rd, T9755 6046, www.hayshedhill.com.au, 1000-1700, is almost next door to **Willespie** (see below), with wines at $15-35. One of the friendliest wineries in the region, with a rare sense of humour. It's one of the prettiest too, occupying a series of large white weatherboard buildings in keeping with the traditional old hay shed. Their flagship wines are a treat, a wonderful Cabernet Sauvignon and the excellent premium block series. If they're not too busy the staff will be happy to help you plan a tasting day. There's also an excellent café serving up refreshingly inventive breakfast dishes until mid-morning and then light snacks; it also sells cheeses and deli meats. In winter it offers mulled wine.

Willespie ① *555 Harmans Mill Rd, T9755 6248, www.willespie.com.au, 1030-1700*, was the first of the wineries and has successfully experimented with a full-bodied Merlot. The first-floor cellar door has a veranda on which its aged wines can be sampled. Wines cost $18-50.

A handful of wineries are now pioneering the area to the east, along the Bussell Highway. **Palandri** ① *T9756 5100, www.palandri.com.au, 1000-1700*, is a powerhouse in the region, serious about providing the whole experience in an innovative hangar-like space. Several ranges and crisp, drinkable wines aimed at a worldwide market. Wines cost $15-35. There is also a café offering unusual breakfasts and light, café-style salads and platters matched to wine varieties (daily 0900-1500). Lots of wine merchandise and playstations to distract the kids.

Treeton Estate ① *Treeton Rd, T9755 5481, www.treetonestate.com.au, 1000-1800*, just outside Cowaramup, has small, rustic wines for around $18-20. Its later opening hours are just one of the reasons to make this the last stop of the day. The whites are extremely drinkable, light summer wines. The friendly owners welcome picnickers.

Cowaramup Brewing Company ① *North Treeton Rd, T9755 5822, www.cowaramup brewing.com.au, 1000-1800*. This family brewery sells five home-brewed standard beers (India Pale Ale, Pilsner, Hefeweizen, Special Pale Ale, Stout) plus one seasonal variety and some Grove wines. A tasting paddle of five beers is $12. They grow nine types of hops and produce hop soap and oil. There is also a restaurant and a playground for the children.

Cowaramup → *Colour map 3, B1. 35 km from Busselton, 10 km from Margaret River.*

Though your nose won't miss the pungent smells of cheese making and dairying, Cowaramup itself is a 'blink and you'll miss it' settlement on the Bussell Highway. It is worth a stop though for a couple of interesting businesses. The **Margaret River Regional Wine Centre** ① *9 Bussell Highway, T9755 5501, www.mrwines.com, Mon-Sat 1000-1900, Sun 1200-1800*, stocks almost every wine made in the region and is willing to ship overseas or within Australia. It can also help plan a wine-tasting itinerary and has tastings daily 1000-1600, often from wineries without a cellar door. The **Sitting Room Gallery** ① *62 Bussell Highway, T9755 9115, www.sittingroom.com.au, daily 1000-1600*, showcases contemporary surf art and there are some great images on display.

Cape-to-Cape Walk Track (2)

The stretch of track from **Wyardup** to **Gracetown** (27 km) is more broken than that to the north and south, a series of rugged cliffs and headlands and a few small sandy coves. The walk mostly follows cliff tops with only a few descents to beaches. To the east there is nothing but vineyards so it is a peaceful stretch with no sealed road access. From Cape Clairault the next 4 km along the cliff top is a good place to see whales and dolphins in season. In the southern half of this section you'll see the 40-m granite-gneiss **Willyabrup Cliffs**, a draw for climbers and abseilers. This section could be walked from Gracetown but it would be a long day (22 km return). With a 4WD it is possible to drive to the end of Juniper Road and walk along the track for about 5 km to the cliffs and return.

Surf's up

As well as linking its name indelibly to the wines between the capes, Margaret River has also become the moniker for the region as a surf destination and it is common to hear or read about 'Margaret River surf breaks', even though only a couple are anywhere near the river mouth itself and none are near the town as it's 10 km inland. Whatever the name, the succession of west-facing beaches between the capes, particularly the northern half, many of which are only accessible by a long walk, are famous for their surf breaks and regarded as the best in Western Australia. The best of the best are around Gracetown, particularly the 'womb', described by one local surfy as the place to go 'if you want a lot of water up your nose'. Others to check out are 'three bears', 'grunters' and 'lefties'.

Gracetown ►► *Colour map 3, B1.*

→ *32 km from Yallingup, 11 km from Cowaramup.*

Gracetown is a tiny coastal settlement due west of Cowarumup. The houses cluster on a hillside, above the white sand and rock outcrops of Cowaramup Bay. The bay is good for fishing from the rocks on a calm day, when the water shimmers with patches of turquoise, but can also put on massive surf when a swell is running. The **Cape-to-Cape Walk Track** follows the coast closely at this point along cliff tops so the views are particularly good and it's only 11 km north to the climbers' playground of Willyabrup Cliffs. Facilities at Gracetown are limited to a **general store** ① *0700-1900*, with petrol and phone and a café, the **Bay Café** (see Eating, page 180).

Cape-to-Cape Walk Track (3)

The third section of the track, 31 km from **Gracetown to Redgate Beach**, passes through several settlements. There's a bit of bush walking in fairly low country and some fine swimming and surfing beaches. After following the beach at Gracetown, the track passes along a cliff top to **Ellensbrook**, where you can look around the Bussells' old homestead and **Meekadarabee Cave**. There's a campsite nearby, beside the stream. The track then continues inland until veering to the coast again near **Cape Mentelle**, a high limestone headland. From here it's not far to the beautiful beach at the mouth of Margaret River. This is a good short walk to do from the rivermouth (3 km return) to see the Cape Mentelle cliffs and Kilcarnup on the northern side. The trail then heads up behind **Prevelly** and **Gnarabup.** The coast is not reached again until 3 km north of Redgate, a picturesque beach with no facilities.

Margaret River and around ►► *For listings see pages 176-184.*

→ *Population: 3000. 100 km from Bunbury via Highway, 55 km from Augusta via Caves Road.*

The Margaret River and around is famous for two things: wineries and surf. The region produces some of Australia's best premium wines and the surf is also exceptional. Contrary to many travellers' expectations, neither are in Margaret River itself, but it does make a convenient base for these attractions. Most of the wineries are to the north, almost as close to Dunsborough as Margaret River, and the beach is to be found at the river mouth near the small settlement of Prevelly.

Margaret River → Colour map 3, B1.

Margaret River town sits on the southern side of the river, 10 km inland from the beach, and a busy street of shops and restaurants has developed along its main street. The town acts as a focus for the talent in the region and has some wonderful restaurants, galleries and accommodation that are the equal of any in the country.

On the northern riverbank is a small **Rotary Park** with BBQs and toilets. The Rotary Park is the trailhead for a walk/cycle trail to **Ten Mile Brook Dam**, a pleasant riverbank trail (15 km return) through karri, blackbutt and jarrah forest to a picnic site by the dam.

There are some talented artists and craftspeople in the southwest region and visiting galleries is an enjoyable experience. Many studios are in the countryside but there are a few galleries in Margaret River that showcase regional work. **Jahroc Gallery** ① 83 Bussell Highway, T9758 7200, www.jahroc.com.au, daily 1000-1700, shows a fine range of painting, sculpture, woodwork and jewellery. The **Melting Pot Glass Studio** ① 91 Bussell Highway, T9757 2252, www.meltingpot glass.com, 0930-1700, sells a wide range of art glassware and there are glass blowing demonstrations Tuesday-Saturday 1000-1600. The **Margaret River Gallery** ① 91 Bussell Highway, T9757 2729, www.margaret rivergallery.com.au, is located next door. The **Tunbridge Gallery** ① T9758 7900, www.tun bridgegallery.com.au, Mon-Sat 1000-1700, Sun 1000-1500, or by appointment, show-cases work from new and established Aboriginal artists from Western Australia and the Northern Territory. Ask the VIC for a list if you wish to go on a gallery crawl.

Margaret River hosts a lively **Wine Festival** ① T9757 9330, www.margaret riverfestival.com, over 10 days in April or May. Events include masterclasses, tastings, art exhibitions, cooking classes and concerts. On some days during the festival special bus routes operate to events at wineries and galleries. The **VIC** ① Bussell Highway, T9780 5913, www.margaretriver.com, 0900-1700, has information on wineries in the region.

Margaret River

Ellensbrook → Colour map 3, B1. 13 km from Gracetown, 13 km from Margaret River.
① House: Sat-Sun 1000-1600, $4, children $2, concession $3; grounds: daily.

One of the earliest houses in the district, Ellensbrook was built by Alfred and Ellen Bussell in 1857. The homestead was part of a farming property and was carefully sited by

Sleeping
Bridgefield 1
Inne Town Backpackers 2
Margaret River
 Backpackers 5
Margaret River
 Guest House 3
Margaret River Lodge YHA 7
Margaret River Resort 4
Prevelly Park Beach Resort 6
Riverglen Chalets 9
Riverview Tourist Park 10
Vintages 8

Eating
Arc of Iris 1
MRH Bistro & Bar 4
Goodfellas 2
Margaret River Bakery 9
Margaret River Fish
 & Chips 3
Sea Gardens 10
Urban Bean 5
Must 6
Wild Thyme Gourmet 11

Bars & clubs
Settlers Tavern 7
Wino's 8

Harmony at Ellensbrook

The Bussell family were one of the first European families in the region and have left their names behind in Busselton and Gracetown. The Bussell brothers arrived at the Swan River Colony in 1830 from England and travelled to Augusta to try and found a settlement there. It wasn't very successful so the settlers explored further north in search of fertile farming land. John Bussell came across Margaret River and is thought to have named it after his cousin. His younger brother, Alfred Bussell, bought land further north, now Busselton. He transported provisions for soldiers from Augusta to Vasse and came to know the region and the local Noongar people very well. Ironically the soldiers were stationed in Vasse to protect new settlers from attacks by the dispossessed Noongars. Much of Alfred's knowledge came from the Noongar people and when he decided to move south with his young family in 1857 he took a Noongar guide who showed him to the freshwater oasis at Ellensbrook, a traditional summer camping place.

Alfred and his family seem to have had a good relationship with local Noongar people and even to have relied heavily on each other. Noongars lived with the Bussells at Ellensbrook and worked on the property, clearing and farming. When two small daughters were lost in the bush for days it was a Noongar boy who found them and saved their lives. Noongar Sam Issacs saved many lives in 1865 when the *Georgette* foundered off Redgate Beach and he galloped for help, finding Alfred and Ellen's daughter Grace. Both were awarded medals from the Royal Humane Society. NgILGI was abandoned at the property as a baby and was brought up and educated with the Bussell children. The family lived at Ellensbrook until 1865, when Alfred built a grander property, Wallcliffe near the Margaret River mouth. Ellensbrook was run by several daughters but Edith looked after it the longest and turned it into a home for destitute Aboriginal children from the northwest, from 1899-1917. Descendants of the Bussells owned Ellensbrook until 1956.

a stream fed by a natural spring. It has been restored by the National Trust and is a fine example of a European pioneer house, built with local materials such as driftwood for beams and paperbark sheets for the roof. In the early days the Bussells established no more than subsistence farming but later had success with beef and dairy cattle. Ellensbrook is a wonderful place to spend a few hours; the immaculate lawn surrounded by trees is a fine picnic spot, there is a beach just down the road and a lovely short walk. The **Meekadarribee Trail** (1600-m loop) is a shady walk through forest, leading along the banks of Ellen Brook to a cave grotto and waterfall. Endangered black cockatoos are often seen by the water.

Prevelly and Gnarabup → *Colour map 3, B1. 9 km from Margaret River.*

Another coastal settlement spilling downhill among dense coastal tea tree, **Prevelly** is Margaret River's closest beach and where the legendary international surf competition, **Margaret River Pro**, is held in April.

Surfers Point, at the northern edge of Prevelly, is a powerful reef break and the surfers' car park there is a great place to watch the action on a big day. Around the corner is a perfect crescent of beach where the eucalypt green of Margaret River meets the aquamarine of the Indian ocean and the only sign of civilization is a small car park. In front of Prevelly itself the beaches are hidden by high sand dunes. At the southern end is

Gnarabup Beach where a humble but picturesque café perches above the water. This is also the site of obtrusive high-density modern housing, a controversial development that goes to the heart of the future of the Capes region. Facilities at Prevelly and Gnarabup are limited to a café and general store.

Southern Margaret River wine area → See map, page 163, for locations.

The small but select number of wineries around Margaret River itself mostly lie along or just off Boodijup Road, the turn-off to which is just south of town.

Leeuwin Estate ① *Stevens Rd, T9759 0000, www.leeuwinestate.com.au, cellar door 1000-1630, tours 1100, 1200 and 1500, restaurant open daily for lunch and Sat for dinner,* may not be the oldest winery in the region, but is the best known. Apart from a stylish restaurant, excellent wines and fascinating art gallery, the key feature is the gently sloping lawned amphitheatre. Here they host the **Leeuwin Concert Series** every February, a few days of mostly classical performances that are the southwest's premier event. Book well ahead for tickets ($100 plus) and accommodation. Wines cost $22-100.

Minot ① *off Exmoor Drive, opposite the Eagles Heritage Centre, T9757 3579, www.minot wines.com.au,* 'cellar door' is simply a modest table outside the owners' bungalow home. They produce a light, refreshing Semillon Sauvignon Blanc, and a rich, velvety Cabernet that is well worth going out of the way for. Call ahead. **Redgate** ① *Boodijup Rd, T9757 6488, www.redgatewines.com.au, 1000-1700,* is nothing fancy but its range of reds and whites is well respected, and it welcomes picnickers. Wines cost $19-40.

If you want a slightly different winery experience, head to **Swallows Welcome** ① *Wickham Rd (unsealed), T9757 6348, 1100-1700,* a few kilometres east of this core group on the other side of the Bussell Highway. Here Tim Negus will offer you tastings of his wines and you can visit Patricia Negus' studio, her botanical paintings are fantastic. Call ahead. **Voyager** ① *T9757 6354, www.voyagerestate.com.au, 1000-1700, tours ($25) on Tue and Sun 1100,* is arguably the most scenic winery in the region. Landscaped rose gardens and white-washed walls surround a gleaming white Cape Dutch-style cellar door and restaurant. Both wines and the expensive cuisine are multi-award winning. Restaurant open daily 1000-1630. Both it and **Leeuwin** are well signposted a little way past Exmoor Drive. Wines cost $20-60. It also offers grape juice, good for those who are driving.

Xanadu ① *T9758 9520, www.xanaduwines.com, 1000-1700, tapas from 1000, meals 1200-1600 and on Sat 1700-2100,* is first on the right, after about 4 km. Everything about this place is smart and savvy, but casual. The three ranges of wines hit both palate and wallet in the right place and the mid-range meals, served inside the huge, heavy beamed and earthy building, or in the large grassy courtyard, are the equal of those you'll get at much pricier establishments (three courses for $65). Children also have an outdoor playground and indoor games. Wines cost $18-80. Recommended.

If all that wine has been a bit much, visit **Yahava Koffee Works** ① *corner Bussell Highway and Rosa Brook Rd, T9757 2900, www.yahava.com.au, daily 0900-1700, tastings 0900-1630,* which is not far from Swallows Welcome. Yahava import, blend and roast about a dozen coffees.

Eagles Heritage Centre

① *Boodijup Rd, T9757 2960, www.eaglesheritage.com.au, Sep-May 1000-1700, Jun-Aug 1000-1600, flying displays 1100 and 1330 (1 hr), $12, children $6, concessions $10.*

Dedicated to rescuing and rehabilitating birds of prey, this is currently the only wildlife park of its kind in Australia. Those fully rehabilitated are released back into the wild, those permanently damaged, either physically or psychologically, are cared for at the centre for the rest of their lives. Incredibly, many of the beautiful birds brought in have been deliberately harmed, shot or poisoned. In every state except NT it is actually possible to obtain a licence to shoot wedge-tailed eagles. These are Australia's largest bird of prey and down to less than 10,000 breeding pairs after decades of deliberate, government-sponsored persecution, the result of an erroneous belief that they prey on sheep. A century ago there were around a million pairs and the birds were a major factor in keeping down populations of feral mammals, they are now listed as endangered. Although you can stroll around the aviaries, try to time a visit for one of the wonderful flying displays.

Cape-to-Cape Walk Track (4)

The fourth section of track from **Redgate to Hamelin Bay** (29 km) is one of the best because it offers a lot of variety and traverses a wide section of the Leeuwin-Naturaliste Park so feels much more remote than the last section. If you're walking south it also has the advantage of finishing at Hamelin Bay where there are the comforts of a caravan park (T9758 5540), shop and stunning swimming beach. Following the coast closely from **Redgate**, the section from the cliff and caves of **Bob's Hollow** to **Conto's** is magnificent. You are close to the edge of high cliffs with excellent views back to Redgate and south to Cape Freycinet. When you reach Conto's there is a campground and you can also walk up to **Caveworks**, where you can explore Lake Cave and visit the café. After leaving Conto's the track passes through the beautiful karri trees of **Boranup Forest** for 8 km, before rejoining the beach for 5 km along sand to **Hamelin Bay**. Redgate to Conto's makes a spectacular short walk (8 km) but ideally with a pick-up at one end.

Caves Road to Augusta

→ *Cave Works 17 km from Margaret River.*

Boodijup Road comes out on Caves Road, 2 km north of the turning to **Redgate Beach**. This white-sand beach has many offshore reefs creating rock pools suitable for swimming and snorkelling. Thanks to its isolation and lack of facilities it's also one of the quietest of those accessible by sealed road. It was the scene of a dramatic rescue in 1865 when Grace Bussell and Sam Issacs rode a line out to the *Georgette*, a ship in severe distress in heavy surf, and rescued every one of those still aboard. Three km south of the turn-off Caves Road passes **Calgardup Cave** ① *T9757 7422, 0900-1615, self-guided, allow 1 hr, $15, children $8*, the first of a series of caves for which the road was named. There are 300 known caves in the region, riddling the limestone base like holes in cheese, but less than a dozen are open to the public. If you want to visit the three main caves (Mammoth, Lake and Jewel) you can buy a Grand Tour Pass for $48, children $22, and it is valid for seven days. Alternatively, you can splash out on an Ultimate Pass for another $7, which also includes entry to the lighthouse. Calgardup, managed by DEC, is a relatively shallow cave and so easily accessed with all routes inside via boardwalks. It has an array of coloured decorations, a lake and a stream. Just around the corner is **Mammoth Cave** ① *T9757 7411, 0900-1700 (last entry 1600), allow 45 mins, $20, children $10*, one of several managed by the **Augusta Margaret River Tourism Association** (AMRTA). With a huge opening chamber the cave was a long-standing shelter for Aboriginal tribes and many species of animals. Over 10,000 fossil fragments have been found here, including bones from several extinct animals. Not the most spectacular of caves, entry is self-guided via boardwalks, includes a personal audio, and some of the cave is accessible to wheelchairs.

Some 3 km south of Mammoth is a right turn into Conto Road. This is sealed the short distance to **Cave Works** ⓘ *T9757 7411, www.margaretriver.com, 0900-1700, free with any AMRTA cave ticket, otherwise $2,* the local cave interpretation centre. The displays describe the geology of the region and how the caves formed, the fossils found in the caves and the scant life that still occupies them, and has a mock-up of a small cave. Cave Works is also the entry point for **Lake Cave** ⓘ *entry by tour, on the ½ hr 0930-1530, allow 1 hr, $20, children $10,* a relatively small but beautiful chamber whose entire floor is covered by a shallow lake. Due to its depth most of the decorations are almost pure white. An unusual feature is the 'suspended table', a section of horizontal flowstone that has had its foundation washed away and hangs just above the lake, held by two 2-m columns. Access is via 300-odd steps.

Conto Road becomes unsealed after Cave Works and heads 3 km down to **Conto's Beach** and the bush campground of **Conto's Field**, the closest such campsite to a beach in the region. It is a stunning piece of coast and you are unlikely to have to share it with anyone if you explore a bit. Back on Caves Road, 2 km south of Conto's Road, is **Giants Cave** ⓘ *T9757 7422, 0930-1530 during school and public holidays, self-guided, allow 1 hr, $15, children $8,* another self-guided cave (you can explore for as long as you like) with a series of massive chambers. This is one of the more adventurous with several ladders and some scrambling required – wear stout shoes.

Just south of Giants Cave is the start of an unsealed scenic drive that runs parallel to Caves Road for 14 km. It winds through the heart of the **Boranup Forest** ⓘ *T9757 2322, camping $7, children $2, facilities include toilets, picnic tables, fireplaces and wood,* a large area of karri forest that was clear-felled in the 1800s and has been allowed to grow back naturally. Though no really massive trees remain the regrowth is impressive and the drive is worth the extra 15 minutes it takes. Towards the far end is a lookout over the forest to the plains beyond, and a bush campground. If, instead of hitting the dirt, you stick to the bitumen you will pass **Boranup Gallery** ⓘ *www.boranupgallery.com, 0930-1700,* almost immediately on the left, the best general gallery for both art and woodwork in the region. It is an impressive showcase for the beauty of West Australian hardwoods and the skill of local craftspeople.

The quickest route to Augusta from this area is to head for **Karridale** and then south. There are a handful of services at Karridale, including the last fuel before Nannup some 75 km away, plus **Fox Studio Glass**, about 200 m down the road east to Nannup. It is a small gallery of the work of Alan Fox, a master glass artist who has been refining his skills for almost 30 years (he reckons on 20 years' practice just to become competent in glass blowing). The longer route, continuing on Caves Road, heads past the turning for Hamelin Bay, and then passes Jewel Cave.

Hamelin Bay, 40 km from Margaret River, 20 km from Augusta, is a long beach suitable for 4WD vehicles, it has a boat ramp and extensive caravan park, and is accessible via sealed road. This generally makes it the busiest of beaches south of Margaret River. However, it's also the best place to see the **stingrays** that will often come in for a feed. A small colony of them practically live around the boat jetty and can easily be enticed in with a small amount of fish bait. The **caravan park** (T9758 5540, **D**) has on-site vans, cottages and cabins, and a small, scantily-stocked shop (larger range of good during peak times).

South of the bay, 9 km by partially unsealed road and 5 km via the Cape-to-Cape Track, are a couple of the most beautiful beaches in this part of the world. **Cosy Corner** is a 2-km-wide bay sheltered by a series of off-shore rocks and reefs. The near part of the bay is a long, wide beach of the finest white sand, sloping off into a maze of seaweed-covered reefs and deep sandy troughs. Further around a long rocky shelf sits at the base of the high dunes that surround the bay. This shelf is punctuated by holes that become a series of spectacular blowholes during heavy seas. Thanks to its lack of facilities and unsealed access, Cosy Corner and its smaller adjacent bays can be virtually deserted even when Hamelin Bay is heaving.

Jewel Cave ① *T9757 7411, entry by tour, every hour 0930-1530, allow 1 hr, $20, children $10*, is 9 km from Augusta. If you only see one cave, make it this one. It is the largest and one of the deepest open to the public. The decorations are fantastic, especially the helictites and straws. There is also a good short walk through karri trees.

Cape-to-Cape Walk Track (5)

The last section from **Hamelin Bay to Cape Leeuwin** (29 km) is one of the wildest and most remote. There is a caravan park at the start but no other settlements along the route. Starting at Hamelin Bay the trail follows the beach before climbing up to the headland and Foul Bay Lighthouse, then dropping to the idyllic Cosy Corner beach. This section from Hamelin Bay to Cosy Corner makes a wonderful **day walk** (6.5 km one way). Following the coast past the blowholes and Cape Hamelin, the track then traverses a long and utterly lonely beach before heading uphill closer to the cape and reaching good lookouts. From Skippy Rock it is a short walk over rocks, beach and bush to the waterwheel at Cape Leeuwin. This section (3 km) passes some interesting 'gour' pools, layers of scalloped stone, and is a pleasant **short walk** to do from Augusta. If you've walked the whole Cape-to-Cape track hobble immediately to the Augusta pub (8 km) or persuade someone to give you a lift. Unfortunately there is no public phone at the Cape. Alternatively use the phone at Hamelin Bay to book accommodation in Augusta and ask to be picked up.

Augusta → *For listings, see pages 176-184. Colour map 3, B1.*

→ *Population: 1500. 90 km from Nannup, 125 km from Pemberton.*

Augusta hugs the west bank of the **Blackwood River** mouth, the region's largest river, and continues a little way down the eastern side of Cape Leeuwin. The town claims to be one of Western Australia's first settlements, but in fact almost all the original 1830 settlers, including the industrious Bussells, had cleared out by 1840 leaving the place to the sealers and whalers. It only got going again in the 1860s. The town's interesting history is illustrated by the many exhibits and photographs in the **Augusta Historical Museum** ① *Blackwood Av, T9758 0465, Sep-Apr 1000-1200, 1400-1600 and May-Aug 1000-1200, $3, seniors $2, children 13-16 years $1.50, children under 12 $0.50*, including a fascinating section on the mass strandings of whales that happened here. In May 1986, 114 false killer whales beached themselves just outside the river mouth and hundreds of volunteers succeeded in rescuing 96 of them. This is thought to be the most successful large-scale rescue of its kind to have happened anywhere.

Although it has most services, including an ATM, Augusta has a friendly, small-town feel. The main street is on a rise above the riverbank, looking down on the town jetty, though a better spot to sit and gaze about the river is actually a few hundred metres further south at Turner Street Jetty where **stingrays** will sometimes come in to feed if a little bait is dropped in the water, and pelicans and seagulls will already be waiting. The grassy foreshore has picnic tables, and an excellent café and takeaway are just across the road. The best spots for a swim at any time of year are 2 km south of town at **Flinders Bay**

Settlement. By the jetty is popular, though nearby **Granny's Pool**, a shallow area enclosed by rocks, is safer still. The helpful **VIC** ① *T9758 0166, www.margaretriver.com, daily 0900-1700*, is at the far end of the main shopping drag

Cape Leeuwin ▸ *Colour map 3, B1.*

Most of Cape Leeuwin, the southern end of the capes' low coastal hill range, is part of the national park and so free of development. The cape marks the geographical point at which the Southern and Indian Oceans meet, though there is seldom any physical sign of meeting currents. As the most southwestern point of the Australian mainland, it was often the only part of Australia ships saw (and still see) before reaching their final port, making the many offshore reefs and rocks a huge danger to shipping.

The kilometre-long promontory at the end of the cape was long seen as an ideal place for a **lighthouse** ① *T9758 1920, daily 0845-1645, ground fee $5, children $3, lighthouse tours every 40 mins 0900-1620, $15, children $7, 8 km from Augusta, may not run if very windy, phone first to check*, though interstate financial arguments delayed building until the 1880s. The still-functioning lighthouse is the fourth tallest in the country yet, as a guided tour reveals, after it was built the reefs still proved dangerous. Just two years before the sinking of *Titanic* the White Star Line lost another liner, the *Pericles*, here in almost dead calm seas, possibly because the skipper was trying to cut the corner. Luckily good weather and sufficient lifeboats enabled all the 463 souls aboard to get safely to shore. There is not a great deal to see on the tour except the excellent views from the top, but the guides' plentiful tales make it well worth the trip. There is also a café here that bills itself as the "last eating house before the Antarctic" and offers teas, coffees and light snacks. Still on the promontory shore, though outside the lighthouse precinct, is the 100-year-old **waterwheel** that used to supply the keepers' cottages with fresh water. Now partly calcified and covered in moss, it is a favourite spot for local photographers. For an excellent view over the entire promontory take the unsealed scenic drive 1 km before the waterwheel car park. The main lookout is about 1 km along this road on the left.

◉ Cape to Cape listings

For Sleeping and Eating price codes and other relevant information, see pages 28-34.

● Sleeping

Cape Naturaliste *p161, map p163*
L-D Wise, Eagle Bay Rd, Eagle Bay, T9756 8627, www.wisewine.com.au. This winery has 4 lovely self-contained chalets that are very good value, especially the romantic (**D**) 'Dolls House' for 2. All have outdoor dining tables and pot belly stoves or fireplaces for winter, linen provided. Good restaurant.

Yallingup and around *p163, map p163*
Coastal prices soar in the peak Dec-Jan period when even an unpowered tent site will set you back over $40. In terms of luxury accommodation, there are a couple of treats in store. If you want to stay in Yallingup for a week or more try the local real estate agent for a huge range of holiday home rentals.
LL-L Cape Lodge, 3341 Caves Rd, T9755 6311, www.capelodge.com.au. Cape-style boutique hotel with beautiful grounds, within which are discreetly placed half a dozen garden and lake suites. Rooms are contemporary and comfortable, the friendly

service cannot be faulted, and the small conservatory restaurant simply enhances the experience. There is a cooking school as well, which welcomes beginners and experienced chefs, lessons are 3 hrs and are rounded off with a 5-course meal in the restaurant.

LL-L Empire Retreat, Caves Rd, Yallingup, T9755 2065, www.empireretreat.com. Private and luxurious resort in bushland. 10 suites are decorated in sumptuous contemporary style with Indonesian and Japanese influences (and if you like it you can buy it!). Most with spa and balcony. There's also a guest lounge, kitchen, BBQ, spa and plenty of bushwalks.

LL-L Windmills Break, 2024 Caves Rd, T9755 2341, www.windmillsbreak.com.au. A relaxing choice, isolated but near enough to Dunsborough by taxi. There is a gym, swimming pool, tennis court and a bar to keep guests occupied, as well as a huge DVD library. Rooms are tastefully decorated and the service is excellent. There is no restaurant on site but the bar offers snacks and platters until 2000.

L Erravilla, Blythe Rd, T9755 1008, www.erra villa.com. Peaceful mansion in 54 ha of bush with 6 spa suites. Each room is spacious and decorated in earth tones with fine textiles and furniture. Warm hospitality, excellent, personal service and a good location close to major wineries and beaches. Substantial healthy gourmet breakfast included.

L-A Rivendell Winery, T9755 2090, www.rivendellwines.com.au. Accommodation in a large self-contained log chalet sleeping up to 20. Minimum 2 nights and 6 people. Also offers self-contained villas, minimum stay 3 nights (7 nights during high season).

L-B Wildwood Valley, Wildwood Rd, T9755 2120, www.wildwoodvalley.com.au. 5 comfortable B&B rooms, all with en suite or private bathroom. Extensive guest areas and facilities include a snooker room, outside BBQ area with pizza oven, gazebo, massage treatment room and laundry.

Full cooked and continental breakfast is included, and as both owners are chefs this is one of the highlights. Evening meals and cookery courses are also available. In addition to the B&B there is an apartment which sleeps 5, and 2 cottages. Honeybee is the smaller cottage (sleeps 2) and is delightful. It's nestled at the back of the property and offers a great deal of privacy, rates for this include a breakfast hamper. Recommended.

A Chandlers Smith Beach Villas, Smiths Beach, T9755 2062, www.chandlerssmiths beach.com.au. 3 widely separated tiers of rammed-earth-and-wood self-contained villas, all with views over Smiths Beach, a 5-min walk away. Each sleeps 4-6. Facilities include gas BBQs and laundry. Minimum stay of 2-4 days during high season school holidays.

A-C Canal Rocks Beach Resort, Smiths Beach, T9755 2116, www.canalrocks.com.au. Has 15 comfortable self-contained spa apartments including studios and 2- to 3-bedroom options. All have ocean views, share BBQs and it's a short walk to the beach.

A-D Yallingup Beach Holiday Park, T9755 2164, www.yallingupbeach.com.au. This holiday park has superb views, cabins, on-site vans, kiosk and grassy sites.

Northern Margaret River
wine area *p165, map p167*
There is less accommodation in the Willyabrup Valley area than around the town centres, but the area has the richest concentration of wineries and makes a very good base for exploring the whole region.

L-A Karriview Lodge, 66 Caves Rd, Cowaramup. T9755 5553, www.karrie view.com.au. Set in 48 acres of bush, the place has been designed to have the cosy feel of a ski lodge. 12 rooms decorated in individual country style. There is also a restaurant, tennis court, golf driving range, sauna and outdoor spa.

B-F Gracetown Caravan Park, corner Caves and Cowaramup Bay Rd, Gracetown, T9755

5301, www.gracetowncaravanpark.com.au. Has several spa and park chalets, on-site caravans and shady, powered sites. General facilities include campers' kitchen, gas and wood barbecues, children's playground, tennis, volleyball and basketball courts. No pets allowed. Wi-Fi available.

C Noble Grape, 29 Bussell Highway, Cowaramup, T9755 5538, www.noblegrape.com.au. 6 comfortable en suite rooms arranged around a pretty garden courtyard and decorated with florals and reproduction antiques. More character then usual. Buffet-style continental breakfast included.

C Tasty Olive B&B, North Treeton Rd, Cowaramup, T9755 5658, www.tasty olive.com.au. A welcoming Mediterranean-style B&B surrounded by olive trees. 2 double rooms and 1 twin bedroom that shares a bathroom with one of the doubles. The guest lounge has a TV and wood fire. A complimentary platter of home-grown olives on arrival. Continental breakfast or a cooked one on request. Very good value. Recommended.

C-D Taunton Farm Caravan Park, Bussell Highway, Cowaramup, T9755 5334 and T1800 248777, www.tauntonfarm.com.au. A friendly place with a few spacious, well-priced cottages alongside the shady, lawned sites. A Big4 but still a working dairy and sheep farm, the campground is far enough from the highway that the only sound you'll hear is mooing. Recommended.

Margaret River and around
p169, map p170

L-B Margaret River Resort, 40 Wallcliffe Rd, T1800 686356, www.mrresort.com.au. Various types of accommodation ranging from spacious self-contained villas and 1-bed spa suites to hotel rooms in classical English style. Facilities include an on-site restaurant, pub, tennis court, children's playground and a resort pool centre with sauna. There is also a wine centre here.

L-C Riverglen Chalets, corner of Bussell Highway and Carters Rd, T9757 2101,

www.riverglenchalets.com.au. Spacious timber chalets in a beautifully landscaped bush setting a short walk from town. Some chalets sleep 8, some have spa and woodfire. All have kitchen, balcony, BBQ. Linen included.

A-B Bridgefield, 73 Bussell Highway, T9757 3007, www.bridgefield.com.au. Lovely National Trust listed guesthouse close to the river with 5 jarrah-lined traditional rooms, brass beds and antiques. At the back of the house are an additional 3 rooms in a more modern setting. Warm hospitality and excellent continental breakfast prepared by a French chef who runs **Nathalie's Cuisine** next door. The only flaw is traffic noise, mostly during the day. Excellent value.

A-B Margaret River Guest House, 22 Valley Rd, T9757 2349, www.margaretriverguest house.com.au. A former convent in a quiet side street with a beautiful English garden, this B&B has 7 comfortable rooms, some opening onto the veranda. The full gourmet breakfast is something of an event and you may not need to eat again for days. There is also a freshly baked cake every day to welcome you back from your day of sightseeing or touring. Off-road parking available.

A-B Vintages, corner of Willmott Av and Le Souef St, T9758 8333, www.vintagesmargaret river.com.au. A cross between a hotel and a guesthouse. 12 en suite rooms, one with disabled facilities, all opening onto a large outdoor courtyard or a balcony. If guests stay 3 nights they're treated to a complimentary trip to a winery in a 1956 Chevy. Bike hire available and a continental breakfast can be requested.

B-E Riverview Tourist Park, 8 Willmott Av, T9757 2270, www.riverviewtouristpark.com. The nearest caravan park to town. Range of cabins but only the most expensive ones have cooking facilities and views of the river.

C-E Surf Point Resort, Riedle Dr, Gnarabup Beach, T9757 1777, www.surfpoint.com.au. Has a luxurious 'hostel' section, which has backpacker accommodation with dining and cooking facilities and chic TV room. It also has good-value en suite doubles. Bike and boogie board hire. Watch out for extras like DVDs, swimming pool and internet.

C-F Prevelly Park Beach Resort, 99 Mitchell Dr, Prevelly Beach, T9757 2374. The nearest campsite to the beach offering cabins and tent sites, and with a shop and a restaurant next door. You'll still need to walk a fair way or jump in a car to reach the water though.

D-E Margaret River Lodge YHA, 220 Railway Terr, T9757 9532, www.mrlodge. com.au. Backpackers in quiet bush location about 2 km from town centre. This place also has a good vibe and lots of ideas and activities. Rammed-earth buildings, pool, BBQs and bike hire. Pick-ups from coach stop. Also has a bar and internet access.

D-F InneTown Backpackers, 93 Bussell Highway, T9757 3698, T0488 135290, www.mronline.com.au/accom/innetown. Small hostel that has the major advantage of being in the centre of town at the end of the main street. Dorms and doubles, mountain bike hire, free tea/coffee, BBQ and internet. Hard-working managers; good atmosphere.

E Margaret River Backpackers, 66 Townview Terr, T9757 9572, www.margaretriverback packers.com.au. Owned by the same people as **Margaret River Lodge**, this is their town centre operation with dorms of varying sizes (including a female-only one). It may be lacking in character but has impressive communal spaces including a large lounge area and outside deck.

Augusta p175

LL-L Blackwood River Houseboats, T9758 0181, www.blackwoodriverhouse boats.com.au. A choice of 3 boats, from small (4-6 berth) to large (8-10 berth). This is an expensive option for 2 people, but great if you can persuade some friends to come along. Spacious and with shade, float down the Blackwood River and do some fishing. 1-hr training session before you're let loose.

A-B Augusta Sheoak Chalets, Hillview Rd, T9758 1958, www.sheoakchalets.com.au.

Well-appointed wooden chalets in a quiet inland spot. Sleeping 2, 8 or 16, the chalets have wonderful views across pasture and forest to the Blackwood River. Each chalet has a fully equipped kitchen, TV, laundry facilities and BBQ.

B-E Augusta Hotel Motel, Blackwood Av, T9758 1944, www.augusta-resorts.com.au. Resort-style pub hotel with a large rear lounge bar, terrace and tiered beer garden with sweeping views across a couple of paddocks to the river and beyond. Over 50 motel rooms, a couple of self-contained 2-bedroom cottages, and a newly refurbished backpackers lodge that sleeps 19. Counter meals are available every day, plus a mid-range restaurant in summer.

D-E Flinders Bay Caravan Park, Albant Terrace, T9758 1380, www.flindersbay park.com.au. Out towards the lighthouse, this caravan park is on the beachfront. On-site vans and powered and unpowered sites.

D-E Westbay Retreat Caravan Park, T9758 1572. Powered and unpowered sites, plus the most stylish toilet block you're ever likely to see.

D-F Baywatch Manor YHA, Heppingstone View, T9758 1290, www.baywatchmanor. com.au. A clean, friendly, purpose-built hostel built on the lines of a large house. Most of the 36 beds are in comfortable singles, twins and doubles. 2 rooms are en suite (**D**) and have good views. There are 2 small single-sex dorms with dorms and single beds. Linen included. Communal facilities are excellent, including 24-hr internet access, a garden, and upstairs balcony with extensive views. Bikes are also available to borrow.

E Turner Caravan Park, 1 Blackwood Av, T9758 1593, www.turnerpark.com.au. Close to both the river and the ocean, and has a boat ramp, campers' kitchen, BBQ and laundry facilities. Unpowered and powered sites but no chalets or cabins. A good place to watch the pelicans, fish or feed the stingrays.

● Eating

Cape Naturaliste *p161, map p163*
▐▐▐ Wise, Eagle Bay Rd, Eagle Bay, T9755 3331, www.wisewine.com. Modern Australian cuisine, breakfast and lunch daily from 0900, dinner Fri-Sat from 1800. The only winery in the southwest with ocean views, though a distant backdrop to vines and forest. A beautiful restaurant with outdoor terrace has been built to fully appreciate it. Book at weekends or for a balcony table. The cellar door (open 1000-1700) offers a range of crisp, fruity whites and spicy reds, priced from $14-55. Also offers accommodation, see Sleeping.
▐ Bunkers Beach Café, Farm Break Lane, Bunker Bay, T9756 8284, www.bunkersbeach cafe.com.au. Open 0900-1700, shorter hours in winter. A beachfront licensed café with a casual atmosphere, but don't let that fool you as the food here is not your usual café fare. Open for breakfast and lunch, Bunkers serves up fresh, local seafood, Margaret River venison and Yallingup Marron. Breakfast can be a traditional fry up, bubble and squeak or parmesan polenta.

Yallingup and around *p163, map p163*
See also the wineries, pages 165-168.
▐▐▐ Lamont's, next to Gunyulgup Gallery, T9755 2434. Thu-Mon 1130-1700, dinner on Sat. The food here is some of the best in the region. An open modern space and tables on a deck overlooking a lake. Fusion food using fresh, seasonal ingredients. Recommended.

Northern Margaret River wine area *p165*
See also the wineries on pages 165-168, and Shopping, below, for other foodie treats.
▐ Bay Café, 4 Bayview Dr, Gracetown, T9755 5000. Daily for breakfast and lunch. A casual restaurant with bay views and a shady outdoor terrace. Uncomplicated food such as salads, pasta, fish and steak.

▐ Udderly Divine, 22 Bussell Highway, Cowaramup, T9755 5519. Mon-Fri 0830-1630, Sat to 1600, Sun 0900-1600. A small café with a few pleasant outdoor tables serving good coffee, teas, smoothies and a selection of tasty, light meals. Generous servings and friendly service. Recommended.

Margaret River and around
p169, map p170
See also Bars and clubs, below.
▐▐▐ Must, 107 Bussell Highway, T9758 8877, www.must.com.au. Daily 1200-late. A stylish place with an interesting menu that changes regularly. There are lunch deals of 2 and 3 courses, as well as cocktails and an extensive wine list. Also arranges nights such as 'Ransack the Cellar Tuesdays'. Warm, unstuffy service and original contemporary decor.
▐▐▐-▐▐ Arc of Iris, 151 Bussell Highway, T9757 3112. Tue-Sun from 1800. This retro-style bistro is a long-standing locals' favourite for tasty, interesting and good-value food. BYO only.
▐▐▐-▐ MRH Bistro & Bar, Margaret River Hotel (see Bars and clubs), T9757 2655, www.margaretriverhotel.com.au. Sun-Thu 1730-2030, Fri-Sat 1700-2100. A sophisticated bistro with a large outdoor courtyard serving wood-fired pizzas, a mix of grills, seafood, 'Mediterrasian' dishes.
▐▐▐-▐ Goodfellas, 97 Bussell Highway, T9757 3184. Mon-Fri 1730-2030 (1600 for takeaway), Sat-Sun 1200-2030. Lively pizza-and-pasta restaurant with an upstairs balcony.
▐ Margaret River Fish & Chips, Town Square, T9757 3808. Mon-Thu 1700-2030, Fri-Sat 1200-2100, Sun 1200-2030. Set back from the street in Town Sq, this is a top-quality fish and chip joint.
▐ Sea Gardens, Prevelly Park, T9757 3074, www.seagardens.com.au. Get away from Margaret River and come here for breakfast lunch or dinner. Think smoked salmon bagels, chilli mussels and pizza (which can also be ordered to take away).

Cafés

Margaret River Bakery, 89 Bussell Highway, T9757 2755. A popular place serving filling food, with a terrace tucked away from the road.

Urban Bean, 157 Bussell Highway, T9757 3480. Daily 0700-1700. Deservedly popular, the outdoor terrace is always filled with people watching the street action. The casual café serves great coffee, cakes, sandwiches and salads from the counter. Also sells a range of local produce.

Wild Thyme Gourmet, 72 Wilmott Av, T9757 2237. Mon-Fri 0730-1530, Sat 0800-1530. Interesting healthy and veggie meals, as well as pancakes or sausage rolls. Breakfast, wraps, curries and smoothies. Takeaway available.

Augusta *p175*

♥ **Colourpatch**, Albany Terr, T9758 1295. Café open daily 0900-1700, takeaway daily 0900-1900. A short distance from the town centre, this is a simple, cheerful place with a terrace overlooking the river. BYO. Also has a fish and chip shop section and does takeaways.

♥ **Deckchair Gourmet**, Blackwood Av, T9758 0700. Serves up coffee, cakes and deli dishes. Wi-Fi is available. Also offers accommodation.

🕎 Bars and clubs

Willyabrup Valley *p166*

Bootleg Brewery, Puzey Rd, at the northern tip of the area, just off Johnson Rd, T9755 6300, www.bootlegbrewery.com.au. Daily 1100-1630, wholesome lunches 1200-1500. The European-style beers include brown ale, wheat beer, pilsner and a more Australian light. They are available for tasting at the large bar, and for purchase by the glass or large stubby. A large beer garden is a pleasant spot to quaff a beer, particularly on a Sat when a band gets going and the place stays open to 1800. There is also a playground for the kids.

Margaret River and around
p169, map p170

Margaret River Hotel, Bussell Highway, T9757 2655, www.margaretriverhotel. com.au. Daily 1200-late, Thu-Sun live music. A classy and civilized pub with lots of outdoor terrace tables. There are also some pleasant holiday suites and hotel rooms upstairs (all en suites) but these can be noisy (**B-C**).

Settlers Tavern, 114 Bussell Highway, T9757 2398. Mon-Sat 1200-2400, Sun 1200-2200. A traditional Aussie pub with no frills. A spacious beer garden on the streetfront, pool tables, TVs and TAB. A refuge for those who dislike the town's increasing yuppieness, it's also a busy live music venue Wed-Sun, see blackboards for current programme, and Mon is karaoke night. They do good food here too.

Wino's, 85 Bussell Highway, T9758 7155. Daily 1500-late. Hip wine bar full of understated art. It's not snooty though – the emphasis is on having fun with wine and food and the staff are very friendly and knowledgeable. Huge range of local wines by the glass and a 'grits' menu, lots of small $5 nibble dishes, so you can eat as much as you wish. Also mezze-style mains for sharing.

🔺 Activities and tours

Margaret River and around
p169, map p170
Adventure sports

Outdoor Discoveries, T0407 084945, www.outdoordiscoveries.com.au. Different sorts of adventure activities for groups, including abseiling, caving and climbing. All the equipments is provided.

Brewery tour

Taste the South, T0438 210373, www.tastethesouth.com.au. For those who don't like wine or have tried enough for one trip, Siegbert and Sabine Schaaf offer a brewery tour. Visit 4-5 microbreweries for tastings, price includes lunch and transfers. $130 for one person or $125 for 2. German

The curious cape cruisers

Humpback and southern right whales cruise past the capes during their yearly migration north from Antarctica. They hang about Cape Leeuwin from around June to August, then head up the coast, coming close to shore at Gracetown and Sugarloaf, before spending another three months or so around Cape Naturaliste. There are whale-watching boat tours from Augusta (June to September) and Dunsborough (September to December), which often get very close to the whales due to their great curiosity. If you can pick your time then head south, as during this period the humpbacks are particularly active, often breaching, spy-hopping and waving to tourists.

and English spoken. See also Dunsborough Activities and tours (page 160).

Canoeing

Bushtucker Tours, T9757 9084, www. bushtuckertours.com. Runs one of the most interesting and fun tours in the southwest. The 4-hr trip ($85, children $40), which leaves the river mouth daily at 1000, takes in a bit of a paddle, a short bushwalk, a cave tour and a bushtucker picnic. The guides are bursting with information and the finale will leave you gasping. Bushtucker also run full-day wine tours (rounded off with a visit to a brewery), which maintain the high quality of the original ($85, children $40).

Family

Sunset Kangaroo Safari, T9757 2747, www.margaretriver-mcleodtours.com. Popular with Aussies and internationals alike, this is a kangaroo safari on the back of a 4WD Bedford Truck. Leaving 2½ hrs before sunset, the group go in search of western grey's, take some photographs and enjoy Billy tea and Neil's famous home-made orange cake. $45 and children $30. Also runs wine tours.

Kitesurfing

Margaret River Kitesurfing & Windsurfing, T0419 959053, www.mrkiteandsail.com.au. Hires and sells equipment. Kitesurfing lessons from $110 per hr (minimum 2 hrs) and windsurfing lessons from $75 per hr (minimum 2 hrs).

Mountain biking

Dirty Detours, T9758 8312, www.dirty detours.com. Mountain bike rides from beginner to advanced. Refreshments, bikes, helmets and gloves all supplied. Also offer a Sip 'n' Cycle ride, a winery tour with a difference. A wine specialist takes riders on a half-day tour round 4 or 5 wineries, lunching at the last stop. If participants buy wine en route the tour company or the winery will arrange to get it back to the accommodation. All tours $80. Longer rides, including of the Munda Biddi Trail, can be organized.

Surfing

Beach Life Surf Shop, 117 Bussell Highway, T9757 2888. Surfboard hire $40 per day, bodyboard $30 per day, snorkelling gear $15. Also book lessons here for **Margaret River Surf School**, T9757 1111, www.margaretriver surfschool.com. Group lessons $50 per person with equipment (2 hrs). A 3-day course costs $120 ($180 for couples or small groups. Drop in or phone the shop for local surf updates.
Margaret River Surf Shop, corner of Wallcliffe Rd and Resort Place, T9757 1111, T0427 572149.

Swimming

Margaret River Recreation and Aquatic Centre, T9780 5620. Pool open Mon-Thu 0545-1930, Fri 0545-1900, Sat-Sun 0900-1700. An 8-lane 25-m lap pool for those who want to work off some wine and chocolate calories. Also has a gym and group fitness classes.

Walking and cycling
A free brochure on walking and cycling trails is available at the VIC.

Wine tasting
There are a number of wine tasting tours, see the VIC for details of others.
Margaret River Tours, T0419 917166, www.margaretrivertours.com. Offers several half-day and day tours, all of the latter include lunch. Prices range from $70 to $160. Personalized tours for small groups (maximum 5 people) also available.
Wine for Dudes, T0427 774 994, www.winefordudes.com. A relaxed wine tasting option. The day tour ($80) is available 7 days a week, includes lunch and lets you create your own wine during the exclusive wine-blending session.

Augusta p175
Boat cruises/hire
Augusta Marine, T9758 0808, T0419 952038. Hires out a variety of motor boats.
Blackwood Explorer River Cruise, Miss Flinders Jetty, Ellis St, T0409 377809. Cruises Tue and Thu at 1000 ($40, children $20, concessions $30. Trips take 3 hrs and the price includes billy tea and damper. Book at the VIC or ring the number above.
Blackwood River Eco-Cruises, Miss Flinders Jetty, Ellis St, T9758 4003, T0419 759562. The Sea Dragon cruises daily at 1100 ($40, children $10). Trip takes 1½-2 hrs. Also hires out kayaks.

Golf
There is a 9-hole par-3 course on Allnutt Terr ($5, honesty box) or an 18-hole course on Hillview Rd ($15 for visitors).
Augusta X-Treme Outdoor Sports, Blackwood Av, T9758 0606. Hires out clubs for $15 a day.

Kayak hire
Kayaks are available for hire outside the Colourpatch Café (see Eating). $10 per hr; if there's no one there, pay in the café.

Scenic tours
Barry's Eco Scenic Tours, T9758 0946. Barry runs a variety of half- and full-day tours exploring the local area, $65-160. Augusta based but pick-ups from Margaret River can be arranged. Rates including morning or afternoon tea, or both.

Whale watching
Naturaliste Charters, T9725 8511, www.whalesaustralia.com. Head out daily at 1000 and 1400, Jun-Dec, and see whales almost every day (2-3 hrs, $75, children $35, concessions $65), light refreshments included. Do not miss this tour if there are whales around.

O Shopping

Northern Margaret River
wine area p165
Candy Cow, corner of Bussell Highway and Bottrill St, Cowaramup, T9755 9155, www.candycow.com.au. Daily 1000-1700. Fine fudges, nougat and boiled lollies (sweets). There is a window from the shop into the kitchen.
Margaret River Cheese Company, Fonti Farm Bussell Highway, Cowaramup, T9755 5400, at the end of Harmons Mill Rd. Daily 0930-1700. Here, the best-known dairy in WA produces a range of rich cheeses, yoghurts, and ice cream. This is just a sales outlet but there is a window that allows you to see the action in the dairy.
Margaret Riviera, Bottrill St, Cowaramup, T9755 9333, www.margaretriviera.com.au. Located next door to the Candy Cow, this friendly gourmet shop offers a good range of organic, local deli products.

Margaret River and around
p169, map p170

There are a number of clothes shops on the main street as well as some interesting small food outlets.

Down South Camping & Outdoors, 40 Station Rd, T9758 8966. Next door to the Margaret River Tourist Park, camping equipment but no hire.

Margaret River Book Exchange, Town Sq, Bussell Highway, T9758 8810. Mon-Fri 0930-1700, Sat 0900-1530, Sun 0900-1500. Second-hand books.

Margaret River Bookshop, 109 Bussell Highway, T9757 3331, www.margaretriver bookshop.com.au. Mon-Sat 0900-1800, Sun 1000-1700. A well laid-out independent bookshop selling new books and offering self-serve coffee and internet access.

⊖ Transport

Margaret River and around
p169, map p170

Bus TransWA northbound bus services leave from Charles West Rd Mon, Wed and Fri 0915, Tue, Thu and Sun 0905, Sun-Fri 1535. Services south depart Sun-Thu 1745, Sun-Fri 1405, Fri 0944. Some buses continue on to **Nannup** and **Pemberton**.

Taxi T9757 3444.

Augusta *p175*
Bus TransWA northbound bus services leave opposite the newsagents Mon, Wed and Fri 0830. Services to **Nannup** and **Pemberton** depart Sun-Thu 0615, Sun-Fri 1435 and Fri 2215.

❶ Directory

Margaret River *p169, map p170*
Banks Major bank branches and ATMs on Bussell Highway. **Internet** Cybercorner Café, off Willmott Av behind Wild Thyme Gourmet, T9757 9388. Mon-Fri 0800- 2000, Sat-Sun 0900-1700. A quiet and comfortable internet café with Wi-Fi access and terminals and cake. **Medical services** Margaret River Pharmacy, 146 Bussell Highway, T9757 2224. Daily 0800-1800. **Police** 20 Willmott Av, T9757 2222. **Post** Corner of Willmott Av and Town View Terr. **Useful addresses** Margaret River Environment Centre, 50 Townview Terr, T9758 8078. Community centre where you can learn about local environmental issues.

Contents

Footprint features

Timber towns

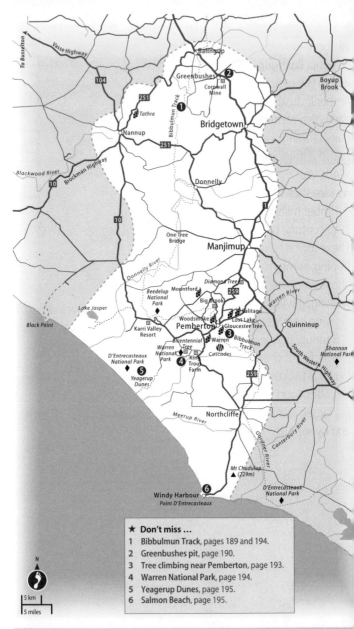

★ Don't miss ...
1 Bibbulmun Track, pages 189 and 194.
2 Greenbushes pit, page 190.
3 Tree climbing near Pemberton, page 193.
4 Warren National Park, page 194.
5 Yeagerup Dunes, page 195.
6 Salmon Beach, page 195.

In stark contrast to the red, barren earth of the north, this area is all about growth and forests of very tall trees. The timber towns of Nannup, Balingup, Bridgetown, Manjimup and Pemberton all sit within the region's vast expanse of forest and grew up when a timber industry developed in the southwest in the late 19th and early 20th centuries. Many areas were cleared and opened up for dairy farming and agriculture by the group settlers of the 1920s; British immigrants were persuaded to settle here after the First World War by promises of free land to farm. Most of them had no idea they would have to clear it first.

Timber mills provided work and prosperity for much of the 20th century, but the few mills left now operate on reduced hours. These towns have suffered in the last few decades and are now hoping, some reluctantly, that tourism will keep them alive. Those who visit these days will be able to enjoy magnificent walking, driving through tall karri forests and climbing to dizzying heights on a few of the giant fire-spotting trees.

Nannup, Bridgetown and Pemberton are the most attractive towns, full of characteristic timber workers' cottages or restored heritage buildings. They are still small and fairly undeveloped, but offer good facilities in beautiful surroundings. Manjimup is a larger, less interesting place that has survived on agriculture and by supplying regional services.

Ins and outs

TransWA has daily bus services from Perth railway station (train to Bunbury then coach) to Balingup, Greenbushes, Bridgetown, and Manjimup that leave at 0930. On Monday, Tuesday, Thursday, Saturday and Sunday it also calls at Pemberton (5½ hours) and Northcliffe. Nannup is reached by a service between Pemberton and Augusta in the Capes region. During the week, **South West Coachlines** buses leave from the City Bus Port, Perth, and call at Balingup, Greenbushes, Bridgetown and Manjimup.

Nannup and around ⇤ *For listings, see pages 196-202.*

Nannup → *Colour map 3, B2. 60 km from Busselton, 90 km from Augusta. Population: 1200.*
A pretty, historic town by the banks of the Blackwood River, Nannup sits in an idyllic green valley surrounded by forest. The main street, Warren Street, is full of trees and timber cottages with bull-nosed tin verandas. Europeans settled here by the river, where they found a ford useful for travellers to rest and water their horses or bullocks. It is a sleepy and peaceful place to unwind but is likely to develop rapidly in the next few years when the Mowen road is sealed, providing a short cut to Margaret River. It is now a stop on the **Munda Biddi Trail**, www.mundabiddi.org.au, a cycle trail that may see more visitors passing through. Canoeing on the Blackwood or walking in the forest are the main things to do and there are a few excellent places to stay. The busiest time of year is during the **Nannup Music Festival**, held on the Labour Day weekend in early March. Nannup is also noted for its flowers, particularly in spring (August-September) when masses of tulips blossom and wildflowers carpet the forest.

One sight you won't see is the Nannup tiger. Some locals believe that *Thylacines*, better known as the extinct Tasmanian Tiger, live in the jarrah forest around Nannup. Needless to say there has been no proof of this but several businesses in town use the tiger as a logo. The town does have one old survivor though, one of the few timber mills still operating in the region, the **Nannup Timber Processing Mill**. There is a **Gemstone Museum** ⓘ *125 Warren Rd, T9756 1182, open daily but best to call ahead*, just north of the Mill, which holds a small amateur collection of rocks, gems, bottles and badges. It's really only for the dedicated rock hound. Gardeners will enjoy **Holberry House** ⓘ *14 Grange Rd, T9756 1276, www.holberryhouse.com, $4 per person*, whose garden is open to the public and offers abundant flora, birdlife and art. In the main shopping area on Warren Street there are a few antique and timber furniture shops.

Just outside the town centre are a few lovely spots for walking or camping in the forest. Cross the river, heading north, and take the first left into Mowen Road. In wildflower season turn left again into Barrabup Road to access the **Wildflower Drive**, a pretty short loop through forest, banksia, orchids and other wildflowers. Continue along Mowen Road and follow signs for **Barrabup** and **Workers Pools** (9 km from Nannup), tranquil emerald green swimming holes surrounded by forest. Each has campsites, picnic tables and BBQs. The **Timberline Walk Trail** links the two pools. Visit the **VIC** ⓘ *4 Brockman St, T9756 1211, www.nannupwa.com, 1000-1600*, for more walking suggestions. It is housed in the former police station at the northern end of town by the riverbank and bridge. On the Vasse Highway, 12 km north of Nannup is **Cambray Sheep Cheese** ⓘ *T9756 2037, www.cambray sheepcheese.com.au, daily 1000-1630*, where there are tastings of both hard and soft cheese (think Brie, Boursin, Feta and Manchego-style). If arranged in advance visitors can also come and see the sheep being milked, and there are two self-contained cottages on the property.

Routes from Nannup

Nannup sits on the confluence of several major roads and highways. The Vasse Highway runs directly from Busselton (see page 153) and the Brockman Highway from Augusta (see page 175) both in the Southwest. In addition to these the still partly unsealed Mowen Road comes almost directly from Margaret River. The Vasse continues south through the Karri Valley to **Pemberton** (75 km), though there is a slightly longer option via the much forested Brockman Highway, turning right at Sears Road through **Donnelly** and then **Manjimup** (85 km). The Brockman itself passes through a small stand of karri trees just after the turn, and then carries on to **Bridgetown** (45 km). The most scenic road north of the town is via the Blackwood Valley to **Balingup** (40 km). This valley, a patchwork of forest, plantations and pasture, is often quite steep-sided and the road hugs the river the entire way.

Donnelly → *Colour map 3, B2. 32 km from Nannup, 27 km from Manjimup.*

In the middle of extensive jarrah and karri forests, Donnelly is a timber milling town that closed down in the early 1970s. The 36 former workers' cottages, each with their own small garden and front veranda, are spaced evenly around a loop road in the forest and are now all available for holiday rental. Facilities are scant, the small shop doubling as reception and tearooms, but there are a few sporting activities available, including tennis and a flying fox. The real attraction is the forest itself, and the wildlife. For good or ill, emus and kangaroos have been hand fed over the years and are now more or less tame. Pellets can be bought from the shop, but even without them you are likely to have several guests in the garden. Birdlife is also prolific, particularly kookaburras, 28s (the green parrots with a yellow collar) and black cockatoos. **Donnelly River Holiday Village** ① *T9772 1244, www.donnellyriverholidayvillage.com.au, 0830-1700*, is where to go for bookings. Linen and towels not supplied. The Bibbulmun Track passes close to the village.

Bibbulmun Track → *See also pages 119, 194, 206 and 211.*

This is one of the most tranquil, appealing and easy sections of the 'Bibb'. Soon after leaving the quaint wooden houses of Donnelly, the track begins to follow the Donnelly River past its attractive falls, pools and log bridges. Further south, after leaving the Donnelly River Valley, the track passes through Beedelup National Park by Beedelup Falls, then the Big Brook Dam and Arboretum just before reaching Pemberton. This southern section can make a good two- to three-day walk: it is 11 km from Pemberton to **Pemberton Forest Stay** near the Big Brook Dam, and a further 13 km from here to the campsite in Beedelup National Park.

Balingup to Bridgetown ›› *For listings, see pages 196-202.*

Balingup → *Colour map 3, B2. Population: 442. 65 km from Bunbury, 26 km from Bridgetown.*

Not yet in the heart of the timber region, tiny Balingup is surrounded by hilly pastoral country. For those walking the **Bibbulmun Track**, which passes through the town, Balingup is a very welcome stop. There is not a great deal to do here but there are a lot of places to eat. The Packing Shed on the main street is a surprising sight, with the French patisserie (there's also a French restaurant in town) patrons sitting outside sipping their coffee, the fruit wine stand and other small and eclectic boutiques Have a look around the **Old Cheese Factory Art & Craft Centre** ① *Blackwood River Tourist Dr, T9764 1018, daily 0930-1630*, which claims to have the biggest collection of craft in Australia. The extensive premises are indeed full of a wide range of items, such as carved wombats – cute little momentos in various timbers costing $30-300. There is also a cheap café. The **VIC** ① *T9764 1818, www.balinguptourism.com.au, 1000-1600*, is just off the main street. Check here for details of walks around the town. There are good views over the pretty vale Balingup sits in from the top of the track leading to **Balingup Heights**, www.balingup heights.com.au.

Greenbushes → *Colour map 3, B3. 10 km from Balingup, 16 km from Bridgetown.*

With the distinct feel of a ghost town, there would be little reason to visit Greenbushes if it wasn't for the **Cornwall Mine**. This open-cast pit, dug to extract various metals including lithium, tin and tantalum, is over 300 m deep and a little over that across. There are good views of it from the lookout, open daily 0800-1700. The town also has an **Eco-cultural Discovery Centre** ① *T9764 3883, Wed, Fri, Sat and Sun 1000-1400, $5, children $2*, giving an overview of the environment in the southwest. It also has information on local bushwalks. If the Discovery Centre is closed, trail maps can be obtained from the **Community Resource Centre** or the **Exchange Hotel**.

Bridgetown → *Colour map 3, B3. Population: 4090. 46 km from Nannup, 37 km from Manjimup.*

A service town for the local agricultural area, Bridgetown nestles alongside the Blackwood River, and is not without its charms. The surrounding, sharply undulating hills, partly forested, are very scenic. During the second week of November major garden and blues festivals run nearly back-to-back here, and the rest of the time it's a nice relaxing spot to spend some time.

 Bridgedale House ① *T9761 1740, entrance fees may apply; run by volunteers and times may vary, so call the VIC for more information*, encapsulates the spirit of much of Bridgetown's history, and that of the timber region. It was the first house in the district, built in 1862 by John Blechynden who was shown the valley by local Aborigines, and enlarged over time. After almost being lost to the bulldozers in the 1960s it has been restored by the National Trust. Entry includes an informative tour of the house. Just over the bridge from the house is a riverside park, and adjacent to this the **Bridgetown Caravan Park**, which hires out canoes (see Sleeping, page 198). **Centenary Outdoor Pool** ① *corner of Steere and Gifford Sts, daily Nov-Easter, Mon-Fri 1000-1800, Sat-Sun 1100-1800. $3, children $1.70*, is a welcome spot on a hot day. The **VIC** ① *154 Hampton St, T9761 1740, www.bridgetown.com.au, Mon-Fri 0900-1700, Sat 0900-1500, Sun 0900-1300*, houses a small artefact museum and a collection of framed jigsaws (gold coin donation).

Manjimup and around ›› *For listings see pages 196-202. Colour map 3, B3.*

→ *Population: 5000. 120 km from Walpole, 160 km from Mt Barker.*

Manjimup is the major service town for the central timber region. The area has a fruit and vegetable industry, and grows tree seedlings and plantation trees such as Tasmanian blue gum for paper pulp. There is not much to interest travellers, but if you have the time and inclination a visit to the **Manjimup Regional Timber Park** ① *corner of Rose and Edwards Sts, 0900-1700*, can be interesting. There is an Age of Steam museum, timber museum, historic hamlet, lookout tower, pleasant grounds and a good café. Wood turning demonstrations take place on Wednesdays and Thursdays 1000-1400 and Sundays 1000-1500. The **VIC** ① *Giblett St, T9771 1831, www.manjimupwa.com, daily 0900-1700*, is in the centre of town by Coronation Park.

About 20 km west of Manjimup are the **Four Aces**, four karri giants 67-79 m high, and a short forest walk. **One Tree Bridge** is another picnic and walking site around a pioneer bridge but both of these areas are pretty out of the way unless you are walking the Bibbulmun Track. **Perup Ecology Centre** ① *T9771 7988*, is open to tours and groups only. Some 50 km east of Manjimup, it is worth the trip for anyone who loves wildlife. About 30 mammal species native to the southern forests can be found here, observed from hides and walk trails, and there are also daily tours and spotlighting night tours. Call for details of tour operators taking trips to the centre. If staying overnight, accommodation is in rammed-earth houses with a shared kitchen.

About 9 km south of Manjimup, just off the main highway, the **Diamond Tree** is one of the original fire-spotting trees. Standing 51 m high, several metres above the surrounding canopy, there are all-round views from the platform at the top. Two great things about the Diamond Tree are that you don't need to pay to get into a national park to get to it, and it's less well known than either the Gloucester or Dave Evans Bicentennial Trees, so draws fewer people.

The South Western Highway continues on to Walpole, and if you are heading for Pemberton there are three roughly equidistant routes. By taking Channybearup Road, 1 km before the Diamond Tree, and then left into the unsealed **Tramway Trail**, you can drive right through some of the most beautiful parts of the local karri forests, and past either **Big Brook Arboretum** or **Big Brook Dam**. Immediately before the Diamond Tree, Eastbourne Road winds mostly through pastoral country before coming out just north of Pemberton. Alternatively the Vasse Highway, 6 km beyond the tree, passes a couple of wineries, including **Salitage** (see page 192), on the way to the town.

Pemberton ►► *For listings, see pages 196-202. Colour map 3, B3.*

→ *Population: 920. 31 km from Manjimup, 31 km from Northcliffe.*

Pemberton sits in a valley surrounded by tall karri, jarrah and marri trees and national parks. Like most of the timber towns it grew up around a timber mill and the town is full of identical wooden workers' cottages that lend Pemberton a quaint toy-town feel. The mill still operates, although it is on reduced hours and many workers have lost their jobs. It is likely to close in the next few years and the town is slowly shifting its focus towards tourism and other ventures. Pemberton is central to an emerging wine region, a couple of superb woodcraft galleries and some wonderfully scenic bushwalking and driving country amid the soaring forests.

Sights

Most sights revolve around forest and fishing. One of the most popular ways to see the forest is to take a **Pemberton Tram** ① *Railway Cres, T9776 1322, www.pemtram.com.au, 1045 and 1400 to Warren River ($18, child $9, 1 hr 45 mins)*. The trams run along disused train lines to Warren River Bridge and Northcliffe. There are a couple of stops where you can get out and wander in the forest. There are also steam train trips 21 km north to Lyall on weekends (April-October). Trainspotters can enquire about driving courses. To see what can be done with all this timber don't miss the **Fine Woodcraft Gallery** ① *Dickinson St, T9776 1399, www.finewoodcraft.com.au, 0900-1700*, one of the best in the region with its superb collection of timber furniture and homewares. **Peter Kovacsy Studio** ① *Jamieson St, T9776 1265, www.peterkovacsy.com, Mon-Sat 0900-1700, $5 per group*, displays modern glass sculpture and offers the opportunity to talk to the artist. Look out for his new project, black and white photographs of Pemberton. The efficient **VIC** ① *0900-1700, T9776 1133, www.pembertontourist.com.au*, is on the main street that becomes Brockman Street where the Vasse Highway passes through the town centre. It has leaflets on walks in the area. The VIC has a **Pioneer Museum** ($2) and the **Karri Forest Discovery Centre**, which aims to reveal the secrets of the karri forest. It's looking pretty tired but has an interesting short film about life in the forest.

Around Pemberton ▸▸ *For listings, see pages 196-202.*

This is a large area, but there are many worthy attractions around. The Karri Forest Explorer Drive will take you past a lot of them, pick up a map from the VIC or look for the signs and tune in to 100FM for a commentary. The Pemberton wine region lies in a cooler, wetter area than the Margaret River wine region so cool climate varieties such as Sauvignon Blanc, Semillon, Pinot and Merlot dominate. There are about 10 cellar doors, a few with good restaurants, and they are often picturesque with rows of vines rolling downhill to meet karri forest. The Bibbulmun Track passes through the Pemberton, on its way down to the coast. The knee-wobbling climbing trees are also good fun and beyond the forest, lies the coastal D'Entrecasteaux National Park, an untouched wilderness of monster sand dunes and wild shores.

Wineries

Lost Lake ① *Vasse Highway, T9776 1251, www.lostlake.com.au, daily 1000-1600, lunch Wed-Sun 1130-1430, dinner Fri-Sat 1830-2100*, has a particularly good Pinot Noir and Chardonnay. Wines cost $8-35. The restaurant opens onto a deck and offers local produce like marron and trout.

Mountford ① *Bamess Rd, T9776 1345, www.mountfordwines.com.au, daily 1000-1600*, is one of the region's oldest vineyards so wines have more intensity and complexity than some. All wine is grown, made and bottled on the estate so these are pure Pemberton wines using the region's classic white and red varieties. There's a lovely timber and rammed-earth cellar door, an art gallery and, unusually, they also make traditional English cider including an organic scrumpy from the barrel. Wines cost $16-45.

Salitage ① *Vasse Highway, T9776 1195, 1000-1600*, 10 km east, is Pemberton's grandest winery with some of the best of the region's wines, costing $17-40. There are daily winery tours at 1100.

Warren ① *Conte Rd (unsealed), 3 km from Pemberton, T9776 1115, www.warren vineyard.com.au, 1100-1700*, is a small family-owned winery producing superb wines specializing in reds that are made for cellaring. Such is their belief in ageing the wine properly that they don't make it available for tasting or sales until it's at least five years old. Wines cost from $12. B&B accommodation is also available.

Wood Smoke Estate and Jarrah Jacks Brewery ① *Kemp Rd, T9776 0225, T9776 1333, www.woodsmoke-estate.com.au, www.jarrahjacks.com.au, Mon-Fri 0900-1700, Sat-Sun 0900-1800*, is a winery producing Sauvignon Blanc, Cabernet Merlot, Merlot and Semillon, and also a micro brewery offering up ale, bitter and porter. Wines cost $13-35. There is a café, playground and an indoor play area.

Living towers

From the 1950s to the mid-1970s, when aerial observation became the preferred method of fire-spotting in the region, there were eight fire-spotting towers around Manjimup and Pemberton used by the local communities to pinpoint fires when smoke was seen. These were not, however, constructed from the ground up, but used living karri trees as enormous central pillars. The trunks were stripped of branches and metal rungs pinned in, curling around and up the trunk to form a sloping ladder. The tree was then topped at a point at which the trunk was still strong and a platform constructed atop it. As well as still being a back-up to the planes, two of the original trees are now open to the public, the 64-m **Gloucester Tree**, in Gloucester National Park, and the 51-m **Diamond Tree**. In 1988 another was 'constructed', with less damage to the tree, in Warren National Park: the **Dave Evans Bicentennial Tree**. At 75 m this is the most challenging, but also the most rewarding. All three will give most people the willies, particularly on the way down when you have to look down at your feet (and thus the ground) the whole way. Only four people are allowed at the top of each tree at one time, so try to avoid the crowds by arriving in the early morning or late afternoon. Climbing can be dangerous in the wet or when windy so watch your step. There is enough clearance around all three to get a good photo of each but you will need a fairly wide-angle lens, about 28 mm.

Gloucester National Park → Colour map 3, B3. Vehicle entry $11.

This relatively small park marks Pemberton's southern boundary and also extends to the east. From Pemberton's main street, a 3-km route, which doubles as the Bibbulmun Track, is clearly signposted to the park's first access point, the site of the **Gloucester Tree**. One of the eight original fire-trees used in the mid-20th century, it reaches 64 m and was named for the visiting Duke of Gloucester who helped drill some of the holes. There are toilets and several picnic tables here. The park's second public access point is 6 km out on the Northcliffe Road, an unsealed 2-km road to the **Cascades**, a series of rocky rapids in the East Brook – impressive after heavy rain in winter, disappointing if it's dry. There are a few short easy walks from the tree.

Big Brook

Just north of town the Big Brook dam supplies water for the town and the trout hatchery. It is a beautiful stretch of water surrounded by tall karri forest and a lovely spot for a picnic or drive. There are usually lots of parrots and fairy wrens flitting about and the route gives the feeling of being deep in the forest. The road is unsealed and mostly one way, forming a loop of about 12 km off Stirling Road. There is a walking circuit of the dam (4 km) and picnic tables by a small stretch of sand. The **Rainbow Trail** is part of the loop and passes through an arboretum planted in the 1920-1930s of Californian redwoods, cyprus and Victorian mountain ash. The **Bibbulmun Track** passes along the dam to Pemberton and it is a very pleasant walk from town along the track (about 6 km one way).

Founders Forest

The Founders Forest is another pretty picnic and walking spot surrounded by karri trees. The forest is significant because it was visited by government minister Lane-Poole in 1913. He knew the land had been cleared in 1875 yet there was a 'fine crop of karri' standing almost 40 years later. This proved to a sceptical government that karri could be successfully regrown and should be kept as forest and not cut down for agriculture. The area became the first under management of the Forestry Department. It is reached by following Pemberton Road North for 9 km, then continuing along the unsealed Smiths Road for a couple of kilometres.

Bibbulmun Track → *See also pages 119, 189, 206 and 211.*

Walking from **Pemberton to Walpole** would take you about 10 days (192 km) but this is a fascinating transitional section, changing gradually from tall karri forest to the low vegetation of sandplains and the rugged southern coastline. Just outside Pemberton the track passes the **Gloucester Tree** (3 km) and the **Cascades** (8 km), both of which make pleasant day excursions from town. Following old rail trails, the track descends into the Warren River Valley and reaches **Warren campsite** on the valley rim with lovely views of the forest canopy (22 km from Pemberton). Around **Northcliffe** the track becomes less wild, skirting farmland and logging areas before finding the quiet Gardner River and entering **D'Entrecasteaux National Park** (see below), reaching **Gardner campsite** 15 km from Northcliffe. The vegetation changes to jarrah woodland and low swampy areas deeper into the park where there is a delightful campsite by **Lake Maringup** (15.5 km from **Gardner campsite**). Swinging east, the track enters the **Shannon National Park** before traversing the **Pingerup Plains** with its granite outcrops and views to Broke Inlet and the coastal dunes beyond. From the blocky granite **Woolbale Hills campsite** it is 11 km down to the coast at **Mandalay Beach**. With your own transport, this would make a fine day or overnight walk (road access at the beach). From Broke Inlet Road, off the highway, you can access the Pingerup Plains and climb **Mount Pingerup** (7 km return).

Warren National Park → *Colour map 3, B2.*

ⓘ *Vehicle entry $11, camping $7 per person per night.*

The unsealed Old Vasse Road, which runs from 12 km west of Pemberton to 8 km south, passes right through the heart of another reserve of old growth karri forest, now encompassed by Warren National Park. Nearer the Northcliffe Road end is the **Dave Evans Bicentennial Tree**, the 75-m living lookout constructed in 1988. There are wonderful views over the surrounding canopy at the top and a guarantee of wobbly legs for those who make it up there. The **Warren River Loop Walk** (10.5 km) starts near the base of the tree and meanders through karri forest to the **Warren Lookout**. Also off the through road is a 12-km one-way loop scenic drive called the **Heartbreak Trail**, which runs down to the banks of the Warren River, then follows its course among the stately karri trees for about 5 km. There are beautiful riverside camping and picnic spots along the way. It's worth noting that the road is unsealed and can be steep in places.

Beedelup and Karri Valley → *Colour map 3, B2.*

Beedelup National Park, 20 km west on the Nannup road, is a small park based around a low waterfall. Like the Cascades, the **Beedelup Falls** are a bit of a (not-so) damp squib in the dry. Even in winter the falls are not especially spectacular but there is a pleasant boardwalk loop constructed around the falls (600 m). Car entry to the park is $11. Just

Fruits of the forest

Western Australia's most beautiful hardwood, **jarrah**, grows in the inland region from the Darling Range to Manjimup. It is a deep red wood that is not susceptible to termites, unlike karri, and so has been used extensively as a building material. It is such a fine wood that it is also often used for handmade furniture and woodcraft. The tree grows to about 40 m and has a stringy grey-brown bark. It typically has a leafy crown, creating a large, shady canopy. Before logging and clearfelling the canopy inhibited the growth of seedlings and kept fuel for bushfires to a minimum. Jarrah trees live for about 300 years.

Marri are often found near jarrah. These are also known as redgum for the sticky gum oozing from their rough, grey bark. Their height varies from 10-60 m, depending on the quality of soil. Marri has beautiful white blossoms in summer and is an important food source for bees and birds. Winemakers like to have marri near their vines, so parrots will leave their grapes alone.

The forest of the southern region between Manjimup and Walpole is dominated by **karri**. Growing to 90 m and as slender and smooth as a telegraph pole, karri is the most easily recognizable of the forest trees. It has pale grey bark that peels in strips, revealing a peachy pink trunk. Karri only grows on red clay loams that receive more than 750 mm of rain a year. It is the third-tallest hardwood in the world and lives for 250 to 300 years. The timber looks very similar to jarrah, a dark red colour, but is not used for construction as termites, or white ants, love it. This hasn't stopped it being cut down, though, as it can still be used for woodchips.

beyond the park is an area known as Karri Valley, a stand of old growth forest, and the **Karri Valley Resort** (see Sleeping, page 199).

D'Entrecasteaux National Park → *Colour map 3, C2.*

This is a large area of wilderness along the coast south of Pemberton. Stretching 130 km from Black Point south of Nannup to the border of the Walpole-Nornalup National Park in the east, the park was reserved on the request of local foresters to stop coastal development. Most of it is inaccessible and all except one route require extensive 4WD experience. However, there are good tours into the park with operators in Pemberton and Walpole. If you can get there, it is a stunning area of almost untouched beaches, cliffs, heathland and forest. Immediately south of Pemberton are the **Yeagerup Dunes**, a spectacular place where the forest abruptly meets high creamy dunes. In fact the dunes are mobile and fast swallowing the forest. **Lake Jasper** is the largest freshwater lake in the southwest and the subject of controversy. Environmentalists are aghast at plans to mine the area for ilminite, a mineral sand. The area is ecologically fragile and contains a significant archaeological site (4000-year-old stone artefacts) but mining may still go ahead.

For park access by sealed road, head for Northcliffe, then south to **Windy Harbour** (25 km) where there is a fishing shack settlement and campground ($7). From here, take scenic D'Entrecasteaux Drive (6 km, sealed road) to **Salmon Beach** via **Point D'Entrecasteax** and **Tookalup Lookout**. There is a short walk at the point, around the lighthouse, but the highlight is Salmon Beach, a perfect long stretch of sand below high, rugged cliffs. Picnic tables and toilets by the car park are the only facilities. You can also walk to Point D'Entrecasteaux and Tookalup from Windy Harbour. **Mandalay Beach** is another beautiful beach at the eastern end of the park, just 12 km from Walpole. There is a DEC campground just after the highway turn-off to this beach, called **Crystal Springs**. Another 5.5 km down Mandalay Beach Road there is a turnoff for another campground (4WD only) called **Banksia Camp**. Vehicle entry into the park is $11, camping $7 per person per night, note that a national park permit is not required to camp at Crystal Springs.

Northcliffe → *Colour map 3, C3. 31 km from Pemberton, 100 km from Walpole.*

The timber mill no longer operates at Northcliffe but there is still a small population supporting a few services, and a large forest park in the centre has several pretty picnic areas. As well as some accommodation, the settlement also has a supermarket, café, petrol station and a VIC with adjacent **library** ① *T9776 7203, www.northcliffe.org.au, Mon-Fri 0830-1600, Sat-Sun 0900-1600.* Behind the VIC you will find **Understory – Art in Nature** ① *www.southernforestarts.com.au, daily 0900-1600, $11, children $6, concessions $8*, a 1-km art trail through the forest. The **Pioneer Museum** ① *daily 1000-1500, gold coin donation,* on the main street is worth a look. It houses artefacts relating to the town and a very impressive rock and fossil collection.

Shannon National Park → *Colour map 3, B3.*

Sitting astride the main highway south to Walpole, and named after the river that runs north–south through it, Shannon was a karri logging settlement in the 1940s with a mill employing 160 men. The mill closed in 1968 and logging stopped in 1983 but amazingly there is hardly a trace of this activity now. The park is best known for the **Great Forest Trees Drive** ① *T9776 1133 for information,* a 48-km one-way unsealed loop road through varied forest country, linked to radio stops telling tales of the timber-cutting days. It crosses the highway at two points so you can just do half of it. The southern half, the first turn you see if driving south, is the best as it takes you to **Big Tree Grove** within 5 km, a small but impressive cluster of karri trees around 85 m high and over 300 years old. At the far end of this part of the drive, near the highway, is a peaceful campsite and basic eight-bed lodge. Call **DEC** ① *T9776 1207,* for bookings. There are also some walking trails in the park, see the information board at the campsite. Car entry is $11 and camping $7 per person.

◉ Timber towns listings

For Sleeping and Eating price codes and other relevant information, see pages 28-34.

● Sleeping

Nannup and around *p188*

LL-L Holberry House, 14 Grange Rd, T9756 1276, www.holberryhouse.com. A large, stone guesthouse on a hillside above Nannup in beautiful grounds. Traditional country style, 6 rooms, spacious guest lounge and conservatory. Continental breakfast is included, cooked breakfast available. Friendly, knowledgeable hosts and plenty of books and newspapers. Outdoor pool and beautiful, flowing garden. Recommended.

A-B Blackwood River Cottages, 7 Nevermann, 2 km southwest of Nannup on road to Augusta, T9756 1252, www.blackwoodrivercottages.com.au. Self-contained accommodation, secluded timber cabins surrounded by bush. Linen provided.

B Redgum Retreat, Balingup Rd, T9756 2056, www.redgum-hill.com.au. One of the few licensed guesthouses with 3 en suite rooms, each opens to the veranda. Country breakfast included. Also offers 2 self-contained cottages away from the main house.

C Loose Goose Chalets, Barrabup Rd, 2 km north of town, T9756 1170, www.loosegoose. com.au. Good self-contained accommodation overlooking the lakes. Breakfast hampers can be provided on request.

C-D Nannup Hotel Motel, 12 Warren Rd, T9756 1080. The town's workmanlike pub has motel units and rather bare hotel rooms improved by old timber furniture and floors. Some en suite, cheaper option with shared facilities. General facilities include an on-site restaurant and bar with pool tables.

D Black Cockatoo, 27 Grange Rd, T9756 1035, www.nannuplodge.com. Nestled in secluded spots around the huge garden are 2 safari tents sleeping up to 3 people, complete with lamps and heaters, and individual campers kitchens. There is a chalet, again with its own cooking facilities or a more luxurious cabin for people who'd rather eat out. If you want a twin room, try the brightly painted caravan. All share a bathroom near the main house.

Caravan parks and campsites

There are 2 caravan parks by the river, run by the VIC. Sites and 1 cabin. Campers should also consider the sites at **Barrabup Pool**; and, close to Balingup on the Nannup to Balingup road, **Wrights Bridge**, a campground ($7 per person) and picnic site in a forested loop of the river. Facilities include fireplace BBQs and toilets, and swimming is allowed.

Balingup p189

A-B Balingup Heights, 1 km off the Nannup Rd, up a steep unsealed road, T9764 1283, www.balingupheights.com.au. 5 self-contained wooden cottages of varying size, each isolated from the others and cleverly contrived to be both in a forest setting and have expansive views over neighbouring valleys.

B Balingup Rose B&B, 208 Jayes Rd, T9764 1205, www.balinguprose.com.au. A friendly B&B 1.7 km from the town centre. 3 en suite

double rooms, in a 1927 cottage with jarrah floors and pressed-tin ceilings.

D Balingup Backpackers, 26 Brockman St, T9764 1049. Also known as 'The Hikers Hideaway', this is simply a self-contained extension to the post office with 10 beds in 4 rooms. Large lounge with TV and adequate kitchen. There are also laundry facilities.

Greenbushes p190

C-E Exchange Hotel, T9764 3509. A friendly pub built in 1907, renovated in keeping with its history and recently refurbished. Both the cheap counter and mid-range brasserie meals are a cut above average pub fare and the hotel rooms are good value. Meals 1800-2000.

Bridgetown p190

A-B The Bridgetown Hotel, 157 Hampton St, T9761 1034. A restored 1920s hotel with 8 luxurious en suite rooms. Continental breakfast during the week but a full cooked breakfast at the weekend. There's a public bar, a restaurant and a café. Meals are served 1200-1430 and 1800-2030.

A-C Ford House, Eedle Terr, T9761 1816, www.fordhouse.com. This 1896 former magistrate's cottage has seen hardly any changes since it was built, but has been very well maintained. 4 en suite doubles, 2 other doubles and 2 singles share a bathroom. All rooms are comfortably furnished in keeping with the house's style. The owners have built 2 additional houses offering 4 more en suite rooms, and a small self-contained studio sits at the rear of the property. Breakfast is served in the café on a big round table, and don't miss the shelves crammed with preserved fruit from the property's many trees.

B Tortoiseshell Farm, 12 km east of Bridgetown, partly via unsealed roads, T9761 1089. A modern B&B farmhouse with serious character, wonderful hosts and sweeping veranda views. Rough red stone walls enclose an open-plan jarrah-floored living area, complete with pool table, old tin ads and 1-armed bandits. Fully cooked breakfast is served and brought up to the room if wished. Dinners by pre-arrangement. There are also 2 self-contained cottages available. Call ahead for directions. Recommended.

Caravan parks and campsites

If heading to Nannup, there is Maranup Ford, 15 mins west of town, T9761 1200, which is a working farm and caravan park.
C-F Bridgetown Caravan Park, South West Highway, T9761 1900, www.bridgetown caravanpark.com. The only caravan park in town is on the far bank of the river, 1 km from the centre. On-site vans and cabins available. Owners are friendly and offer canoe and kayak hire ($30 and $20 per hr respectively).

Manjimup and around *p190*

B-F Fonty's Pool and Caravan Park, Seven Day Rd, off the South Western Highway to Pemberton, T9771 2105, www.fontyspool. com.au. Has cottages, on-site cabins and shady sites. Facilities include campers' kitchen, BBQ area and a large freshwater swimming pool. Closed in Jul and Aug. The adjacent winery does tastings, daily 1200-1600, T9777 0777, www.fontyspoolwines.com.au.
D Manjimup Hotel, Giblett St, Manjimup, T9771 1322, www.manjimuphotel.com.au. Has a smart lounge bar and serves cheap but filling counter meals, Both single and double hotel and motel rooms available. Meals Mon-Sat 1200-1400, daily 1830-2030.
D-E Manjimup Lodge and Backpackers, 59 Rose St, Manjimup, T9771 8077, www.manjibackpackers.com.au. Double rooms, some with en suite, and dorms sleeping 4-12 people. Wi-Fi available.

Pemberton *p191*

The busiest period is in Jan. It's often quiet in winter when you may get a good discount. Accommodation in the area is dominated by self-contained cottages, usually timber or rammed earth and surrounded by bush.

A-C Pemberton Hotel, Brockman St, T9776 1017, www.pembertonhotel.com. 30 luxurious rooms in shades of navy and taupe furnished with modern art and timber furniture, some with spa, balcony and kitchenette. Internet available.
B Lavender Berry Farm Cottages, Browns Rd, 4 km from town, T9776 1661, www.lavenderberryfarm.com.au. 4 comfortable self-contained rammed-earth cottages overlooking a lake and the berry farm. 2 bedrooms, wood fires, leather couches, BBQs.
B-C Treenbrook Cottages, Vasse Highway, 5 km northwest of town. T9776 1638, www.treenbrook.com.au. 4 charming, rustic cottages made of mud brick and local timbers. 1-3 bedrooms, full kitchen, woodfire, BBQ, and lots of bushwalk trails in the adjoining forest. Linen is provided, undercover parking available. Breakfast baskets can be arranged for $12.50-15.
B-E Pemberton Caravan Park, 1 Pump Hill Rd, T9776 1300, www.pembertonpark. com.au. En suite and budget cabins, bungalows and tent sites. No pets allowed.
E Pemberton Backpackers YHA, 7 Brockman St (8 km from town), T9776 1105, www.pembertonbackpackers.com.au. Dorms, doubles, singles and budget self-contained cottages along with free BBQs, friendly roos and advice on walks and hikes in the region.

Big Brook *p193*

C-D Pemberton Forest Stay, Stirling Rd. T9776 1153, www.pembertonforeststay.com. Peaceful hostel-style accommodation in bush near the dam. Beds are in 6 former timber workers' cottages, each with 2 bedrooms, own kitchen, lounge, fireplace. General facilities include outdoor BBQ shed, bike hire, volleyball court, free laundry and rescued kangaroos to feed. If you want to splash out, take the Zamin cottage ($90 double) exclusively.

Warren National Park p194

Camping is possible here.

A Marima Cottages, Old Vasse Rd (unsealed), T9776 1211, www.marima. com.au. Offers 1- to 2-bedroom spa chalets, each set at the boundary between the encircling forest and a modest paddock. Very smart, with potbelly stoves and wide verandahs. A favourite evening haunt of kangaroos and very near the bicentennial tree. Minimum stay 2 nights. The owners also run the nearby Wine Centre, which offers tastings.

Beedelup and Karri Valley p194

A Karri Valley Resort, T1800 245757 or T9776 2020, www.karrivalleyresort.com.au, on the shores of Lake Beedelup to the west of Pemberton. Has a series of wooden self-contained chalets, motel-style rooms and a restaurant. Though the experience isn't cheap, it is possible to fish for trout straight off some verandas here. The office is open daily 0900-1800 and a wide range of generally inexpensive activities, all open to non-residents, include mini golf, guided bushwalking, canoeing, trout fishing, animal night-spotting and bike hire. It is also where the **Donnelly River Cruises** bus (see page 201) makes its pick-ups. There is no mobile phone reception or internet access here.

Northcliffe p196

C Bibbulmun Break Motel, 14 Wheately Coast Rd, T9776 6060, www.bibbulumbreak motel.com. This small hotel has 4 smart en suite rooms. Continental breakfast is included in the price and Bibbulmun Track pick-ups and drop-offs available if organized in advance.

D-E Roundtu-it Eco Caravan Park and B&B, T9776 7276. In forest surroundings, offers B&B rooms, on-site vans, tent sites and backpacker beds. The Bibbulmun Track passes nearby and there is also bike hire available.

Eating

Nannup and around p188

Nannup Bridge Café, 1 Warren Rd, T9756 1287. Breakfast, lunch and dinner Wed-Sun 0900-1400, 1800-2000; lunch on Tue 0900-1400. Sit out the front and watch the world go by, or enjoy the dappled shade on the peaceful back veranda. BYO and licensed.

Tathra, Blackwood River Tourist Dr, T9756 2014, www.tathra.net. A fruit winery with a restaurant serving lunch, morning and afternoon teas (Thu-Tue 1100-1630) and a humble 19th-century woodman's slab cottage, furnished much as it was when first built. It also rents out B&B apartments (T9756 2040).

Chip 'n' Gales, 42 Warren Rd, T9756 1147. Tue 1200-1400, Thu-Sun 1130-1430, Thu-Tue 1700-2000. Good fish and chips, with options such as marron, snapper, red emperor and hake.

Cafés

Blackwood Café, 24 Warren Rd, T9756 1120. Daily 0830-1630. Good food and great cakes that can be enjoyed in the large shaded garden overlooking the main street. Runs a pizza and pasta night on Wed from 1830-2030.

Blackwood Wines, Kearney St, a 30-min walk from the VIC along the riverbank, T9756 0077, www.blackwoodwines.com.au. Bistro open Thu-Sun 1130-1430, cellar daily 1000-1600. A good place for lunch, do a good sharing platter and home-made quiches, salads and soups.

Good Food Shop, Warren Rd. Mon-Sat 0930-1600, Sun 1000-1600. Wholesome snacks and lunches.

Balingup p189

Balingup Bronze Café, corner of South West Highway and Forest St, T9764 1843, www.ballingupbronzegallery.com.au. Daily 1000-1600 and on Fri offers a takeaway menu from 1800-2000. An art gallery and a 100% gluten free café. Menus change regularly but look out for some good vegetarian options, seafood dishes and a curry or 2.

The Mushroom Café, 61 South West Highway, T9764 1505. Daily 0830-1500. Specializes in pies and there are a good number to choose from, including 4 vegetarian options. Also offers daily specials, breakfasts and sandwiches.

Bridgetown *p190*
Red Panda, 122 Hampton St, T9761 2888. Mon-Sat 0900-1630. Breakfasts, lunches and coffees and cakes, Free Wi-Fi on purchase. On Fri and Sat evenings (1800-2200) serves up Asian-inspired meals. BYO.
Barking Cow Café, 88A Hampton St, T9761 4919. Mon-Fri 0800-1500 and Sat 0830-1300. Offers wholesome breakfast and lunch.
Cidery, 43 Gifford St, T9761 2204, www.thecidery.com.au. Daily 1100-1600. Sells its own strong-brewed ciders and beers from a large barn. Ask for a cider tasting and try everything from pure apple juice, to Sweet Rosie (3.5%), to Scudamore's Scrumpy (8%). It's a good place to stop for lunch, and if you're in town on Fri pop down for the Sundowner (1700-1900) when there's live acoustic music, cheese and pâté platters and beer, cider and wine.

Manjimup and around *p190*
Blue Tiger Café, Rose St, T9777 2555. Mon-Sat 0900-1600. Burgers, wraps and all day breakfast.
Food Kultur, 5C Brockman St, T9777 1879. Tue-Thu 0900-1900, Sat 0900-2000. This café offers the usual fare of burgers and breakfast, Also serves coffees and cakes, and sandwiches can be made to order. Take away fish and chips.
Graphiti Café, T9772 1283, out towards One Tree Bridge. Wed-Sat 1000-1700, Sun from 0900. A nice café that serves cakes and lunch plus breakfast on Sun. BYO.

Pemberton *p191*
The wineries around the town provide some of the best food in and around Pemberton and some may be open for evening meals at weekends, see section for details.

Shamrock Restaurant, 18 Brockman St, T9776 1186, www.shamrockdining.com.au. Tue-Sun from 1600. Serves up a variety of seafood dishes and local Marron specialities. BYO. Booking advised.
Pemberton Hotel, T9776 1017, www.pembertonhotel.com. A traditional old place with a huge modern café and accommodation wing. Hotel meals are cheap and standard favourites are served from 1200-1400, 1800-2000. There is also a more modern café for light snacks.

Cafés
Lavender Berry Farm, Browns Rd, T9776 1661, www.lavenderberryfarm.com.au. Daily 0930-1700. Has a fragrant garden and a café with wholesome food such as pies, toasties and Devonshire teas. It also serves sweet treats such as scones with berry jam, lavender or honey ice cream, and is renowned for its berry pancakes with ice cream. You can also pick your own berries.
Pemberton Millhouse Café, 14 Brockman St, T9776 1122, offers a good range of soups, light meals, cakes, award-winning ice cream, coffee and tea. From the end of the year they will also be open for evening meals on Fri and Sat. Enquire here about tours of the Pemberton mill.

Beedelup and Karri Valley *p194*
Karri Valley Resort, T9776 2020. The restaurant is open 1100-2030, serves cheap light lunches, cream teas and very good evening meals (expensive). The views across the lake are great but there is no deck or outside tables. However, opposite the adjacent Activity Office there's a small lakeside grassed area, teeming with ducks and swans, which has a free BBQ and picnic tables.
King Trout Café, Northcliffe Rd, 8 km south, T9776 1352. Fri-Tue 0930-1700. Both trout farm and log-cabin café so they'll happily cook the fish you catch. There are several good seafood options including a good-value 'trout taster'.

Gone fishing

There are several places around Pemberton that farm trout in large dams and offer the opportunity to catch a fish or two for supper. Such is the density of fish stocks that you usually don't need to be an expert angler to get a bite. There is normally a hire charge for the rod, possibly a fishing charge, and any fish caught are charged at around $15 per kg. A reasonably sized fish, enough to feed one person, is around 300-400 g.

Although more patience and/or skill will be required at Beedelup Lake, fish caught here are free. There is a limit of two fish per person per day and rod hire for the resort Activity Office is $10.

You can also fish for trout, perch and marron in any of Pemberton's rivers and streams if you have your own gear but you need a licence (obtain at the post office). The VIC can give more information on licensing, sizing and locations. Marron is a small freshwater crayfish that carries a lot of meat for its size and is absolutely delicious. Marron season is January-February, trout September-April.

Northcliffe p196

♥ **The Dairy Lounge Café**, Bannister Downs Farm, Muirillup Rd, T9776 6266. A little way out of town, serves coffees, cakes and light meals. Whilst tucking into apple pie visitors can watch the dairy at work through the window opening onto the processing plant.

▲ Activities and tours

Nannup and around p188

Blackwood River Canoeing, T9756 1209. A quick paddle (less than 2 hrs) for $17.50, twilight paddles ($35) or extended trips with equipment and transport to canoe a section of the river for 2-4 days (from $35 day). Bookings are essential.

Manjimup and around p190

Donnelly River Cruises, T9777 1018 and T0427 771018, www.donnellyrivercruises. com.au. Offers morning and afternoon cruises for $55, children $35. Pick-ups at Manjimup VIC are possible by prior arrangement.

Pemberton p191

For tours of the mill, contact **Pemberton Millhouse Café** (see Eating, above).

Pemberton Discovery Tours, The Discovery Shop, Brockman St, T9776 0484, www.pembertondiscoverytours.com.au. Eco-certified, excellent 4WD trips into D'Entrecasteaux National Park and the Yeagarup Dunes and Warren National Park. Beaches, river and forest with a lively and flexible guide. Also winery tours. Tours include lunch or afternoon tea and park fees. Depart daily 0900 and 1400. Bibbulmun Track drop-offs are available.
Pemberton Hiking & Canoeing, T9776 1559, www.hikingandcanoeing.com.au. Guided walks with knowledgeable locals and environmentalists. Also canoeing on the Warren, Yeagarup Dunes on foot, night walks and 2- to 5-day wilderness walks. Can plan any tour to suit and caters for those with special needs.

Beedelup and Karri Valley p194

Karri Valley Resort runs a wide range of activities, all available to non-residents, including horse riding (see Sleeping, above).

⊖ Transport

Bridgetown *p190*
Bus TransWA buses leave from the Boat Park for stops to **Bunbury** daily at 1247 (change to *Australind* train for **Perth** if necessary). **Pemberton** buses depart Mon, Tue, Thu, Sat, Sun 1317 and Fri 1702. There are daily 1317 services that continue on to **Albany** (the Wed and Fri buses don't call at Pemberton). **South West Coachlines** heads to **Perth** Mon-Fri at 0700, and to **Manjimup** Mon-Fri at 1800.

Pemberton *p191*
Bus TransWA buses leave from the VIC for stops to **Perth** on Mon, Tue and Thu at 0845. Buses to **Northcliffe**, **Walpole** (2 hrs), **Denmark** and **Albany** (3½ hrs) leave Thu-Tue at 1441 and Fri at 1816. Its **Nannup** and **Capes** region buses depart Mon, Wed and Fri at 0630.

❶ Directory

Bridgetown *p190*
Banks Commonwealth, Westpac and Bankwest ATMs on Hampton St. **Internet** Community Resource Centre, 150 Hampton St, near the post office, T9761 2712. Mon-Fri 1000-1600. Internet access is also available at the VIC. **Medical services** Chemists: Bridgetown Pharmacy, 127 Hampton St, T9761 1004, Mon-Fri 0830-1800, Sat 0830-1300. **Police** Steere St, T9761 1666. **Post** 142 Hampton St.

Pemberton *p191*
Banks Bankwest ATM on Brockman St. **Internet** Community Resource Centre, next to VIC, 29 Brockman St, T9776 1745. Mon-Fri 0900-1700, Sat 0900-1200. **Laundry** Pemberton Wash House, Brockman St. **Medical services** Chemists: Pemberton Pharmacy, Brockman St, T9776 1054, Mon-Fri 0900-1730, Sat 0900-1200. Hospital: Hospital Av, T9776 4000. **Police** Ellis St, T9776 1202. **Post** Corner of Brockman St and Ellis St, T9776 1034.

Contents

Footprint features

South Coast

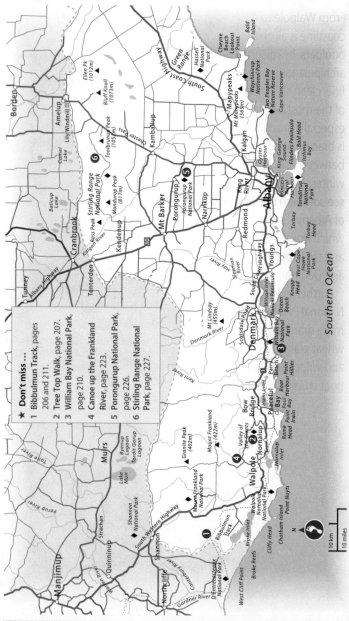

★ Don't miss ...

1 Bibbulmun Track, pages 206 and 211.
2 Tree Top Walk, page 207.
3 William Bay National Park, page 210.
4 Canoe up the Frankland River, page 223.
5 Porongurup National Park, page 226.
6 Stirling Range National Park, page 227.

Southern Ocean

From Walpole to Albany and beyond, the long southern coastline is all about granite. Weathered into smooth rounded boulders, headlands and islands, granite forms striking bays and archipelagos on this coast. It also breaks down into impossibly fine, clean sand, leaving the water as clear as liquid glass. Some of the most beautiful beaches in the country are found here, especially around Denmark and Albany. The catch is that the water is bracing at best – this is the southern ocean and there's nothing between you and Antarctica. This makes summers mild and winters surprisingly cold, although the latter is the best time to see southern right whales, which sojourn near the historic town of Albany. The south coast also receives relatively high rainfall, which nourishes the rare tingle trees of the Valley of the Giants and tall karri forests down to the shoreline around Walpole and Denmark.

Further inland, the low granite range of the Porongurup National Park provides gentle walks and good views of the more dramatic Stirling Ranges, rising above the state's vast wheat plains. This magnificent region of forest, hills, beaches and wilderness offers superb walking, as well as canoeing, boat cruises and coastal drives.

Walpole to Albany

The most striking thing about this stretch of coast is its abundance of natural attractions and how few people there are visiting them. Most of your exploring – whether in forests, up granite knolls, down quiet rivers or along white-sand beaches – will be uninterrupted by other people. The only exception is the Valley of the Giants, a preserved area of soaring old growth forest with both tree-top and forest floor walks, but even here you'll not exactly be crowded out. ►► *For listings, see pages 217-224.*

Walpole and around ►► *For listings, see pages 217-224.*

Walpole → *Colour map 3, C4. Population: 512. 120 km from Pemberton, 65 km from Denmark.*

Walpole is a tiny town, with the minimum of services, that sits on the northern shore of Walpole Inlet, itself a watery outpost from Nornalup Inlet. The main street shops hug one side of the highway, while the foreshore area is undeveloped. The scantiness of the town often causes travellers to suppose that the only reason to visit the area is the Tree Top Walk (see below). In actual fact the natural forest and coastal attractions are such that many who come for a night end up staying several.

The inlets and the town are almost entirely enclosed by the **Walpole-Nornalup National Park**, which extends for several kilometres in each direction and encompasses one of the best preserved coastal forest and heath areas in the state. The Walpole Wilderness Area is a recently formed conservation region that incorporates a number of nearby national parks and reserves, including Walpole-Nornalup. The Bibbulmun Track runs right through the area and town, and several sections of it, some of the best on its entire course, can easily be done as day walks using the town as a base. A shorter 2-km loop walk through karri forest runs directly from behind the VIC. The extremely helpful **VIC** ① *T9840 1111, www.walpole.com.au, Mon-Fri 0900-1700, Sat-Sun 0900-1600,* is opposite the main shopping strip on the South Coast Highway.

Bibbulmun Track → *See also pages 119, 189, 194 and 211.*

The walks around Walpole are some of the best on the track, combining magnificent tall karri and tingle forest with coastal scenery and riverside and beach walking. It is also a convenient place to attempt short sections. **Mount Clare to Walpole** is 10 km and descends gradually to the town with good views over the Walpole-Nornalup Inlet. The next section from **Walpole to Frankland** (17.5 km) follows the shore of the inlet before rising to Hilltop Lookout and passing by the Giant Tingle Tree (see below). Walking through stunning forest follows until you reach the campsite at Frankland River, an isolated and pristine spot. From **Frankland to Giants** (13.5 km) is another fine forest section that passes the Valley of the Giants treetop walk before ending at a campsite nearby. The next section, **Giants to Rame Head** (15.5 km) moves through forest, through the renowned patch of red flowering gum to the coast at Conspicuous Cliff and a campsite on the headland. Also consider a long-distance walk from **Walpole to Denmark** (115 km, six to seven days), easily accessible by public transport.

Giant Tingle Tree and Circular Pool

Opposite the turn to Coalmine Beach is another unsealed road to the fair but unremarkable **Hilltop Lookout**, and then, 5 km from the highway, to the **Giant Tingle Tree**, a 400-m walk

Shiver me tingles

There are three types of tingle tree: the red, yellow and rates tingle. The one most commonly referred to simply as tingle is the red tingle. It has grey stringy bark similar to jarrah but can be distinguished by its height and wide-buttressed trunks. Red tingle reaches 70 m high and 20 m wide at the base, although the bases are often burnt out and hollow. These trees are only found in a tiny patch of the country around Walpole, close to the Deep, Bow and Frankland rivers. The tingle are believed to be relict species from the Gondwanan period, 65 million years ago when the climate was wetter, and have only survived in the wettest areas of the southwest. These rare stars of the Tree Top Walk are not harvested for the timber industry. The yellow and rates tingle can only be distinguished by looking at their leaves and gumnuts closely, but both are generally smaller trees.

from the carpark. This is said to have the widest girth of any living tree in Australia, but is burnt out, hollow and seems to cling precariously to life. It is a magnificent old survivor but perhaps less impressive than a circumference of 25 m suggests. Just beyond the tree the road hits a T-junction. The one-way right turn deposits you back on the highway near Nornalup, the one-way left heads the long way back to Walpole with an optional 8-km loop up to **Circular Pool**, a picturesque part of the Frankland River, overhung by giant karri and a good place for a swim.

Valley of the Giants → *Colour map 3, C4.*
① *T9840 8263, walkway 0900-1700, last entry 1615, guided walks 1015, 1130 and 1400, $8, children $4, concessions $6.*
On the other side of Nornalup, 12 km from Walpole, the Valley of the Giants is an area of forest with a high density of good-sized karri, tingle and other trees. In 1996 DEC opened the 600-m **Tree Top Walk**, a sloping steel walkway suspended up to 40 m above the forest floor and passing several forest giants at canopy level. Although the walkway does sway, the sense of awe most people feel is enough to make them forget their vertigo, and the clever design means no steps are involved, making the entire walk wheelchair accessible. A separate forest floor walk, the **Ancient Empire**, identifies several species of giant forest tree and introduces you to a few striking individuals, notably Grandmother Tingle.

Peaceful Bay, Mandalay Beach and Conspicuous Cliffs → *Colour map 3, C4.*
There are two ocean beaches accessible by unsealed road within 25 km of Walpole, and another at **Peaceful Bay**, that can be reached via sealed road. **Mandalay Beach** is reached via **Crystal Springs** bush campground and national park entry fees apply ($11 per car). The beach at **Conspicuous Cliffs** is the most beautiful in the area – a long sweep of broad sand with the cliffs a towering eastern backdrop – that can be reached without a 4WD. The unsealed Ficifolia Road connecting the cliffs with Peaceful Bay is named for the many red flowering gums that line it. These eucalypts flower in a range of vibrant oranges, reds and pinks during summer. The tree has been introduced all over the world, but its origin is in this area of bush. Other wonderful beaches and bays in the area include **Shell Beach** and **Blue Holes**, the site of the annual **Salmon Camp**, only accessible by 4WD or boat. Some can be visited as part of a tour.

Dinosaur World and Parrot Jungle Bird and Reptile Park

ⓘ T9840 8335, www.dinosaurworld.com.au, 1000-1630 (last entry 1600), $12, children $6, concessions $10.

On the road to Denmark, 300 m off the highway, this modest-sized discovery centre, where you can get up close to some of history's biggest carnivores, exhibits several dinosaurs. It also has an excellent collection of some of the world's most brightly coloured parrots and macaws. The birds are well cared for and held in large cages in a pleasant, grassy garden and in a walk-in aviary. Some of the rescued and hand-reared birds roam free about the park and visitors are invited to have a bird perch on them, a memorable opportunity. Reptile handling daily at 1100 and 1400.

Swarbrick and Mount Frankland → *Colour map 3, C3. 8 km and 30 km from Walpole (10 km of which are unsealed).*

Inland from Walpole, both of these areas are off the beaten track and little advertised. Watch carefully for very small signs at the turnoffs. **Swarbrick** is a 500-m sealed loop walk in the forest amid sculptures designed to challenge your perceptions. At the entrance to the walk there is a striking mirrored wall. Quiet and contemplative, Swarbrick is well worth a quick detour. Further up the road, **Mount Frankland** is a bare lump of granite sticking out of the forest like a bald man craning to see above a crowd. The 15-minute ascent to the summit, via concrete steps and a metal ladder, seems over before you've started, leaving all the more time to admire the 360-degree views. To the south the inlets can be distantly glimpsed, to the north the forest seems to stretch away forever, broken only by a few other peaks. By taking the **Loop Walk** on the way back down you extend the total walk to a little over an hour, hiking right around the base of the exposed granite cap, threading your way between towering karri trees. There are fireplace BBQs and a toilet back at the car park. This is an amazing spot to see either sunrise or sunset but camping is not permitted. The nearest campground is at **Fernhook Falls**, 20 km west of Mount Frankland, on Beardmore Road.

Denmark and around ⇥ *For listings, see pages 217-224.*

The small, appealing town of Denmark lies on the western bank of the Denmark River as it flows into Wilson Inlet. The hills above the inlet are cloaked in karri trees and outside its narrow entrance lie some of the most stunning beaches and headlands on the southern coast. William Bay National Park, 18 km to the west of Denmark, includes the magical Greens Pool, Elephant Rocks and Madfish Bay, scattered with leviathan granite boulders. The picturesque, temperate location has attracted artists and winemakers and their galleries and cellar doors are found along the Scotsdale and Mount Shadforth roads in the hills above town.

Denmark → *Colour map 3, C5. Population: 5000. 55 km from Mt Barker, 55 km from Albany.*

Denmark is fast losing its alternative edge and is a now a sophisticated small town, a rival to Margaret River, with a new visitor centre, classy galleries, cafés, bookshops and gourmet food specialists. The commercial centre is limited to the junction of the highway and Strickland Street and the grassy banks of the wide river have been left to picnickers and walkers. The attractions of Denmark are mostly natural ones, or outside the town centre. Within town, the small **Historical Society Museum** ⓘ *Mitchell St, T9848 1781, Thu 1000-1200, Tue, Thu and Sun 1400-1600, or by appointment, entry by donation,* is dedicated to the lives of early settlers in Denmark. **Denmark Environment Centre** ① *25 Strickland St, T9848 1644, Mon-Fri 1000-1600, Sat 1000-1300,* is a focus for conservationists and greenies in the area and is a good place to go to pick up publications on flora and fauna or information on any green events. The impressive **VIC** ① *T9848 2055, www.denmark. com.au, daily 0900-1700,* is on the corner of the highway and Ocean Beach Road, just north of the shopping area. Its tower houses the world's largest water barometer and stocks a range of locally made arts and crafts.

Wilson Inlet and Ocean Beach → *Colour map 3, C5. 11 km from Denmark.*

Ocean Beach Road heads straight down to Wilson Head, though a slightly more scenic option is to detour via Hollings Road to **Rivermouth**, and then via **Poison Point**. There is a lookout here and a 300-m walk down to the tiny deserted promontory – a good place to see the many water birds living on the inlet, including black swans and pelicans. A spit of sand usually blocks the ocean entrance to Wilson Inlet and this extends round the external Ratcliffe Bay in a long sweep. The near-side section, **Ocean Beach**, is popular with locals and holidaymakers alike. The sealed road ends at the lookout just above Ocean Beach; continue along the unsealed road for a succession of ever better views. Where the road ends you can look directly south at **Wilson Head** where a shelf of rock, extending

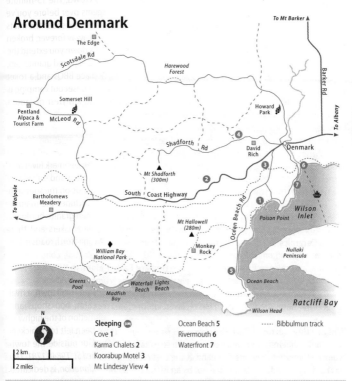

Around Denmark

The Edge

Scotsdale Rd

Harewood Forest

To Mt Barker ▲

Barker Rd

To Albany

Somerset Hill

Pentland Alpaca & Tourist Farm

McLeod Rd

Howard Park

Shadforth Rd

David Rich

Denmark

❹

Mt Shadforth (300m)

❷

❸

❻

❼

South Coast Highway

To Walpole

Bartholomews Meadery

Mt Hallowell (280m)

Monkey Rock

Ocean Beach Rd

Poison Point

Wilson Inlet

❶

Nullaki Peninsula

William Bay National Park

Greens Pool

Waterfall Beach

Lights Beach

Madfish Bay

❺

Ocean Beach

Wilson Head

Ratcliff Bay

N

2 km

2 miles

Sleeping 🛏

Cove **1**
Karma Chalets **2**
Koorabup Motel **3**
Mt Lindesay View **4**

Ocean Beach **5**
Rivermouth **6**
Waterfront **7**

----- Bibbulmun track

some 100 m east, creates fantastic waves. The view gets better if you scramble the 200 m down the path to the boulders below.

Mount Shadforth and Scotsdale scenic drives → *Full loop about 45 km.*

From Denmark two roads heading northwest have been designated as tourist drives – you can drive both as a continuous loop, though this involves an unsealed section. **Mount Shadforth Road** winds west along the range of hills culminating in Mount Shadforth (300 m) after 10 km. There are a succession of excellent views both inland and south over the inlets. It's hardly worth the trouble going out to the official lookout, especially if you stop for a coffee at the **Southern End Restaurant** (see Eating, page 221).

Beyond Mount Shadforth an unsealed section leads to McLeod Road. A left turn here runs down to the highway, almost opposite the turn-off for **William Bay National Park**, see page 210, and close to **Bartholomews Meadery** ① *T9840 9349, www.bartholomews meadery.com.au, 0930-1630*. This honey farm produces a selection of meads (honey wines), honey, honey ice cream and beeswax products, and has a buzzing see-through hive right by the counter.

Backtracking, the right turn off the unsealed section of Mount Shadforth Road onto McLeod Road heads up to the western end of the 'tourist' section of **Scotsdale Road** after passing **Somerset Hill Winery** ① *T9840 9388, www.somersethillwines.com.au, Dec-Jun 1100-1600, Aug-Nov 1100-1700*, a true cellar built on Mediterranean lines, with the bubbly ageing on a series of racks. Wines cost $19-39 and include the top-end Methode Champenoise. Almost on the Scotsdale Road junction is **Pentland Alpaca Stud Animal Farm and Wildlife Park** ① *2019 Scotsdale Rd, T9840 9262, www.pentlandalpacafarm. com.au, 1000-1600, $12, children $6, concessions $10*, a rustic attraction with paddocks and pens containing farm and native animals, including koalas. Visitors can enter many of the areas. Koala feeding is at 1000 and bottle feeding of the baby animals takes place at 1500.

The 20-km drive back to Denmark heads through a mix of pastoral and forest country, and passes many wineries and galleries along the way. There is the **Denmark Farmhouse Cheese** ① *1678 Scotsdale Rd, T9840 9844, daily 1000-1600*, where visitors can try cheese, handmade fudge and, of course, wines. The cheese platters are good for sharing. **Rickety Gate Wines** ① *RMB 1949 Scotsdale Rd, T9840 9503, www.ricketygate.com.au, Fri-Mon 1100-1600, wines $15-40*, has good platters in their café, as does **The Lake House** ① *106 Turner Rd, T9848 2444, www.lakehousedenmark.com.au, daily 1100-1600, wines $19-45*. If you need something more substantial, brave the 4.5 km of unsealed road and make your way to the Whitfield Estate where you'll find the **Picnic in the Paddock Café** ① *T9840 9016, www.whitfieldestate.com.au*. As well as tasting wine, local cheese and chocolates there is the opportunity to tuck into some very good home-made food. **Jonathon Hook Studio Ceramics** ① *Lantzke Rd (5 km from town, from Redman Rd off Scotsdale Rd), T9848 1436, www.jonathonhook.com, Mon-Fri 1000-1700*, produces elegant contemporary ceramics, and close to the town centre is the **Howard Park & Madfish Wines** ① *T9848 2345, www.howardparkwines.com.au, www.madfishwines.com.au, 1000-1700, wines $14-85*. These people regularly make some of the best wines in the region, including their 'drink-now' range, *Madfish*, which has received international recognition.

William Bay National Park → *Colour map 3, C4. Greens Pool 18 km from Denmark.*

The granite that makes up much of the south coast takes on some of its most spectacular sculpted forms in the gentle headland at the east end of William Bay. Mesmeric **Greens Pool** is a clear sandy bay, sheltered not by an island or reef but by a collection of domed boulders scattered for several hundred metres about 100 m offshore. At the end of the sealed road and a safe swimming beach, the pool is a very popular family destination. Parking in the Elephant Rocks car park, just 50 m along the unsealed section, gives just as quick walking access to the pool, but also to **Elephant Rocks**, a cluster of gigantic boulders nuzzling the nearside of a tiny sandy inlet, more like beached whales than elephants. The whole ensemble never fails to awe, in fair weather or foul. The unsealed road leads, after 3 km, to **Madfish Bay**, a broad sandspit connecting the mainland to a long rock island. In strong seas waves come around both ends of the island to meet at the middle of the spit. Not always recommended as a swimming spot, this is nevertheless well worth a visit.

Bibbulmun Track → *See also pages 119, 189, 194 and 206.*

The section west of Denmark makes an excellent short-day walk or overnight walk. From **Wilson Inlet Holiday Park**, 6 km south of town, the track rises through huge granite outcrops to **Mount Hallowell**, where there are great views of the inlet (6 km one way). After descending to the coast you reach a campsite close to the beautiful beaches of **William Bay** (15 km from Denmark). Another good section is the track through **West Cape Howe National Park**, where there are not only spectacular coastal views but views inland to the Porongurups and Stirling Ranges. If a pick-up can be arranged, the ideal section would be from Tennessee Road South car park to **Cosy Corner** car park (21 km to Torbay campsite, 2.5 km to Cosy Corner the following day). Walkers heading straight through need to get over the inlet to (or from) the Nullakai Peninsula.

Denmark to Albany

There are two routes between these settlements and taking the more scenic Lower Denmark Road rather than the South Coast Highway provides views of the coastline and access to **West Cape Howe National Park** ⓘ *South Coast Highway, T9845 2028, Fri-Tue 1000-1600.* The area is known as **Torbay**, after Torbay Head in the national park. Just before the road splits there is a fine gallery, **Woodworks**, showing the impressive work of Dean Malcolm, as well as other local artisans.

After turning down the Lower Denmark Road there is a right turn almost immediately onto Eden Road. This leads down to the shores of Wilson Inlet and meets the Bibbulmun Track. Back on the main road, there is a general store 2 km further on at **Youngs Siding**, a reminder of the days when Denmark and Albany were connected by a railway line that followed the route of this road. The line was used to transport timber felled in the Torbay region in the late 1890s. The next turn-off leads to Lowlands Beach at the western edge of West Cape Howe National Park. Tennessee South Road is sealed for 4 km but unsealed for the last few kilometres to the beach. A little further on is Piggot Martin Road, which leads to **The Bushfood Factory and Café**, where you can sample foods make from bush fruits and spices (see Eating, page 221).

West Cape Howe National Park is a small park with cliff and coastal scenery, most of it is only accessible to walkers and 4WD vehicles. The main entrance is further east, along the sealed Cosy Corner Road, from Lower Denmark Road. At Cosy Corner beach there is a general store. Continue along the unsealed road to **Shelley Beach**. There are great views from the hang-gliding ramp above the long sandy beach. The Bibbulmun Track passes both beaches and these can be a good start or finish point if you can arrange transport. From the Cosy Corner turn-off it is a further 26 km east to Albany.

⇢ *Population: 33,000. 385 km from Margaret River, 410 km from Perth, 480 km from Esperance.*
Albany has a small city centre making it a relaxed and friendly place and many enjoy the mild climate (Albany is often 10°C cooler than Perth in summer). There are great national parks in every direction but Torndirrup National Park is the closest and has some impressive granite rock formations, cliffs and a range of magical ocean beaches. The main activity in winter is whale watching, and, perhaps strangely, one of Albany's busiest attractions is the whaling station where the giants were chopped up as recently as 1978.

Ins and outs
The **VIC** ⓘ *Proudlove Parade, T9841 9290, www.albanytourist.com.au, 0900-1700*, is housed in the former railway station on the waterfront, a timber building constructed in the 1880s. ⇢ *See Transport, page 224.*

History
Albany is the site of the first European settlement of Western Australia, thanks to the state's finest natural harbour, Princess Royal Harbour within King George Sound. The sound was officially discovered by George Vancouver, captain of the *Discovery*, in 1791, who landed on a beach with a freshwater stream "the colour of brandy but exceedingly well tasted". He laid claim to the land in the name of King George III and named the inner harbour after the Princess Royal as it was her birthday. He sailed away shortly afterwards to explore the far west coast of North America but his charts led Matthew Flinders to enter the harbour in search of shelter in 1801. Flinders wrote detailed notes on the Aboriginal people he met, describing their kangaroo-skin capes and their fascination with his red-coated soldiers.

The French arrived two years later on Baudin's voyage of exploration and indirectly caused the British settlement of Albany. In NSW and in England the activities of the French were watched anxiously for fear they would claim and settle parts of Australia. In the same way that Tasmania and Victoria were settled immediately after Baudin's expedition, in 1825 the British authorities decided to order settlement of King George Sound to forestall the French who were reported to be continually present in the southern coastal waters that year. In 1826 Major Edmund Lockyer set out from Sydney in the *Amity* with a small party of soldiers and convicts and established a town site in Princess Royal Harbour that he named Frederickstown. When James Stirling founded a new colony at Swan River (Perth) in 1829, control of the southern settlement passed from Sydney to Perth and the name was changed to Albany. The town's position on the main shipping route to the eastern states ensured its survival and it became a busy port. However, its importance quickly declined after Fremantle's harbour was built in the 1890s. Whaling and the harvesting of karri, jarrah and sandalwood timber were important industries, although all were eventually exhausted and replaced by agriculture.

Sights
Despite the advanced age of Albany in Western Australian terms, the first impression is not of its heritage but its beautiful natural harbour. The city sits on the northern shore of Princess Royal Harbour and King George Sound and overlooks both the curving arm of the peninsula and the granite islands of the sound. The main street, York Street, runs downhill to the waterfront and it is here that Albany's history becomes more visible, in

the simple Residency and Gaol by a 19th-century sailing ship and the Victorian buildings of Stirling Terrace.

The earliest settlement in Albany was established on the waterfront, just to the west of the modern port facilities. Major Lockyer's party stepped ashore at the spot where the Residency still stands and the first encampment was made on flat high ground just above, now called Foundation Park. A replica of Lockyer's ship, the **Brig Amity** ① *T9841 6885,*

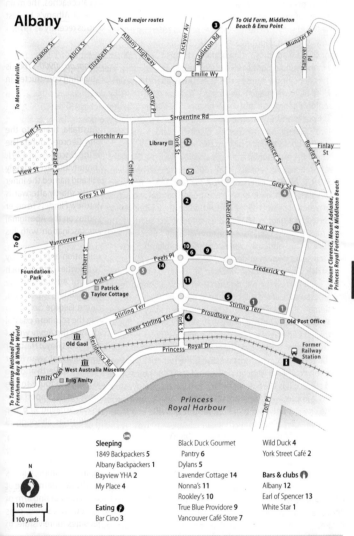

Albany

To all major routes

❸ *To Old Farm, Middleton Beach & Emu Point*

To Mount Melville

To Mount Clarence, Mount Adelaide, Princess Royal Fortress & Middleton Beach

To Torndirrup National Park, Frenchman Bay & Whale World

Foundation Park

Princess Royal Harbour

N

| 100 metres |
| 100 yards |

Sleeping 🛌	Black Duck Gourmet	Wild Duck **4**
1849 Backpackers **5**	Pantry **6**	York Street Café **2**
Albany Backpackers **1**	Dylans **5**	
Bayview YHA **2**	Lavender Cottage **14**	**Bars & clubs** 🍸
My Place **4**	Nonna's **11**	Albany **12**
	Rookley's **10**	Earl of Spencer **13**
Eating 🍴	True Blue Providore **9**	White Star **1**
Bar Cino **3**	Vancouver Café Store **7**	

0930-1600, $6, children $2, concessions $4, access from museum, has been built and stands roughly in the place that the original ship moored in 1826. At the time the brig was owned by the colonial government in Sydney and used as a government supply vessel. She carried a party of about 45 people, as well as supplies and livestock for the new settlement, although today the boat looks hardly big enough for one family. The *Amity* was reconstructed by local boat builders in time for the 150th anniversary of its arrival in 1976. Visitors can clamber all over the boat and below deck to see the cramped living conditions of sailors of the 19th century.

The **Residency**, just next door, was built in 1850 and originally used as a storehouse for the convict hiring depot nearby. In 1873 it became the home of Government Residents, responsible for administration of the settlement and exploration of the area. Magistrates lived in the building until 1953 when the last moved out complaining of damp and cold. The Residency now houses the **West Australian Museum – Albany** ① *Residency Rd, T9841 4844, www.museum.wa.gov.au, Thu-Tue 0930-1630, by donation*, and displays on the region's geological and social history. The site includes the Eclipse Building, housing the Eclipse Island lighthouse optic and displays related to the ocean. There is also an Artisans' Gallery, selling leather products, and a museum shop selling a range of interesting books on local history and wildlife.

Behind the museum lie the high, spiky walls of the **Old Gaol** ① *Stirling Terr, T9841 6174, www.historicalbany.com.au, 1000-1600, $5, children and concessions $2.50; night tours Fri or Sat 1930, booking essential T0407 387 484, $20, concessions $15, children $10*, set with broken glass to dissuade nimble escapees. The gaol was actually built in 1852 as a convict depot where convicts were housed while they laboured on the town's roads. It was converted to a gaol in 1873 and used for police quarters. The Albany Historical Society now runs the Old Gaol as a museum of early European local history. Some cells have displays on the ghoulish crimes of their inhabitants, such as Frederick Bailey Deeming, who put several wives under concrete.

Patrick Taylor Cottage ① *Duke St, T9841 5403, www.historicalbany.com.au, 1100-1500, $2*, is just up the hill, on the street behind Stirling Terrace. This is considered to be the oldest wattle and daub building in the state. Built in 1832 it was purchased by a British gentleman, Patrick Taylor, in 1834. He married Mary Yates Bussell, whom he had met on the voyage from England. Mary was a member of the Bussell family who settled in the Southwest Capes region. The humble and cosy cottage has been furnished with clothing and furniture of the period. There are also many historic buildings along Stirling Terrace, east of York Street. The most striking is the red brick **Old Post Office** with its turrets and clock tower. The 1870 building housed the courthouse, mail room, customs office and bond store. It has been occupied by the University of Western Australia to be used as the Albany campus.

The city sits between two hills, **Mount Melville** and **Mount Clarence**, both of which have impressive viewpoints that can be driven to (within 100 m or so). Mount Clarence was the site of Australia's first dawn ANZAC Day service in April 1930. Further to the east, forming the northern headland of the Ataturk Entrance, is the city's third major hill, **Mount Adelaide**. It is atop Mount Adelaide that the city's defences were chiefly constructed at the end of the 19th century. **The Forts** ① *T9841 9369, daily 0900-1700, $9, children $3, concessions $6, café Tue-Sun 0900-1600*, is the common name for the **Princess Royal Fortress**, actually less a fortress and more a barracks and gunnery station. Gun emplacements were first put into place at the end of the 19th century to guard against the imagined threat from both France and Russia, and were beefed up for the duration of the Second World War, though a shot was never fired in anger. Many of the dozen or so existing buildings, from barracks to ammunition storage pits, have been restored and either convey their original use or have been converted to museums, notably of the Australian Light Horse. The extensive grounds also contain a couple of good lookouts and two large gun turrets from Second World War naval vessels, including one from *HMAS Sydney*, which are open for inspection. The tearoom serves light lunches and cream teas.

The Old Farm at Strawberry Hill ① *Middleton Rd, T9841 3735, 1000-1600, $5, children and concessions $3, National Trust*, between the city centre and Middleton Beach (see below) was the very first farm in WA and the small complex sports a number of buildings from the 1830s. One original cottage is now a tearoom, very much in the English style. The main two-storey building, dating from 1836, was the family home of Captain Sir Richard Spencer, Albany's Government Resident of the time, and is now furnished as it might have been a century or so ago.

The nearest decent beach to the city, **Middleton Beach**, is at the northern base of the hill, 4 km from the city centre via road or 5 km via the pleasant walking track that comes around the headland from the end of Princess Royal Drive. This beach has a grassy foreshore with a BBQ and picnic tables, toilets, showers and changing rooms. The small adjacent suburb boasts a couple of cafés, a large hotel and several other accommodation options. Another 4 km north along the shore of Middleton Harbour is **Emu Point**, the western headland at the entrance to **Oyster Harbour**. On the harbour side of the point is a small, more sheltered beach with a safe swimming enclosure and boat hire. The beach also has a grassy foreshore with BBQs, picnic tables and toilets, plus an adjacent café and restaurant.

Around Albany ›› *For listings, see pages 217-224.*

Torndirrup National Park → *Colour map 3, C5. Return drive around 60 km.*

Occupying the ocean-side part of the peninsula that forms the southern arm of both Princess Royal Harbour and King George Sound, Torndirrup protects one of WA's most striking stretches of granite coast. The final 6 km of Frenchman Bay Road winds through the inland part of the park, with a series of side roads, mostly sealed, leading to the coast's most spectacular landmarks. The first of these, **Sharp Point**, is accessed by an unsealed road just past an '80 km' sign and shortly before the ranger's residence. A short loop walk at the point gives excellent views up and down the coast. The first sealed turn-off, after the information bay, leads to the **Gap** and **Natural Bridge**. The first is a 25-m-deep chasm perpendicular to the cliff edge, a real wave trap that sees the sea thumping into the rocks, shooting spray sometimes up as far as the lookout (take care to stay behind the rails when the seas are heavy). A similar chasm 50 m away is bridged at the end by a massive natural arch. The third access road is for the **Blowholes**, a series of cracks in the granite foreshore that in heavy seas can erupt into geysers of spray and foam. At quieter times the 30-minute return walk is worth it for the views up and down the coast, including the impressively bulbous promontory of **Peak Head**. There is a 2½-hour return walk to the head from **Stony Hill**, a couple of kilometres from the Blowholes. Views from the hill range over much of the park. Salmon Hole Road leads to **Salmon Holes**, a beautiful sandy beach below a ring of protective low hills. An offshore reef creates a beach-side pool, said to shelter migrating salmon in rough seas. Also off this road, an unsealed turn heads down to **Misery Beach**, a beautiful white-sand cove on the sheltered side of the peninsula, and **Isthmus Hill**. A path leads up over the shoulder of the hill (20 minutes return), with views over Salmon Holes and King George Sound, and then on another 5 km to the end of the peninsula at Bald Head. Allow six hours return for this excellent hike. Frenchman Bay Road ends at **Frenchman Bay**, with its lovely little beach, complete with BBQs and picnic tables. There are places you can stay here.

Whale World

ⓘ *Frenchman Bay Rd, 20 km from Albany, T9844 4021, www.whaleworld.org, 0900-1700, tours on the hour 1000-1500 (40 mins), $25, children $10, concessions $15-20. Walk on the Wild Side, $10, children $5, concessions $9; nocturnal tours $35, children $10, concessions $30.*

This former whaling station turned museum treats its history and subject matter in a laudably even-handed way, offering a rare glimpse into the inner life of this emotive industry. Most of the extensive complex comprises the old whale-processing buildings, preserved more or less as they were the day the station closed in 1978. These include the open-air cutting and flensing decks, cooking rooms, oil processing and storage facilities, and even one of the last hunting ships, now dry-docked. All allow virtually full access. One shed houses various skeletons and pickled remains. Displays, films and dioramas leave

Around Albany

little (except, thankfully, the notorious smells) to the imagination, so this may not be for you if you're squeamish, but a fascinating couple of hours can be spent here. The main building also houses a wonderful collection of prints by wildlife artist Richard Ellis, depicting over 60 marine mammals, plus a gift shop and cheap café with indoor and terrace tables overlooking the harbour. There is also a picnic area with children's playground and free BBQs.

New to Whale World is **Walk on the Wild Side**, a fauna park offering visitors the chance to discover some of Australia's lesser seen marsupials and reptiles. Tours are self-guided during the day, or there are nocturnal guided tours (times advised on booking) when you can watch the animals being fed.

Two Peoples Bay Nature Reserve → *Colour map 3, C6.*

① *T9846 4276, visitor centre open Dec-May daily 1000-1600, Jun-Nov Wed and Sat 1000-1600.*
Just to the east of Albany, about 35 km by road, is another magical bit of coastline, **Two Peoples Bay**, where granite domes slope into the sea and sand. The bay got its name from a meeting between Frenchman Captain Ransonnet of Baudin's exploratory expedition and James Pendleton, captain of an American brig that had just arrived for sealing and whaling. The pair are thought to have had a good whinge about the British and then named the bay 'Baie des Deux Nations' in memory of the meeting. The reserve has some rare fauna, in fact two species previously thought to be extinct have been found here, the noisy scrub bird and Gilbert's potoroo. The potoroo is a distant relation of the wallaby and is a small nocturnal creature that digs for truffles. You are unlikely to see either of these creatures but there is a good visitor centre where you can learn more about them. **Little Beach** tends to be more peaceful than the fine beaches of Frenchman Bay. At the picnic ground by the visitor centre there is a 2-km walk with several lookouts providing views over the bay and towards Mount Manypeaks. The road is not sealed but fine for 2WD. Camping is not allowed.

◉ Walpole to Albany listings

For Sleeping and Eating price codes and other relevant information, see pages 28-34.

● Sleeping

Walpole and around *p206*

L Houseboat Holidays, T9840 1310, www.houseboatholiday.com.au. Has 10-, 6- and 4-berth boats available, expensive for 2 people, but around $150-200 per person per night if you fill them up.
B Riverside Retreat, South Coast Highway, near Nornalup, T9840 1255, www.riverside retreat.com.au. Good location, with splendid views over the Franklin River. The 6 chalets are clean and comfortable rather than luxurious, and sleep up to 8. Facilities include use of tennis court and canoes.

B-C Tree Top Walk Motel, Nockolds St, T9840 1555, www.treetopwalkmotel.com.au. 35 standard motel rooms. There is also a restaurant (daily 1830-2100) and an outdoor pool. Reception hours daily 0700-2200.
C Inlet View, 58 Walpole St, T9840 1226. Not an outstanding B&B, but the welcome is warm and it has good views over Walpole Inlet. Continental breakfast provided.
C Stargazers, 51 Jacksonii Av, off Allen Rd 5 km from Walpole, T9840 1553, stargazers@ wn.com.au. Another unremarkable, modern B&B, but with very friendly hosts and a great position overlooking a dam and forest. All meals can be prearranged, telescope available for stargazing. A full English breakfast is served, a 'healthy option' can be requested.

C Tingledale Cottage, off Hazelvale Rd, T9840 8181, www.tingledalecottage.com. Charming, isolated wooden cottage for 2 in a forest setting with outdoor spa. Semi-self-contained, all meals can be arranged, country-style cooked breakfast included. 2 nights minimum.

D-E Tingle All Over YHA, 60 Nockolds St, T9840 1041, tingleallover2000@yahoo.com.au. Clean budget rooms, shared bathroom and superb kitchen. Linen provided, free pick-ups available. Car hire and bike hire can be organized here.

D-E Walpole Lodge, corner Pier St and Park Av, T9840 1244, www.walpolelodge.com.au. Dorms, singles, en suite doubles and family rooms. TV, pool table, BBQ, disabled facilities.

Caravan parks

B-E Coalmine Beach Holiday Park, T9840 1026, www.coalminebeach.com.au. Very close to Nornalup Inlet. Cabins, but no on-site vans. Powered and unpowered sites.

D-F Peaceful Bay Caravan Park, T9840 8060. Near the ocean, offering on-site vans and powered and unpowered sites.

D-F Rest Point Holiday Village, Rest Point Rd, T9840 1032, www.restpoint.com.au. The best location, overlooking Walpole Inlet, about 5 km from town.

E-F Valley of the Giants Eco Park, South Coast Highway, Nornalup, T9840 1313, www.valleyofthegiantsecopark.biz. Only 6 km from the Tree Top Walk. Unpowered and powered sights as well as on-site van hire.

Denmark *p208, map p209*

There's a lot of accommodation around Denmark, particularly self-contained chalets and cottages. Contact the VIC for more.

A-B Karma Chalets, 1572 South Coast Highway, T9848 1568, www.karmachalets.com.au. 8 luxury houses on stilts, most with spas, backing onto karri forest. Each with private balcony and BBQ. Superb views.

B The Cove, Payne Rd, T9848 1770, www.thecovechalets.com. Sits on about 20 ha of mixed karri, jarrah and tingle forest, threaded through with bushwalks that wind directly down to the inlet. 5 hand-built wooden cottages sleeping 2-20, 'Sanctum' and 'Tingle', are particularly charming. Happy to do Bibbulmun drop-offs and pick-ups.

B Mt Lindesay View, corner of Mt Shadforth and McNabb Rds, T9848 1933, www.members.westnet.com.au/mtlindesayview. Modern bungalow B&B with 3 comfortable en suite rooms and views over the valleys to the north. The welcome extends to a cooked breakfast, and complimentary port and chocolates.

B-D Waterfront, 63 Inlet Dr, T9848 1147, www.denmarkwaterfront.com.au. A good range of accommodation in this complex among karri trees on the inlet shore 2.5 km from town. 2 level studios with balcony and motel rooms are all bright and cheery and built in a rustic timber and earth style.

C Koorabup Motel, South Coast Highway, T9848 1044, www.koorabup.com.au. 1- to 2-bedroom apartments with fully equipped kitchen, plus motel rooms with bush-view balconies. The family rooms are good value. Continental breakfast available ($8).

D-E Blue Wren Travellers' Rest YHA, 17 Price St, T9848 3300, www.denmarkbluewren.com.au. 20 beds in backpacker hostel, in an old timber worker's cottage extended for modern dorms and bathrooms. Clean with central location. Bike hire and internet available.

Caravan parks

A-E Ocean Beach, T9848 1105, www.denmarkobhp.com.au. Big 4 caravan park in a beautiful location near the mouth of the inlet. Accommodation types range from chalets with ocean view, to on-site cabins and powered tent sites. BBQs, campers' kitchen, mini golf, tennis court and children's playground.

C-F Rivermouth, Inlet Dr, T9848 1262, www.denmarkrivermouthcaravanpark.com.au. On-site vans, en suite and budget cabins.

Denmark to Albany *p211*

Contact the Denmark VIC for more information about accommodation in West Cape Howe National Park.

A-B Cape Howe Cottages, Tennessee South Rd, western edge of West Cape Howe National Park, T9845 1295, www.cape howe.com.au. 2-bedroom cottages, a luxury retreat and more modern lodge. All are self-contained and linen and towels included. Bibbulmun Track drop-offs and pick-ups by arrangement. Fishing rods for hire.

B Tennessee Hill Chalets, Piggot Martin Rd, T9845 2359, www.tennesseehillcom.au. 2 private self-contained chalets with wonderful views from their spots on the hillside. Linen and towels included. The owners also run **The Bushfood Café** (see Eating, below).

Albany *p212, map p213*

Albany VIC can provide information on accommodation options, including some free camping spots by the beaches on the outskirts of town. These are very popular so arrive early.

LL-A Maitraya, 1320 Nanarup Rd, T9361 90444, www.maitraya.com. A luxury private residence 30 mins outside of Albany, this is the place to treat yourself if there are a number of you (the house sleeps 16) and it's a special occasion. The main house has an indoor pool, gym, cinema room and there are tennis courts and an orchard nearby. However, if you want the seclusion without breaking the bank, you can rent the Airstrip Cottage (**A**) for a minimum stay of 2 nights. The cottage is small but comfortable and you're really paying for the breathtaking views and access to the lake and the beach.

L-B The Terrace, 36 Marine Terr, Middleton beach, T9842 9901, www.members.westnet. com.au/theterrace. Types of accommodation include en suite B&B rooms (country-style or continental breakfast included), spacious 3-bedroom villas with full kitchen and a 4-bedroom villa that sleeps up to 9.

L-E Middleton Beach, 28 Flinders Parade, Middleton Beach, T9841 3593. Excellent but

pricey Big4 caravan park with villas, chalets, cabins, spa and good communal facilities.

A-B Hideaway Haven, 21 Yokanup Rd, Bayonet Head, T9844 9417, www.hideaway-haven.com.au. Set amidst bushland, this luxury B&B offers 2 queens and 1 twin room, all en suite and with balconies. Very peaceful with great views, a jacuzzi on the deck and excellent birdwatching opportunities. Fully-equipped kitchen and a BBQ, gourmet breakfast is provided and includes home-made bread.

A-E Rose Gardens, 45 Mermaid Av, Emu Point, T9844 1868, www.acclaimparks. com.au. Caravan park with on-site vans, beachfront villas, budget chalets, numerous tent sites, a store and fuel.

B My Place, 47 Grey St East, T9842 3242, www.myplace.com.au. 8 spacious and clean units with full kitchen, laundry and BBQ.

C-E Kalgan River Chalets and Caravan Park, 247 Nanarup Rd, T9844 7937, www.kalganrivercaravanpark.com.au. Located outside town on the Kalgan River, this caravan park has a range of self-contained chalets sleeping 2-12 people. Facilities are excellent and kangaroos are regular visitors to the 9-hole golf course. Recommended.

D-E 1849 Backpackers, The London Hotel, entrance on Duke St, T0405 179 977. Recently opened backpackers still in its infancy with small dorms and some en suite doubles. The downstairs is currently being renovated and should soon house a big screen TV and a restaurant.

D-E Discovery Inn, 9 Middleton Rd, 200 m from beach, T9842 5535, www.discovery inn.com.au. Guesthouse with 14 rooms, including a couple of small 'backpacker' dorms. Full-cooked breakfast ($8.50) can be taken in the pleasant central courtyard. Laundry and internet facilities (10 mins free).

D-F Bayview YHA, 49 Duke St, T9842 3388, www.yha.com.au. Friendly, quiet backpackers with lots of space, sea views and good facilities. Doubles, twins and family rooms have TVs and fridges and DVDs are available to borrow from reception. Bike and snorkel hire. Free bread. Wi-Fi available, the more you buy the cheaper it gets.

E-F Albany Backpackers, corner of Stirling Terr and Spencer St, T1800 260 130, T9841 8848, www.albanybackpackers.com.au. Lively, central hostel with some vivid wall paintings and spacious communal areas. Activities arranged, such as BBQ, pool and movie nights. Free coffee and cake every night at 1830. Wi-Fi available or there's an internet café downstairs. Also offers bike hire.

❶ Eating

Walpole and around *p206*
Ⅲ-Ⅱ Tea House, 6684 South Coast Highway, Nornalup, T9840 1422, www.nornaluptea house.com.au. Wed-Mon 1130-2100, booking essential. This is an essential stop on your trip for some of WA's best cuisine, serving inventive Modern Australian dishes using seasonal local produce. The friendly service, gourmet coffee and wines match its food. Fully licensed and BYO. Recommended.
Ⅲ-Ⅱ Top Deck, Nockolds St, T9840 1344. Tue 0900-1600 and Wed-Sat 0900-2100. Takes care to serve consistently good food. Fully licensed.

Denmark *p208*
It's best to go out for lunch in Denmark as places to have dinner are thin on the ground. It's also worth considering eating at one of the wineries, see section.
Ⅲ-Ⅱ Denmark Hotel, Hollings Rd, T9848 2206. Daily 1200-1400 and 1800-2100. The pub has a large, modern dining room overlooking the river and does pub meals a cut above the usual, including Peri Peri crocodile and Scotch Marron.
Ⅲ-Ⅱ Denmark River Bistro, 6 Hollings Rd, T9848 2217. Mon-Sat 0800-1600 and 1800-2100, Sun 0830-1500 and 1800-2100. Filling options for breakfast, lunch and dinner.
Ⅲ-Ⅱ Forest Hill Vineyard, South Coast Highway (4 km west of town), T9848 1922.

Cellar door daily 1000-1700, restaurant daily 1100-1400 and Fri 1800-1900. Superb regional produce in a modern space overlooking the forest and ocean. Recommended.
Ⅲ-Ⅱ Denmark Pizza, corner Walker and Strickland St, T9848 2479. Cheap and cheerful, serving very good pizzas. Cash only.
Ⅱ Bento Box, corner South Coast Highway, opposite Berridge Park, T9848 1163. Mon-Thu 0800-1930, Fri-Sat 0800-2100, Sun 0800-2000. Bento boxes, fresh sushi, soups and Italian dishes such as lasagne and cannelloni. Eat in or takeaway.

Cafés
Bibbulmun Café, corner South Coast Highway and Strickland St, T9848 1289. Mon-Fri 0700-1600, Sat 0730-1500, Sun 0800-1400. Good range of organic dishes, coffee and pastry. Breakfast is served every weekday until 1100 and weekends until midday.
Café 8, Fig Tree Square, 27 Strickland St, T9848 2051. Daily 0830-1700. Located a bit off the main strip, this popular spot has outdoor tables, good breakfast and lunch options.
Denmark Bakery, 8 Fig Tree Square, 27 Strickland St, T9848 2143. Daily 0700-1700. An award-winning bakery offering a variety of tasty pies including Vindaloo Roo. Also serves cakes and coffees and other bakery staples.
Denmark Chocolate Lounge, 2023 South Coast Highway, 9 km west of Denmark, T9840 9708, www.denmarkchocolate.com.au. Daily 1000-1630. A little way out of town, this licensed café is a great place to unwind. Sit outside on the veranda or lounge in the comfortable chairs and enjoy the handmade chocolates. Local wines, stouts, ales, fruit beers from Belgium and liqueurs have been carefully chosen to complement the milk and dark chocolates. The hot chocolate on offer is also quite something.
McSweeneys Gourmet Café, 5B Strickland St, T9848 2362. Open 0700-1700 (no hot food after 1530). Small, rustic establishment with outside tables and serving the best café food in Denmark. Recommended.

Mount Shadforth and Scotsdale scenic drives p210

♔♔-♔ The Southern End Restaurant, Karri Mia, 427 Mt Shadforth Rd, T9848 2600, www.southernend.com.au. Sun buffet breakfast 0830-1030, lunch Thu-Mon 1130-1400, and dinner Thu-Sat 1730-2100. Stylish dining room and an outside deck, both with superb views. Not particularly inventive menu but the food is excellent, using locally grown products and specialising in seafood. Mid-range, light lunches, more formal in evening. Deck overlooking the ocean. Also runs Denmark Brew and Ales microbrewery from here, beers are available for tasting.

Denmark to Albany p211

♔ The Bushfood Factory and Café, 233 Piggot Martin Rd (off Lower Denmark Rd), T9845 2359, www.anbp.com.au. At the top of Tennessee Hill amidst a bushfood plantation is a café that offers home-cooked food using native ingredients. Sit on the terrace and enjoy the view whilst tucking in to a crocodile burger, witchetty grubs or lemon myrtle fishcakes. Also serves up very popular curries and a selection of cakes. Can cater for vegetarians and vegans.

Albany p212, map p213
See also Bars and clubs, below.

♔♔♔ The Wild Duck, 112 York St, T9842 2554, www.wildduckrestaurant.com. Wed-Sun from 1800-2100. Considered by foodies to be the best restaurant in the region, the simple and serious interior is a stage for sophisticated and imaginative cooking. Degustation menu $90 per person. Bookings essential.

♔♔♔-♔♔ Mean Fiddler, 132 York St, T9842 1852. Mon-Sat 1800-2200. A child-friendly Italian restaurant with a bright interior. Licensed and BYO.

♔♔ Lavender Cottage, 55 Peels Place, T9842 2073. Mon-Fri 1130-1330, Fri dinner 1830 until late. A cosy and extremely welcoming place that serves tasty lunches and a French-style gourmet dinner on Fri (booking advised).

♔♔ Nonna's, 135 Lower York St, T9841 4626. Mon-Fri 1100-2200, Sat 1700-2200. Relaxed

restaurant serving a range of seafood, pasta and meat dishes.

♔ Dylans, 82 Stirling Terr, T9841 8720, www.dylans.com.au. Tue-Sat 0700-2030, Sun 0800-1600. Casual place that does breakfasts, burgers, pancakes and dinners. BYO.

Cafés
Bar Cino, 338 Middleton Loop, T9841 5550, www.barcino.com.au. Mon-Fri 0800-1600. Sleek joint at the top end of town, with a good range of rolls, salads and stylish casual food. Free wireless internet with purchase.
Black Duck Gourmet Pantry, 34 Peels Place, T9842 1433. Mon-Wed 0830-1700, Thu 0830-1730, Sat 0830-1500. Next door to Rookley's, this deli sells chutneys, sauces, cheeses and sweets to take away. Alternatively, grab a piece of cake and coffee or a sausage roll and relax in the sun.
Rookley's, 36 Peels Place, T9842 2236. Mon-Fri 0800-1600, Sat 0830-1400. The best position and outdoor terrace tables to watch the action on York St. Good range of pastry and some light meals.
The Squid Shack, Emu Point Boat Ramp. BYO. Wed-Sun 1000-1900 (summer), 1000-2100 (winter). No-frills fish and chips, but could be the best you've had in years.
True Blue Providore, 14 Peels Place, T9841 1815. Mon-Fri 0630-1430, Sat 0630-1130. All-day breakfast menu and tasty and diverse lunch options. Sells smoked meats, including kangaroo, to take away and sources a lot of its produce locally. Check out the blackboard for details of how far things have travelled to your plate.
Vancouver Café Store, 65 Vancouver St, T9841 2475. Daily 0730-1530. Tucked away a short walk from York St, this popular café is worth seeking out for the atmosphere as much as the food. The produce is fresh and locally sourced, and there's a specials board behind the counter. Recommended.
York Street Café, 184 York St, T9842 1666. Mon-Sat 0830-1600 and Wed-Sat 1800-2100. Another great spot on Albany's main street to enjoy great coffee and excellent, inventive

food in a modern setting. Friendly service and the best iced chocolate in town.

Around Albany *p215, map p216*

⏝⏝⏝ **Cello's of Church Lane**, corner of Hassell Highway and Church Lane Rd, 25 km from Albany, T9844 3370. Thu-Sun 1030-1700, Fri-Sat 1800-2030. Considered the best in the region, imaginative food served in a historic homestead overlooking the Kalgan River. BYO. Recommended.

🌓 Bars and clubs

Albany *p212, map p213*

Albany, 244 York St, T9842 3337. The street terrace of this busy pub is one of the town's most popular spots on a sunny day. Restaurant meals 1130-1430, 1800-2030.

Earl of Spencer, corner of Earl and Spencer Sts, T9841 1322. Built in the 1870s this fine pub has seen stints as a boarding house, ale house and grocery store. Its cosiness, traditional decor, English and Irish beers, and excellent food make it about as close to a real English pub as you'll find in WA. Cheap meals daily 1200-2100. Lovely courtyard. Recommended.

The White Star, 72 Stirling Terr, T9841 1733, www.whitestarhotel.com.au. Modern bar, brewery and restaurant with patio at the rear. Cheap and filling bar food, beer tasting trays, big screen for live sport and live music Thu-Sun. Meals Mon-Thu 1100-1500, 1700-2200 and Fri-Sun 1100-2200.

⭘ Shopping

Albany *p212, map p213*

Albany Farmers Market, Collie St, T9841 4312, www.albanyfarmersmarket.com.au. Sat 0800-1200. Delicious regional produce.

Albany Boatshed Markets, Albany Boatshed, Princess Royal Dr, www.albanyboatshed markets.com. Sun 1000-1300. Fresh fish seafood and produce.

Camping World, 173 Chester Pass Rd. Camper trailer, tent and equipment hire.

Gemini, 150A York St, T9841 7711. Mon-Fri 0900-1700, Sat 0900-1500, Sun 1000-1500. Second-hand books and exchange.

Mountain Design, 222 York St, T9841 1413. Mon-Wed, Fri 0900-1715, Thu to 1900, Sat to 1230. Outdoor, trekking and camping equipment.

Denmark *p208*

Dark Side Chocolates, 10 Hollings Rd, T0407 984820. Wed-Fri 0930-1700, Sat 0930-1200. Handmade chocolates ranging from the more mainstream to Beetroot and Shiraz or Balsamic and Blackberry.

Denmark Health Shop, 4/39 Strickland St, T9848 1039. Stocks a range of organic beauty products and also has self-serve grains and pulses.

Odyssey Bookshop, 8/21 Strickland St, T9848 3344. A lovely little second-hand bookshop, which also stocks some new books.

Old Butter Factory Galleries, 11 Mt Shadforth Rd, T9848 2525. Daily 1000-1630. Largest gallery in Denmark with the best range of jewellery, pottery and artworks. Also luxurious Alpaca products.

The Source – Real Food Store, Fig Tree Square, 27 Strickland St, T9848 1183 www.thesourcerealfoodstore.com.au, Wed-Mon 0900-1700 (Sun 1400). Amazing range of organic, local and imported food that will be appreciated by self-caterers. Sat morning is the best time to pop in for fresh produce, as it comes direct from Albany Farmer's Market. If you're staying in town over the weekend, place your order for seasonal produce on the Fri and then come and pick it up.

▲ Activities and tours

Walpole *p206*

Going Wild Bushcraft and Survival, Jacksonii Av, T0458 076 503. Can you find food? Can you build a shelter? Anthony Thompson answers these questions and more during his 4-hr workshop (1300-1700). It takes place on his 6 ha of bush and includes bush plant ID, a trapping demonstration, shelter building, fire lighting and a trip to try and catch Marron. Call in advance, $80, children $40 (less if accompanied by a paying adult).

Naturally Walpole Tours, T9840 1019, www.naturallywalpole.com.au. Several 4WD tours in the region including refreshments and cakes (half day from $75, children $40).

WOW Wilderness, T9840 1036, www.wow wilderness.com.au. Enthusiastic, informative and entertaining boat cruises around the inlets (2½ hrs, $40, children $15) or, in summer, memorable trips up the Frankland River (3½ hrs, $35, children $15). Morning tea included, BYO lunch. Departures 1000 and 1230 daily from the jetties near the pub. Enquiries at the VIC. Book the day before as it's very popular.

Denmark *p208*

Ashburton Air Service, T9848 2133 and T0408 846041, www.ashburtonairservice. com.au. Offer a variety of flexible scenic flights (30 mins) and aerial safaris departing from and returning to Jandakot Airport. Pick-ups and drop-offs at other airport throughout the state also possible. Minimum 2 people.

Out of Sight Tours, 8A Hollings Rd, T9848 2814 and T0427 234 388, www.outofsight tours.com. This eco-friendly company offers a wide range of tours around Denmark. 5 different adventure tours take small groups of people to remote parts of the region's national parks, the Quarram Nature Reserve, West Cape Howe National Park and the Valley of the Giants. Wine-tasting tours (half day $75, full day from $95) and guided walks along the Bibbulmun Track (from $95 including lunch) are also available. Enquire here about kayak, canoe and bike hire as well.

Wilderness Getaways, T9848 2814, www.wildernessgetaways.com.au. Offers a range of packages with chalet accommodation, including guided walks along the Bibbulmun Track.

Wilson Inlet and Ocean Beach *p209*
South Coast Surfing, T9848 2057 and T0401 349854, Ocean Beach. Board hire ($20 per hr). Private lessons $80 for 2 hrs. 1-day group lessons $50 per person including wetsuit and board hire.

Albany *p212*

At Emu Point you can hire pedalos, surfcats, paddle boats and kayaks at weekends and daily during school holidays, T9842 9798.

Albany Scenic Flights, T0437 194354, www.heliwest.com.au. Based at Whale World, Heliwest offers helicopter scenic flights of varying lengths (from 8 mins to 1 hr).

Albany Tailor Made Tours, T0401 594794, www.albanytailormadetours.com. Customized tours for 1-6 people, including town tours, scenic coastal tours and winery visits.

Albany Whale Tours, T0409 107180, www.albanywhaletours.com.au. Whale-watching trips (Jun-Oct) daily at 0930 (3 hrs) and at 1330 by appointment. In summer organises scenic (3 hrs) and sunset cruises.

Kalgan Queen, T9844 3166, www.albany australia.com. Half-day cruises from Emu Point up the Kalgan River in a glass-bottom boat to explore Albany's history and wildlife. Wine-tasting at no extra cost. Tea or coffee and a hot damper. Half day for $65, children $35. Sep-Jun.

Silver Star Cruises, T0428 429 876, www.whales.com.au. Heads out daily, Jun-Oct, at 0930 and 1300 for 2½-hr whale-watching trips. Daily scenic cruises (2½ hrs) depart all year at 0930.

Spinners, T9844 1906, www.spinners charters.com.au. Offers full-day ocean fishing, all equipment supplied..

⊖ Transport

Walpole *p206*
Bus TransWA buses leave from the Visitor Centre parking bay for the **timber towns** and **Bunbury** Tue, Wed, Fri, Sat, Sun at 0943, and Mon and Thu at 1018 (the latter Mon and

Thu services do not stop at **Northcliffe** or **Pemberton**). All have immediate onward connections to **Perth**. Eastbound buses to **Denmark** and **Albany** depart Mon, Tue, Thu, Sat, Sun at 1627, Wed at 1552 and Fri at 1552 and 2002.

Car servicing Walpole Mechanical and Tyres, Vista St, T9840 1297. Mon-Sat 0800-1700, Sun 0800-1200.

Denmark *p208*
Bus TransWA buses leave from Strickland St for **Walpole**, the **timber towns** and **Bunbury** Tue, Wed, Fri, Sat, Sun at 0847, and Mon and Thu at 0922 (the latter services do not stop at **Northcliffe** or **Pemberton**). All have immediate onward connections to **Perth**. Eastbound buses to **Albany** depart Sat-Tue and Thu at 1723, and Wed and Fri at 1648.

Car servicing Talisman Motors, South Coast Highway, corner of Welsh St, T9848 1372.

Albany *p212, map p213*
Air Skywest flies daily to **Perth**.

Bus Love's Bus Service, T9841 1211, operates a handful of services around the northern city suburbs, all starting and terminating at Peels Place. The 301 heads out along **Middleton Road** to **Middleton Beach** and **Emu Point** Mon-Fri at 0845, 1045, 1300 and 1440, and Sat at 1030 and 1200. TransWA buses leave from the VIC for **Denmark**, **Walpole**, the **timber towns** and **Bunbury** Tue, Wed, Fri, Sat, Sun at 0800, and Mon and Thu at 0835 (the latter Mon and Thu services do not stop at Northcliffe or Pemberton).

Car Car hire from: Albany Car Rentals, 386 Albany Highway, T9841 7077. Budget Rent-A-Car, 360 Albany Highway, T9841 7799, www.budget.com.au. Avis, 557 Albany Highway, T9842 2833, www.avis.com.au. King Sound Vehicle Hire, 6 Sanford Rd, T9841 8466, www.kingsoundcars.com. Rainbow Coast Car Rental, 33 Campbell Rd, T9841 7130.

Car servicing from De Jonge Mechanical Repairs, 52 Cockburn Rd, T9842 2293.

Taxi T9841 7000.

Around Albany *p215*
There are no public services to Torndirrup National Park.

● Directory

Walpole *p206*
Banks There is an ATM in the local IGA supermarket on Nockolds St. **Internet** Community Resource Centre, T9840 1395. Mon-Fri 0900-1700, Sat 1000-1200. **Laundry** Vista St. **Medical services** Walpole Pharmacy, Nockolds St. Mon-Fri 0900-1700, Sat 0900-1200. **Post** Main St, Mon-Fri 0900-1700. **Useful contacts** DEC, Main St, T9840 0400. Mon-Fri 0800-1630.

Denmark *p208*
Banks Several banks and ATMs on Strickland St. **Internet** Spot News, 39 Strickland St, T9848 1362. Mon-Fri 0800-1700, Sat 0815-1300 and Sun 0830-1230. **Community** Resource Centre, Strickland St, T9848 2842. Mon-Fri 1000-1600. **Medical services** Chemists: Denmark Pharmacy, 20 Strickland St, T9848 2553. Mon-Fri 0900- 1700, Sat 0900-1200. Hospital: Denmark Hospital and Health Service, 50 Scotsdale Rd, T9848 0600. **Police** South Coast Highway, T9848 1311. **Post** Stickland St, Mon-Fri 0900-1700.

Albany *p212, map p213*
Banks Several banks and ATMs on York St. **Internet** Several, including Public Library, 221 York St. **Medical services** Chemists: Amcal, 262 York St, T9842 2036, daily 0900-2100. Hospital: Albany Regional, Warden Av, T9892 2222. Medical centre: Southern Regional Medical Group, 32 Albany Highway (near York St roundabout), T9841 2733. **Police** 210 Stirling Terr, T131 444. **Post** 218 York St.

Mount Barker and around

Mount Barker is a service town for the surrounding agricultural region. The area was explored by Europeans in the 1830s, mostly settlers from Albany looking for good agricultural land. In the past the region was known for apples, sheep and cattle but now, like much of the southwest, the earth is fast being covered by vines. Wildflowers are also grown commercially and there are many young plantations of Tasmanian blue gums that will be used for paper and woodchips. The main appeal for visitors is Mount Barker's location just west of the Porongurup National Park and south of the Stirling Range National Park. Both are beautiful forested hill ranges with great peak walks and the Stirling Ranges, in particular, has an incredible diversity of flora. The wildflowers in spring are wonderful. ➤➤ For listings, see pages 228-229.

Ins and outs

The **VIC** ① T9851 1163, www.mountbarkertourismwa.com.au, Mon-Fri 0900-1700, Sat 0900-1500, Sun 1000-1500, is in the old railway station on the Albany Highway. It's very efficient and can provide maps for a driving route around the region, taking in wineries, wildflowers and St Werburgh's Chapel. ➤➤ See Transport, page 229.

Mount Barker → Colour map 3, C5. Population: 1700. 50 km from Albany.

Just north of the town centre is a cluster of some of Mount Barker's oldest buildings, now restored. The **Old Police Station** was built by convicts in 1867 from local ironstone cemented with mud. For 20 years, until a lockup was added to the stables building, prisoners were tied to a log out front during the day and if required to spend a night in custody, the prisoner would be firmly secured to the leg of the police constable's kitchen table. The buildings are now used as a **museum** ① T9851 1631, Albany Highway, 500 m north of VIC, Sat-Sun and daily during public holidays 1000-1500 or by appointment (T04-0999 3472), $5, under 12s free, by the local historical society.

During the wildflower season it is well worth visiting the local **Banksia Farm** ① Pearce Rd, off Muir Highway, T9851 1770, Aug-Nov daily 0930-1630, Mar-Jun Mon-Fri 0930-1630, self-guided garden walks $11, children under 14 free, fully guided walks Aug-Nov 1000 $25, children under 14 $5, which displays an impressive collection of these unique Australian flowers. The garden walk encourages the visitor to touch and smell the plants and the five-minute talk beforehand offers tips on what to look out for. In Spring there are early morning bird lover walks (by appointment). Banksia Farm also operates a B&B (see Sleeping, page 228) and has a café and gallery. To the southwest of town, the lovely old **St Werburgh's Chapel** ① St Werburgh's Rd, off Muir or Albany Highways, visitors welcome, was built for the local settlers in 1872 from local timber and clay. Services are still held there today by candlelight. For those with the time, 60 km along the Muir Highway towards Manjimup is the **Uralla Wildlife Sanctuary** ① T9856 1065, mandyroo@ westnet.com.au. This is a centre that cares for sick and orphaned animals with an aim to release them back into the wild. Call before you set off as it's quite a way, but there's basic camping available when you get there and a cottage for those who want a bit more comfort. There are opportunities to volunteer if you contact them in advance.

Wineries

The first vines were planted in 1867 but most vineyards in the region were established much more recently. Riesling has been the most successful variety, although Chardonnay and Shiraz are doing well. There are around 20 cellar doors around Mount Barker and most are fairly small and friendly places. A number can be found on Porongurup Road and the Muir and Albany highways.

West Cape Howe ① *Muir Highway, T9892 1444, www.westcapehowewines.com.au, daily 1000-1700,* has relocated from Denmark to Mount Barker and is an impressive, modern cellar door, 10 km south of town. A good range of whites and reds. Good coffee available as well as good wine and there's a café coming soon. Wines cost $10-28.

Plantagenet ① *Albany Highway, T9851 3111, www.plantagenetwines.com, daily 0900-1700,* is right in town so ideal for those without transport. The first winery established in the region, it offers tastings of dry whites, dry reds and a few fortifieds. Wines cost $13-40.

Porongurup National Park → *Colour map 3, C5. 22 km from Mt Barker, 50 km from Albany.*

① *Vehicle entry $11 payable at the entrance, park ranger, T9853 1095. It's worth noting that purchasing a day pass will give you access to Porongurup and the Stirling Ranges*

Despite the proximity of the Porongurup Hills to the Stirling Range, these massive **granite domes** have a very different geological background to their taller neighbours and are thought to be about twice their age. The national park is a small area of forest encompassing the Porongurup Range, only about 12 km long and a few kilometres wide. The range rises out of tall **karri forest**, a relic from a wetter climate that has managed to survive in the conditions provided by the ranges. Karri usually grows further south, between Manjimup and Walpole. The typical karri forest understorey flora and fauna has also survived here and wildflowers stage a brilliant display in spring. Walking in the Porongurup range is very enjoyable as most walks include both gentle forest trails and fantastic views of the Stirling Range and King George Sound from the top of sheets and boulders of granite. You also have a good chance of seeing western grey kangaroos, brush wallabies and lots of birds if you walk quietly, particularly in the late afternoon. There are two main entry points, both from the northern side. Bolganup Road leads from the main settlement area to a shady clearing where there are picnic tables and BBQs. This is the start of several walk trails. The next entry point is Castle Rock Road, unsealed but only 1 km long, about 6 km further east, and gives access to the **Castle Rock** and **Balancing Rock** trail only.

One of the park's attractions is **Tree in the Rock**, a karri that appears to be growing from the centre of a large boulder. The tree is only about 100 m from the Bolganup picnic area and you will pass it if you walk the **Nancy Peak Circuit**. This is a steady uphill walk through forest up to three peaks: Hayward, Nancy and Morgans. The highest is Nancy at a little over 600 m. Once you reach the first peak you walk along the ridge and there is little further uphill walking. The southern coast and the Stirling Range are clearly visible from the top. There is a short, steep descent from Morgans and then a wide forest path back to the picnic area (5.5 km, two hours). This is a good walk but if you only have time for one, then head for **Castle Rock**. An easy uphill walk through forest leads to Balancing Rock, a huge 180-tonne boulder that appears to be sitting on its narrowest point, like an upstanding egg. From here you can access the top of adjacent Castle Rock, though it is a bit of a scramble. You need to squeeze through two sets of massive rocks to reach a ladder. Climb the ladder to a platform and you are in the 'castle', a tall group of boulders that enclose you. There are magnificent views of the Stirling Range, laid out on the horizon like a Hollywood set and you will want to stay up here for ages. Return by the same route (4 km; 1½ hours return).

Stirling Range National Park → *Colour map 3, B5. Loop drive (some unsealed) approximately 180 km from Mt Barker, 260 km from Albany.*
① Vehicle entry $11 payable at Bluff Knoll turn-off, park ranger, T9827 9230.

The Stirling Range is an island of pointy bush-clothed peaks, rising sharply from an endless expanse of flat, cleared farmland. The ranges are formed from uplifted quartzite, sandstone and shales and were once ancient seabeds. Rippled stone found all over the ranges is a reminder that they lay under a shallow sea about 500 million years ago. The park is particularly noted for its incredible diversity of flora: there are over 1500 plant species within the park, an area about 65 km by 20 km. The wildflowers are wonderful here in spring and the park has some unusual species of orchids and mountains bells (Darwinias). The park has many peak walks giving views over the surrounding plains and a scenic drive running east–west through the ranges. This unsealed drive (50 km) is best done westward in the morning and eastward in the afternoon. It is also worth a drive up the sealed road to the Bluff Knoll car park for good views of the ranges, even if you don't walk. There are a few picnic areas and lookouts but essentially the park is undeveloped. Dieback (a condition in which branches or shoots die from the tip inwards due to disease or environmental conditions) is a problem here, requiring some areas to be closed to visitors, as are bushfires caused by lightning strikes. There is still much evidence of the bad fires of 1996.

Walking in this national park is really for those who enjoy climbing peaks. Most of the highest peaks can be climbed but two stand out. **Bluff Knoll** (1073 m), the distinctive prow-like peak at the eastern end of the park, is the highest point in the southwest (second highest in WA) and for many visitors this is the one to tick off, if only because it is the only one accessed via a sealed road. The walk starts at the car park and ascends 656 m to the summit. It is a steady uphill walk, along a good formed path, through scrub to a saddle, before swinging around to the summit plateau. The wildflowers are ever present but fantastic in spring, and there are good views of the coast from the saddle (5 km, two to three hours return). The best views in the park are, however, from **Toolbrunup Peak** (1054 m). This narrow conical hill, with two prominent shoulders, can be seen from Bluff Knoll though is more impressive from the scenic drive. It is a more challenging and interesting walk (ascending 630 m) but only for those who are fit, agile and enjoy scrambling over large boulders. Despite the daunting look of the peak from the western side, the route approaches from the east and is tiring. The first half ascends through forest along scree and gravel paths before reaching a boulder field. After an extended, steep scramble the route reaches a saddle and from there it is a short clamber up to the summit, where you can enjoy 360-degree views across the whole of the Stirling Range, Porongurups and the surrounding plains.

There is a two- to three-day wilderness walk, **Stirling Ridge Walk**, from Ellen Peak to Bluff Knoll but you should talk to the DEC ranger (T9827 9230) if considering this. **Stirling Range Retreat** can arrange pick-ups and drops-offs for day walks or extended walks. They also run good-value short guided walks and slide nights during the wildflower season (September to October). Carry plenty of water and check the forecast. Weather can change rapidly on the high peaks and low cloud can cause wind chill and obscure the route.

❂ Mount Barker and around listings

For Sleeping and Eating price codes and other relevant information, see pages 28-34.

🛏 Sleeping

Mount Barker *p225*

The busiest time in Mt Barker is wildflower season from mid-Aug to Oct.

B-C Banksia Farm, Pearce Rd, T9851 1770. Relax on the grounds of the farm or indulge in a spot of birdwatching, whilst staying in this stone house overlooking the Porogurup Ranges. 1 queen room and 1 double, and breakfast is served in the farm's café. For music lovers there's a piano in the large living room and a collection of old vinyl to pop on the record player.

C-D The Jolly Frog B&B, 260 Mt Barker Rd, T9851 1182. B&B that contains 1 queen room and 1 twin. Set in large spacious grounds with a number of small farm animals to visit. Pick-ups available by appointment.

D Plantagenet, 9 Lowood Rd, T9851 1008. Standard hotel rooms above the pub with shared facilities and slightly more expensive self-contained motel rooms.

D-E Mount Barker Caravan Park, Albany Highway just north of town, T9851 1691, www.mtbarkercaravanpark.com. Cabins, on-site vans and basic dongas. Facilities include campers' kitchen and BBQs.

Porongurup National Park *p226*

Porongurup settlement is little more than a shop and service station, which triples as a tearooms and a small, simple hostel. There is no camping permitted in the Porongurup National Park.

A-C Karribank Country Retreat, Porongurup Rd, T9853 1022, www.karribank. com.au, this is the area's upmarket option, an old farm turned guesthouse. A genteel retreat with some beautifully furnished century-old cottage rooms and several cheaper chalets.

C Bolganup Homestead, Porongurup Rd, T9853 1049, www.bolangup.com.au. Next to the shop, a classic farm homestead has been split into 3 large self-contained apartments. Good value for 2, bargain for 4-6. There is also a 3-bed cottage on the property (**A**).

D-E Porongurup Range Tourist Park, 1304 Porongurup Rd, T9853 1057, www.poronguruprangetouristpark.com.au. Has on-site vans and cabins, plus an excellent campers' kitchen and common room. Facilities include swimming pool, tennis court and free gas BBQs.

Stirling Range National Park *p227*

There is camping available at Moingup Spring campground ($7, children under 16 $2, concessions $5), facilities are limited and the spaces fill up quickly so arrive early. A ranger will come round to collect the fees.

B The Lily, Chester Pass Rd, 12 km north of Bluff Knoll turn-off, T9827 9205, www.thelily.com.au. No visit to the Stirlings is complete without a trip here. This inspiring mini 'complex' of rescued and hand-built buildings includes a fully working replica 16th-century Dutch windmill, various 'outbuildings' with elegant and homely rooms and an excellent restaurant in a transferred and restored 1924 railway station. The buildings sit on a slight rise on a wide plain with fantastic views to the ranges. Guests are treated to home-cooked dinners and a breakfast basket to enjoy in their individual houses. There are windmills tours available (minimum 4 people and ring in advance), $10. Recommended.

B-E Stirling Range Retreat, Chester Pass Rd, opposite Bluff Knoll turn-off, T9827 9229, www.stirlingrange.com.au. Self-contained chalets, cabins, vans, hostel rooms and campsites. General facilities include a swimming pool (Nov-Mar), playground and gas BBQs. Friendly staff can advise on walking and arrange pick-ups and drop-offs. Managed as bush retreat for native animals so can be a good spot to see wildlife. Free guided bush walks are held by arrangement and there are Spring bird walks. Internet access available.

E-F Mount Trio Bush Camping and Caravan Park, T9827 9270, www.mounttrio.com.au. Powered and unpowered sites ($14/12 per person), campers' kitchen, hot showers, free gas BBQs and log fire area. There's even a table tennis area. Self check-in.

🍴 Eating

Mount Barker *p225*
The **Banksia Farm** on Pearce Rd (see Sleeping, above) has a café serving home-cooked meals such as soup, quiche and lasagne.

♦♦♦-♦♦ Fio's Restaurant, 34 Albany Highway, T9851 1974. Wed-Sun dinner from 1800, Sat for lunch from 1100. Serves good lunches and slightly more expensive seasonal à la carte dinner. Fully licensed. Every Sun there's a roast on offer for $12.95.

♦♦ Plantagenet, see Sleeping. Mon-Thu from 1500-late, Fri-Sun 1200-1400 and 1800-2000. Pub has a good reputation for its food, particularly steak, served in a very ordinary dining room.

♦ Old Station House Café, 11 Albany Highway, T9851 2084. Tue-Thu 1000-1600, Fri 1000-2100, Sat 1200-1600 and Sun 0900-1600. Thu and Sat evenings by appointment. Very popular and serves up good breakfasts, light meals, cake and coffee. It also does takeaways.

Porongurup National Park *p226*
♦♦♦ Maleeya's Thai Café, 1376 Porongurup Rd, 6 km west of Porongurup, T9853 1123. Fri-Sat 1130-1500, 1800-2100, Sun 1130-2030. Wonderful authentic Thai food at this bamboo nursery and souvenir shop.

Stirling Range National Park *p227*
See also **The Lily**, in Sleeping, above.
♦ Bluff Knoll Café, Chester Pass Rd, almost opposite **Stirling Range Retreat**, T9827 9293. Mon 1000-1500, Thu-Sun 1000-1500, 1730-2000. A pleasant café with good food and friendly service.

🚌 Transport

Mount Barker *p225*
Bus From Albany, northbound buses to **Perth** go via **Mount Barker** Mon-Thu at 0939, Fri at 0939 and 1809, Sat at 0939 and 1139 and Sun at 1539.

The route east

Albany to Esperance → *Distance: 480 km.*
The road to Esperance is a long and mostly featureless one, but there are a few places where you can break the journey up and enjoy the magnificent wilderness within the **Fitzgerald River National Park**. Petrol stations are roughly every 100 km.

At **Ravensthorpe**, 290 km from Albany, the South Coast Highway meets the meandering route back to Perth, which heads through the wheatbelt and can take in **Wave Rock** at Hyden. Ravensthorpe has a VIC, pub and caravan park.

Hopetoun, 50 km off the highway due south of Ravensthorpe, is a little coastal town that provides the best access to Fitzgerald River. Tourist information is available from the **VIC** ① *T9838 3258*, on Veal Street. You can sleep at **Hopetoun Motel and Chalet Village** (T9838 3219) and the pub on the foreshore, **Port Hotel** (T9838 3053). Hopetoun also has a supermarket, fuel and caravan park.

The wilderness of **Fitzgerald River National Park** ① *$11 car, camping at Point Ann and Hamersley Inlet, for more information contact DEC ranger, T9835 5043*, stretches between Bremer Bay and Hopetoun, and inland almost as far as the highway. It is one of the state's most important national parks and has been registered as a UNESCO international biosphere reserve. It contains about 1900 plant species in an area of almost 330,000 ha. Most of the park is covered in low scrub leading to a string of granite ranges and peaks close to the coast. Hammersley Drive passes south of **East Mount Barren**, 12 km west of Hopetoun, and you can climb to the top (3 km, 2½ hours) along a ridge for views along much of the park's coastline.

The last town on the south coast is **Esperance**, a port town dominated by an industrial wharf. The town overlooks the **Archipelago of the Recherche**, a beautiful wide bay full of more than a hundred granite islands. It is one of the most isolated towns in the state and a practical place, with few frills or buildings of character. What draws visitors are the stunning beaches and coastal scenery both to the west on Great Ocean Drive and, further out, to the east of the town in the **Cape Le Grand National park** and **Cape Arid National Park**. The contrast of snow-like sand and aquamarine water deepening to sapphire blue has captivated visitors since Captain Jean Michel Huon de Kermadec discovered this coast in 1792 in *L'Esperance*. For more information contact the **VIC** ① *Dempster St, T9083 1555, www.visitesperance.com, Mon, Tue, Thu 0900-1700, Wed, Fri 0800-1799, Sat 0900-1400, and Sun 0900-1200.*

Across the Nullabor and beyond
From Esperance it's 200 km north to the small gold-mining town of Norseman and from there 720 km east to the WA border. If you are heading to the eastern states take a deep breath because it's a further 1265 km from the WA/SA border to Adelaide. For brief details of **Norseman**, and the trip across the **Nullarbor**, see page 143.

Contents

Footprint features

Midwest

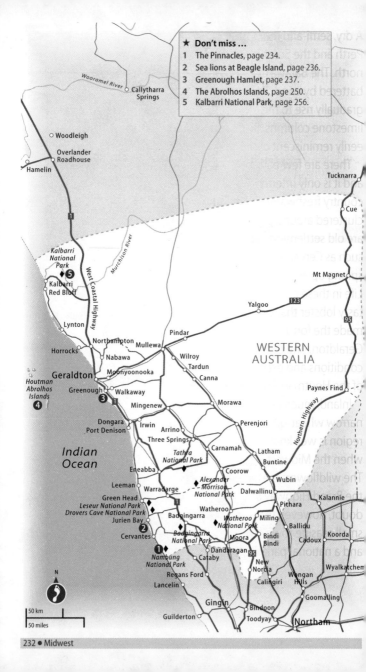

Wooramel River

Callytharra Springs

○ Woodleigh

Overlander
Roadhouse

Hamelin

Tucknarra

Cue

Kalbarri
National
Park

♦ 5

Murchison River

Kalbarri
Red Bluff

Mt Magnet

Lynton

West Coastal Highway

Yalgoo

123

Horrocks

95

Northampton
Nabawa

Mullewa

Pindar

Wilroy

WESTERN
AUSTRALIA

Houtman
Abrolhos
Islands

4

Geraldton

Moonyoonooka

Tardun

Canna

Paynes Find

Greenough

Walkaway

3 1

Mingenew

Morawa

Dongara
Port Denison

Irwin

Arrino

Perenjori

Indian
Ocean

Three Springs

Carnamah

Latham

Tathra
National Park

Coorow

Buntine

Eneabba

Alexander-
Morrison
National Park

Dalwallinu

Wubin

Leeman

Warradarge

Green Head

Leseur National Park
Drovers Cave National Park

Jurien Bay

2

Cervantes

Badgingarra

Watheroo

Watheroo
National Park

Miling

Ballidu

Pithara

Kalannie

Koorda

Northern Highway

Badgingarra
National Park

1

Nambung
National Park

Dandaragan

Moora

Bindi
Bindi

Cadoux

Wyalkatchem

Regans Ford

Cataby

New
Norcia

Calingiri

Wongan
Hills

Goomalling

Lancelin

Gingin

Bindoon

Toodyay

Guilderton

Northam

N

50 km
50 miles

A dry, semi-arid region, the Midwest divides the green hills of Perth and the Southwest from the near-desert regions further north. The Batavia Coast is a long, straight stretch of coastline battered by wind. The narrow beaches and high white dunes gradually rise to the limestone cliffs of Kalbarri. At Cervantes, limestone columns, the Pinnacles, protrude from the sand, eerily reminiscent of the stone circles of northern Europe.

There are few bays and natural harbours along this coastline, and it is only interrupted by slow-flowing rivers. In such dry country freshwater is the key to survival, so almost every town is clustered around a river mouth. Some of these, such as Dongara, are old settlements, used as ports by early pastoralists. Others, such as Cervantes and Kalbarri, are relatively young towns that sprang up as a collection of fishing shacks in the last 50 years. Life in these coastal towns is dominated by the crayfish, a small tasty lobster that commands high prices overseas and has made the fortune of many a local fisherman. The major port of Geraldton, one of the state's largest cities, has superb windsurfing conditions and excellent diving and snorkelling on the coral reefs of the Houtman Abrolhos Islands, 60 km offshore.

Inland, much of the country has been cleared and there is a narrow wheat-growing area as far north as Northampton. This region is well known for its spectacular wildflowers in spring when the Midwest is carpeted in flowers after good winter rains. The wildflowers are best seen just inland but are also found along the Brand Highway and in the Kalbarri National Park. There is no doubt, however, that Kalbarri is the queen of the Midwest. This small seaside town can boast a beautiful location, fine beaches, and a national park with stunning river and coastal gorges.

Batavia Coast

This coastline got its name from the Batavia, a Dutch trading ship that was wrecked on the Houtman Abrolhos Islands in 1629, close to Geraldton. The Batavia is famous for the gruesome behaviour of its survivors, but it is only one of many shipwrecks on this coast. Strong westerly winds and an absence of safe, sheltered harbours meant ships were regularly smashed onto the reefs and rocks of this unforgiving coastline. The settlements of Cervantes, Jurien Bay, Leeman and Green Head are all crayfishing towns of utterly functional architecture. They hold little of interest except for the Pinnacles in the Nambung National Park, near Cervantes, and the possibility of swimming with sea lions at Jurien Bay and Green Head. The Highway extension between Lancelin and Cervantes was due to be completed in mid-2011 and this will change these sleepy hamlets forever, as more visitors pass through. Further north, the old twin towns of Dongara-Port Denison are good places for a relaxed overnight stop and the historic settlement on the Greenough Flats is worth exploring. Geraldton is a large city where you can stock up on supplies and explore an excellent maritime museum focusing on the story of the Batavia. It is also good for watersports: the windsurfing is known worldwide and there is excellent diving and snorkelling both on a brand-new artificial reef and on the coral reefs of the Houtman Abrolhos Islands, 60 km offshore. ➤➤ *For listings, see pages 238-240.*

Cervantes ➔ *Colour map 4, B1. Population: 900. 225 km from Perth, 25 km from Jurien.*

Cervantes is a small crayfishing community built in the last 30 years on flat sandy land by Ronsard Bay, sheltered by an offshore reef. The town has the good fortune of being the closest to Nambung National Park and its famous Pinnacles, although most people visit the park on a day trip so the town remains essentially undeveloped. The most exotic thing about Cervantes is its Spanish street names. The town was named after an American whaling ship wrecked just offshore in 1844 but the street names were chosen from *Don Quixote* (by Miguel de Cervantes). There is a **VIC** ① *T9652 7700, www.visitpinnaclescountry. com.au*, in the newsagents on Cadiz Street, and nearby is a general store, fish and chip shop and surfwear boutique. Just 1 km from the town centre are the stromatolites at Lake Thetis, where there is a boardwalk so visitors can get a good look at these living fossils (for more on stromatolites, see Hamelin Pool, page 264).

Nambung National Park and the Pinnacles ➔ *Colour map 4, B1. 19 km from Cervantes. The park entry fee is $11 per car.*

This national park protects an otherworldly forest of spiky rocks rising out of a yellow sandy desert. The Pinnacles are one of the most recognizable images of Western Australia and they are certainly a striking sight, one well worth making a detour for. Dutch sailors passing by in the 17th century marked them on their charts and likened them to the crumbling remains of an ancient city. The rock formations are surprisingly extensive, covering an area of several square kilometres, and there are thousands of them, taking varied forms from narrow towers 5 m high to modest stubs. There is some debate about the geological origin of the Pinnacles but the consensus is that deep cracks and hollows created by plant roots filled with a hard quartz limestone. These shapes and columns were left exposed when much of the vegetation cover and top sands eroded away some 20,000 years ago. The best time to see the park is in the soft light of early morning or at sunset, although sunset is quite busy with tour groups. A 4-km one-way loop road (sandy but hard packed and so suitable for 2WD) traverses the main area of formations and you

The Batavia

The *Batavia* was some ship: twice as big as the later *Endeavour*. It embarked on its maiden voyage to the Dutch East Indies in 1628 with a rich cargo of currency, jewels, provisions and, as it turned out, mutineers. The ship rounded Cape Horn and headed east, setting out over the Indian Ocean and planning to turn north after sighting the 'Southland'. That was Commander Pelsaert's plan at any rate. Skipper, Jacobsz, and the senior merchant, Cornelisz, had other ideas. Previous animosity with the commander and rampant greed persuaded them to a new plan: to murder all but a handful of like-minded crew and take to a life of piracy.

Before the mutiny was sprung, however, fate intervened. On 4 June 1629 the ship ran permanently aground on the reefs of the Abrolhos islands, though no life was lost. At first the situation was dire, much of the water was spoiled and little food was recovered. The ship carried two boats, each capable of carrying 50 or so people. In a shameful move the commander and Jacobsz slipped away in these under cover of darkness, with 40-odd able crew and the lion's share of the water and provisions. Pelsaert intended to return as quickly as possible with a larger ship, but in his heart must have assumed none would survive to be rescued.

Some did indeed die of thirst, but within days a great storm dumped rain by the bucket load onto the islands. Their new inhabitants were able to channel much of it into barrels, while at the same time discovering that the islands offered plentiful food in the way of fish, shellfish and seals. Survival seemed possible, even probable.

They hadn't, however, reckoned on one of their own number. Cornelisz harboured plans of taking over the expected rescue ship, recovering the *Batavia*'s treasure and still living a piratical life. But that meant eliminating the majority of the survivors before the rescue ship arrived. He re-recruited his fellow mutineers and began a campaign of terror that makes *Lord of the Flies* seem like a tea party. About 125 people were gradually isolated and murdered; one young boy was decapitated simply to settle a bet on the sharpness of a sword. When Pelsaert did eventually return, it was to discover Cornelisz and his well-armed band besieging a larger and unarmed, though admirably resourceful group led by a common soldier, Weibbe Hayes.

Cornelisz and the other most dangerous ringleaders were hung by Pelsaert on the spot, though some mutineers were brought back to the *Batavia* for more visible punishment. Two were given a last-minute reprieve by the commander and marooned on the mainland, their fate still unknown. Pelsaert was dead within a year, some say of shame, but his career would certainly have ended shortly after. Jacobsz was arrested and was last heard of rotting in a Javan prison, unwilling to confess his planned role in the mutiny despite the testimonies of several co-conspirators. Weibbe Hayes received a handsome promotion and has become something of a Dutch legend. Relics from the wreck of the *Batavia* are housed in the Western Australian Museum in Geraldton and the ship's hull is preserved in the Maritime Museum in Fremantle.

can stop along the way and walk among them. There is also a **Desert View Walk** (1.2 km), clearly signposted through a section of the Pinnacle Desert. The Interpretative Centre has information on the wildlife that lives in the Nambung National Park as well as details on how the Pinnacles are thought to have formed and the history of the area. There are two picnic spots by the beach on the way out, at **Kangaroo Point** and **Hangover Bay**; the latter is the best for swimming and has gas BBQs.

Cervantes to Dongara → *Distance: 160 km.*

This coastal route passes through sand dunes with the occasional glimpse of the ocean or a few fishing shacks, and the small fishing communities of Jurien, Green Head, and Leeman. The coastline is long and flat here and the largest of the three townships, Jurien Bay, has created an artificial boat harbour for safe anchorage. Swimming, windsurfing, snorkelling and surfing are all popular activities along this stretch of coast, although you'll need your own gear. All of the towns are very similar; a collection of functional shacks and bungalows, boat ramps and jetties, and a few basic services.

Jurien Bay has a shopping centre on the corner of the main street, Bashford Street, and Roberts Street. Tourist information is available from the **Shire Office** ① *Bashford St, opposite the Shopping Centre, T9652 1911, www.turquoisecoast.org.au*. There is a supermarket (open 0800-1800) with an ATM and a pleasant café. The main appeal of this area for visitors is the chance to swim with sea lions, who live in large colonies on **Fisherman Islands**, north of Jurien, and **Beagle Island**, north of Leeman.

Between Jurien and Green Head there are three national parks, all strictly 4WD only, with rough sandy and rocky tracks. **Drovers Cave National Park** and **Stockyard Gully National Park** have limestone caves (without decoration) and the latter a 270-m riverbed tunnel that you can walk through. **Lesueur National Park** has over 900 species of plants, one of the most diverse collections of flora in the state. There is a short walking track up **Mount Lesueur** (3 km return), a low flat-topped laterite mesa. For more information, contact the Cervantes DEC, T9652 7043.

Green Head has little more than a general store, a café and a **caravan park** ① *9 Green Head Rd, T9953 1131*, with on-site vans, but it does have a lovely swimming and picnic spot at **Dynamite Bay**. The bay is a tiny cove with rocky limestone headlands and there are covered picnic areas, showers, toilets and BBQ. **Leeman** is slightly larger, housing workers from a mineral sands mining venture at Eneabba. The foreshore area has a few picnic tables and BBQs. There are basic shops on Nairn Street, parallel to the main coast road and Spencer Street, between Nairn Street and the foreshore. Leeman also has a Community Resource Centre on Spencer Street, for internet access, and a caravan park (see Sleeping, page 238).

Badgingarra to Dongara → *Distance: 155 km.*

Badgingarra, 200 km out of Perth and a few kilometres past the Cervantes turn-off, is many people's first stop north on the Brand Highway if they're not going via the coast. **Badgingarra Roadhouse** ① *T9652 9051, 0600-2000*, is all that most people see of the tiny town, and frankly all they need to. The roadhouse has a tearoom. The town sits amidst the much bigger **Badgingarra National Park**, a wildflower wonderland in season. There are few trails in the park, but there is a short walk that's worth the time, especially in spring – it heads a short way east from the highway opposite the roadhouse turn-off.

From Badgingarra the highway continues 75 km north to **Eneabba**. Along the way is **Hi-Vallee Farm** ① *T9652 3035*, a good stop in wildflower season as they leave a large section of their farm uncleared. The owners also offer trips to Lesueur National Park and have some accommodation available. Call before stopping in. Eneabba itself is another tiny settlement, with a pleasant surprise. As well as the **roadhouse**, 0630-1930, and pub, its outdoor community **swimming pool** ① *Nov-Mar Mon-Wed 0600-1000, 1400-1900, Fri 0600-1000, 1400-2000, Sat 1000-1200, 1400-2000 and Sun 1000-1200, 1400-1900*, can provide a welcome break on a hot day. Dongara is a further 80 km up the road, with a short diversion via Port Denison signposted a few kilometres before.

Dongara and Port Denison → *Colour map 4, A1. Population: 3700. 65 km from Geraldton.*
Dongara and its sister town **Port Denison** are sited 3 km apart at the point at which the Irwin River meets the Indian Ocean. Dongara is a historic town, retaining many buildings over a century old and with a picturesque main street lined with huge mature Moreton Bay fig trees. It was first settled in the 1850s as the centre of a new agricultural area. From its earliest days the river mouth was used as a stop-gap port and a jetty was built in the 1860s to ease transport of goods. The present day port exhibits much less of its history and is dominated by an extensive modern harbour. There are beaches north and south of the towns, **Harbour Beach** being very sheltered and **South Beach** a kilometre-long expanse of hard-packed sand on which vehicles are allowed. Town services are comprehensive, including banks and a hospital.

The **Irwin District Museum** ⓘ *Waldeck St, T9927 1323, adjacent to the VIC, Mon-Fri 1000-1200, Sat 1000-1130 when volunteers are available, $2.50, children $2,* has photographic displays and memorabilia that explore local history, shipwrecks and, somewhat oddly, the phenomenon of rabbits in Australia. It also manages **Russ Historic Cottage** ⓘ *corner of Point Leander Dr and St Dominics Rd, Sun 1000-1200 and by appointment at the VIC, $2.50, concessions $2, children $0.50,* a pioneer dwelling built in the 1870s and now restored and furnished in keeping with the period. The **Old Mill** (1894), visible from the highway, is currently being restored. The **VIC** ⓘ *9 Waldeck St, T9927 1404, www.irwin.wa.gov.au, Mon-Thu 0900-1700, Fri 0900-1630, Sat 0900-1200,* occupies part of the Old Post Office, which also houses the library.

Greenough → *Colour map 4, A1. 41 km from Dongara, 24 km from Geraldton.*
Greenough Flats is a long flat area of relatively fertile ground, sandwiched between the coastal dunes and a low inland limestone ridge, and extending about 30 km south of Geraldton. From the south the area of principal interest starts at the **S Bend roadhouse and caravan park** ⓘ *T9926 1072.* Here the main highway turns sharply to the right while the old road carries straight on for about 6 km before a right turn into McCartney Road heads over a convict-built bridge and back on to the highway. Don't be fooled by the unsealed turn-off, it reverts to tarmac within 50 m. Taking this diversion misses nothing, and takes you past the **Hampton Arms**, a characterful 1863 pub that incorporates the **Rare & Antique Bookshop**. Opposite McCartney Road a 2-km unsealed track leads to **Lucy's Beach**, a wild and windswept stretch of coast, much favoured by fishers and surfers, with some impressively spiky weathered rocks exposed at low tide. The last 600 m of the track are 4WD-only or a walk.

Greenough Hamlet
ⓘ *T9926 1084, www.greenough.wa.gov.au, 0900-1700, $6, children $3, concessions $5.*
On the other side of the highway from McCartney Road is Greenough Hamlet. This settlers' village, dating back to the 1860s, is now uninhabited and maintained as an open-air museum by the National Trust. The dozen buildings include two churches and several cottages, half of them accessible and furnished to lesser and greater degrees as they might have been over a hundred years ago. Most interesting is the court and gaol building, the cells of which powerfully demonstrate the contempt in which Aboriginals were held. There are several displays in the entry building that inhabits the VIC and also a small café serving a variety of snacks and afternoon teas.

The road behind the Hamlet leads, after 15 km of bitumen and 5 km of unsealed road, to **Ellendale Pool**, a picturesque and shaded swimming waterhole and camping spot

($5 per vehicle), with basic toilets. Further up the highway, past the wind-tortured leaning trees is the **Pioneer Museum** ⓘ *T9926 1058, daily 0930-1530, $4.50, children and concessions $3.50*, another of the Flats pioneer homes and now a folk museum stuffed full of everyday artefacts from the late 1800s. It gives a good idea of how a well-to-do family of the period lived. There are sheltered picnic tables out the front.

Greenough Rivermouth

Greenough River winds down from the Moresby Ranges to meet the ocean 12 km south of Geraldton at Greenough Rivermouth. A sandbar turns the lower reaches of the river into one long lake most of the time and there are walking trails up along both banks for several kilometres. At the beach are toilets and some shelter.

⓪ Batavia Coast listings

For Sleeping and Eating price codes and other relevant information, see pages 28-34.

⊜ Sleeping

Cervantes *p234*
B-C Cervantes Pinnacles Motel, Aragon St, T9652 7145, www.cervantespinnacles motel.com.au. Large modern motel with standard and self-contained rooms. Facilities include pool, bar and restaurant.
C-E Cervantes Lodge & Pinnacles Beach Backpackers, 91 Seville St, T9652 7377, www.cervanteslodge.com.au. Clean, comfortable, attractive and welcoming hostel, with a range of rooms from dorms to en suite doubles. Facilities include a licensed café, the *Don Quixote*. Internet access is available. Recommended.
D-E Pinnacles Caravan Park, Aragon St, T9652 7060, www.pinnaclespark.com.au. Has cheap, clean cabins, on-site vans and grassy sites. There is also an on-site shop.

Cervantes to Dongara *p236*
Jurien Bay
C Jurien Bay Hotel Motel, 5 White St, T9652 1022. Self-contained units, swimming pool and à la carte restaurant. There's also a pub that serves counter meals.
C Jurien Beachfront Holiday Units, corner of Cook and Grigson Sts, T0438 753964, www.jurienbeachfrontunits.com.au. Offers 4 units near the beach, each with 2 bedrooms.

C-F Jurien Bay Tourist Park, Roberts St, T9652 1595, www.jurienbaytouristpark.com.au. Centrally located caravan park with chalets, on-site vans, shady tent sites, kitchens, BBQ areas as well as a restaurant and café.

Leeman
C-D Leeman Holiday Units, corner of Tamarisk and Nairn Sts, T9953 1190, www.leemanholidayunits.com. Range of self-contained units. Laundry and BBQs.
C-E Leeman Caravan Park, Thomas St, T9953 1080, www.leemancaravan park.com.au. At the southern end of town near the beach. Units, cabins and shaded camping spots. Has a good camper's kitchen with free BBQs.

Badgingarra to Dongara *p236*
C Coomallo Park Chalets, Nylagarda Rd, Badgingarra, T9652 6018, www.ecology. com.au. Fully equipped units that sleep up to 4 people, surrounded by bushland. Each chalet has a kitchen, a/c and solar hot water service. Cakes, tea, coffee and excellent handmade bread available. Meals on request. They also hire out Nordic walking equipment.
C-E Western Flora Caravan and Tourist Park, 22 km north of Eneabba, T9955 2030, http://members.westnet.com.au/westernflor a.tinker. A caravan park on the Brand Highway. Great place if you are a wildflower enthusiast as it's just west of the wildflower district and during the season there are

guided wildflower walks every day at 1630. Chalets, vans, and backpacker beds. There is also an on-site shop, BBQ area and laundry facilities. Meals available on request.

Dongara and Port Denison p237
Dongara is blessed with a range of extremely good-value accommodation.
B-D Priory Hotel, 11 St Dominic's Rd, T9927 1090, www.prioryhotel.com.au. An old colonial inn, with a restaurant, a public bar and a beer garden opposite the river. 21 spacious, doubles and singles with high- ceilings and plain decor, some en suite. One self-contained apartment. Backpacker accommodation and discounts available. There is also a swimming pool and internet access.
C Charlotte's Cottage B&B, Brand Highway, T9927 2324. This B&B in a historic limestone cottage has comfortable en suite rooms in French country decor and provides a full gourmet breakfast.
C Dongara Hotel Motel, 12 Moreton Terr, T9927 1023, www.dongaramotel.com.au. Standard motel rooms with free Wi-Fi. Also has a large bar and separate restaurant.
C Lazy Lobster, 49 Hampton St, Port Denison, T9927 2177, www.lazylobster.net.au. Self-contained chalet and units.
C-E Dongara Tourist Park, 8 George St near South Beach, T9927 1210, www.dongara touristpark.com.au. One of 5 caravan parks here with cabins, chalets, on-site vans and sites in a shaded bush setting. Some sites overlook the ocean. There is a campers' kitchen as well as a children's playground.
D Gracelyn B&B, 6 Delmage St, T9927 1938, www.gracelynbedandbreakfast.com.au. B&B with good-value double and twin rooms, outdoor area with BBQ, swimming pool and wood fire. Continental breakfast is included.

Greenough p237
C Bentwood Olive Grove, T9926 1196, is set back off the Brand Highway. Has a single, self-contained cottage. Private garden with BBQ, access to the family pool (unheated) and optional breakfast. One double, one

4-bunk room. Comfortably and cheerfully furnished, and excellent value. The café serves home-made cakes, light meals and coffee from May-Dec.
C Hampton Arms, Company Rd, T9926 1057, www.hamptonarms.com.au. One of WA's great historic pubs, the bookshop simply adding to the feel of antiquity. There's a small bar, a ballroom turned mid-range restaurant, and 5 suitably characterful rooms. Rates include continental breakfast.
C-F Greenough Rivermouth Caravan Park, T9964 9845, just back from the mouth of the river. On-site vans and cabins, as well as chalets, dongers and caravan sites.
D Rock of Ages B&B, T9926 1154, rockofages@westnet.com.au. An 1857 thick, stone-walled cottage, opposite the Pioneer Museum, originally built by WA's convict no 2, John Patience. It's been beautifully restored, furnished mostly in period as a B&B, and has a small garden with gazebo spa and BBQ. 3 double rooms share a bathroom. Continental breakfast included, cooked breakfast available for a small charge. Recommended.

🍴 Eating

Cervantes p234
There is a small shopping centre with a general store and fish and chip takeaway shop near the Tavern.
🍴 **Ronsard Bay Tavern**, Cadiz St, T9652 7009. Daily 1800-2030, Mon-Thu 1200-1400, Fri-Sun 1200-1430. Has a large dining room and a public bar, with roast offered on Sun.

Cervantes to Dongara p236
Jurien Bay
🍴 **Seaside Café**, at the shopping centre, T9652 1325. Daily 0700-1700. Does all-day breakfasts, light meals and coffee.

Badgingarra to Dongara p236
🍴 **Eneabba Sands Tavern**, Eneabba, T9955 1077. Daily 1600-2100. Has pool and table tennis tables and serves bar snacks and grills.

Dongara and Port Denison *p237*

♥♥♥-♥♥♥ Priory Hotel, see Sleeping. Meals Mon-Sat 1800-2030, Sun 1700-2000. Has a public bar where counters meals are served but if diners want a more refined environment there is the 1881 restaurant. Here, the food on offer includes grilled fish, kangaroo salad and a large selection of steaks. Roasts available on Sun, live regular weekend live music.

♥♥ Southerlys, 60 Point Leander Dr, Port Denison, T9927 2207. Meals daily 1200-1400, 1800-2030. A smart, casual, modern bar and restaurant with a large front terrace over the road from the foreshore. diners can choose to eat in the bar on in the restaurant area.

♥♥-♥ Dongara Hotel Motel, see Sleeping. Bar meals 1200-1400, evening meals in the restaurant from 1800-2000. Has a large bar and a separate restaurant serving light meals, seafood and Asian cuisine. On Fri evenings they have bands in the bar.

♥ The Little Starfish, White Tops Rd, South Beach, Port Denison, T0448 344215. Wed-Mon 0800-1600. In a great location, right next to the beach. Patrons tuck in to breakfast or lunch (dinner on request) listening to the waves, sheltered from the sun and the wind. Coffee, home-made cake, toasted sandwiches and specials such as Mexican stew. There are even favourites like jam or nutella sandwiches.

♥ The Season Tree, 8 Moreton Terr, T9927 1400. Daily 0830-1500, 1700-2100. Has a small terrace under one of the larger fig trees and is a pleasant spot to sit and watch the world go by. All-day breakfast, Asian food, coffee and good cake.

Greenough *p237*

♥♥ Hampton Arms, see Sleeping. Tue-Sun 1200-1430, Fri-Sun 1800-2100. Has a small bar, a ballroom turned mid-range restaurant serving simple grills, seafood and gourmet pies, 5 rooms and a covered rear courtyard. The hotel also contains a big and well-stocked bookshop.

▲ Activities and tours

Cervantes *p234*

A number of tours are available from Perth. **Turquoise Coast Enviro Tours**, 59 Seville St, T9652 7047, www.pinacletours.info. Ex-ranger Mike Newton offers personalized tours of the Pinnacles. Tours leave Cervantes at 0800, 1200 and 2½ hrs before sunset (3 hrs).

Cervantes to Dongara *p236*
Jurien Bay

Jurien Charters, T9652 1109, www.jurien charters.com. Swimming with sea lions. Prices vary according to size of party. Mornings are usually the best time for a tour and there is a minimum number requirement. Also arranges sea fishing, whale watching (Oct-Dec) and diving. Hires out fishing gear and boats.

Dongara and Port Denison *p237*

Aqua Jack Fishing & Charters, T9927 2200, T0419 967615. Offers various sightseeing, deep-sea and inshore fishing trips.
Icon Charters, T9927 1256. Organizes fishing trips, overnight trips to the Albrolhos Islands (bring your own sleeping gear) and an Experience Rocklobster fishing tour ($50). The latter 2 trips are seasonal (Mar-Jun).

Greenough Rivermouth *p238*

Greenough River Cruises, T9926 1717, cruise@wn.com.au. Leaves the mouth most days for cruises up river. Tue-Sun 1030, other times as per demand. Morning or afternoon tea, or sunset BBQ included.

⊖ Transport

The Batavia Coast *p234*

Bus TransWA passes through the region on 3 routes. The main (N1) services to Geraldton (6 hrs) leave East Perth terminal Mon-Sat at 0830, Fri at 1630 and Sun at 0930, stops include **Gingin**, **Dongara** and **Greenough**. The morning Mon, Wed and Fri services continue on to **Kalbarri**.

Geraldton and around

Many West Australians dismiss Geraldton as a large and uninteresting port city. It is true that the city's emphasis is firmly on industry and it hasn't developed with aesthetics in mind; an enormous silo and industrial wharves dominate its southern end and a series of functional rock groynes obscure the coastline. It does, however, have a fantastic sunny climate and strong, reliable westerlies make it a mecca for windsurfers. It is also the base for dive and snorkel tours out to the Houtman Abrolhos Islands, a remote group of coral islands teeming with fish and only inhabited for a few months a year by local crayfishermen. Geraldton itself has many interesting sights and all the services of a large town – if you're heading north this will be the last place to find such services for many hundreds of kilometres. ▶▶ *For listings, see pages 245-248.*

Ins and outs
The **VIC** ① *T9921 3999, www.geraldtontourist.com.au, Mon-Fri 0900-1700, Sat-Sun 1000-1600,* is located in the Bill Sewell Complex, along with a simple café and a backpacker hostel. The fine two-storey sandstone buildings were part of a district hospital built in 1884. ▶▶ *See Transport, page 248.*

Geraldton ▶▶ *For listings, see pages 245-248. Colour map 4, A1.*

→ *Population: 20,000. 425 km from Perth, 480 km from Carnarvon.*
Geraldton can make the welcome claim that many of its main tourist attractions are free, or involve a token donation. Some, notably the gallery and museum, are of a high standard. The waterfront area around the museum is being developed into a townhouse and marina complex and is likely to become an attractive part of the city.

Sights
Lighthouse Keeper's Cottage ① *Chapman Rd, Bluff Point, 3 km north of town centre, Mon-Fri 1000-1500, Sun 1300-1600, $2, tours by appointment (contact the VIC),* houses the main research office of the Geraldton Historical Society, and is stuffed full of their records and pictures. Public access is restricted to a couple of rooms in this unusual 1876 blend of lighthouse and keeper's cottage. There used to be another lighthouse on the beach and the two were used as a line-of-sight by shipping to guide them through the difficult mouth of the harbour.

Old Geraldton Gaol Craft Centre ① *Chapman Rd, T9921 1614, Mon-Sat 1000-1530, entry by donation,* located just south of the Bill Sewell tourist complex, is a whitewashed old gaol built in 1858 and last used in 1986. There are 16 cells along a central corridor and several exercise yards. Information sheets along the corridor explain some of the history of the gaol including amusing correspondence between the gaoler and his boss. The gaol is rather run down but has been taken over by an army of craftspeople who look after it and sell their work from the cells. Exhibitions are sometimes held in the adjacent former police quarters. Teddies, pottery, jewellery and baby clothes are some examples of the craftwork produced.

Western Australian Museum Geraldton ① *1 Museum Place, T9921 5080, www.museum. wa.gov.au, Thu-Tue 0930-1630, by donation,* is an impressive museum focusing on the maritime and so appropriately has been built next to the sea. A wall of glass overlooks the ocean and the floor of warm, polished timbers is evocative of a ship's deck. The hangar-like museum has an open central space where there is an exhibition on the Midwest, charting its history from Aboriginal trade routes, to pioneers to modern day industry. This leads into the Shipwreck Hall, the heart of the museum's collection. The dimly lit space contains relics from the wrecks of the *Batavia* and *Zuytdorp* and tells the stories of those ships and others of the Dutch East India company wrecked on the Midwest coast or the Abrolhos Islands in the 18th century (see box, page 235). The deliciously chilling tale of the *Batavia* wreck is borne out by a skull bearing axe marks. Temporary and touring exhibitions can be found in adjoining galleries. The museum shop stocks an exceptional range of books on the sea, wildlife, aboriginal issues and local history.

HMAS Sydney Memorial ① *Mt Scott, accessible from car park on Gummer Av*, on a small rise overlooking the city, is a beautiful landmark built in 2001 to remember the victims of the *HMAS Sydney* tragedy. This Australian naval ship was lost in 1941 when it engaged a German raider, the *Kormoran*, disguised as a Dutch merchant ship. None of the 645 crew survived and, despite many extensive searches, the ship was not found until March 2007, 240 km west of Shark Bay at a depth of about 2500 m. The loss was more keenly felt because the *Sydney* was already famous, having sunk an Italian ship off Crete in the first year of the Second World War. The crew paraded as heroes through the streets of Sydney, feted by thousands, less than a year before the tragedy. Each aspect of the memorial carries significance. The silvery dome is a filigree of 645 seagulls, traditional symbols of the souls of lost sailors. The design was inspired by a flock of silver gulls that swooped over the crowd during the mournful notes of the Last Post when the site was dedicated in 1998. The stele represents the prow of the *Sydney* and echoes the form of a standing stone, used in ancient British times as grave markers. Naturally, there are also excellent views of Geraldton from the site. There are guided tours daily at 1030 (30 minutes, $5), contact the VIC, T9921 3999, for more information.

Geraldton Regional Art Gallery ① *24 Chapman Rd, T9964 7170, Tue-Sat 1000-1600, Sun and public holidays 1300-1600, free*, is housed in the former Town Hall, built in 1907. A public campaign in the 1980s saved this elegant civic building from being demolished and shortly afterwards it was converted into the gallery. A large contemporary space on the ground floor is used for regular touring exhibitions, while the small permanent City of Geraldton collection is usually hung upstairs. This contains contemporary art of the 1990s focusing on Geraldton and the Midwest or local artists. Earlier artworks include paintings by Elizabeth Durack, a Hans Heysen and Robert Juniper's *Pilgrimage* (1962). The gallery's wonderful shop stocks high-quality art, craft, ceramics and jewellery made by local artists and from countries such as Morocco and India.

St Francis Xavier Cathedral ① *open daily, guided tours Mon, Wed and Fri 1000, $5*, the town's Catholic cathedral, is a splendid edifice in golden stone built between 1916 and 1938, and designed by the indefatigable Monsignor John Hawes (see box, page 244). To some, the inside of the building, with its grey and orange stripes, will seem fairly psychedelic.

At the **Fisherman's Harbour** during the crayfishing season it is possible to tour the **Live Lobster Factory** ① *T9921 7084, Nov-Jun, Mon-Fri 0930, $10, children $5, closed shoes must be worn, 3 km from the town centre on West End's northern shore*, to find out more about this valuable industry. The one-hour tour includes an explanatory video and you'll get to see the unloading and sorting of the crays, plus the live holding tanks. **Point Moore Lighthouse**, at the far end of West End, is a rare all-steel building and was imported from

England in sections in 1878. It was commissioned after the *Africa* ran aground on a reef (now called African Reef) off Point Moore in 1863, though failed to prevent at least two other vessels coming to grief in later years. Closed to the public, it is nonetheless an impressive structure.

There are plenty of beaches around the town. **Pages Beach**, on the north shore of West End, is the most family orientated with safe swimming, toilets, BBQs, playground and a large grassed area for picnics. Those at **Point Moore**, at the end of West End, get the brunt of the wind and are generally the preserve of windsurfers. To the south of the point, **Greys Beach** is pretty scruffy but things improve past Separation Point where **Back Beach** and **Tarcoola Beach** have decent stretches of white sand and offer good surfing, though swimming can be dangerous. **Town Beach**, accessed via Foreshore Drive, is, as the name suggests, the nearest beach to the centre of town. Sheltered, it's perfect for a cooling afternoon dip. A long series of beaches also stretch north from town, offering surfing breaks at **Bluff Beach** and beyond.

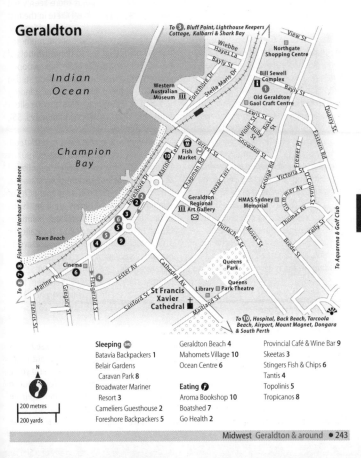

Geraldton

Sleeping
Batavia Backpackers **1**
Belair Gardens
  Caravan Park **8**
Broadwater Mariner
  Resort **3**
Cameliers Guesthouse **2**
Foreshore Backpackers **5**

Geraldton Beach **4**
Mahomets Village **10**
Ocean Centre **6**

Eating
Aroma Bookshop **10**
Boatshed **7**
Go Health **2**

Provincial Café & Wine Bar **9**
Skeetas **3**
Stingers Fish & Chips **6**
Tantis **4**
Topolinis **5**
Tropicanos **8**

Heavenly toil

Monsignor John Hawes is an interesting Midwest figure who left his imprint on the region with a series of distinctive and original church buildings. Hawes was born in Richmond, Surrey in 1876, the son of a London solicitor, and was inspired as a boy by the architecture of Canterbury Cathedral. He trained as an architect during the time that the Arts and Craft movement was advocating a return to simple organic decoration and natural materials. In 1901 he converted to High Anglicanism and was ordained two years later. His lifelong task of helping others began in the London slums, before he sought missionary work in the Bahamas. After a few years Hawes converted to Catholicism and it was when he was in Rome studying for the priesthood that he met Geraldton's Bishop Kelly, who was there on a recruiting drive. Hawes agreed to move to Western Australia and was allocated the Murchison Goldfields region.

Arriving in 1915, he brought the plans for a new cathedral for Geraldton with him and construction began the following year. Because of delays and the scale of the work, the Cathedral of St Francis Xavier was not completed until 1938. In the meantime Hawes led a hardworking life as parish priest in Mullewa and designed many church buildings in the region. It is possible to see his work in the Midwest towns of Mullewa, Morawa, Yalgoo, Northampton, Perenjori and Tardun. All of his buildings were made of local stone and are quite different from each other but he aimed to catch 'the rhythm of a poem in stone' with his solid Mediterranean style buildings with their domes, tiles, round arches and simple whitewashed interiors. Hawes constructed some of the smaller buildings with his own hands, "tormented with flies and scorching summer sun" as he put it and worrying that his cracked hands would catch on his silk vestments on Sunday. He always lived among very humble surrounds but as he aged he began to long for a simpler monastic life of Franciscan poverty. He also wanted to leave Australia, writing: "I shall be only too glad to leave this prosaic and mundane land full of hotels, beer, wool and sheep."

At 64, feeling worn out, he told his bishop he was going on holiday to Europe and never came back. He settled on the Bahamas where he became a hermit known as Father Jerome, but even there the local bishop pestered him to design churches and colleges. He was buried on Cat Island in the Bahamas in 1956. Brochures on the *Monsignor Hawes Heritage Trail* can be purchased at the Geraldton VIC.

Around Geraldton

Houtman Abrolhos Islands → *Colour map 4, A1.*

The Houtman Abrolhos Islands (commonly just called the Abrolhos) are a maze of low coral islands lying 60 km west of Geraldton. Essentially built-up reefs, they are uninhabited, except for a few crayfishermen in the short island season (March to June). Their low-lying nature and treacherous outlying reefs mean they are very difficult to spot and they are the final resting place of at least 19 vessels, including the ill-fated *Batavia*. Indeed the name Abrolhos is thought to be a corruption of the Portugese words for 'keep your eyes open'. The principal attraction for visitors however, are the crystal-clear waters and huge diversity of sealife. As the recipient of the final gasp of the warm tropical currents that spill down Australia's west coast, the islands encompass the world's most southerly coral reefs but also have a rich variety of more temperate species, a mix quite fascinating to marine biologists. They are also home to sea lions, turtles and dozens of species of sea birds. Snorkelling and diving here is outstanding for coral gardens and many types of reef and pelagic fish. The islands can be reached either via air or sea, but air is the better option for a short trip as the views are wonderful and the sea crossing can be a bit rough.

Geraldton to Northampton → 52 km via coast road.

There is little of particular interest on the main coast road, except the **Oakabella Homestead** ⓘ *T9925 1033, Mar-Jan 0900-1600, tours $10, 20 mins, usually conducted on demand*, 3 km down an unsealed side-turn 32 km out of Geraldton. The century-old homestead, largely furnished in keeping and reputedly haunted, is open for tours that also take in the grounds and a small folk museum housed in an unusual and historic barn. The pleasant tearoom, in a modern but sympathetic building, serves light lunches as well as cream teas. There is also camping available here for $8 per person, with facilities including hot showers and laundry.

An alternative route, about 20 km longer than the coastal route, heads up along Chapman Valley Road via Nabawa. Along the way is **Chapman Valley Wines** ⓘ *Howatharra Rd, 3 km off on an unsealed side-road, T9920 5148, www.chapmanvalleywines.com.au, Mon-Fri 1000-1600, Sat and Sun 1000-1700*, one of WA's nothernmost wineries.

◉ Geraldton and around listings

For Sleeping and Eating price codes and other relevant information, see pages 28-34.

● Sleeping

Geraldton *p241, map p243*
The VIC can advise on and book other motels.
A-B Broadwater Mariner Resort, 298 Chapman Rd, a 5-min drive out of town, T9965 9100, www.broadwaters.com.au. Offers spacious self-contained accommodation, which ranges from studios to 3-bed apartments. There's a large swimming pool, communal BBQ areas and secure parking. Guests are sure to enjoy the large double showers. There's also an adjoining restaurant, which serves good à la carte meals.
A-B Ocean Centre Hotel, corner of Foreshore St and Cathedral Av, T9921 7777, www.oceancentrehotel.com.au. Right on the foreshore in the middle of town, with lots of balcony rooms overlooking the harbour, an upmarket, motel-style set-up with expensive

restaurant and bar. All rooms en suite, some with spa.
B Mahomets Village, Willcock Dr, T9921 6652, www.mahometsvillage.com. 13 self-contained, well-equipped villas that sleep 4-7, a short walk from Back Beach. Wi-Fi available.
D Geraldton Beach Hotel, 15 Fitzgerald St, T9921 4444. One of several pubs offering accommodation. Singles, doubles twins, a bar and bottle shop.
D-E Batavia Backpackers, on the corner of Chapman and Bayly Sts behind the VIC, T9964 3001. A clean and friendly, if somewhat spartan, 100-bed hostel in a heritage building with large verandas. Good private storage space and close to bus stop.
D-E Cameliers Guest House, 92 Marine Terr, T9964 3725. Another budget option, very basic but cheap.
D-E Foreshore Backpackers, 172 Marine Terr, T9921 3275, www.foreshoreback packers.bigpondhosting.com. A good place to relax for a few days, this homely 50-bed

hostel in a spacious old house faces a small swimming beach. There are sunny, enclosed verandas, hammocks, and 3-, 4- or 6-bed dorms, as well as single and double rooms, all with lovely old wooden furniture. Recommended.

Caravan parks
B-E Belair Gardens Caravan Park, Willcock Dr, T9921 1997, www.belairgardenscaravan park.com.au. The best positioned caravan park, with units, cottages, chalets and camping sites. It has a good range of facilities.
C-E Batavia Coast Caravan Park, 239 Hall Rd, T9938 1222, www.bataviacoastcp.com.au. Located a short distance outside the city centre, this is a small but friendly caravan park with cabins, chalets, on-site vans and a cottage. Facilities including a pool and a shop. Reception is open until 1700, 24-hr check-ins possible by prior arrangement.

Eating

Geraldton *p241, map p243*
In contrast to Geraldton's relatively cheap accommodation and many free sights, the restaurants in town are generally pretty pricey. As well as those listed below, see Broadwater Mariner Resort, under Sleeping.
ŸŸŸ Boatshed, 357 Marine Terr, T9921 5500, Mon-Sat 1800-2030. The town's seafood specialist, with a nautically themed dining room and a more atmospheric stone-walled courtyard. Licensed and BYO.
ŸŸŸ-ŸŸ Skeetas Restaurant, 101 Foreshore Dr, T9964 1619, www.skeetas.com.au. Daily 0700-2130. An airy restaurant with ocean views and an outdoor terrace serving mainly Modern Australian and Mediterranean cuisine. It also has a good range of seafood dishes. Licensed.
ŸŸŸ-Ÿ Topolinis, 158 Marine Terr, T9964 5866. Daily 1100-late. A pleasant and airy restaurant serving good breakfast, café food and delicious, authentic Italian dishes. Takeaways are also available. Recommended.

ŸŸŸ The Provincial Café & Wine Bar, 167 Marine Terr, T9964 2681. A relaxed and funky café and bar that offers bistro food, wood-fired pizzas, light meals and all sorts of coffee.
Ÿ Stingers Fish & Chips, 239 Marine Terr, next to the cinema, T9964 7484. Daily 1100-1400, 1700-2100. Offers a good range of seafood snacks and burgers.
Ÿ Tantis, 174 Marine Terr, T9964 2311. Mon-Sat 1700-2100, Wed-Fri 1130-1400. Of a number of Thai and Chinese restaurants try this one. Good-value 3-course set meals, BYO. It also does takeaways.
Ÿ Tropicanos, Point Moore, T9923 9776. Daily 0900-2100 (closed Mon-Tue in winter). A cheap café with views across to the ocean. Substantial, cheap breakfast (good buffet on Sun), lunches and evening meals. Mediterranean-style cuisine. BYO only.

Cafés
Aroma Bookshop, 55 Marine Terr, T9921 4600. Mon-Fri 0900-1700, Sat 0900-1200. A cosy bookshop with wooden furniture that also serves coffee and cakes.
Go Health, 122 Marine Terr, T9965 5200. Mon-Fri 0830-1500, Sat 0830-1400. A juice and sandwich bar with internet.

Bars and club

Geraldton *p241, map p243*
Much of the scene revolves around 2 pubs, both at the northern end of the main shopping area.
Breakers Bar & Café, 41 Chapman Rd, T9921 8924. Sun-Wed 1100-2100, Thu 1100-2400, Fri-Sat to 0100. Mid-range meals, mainly seafood, are served daily 1200-1400 and 1800-2100. Stages a variety of live bands in its single large bar, every Fri-Sat, and often Wed-Thu.
Freemasons Hotel (the Freo), 79 Marine Terr, T9964 3457. Sat 1100-2400, Sun 1100-2200. Has 3 main bars, one café style, the others with an Abrolhos theme. It has live bands or DJs every Fri-Sat and a local jam session on

Thu. The bar meals are excellent, daily 1200-1430, 1800-2030. The accommodation upstairs has a few bunkbeds, mostly in twins or quads, veranda access and a small lounge/kitchenette.

🎭 Entertainment

Geraldton *p241, map p243*
Queens Park Theatre, Cathedral Av, T9956 6662, www.queensparktheatre.com.au. Box office open Mon-Fri 0900-1700. An impressive, modern theatre designed on traditional lines. It hosts visiting and local productions from dance to comedy, bands to pantomime. A grassed outdoor amphitheatre is the venue for open-air evening films from Jan-Apr.

🛍 Shopping

Geraldton *p241, map p243*
Marine Terr, between Fitzgerald St and Forrest St, is the main shopping precinct in town, though a large mall with a **Coles** and **Target** budget department store, is just north of the VIC at Northgate. Also check the museum shop for a good selection of new books. There are shops selling street surfwear, and some even selling boards, along Marine Terr. There is a farmer's market on Sat at Maitland Park from 0800-1200.
Barlo's Tackle World 20 Anzac Terr, T9921 6822. Sells a range of fishing, snorkelling and camping gear. There is another good fishing shop on Marine Terr.
Geraldton Fish Market, 365 Marine Terr. Mon-Fri 0830-1730, Sat 0830-1200. Fresh seafood, including crays, can be purchased at the supermarkets or here.

⛰ Activities and tours

Geraldton *p241, map p243*
Aerial tours
Geraldton Air Charter, T9923 3434, www.geraldtonaircharter.com.au, and **Shine Aviation Services**, T9923 3600, www.shineaviation.com.au. Both fly regular tours to the **Abrolhos**. On some of these they land on 1 or more of the main islands, allowing a closer look and perhaps some snorkelling. Minimum of 2 passengers, flights start at around $1750 for 1½ hrs. Both companies also offer excursions up coast to **Kalbarri** and **Shark Bay**.

Diving
The clean waters off Geraldton can be excellent for diving, but winds and silt from the Chapman River also often ruin visibility. The best time is mid-Feb to mid-May. The waters are also now the home of Australia's newest artificial reef, the *South Tomi*, an illegal fishing boat that was seized by Australian Fisheries.
Batavia Coast Dive Academy, 153 Marine Terr, T9921 4229, www.bcda.com.au. Mon-Fri 0900-1700, Sat 0800-1400, Sun 1000-1200. Phone ahead for current dive conditions. Hires out scuba gear and run shore and boat dives, according to demand and conditions. Also offers snorkelling and Open Water courses. The classrooms and swimming pool are on site.

Fishing
Chapman Valley Fishing Park, 338 Hickey Rd, 25 km north, T0400 618484. Sat-Sun and public holidays 0930-1600. Come and catch your lunch. Fish here for silver perch and barramundi, or set a net in the yabbie dam. There are BBQs available for cooking your catch. Entry is $7, children $5 and you pay for the fish.

Golf
Geraldton Golf Club, Pass St, T9964 1911. The closest course to the town centre and welcomes visitors. Club hire.

Surfing and windsurfing
Geraldton calls itself, not unreasonably, Australia's windsurfing capital, and there are good wind and water conditions for most of the year.
Midwest Surf School and Tours, T0419 988756, www.surf2skool.com. Offers surf courses ($60 for 1½ hrs) and equipment hire. Pick-ups are available.
Sail West, Point Moore, T9923 1000, www.sailwest.com.au. Mon-Fri 0900-1700, Sat-Sun 1000-1700, when the wind is above 20 knots. Hires out windsurfers and surfboards from their shop next to the lighthouse.

Swimming
Aquarena, Pass St, T9921 8844. Mon-Fri 0530-2000, Sat 0900-1900, Sun 0900-1500 (shorter opening hours in winter). A large complex with indoor and outdoor pools, slide, spa and steam room.

⊖ Transport

Geraldton *p241, map p243*
Air
Skywest has daily flights to **Perth**.

Bicycle hire
Bike Force, 58 Chapman Rd, T9921 3279. Mon-Wed, Fri 0830-1730, Thu 0830-1900.

Bus
Local There are local bus services to and from Anzac Terr, T9923 1100. The circular 800 service is free, as are the 201 and 501 services between the terrace and Northgate Shopping Centre (adjacent to the VIC). Services run Mon-Sat, 2-5 times a day, the 800 service more frequently in the mornings.

Long distance There is at least 1 daily TransWA service to **Perth** from the railway station, many leaving at 0830 (Sun 0930). The **Northampton** and **Kalbarri** service leaves Mon, Wed and Fri at 1430. **Greyhound** northbound services leave the VIC Mon, Wed and Fri at 1415. **Perth** buses depart Tue, Thu and Sat at 1015.

Car
Parking is metered and restricted in town centre. Free and unrestricted at the railway station. Car servicing at **Axis**, 284 Marine Terr, T9921 2411. Fill up with cheap fuel at the **440 Roadhouse**, 10 km north of town. Cheapest at **Gull**, opposite VIC; 24-hr services at **BP Tarcoola**, Brand Highway, and **Gull 440 Roadhouse**, North West Coastal Highway.

Taxi
Call T9921 7000.

ⓘ Directory

Geraldton *p241, map p243*
Banks Along Marine Terr or Chapman Rd.
Internet Free internet access and Wi-Fi at the library (booking required). Otherwise try Go Health (see Eating) or **Sun City Books & Internet**, 49 Marine Terr, T9964 7258, Mon-Fri 0900-1700, Sat 0900-1300. **Medical services** Chemists: Chemmart, 113 Marine Terr, T9921 1755, daily 0800-2000. **Hospital:** Geraldton Regional, Shenton St, T9956 2222. **Police** Marine Terr, T9923 4555. **Post** 50 Durlacher St.

Kalbarri and around

Although Kalbarri is a very young town, the surrounding district is notable for its part in early West Australian settler history. Northampton is an old mining town, partly built by the labour of convicts based at nearby Lynton. Port Gregory, and Horrocks further south, are now both just sleepy beach settlements popular with locals for cheap holidays. Lynton guards much of what little early European history survives in the area, while the rock art near Horrocks harks back to an even earlier era. This lovely town has plenty to keep you occupied for days, and is also a beautiful spot for doing nothing at all. ▸▸ *For listings, see pages 253-257.*

Northampton → *Colour map 4, A1. Population: 1000. 105 km from Kalbarri, 225 km from the Overlander Roadhouse.*

This historic town on the Nokanena Brook was the first of Western Australia's mining towns. Galena (lead ore) was found in the bed of the Murchison River in 1848 and the following year the Geraldine Mining Company was formed to exploit deposits of lead and copper in the area. Welsh and Cornish miners were brought out from Britain for their expertise and many of their descendants still live in the area. Port Gregory was used to export the lead to Britain and a convict-hiring depot was established at Lynton for convict labour on roads, buildings and in the mines. Port Gregory wasn't the safest anchorage though so a new lead port was opened at Geraldton in 1861 and a 54-km railway linking Northampton and Geraldton, built in 1879, was the first government railway in WA. The town still has many fine old-stone buildings, but little is made of them. Northampton exists to service the surrounding wheat district and lies on the main highway north. However, its passing trade has dropped off significantly since the coast road to Kalbarri was sealed in 2000 and there are few facilities for visitors. The liveliest times to be in Northampton are **Purple Bra Day** in June and the **Airing of the Quilts** in October. Purple Bra Day sees purple bras hung from all the shop fronts and along the main road, stalls are set up selling cakes and bric-a-brac, and there's live music. The town takes on a carnival atmosphere, all in aid of raising money for breast cancer. The Airing of the Quilts, is when colourful handmade quilts festoon the verandas of the town and it's quite a sight. Check the dates with the **VIC** ① *Old Police Station, Hampton Rd, T9934 1488, Mon-Fri 0900-1500, Sat 0900-1200*. It also has brochures for a heritage walk.

At the southern end of Northampton, the long stone building is the former home of Captain Samuel Mitchell and now the site of the **Chiverton House Museum** ① *Hampton Rd, T9934 1215, Fri-Mon and Wed 1000-1200, 1400-1600, $3, children $0.50, guided tours are available on request*. Mitchell was the mining engineer for the Geraldine Mine and a respected member of the community with 14 children. He had the house built by convicts around 1868. The museum has a sprawling, ordinary and dusty collection of domestic equipment, photographs, clothes, and farm machinery. Further up the main street is a fine Catholic church, **St Mary in Ara Coeli**, built in 1936 to a design by talented architect-priest Monsignor John Hawes. Its rough-hewn stone and restrained decoration is typical of Hawes' work, although he had originally planned a more Byzantine style. The Priest of Northampton, Father Irwin, insisted on a Gothic design and Hawes agreed but the whitewashed interior with its round arches and shutters retains a Mediterranean feel. The jarrah roof is particularly fine. The impressive two-storey building next door is the former **Sacred Heart Convent** and was also designed by Hawes.

Horrocks → *Colour map 4, A1. 24 km from Northampton 55 km from Lynton.*

Horrocks is a tiny fishing and family orientated tourist town at the end of an 18-km off-shoot from the Northampton–Kalbarri road. Nestled amidst high sand dunes, the settlement crowds around a grid of former squatters huts, now made more respectable by formal legislation and the permanency that comes with it. They face a long beach, remarkably sheltered for this coast because of a reef about 200 m from the shore, which makes this a good spot for safe swimming and snorkelling, though the natural harbour is also used by a small fishing fleet. Aside from many happy children in summer this is a quiet spot. A grassy foreshore has BBQs and covered picnic tables. The general store has a limited supply of groceries, fuel (much more expensive than Geraldton) and also operates as a takeaway. Other facilities include tennis courts and a nine-hole golf course.

Around Horrocks

About 2 km back towards Northampton is an unsealed right-hand turn to **Bowes Beach**. After a rough 3-km drive it leads to a beach very popular with both surfers and fishermen, and bush camping is allowed. It's well worth stopping just 50 m down the track, even if a beach visit isn't in your plans, as a very short path up the slope leads to the **Willigulli Rock Art Site**. Of undetermined age, there are several images, mostly of stencilled objects created by the blowing of white, yellow and red pigments. Hands are ubiquitous, but the images also include the local native yams and boomerangs. They were made by the Nanda and their ancestors, a peaceful people who, on the arrival of Europeans, were already living a settled existence with stone huts, deep wells and the beginnings of an agriculture based on yams. It has been suggested, controversially, that they learnt some of their ways from Wouter Looes and Jan Pelgrom, the two men from the *Batavia* marooned on this coast back in 1629.

Lynton → *Colour map 4, A1. 40 km from Northampton, 65 km from Kalbarri.*

Squeezed between the low Menai Hills and the coastal sandhills, a rosy future was anticipated for the township of Lynton. Captain Henry Ayshford Sandford was the first arrival, setting up a considerable farm property in 1852. His house, now being gradually restored, sits prominently on the side of the hill, the upstairs veranda begging a tearoom. The house, plus the original flour mill and impressive stables, can be visited for a gold-coin donation. It's a 10-minute scramble from the main property up to the top of the Menai Hills. From here there's a view over the dunes to the ocean and north up to the **Pink Lake**, an aquaculture farm harvesting the intensely red algae *Dunaliella salina*. By the main entrance are the remains of the **Lynton Convict Settlement**, established in 1853 to hire out convicts to the surrounding mines but abandoned just three years later.

Kalbarri → *Colour map 4, A1. 155 km from Geraldton, 250 km from Overlander roadhouse.*

The most picturesque coastal town in the state, Kalbarri sits at the mouth of the Murchison River where it winds through shoals of sand to the ocean. At the entrance a triangular rock rises above the surf and marks the difficult zigzag passage through the reef to the ocean. The reef protects the calm waters of the inlet, forming a safe harbour for the crayfishing fleet moored here and a tranquil place for swimming, sailing and fishing. A long grassy foreshore lines the riverbank and the town is laid out along the foreshore, facing the sparkling blue water of river and ocean.

    Kalbarri Wildflower Centre ① *1 km north of town, behind the tourist info bay, T9937 1229, Jul-Nov, Wed-Mon 0900-1700, $5, children free, guided tours by appointment*, has a large number of the local wildflowers in a small area bordering the national park. A 2-km trail takes in hundreds of species, bursting into flower from July to October.

Kalbarri Oceanarium ① *north end of Grey St by the marina, T9937 2027, www.kalbarri explorer.com.au/oceanarium.htm, Mon-Sat 1000-1600, $7, children $5*, is a modest-sized but well-stocked outfit with a dozen tanks featuring most of the species of fish and crustaceans that can be found in the sea off Kalbarri. Includes a tank of seahorses and a children's touch pool.

Rainbow Jungle ① *3 km south on Red Bluff Rd, T9937 1248, www.rainbowjungle kalbarri.com, Mon-Sat 0900-1700, Sun.1000-1700, $13.50, concessions $11.50, children $5,* claims to be the foremost Australian parrot breeding centre and is certainly one of the more impressive aviaries in the country. Privately developed, most of the many parrots fly around in large enclosures, well watered and with lots of ferns and other plants. Visitors get to stroll amongst them, and can stay for a picnic and make use of the BBQs. Worth a visit even on a hot day. It is also home to **Cinema Parrotiso**, an outdoor cinema with wood-fired pizzas and a licensed bar (operates seasonally).

Opposite Rainbow Jungle is a parking bay for an ocean **beach**. Once on the sand it is about 4 km north to **Chinamans Rock** and beach at the mouth of the Murchison River, and 800 m south to **Jakes**, Kalbarri's well-known surf break. This is not recommended for beginners, though the bay just before it is great for boogie-boarding, as is **Red Bluff beach** 1 km further south.

Murchison House Station ① *T9937 1998, www.murchisonhousestation.com.au, access to the station is via tour only (4 hrs, can be booked through the VIC), which leave most days Jul-Dec and include morning tea, also offers guided self-drive 4WD tours to the homestead,* is one of WA's most historic properties. It was established in 1848 by Charles Von Bibra to grow supplies for his convict lead-miners and also breed horses for the Indian Army. The station has had a colourful history, witnessing the fatal crash of one of the three planes involved in WA's first commercial flight, and later as the home and playground of Prince Mukramm Jah, the eighth Nizam of Hyderabad. Most of the station's income now comes from feral goats and Brahmin cattle. The original homestead and old woolshed are still standing and the area around the current homestead is littered with the prince's playthings, including several decrepit military vehicles and gigantic earth-movers. A visit is recommended.

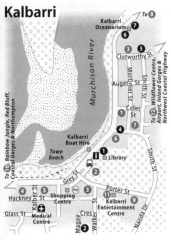

Kalbarri

To 8

Kalbarri Oceanarium 7 6

Murchison River

Clotworthy St 3 5

Mortimer St
Auger St

Shith St

To 9 Wildflower Centre, Airport, Inland Gorges & Northwest Coastal Highway

Coles St

Kalbarri Boat Hire

To 10 Rainbow Jungle, Red Bluff, Coastal Gorges & Northampton

Town Beach

4
6
1 Library
2

Grey St

Porter St

Hackney St

Shopping Centre

3
11 Kalbarri Entertainment Centre 9

Smith St

Nanda Dr

Glass St Medical Centre

Magee Cres

Walker St

N

↑

300 metres
300 yards

Sleeping
Anchorage Caravan Park **8**
Gecko Lodge **10**
Kalbarri Beach Resort **3**
Kalbarri Edge Resort **11**
Kalbarri Motor Hotel **2**
Kalbarri Riverfront **4**
Kalbarri Riverfront
  Budget Units **5**
Lola-Rose B&B **12**

Murchison Park **6**
Pelican's Nest & Kalbarri
  Backpackers YHA **7**
Seafront Villas **1**
Tudor Holiday Park **9**

Eating
Black Rock Café **1**
Finlays **2**
Gorges Café **7**
Grass Tree **4**
Jakes **5**
Jetty Seafood Shack **6**

Bars & clubs
Gilgai Tavern **3**

The **VIC** ① *70 Grey St, T9937 1104 or T1800 639468, www.kalbarriwa.info, 0900-1700*, is opposite the foreshore.

Kalbarri National Park → *Colour map 4, A1.*

① *For information call the DEC ranger, T9937 1192, $11 per vehicle (inland gorges only). Note that there is no drinking water available in the park, so if walking in the summer months make sure you bring enough as it can get very hot in the gorges.*

The Murchison River meanders through deep gorges of spectacular red and white banded rock with the most striking formations and tight loops of riverbed enclosed within the park. In winter and spring, the park is also renowned for its beautiful display of wildflowers. On the route running east to the highway, you can see many blooms including banksias, grevilleas, kangaroo paws, the appropriately fluffy lambswool and brightly coloured featherflowers. The park also extends along the coast and contains high coastal cliffs, gorges and magical sheltered coves. Along the coast road, the heath is dominated by the waving stems of white plume grevillea, also called smelly socks for its less than pleasant locker-room fragrance. The dramatic gorges and cliffs, cut by the sea into rugged notches and rock platforms, are quite different from the inland gorges. This wealth of natural beauty in the park is complemented by a great range of tours, activities and services. There are many excellent lookouts over the gorges and a few walking tracks aimed at reasonably agile walkers.

Coastal gorges South of the river mouth, the ocean beaches gradually rise to a long stretch of golden sandstone cliffs. This southern coastline is also part of the national park and there are a series of excellent lookouts and tracks down the rock platforms and beaches. **Red Bluff** is the imposing knoll that can be seen from the town beaches and is the first of the park lookouts, 5 km from town. There is an 800-m return walk to the top of the bluff from where you can see the whole coastline and this is also a great spot in calm weather for whale watching in winter. A loop walk from **Mushroom Rock** to **Rainbow Valley** takes one to 1½ hours and allows you to explore the rock platforms and the arid hillside. **Pot Alley Gorge** is a delightful narrow gorge with interesting rocks and a pretty beach – the ideal place for secluded swimming or sunbathing. **Eagle Gorge** also has a good sandy beach reached from a track by the lookout but less protected, and extensive rock platforms to explore (8 km from town). **Shellhouse Grandstand** is named for a rock that looks like the Shell service station sign if you see it from a boat and a natural amphitheatre formed by rock platforms. Towards the southern end the cliffs become higher and less accessible but more impressive. The last two lookouts, **Island Rock** and **Natural Bridge**, are both remnants left behind by the cliffs as they retreat before the waves, and are particularly beautiful at sunset.

Inland gorges There are three main points to access the inland gorges, all situated at scenic bends and loops in the river's course, and all via unsealed roads. Shortly after leaving town there is also a great lookout over Kalbarri called **Meanarra Hill**, reached by a short walk from the car park. After a further 11 km the first park turn-off is on the left. This leads to Nature's Window (26 km) and Z-Bend (25 km). **Nature's Window** is a rock arch that overlooks a tight bend in the river called **The Loop**. The walk around the Loop is excellent, following the ridge at first and then dropping down to the riverbed (8 km, three hours). At **Z-Bend** (a few kilometres drive away) there is a lookout over a right angle in the gorge and with some careful rock hopping you can get down to the river and explore. Take the unmarked but well-used track to the right of the lookout. This is also a lovely place for a swim as the river does not flow all year round and is often a series of calm shallow pools. You need to return to the main road and travel another 24 km to get to **Hawks Head** and **Ross Graham**. These are both good lookouts and there are easier tracks down to the river. It is possible for experienced walkers to tackle the 38 km (four days) from Ross Graham Lookout to The Loop or shorter two-day walks, but you must notify the ranger and plan carefully. There are picnic tables and toilets at all the car parks. Nature's Window and Z-Bend also have gas BBQs.

⊕ Kalbarri and around listings

For Sleeping and Eating price codes and other relevant information, see pages 28-34.

⊜ Sleeping

Northampton *p249*

C Railway Tavern, T9934 1120. Offers 9 double rooms, some en suite. Dinner served Wed-Sun from 1800.

D Jidamya Ostriches Farm Stay, Barron St, just outside town, T9934 1024, www.members.westnet.com.au/jidamya. A continental breakfast and interaction with their large feathered stock. Single occupation and evening dinners (by pre-arrangement) are great value.

D-E Miners Arms, main street, T9934 1281. This top pub is marginally the most characterful of 3 very ordinary establishments. Serves meals Mon-Sat 1200-1330, 1800-2000. En suite motel rooms at the back too.

E-F Northampton Caravan Park, main street, T0439 979489, www.northampton caravanpark.com. On-site vans and powered and unpowered sites. Fri night sausage sizzle, $5. Railway carriage open for inspection by appointment. Cash only.

E-F Old Convent, main street, T9934 1692, www.railwaytavern.com.au. Looks impressive from the road but inside is a bit stark and functional. It sleeps 40 in a variety of rooms from one double and a 10-bed dorm, and has a clean communal kitchen and lounge area. Some rooms are accessed from the wide 1st-floor veranda.

Horrocks *p250*

D Horrocks Beachside Cottages, 5 Glance St, T9934 3031, www.northampton accommodation.com.au. Not exactly beachside, but only a very short distance away. These simple self-contained cottages are a good budget option and are cheaper if you choose the non-a/c option.

D Killara Cottages, T9934 3031. Has 12 large, basic but well-equipped cabins. Good value, but in peak holiday season you can only take them for a week, and you'll need to book.

D-E Horrocks Beach Caravan Park, T9934 3039, www.horrocksbeachcaravanpark. com.au. Has cabins and on-site vans as well as sites, also a small café, and tennis and golf hire.

Lynton *p250*

B-E Lynton-on-Sea Farmstay, T9935 1040. The property owners are now Lynton's entire population. A small number of simple but clean twin dongers, a self-contained modern cottage with 2 twin bedrooms and a 3-bed farm house. Own linen required. Bookings essential.

Kalbarri *p250, map p251*

The bulk of accommodation available is in complexes of self-contained units, all very much designed to a common plan and mostly located on the foreshore. The competition means high standards, generally well-equipped kitchens, good laundry facilities and many have on-site pools. Almost all are designed for families, with 2 or 3 bedrooms. Prices can drop considerably in low season.

L-A Kalbarri Edge Resort, 22 Porter St, T9937 0000, www.kalbarriedge.com.au. Self-contained accommodation from studios to 2-bed apartments. All have Wi-Fi, and some have washing machines and balconies. There is a pool, a gym and even giant chess. The restaurant on-site serves Modern Australian fare with emphasis on seafood.

A-B Gecko Lodge, 9 Glass St, T9937 1900. Offers 4 very clean rooms that open out onto the pool courtyard (each with their own entrance). Muffins await in the afternoon, and port and chocolate in the evening. The owner, Sharyn, is on hand to recommend somewhere for dinner. Free Wi-Fi, and off street parking available. Continental breakfast included, or guests can choose from a menu of cooked options the night before.

A-B Kalbarri Beach Resort, 1 Clotworthy St, T9937 1061, www.kalbarribeachresort.com. Has over 100 units with 2 and 3 bedrooms. General facilities include 3 spas, table tennis, swimming pool, tennis and volleyball courts, BBQs, Wi-Fi and on-site restaurant (Jakes, see Eating, below).

A-B Seafront Villas, 108 Gery St, T9937 1025, www.kalbarriseafrontvillas.com.au. One of the better examples with swimming pool, BBQ and internet access. The units sleep 2-8 people and there are studio apartments and a 4-bedroom townhouse.

B-C Kalbarri Motor Hotel, 188 Gray St, T9937 1000. This is the only motel in town and has a few doubles, twins and family rooms, all en suite. There is also a pool and a restaurant.

B-E Pelican's Nest and Kalbarri Backpackers YHA, corner Mortimer and Wood Sts, T9937 1430, www.pelicansnestkalbarri.com.au. En suite motel and studio rooms with private balcony as well as self-contained chalets. Backpacker accommodation next door with pool, BBQ and internet facilities. The hostel is large but friendly, has en suite dorms, free

boogie board and snorkel hire. Bicycle hire for $20 per day and cycle tours also available. Recommended.

C Kalbarri Riverfront, 16 Grey St, T9937 1032, www.westnet.com.au/fg. Has a completely furnished 2-bedroom unit that sleeps up to 5.

C Kalbarri Riverfront Budget Units, 26 Grey St, T9937 1144, www.riverfrontbudget units.com.au. The only budget units on the foreshore, which are considerably more pleasant inside than they look from the outside. Fully self-contained 2- to 3-bedroom cottages. No linen provided.

C Lola-Rose B&B, 24 Patrick Crescent, T9937 2224. Slightly set back from the main street, this B&B offers 3 en suite rooms (2 double, 1 single) and 3 with shared facilities. A continental breakfast is included in the price. Cash only.

Caravan parks

B-E Murchison Park, corner of Grey St and Wood St, T9937 1005, www.murcp.com. The most central of those in town, some sites have waterfront view. Cabins (some en suite), on-site vans and a good range of facilities.

B-E Tudor Holiday Park, Porter St, T9937 1077 or T1800 681 077, www.tudorholiday park.com.au. Has the best-value cabins (backpacker, standard and en suite). There are also motel and brick units, a swimming pool and a campers' kitchen. Spring water is available on site.

C-E Anchorage Caravan Park, River Rd and Anchorage Lane, T9937 1181, www.kalbarri anchorage.com.au. Located at the north end of town, with views of the Murchison River from some sites. This caravan park has cabins, park homes, a pool and a children's playground. Also does a Thu night BBQ.

🍴 Eating

Northampton *p249*
🍴 **Northampton Café**, at the northern end of town, T9934 1650. Mon-Fri 0830-1600 and Sat to 1400. Has a selection of simple sandwiches, burgers and drinks.

Kalbarri *p250, map p251*
The 2 pubs provide the other options for a substantial lunch. Both do cheap to mid-range meals daily 1200-1400 and 1800-2030.
🍴🍴-🍴🍴 **Black Rock Café**, 80 Grey St, T9937 1062, www.blackrockcafe.com.au. Tue-Sat 0700-2000 and Sun for breakfast only from 0700. The best spot in town. Dinners can verge on the expensive and breakfast and lunch are also pricey but the foreshore location, consistently good food and unhurried, friendly service always make it a good spot. Licensed. Recommended.
🍴🍴-🍴🍴 **The Grass Tree**, 94 Grey St, T9937 2288. Mon 0900-1400, Tue, Fri-Sun 1000-1400, Mon-Tue, Fri-Sun 1800-late. Gives **Black Rock** a good run for its money. Fully licensed and BYO.
🍴 **Finlays**, Magee Cres, off Walker St, T9937 1260. Provides a BBQ feed with plenty of outdoor seating. Deliberately a bit rough and ready, the seafood and salads may not sensationalize your tastebuds but they will satisfy your stomach. Gets very busy with tourists in summer and you can't book so get there early at busy times. BYO only.
🍴 **The Gorges Café**, opposite the marina, T9937 1200. Mon, Tue, Thu-Fri 0800-1600, Sat-Sun 0800-1400. In a quieter spot than the others, with views of the Murchison River. Offers breakfast and lunch, as well as coffee and cake. Takeaway available. Internet access and BYO (no corkage fee).
🍴 **Jakes Family Restaurant**, in the grounds of the **Kalbarri Beach Resort**, T9937 2222. Daily 1700-2100. Serves substantial, good-value food. Buffet roast on Sun.
🍴 **Jetty Seafood Shack**, opposite the marina, T9937 1067. Mon-Sat 1630-2100, Sun

1130-1430 and 1730-2100. Offers the best value portion of fish 'n' chips. Alfresco dining or takeaway, BYO.

🍸 Bars and clubs

Kalbarri *p250, map p251*
Gilgai Tavern, 12 Porter St, near supermarket, T9937 1083, www.gilgaitavern.com. The town's quieter option, but has occasional live music. It serves up mid-range lunch and dinner, daily 1200-1400 and 1800-2030. 12 tap beers, pool table and good happy hours Sat-Thu 1700-1800, Fri-Sun 1200-1300.
Kalbarri Motor Hotel, see Sleeping. Is the larger place with a dancefloor, large bar and restaurant area, betting shop, bottle shop, plenty of covered outdoor tables and is the social hub of the town, has occasional live music. Restaurant meals, mainly seafood and steak, are served daily 1200-1500 and 1800-2030. There's also a good range of cheap bar meals available daily.

🎭 Entertainment

Kalbarri *p250, map p251*
Kalbarri Entertainment Centre, 15 Magee Cres, T9937 1105, www.kalbarripirate.com. Has a crazy golf course and children's trampolines. It also hires out bicycles for $20 a day.

🛍 Shopping

Kalbarri *p250, map p251*
Black lip oysters are farmed off the Abrolhos Islands and local jewellers along the coast create some very interesting pieces of jewellery that incorporate them. Local gift shops stock some fine examples.
There are 2 supermarkets in town, both open daily, and also meat and seafood specialists.

▲▲ Activities and tours

There are dozens of river, sea and bus tours available, plus a good many adventure activities. All can be booked via the VIC. Some can be very demanding in hot weather, check what is supplied and be well prepared with drinks and for the sun.

Kalbarri *p250, map p251*
Boat cruises/hire
Kalbarri Boat Hire, on the beach opposite the VIC, T9937 1245, www.kalbarriboathire.com. Open daily with a wide variety of boats, from canoes to small motor boats, windsurfers to paddlebikes. Prices from $15-50 per hr.
Kalbarri Wilderness Cruises, T9937 2259, www.kalbarricruises.com.au. Sunset and 2-hr wildlife cruises starting from $35, children $25.
Murchison Boat Hire, T9937 2043, www.murchisonboathire.com.au. Has larger sea-going motor boats for DIY fishermen and divers, from $304-610 per day. Fishing gear hire available. Accommodation and boat hire packages.

Canoe trips
Kalbarri Adventure Tours, T9937 1677, www.kalbarritours.com.au. Runs more adventurous day trips into the inland gorges ($90), tours depart Mon, Wed, Fri and Sun. This is a great way to see what the national park has to offer if you have just a day to do so. They also offer hike-only-tours to the park's most famous and beautiful spots. Bring lunch. Recommended.
Kalbarri Boat Hire, see Boat cruises, above. Takes groups a short way up the Murchison for a gentle paddle around the lower reaches of the river. Breakfast and lunch canoe trips for $65, children $35-45 (including meals).

Dive and fishing
Kalbarri Explorer, T9937 2027, www.kalbarri explorer.com.au. Runs day sea-fishing trips for $230 and whale-watching for $65 (Jun-Dec).
Kalbarri Sports & Dive, Kalbarri Arcade, T9937 1126. Fishing tackle ($10-15 per day),

snorkel ($15), scuba gear ($70), golf clubs $15 available, Mon-Sat 0830-1730, also Sun in summer. Tank refills $7.
Reefwalker, T9937 1356, www.reefwalker. com.au. Runs sea-fishing day trips for $230, shared line $290. They also do lobster tours, coastal cliff, whale-watching and dolphin cruises (in season).
The Specialists, T9937 1050, www.the specialists.com.au. Tours include 6-8 hrs of fishing and a light BBQ lunch, $210, share line $270. They also run sunset and whale-watching (Jul-Dec) cruises, kite surfing tours and 3-day trips to the Abrolhos Islands.

Golf
Golf & Bowling Club, Haselby St, T9937 1499. An 18-hole course set within the Kalbarri Nature Reserve. Green fees $15.

Pelican feeding
A number of pelicans come to the grassy foreshore area opposite the **Grass Tree Café** to be fed daily at 0845. This is a good opportunity for those who want to get up close to these majestic birds and learn a bit more about them.

Tour operators
Big River Ranch, 2 km north of town, T9937 1214, www.bigriverranch.net. A range of bush and beach horse rides from 1-2 hrs for all levels. A 1-hr ride costs about $55, 20-min pony rides for about $20. Also offers farm stay accommodation and camping.
Kalbarri Abseil, T9937 1618, www.abseil australia.com.au. Head out most mornings to the Z-Bend gorge and conduct abseils on the red cliffs above the river. Half-day $80, children $70.
Kalbarri Safari Tours, T9937 1011, www.kalbarrisafaritours.com.au. Runs quad bike tours in the region ($59 per hr).
Kalbarri Sandboarding, T9937 2377, www.sandboardingaustralia.com.au. Runs sandboard trips ($60) daily.
Kalbarri Scenic Flights, Grey St, T9937 1130, www.kalbarriaircharter.com.au. Offers a range

of flights from a 20-min zip along the coast cliffs ($59, children $44) to an excellent morning excursion up to **Monkey Mia** ($285, children $199). Also hires bikes and scooters.

⊖ Transport

Kalbarri *p250, map p251*
Bicycle/scooter hire From end to end Kalbarri is 2 km, and the coastal gorges are 5 km south. Bicycles and tandems can be hired at **Kalbarri Entertainment Centre**, 15 Magee Cres, T9937 1105. **Kalbarri Scenic Flights** hires bikes ($20 a day) and scooters ($85 a day).

Bus The main (N1) services to Geraldton (6 hrs) leave East Perth terminal Mon-Sat at 0830, Fri 1630 and Sun 0930; Mon, Wed and Fri services go to **Kalbarri**. TransWA services leave the VIC for **Northampton**, **Geraldton** and **Perth** Tue, Thu and Sat at 0710.

Car Car servicing from **Kalbarri Auto Centre**, Atkinson Cres, T9937 1290 and T0403 017956 (24-hr mobile). An RAC roadside assistance contact which offers a 24-hr towing service. Car hire also possible.

Taxi Call, T9937 1888.

⊙ Directory

Kalbarri *p250, map p251*
Banks There are a number of ATMs around town, including in the Kalbarri Arcade, the Kalbarri Motor Hotel and down at the marina. **Internet** Community Resource Centre, Hackney St, T9937 1933. Mon-Fri 0900-1500. Also at several cafés. **Medical services** Chemists: Kalbarri Arcade, T9937 1026. Open Mon-Fri 0900-1700, Sat 0900-1230. Medical centre: Glass St, T9937 0100. **Police** Grey St, T9937 1006. **Post** Marina Complex, next to the Jetty Seafood Shack, T9937 1175.

Routes north

Northampton to the Overlander Roadhouse → *Distance: 225 km.*

From Northampton the **North West Coastal Highway** leaves the northern end of the wheat belt and plunges into native scrub, now largely utilized for keeping stock animals such as sheep and cattle. The vast paddocks are not fenced off from the road so this is not a stretch of road to undertake at dawn or twilight. For several hundred kilometres the drive is remarkable only for its uniformity – only wildflowers in season save it from serious monotony. The last hint of interest is the picnic spot (24-hour rest stop) at Galena bridge over the Murchison River, about 60 km from Northampton, and just past the Kalbarri turn-off. From there it is another 120 km to **Billabong**, the site of a roadhouse and hotel.

The Wildflower Way → *See page 370 for an overview of WA's wildflowers.*

During the months from July to September, it is well worth considering the route from Perth to Moora (preferably via New Norcia), and from there to Mullewa via Carnamah, Perenjori, and Morawa to Mullewa. The quality and richness of the wildflowers along the way varies from year to year, depending chiefly on the amount of rainfall the region receives the preceding winter, but can be quite fantastic. The VICs at Mullewa and Morawa are happy to advise on the year's blooms and the best places to seek them out on your way through. In this region you can see orchids, everlastings, grevilleas, smoke bush and many other species but it is particularly known for the unusual wreath flower, *Lechenaultia macrantha*. This region is also interesting for the unusual church architecture of Monsignor John Hawes.

Morawa is a wheat-growing area where 70% of native vegetation has been cleared, but great diversity in flora remains in reserves and on roadside verges. The Church of the Holy Cross in Davis Street is one of John Hawes' designs (see box, page 244), of local stone with Cordoban roof tiles and green tropical shutters. Contact the **VIC** ① *main street, T9971 1204, or shire office on Prater St, T9971 1004, Jun-Sep only.*

Mullewa, 550 km from Perth, 100 km from Geraldton, has one of Hawes' finest works, The Church of Our Lady of Mount Carmel, a romantic Mediterranean style with solid stone walls to keep out the sun. The Priest House nearby is maintained as a museum of Hawes' life. For more information contact the **VIC** ① *Jose St, T9961 1500, www.mullewatourism. com.au, Oct-Jun Mon-Fri 0830-1630, Jul-Sep Mon-Fri 0830-1630, Sat-Sun 0900-1630, or the shire office on Padbury St, T9961 1007, Mon-Fri 0900-1630.*

From Mullewa you can choose to head out to the North West Coastal Highway at Geraldton or inland to Mount Magnet (245 km) and the Great Northern Highway. If heading inland, **Yalgoo**, 120 km east of Mullewa, is a charming old gold-mining town with a lovely John Hawes' chapel, the Dominican Chapel of St Hyacinth. Ask at the shire office for the key and a heritage trail booklet to explore Yalgoo.

Great Northern Highway → *Mt Magnet 345 km from Geraldton, 200 km Meekatharra.*

If you're heading north towards the central Pilbara or the Kimberley, the Great Northern Highway can save a few hundred kilometres when compared to the coastal highways. The route splits from the Brand Highway just north of the Swan Valley and continues via **New Norcia** through wildflower country to the vast inland plains beyond the small town of **Wubin**, 270 km from Perth. From here towns and fuel become considerably more scarce, the 290 km to Mount Magnet interrupted by just one fuel-stop midway at Paynes Find.

Mount Magnet is one of the most active of the Midwest goldfield towns, though there is still activity at both Cue and Meekatharra further north. The Pilbara town of Newman, 430 km north of Meekatharra, marks the start of the rich iron-ore mines of the northwest.

⊙ Routes north listings

For Sleeping and Eating price codes and other relevant information, see pages 28-34.

⊜ Sleeping

Northampton to the Overlander Roadhouse *p258*

C Billabong Hotel Motel, Billabong, T9942 5980, www.billabonghotelmotel.com. Modern, with a bar and café, motel rooms, caravan sites but no kitchen. Rooms are en suite and have a/c. Internet $5 for 30 mins.
C Billabong roadhouse, Billabong, T9942 5919, next to the Billabong Hotel. A friendly place. Its rooms aren't en suite but do have a/c. Standard cheap meals available at both from 0630 to 2000. Bar and fuel until around 2200.
C-F Overlander, Northwest Coastal Highway, T9942 5916. A friendly roadhouse that marks the turn-off to Denham and Monkey Mia. Fuel is no more expensive than at Billabong, and

fractionally cheaper than Shark Bay. It has an ATM, a good range of cheap meals (0500-2400). Accommodation is basic but clean and includes linen and a/c. Backpacker beds are the same without linen. Also caravan sites.

The Wildflower Way *p258*

Morawa has a small motel, T9971 1060, and a caravan park. Mullewa has a site-only caravan park (enquire at Yarrumba service station on Jose St). Yalgoo has a pub, site-only caravan park, hotel (T9962 8031), general store and petrol. There are several station stays nearby.
B Pindar Guest House, in the old pub at Pindar, 26 km east of Mullewa on Mt Magnet Rd, T9962 3024, www.pindarguesthouse.com. 5 rooms, breakfast is included in the price. A 2-course evening meal·is available by arrangement for $30. Open Jun-Oct.
C Railway Hotel, Mullewa, T9961 1050. Motel and hotel rooms.

Contents

The Gascoyne

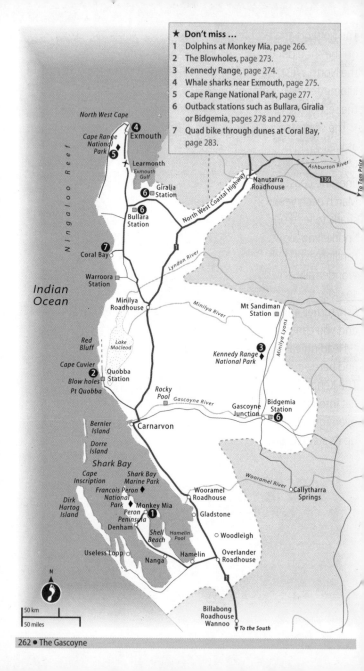

★ **Don't miss ...**
1 Dolphins at Monkey Mia, page 266.
2 The Blowholes, page 273.
3 Kennedy Range, page 274.
4 Whale sharks near Exmouth, page 275.
5 Cape Range National Park, page 277.
6 Outback stations such as Bullara, Giralia or Bidgemia, pages 278 and 279.
7 Quad bike through dunes at Coral Bay, page 283.

The hot and arid Gascoyne region sits between two distinct hooks on the shoulder of the coastline – from Shark Bay in the south to the North West Cape in the north, and inland for a few hundred kilometres. In the waters off this region marine life is abundant; in the rest of the country, only the Great Barrier Reef can rival them.

The sheltered waters of Shark Bay harbour dugongs and turtles as well as dolphins, which come in to shore to be fed by hand at Monkey Mia. Further north, a coral fringing reef – Ningaloo Reef– lines the coast for more than 250 km. When the coral spawns in March each year it attracts the world's largest fish, the whale shark, to feed on this caviar-like soup for several months. Snorkelling alongside them as they feed is one of the most thrilling experiences this great island nation can offer. On a wonderfully accessible level, at some points the reef comes so close to shore that you are able to snorkel among coral, fish, turtles and rays straight off the beach. Come in summer and you can watch the turtles laying and hatching.

Heading east is a landscape of red dirt and open spaces, and here you'll encounter the hospitality of outback country. The Kennedy Range is a rare break in the Gascoyne's relatively flat interior and orientated such that in the early morning overnight campers are treated to a rich morning glow lighting up its steep east-facing cliffs.

Shark Bay

Shark Bay is formed by two long peninsulas lying parallel to the coast, like the prongs of a fork. The middle prong is the Peron Peninsula, and the western prong is formed by the Zuytdorp Cliffs and Dirk Hartog Island. These are the most westerly bits of land in Australia, forming an extraordinary sheltered marine environment in its countless small bays. The waters of Shark Bay are always a startling turquoise and as clear as a swimming pool thanks to its shallowness; the average depth of the bay is 10 m and much of it is no deeper than 1 m. It is most famous for its colony of dolphins, some of which come into shore at Monkey Mia, but there are also dugongs, turtles, rays and sharks living in these waters and all are easily seen on a boat trip or from the shore. The land is also a refuge for wildlife. Although its low arid scrub and red sand looks too harsh and barren for anything to survive, the Francois Peron National Park is the focus for a program to save endangered native species. The small town of Denham and the tourist facilities at Monkey Mia provide comfortable lodging for visitors but most of the Shark Bay region is a wilderness. Shark Bay was declared a World Heritage Area in 1991 for its rare stromatolites, extensive seagrass beds, endangered animals and natural beauty. ►► *For listings, see pages 268-270.*

Overlander Roadhouse to Denham ►► *For listings, see pages 268-270.*

Hamelin Pool → *Colour map 5, C1. 35 km from the Overlander Roadhouse, 105 km from Denham.*
Hamelin Pool is a wide shallow estuary on the eastern side of Shark Bay. It elicits great scientific interest today because of the resident colonies of **stromatolites**. These boulder-like formations are the direct result of sediments becoming trapped by thin organic mats of cyanobacteria over thousands of years. These dark, stumpy colonies, squatting in the inter-tidal area, are about 3000 years old. In pre-Cambrian times, over 600 million years ago, these communities were one of the dominant features of life on earth, but now thrive only in those places where just about every other kind of life finds it very tough going. A boardwalk with interpretative panels extends out over the stromatolites into the bay, and though the action is subdued to say the least, it is striking to consider that this is a window into an almost inconceivably distant past.

In the 1880s this spot was chosen as the site of one of WA's **telegraph repeater stations** ① *T9942 5905, $5 per person, guided tours only*, because of its relative ease of provisioning by sea. The original station is now a modest museum, partly devoted to an explanation of the stromatolites and partly to preserve the heritage of the telegraph system. The shady compound is something of an oasis in the baking hot conditions, and the tearoom is a welcome place to grab a cold drink.

Hamelin Pool to Ocean Park Aquarium
There are a couple of sights worth stopping for on this stretch, first **Shell Beach**, 50 km from Hamelin. At Hamelin you'll have noticed that the white sand underfoot is actually crushed shells. Shell Beach is one of the most accessible examples of a beach entirely made up of tiny white shells, and it slopes gently into the bay for hundreds of metres. The shells are the bivalve cardiid cockle, a type of saline-tolerant cockle only found in Shark Bay. Deep under the beach the shells cement together when rainwater dissolves their calcium carbonate and the resulting coquina limestone has been readily utilized around Shark Bay as a building material. Some 20 km short of Denham a 4-km unsealed side-road leads to **Eagle Bluff**, a 40-m-high headland that has great views. Extensive boardwalks

Predators ousted from paradise

Project Eden aims to make Peron Peninsula (1050 sq km) the largest conservation area in Australia and has had great success since its inception in 1995. It is protected by a 2-m-high electrified fence and a cattle grid has been placed where the fence meets the road. In case any nimble-footed predators are tempted to tiptoe over the grid, there are also recordings of barking dogs, activated by movement, and high-pitched sonar recordings to deter them. About 50,000 baits a year are laid on the peninsula (and nearby stations) to kill foxes and it is thought that there are few, if any, left on the peninsula. Feral cats are more difficult to eradicate as they won't take baits if live marsupials are on the menu. Traps and yummier baits have caught thousands of cats since 1995 and seem to be keeping

numbers down. Native fauna such as emus, echidnas, monitors and many small marsupials have flourished since exotic predators have been almost eliminated, including nine endangered species that were on the brink of extinction a few years ago. The DEC has successfully introduced malleefowl, bilbies and woylies and now hopes to translocate the burrowing bettong (boodie), pale field rat, chuditch, greater sticknest rat and phascogale to the area. In the future DEC intends to provide more ways for visitors to be able to observe these native creatures in the wild but many of the small marsupials are nocturnal so will always be elusive. If you go to the peninsula make sure you visit at around dawn or dusk and be sure to take the time to look for tiny tracks in the sand.

make it easy to find vantage points from which you may spot some of the region's marine life, which includes rays, turtles, sharks and dolphins.

Ocean Park Aquarium

ⓘ 8 km south of Denham, clearly signposted, T9948 1765, www.oceanpark.com.au. $16, children $11, concessions $14. Daily 0900-1600.

Originally started as an aquaculture venture, this is an aquarium where instead of viewing marine creatures through the glass, knowledgeable and enthusiastic tour guides take visitors round a series of open tanks explaining about habitat, feeding and how to identify certain species. In addition to the turtles, eels and sea snakes, there is also shark feeding from an observation deck above the pool. The tiger sharks, lemon sharks and sand bar sharks are not endangered species and are only held and observed for short periods of time for rehabilitation or research, after which they are released back into the ocean. The café, which serves food, has a large veranda and is a great place to have enjoy a glass of wine and a sunset. The aquarium can arrange station stays at **Carbla Station** and also offers 4WD tours to the Francois Peron National Park (see below).

Denham ⤭ For listings, see pages 268-270. Colour map 5, C1.

→ Population: 1200. 375 km from Kalbarri, 330 km from Carnarvon.

Denham is a friendly town that services much of the tourist trade on its way to Monkey Mia, 30 km away on the eastern side of the Peron Peninsula. Denham sits on the western side of the peninsula, well protected from the open ocean by long and narrow Dirk Hartog Island. The main industry is fishing, replacing the one that brought Europeans, Malaysians and Chinese people here in the 1850s: pearling. Recently the industry has been revived and pearl farms have been established in the bay, producing fine black pearls. One such farm offers tours via Monkey Mia (see Activities and tours, page 269). The town has a grassy foreshore, with BBQs and picnic tables, and has fuel and a supermarket. The **Shark Bay World Heritage Discovery Centre** ① *29 Knight Terr, www.sharkbayinterpretive centre.com.au, daily 0900-1800, $11, child $6, concessions $8*, is located in the VIC and the opening hours are the same. The Discovery Centre has some interesting displays, which inform about the history and wildlife of Shark Bay. The film footage is particularly interesting if you want to know more.

Francois Peron National Park ▸▸ *Colour map 5, C1.*

① *For more information contact DEC, 89 Knight Terr, Denham, T9948 1208. $11 car, camping $7 per person. Visitor centre daily 0800-1630.*

Named after a French naturalist who explored Shark Bay as part of Baudin's expedition on the *Geographe* and *Naturaliste* in 1801 and 1803, the Francois Peron covers the northern tip of the Peron Peninsula, from the Monkey Mia road north to Cape Peron, an area of 52,500 ha. A dramatic series of cliffs and bays, where red rocks merge into white sand and turquoise sea, encloses a dry and arid region with many salt-pans (birridas) dotting the low sandy plains. Despite the unpromising look of the land that early European visitors called 'useless', the peninsula was used as a sheep station from the 1880s until 1990, when the government bought the station and created the park. The vegetation here is significant because the flowering plants of the southwest – grevilleas and hakeas – reach their northern limit in the park and meet the acacias typical of northern regions. The park is also notable for **Project Eden**, part of the Western Shield nature conservation programme to reverse the decline of native mammals caused by fox and feral cat predation (see box, page 265). The park is home to malleefowl, bilbies, woylies, bandicoots, the Shark Bay mouse and many other species. This mostly nocturnal wildlife is not often seen but thorny devils are common and dolphins, dugongs and turtles may be spotted from the cliffs at Cape Peron. There is a **visitor centre** at the old station homestead that aims to educate visitors about Project Eden, and an outdoor hot tub fed by an artesian bore that visitors are welcome to use. The homestead is usually accessible by 2WD (10 km, unsealed) but the rest of this peaceful, remote place is only accessible by high-clearance 4WD (check with the DEC for up-to-date road and track information).

Monkey Mia ▸▸ *For listings, see pages 268-270. Colour map 5, C1.*

① *For more information contact DEC, Shark Bay, T9948 1208 or the Monkey Mia Reserve T9948 1366. Day pass $8, children $3, family $15 (valid for 24 hrs). Family holiday pass $30 (valid for 4 weeks).*

Dolphins have lived in Shark Bay for millennia but the current encounters with humans only began in the 1960s when fishermen began to hand feed dolphins. The dolphins were happy to accept a free feed and visited settlements regularly. By the 1980s word began to spread of a place called Monkey Mia where people fed and swam with dolphins. Even though the place is incredibly remote, over 800 km from Perth and 330 km from Carnarvon, the pull of wild dolphins is irresistible and has made the area internationally famous. Each year Monkey Mia seems to get busier and things are very different from the informal encounters of the past. Interaction with the dolphins is carefully managed to keep them wild and

Temptresses and turtles

The clear waters of Shark Bay are home to a far more mysterious creature than the friendly dolphin. This is the sirenia, named for the mythical sirens of the sea luring sailors to their doom. When you see the portly, brown body and broad snout of a dugong it's hard to believe that sailors once mistook them for mermaids, but from a distance their ample figures and mermaid-shaped tail set sailors' hearts pounding.

The dugong is a type of sea cow and is similar to the only other surviving sirenia, the manatee of the Caribbean. An average dugong is about 3 m long, 300 kg and can live more than 70 years. About 10,000 dugongs live in Shark Bay, the second largest population in the world. These animals graze on seagrass and they are able to live so successfully in Shark Bay because it has the largest and most diverse seagrass meadows in the world. Over thousands of years the seagrass has had a powerful influence on the environment of the bay. For starters the meadows inhibit tidal flow, a factor in the hypersaline conditions that have resulted in the growth of stromatolites and tiny bivalve cockles. Seagrass also provides food and shelter for hundreds of animals in the food chain, creating Shark Bay's rich marine environment.

The turtle is another magnificent animal that feeds on the seagrass and there are estimated to be about 6000 in the world heritage area; mostly green turtles and the endangered loggerhead turtles. The loggerheads breed and nest on Dirk Hartog Island from August to January and their hatchlings emerge in around February to March. Green turtles and dugongs are often seen from boats, although dugongs are shy. Also look out for turtles around the jetty at Monkey Mia and while you're swimming as they're often seen close to shore.

minimize the impact of hundreds of visitors a day. One of the best things to do in Monkey Mia is to leave the beach and take a boat cruise and see the dolphins in their own environment, as well as many other incredible animals such as dugongs and turtles. Despite the number of visitors, Monkey Mia itself is just a small low-key resort. The visitor centre overlooking the beach where the dolphins swim into shore has displays on the biology and behaviour of dolphins and shows videos on marine life.

Dolphin encounters

Free spirits wanting to commune with nature may be a little disappointed with the Monkey Mia experience. This is how it works: the dolphins swim into a section of beach by the jetty that is closed to boats and swimmers. When the dolphins arrive people line up along the beach, perhaps for 100 m or more. You are not allowed to enter the water beyond your knees, and a DEC officer will stand in the water making sure that the dolphins are not disturbed. The dolphins are often only a few feet away and nuzzle the officers' calves while the officers chat about them. When the DEC officers decide to feed the dolphins everyone is asked to step out of the water and a few lucky souls are picked to come forward and give a dolphin a fish. Only mature female dolphins are fed and they get no more than a third of their daily requirements so they will not become dependent on handouts. Once the feeding is finished the dolphins usually swim away, but if they don't you can step back in the water to your knees again. Even in such crowded and controlled conditions it is wonderful to be so close to these wild dolphins. When they roll on their sides and look up at you can't help feeling that these creatures really are as curious about you as you are about them (or maybe they're just wondering where you're hiding the fish).

To get the best out of the experience plan to spend the whole day at Monkey Mia or make it an overnight trip. The dolphins usually arrive about 0800 and after they have been fed the main crowds disappear. Dolphin feeding is allowed three times between 0800 and 1300 and there is a good chance that the dolphins will reappear and you'll have a more intimate encounter. Take an afternoon and sunset cruise and you can't fail to have an awesome day.

It is possible to do volunteer work with the dolphins (for a minimum of four days and a maximum of two weeks). Contact **DEC** ① *T9948 1366,* or email monkeymiavolunteers@westnet.com.au.

◉ Shark Bay listings

For Sleeping and Eating price codes and other relevant information, see pages 28-34.

● Sleeping

Hamelin Pool *p264*
C-F Hamelin Station, T9948 5145, hamelinstationstay@bigpond.com. Only 5 km from Hamelin Pool, this station offers accommodation in refurbished shearer's quarters as well as some self-contained units, Campsites are also available. There's a campers kitchen and free BBQs.
E Hamelin Pool Caravan Park, T9942 5905. Campers can use the lawns and there are powered caravan sites.

Denham *p265*
There is a fair range of reasonably priced accommodation here, mostly in self-contained units and caravan parks. The busiest season is Jul-Oct, but all school and public holidays and the Dec-Jan period are usually booked out well in advance.
B Denham Villas, Durlacher St, T9948 1264, www.denhamvillas.com. Has some of the best presented and equipped self-contained units close to the ocean.
B Heritage Resort Hotel, corner of Knight Terr and Durlacher St, T9948 1133, www.heritageresortsharkbay.com.au. Large hotel with 27 en suite rooms, some with ocean views and small balconies. There is also a swimming pool and an on-site restaurant.

Scooter hire is possible for $50 per day and there's car hire available.
B Oceanside Village, 117 Knight Terr, next to the YHA, T9948 3003 and T1800 680600, www.oceanside.com.au. 22 well-equipped, self-contained chalets that sleep up to 6, some with ocean view. Facilities include free Wi-Fi, swimming pool, BBQs and DVD library. Recommended.
B-C Shark Bay View B&B, 58 Durlacher St, T9948 1060. A/c doubles and singles in a modern Mediterranean-style building. Continental or hot breakfast included.
C-E Bay Lodge YHA, Knight Terr, T9948 1278, www.baylodge.info. Has motel rooms, some facing the ocean, self-contained chalets, and several units grouped around the pool set aside as good-value 3- to 5-bed backpacker apartments with small kitchens, a TV area and bathroom. Also BBQ, laundry and free shuttle to Monkey Mia, 0745.
C-E Denham Seaside Tourist Village, at the northern end of Knight Terr, T9948 1242 and T1300 133733, www.sharkbayfun.com. The best positioned of 3 caravan parks, with good facilities. Offers en suite powered sites, as well as a range of self-contained cabins.

Monkey Mia *p266*
Facilities at the **Money Mia Resort** include a pool, hot tub, good-sized campers' kitchen, BBQs, tennis and volleyball courts, and internet access. The complex also has a few shops, a bar and food outlets. These are accessible to

everyone. In addition to the accommodation outlined below, camping is also available on powered and unpowered sites.

L-A Dolphin Resort, T9948 1320 and T1800 653611, www.monkeymia.com.au. Has a few very comfortable beachfront and garden villas.

C-E Dolphin Lodge, T9948 1320 and T1800 653611, www.monkeymia.com.au. The budget accommodation in Monkey Mia, offering shared en suite rooms and dorms.

🍴 Eating

Hamelin Pool *p264*
🍴 **Hamelin Pool Telegraph Station**, T9942 5905. Daily 0900-1630. Serves snack lunches and excellent cream teas.

Denham *p265*
There are a few places on Knight Terr serving takeaway food, snacks and average coffee.
🍴🍴🍴 **Old Pearler**, corner of Durlacher St and Knight Terr, T9948 1373. The most visible example of a building made of shells (coquina limestone blocks) and the only real restaurant in Denham. While it certainly has the most character, the food does not always live up to the cosy rustic interior and is priced well above other places in town.
🍴🍴-🍴 **Heritage Resort Hotel**, corner of Knight Terr and Durlacher St, T9948 1133. Meals 1200-1430, 1800-2100. Cheap light lunches, pizzas and a basic dinner menu. Good views from upstairs restaurant balcony. Live music on Sun.
🍴 **Sunset Mura Mura Café**, 51 Knight Terr, T9948 1047. Mon-Wed 0700-1730, Tue-Sun 0700-2030. By the VIC, this café serves up good coffee and cake, as well as healthy and wholesome light lunches and options for self-caterers to take home and pop in the oven. Wi-Fi available on purchase. Around the back is a takeaway pizza joint (1730-late) that operates in the evenings.

Monkey Mia *p266*
🍴🍴-🍴🍴 **Boughshed**, T9948 1171. Open for breakfast, lunch, dinner, coffee and snacks all day. This serves as the resort restaurant. While the food is OK and it's a great place to sit and watch the beach, you pay for the privilege. Instead, you could grab something from the takeaway, eat on the grass in front of the café and enjoy the same view.
🍴 **Monkey Bar**, T9948 1320. Open 1200-1400 and 1800-2000. A takeaway café/bar serving pizzas and burgers.

▲▲ Activities and tours

Denham *p265*
Films are shown at the Town Hall on Sat nights, what's on is advertised on Knight Terr near the VIC.
Shark Bay Air Charter, T9948 1773, www.sharkbayair.com.au. Flights are a good way to see these peninsulas and sharks, dugongs and dolphins are visible from the air. Flights over Monkey Mia and Peron Homestead, Denham, Francois Peron National Park, Steep Point, Useless Loop and salt lakes, Zuytdorp Cliffs, Hamelin Pool, Coral Bay, Mount Augustus (prices range from $55-595). Also offers a flight to Dirk Hartog Island, which is complemented by a 4WD tour around the island.
Unreal Fishing Charters, T9948 1185, www.sharkbayfishing.com.au. Day trips on the 34-ft *Woomerangee* to Dirk Hartog Island and Steep Point. All gear and lunch provided.

Monkey Mia *p266*
4WD
Monkey Mia Wildsights, T9948 1481, www.monkeymiawildsights.com.au. Runs a day tour around Francois Peron National Park (8 hrs, $189, all fees and lunch included) departing at 0900.

Beach volleyball
Use of the court is free, ask to borrow a ball at the resort reception.

Boat cruises
Aristocat 2, T9948 1446, www.monkey-mia.net. Has a large enclosed cabin, making it

slower to move around, but ideal for those sensitive to the sun. There are underwater observation windows for dolphin and dugong viewing. A range of tours on offer, from a 1-hr mini cruise ($45, child $22) to a sunset cruise (1½ hrs, $59, child, $27) and nature tour (2½ hrs, $75, child $37), which takes visitors out to look for dugongs and also includes a trip to the Black Lagoon Pearl Farm to see how black pearls are grown. **Shotover**, T9948 1481, www.monkeymia wildsights.com.au. An 18-m open catamaran. No central cabin means excellent all-round views, and there are large nets slung between the hulls that you can sit in, as well as plentiful deck seating. Polarized sunglasses are provided, which make it much easier to see underwater. Daily cruises: morning wildlife cruise 0900 (2½ hrs, $69), dugong-spotting cruise 1300 (3 hrs, $84), sunset cruise (1½ hrs, $54).

Boat and snorkel hire
Monkey Mia Boat Hire, on the beach in front of the **Monkey Bar**, T9948 1000. Rents out kayaks, glass-bottom boats and pedal boats. **Power Dive**, at Monkey Mia Resort, T9948 3031. Has snorkelling gear for hire.

Cinema
Research documentaries are shown at the **Theatrette** near the DEC office; the timetable is posted outside.

Cultural tours
Wula Guda Nyinda Aboriginal Eco Adventures, T0429 708847, www.wulaguda. com.au. Enthusiastic guide Capes offers morning, sunset and kayaking tours of Shark Bay ($40-90). Learn about bush tucker and medicinal plants, identifying animal tracks and reading the land, all the while listening to stories, legends and traditions. Recommended.

Walking
A short loop walk around Monkey Mia (2 km) takes you past an ancient Aboriginal site and provides good views from a low ridge. Pick up a walksheet from the DEC office.

⊖ Transport

Denham *p265*
Bus If travelling by **Greyhound**, there is no shuttle to/from the Overlander Roadhouse. Your accommodation may be able to offer pick-ups, so contact them in advance. **Shark Bay Coaches** run a shuttle to **Monkey Mia**, T9948 1081, departing 0745 and returning 1630 ($45 each way).

Car Hire from **Shark Bay Car Hire**, T9948 3032. 4WD hire from $188 a day, allowing exploration of the national park. Must be over 25 and able to prove experience driving a 4WD. Car hire is also available from the **Heritage Resort Hotel**.
    Servicing at **Shark Bay Fuel and Service Centre**, 85 Knight Terr, T9948 1239. Daily 0700-1800.

Scooter hire The Heritage Resort Hotel hires out scooters for $50 per day.

❶ Directory

Denham *p265*
Banks There are a few ATMs scattered around town, including **Bankwest** at Heritage Resort. **Internet** Shark Bay Community Resource Centre, 67 Knight Terr, T9948 1787. Mon and Fri 0930-1430, Tue-Wed 0900-1630, Thu 0900-1530. **Sunset Mura Mura Café** (see Eating) offers Wi-Fi on purchase. **Medical services** Chemists: Shark Bay Pharmacy, 51 Knight Terr, in the newsagents and post office building, T9948 1017. **Hospital:** Emergency care (24 hrs) at Silver Chain Nursing Post, 35 Hughes St, T9948 1213. **Police** Corner Durlacher and Hughes Sts, T9948 1201. **Post** Back of newsagent on Knight Terr, T9948 1220.

The northwest

This area vies with the Nullarbor for the title of Australia's driest stretch of coastline, and so it's something of a surprise to find lush banana plantations surrounding the port town of Carnarvon. This is an anomaly, though, as the rest of the region struggles for water. By far the biggest draw is just offshore from the impressive beaches, the Ningaloo Reef. This runs parallel to the coast from south of Coral Bay to north of the North West Cape and although the reef's corals may not be quite as colourful as other major reefs, the fish and other sealife it harbours are second to none. Coral Bay is still only a small holiday resort, struggling to stretch its resources to cope with the thousands of visitors who come to wade off the beach, to snorkel over the reef and swim with giant manta rays. Exmouth, one of the youngest towns in WA, is on the other side of the Cape to the reef, but acts as the base to explore the pristine Cape Range National Park and the long part of the Ningaloo that lies just metres off the shore. Exmouth is also the base for those wanting to experience one of life's true wonders: swimming with whale sharks. ▶▶ *For listings, see pages 278-286.*

Overlander Roadhouse to Carnarvon

→ *Distance: 200 km.*

The vegetation gets a little more sparse and scrubby but there is little else to enliven this featureless drive. One bright spot is the welcoming **Wooramel Roadhouse** (**F**, 75 km from the **Overlander**, T9942 5910), which pumps relatively cheap fuel, as well as breakfasts, snacks and burgers. It has an ATM, donger rooms with shared facilities and a caravan park with powered and unpowered sites. Meals and fuel are available 0700-1800. Just short of Carnarvon, the highway north is interrupted by a T-junction, the focus of a cluster of 24-hour roadhouses, fruit plantations and caravan parks. Turn left for the town centre, 5 km away, right for the Blowholes, Quobba, the Kennedy Range, and destinations further north.

Carnarvon ▶▶ *For listings, see pages 278-286. Colour map 5, C1.*

→ *Population: 6900. 480 km from Geraldton, 370 km from Exmouth, 360 km from Nanutarra Roadhouse.*

Of many ports set up by settlers in the mid-1800s along the west coast, Carnarvon is one of the few survivors and has consolidated its early prosperity by making the most of the water that flows in great volume down the Gascoyne River. Most of the time the mighty riverbed is exposed as a wide ribbon of sand but the Gascoyne flows deep underground all year round and it is tapped by local fruit growers for irrigation. Consequently, Carnarvon appears as something of an oasis among the dry, scrubby plains to the north and south. Vast plantations of banana and mango trees are mingled with colourful bougainvillea, poinciana trees and tall palms. Other than a couple of plantations with tours and tropical cafés, Carnarvon has few tourist pretensions, but does make a useful base for exploring the rugged coastline to the north, including the Blowholes, and the impressive Kennedy Range, 200 km inland. A lot of Australians and backpackers come to Carnarvon for work, as attested by the many caravan parks.

Sights

On the way into town look out for a big orange building, as this is **Gwoonwardu Mia** ① *146 Robinson St, T9941 1989,* the Gascoyne Aboriginal Heritage and Cultural Centre. Worth a visit to look at the art and craft on display and also for the café (see Eating, page 281), which is one of the best around. The town centre sits by the shore of an artificial ocean inlet, the Fascine. Over the inlet are Babbage and Whitlock Islands, cut off from the mainland by the Fascine and a swampy section bridged by a causeway. **Babbage Island** has an unremarkable ocean beach and the remains of the original port facilities, the long town jetty.

One Mile Jetty ① *T9941 3423 and T9941 4309, $4, children free, train runs Apr-Nov daily 0900-1700, and on weekends from Dec-Mar, $7, children $3, train and walk $5.50, children $1.50*, is the main feature of the town's Heritage Precinct on Babbage Island, curiously named after Charles Babbage, the English mathematician and inventor of the first mechanical computer. The jetty was built at the close of the 18th century and began to fall into disrepair in the 1970s but was rescued by the community in the late 1990s. Visitors can walk along the jetty or catch a train from the adjacent kiosk. Also part of the precinct are a rail shed and the genteel **Lighthouse Keeper's Cottage** ① *daily Apr-Nov 1000-1300, gold coin donation*, now furnished as it might have been in the 1920s.

Close to the main T-junction is an OTC dish, part of a **satellite tracking station** set up in 1963 to assist NASA with communications during the orbital Gemini and Apollo moon-landing programmes. Up to 180 people once worked at the station, which was a crucial part of the communications set-up that guided the space vehicles. The station ceased operations in 1987 after helping to track Halley's Comet but the dish is now one of Australia's most unusual lookouts, with steps up to a first-floor 'landing' giving great views across the surrounding plains, plantations and ocean.

For information contact **VIC** ① *corner of (the main) Robinson St and Camel Lane, T9941 1146, www.carnarvon.org.au, Oct-Apr Mon-Fri 0900-1700, Sat-Sun 0900-1200, May-Nov Mon-Fri 0900-1700, Sat 0900-1400, Sun 0900-1200.*

Around Carnarvon

The **plantations** of Carnarvon are the most attractive and unusual aspect of the town. It is well worth driving along South River Road to see the plantations and buy fruit from roadside stalls. **Gascoyne Fresh Company** has a café and offers light meals using local produce. The water that nourishes the fruit trees is also used to encourage a profusion of trees, palms and flowering plants and café tables are placed under the deep shade they provide. On a hot day it feels at least 10°C cooler here and it's worth stopping for respite from the dull highway. On North River Road visitors will

Carnarvon

Sleeping 🛏
Carnarvon 1
Coral Coast Tourist Park 6
Fish & Whistle 3
Gascoyne 4
Gateway Motel 5
Plantation Caravan Park 7
Sea Change Apartments 2
Wintersun Caravan
& Tourist Park 8

Eating 🍴
Fascine Coffee Lounge 3
Harbourside 2
Old Post Office 4

find **Bumbaks**, the only plantation to offers tours (April-October weekdays at 1000). These are excellent and allow the public to learn something of the industry. The small shop sells home-made preserves, fruit ice creams and dried fruit.

The **Blowholes** are a bit of a drive from Carnarvon, some 75 km, but they are good fun and the road is sealed all the way. This is a very rocky, sharp coastline with waves crashing on jagged shelves and reefs even on a calm day. At the Blowholes site water surges under a rock platform and is forced up a narrow channel to eject a roaring jet of water 10 m high in calm weather, double that in rough weather. You can't miss the sign at the junction of the Quobba Road: 'king waves kill'. So stand well back when looking at the blowholes and watch the ocean carefully.

Just one unsealed kilometre south of the Blowholes is **Point Quobba**, where there are a few fishing shacks and a campsite. The rocky sites cost $5.50 (the ranger will collect the fees); there are toilets but no showers or fresh water. There is also a small sandy beach and an excellent **snorkelling** site, between the beach and an island. You'll need to take your own gear but you'll see lots of colourful fish, coral and even turtles if you're lucky.

Heading north from the junction the road becomes unsealed, reaching the **Quobba Station** ① *T9948 5098, www.quobba.com.au*, after 10 km. This is a working sheep station that provides accommodation and a small shop for the hordes of locals and tourists who love to fish along this coastline. There are self-contained chalets with great views of the ocean (**B-C**), self-contained cottages (**C-D**), and campsites for the more budget-conscious (powered and unpowered). Drop in for a map and advice if you're heading further north. The road continues north for about another 100 km along pale rocky cliffs and scrub-covered dunes. This remote, rugged country is a fishermen and surfers' paradise.

After 21 km, past the second bitumen mining road, is a 3-km station track (2WD) to the cliff edge. There are good views south to **Cape Cuvier** and its salt and gypsum loading facility. You might see sharks in the clear water below the cliffs and the last remnants of the *Korean Star*, a bulk carrier ship wrecked during a cyclone in 1988. Another 25 km north is **Red Bluff**. The long wide beach below the bluff offers sheltered swimming and is a fantastic surfing spot. Accommodation here is in the form of luxury safari tents (**L**) with en suite and kitchenette, en suite bungalows with communal kitchen that sleep up to eight (**B**), palm frond humpies (shacks on the sand) and camping. There's even a spa here offering beauty treatments. Note that camping outside the three spots mentioned is not permitted by the station owners. After Red Bluff you pass into **Gnaraloo Station** ① *T9315 4809 and T9942 5927, www.gnaraloo.com.au*, which has a wide range of accommodation in the homestead, shearers' quarters, fishing lodges, cabanas and swags. It also allows limited camping at **Three Mile Camp** ① *T9948 5000*, close to the beach and provides facilities including a laundry and a basic shop. The surf is so good that major surfing competitions have been held here but it's a long drive on a very rough track.

Working in Carnarvon

The fruit-picking season extends for most of the year from April to January, while the fishing season is from April to September. Getting a job as a deckhand is the better paid, but is harder work. Expect to earn upward of $10 an hour. The backpacker hostel can help find work, otherwise do the rounds of the plantations and boats yourself. If driving round the plantations looking for work keep an eye out for signs at the entrance to the drive, if there's no work available the owners will advertise it. If driving up to the house proceed slowly to avoid kicking up dust.

ⓘ *For more information contact the DEC office in Carnarvon, T9941 3754; road conditions, T9943 0988 or T138138. Entry $11 per vehicle, camping fees $7 per person at Temple Gorge.* Just north of the main Carnarvon T-Junction is an unsealed right turn onto Gascoyne Junction Road. This becomes sealed for a fair way, before becoming unsealed again around about the turn-off for Rocky Pool, 38 km from the highway. This permanent waterhole in the Gascoyne River is a popular camping spot in winter and there is a toilet close by. **Gascoyne Junction** is a tiny, dusty community another 130 km on with a hotel and expensive but very handy fuel. Turn left at the crossroads for the Kennedy Range, straight on for Bidgemia Station.

The Kennedy Range forms a dramatic flame-coloured mesa, 75 km long, running north to south. Sheer sandstone walls rise above a skirt of scree slopes, spreading down to the plains below. The range is all that remains of a plateau that elsewhere has been worn away, down to the current level of the Lyons River Valley plain. The range is a long drive from anywhere on an unsealed road, but this park offers the chance to experience the outback, and perhaps a local station stay. Much of the range is inaccessible, but on the eastern side there are three narrow gorges that can be explored and a campsite right at the base of the 100-m cliffs. Each gorge is less than a kilometre apart and there are short walks along the creek beds. The Kennedy Range contains such interesting rocks that you'll wish you had a geologist with you. In fact, the sheer variety of the rock shapes and colours is so captivating that it is hard to remember to lift your head and look at the stunning cliffs above. The cliffs themselves are at their best at dawn when they can take on some seriously impressive yellow, orange and red hues. The campsite has a toilet but no other facilities. Take plenty of water. Roads are fine for 2WD except after heavy rain, when the roads will be closed.

The **southern gorge** has the longest and hardest walk (3 km return), including an optional scramble up the sides of the gorge to the plateau edge above. The unmarked track passes several rock pools and waterfalls before reaching a final high waterfall. Of course 'waterfall' in this region, much like 'river', doesn't necessarily mean there's much water to be found. The **middle gorge**, Temple Gorge, is an easier, more open walk (1.5 km return). Look for marine fossils in ledge caves above the car park of both walks. The **northern gorge** has a stunning series of cliff faces and rock weathered to honeycomb (500 m). Again, you can climb to the top where there is an unexpected landscape of red sand dunes covered in spinifex and scrub, but there is no path. Take great care if you do this as the sandstone is very crumbly and loose.

Carnarvon to Coral Bay

Minilya → *Colour map 5, B1. 140 km from Carnarvon, 225 km from Exmouth.*
On the south side of the course of the eucalypt-flanked Minilya River is a shady picnic area with BBQs and toilets. Customers of the spotless **Minilya Roadhouse** ⓘ *T9942 5922, just over the bridge, 0600-2100, meals until 2030,* enjoy the air-conditioned bathrooms, a rare treat along this long stretch of road. Dedicated to quality, the roadhouse (**C-E**) serves above-average cheap meals and takeaways, has comfortable donger rooms and lawned caravan sites. It also sells the last relatively inexpensive fuel if you're heading north. Soon after Minilya the highway forks. Take the left turn for Coral Bay and Exmouth, continue right for Karratha and Broome.

Swimming with whale sharks

Imagine swimming with a shark the size of a bus, in water 1 km deep. You stand on the back of the boat all suited up in snorkel, fins and wetsuit and the Dive Master shouts 'go, go, go'. Adrenalin surges and suddenly you're looking at a mouth as big as a cave coming straight for you. Shock paralyses for a second as your mind screams to get out of the way!

Swimming with whale sharks may be one of the most memorable and exciting things you do in your lifetime. The whale shark is a plankton feeder that isn't the slightest bit interested in gobbling you into its wide gaping mouth but is alarmingly huge when you are only a few metres away. These rare, gentle beasts can reach 18 m but are more often seen at 4-12 m. Little is known about them except that they travel in a band around the equator and arrive to feed at the Ningaloo Reef after the coral spawning in March and April. The sharks swim just under the surface as sunlight sparkles on their blue-grey bodies and delicate pattern of white spots. When spotted by a boat,

snorkellers jump in and accompany a shark, just like the fleet of remora fish that hang around its mouth and belly. Some sharks seem mildly curious about their new flapping friends but others seem about as bothered as an elephant by a gnat. However, the interaction has only occurred for about 15 years and it is not known what impact swimmers have.

Fishermen had seen a few on the Ningaloo Reef over the years but it wasn't until the late 1980s that marine biologists began to realize just how unusual but regular these sightings were. During the 1990s tours were developed to take visitors out to swim with the whale sharks and it has become big business in Exmouth. DEC has developed strict guidelines for swimming and boating around them and it is hoped that this will keep the whale sharks undisturbed. Of course these are wild creatures and sightings are not guaranteed (although you will generally get a second trip for free if you don't see any). Experiences can vary from hectic five-minute swims to magical 40-minute floats.

Warroora → Colour map 5, B1. 55 km from Minilya, 60 km from Coral Bay.

An unsealed detour off the main road leads to the coastal sheep station of **Warroora** ① T9942 5920, www.warroora.com, known as 'Worra'. One of four neighbouring stations that have allied to help protect this beautiful piece of coastline and the offshore **Ningaloo Reef**, Warroora has about 50 km of beaches, all accessible by 4WD only. In some places the reef is just metres offshore and there are consequently some wonderful snorkelling and diving spots. Camping is allowed all along the coast ($7.50 per person per day) and there are basic but comfortable twin donger rooms near the homestead (**D**) with an ablution block and BBQs. No linen provided. Water is very restricted and there are no supplies available, so bring your own. Call in to the homestead office to pay your fees and get a map.

Coral Bay ▸▸ For listings see pages 278-286. Colour map 5, B1.

→ 240 km from Carnarvon, 150 km from Exmouth.

This pretty shallow bay is just a notch in a long coastline of white sand, dunes and desert but this is the most accessible spot on the northwest coast where the **Ningaloo coral reef** is within 50 m of the shore. The reef is full of colourful fish, clams, sea cucumbers, rays and even the odd turtle, though the coral itself is more notable for its intricate shapes and forms than any vibrancy of colour. All you need to do is grab a snorkel, mask and fins and wade in. There are also a variety of boat trips that take you further out onto the reef to snorkel or dive with manta rays, turtles and whale sharks, or spot humpback whales, dugongs and dolphins; near-Utopia for anyone who loves marine wildlife. The settlement itself is a small, relaxed beach resort where you can walk barefoot from your door to the beach in two minutes. Coral Bay is changing fast though and each year there are more operators, activities and visitors. There's no independent VIC; half a dozen local tour operators have set up booking offices that sell their own, and usually most of their competitors', tours.

For free information on the Coral Bay environment and wildlife, call into the **Coastal Adventure Tours** office and internet café in the Coral Bay Shopping Centre. Facilities in Coral Bay are modest, but you will find a supermarket, newsagents, a few gift shops, including a good jewellery shop selling handmade pieces and a beauty spa. Fuel is available at the **Coral Bay Shopping Village**, near the People's Park Caravan Village.

Exmouth

Exmouth ⇥ *For listings, see pages 278-286. Colour map 5, A1.*

→ *Population: 2500. 615 km from Tom Price (Karijini), 555 km from Karratha.*

Exmouth sits on the eastern side of the North West Cape, facing the calm waters of the Exmouth Gulf and separated by the low hills of Cape Range from the pristine beaches of the **Ningaloo Marine Park**. Despite the marine riches of the cape, the town doesn't have a coastal feel. It's a practical place that was built to service the local military bases and to withstand the seasonal cyclones. A self-sufficient community of American naval staff lived on the Harold E Holt Naval Communications station from 1967 until 1992 when the Australian Navy took over management of the base. Thirteen VLF towers dominate the northern tip of the cape and are taller than the Eiffel Tower. Until recently some buildings at the station were used for tourism ventures but after the 11 September terrorist attacks security has been tightened and the base is effectively closed for the present.

Exmouth's proximity to the **Ningaloo Reef** and its extraordinary wildlife make it a special place for eco-tourism. It is possible to swim with whale sharks, watch turtles laying and hatching, spot migrating humpback whales, snorkel over coral from the beach, and dive on almost untouched sites. There are also red rocky gorges and

Map labels:
To ③ ⑧, Ningaloo Lighthouse, Cape Range National Park & Ningaloo Reef

Fyfe St
Lockwood St
Bennet St
Library ③
Exmouth Dive Centre ⑤
Payne St
Madison Cres
Maidstone Cres
① ⑤
Shopping Centre
Bonefish St
Swimming Pool
Murat Rd
Willersdorf Rd
Diving Ventures ②
Marsh St
Yardie St
Kennedy St
Carpenter St
Davidson St
Christie St
Broad St
Lefroy St
Huston St
②
⑦
ℹ
Reid St
Carter Rd
Craft St
Pellas St
Truscott St
①
Bookshop
Pellew St

To ⑤ ⑥, Town Beach, Exmouth Gulf & Boat Harbour

N
400 metres
400 yards

Sleeping
Exmouth Cape Holiday Park **1**
Ningaloo Club **6**
Ningaloo Caravan & Holiday Resort **7**
Ningaloo Lighthouse Caravan Park **4**
Ningaloo Lodge **2**
Novotel Ningaloo Resort **5**
Potshot Resort **3**
Sea Breeze Resort **8**

Eating
Blue Lips Fish & Chips **3**
Golden Orchid **1**
Grace's Tavern **2**
Ningaloo Health **5**
Whaler's **4**

campsites by perfect beaches in the Cape Range National Park. The only drawback is the intense heat and aridity of the cape – most people visit in winter when temperatures drop to 25-30°C. Exmouth is well set up for travellers, with a good range of accommodation, tours and activities to make the most of what it has to offer. The helpful **VIC** ① *Murat St, T9949 1176, T1800 287328, www.exmouthwa.com.au, Nov-Mar Mon-Fri 0900-1630, Apr-Oct daily 0900-1630,* is on the main through road.

Cape Range National Park ▸▸ *For listings, see pages 278-286. Colour map 5, B1.*

① *Milyering VIC, T9949 2808. $11 per vehicle, camping $7.*

Cape Range National Park is an unforgiving, rocky strip of land on the western side of North West Cape, adjoining the Ningaloo Marine Park. The low red hills of Cape Range form a spine running down the middle of the cape, gashed by gorges that are all dry as a bone except the tranquil Yardie Creek Gorge, at the southern end. The glittering turquoise sea fringing the park just seems to emphasize its aridity and kangaroos have to seek shade under bushes only knee high. However, this is the place to access the wonderful Ningaloo Reef and at places such as Turquoise Bay the reef is only metres from shore so you can snorkel off the beach among a dazzling parade of fish. On the drive from Exmouth, you will pass the **Jurabi Turtle Centre**, just south of Vlamingh lighthouse. This open-air interpretive centre is well worth a look before you enter the park itself. Educational displays present facts about the turtles as well as conservation strategies. Turtle tours and talks are available during the breeding season. Call the Exmouth VIC for more information. The park's **Milyering Visitor Centre** ① *T9949 2808, open 0900-1545,* is 13 km inside the northern park boundary. It houses an interpretative centre and a small shop with a limited range of drinks and snacks, and souvenirs. **Turquoise Bay**, a beautiful white swimming beach, is a further 10 km south. There are a few shade sails and a toilet here but no other facilities. About 15 km from Milyering is **Mandu Mandu Gorge**, where there is a 3-km (return) walk into the dry gorge. Right at the end of the sealed road is **Yardie Creek**, a short gorge with sheer red walls above the creek and a colony of black-footed rock wallabies. Yardie Creek has a picnic area, a one-hour boat cruise along the creek (check with the VIC for

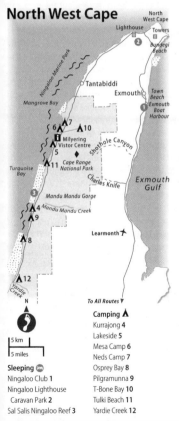

North West Cape

North West Cape

Lighthouse

Towers
②
Bundegi Beach

Ningaloo Marine Park

○ Tantabiddi

Exmouth ○

Town Beach

Exmouth Boat Harbour

Mangrove Bay

▲7
▲6 ▲10
■ Milyering Visitor Centre
▲5
♦ Cape Range National Park
Shothole Canyon
▲11

Turquoise Bay

Charles Knife

Exmouth Gulf

Mandu Mandu Gorge
Mandu Mandu Creek
③
▲4
▲9

Learmonth ✈

▲8

▲12
Yardie Creek

N

To All Routes ▾

5 km
5 miles

Sleeping 🛏
Ningaloo Club **1**
Ningaloo Lighthouse
Caravan Park **2**
Sal Salis Ningaloo Reef **3**

Camping ▲
Kurrajong **4**
Lakeside **5**
Mesa Camp **6**
Neds Camp **7**
Osprey Bay **8**
Pilgramunna **9**
T-Bone Bay **10**
Tulki Beach **11**
Yardie Creek **12**

running times) and a short, rocky track (1.5 km return) along the northern side of the gorge. There are also two gorges that can be accessed from the eastern side of the cape, **Shothole Canyon** and **Charles Knife**. There are great views of the gulf from these rugged gorges but the roads are unsealed and very rough.

Exmouth to Nanutarra Roadhouse ›› *Colour map 5, B2.*

→ *Nanutarra Roadhouse 280 km from Exmouth, 265 km from Karratha, 335 km from Tom Price.*
If heading north there is a sealed short-cut connecting the Exmouth Road with the North West Coastal Highway. Minutes up this road is **Bullara** ① *T9942 5938, www.bullarastation.com.au*, an excellent station that is only 1.5 km off the bitumen and easily accessible to 2WD vehicles. Accommodation is available April-October in a renovated shearer's lodge (**C**). Facilities are shared and include an outdoor shower (with an open roof offering views of the night sky). There is a complimentary breakfast and a well-equipped and comfortable kitchen and lounge area. Camping is available (**F**), with a separate campers kitchen. Visitors can book to go on a station tour, during which they will learn more about the flora and fauna, and the workings of a pastoral station. It is a fascinating insight into life in outback WA; the homemade cake and billy tea overlooking the Gulf is an added bonus. Further along is **Giralia** ① *130 km from Exmouth, T9942 5937, www.giralia.net.au*, which is one of the best station stays in the region (**B-D**). It has air-conditioned en suite B&B rooms located in the main homestead. Rates include a two-course dinner. Close to the main house, completely rebuilt following the devastation of Cyclone Vance in 1999, is a self-contained family cottage that sleeps up to five, budget accommodation in singles and doubles with shared bathrooms and a bush camp (**F**). There are basic kitchen facilities and guests can use the swimming pool. There are several 4WD tracks on the station, some leading to the tidal flats of Exmouth Gulf 30 km north, well known locally for excellent fly fishing.

After the following junction with the main highway the slow greening of the landscape continues and the monotonous flat becomes punctuated with low hill ranges, the first signs of the Pilbara. The change is a sight for sore eyes after the west coast scenery, as is the first appearance of rivers with (some) water in them. Yannarie is the first of these, 45 km from the junction, where bush camping is allowed at the **Barradale Rest Area**. However, it's worth hanging on for the **Nanutarra Roadhouse** ① *T9943 0521*, by the Ashburton River, which always has some decent-sized waterholes. The roadhouse (**D-E**) has a few air-conditioned donger rooms, campsites and a licensed café (meals 0630-2200). Fuel is available until 2400. Note that this roadhouse is known as the most expensive in WA so expect to pay significantly more per litre. It marks one of the north's major junctions, and from here it's 120 km to **Onslow**, 270 km to **Karratha**, and 350 km to **Tom Price**.

⊚ The northwest listings

For Sleeping and Eating price codes and other relevant information, see pages 28-34.

⊜ Sleeping

Carnarvon *p271, map p272*
A-B Sea Change Apartments, 75 Olivia Terr, T0408 785697, www.carnarvonseachange

apartments.com.au. Primarily for the business market, most of the 1- and 2-bed apartments have sea views. Internet access available.
B-C Gateway Motel, 379 Robinson St, T9941 1532. Has 66 motel rooms including 10 family rooms, all with a/c and kitchenette. There is a pool, a bar and an on-site restaurant that serves daily all-you-can-eat dinner buffets.

C-E Fish & Whistle, 35 Robinson St, T9941 1704, www.fishandwhistle.com.au. Basic motel and backpacker accommodation. En suite units with TV and fridge at the back of the property or singles, doubles and 4-bed rooms with shared facilities (no dorms) in the main building. Communal areas are spacious and light. There is off-street parking and the outdoor space is currently being refurbed. Ideal for the solo traveller who wants their own room.

C-D Gascoyne Hotel, 88 Olivia Terr, T9941 1412, www.gascoynehotel.com.au. This pub has 19 en suite hotel and motel units, an inoffensive dining room and shaded rear courtyard. It serves up cheap but good meals daily 1200-1400 and 1800-2030.

D-E Carnarvon Hotel, 28 Olivia Terr, T9941 1181, www.thecarnarvon.com.au. Basic motel rooms with fridge, TV and en suite, as well as backpacker rooms with communal facilities. The pub serves bar meals and there is a restaurant overlooking the water (see Eating).

Caravan parks

B-E Coral Coast Tourist Park, 108 Robinson St, T9941 1438, www.coralcoasttourist park.com.au. The closest of the many caravan parks here. Has a good range of cabins, on-site vans and sites. Facilities include children's playground, swimming pool and bike hire. An extra charge is levied for after hours check-in during peak periods.

B-E Plantation Caravan Park, 589 Robinson St next to the Caltex Petrol Station, T9941 8100 and T1800 261166, www.plantation-caravan-park.wa.big4.com.au. Located a bit outside town next to banana and mango plantations, this Big4 caravan park has grassy sites, en suite cabins, a pool, campers' kitchen with free gas BBQ and internet access. The friendly staff are extremely helpful.

B-E Wintersun Caravan & Tourist Park, 546 Robinson St next to Morels, T9941 8150 and T1300 555585, www.wintersuncaravan park.com.au. A family-run caravan park that has recently been refurbished. Offers en suite chalets, cabins and campsites. Wi-Fi, swimming pool and camp kitchen.

Kennedy Range National Park *p274*
Camping is free at a designated spot in the visitor area. There are also 2 options, which suit most budgets, within 70 km, 1 of these is an outback station stay.

A-D Bidgemia Station, 11 km east of Gascoyne Junction on the banks of the river, T9943 0501, www.bidgemia.com. Has 2 sets of rooms: 5 twins in a spacious Mediterranean-style a/c house within the pleasant homestead gardens, and 5 simple but comfy twins designated as shearers' quarters. Breakfast and dinner available. There is also a campsite by the river. Recommended.

C-F Gascoyne Junction Hotel, T9943 0504. A classic outback tin pub with a friendly bar full of decaying memorabilia, a games room and shady beer garden. All the single and double donga rooms are a/c, and there are also camping sites. Drinks, basic supplies and fuel available 0800-2000.

Coral Bay *p275, maps p276 and p277*
Coral Bay is booked out weeks in advance for school and public holidays. All establishments are on the main street, Robinson St.

LL-A Ningaloo Reef Resort, T9942 5934, www.ningalooreefresort.com.au. The bay's only resort-style hotel, with many rooms having ocean views and direct access to the central pool. There is also an on-site restaurant.

L-D People's Park Caravan Village, T9942 5933, www.peoplesparkcoralbay.com. The more expensive caravan park, as it's nearer to the ocean. Caravan and grassy camping sites, some with views of the bay (the prices are higher). A few en suite, a/c cabins and hilltop villas with views of the reef.

L-E Bayview Coral Bay, T9942 5932, www.coralbaywa.com. A great range of accommodation from self-contained villas with sea views, motel-style rooms, chalets, cabins, on-site vans and a grassy caravan and camping park. All are bright, clean and a/c. The villas and motel rooms have TV and linen is supplied. Facilities include BBQs, campers' kitchen, laundry facilities, swimming pool and an on-site licensed café.

C-E Ningaloo Club, T9385 6655, www.ninga looclub.com. A large hostel arranged around a pool-filled central courtyard with a pleasant communal deck area. The kitchen is small but well equipped. Linen is included, rooms are simple, comfortable and most have a/c. The more expensive doubles are en suite. Internet access, licensed poolside bar (no BYO alcohol) with happy hour, pool tables, ping pong table, TV, BBQ and laundry facilities. Recommended.

Exmouth *p276, maps p276 and p277*
LL-L Novotel Ningaloo Resort, Madaffari Dr, T9949 0001, www.novotelningaloo.com.au. Luxury 68-room resort facing the gulf, with 2-storey apartments and low rise bungalows, all in tasteful shades of sand and wood. There are magnificent views from the pool, around which a large portion of the accommodation is grouped. There's also a restaurant (see Eating), bar, shop, gym and laundry. Note that the resort is a distance from the town centre.
A Sea Breeze Resort, 116 North C St, H E Holt Naval Base, T9949 1800, www.seabreeze resort.com.au. A Best Western with 26 self-contained studios. There is a pool and a fully-equipped outdoor kitchen with BBQ. Airport transfers are available on request. A free shuttle is available for those wishing to dine in town.
A-E Potshot Hotel Resort, Murat Rd, T9949 1200, www.potshotresort.com. The town's largest resort complex, covering a huge area with different accommodation types in brick poolside units. Standard motel rooms, self-contained apartments, as well as modern, well-equipped villas across the road. General facilities include 3 bars and an on-site restaurant, swimming pools, BBQs and laundry. Also runs **Excape Backpackers**, which has modern but characterless a/c en suite dorms, large industrial kitchen, internet access and use of resort facilities.
C Ningaloo Lodge, Lefroy St, T9949 4949 and T1800 880949, www.ningaloolodge.com.au. Comfortable motel with twins and doubles, courtyard pool and communal kitchen, shaded outdoor BBQ area, dining, television and games rooms. Free Wi-Fi.

Caravan parks
The caravan parks here either don't allow check-ins after 1800 during peak periods or will charge extra for it.
A-E Exmouth Cape Holiday Park (Blue Reef Backpackers), corner Truscott Cres and Murat Rd, T9949 1101, www.aspenparks.com.au. A range of a/c, en suite cottages and cabins are available, as are backpacker dorms and double rooms. Also grassed and shady caravan and campsites, a swimming pool, volleyball court and internet access. It also runs the airport/ 'Greyhound' shuttle and the on-site **Whaleshark-n-Dive** centre. Recommended.
A-E Ningaloo Caravan & Holiday Resort, opposite the VIC, T9949 2377 and T1800 652665, www.exmouthresort.com. Set on 23 acres, this caravan park offers a good range of accommodation including self-contained 1- to 3-bedroom chalets and many grassed or paved campsites. **Winstons Backpackers** is based here, offering dorms and doubles. There is also a swimming pool, an on-site restaurant (see Eating), children's playground, gas BBQs and Wi-Fi access.
B-C Ningaloo Lighthouse Caravan Park, 17 km north of town on Yardie Creek Rd, T9949 1478, www.ningaloolighthouse.com. Well-run park with lots of trees and grassy sites and smart self-contained chalets, all with private veranda and BBQ. The 'Lookout' chalets perch high above the park and have wonderful sea views. Also shop, pool, tennis court, laundry facilities, cheap fuel and a popular café open Tue-Sun 1800-2000, which also does takeaways. Well-placed if planning to head in to the national park in the morning.

Cape Range National Park *p277*
LL Sal Salis Ningaloo Reef, T9571 6399, www.salsalis.com.au. The only commercial accommodation within the park itself. It offers luxury en suite safari tents overlooking the ocean and beach. All the power is solar generated and each bathroom has a composting toilet. Herb soaps and eco-shampoos are provided for visitors use. The price includes all meals, drinks and activities

including park fees, guided kayaking, guided gorge walks and snorkelling.

Camping

There are lots of campgrounds within the park, mostly close to the beach and some with bush toilets. There is no fresh water available so bring your own, though drinks are available at Milyering. The VIC and DEC have a comprehensive list that details the qualities of each site. Only **Lakeside**, near Milyering, is close to a good snorkelling site. No bookings are taken so call ahead for availability of spaces during the Apr-Oct peak season, or get to the National Park early and queue.

❷ Eating

Carnarvon p271, map p272

₮₮₮-₮₮ Harbourside, Harbour Rd, at the jetty out of town, T9941 4111. Mon-Fri 1700-2100, Sat-Sun 0900-2100. This is the best place to enjoy delicious fish and seafood in a beautiful setting overlooking the harbour. Fully licensed, indoor and outdoor dining. Takeaway available.

₮₮ Old Post Office, 10 Robinson St, T9941 1800. Tue-Sat 1700-2200, though best to call in advance. This restaurant is a local favourite and serves mostly excellent, mid-range pizza and pasta on the large alfresco deck. Licensed.

₮₮-₮ Yallibiddi Café, Gwoonwardu Mia, see page 271. This café in the Aboriginal Cultural Centre offers excellent coffee and meals ranging from light snacks to restaurant-standard hearty grub. Modern Australian and bush food, such as kangaroo lasagne, slow-roasted goat and tasty salads. The bush tapas plate is a good option for those who can't decide or who want to try some bushtucker.

₮ Fascine Coffee Lounge, Robinson St, near the foreshore. Mon-Fri 0700-1500, Sat 0900-1200, Sun 0730-1200. A small café with outdoor tables offering smoothies, cheap light meals, burgers, fish and chips.

₮ Gascoyne Fresh Company, 340 South River Rd, T9941 9529. Mon-Fri 1000-1600. This plantation café offers good home-made

sandwiches, quiches and cakes. The shop also sells local produce and some crafts.

₮ River Gums Café, Margaret Row, T9941 8281. Wed-Sun 1000-1500 (May-Oct only). Located on the banks of the Gascoyne River in a beautiful setting, this café offers a variety of cakes, muffins, burgers and smoothies. They also sell excellent, home-made tomato relish. Recommended.

₮ Watersedge Restaurant, Carnarvon Hotel, see Sleeping. Fri-Sun 1200-1400, Wed-Mon 1800-2100. Bar meals Wed-Mon 1200-1400, Sat-Thu 1800-2000. The pub has been opened up to the waterfront with glass walls and a beer garden, serving as both bistro and café. The food is simple pub fare, with some more expensive dishes available.

Kennedy Range National Park p274

₮ Gascoyne Junction Hotel, T9943 0504. Serves cheap meals Apr-Oct daily 1200-1400 and 1800- 2000, otherwise the publican will usually see what he can throw together.

Coral Bay p275

All establishments are on the main street, Robinson St.

₮₮₮-₮₮ Fins, Robinson St, T9942 5900. Breakfasts, coffee and snacks all day from 0800, evening dining from 1800. A Greek taverna-style terrace restaurant, shading into expensive, but BYO and easily the best food in town. Daily specials are displayed on the blackboard. Bookings are essential during busy periods.

₮₮-₮ Ningaloo Reef Café is part of Bayview Coral Bay, T9942 5932. Daily 1800-late. This is a colourful, licensed, open space with a simple cheap menu of fish, steak, pasta and pizzas. Also takeaways.

₮₮-₮ Shades Café, T9942 5934. Meals and snacks 0800-2100, happy hour in the main bar Tue and Fri from 1730-1830.

Exmouth p276, map p276

₮₮₮ Mantaray's, at Novotel Ningaloo Resort, see Sleeping, T9949 0003. Daily for breakfast 0800-1000, lunch 1130- 1430 and dinner 1800-2100. Serves an excellent, inventive international cuisine with a slight emphasis on seafood. Also offers cheap lunch, a selection of desserts and coffee. Licensed.

♥♥♥-♥♥ Whaler's, 5 Kennedy St, T9949 2416. The town's main restaurant, with plenty of tables on a covered terrace. Open 0830-1400 for a good range of breakfasts and light lunches, and 1830-late for mostly Italian-influenced meals and fresh seafood. Licensed. Bookings recommended as it gets very busy.

♥♥♥-♥ Pinocchio Restaurant, Murat Rd, Ningaloo Caravan and Holiday Resort, see Sleeping, T9949 4905. Daily 1800-2100. Good pizzas and has some pasta dishes, as well as more substantial Italian meals. Also takeaways.

♥♥-♥ Grace's Tavern, Murat Rd, look for the Thirsty Camel bottle shop and it's next door, T9949 1000. Serves counter and à la carte meals 1200-1400 and 1800-2100. Dishes include Moroccan and Asian fare, prepared by separate chefs.

♥ Blue Lips Fish & Chips, Pelias St, T9949 1130. Daily 1130-1400 and 1700-2030. Try this one for a good serving of fish'n'chips, burgers or casual light meals.

♥ Golden Orchid, main shopping area, T9949 1740. Mon-Fri 1130-1400, and daily 1700-2200, closed mid-Dec to mid-Feb. Chinese restaurant offering cheap lunch specials. BYO alcohol.

Cafés

Ningaloo Health, 3A Kennedy St, T9949 1400, www.ningaloohealth.com.au. Daily 0800-1630. Offers a wide range of gourmet breakfasts, light Thai meals, wraps, salads, wonderful picnic hampers, desserts and home-made cakes. It also does smoothies, lassies and organic coffees.

O Shopping

Carnarvon *p271, map p272*
Gascoyne Growers Market, Carnarvon Civic Centre. May-Oct every Sat 0800-1130. Local food producers sell their wares here. Great for self-caters or just interesting to wander

around and pick up some snacks such as Carnarvon bananas.

Morels, 486 Robinson St, T9941 8368. Daily May-Oct. No trip to Carnarvon is complete without dropping in to Morels for some excellent fresh, seasonal fruit and veg. As well as the staples there are treats on offer, including chocolate covered frozen strawberries.

▲ Activities and tours

Carnarvon *p271, map p272*
4WD
Stockman Safaris, T0400 083900, www.stockmansafaris.com.au. Offers a Carnarvon Town Tour on Mon, Tue, Thu and Fri, as well as a tour of Lake Macleod Salt Mine on Wed. There is an excellent 4WD outback tour that includes a visit to an authentic station homestead and the Kennedy Ranges. Trips cost in the region of $50-130.

Kite surfing
Kitemix, T0400 648706, www.kitemix.com. Offers kite surfing lessons for the beginner or the more advanced student. $70 per hr for 1 person or $50 per hr for 2.

Coral Bay *p275*
There is a profusion of booking offices around town, and most will sell the majority of the tours available, making shopping around a confusing business. It's worth looking in at each place to get an idea of what's on offer.

The caravan on the beach hires out snorkelling gear for $7.50 for a half-day and $15 for a full-day. There are also see-through boogie boards, glass bottom canoes, wet suits and sun shades available.

4WD
Tracks up and down the coast from Coral Bay are 4WD only and tours are available.
Coral Coast Tours, T0427 180568, www.coralcoasttours.com. Runs a full-day 4WD tour around the cape for $185, children

$124, departing at 0800. It also offers 4-day 4WD tours of Karijini for $645.

Boat trips

Coral Bay Adventures, T9942 5955, www.coralbayadventures.com. Very experienced. Glass-bottomed boats. The 2-hr trip at 1200 visits 2 snorkelling spots. A slightly cheaper, option is the 1-hr coral viewing cruise departing at 1000, 1100 and 1400.
Coral Breeze, T9948 5190. A fairly small catamaran that heads out for 4-hr wildlife spotting and snorkelling trips and 2-hr BYO sunset cruises. This is one of the most peaceful and rewarding ways of seeing the bay, and the cruises are excellent value.

Diving

Ningaloo Reef Dive Centre, Coral Bay Shopping Centre, T9942 5824. Open 0730-1730. Daily reef dives (half day $160), snorkelling and diving with manta rays (full day $145-205), dive safaris (full day, 2 dives, $205) and PADI tuition (Open Water courses start every Sat, $550 and can arrange medicals in Exmouth). Also offers whale shark encounters (full day $365). Full gear hire $100 a day, snorkel gear $12 a day.

Fishing

Fish feeding occurs at the main beach every day at 1530.
Coral Bay Ocean Game Fishing Charters, T9942 5874, www.mahimahicoralbay.com.au. Offers full-day ($240, share line $290) game fishing trips. Gear, bait and drinks but no lunch provided. Private charters are also available for groups of up to 10.
Sea Force Coral Bay, T9942 5817, www.seaforcecharters.net.au. Offers a similar full-day trip as above, at same price but leaving at 0710. Half-day trips are $220, shared line $285. BYO lunch.

Kayaking

Ningaloo Kayak Adventures, caravan on the beach, T9948 5034, www.ningalookayak adventures.com. Offers a 2-hr 'taster' kayaking trip at 0900, 1100 and 1300 ($40) or a 3-hr snorkelling and kayaking adventure at 0900 and 1300 ($60). Overnight tours are available and they hire out equipment from here.

Quad bikes

Quad-Treks, T9948 5190. The more experienced of 2 companies operating these 4-wheel motorbikes out along the dunes and beaches. These are fantastic fun and you find yourself spending much of each trip working out how you can afford one when you get home. Options include 3-hr snorkelling trips to some favoured turtle spots ($105), and 2-hr turtle or sunset trips, which include more challenging terrain and the thrill of a return run in the dark for $90.

Snorkelling

Unless you specifically want to see turtles, sharks or rays, then it is hard to beat simply snorkelling straight off the main beach (head out beyond the 5 knot sign just south of the main beach then drift back towards the moorings). If you want to be fairly sure of seeing turtles then head out on the appropriate boat or quad-bike trip. Most boat operators offer a half-day snorkel, including **Coral Coast Tours** (see 4WD) for $90. **Coral Bay Adventures** (see Boat trips) runs 2-hr snorkel trips to 2 good snorkelling spot, daily 1200-1400 ($45). Another option is a 2½-hr snorkel trip with **Eco Tours**, T9942 5885, that departs at 0900 and 1300. Sep-Jan is the breeding season for the local reef sharks, and baby ones can be seen by their dozens during this time in Skeleton Bay, just to the north of the main beach.

Ningaloo Reef Dive Centre and Ningaloo Experience hire out snorkelling gear. Both charge $12 a day ($50 deposit).

Wildlife trips

Manta rays A couple of boats offer snorkelling trips out to swim with these massive but gentle rays. **Coral Bay Adventures** (see Boat trips, above), runs very experienced and good half-day tours for $165. A spotter plane increases the chances of success or you get a 2-hr snorkel trip ($45) on the next day for free. Tours depart at 0900.

Whale sharks Although Exmouth is hailed as the world's whale shark 'capital', a couple of Coral Bay boats do offer snorkelling trips to try and find them in season (Apr-Jun). They include **Coral Bay Adventures** (full day $390).

Whale watching Most of the larger boat operators and **Ningaloo Reef Dive Centre** offer tours to see humpbacks Jun-Nov.

Exmouth *p276, map p276*
4WD
WestTreks Safaris, T9949 2659, www.westtreksafaritours.com.au. Neil and Rhonda McGregor run knowledgeable and enthusiastic 4WD tours into Cape Range National Park, including Shothole Canyon, Charles Knife Rd, 4WD over the top of the range to Yardie Creek and a snorkel at Turquoise Bay. Lunch and tea breaks included (full day, $199, child $150). Recommended.

Bus tours
Exmouth Bus Charters, T9949 4623. Runs trips to Turquoise Bay (minimum 6 people) for $55 per person including park entry and snorkel gear.

Diving
Diving on the Ningaloo can be exceptional, with hundreds of species of fish and coral. There are a number of operators in town, each with their own specialities. Some are run by or associated with accommodation.
Exmouth Diving Centre, Potshot Hotel, T9949 1201, www.exmouthdiving.com.au. Has one of the widest ranges of single-day options starting from about $165. It also runs 5-day Open Water courses ($550) and trips to the Muiron Islands.
Ningaloo Reef Dreaming, T9949 4777, www.ningaloodreaming.com. The only operator currently licensed to dive off the disused navy pier, home to around 200 fish species (single, double and night dives). Offers various scuba-diving courses (Open

Water $600, Advanced $545, Rescue Diver $410, Dive Master $1320). It also runs glass-bottom boat tours, whale shark cruises (late Mar-Jul) with their own spotter plane increasing chances of finding them, and an overnight safari to the Muiron Islands ($495, including all meals).
Ningaloo Whaleshark-n-Dive, T9949 1116, www.ningaloowhalesharkndive.com.au. Offers PADI dive courses from Open Water to Dive Master and organizes trips to the Muiron Islands and Lighthouse Bay. Also runs snorkelling trips and whale shark cruises.

Fishing
Several boats run game-fishing trips, though choice is reduced during whale shark season.
Blue Horizon, T9949 1620, www.makaira. com.au. (Game) fishing trips on *Makaira II*, also diving and island cruises.
Ningaloo Blue Dive, T9949 4129, www.ningalooblue.com.au. Offers bottom and game fishing trips, lunch provided. Also organizes whale shark tours.
Ningaloo Pearls, T0417 944 820, www.ningaloopearls.com.au. Offers half-day ($140) and full-day ($180) deep-sea fishing tours. BYO drinks, gear, bait and light refreshments provided. Also offers whale-watching in season.

Kayaking
Capricorn Seakayaking, T6267 8059, www.capricornseakayaking.com.au. Runs sea kayaking and snorkelling tours Apr-Oct. There's a 3-hr kayaking tour ($79) or a full-day kayaking and snorkelling option ($159). Pick-ups are available from Exmouth accommodation; longer trips available on request.

Mini golf
There is an 18-hole mini golf course opposite **Grace's Tavern**. Open daily 0900-late.

Snorkelling
As always in WA, remember that conditions on the beach are best in the morning before

the wind arrives, particularly for snorkelling when you want a calm, flat sea.

If you have your own transport you can snorkel from many beaches in the Cape Range National Park where you can expect to see a great variety of fish and coral, although the coral is not very brightly coloured, and perhaps turtles, rays and reef sharks (harmless!). The best site is **Turquoise Bay** but take care as there is a very strong current and a break in the reef. From the beach walk south around the corner and another 100 m down the beach before entering the water. The current will drift you north and you should get out at the sandspit on the corner to avoid the channel leading to the gap in the reef. Check conditions at the park entry booth or Milyering before snorkelling here – high tide is the worst time.

Ningaloo Coral Explorer II, T9949 4499, www.bundegi.com.au. 2-hr coral viewing and snorkel tours for $60, children $27, departing at 1300.

Ningaloo Ecology Cruises, T9949 2255, www.ecology.com.au. Runs trips from the Tantabiddi boat ramp. The glass-bottom boat heads out a few hundred metres to the reef and is a good way to see fish, coral and turtles if you don't snorkel. A 2½-hr tour includes 1-hr snorkelling option in the outer reef.

Ocean Eco Adventures, T0427 425925, www.oceanecoadventures.com.au. Snorkel wildlife discovery tours (Apr-Aug), as well as liveaboard options. Also runs whale shark trips, and sunset and whale-watching cruises.

Swimming
The very average town beach is 2 km south of the town centre.

Paltridge Memorial Swimming Pool, Payne St, T9949 1042. Open Sep-May. Aside from the beaches, this outdoor pool is a good spot to cool off on a hot day.

Wildlife trips
Turtle watching Turtles come ashore in the Cape Range National Park to breed and lay eggs and it is possible to have the extraordinary and rare experience of watching them do so. Nesting turtles lumber onto the northern end of the cape (Hunters, Mauritius, Jacobsz and Jansz beaches) during Nov-Feb, at night just before high tide and for 2 hrs afterwards. Hatchlings emerge from Jan-Apr 1700-2000 and scamper to the water's edge. Turtles must not be disturbed by noise, light or touching – it is very important to follow the DEC code of conduct for turtle watching (pick a copy up at their office in town) or the turtles may stop nesting here. Visit the **Jurabi Turtle Centre**, T9949 1176, just south of Vlaming lighthouse, an innovative open-air structure that educates visitors about turtles and how to observe them. Night tours are run from the centre during Dec-Feb, contact the Exmouth Visitor Centre for details. For more turtle info see www.ningalooturtles.org.au.

Whale sharks For many people the sole reason to venture up to Exmouth. A successful swim with a whale shark is simply one of the most awesome experiences Australia has to offer. They come in to feed off the reef from Apr to Jul, though at the fringes of the season they are generally fewer and smaller. Come May-Jun for the best chance of seeing a real biggie (12-m sharks are not uncommon). Half a dozen boats offer day trips to snorkel with them for around $350-400, and most offer a free follow-up trip if they fail to find one first time around. **Exmouth Diving Centre**, T9949 1201, is one of the best operators. Like most operators they use a spotter plane to increase chances of finding the whale sharks and includes the longest diving and snorkelling time. You will need to be comfortable with a snorkel, and be a reasonably strong swimmer if you catch a shark going faster than its 'amble' pace. **Ningaloo Whaleshark-n-Dive**, T9949 1116, www.ningaloowhalesharkndive.com.au. Another excellent operator, with knowledgeable and friendly staff. Welcomes novices as well as experienced snorkellers, and ensure everyone gets the best out of their day with the whale shark.

Whale watching Humpback whales migrate along Ningaloo Reef Jul-Oct, and most of the dive and boat operators run whale-watching trips.

☉ Transport

Carnarvon *p271, map p272*
Air There are regular **Skywest** services to **Perth**. The airport is a 10-min walk from town or a cheap taxi ride.

Bicycle hire Bikes are available from the VIC from $20 but there's a hefty deposit.

Bus Greyhound northbound services leave the civic centre Mon, Wed and Fri at 2035 (**Coral Bay** and **Broome**). **Perth** buses depart Wed, Fri and Sun at 0340.

Car Car hire at the airport: **Avis**, T9941 1357, and **Budget**, T9941 2155.
Servicing from **Carnarvon Mechanical Service**, 92 Boundary Rd, T9941 1624 and the **Tyrepower Auto Centre**, 58 Robinson St, T9941 1604.

Taxi Call T131008.

Coral Bay *p275*
Air A shuttle bus operates between Coral Bay and Exmouth's **Learmonth Airport**, T9942 5955, ($80 per person, minimum 2 people) if booked in advance. However, it's about $20 cheaper to catch the coach to Exmouth then the scheduled buses back down.

Bus Greyhound northbound services leave the Ningaloo Club for **Broome** on Mon, Thu and Sat at 2325. **Carnarvon** and **Perth** buses depart on Wed, Fri and Sun 2435.

Exmouth *p276, map p276*
Air 35 km south of Exmouth, a shuttle, T9949 1101, meets each of the daily Skywest flights on request. **Allen's**, **Budget** and **Avis** hire cars. Skywest has daily flights to **Perth**.

Bus If heading to **Broome** with Greyhound you will need to catch the Greyhound GX602 service from Exmouth VIC at 2230 (Tue, Thu and Sun), which will drop you at the Giralia turn-off for your connection. If coming the other way, catch the GX601 but ring Greyhound in advance to let them know you need picking up from Giralia. This service will stop at both the airport and Exmouth VIC.

Car Car hire from both **Allen's**, 24 Nimitz St, T9949 2403, and also from **Ningaloo Dreaming**.
Car servicing from **Exmouth Automotive & Boating**, Griffiths Way, T9949 2795.

Taxi Call T0409 994933.

❶ Directory

Carnarvon *p271, map p272*
Banks Major banks and ATMs on Robinson St. **Internet** at the Library, Stuart St, T9941 1708. **Medical services** Chemists: Amcal, Boulevard Centre, T9941 1547. Mon-Fri 0830-1800, Sat 0830-1300, Sun 0900-1300. Hospital: Carnarvon Regional, Cleaver St, T9941 0555. **Police** 11 Robinson St, T9941 1444. **Post** 14 Camel Lane, T9941 1122.

Exmouth *p276, map p276*
Banks 1 bank branch, plus ATMs in the Caltex and the VIC. **Internet** Available at a number of places in town, including the Library, Maidstone Cres. Mon-Thu and Sat 0900-1200, Mon, Tue and Thu 1300-1600, Wed 1500-1800. **Medical services** Chemists: Exmouth Pharmacy, main shopping area, T9949 1140. Mon-Fri 0900-1730, Sat 0900-1300. Hospital: Lyon St, T9949 3666. **Police** Riggs St, T9949 2444. **Post** Maidstone Cres, T9949 1265. **Useful contacts** DEC, T9947 8000. Brochures and park advice. Cyclone Warning Movements, T1300 659210. Road Condition Report, T1800 013314.

Contents

The Pilbara

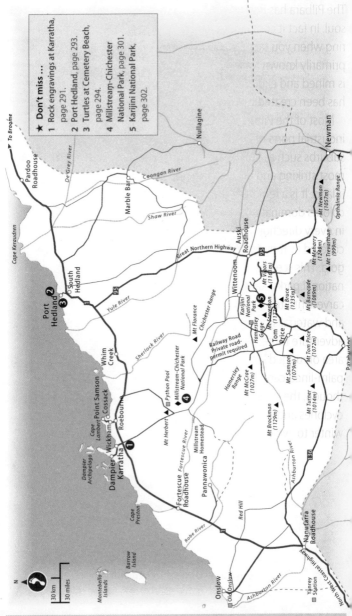

★ Don't miss ...

1 Rock engravings at Karratha, page 291.
2 Port Hedland, page 293.
3 Turtles at Cemetery Beach, page 294.
4 Millstream-Chichester National Park, page 301.
5 Karijini National Park, page 302.

The Pilbara has iron in its ancient dark-red stone and its very soul. In fact it contains so much iron that some rocks give a dull ring when you tap them, and it is this mineral that the region is primarily known for. More than half of Australia's mineral wealth is mined and exported from the region and almost every town has been created by mining companies in the last few decades.

Most of the Pilbara's population lives on the coast in the industrial ports of Dampier and Port Hedland or residential suburbs such as Karratha, Wickham and South Hedland, but the most striking and distinctive landscapes of the Pilbara are found inland. It is a region of stark beauty and grandeur where just two colours dominate – red and gold. Stony, rounded ranges extend in every direction, sitting like pincushions across the landscape, covered as they are in spinifex grass and bleached to a mellow gold. This scenery is seen at its best in one of Australia's finest national parks, Karijini. Here, deep, narrow gorges have been carved into the Hamersley Range to create an oasis of rock pools and waterfalls, some reached only by fantastic nerve-jangling adventure routes. Millstream-Chichester National Park is another area of rugged landscape relieved by water and has idyllic, palm-lined campsites by spring-fed pools. It's not all roses though; the locals also have to take the Pilbara's isolation, cyclones and unrelenting heat in their stride. Try to visit in winter to avoid the latter two.

Pilbara coast

The tidal flats and mangrove swamps of this section of the West Australian coast wouldn't win any beauty contests, but the coastal towns of the Pilbara are impressive in their own way. Some 60% of Australia's mineral wealth is exported from these towns and the scale of operations required is staggering. Much can be seen from viewing platforms or on mine site tours. The services provided for workers are excellent and useful for travellers, so these towns are convenient places to rest and replenish supplies. However, the main focus lies on the local industries and their workers. Accommodation can be expensive and activities are limited. The offshore island groups, the Mackerel and Montebello islands, and the Dampier Archipelago, offer excellent fishing, diving and snorkelling in clear turquoise water. They're not easy to get to, but a trip out can be quite an experience for those who make the effort. ►► For listings, see pages 296-300.

Onslow and around ►► *For listings, see pages 296-300. Colour map 5, A2.*

One of Western Australia's most isolated coastal towns, tiny Onslow is a favoured spot for recreational fishing and gets very busy in winter. Other visitors are attracted by the opportunity to live for a while on a true desert island as there are a few off the coast on which the enterprising locals have built accommodation.

Onslow and Old Onslow → *140 km from Nanutarra Roadhouse, 310 km from Karratha.*
The town's few attractions include a folksy museum (part of the VIC), the 'sunset' beach, 2 km north, which is also the site of a salt-loading jetty and surprisingly attractive at night, and the abandoned remains of **Old Onslow**, a 50-km 4WD excursion off the main road. Old Onslow was a pearling port dating from 1863, but the town site was moved in 1925 and many buildings relocated. Only the crumbling courthouse and gaol buildings survive at the original site. Services include a post office, supermarket (closed Sunday afternoon) and fuel. The **VIC** ① *Second Av, T9184 6644, Mon-Sat 0900-1200 and 1300-1600, Sun 1000-1400, museum gold coin donation,* is helpful.

Mackerel and Montebello islands → *Colour map 5, A2.*
These island groups are more or less due north of Onslow at a distance of 20 km and 110 km respectively. Both are surrounded by rich and pristine coral reefs, providing spectacular opportunities for fishing, snorkelling and diving. Whales, dolphins, dugongs and turtles are often seen in these remote waters. The Montebellos were used by the British government for nuclear weapon tests in 1952 and 1956. Some low-level radiation exists but the islands are considered perfectly safe. There are currently three options for staying on or near the islands – including one where you get a whole island to yourself.

Fortescue Roadhouse → *Colour map 5, A2.*
Alongside the wide Fortescue River the **Fortescue Roadhouse and Tavern** ① *T9184 5126,* is the only stop on a long and lonely stretch of highway. It has cheap dongas and campsites, and serves fuel and snacks from 0630-2030. The bar is open until midnight. Fuel is considerably cheaper than at Nanutarra (160 km away), and usually on a par with Karratha (110 km).

→ *Populations: Karratha 12,756, Dampier 2000. Karratha 635 km from Carnarvon, 245 km from Port Hedland.*
The industrial towns of Karratha and Dampier, 20 km apart, were created in the late 1960s to service the mining of Pilbara iron ore, salt and natural gas and oil. Dampier was established first by the mining company Pilbara Iron and, although it remains a major industrial port, its residential space was quickly outgrown. Karratha was therefore chosen as a better place for a regional capital. Karratha is now a thriving mining and administrative centre between the tidal flats of Nickol Bay and the low dark red Karratha Hills. There is little to interest visitors in Karratha itself, except the large air-conditioned shopping mall, **Karratha City**, which has the interesting **Pilbara Fine Art Gallery**. Karratha is a useful base, however, for trips to the Millstream-Chichester and Karijini national parks, and the islands of the Dampier Archipelago just offshore. There are also ancient aboriginal rock carvings to see in the Karratha Hills and on the Burrup Peninsula, where you can also take in the mind-boggling scale of Dampier's port facilities and natural gas plant.

Sights

The Aboriginal Jaburara people, who were custodians of the land from the Burrup Peninsula to an area west of Wickham at the time of European settlement, produced thousands of **rock engravings** in the area, thought to be about 6000 years old and now the only remaining trace of the people and their culture. The **Jaburara** ('Yabura')

Karratha

Sleeping 🛏
All Seasons **6**
Karratha Apartments **3**
Karratha Backpackers **1**
Karratha Caravan Park **4**
Karratha International **2**
Pilbarra Big 4 Holiday Park **5**

200 metres
200 yards

Heritage Trail has been developed in the hills behind the VIC and this is a very accessible place to see some of the engravings. The walk is 3.5 km one way and very hot and exposed so try to do it before 0800 or after 1600. From the car park by the water tanks, you can find engravings within 500 m but the best are halfway along at the **Rotary Lookout**. If you can't arrange a pick-up at the far end of the trail, you won't miss much by just reaching this lookout and then retracing your steps to the VIC. The engravings are very faint and not signposted so you will have to look carefully for figures such as fish and kangaroos on large rock faces.

The other main sights in these towns are not exactly traditional. There's a lookout and interesting visitor centre at the **North West Shelf Gas Venture** ① *T9158 8292, Apr-Sep Mon-Fri 0900-1600; Oct-Mar Mon-Fri 0900-1300*, with lots of information and cool models. The project is the biggest of its kind in the country and it is worth the drive out to see it if you're in the vicinity. It's halfway up the **Burrup Peninsula** (signposted 'North West Shelf Venture'), a range of red shattered hills extending out into the Indian Ocean, and marks the end of the sealed road. There are some great beaches further up but this is 4WD territory only. Over 10,000 rock engravings still exist on the Burrup Peninsula, but few are easily found. The best collection is in the evocative **Deep Gorge**, reached via a short, rough unsealed track off the road to **Hearson's Cove**, a fairly average beach and not good at low tide. The right turn to the gorge is just before where the sealed road ends.

There are 42 rocky islands in the **Dampier Archipelago**, about 20 km west of Karratha, and a wonderfully rich marine life. Turtles nest on the beaches and whales, dolphins and dugongs inhabit island waters. Fringing coral reefs provide great diving and much of it has hardly been explored. DEC has estimated that there are 600 species of fish in the archipelago and naturally this is a popular local fishing ground. There are current plans to create a marine conservation reserve for the area from the Dampier Archipelago to Cape Preston but the state government is yet to make a decision on the proposal. A shipping channel has been included in the proposal but it is thought that locals may oppose any limits on fishing in the archipelago. For fishing and diving charters out to the islands, see Activities and tours, page 299.

The **VIC** ① *Karratha Rd, T9144 4600, www.pilbaracoast.com, Apr-Oct Mon-Fri 0830-1700, Sat-Sun 0900-1500, Nov-Apr Mon-Fri 0900-1600, Sat 0900-1300*, is found just by the main junction into town. If coming from the west take the second left-hand turn off the main highway signposted Karratha.

Roebourne and around » *For listings, see pages 296-300.*

European settlement of the Pilbara was first established in this area and the sleepy remnants of the 19th century can still be found in Cossack and Roebourne. Cossack is not even a town anymore; just a charming group of old buildings maintained by caretakers that make an unusual and peaceful overnight or lunch stop. Many of Roebourne's grand buildings are still used for their original purpose, such as the police station, Holy Trinity Church and the post office, but aside from these the town lacks any attraction. The largest town is Wickham, in the centre of the peninsula, built to house iron-ore workers for the nearby loading facility. At the end of the peninsula is the laid-back seaside village of Point Samson where life revolves around fish, fishing and fish and chips.

Roebourne → *Colour map 5, A3. Population: 1400. 40 km from Karratha, 205 km from Port Hedland.*
The original regional capital when the first pastoral leases were granted in the 1860s, Roebourne has declined to a small scruffy junction town straddling the main highway. Some impressive colonial buildings survive, notably the gaol, which is now a **museum** and the area's **VIC** ① *Queens St, T9182 1060, www.pilbaracoast.com, May-Oct daily 0900-1600, Sat-Sun 0900-1500, Nov-Apr Mon-Fri 0900-1500, museum entry by gold coin donation.* The gaol is notable for an unusual hexagonal design, the work of innovative government architect George Temple Poole, who also designed the bond store in Cossack and other interesting buildings in York, Albany and Perth. The gaol holds a small collection of historical photos and prison memorabilia and sells local arts and crafts.

Cossack → *Colour map 5, A3. 12 km from Roebourne.*
Once a thriving port servicing Roebourne and the surrounding pastoral stations, Cossack declined dramatically in the early 1900s and now only a handful of colonial government buildings remain. These are all magnificently solid buildings of the 1890s, made from the

local bluestone, which have survived years of cyclones to give Cossack an air of faded dignity. The settlement is part-way along a rocky promontory that protrudes east through sand-flats and mangrove swamps, and it's well worth driving or walking the 2 km out to the lookout at the far end. Since the 1980s the remaining buildings have been gradually restored and have now been put to use. The old courthouse is now a **museum** ① *0900-1600, gold coin donation,* with an interesting collection of local memorabilia and photographs. Other buildings are now an aboriginal **art workshop** and a **gallery**. The police quarters have been converted into the peaceful **Cossack Backpackers**, run by the Shire. For more information or enquiries contact the caretaker on T9182 1190. This is a great place to relax as there's little to do but wander the museum, watch the tides change from the jetty, or go swimming and fishing.

Wickham → *Colour map 5, A3. Population: 1600. 12 km from Roebourne, 5 km from Cossack.*

A service town for the local iron-ore loading facility, Wickham has nothing to offer visitors except a good supermarket, an ATM and the **Red Rock Café**. A private company road leads out to Cape Lambert where Robe has built one of the largest piers in Australia, visible from Point Samson. **Robe** ① *T9182 1060, departs the Robe VIC May-Oct on Mon, Wed and Fri at 0930 (2 hrs), $10,* runs tours around the peninsula (including Cossack) and out to their modern port facilities.

Point Samson → *Colour map 5, A3. Population: 400. 20 km from Roebourne.*

This small community on the eastern edge of the peninsula is a commercial fishing port and mellow seaside home for those working in other parts of the region. It attracts many recreational fishermen and is well known for great fish and chips at **Moby's Kitchen**. The sandy beaches of **Honeymoon Cove**, **Back Beach** and **Main Beach** are good for swimming but Point Samson has a tidal range of about 5 m and you can only swim at high tide. At low tide you can snorkel at Honeymoon Cove on coral reef 20 m from shore or explore the rock pools at the other beaches. There are no hire facilities so bring your own snorkel gear and make sure you wear shoes on the rocks as stone fish and other nasties are found on the Pilbara coast. If you want to head out into deeper water, charters are available.

Roebourne to Port Hedland

The only stop on this route is the **Whim Creek Hotel** (**C-F**, T9176 4914), a great old two-storey pub of corrugated iron, with loads of atmosphere. It dates back to the 1870s when **Whim Creek** was a copper mining town, but nothing else but ruins survive from that time. The pub boasts a warm welcome, excellent food, a shady beer garden and even has orphaned kangaroos wandering about. Meals of burgers, steak and fish are served from Tuesday-Saturday at 0730-1430 and 1800-2000, Sunday 0730-1500; they include the 'Barra Burger', a towering mouthful of barramundi and bun. Hotel rooms have air-conditioning, TV and fridge and there are also cheap backpacker rooms (without air-conditioning, so only bearable May-September). Beyond the hotel the scenery becomes very dull.

Port Hedland ‣ *For listings, see pages 296-300. Colour map 5, A3.*

→ *Population: 15,000. 265 km from Auski Village (Karijini), 610 km from Broome.*
Named after its discoverer in 1863, Port Hedland was soon pressed into service as a port servicing the local pastoral and small-scale mining industries, while also developing its own pearling fleet. It remained a relatively small town until 1965 when it was earmarked

as a major terminal for the export of the considerable tonnage of ores that was starting to flood out of the Pilbara. Today several 300-m-long ore carriers visit the port every day, and watching them creep in and out of the harbour is a favourite pastime for locals and visitors alike (a noticeboard outside the VIC advises their movements and size). Port Hedland is dominated by huge stockpiles of ore, heavy industry and loading facilities. Some of these can actually prove quite fascinating sights, however, and Port Hedland also makes a very good base for taking a tour into the Karijini National Park (see page 302), 250 km to the south. There is certainly enough to fill a day or two while waiting for, or recovering from, a bush trip. Port Hedland is mainly a service town for the local industry and tourism takes a back seat to the riches that flow from mining. Its sister town, **South Hedland**, 20 km inland, was established as a dormitory town for the burgeoning industry and is now several times bigger than Port Hedland itself.

Sights

Dalgety House ① *Anderson St, Apr-Oct Mon-Fri 1000-1400, Sat-Sun 1100-1300, gold coin donation*, is the restored former manager's residence of Dalgety & Co, the company that for generations handled much of the importation of the area's supplies and the export of commodities such as wool. It is now a museum cleverly portraying the town's history prior to the advent of large-scale mining. The **Courthouse Gallery** ① *16 Edgar St, T9173 1064, Mon-Fri 0900-1630*, exhibits usually good-quality local art and craft.

Cemetery Beach, opposite the All Seasons, is the scene of flatback turtle nesting and hatching from November-February, a must-see if you're in the vicinity. Activity coincides with high tide, contact the VIC for guidance on seeing the turtles. The green turtles can be found throughout the whole year if you're lucky. Adjacent to the Shell station on Wilson Street, **Don Rhodes Open-air Mining Museum**, is a simple collection of vehicles, including giant diesel train engines, used in various local mining operations over the last few decades. It's worth stopping by on the way past. Both the **Royal Flying Doctor Service** ① *T9172 0700, Mon-Fri 0900-1400*, and **School of the Air** are based at the airport. Visitors are welcome – call ahead or contact VIC to find out the best visiting times for the school. The best time for the Flying Doctors is 0900-1030.

Port Hedland

Sleeping 🛏	Eating 🍴
All Seasons **1**	Kath's Kitchen **1**
Bruno's Ocean Lodge **2**	Bernie's Place **2**
Esplanade **3**	

300 metres
300 yards

The **VIC** ⓘ *Wedge St, T9173 1711, May-Oct Mon-Fri 0830-1630, Sat 1000-1400, Sun 1000-1200, Nov-Apr Mon-Fri 0900-1600, Sat 1000-1400,* has limited though helpful and well-organized information.

Port Hedland to Broome ⟩⟩ *For listings, see pages 296-300.*

This is one of the most tedious stretches of road in WA, particularly the last 300 km or so. There are sections where the vegetation struggles to get above knee-high, and the endless flat vista can be quite mesmerizing. Take plenty of water, even if you don't plan on any stops, and allow a full day.

The first roadhouse, **Pardoo** ⓘ *150 km from Port Hedand, T9176 4916, www.pardoo.com. au,* **(C-F)**, has air-conditioned singles and doubles in the usual dongas, is open for fuel 0600-2200, has a bar, a small range of supplies and serves meals until 2000. Drinkable (bore) water is available (20 litres maximum) and there is also a campsite with swimming pool. The roadhouse is close to the junction with two unsealed roads. To the north is the 14-km track to the wide inlet of **Cape Keraudren**, an exposed camping area very popular in winter with fishing families. Facilities are limited to drop toilets; camping is $5 per night. The unsealed road heading south winds its way to **Marble Bar** via Shay Gap, half the distance of the 300-km sealed route for those travelling down from Broome. Ask the roadhouse for directions and phone the Marble Bar police or your accommodation to let them know you're coming.

The next place of interest on the road is **Eighty Mile Beach**, 10 km (unsealed) off the highway and 105 km from Pardoo. The beach stretches as far as the eye can see in either direction and slopes gently down to the water, a favoured fishing spot though not recommended for a swim. One of the beach's chief claims to fame is its number and variety of shells, and many collectors will head down at low tide for the pick of the day's offerings. Adjacent to the beach is the **Eighty Mile Beach Caravan Park**.

The **Sandfire Roadhouse** ⓘ *T9176 5944,* 140 km from Pardoo, is the last before the junction with Broome Road, 290 km up the track, so make sure you have enough fuel. Accommodation is in simpler dongas **(E-F)**. There is also a campground and a licensed restaurant; fuel and meals are available 0700-1900.

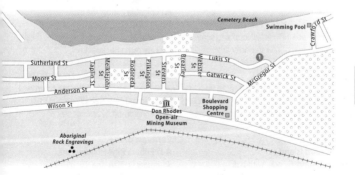

◉ Pilbara coast listings

For Sleeping and Eating price codes and other relevant information, see pages 28-34.

◉ Sleeping

Onslow and Old Onslow *p290*
There are 2 motels and a couple of caravan parks in Onslow.
A Onslow Mackerel Motel, Second Av, T9184 6586, www.onslowmackerelmotel.com.au. Top of the range with some pleasant foreshore units, continental breakfast included.
B Sun Chalets, Second Av, T9184 6058, www.onslowsunchalets.com.au. Has a few well-presented motel units with ocean views, several shabbier self-contained chalets and a swimming pool.
D-E Ocean View Caravan Park, at the north end of the main street, T9184 6053. The principal caravan park, and has a/c cabins and on-site vans with communal facilities.

Mackerel and Montebello islands *p290*
To stay on either of the islands contact T9184 6444, www.mackerelislands.com.au. Both require a minimum 3-night stay.
LL Montebello Island Safaris, T0419 091670, www.montebello.com.au. Takes parties of up to 14 out to the Montebello Islands on their houseboat for week-long trips. Safaris run Apr-Oct and leave from Exmouth. Price includes all food and some activities. Very popular so book early.

Direction Island
Has a single A-frame cabin, sleeping up to 8, as its only man-made structure! This can be hired at a weekly rate depending on season. Bring bed linen and food.

Thevenard Island
Has a 30-room 'village' with bar, restaurant and a few self-contained cabins, sleeping up to 10 (from $130 per person per night), whilst the 'village' accommodation is $185 for a double and includes meals.

Karratha and Dampier *p291, map p291*
There are a handful of expensive, high-standard motels in both Karratha and Dampier (generally cheaper in the latter) catering for the large business market and the mining industry. Karratha has 3 caravan parks, none close to the town centre, and Dampier has a sites-only park.
LL-L All Seasons, Searipple Rd, Karratha, T9185 1155, www.accorhotels.com. 60 a/c rooms in the town centre. Facilities include a shaded swimming pool, bar, on-site restaurant and Wi-Fi.
LL-L Karratha International, corner of Hillview and Millpoint Rds, Karratha, T9187 3333, www.karrathainternational.com.au. Sets the benchmark for the region with excellent rooms and facilities.
L Karratha Apartments, Galbraith Rd, 2 km from Karratha, T9143 9222, www.karrathaapartments.com.au. Has 10 self-contained, spacious chalets grouped around a pleasant pool and BBQ area.
A Dampier Mermaid Hotel & Motel, The Esplanade, Dampier, T9183 1222, www.dampiermermaid.com.au. Has 68 comfortable a/c hotel rooms and motel units, the more expensive ones with ocean view. There is also a pool, a bistro and a licensed bar.
A Peninsula Palms, The Esplanade, Dampier, T9183 1888. En suite rooms and more expensive motel units, price includes meals.
C-D Karratha Backpackers, 110 Wellard Way, Karratha, T9144 4904. A cheerful hostel, which is a brick ex-motel with 30-odd beds in 10 rooms, including 1 double. Courtyard BBQ, games room, free airport and bus pick-up/drop-off by arrangement.

Caravan parks
A-D Pilbara Big4 Holiday Park, Rosemary Rd, Karratha, T9185 1855, www.pilbara-holiday-park.wa.big4.com.au. Lots of spacious cabins, motel units and en suite powered sites. There's a pool and shop with takeaways available.

B-E Karratha Caravan Park, near the industrial estate off Karratha Rd, Karratha, T9185 1012, www.karrathacaravan.com.au. Has cheaper on-site vans and cabins.

Roebourne p292
E Harding River Caravan Park, on the far side of the river from the town, T9182 1063, www.hardingrivercaravanpark.com.au. It has shaded caravan and camping sites, a shop and a pool.

Cossack p292
Cossack Backpackers, T9182 1190, see page 293.

Point Samson p293
LL-L Point Samson Resort, T9187 1052, www.pointsamson.com. Has 12 pricey but comfortable self-contained garden chalets, which are studios or spa suites. There's a pool and an expensive alfresco restaurant and cocktail bar, TaTa's, open to non-residents daily for dinner, 1800-2100. Asian-influenced seafood, curries and soups are specialities.
A-E The Cove Caravan Park, McLeod St, T9187 0199, www.thecovecaravanpark. com.au. Has a good spot overlooking the beach, with sites and en suite cabins. The place seems to be almost constantly full so book ahead, particularly in winter.
B Delilah's Bed & Breakfast, T9187 1471. Opposite the sea and a short walk to the pub and **Moby's**. Rooms are small but clean and have a/c and well-stocked fridges. The cooked breakfast is excellent and is best enjoyed in the garden. Recommended.

Port Hedland p293, map 294
Contact the VIC for additional options in South Hedland. Note that accommodation becomes very busy during the winter months Apr-Sep.
LL The Esplanade Hotel, 2 Anderson St, T9173 2783, www.theesplanadeporthedland. com.au. In the centre of town, The Esplanade has been recently restored and offers en suite rooms that are clean and well-equipped,

most with access to large communal balconies. The ones in the original hotel, however, may seem a bit small for the price. There is an on-site restaurant (see Eating) and a bar. Additional rooms in a new block should be available in early 2011, as will a pool.
LL-L All Seasons, corner Lukis and McGregor Sts, T9173 1511, www.accorhotels.com. Has one of the best spots on the northern foreshore. It's well maintained, has a pool and a patio dining area overlooking the sea. Mid-range meals are generally the best in town, available 0530-0900, 1200-1400 and 1800- 2100. Of the 65 rooms it's the slightly smaller older ones that have ocean-view balconies. Internet access available.
L-A The Lodge Motel, 13 Hawke Place, South Hedland, T9172 2188, www.thelodgemotel.com.au. Simple a/c motel units. Swimming pool, buffet restaurant and bar. Prices include in-house movies, buffet breakfast, packed lunch and buffet dinner. Mostly for long-term stays and seasonal workers.
A-D Cooke Point Caravan Park, Athol and Taylor Sts, T9173 1271, www. cooke-point-holiday-park.wa.big4.com.au. This Big4 is the closest caravan park to town. It has chalets, motel units, backpacker accommodation and a number of campsites. Swimming pool, children's playground, campers' kitchen and internet access.
A-B Bruno's Ocean Lodge, Richardson St, T9173 2635. Has the best value motel-style a/c en suite rooms in town. Nothing fancy, but clean, comfortable and well-equipped.

Port Hedland to Broome p295
There are a surprising number of accommodation options along this road and all are very close to the ocean. **Barn Hill**, which is the nearest to the Highway, offers mainly camping, T9192 4975, whilst **Port Smith Carvan Park** has more options such as dongers and chalets, T9192 4983. If you're feeling flush, the **Eco Beach Wilderness Resort** is out this way too, www.ecobeach.com.

B-E Eighty Mile Beach Caravan Park,
T9176 5941, www.eightymilebeach.com.au.
Adjacent to Eighty Mile Beach, has a few
en suite a/c cabins and hundreds of shady
camping sites. Facilities are surprisingly good,
including free gas BBQs, laundry, campers'
kitchens, a small store and takeaway. Book
well ahead for the Jun-Sep peak season.

⑦ Eating

Onslow and Old Onslow *p290*
†† **Nikki's**, 336 First Av, T9184 6121. Mon-Fri
1800-2000. The town's only restaurant and
has a wide deck overlooking the ocean.
The mid-range menu is understandably brief,
but a high standard is thereby maintained,
and the seafood is very good. Licensed.
† **Coastal Café**, back on the main street.
Breakfasts Mon-Sat from 0730, Sun 0830,
snacks and takeaways until 2000. A standard
takeaway with a few tables.
† **Fish Shack**, a few kilometres east, by
Beadon Creek wharf. Fri-Sun 1730-2030.
A fish and chip takeaway and BYO café.

Karratha and Dampier *p291, map p291*
A couple of the motels in Karratha have
bistros. There are licensed Chinese restaurants
in both Dampier and Karratha. Karratha has
the better cafés.
††† **Etcetera**, Karratha, T9187 3333, at the
Karratha International, see Sleeping. Meals
Mon-Fri 0600-0930, Sat-Sun 0700-1000,
Mon-Sat 1800-2200. The area's undisputed
best bistro, a contemporary open space
overlooking the hotel's central pool
courtyard. An extensive menu of rich and
sophisticated modern food complements
the excellent service.
††† **Gecko's**, Karratha International, see
Sleeping. Mon-Sat 1200-2100. The best of
Karratha's watering holes. Unpretentious,
serves counter meals
† **Universal Chinese Restaurant**, Balmoral
Rd, Karratha, T9185 4333. Mon-Sat for lunch
1130-1400 and daily for dinner from 1700.

Has a good range of cheap meals and
lunch specials Mon-Sat. BYO.

Café
Jamaicablue, in the Karratha City shopping
centre. Serves up wraps, sandwiches, scones,
cakes, tea and coffee.

Cossack *p292*
Cossack Café, in the Customs House. Opens
as a café May-Oct daily 1000-1400. Snacks,
drinks and wonderful scones.

Wickham *p293*
† **Red Rock Café**, Wed-Sun 1700-2200.
A friendly little café serving cheap pizzas,
pasta, salads, curries and seafood.

Point Samson *p293*
††† **Point Samson Lodge**, see Sleeping,
T9187 1052. Has an expensive alfresco café,
TaTa's, open to non-residents daily for dinner,
1800-2100. Asian-influenced seafood, curries
and soups are the specialities.
† **Moby's Kitchen**, Bartley Court, T9187 1435.
daily 1200-1400, 1800-2000, Sun 0800-1000.
The town is best known for this place. It's a
legendary spot for the freshest, tastiest fish
and chips imaginable, served at outdoor
wooden benches overlooking the sea.
BYO but you can buy drinks upstairs.
Recommended.
† **Samson Beach Tavern**, T9187 1503. Meals
daily 1130-1430, 1800-2100. Worth going out
of your way for the pub upstairs. Relaxed,
friendly veranda bar that appeals to both
locals and visitors alike.

Port Hedland *p293, map 294*
Eating out in Port Hedland, even at the
All Seasons, falls quite a way short of what
most folks would call fine dining, but it is
generally good quality.
†††-†† **Bloomoons Restaurant**, The
Esplanade Hotel, see Sleeping. Tapas Sun
lunchtime. Mon-Fri 0600-2100, Sat-Sun
0600-2200. Offers Modern Australian cuisine
in comfortable surroundings. There are

alfresco tables, where live music can be enjoyed once a month. The main menu changes seasonally, but there are also theme buffets, such as Asian, Indian and the very popular Ribs night.

† **Bernie's Place**, Hedland Arcade, Edgar St, T9173 4342. Mon-Fri 0900-1500. Quick and filling Asian food in a tiny tucked away café, see the chalkboard for daily specials. There's good homemade chilli sauce for sale.

† **Dynasty Gardens**, Throssell Rd, South Hedland, T9172 1000. Open for lunch Mon-Fri 1130-1400 and daily for dinner 1700-2100. Offers a wide range of Chinese meals and good-value lunch and dinner specials. It also does takeaways.

† **Kath's Kitchen**, Wedge St, opposite the VIC, T9173 2128. Mon-Fri 0700-1500. A simple, unpretentious café that serves burgers, fresh juices and sandwiches. Also takeaway.

† **Port Hedland Fish & Chip Shop**, Keesing St, T9173 1200. Fish and chips, burgers and casual meals.

▲ Activities and tours

Mackerel and Montebello islands *p290*
The Mackerel Islands offers great fishing, snorkelling and diving. It's possible to do the PADI Open Water here for $595 or there are guided snorkel tours for $665. For information on what's on offer, see www.mackerelislands dive.com.au.

Dampier *p291*
Boat hire and boat trips
Dampier Trailer Boat Hire, 32 DeGrey Cres, Dampier, T0408 801040. Hires out 4.9-m plaka boats, but visitors need to have their recreational skippers ticket. Also runs day yacht cruises to the island, which include snorkelling, swimming, beach walks ($90), sunset cruises are $70.

Cinema
Karratha Cinemas, Sharpe Av, at the shopping centre, T9143 1155, www.karratha cinemas.com.au. Shows the latest (mainstream) movies.

Fishing
Oceanus Fishing Charters, T9144 4322. Operates a large boat for up to 10 passengers.

Swimming
There's an excellent outdoor municipal pool with gardens and BBQs on Sharp Av, T9186 8527, Karratha. 0900 or earlier to 1700 or later. $3.90, children and concessions $2.80.
Karratha International (see Sleeping) allows daytime customers at the pool-side bar to take a dip.

Roebourne *p292*
Port to Port Tour, T9182 1060. Departs from the VIC and takes in the old gaol before visiting Cape Lambert Iron Ore facility and Cossack. Runs May-Oct on Mon, Wed and Fri in the morning. Wear long sleeves shirts, long trousers and closed-toe shoes, and bring lunch.

Wickham *p293*
Pete's Parachuting, T0417 180064, www.australianskydivingadventures.com. Offers excellent tandem and solo jumps above the stunning coastline. You can stay for free at the **Wickham Skydiving Clubhouse**.

Port Hedland *p293, map 294*
Bus and walking tours
The VIC organizes a few informative tours, including:
BHPB Iron Ore Tour, which departs Mon, Wed and Fri at 0930, taking in the impressive port loading facilities and stockpiles. $26, children $20, concessions $24.
Town Discovery Tours, guided walks depart the VIC Apr-Oct Mon-Fri at 1400.

Swimming

None of the beaches are particularly inviting, and can be dangerous thanks to stone fish, octopuses and even salties.

Gratwick Memorial Swimming Pool, T9173 3303. Preferable to an indoor pool, open-air, open every afternoon, Sep-Apr. Entry $4, concessions $1.70. No children allowed.

⊖ Transport

Karratha and Dampier *p291, map p291*
Air Karratha Airport, roughly between the 2 towns, is one of Australia's busiest domestic airports, handling about 500 people a day, mostly workers. There's a bar, café and all the major hire car companies have desks. A taxi to Karratha will be about $30. **Qantas** and **Skywest** have daily flights to **Perth**.

Bus The Greyhound **Perth** to **Broome** service leaves the Coach Bay near McDonalds for **Port Hedland** Tue, Thu and Sat at 0635. The Perth-bound service departs Tue, Thu and Sat at 1830.

Car Car hire from **E-Go Car Hire**, Croyden Rd, T9144 1301, or **McLaren Hire**, Mooligunn Rd, T9185 6383, www.mclarenhire.com.au. Other options include **Avis**, T9144 4122, **Budget**, T132727, and **Thrifty**, T9143 1711.

The cheapest fuel in the region is generally at the Shell roadhouse on the highway opposite the airport.

Car servicing at **North West Mechanical**, T9185 1111. Tyres and parts from **Opposite Lock/Tyre Power**, 5 Crane Circle, T9144 4222.

Taxi Call Swan Taxis, T131330.

Port Hedland *p293, map 294*
Air Qantas and Skywest operate flight between Port Hedland and **Perth**.

Bus

Local Hedland Bus Lines, T9172 3194, www.hedlandbuslines.com, runs a number of services around Port and South Hedland. Its 501 bus between the 2, stopping at the Boulevard Shopping Centre and South Hedland, runs 4-5 times a day, Mon-Fri and twice on Sat.

Long distance The Greyhound **Perth** to **Broome** service leaves the VIC Tue, Thu, Sat at 1000. The Perth-bound service departs Tue, Thu and Sat at 1425.

Car Car servicing at **Pilbara Automotive Services**, Hardy St, T9173 1815. The VIC can supply a list of car hire companies.

Taxi Call T9172 1010 or T9140 1313.

❶ Directory

Karratha and Dampier *p291, map p291*
Banks All the major banks, with ATMs, on Hedland Pl, Karratha town centre.
Internet At the VIC. **Medical services** Chemists: Karratha Pharmacy, Karratha City, T9185 1316. Mon-Fri 0900-1730, Thu to 2100, Sat 0830-1700. **Hospital:** Nickol Bay, Dampier Rd, Karratha, T9144 0330.
Police Welcome Rd, T9144 2233.
Post Opposite Karratha City, off Welcome Rd.

Port Hedland *p293, map 294*
Banks Main banks and ATMs in Wedge St.
Internet Access at the VIC. **Laundry** Wedge St, T9173 5130. **Medical services** Chemists: Soul Pattinson, Wedge St, T9173 1132. Mon-Fri 0700-1730, Sat 0800-1700, Sun 1000-1600. **Hospital:** Sutherland St, T9158 1666. **Police** T9173 1444. **Post** Wedge St, T131318.

Pilbara interior

Despite a couple of mining towns, Aboriginal communities and a handful of stations, inland Pilbara is one of the least populated but still accessible regions in the country. This glorious emptiness makes exploring the ancient ranges a real adventure: it is quite possible to head along the roads from Karratha, through Millstream, Karijini and Marble Bar and back to the highway without seeing another vehicle. Care is required, however. The iron-rich stone fractures to create small sharp shards, and it is these that make up the surface of many of the region's unsealed roads. Punctures are the norm, not the exception, and you should expect and prepare for at least one during an extended drive around the area. ▸▸ *For listings, see pages 305-306.*

Millstream-Chichester National Park ▸▸ *Colour map 5, A3.*

ⓘ *Python Pool 125 km from Karratha, 90 km from Roebourne. For more information contact DEC, Karratha, T9182 2000, or the park T9184 5144, park fees $11 per vehicle, camping $7 per person, water available but must be treated, phone at homestead (takes cards only).*

As you approach this national park from the north you pass through classic Pilbara landscape and begin to see the unusual grandeur and beauty of this region. Flat-topped ranges and hills the colour of dried blood are dotted with yellow pincushions of spinifex grass. The flat expanse of the plains below is broken only by green ribbons of white-barked gum trees along the banks of stony creek beds. This park is a true oasis fed by a 2000 sq km underground aquifer. The new sealed road has made the park more accessible to visitors coming from Karratha and so with numbers rising, improvements are being made to the facilities. The park is managed jointly by the DEC and the local Yindjibarndi and Ngarluma people of the Millstream Park Council.

Ins and outs

There is a sealed 90 km road from Karratha to Millstream, however it does not yet run all the way through the park. Those who want to carry on to Tom Price will have to navigate the unsealed section and then take the Private Pilbara Rail Access Road, for which a permit is required (contact the Karratha VIC). Eventually the route will be sealed the rest of the way from Millstream to Tom Price. During the wet season the roads may be closed due to flooding. Ask for current conditions at the Karratha VIC.

Sights

The park itself has two distinct visitor areas. The northern end provides stunning views over the landscape described above, from **Mount Herbert**, just beyond **Python Pool**, a deep pool below a sheer rock wall. The view from Mount Herbert is best at sunset and Python Pool is wonderful at sunrise so it's a good place to spend a night, although the Snake Creek campground is stony and shadeless.

Once your vehicle has climbed past Mount Herbert, you'll reach a plateau and travel 60 km over fairly featureless country to the freshwater oasis of Millstream, 145 km from Karratha, 220 km from **Auski Roadhouse**, at the southern end of the park. Here there are permanent spring-fed pools in the Fortescue River, lined with palm trees, rushes and tall gums – idyllic swimming and camping spots. This area was under a pastoral lease from 1865 until the 1960s and the park visitor centre is situated in the old farm homestead. The centre is normally unattended but has interesting displays on the history and environment of the park and a box to put your park fees in. Kangaroos often rest in the shade of the homestead grounds, where there is also a pretty picnic spot. There is a campground, **Miliyanha**, near the Homestead Visitor Centre, as well as camping at **Stargazers Campground** (seasonal). **Crossing Pool** also has a shady campsite with toilets, BBQs and ladders into the river if you feel like a swim (you will). **Deep Reach Pool** is another good place for a dip. There are walks detailed in the free park brochure including a short walk around the homestead, a 6.8-km trail to Crossing Pool and a trail from Mount Herbert to **Python Pool** (16 km return).

Tom Price ➤ *For listings, see pages 305-306. Colour map 5, B3.*

→ *Population: 6500. 335 km from Nanutarra, 155 km from Auski Roadhouse.*

Owned by Pilbara Iron, a subsidiary of one of the world's largest mining companies, Rio Tinto, Tom Price is an attractive company town surrounded by the **Hamersley Ranges**. Brilliant green grass and palm trees have been cultivated, which makes a change from the film of red dust that coats most mining towns. Although increasingly employees prefer to work on a fly-in fly-out basis from Perth, the company tries to make life as comfortable as possible for the young families of Tom Price. This is good news for travellers as the huge supermarket contains the kind of goodies you may have forgotten existed. There is also a drive-in cinema showing films at weekends.

Day tours operate out of Tom Price to **Karijini National Park** and there are regular tours to the Rio Tinto open-cut mine. There are fantastic views of the area from **Mount Nameless**, actually called Jarndrunmunhna for countless years, accessible both by foot and 4WD from the road to the caravan park. The walking track from the caravan park to the summit (1128 m) takes about two to three hours return (and if you park here you'll avoid the very rough unsealed 2-km access road to the trail car park). Tom Price is the highest town in WA at 747 m above sea level so the ascent of Mount Nameless is not too arduous. The **VIC** ⓘ *Central Rd, T9188 1112, www.tompricewa.com.au, Jun-Oct Mon-Fri 0830-1700, Sat-Sun 0830-1230, Nov-May Mon-Fri 0930-1530, Sat 0900-1200,* is very helpful and knowledgeable.

Karijini National Park ➤ *For listings, see pages 305-306. Colour map 5, A/B3.*

→ *Central gorges 80 km from Tom Price, 110 km from Auski roadhouse.*

ⓘ *For more information contact the VIC, T9189 8121, Apr-Oct daily 0900-1600; Nov-Mar daily 1000-1400 or the DEC Pilbara T9182 2000. Park fees $11 per person, camping $7 per person. Water available but must be treated.*

Northern and central Australia contain so many impressive red-walled gorges that some visitors get gorge fatigue, but Karijini's gorges are the dessert course you'll find you still have room for. The park contains extraordinarily deep and narrow gorges full of waterfalls, swimming pools and challenging walks, yet it is hardly known, even within Australia. The park sits within the heart of one of the world's most ancient landscapes, the **Hamersley Plateau**, where creeks have carved 100-m-deep chasms into layers of 2500-million-year-old sedimentary rock. You enter the park from the plateau and descend into the gorges, which means there are excellent lookouts. The most spectacular view can be seen from **Oxers Lookout**, where four gorges meet below the golden spinifex and crooked white snappy gum trees of the plateau.

Ins and outs

Getting there If travelling northeast along the coast, turn off at the **Nanutarra Roadhouse** to reach Tom Price, close to Karijini's western border. Another alternative is to continue north to Karratha and take the sealed route to Millstream-Chichester National Park, continuing along the unsealed road from the park to join the sealed Private Pilbara Rail Access Road (a permit is required, which can be obtained from the Karratha VIC). No petrol is available on either route. If travelling southwest, take the Great Northern Highway south shortly after Port Hedland to **Auski Roadhouse** and turn right after 35 km onto Karijini Drive. If you're comfortable with unsealed roads a pretty alternative is through Marble Bar. A tour is a good way to see Karijini, especially if you want some adventure, but choose carefully, checking that the age and activity level will suit you.
▶ *See page 306 for tour operators.*

Getting around Although this is the state's second largest park, all of the facilities and walks are found fairly close to each other in the northern section of the park, above Karijini Drive. Head first for the innovative **visitor centre**, built with curved walls of rusted iron that both mirror and disappear into its landscape. An interpretive display explains the history and geology of the park and the viewpoint of its Banyjima, Yinhawangka, and Kurrama traditional owners. Maps, drinks and souvenirs are available and there are toilets, showers and phones. The park is generally open all year round, although most pleasant April-September. The main roads into the park are sealed, others are unsealed and rocky (2WD but remote driving rules apply and punctures are common).

The gorges

Walking and swimming are the main activities but Karijini is also known for some very exciting adventure trails. Because some gorges are just 1-2 m wide, or filled with water, you cannot walk between the gorge walls but have to clamber along the steep sides on narrow ledges of dark red ironstone, swimming through difficult sections. Follow the circular walk markers, as these designate the best route to take. The routes beyond Kermits Pool in **Hancock Gorge** and Handrail Pool in **Weano Gorge** should only be attempted with a guide. There are easy walks but you will not be able to see the best of this awesome park unless you are reasonably fit and agile.

There are two main areas to visit in the park. **Dales Gorge** is 10 km east of the visitor centre, where you can walk up the gorge to a wide cascade, **Fortescue Falls**, and beyond the falls to **Fern Pool**, a lovely, large swimming hole (1 km). Return to the top of the gorge by the same path or walk down the centre of the gorge and turn left at the end to join the trail to **Circular Pool**, a lush rock bowl dripping with ferns. At the point where you turn, a steep path joins the car park to the pool (800 m) so you don't need to retrace your steps. There is also an easy rim trail overlooking Dales Gorge and Circular Pool (2 km).

The other main area is 29 km west of the visitor centre, at the junction of **Weano, Joffre, Hancock** and **Red gorges**. There are lookouts here, including **Oxer Lookout**, and trails into Joffre (3 km), Knox (2 km), Weano Gorge (1 km to Handrail Pool) and Hancock Gorge (1.5 km to Kermits Pool). These all involve some scrambling, but the latter two offer a taster of Karijini adventure that most people can manage without a guide.

One of the prettiest gorges to visit is **Kalamina Gorge**. The turn-off is 19 km west of the visitor centre, and it is also one of the easiest to explore. A short, steep track leads to the base of the gorge and a permanent pool. If you turn right and walk for a short distance you'll reach a small, picturesque waterfall, if you turn left there is a lovely and flat walk downstream to **Rock Arch Pool** (3 km return).

Hamersley Gorge is another delightful spot, although on the far western border 100 km from the visitor centre. This is a large, open gorge with dramatically folded rock walls in shades of purple, green and pink. Fortescue River flows through the gorge, creating beautiful pools and waterfalls. If you head upstream you'll pass a deep 'spa' pool on the way to the fern-lined **Grotto** (1 km, difficult). To get a bird's-eye perspective on the whole landscape you can climb **Mount Bruce**, WA's second highest mountain at 1235 m. This is the island peak visible from the western end of Karijini Drive and the track is a long but rewarding slog up the western face (9 km, six hours return).

Marble Bar ›› *For listings, see pages 305-306. Colour map 5, A4.*

→ *Population: 357. 200 km from Port Hedland, 250 km from Auski roadhouse.*

You'll know by now that Australians often take a perverse pleasure in their continent of extremes and proudly boast of its isolation, dangerous creatures or whatever else is big, bad and ugly. The people of the Pilbara can really win at this game, with their huge ships, trucks and trains, and those of Marble Bar are no exception. They gladly proclaim that they live in the hottest town in Australia. In the summer of 1923-1924 there were 160 days over 38.7°C, but any typical summer could boast at least a few months of days sweltering in the high 30s. Despite this, Marble Bar is quite an attractive, if tiny, outback town with a wide main street. The town is surrounded by spectacular Pilbara scenery of low spinifex-covered ranges and dark red ironstone ridges.

Ins and outs
The main route to the town heads south off the Great Northern Highway, 40 km east of Port Hedland, and is sealed all the way through to Marble Bar (150 km). If coming west from the Kimberley there is an unsealed alternative 50 km past Pardoo. Take this left-hand turn, then right over the railway line after a couple of kilometres. This scenic road joins with the Marble Bar Road after 75 km, 50 km from the town, saving about 70 km off the sealed route. Watch for slippery concrete beds on a couple of creek crossings. The unsealed Hillside Road links Marble Bar to the Great Northern Highway (155 km). This is a remote route, but one of the most scenic in the Pilbara. Also unsealed, the Marble Bar Road to the south connects the town with Newman (300 km).

Sights
Marble Bar was founded in 1893 after discoveries of alluvial gold nearby and had a population of 5000 at its peak. The fine stone government buildings (1896) at the end of the main street are an indication of the optimism of the time. Just outside Marble Bar is the beautiful rock bar of jasper across the Coongan River that gives the town its name and **Chinaman's Pool** nearby where you can swim. Samples of jasper cannot be taken from the Marble Bar but there is a quarry (signposted **Jasper Deposit**), 4 km from town on the Hillside Road where you can chip away. On the same road, 8 km from town, is the **Comet Gold Mine** ① *T9176 1015, 0900-1600, $3.* This mine operated from 1936 until 1955, and is now run as an interesting historic site, mineral display and gem shop. There are some other attractive natural sights around Marble Bar only accessible to 4WD, such as **Coppins Gap** and **Glen Herring Gorge**. Ask for directions at the Shire office in the main street.

For Sleeping and Eating price codes and other relevant information, see pages 28-34.

😴 Sleeping

Tom Price *p302*

B Tom Price Hotel, Central Rd, T9189 1101. Basic motel-style rooms. Probably not the first (or best) choice of accommodation. Counter and restaurant meals available.
B Windawarri Lodge, Stadium Rd, T9189 1110. Caters mainly for the mining industry and the corporate partners but has some standard en suite rooms and a buffet restaurant. Price includes meals.
C-E Tom Price Tourist Park, 2 km from town, T9189 1515. Has self-contained A-frame units, 4-bed dorms in dongas, and a campers' kitchen and shop.

Karijini National Park *p302*

A-E Karijini Eco Retreat, Savannah Campground, off Weano Rd, T9425 5591, www.karijiniecoretreat.com.au. This is the only commercial accommodation within the park and 100% Gumala Aborigine owned. The camp consists of deluxe en suite eco tents with king or twin beds, and campsites with share facilities and a communal kitchen. Guided walks at selected times. There is also a restaurant and bar open during peak season.
B-E Auski (Mujani) Roadhouse, T9176 6988, on the Great Northern Highway, 265 km from Port Hedland, 200 km from Newman. On the northeastern border of the park, the roadhouse is a coach stop and a useful meeting point for tours. 20 comfortable motel rooms, budget twins without en suite, and powered and unpowered sites. Internet access is available.

Camping

Dales Camping Area, 10 km east of the visitor centre, is a simple campground. Dingoes are common here, so ensure you store all food in your vehicle.

Marble Bar *p304*

B Iron Clad Hotel, 15 Francis St, T9176 1066. One of the town's landmarks and much smarter inside than the corrugated-iron exterior suggests. It has recently been refurbished and offers motel rooms, a beer garden, restaurant (May-Sep) and bar. Counter meals available lunch and dinner.
B Marble Bar Travellers Stop, Halse Rd, T9176 1166. A roadhouse with motel and donger rooms, a licensed à la carte restaurant and a shop that does takeaways, open daily 0600-2100.
E-F Marble Bar Holiday Park, T9176 1569. Has sites only.

🍴 Eating

Tom Price *p302*

The town also has a range of takeaways, a bakery and a **Coles** supermarket (open daily).
❤️ Red Breeze Bistro and Café, Stadium Rd, T9189 6529. Tue-Sun 1100-1400 and 1700-2100, Sat-Sun 0900-1100. A licensed restaurant for Thai and Chinese, also takeaway.
❤️ Moon Palace, Stadium Rd, T9189 1331. Wed-Sun 1130-1430, Fri-Sat 1700-2200, Sun-Thu 1700-2100. Offers a wide selection of Chinese dishes, dine-in or takeaway. BYO.
❤️ Nameless Coffee House, Stadium Rd, opposite the VIC but tucked around the corner, T9188 7168. Mon-Fri 0800-1600, Sat 0900-1300. Serves up cheap breakfasts, light meals, focaccias, nachos and average coffee. Also offers internet access.
❤️ Windawarri Lodge, Stadium Rd, T9189 1110. Has a buffet restaurant.

Marble Bar *p304*

❤️ Iron Clad Hotel, see Sleeping, T9176 1066. Meals 1200-1400 and 1800-2000. The pub does counter meals for lunch and dinner and has an à la carte restaurant open May-Sep.
❤️ Marble Bar Travellers Stop, T9176 1166. Has a reasonable restaurant. Licensed.

▲▲ Activities and tours

Tom Price *p302*
Many Perth-Broome tours stop into Karijini and these tend to include 2-3 nights camping in the park.
Lestok Tours, T9189 2032, www.lestoktours. com.au. Operates daily coach tours of the Pilbara Iron Mine (1½ hrs, $25, children $15). Contact the VIC for departure times. Also runs a regular day trip into Karijini, departing at 0800 ($145, children $80).
Pilbara Gorge Tours, T9188 1534, www.pilbaragorgetours.com.au. Runs half-($125, children $60) and full-day ($145, children $60) tours to the main attractions of Karijini National Park.
West Oz Active, T0438 913713, www.westozactive.com.au. For those who want a more extreme Karijini experience, trips include hiking, climbing, swimming and abseiling. Prices range from around $140-220, and the tours only run during summer.
Wilanah Walkabouts, contact the VIC, T9188 1112. A 2-hr guided bush walk, learning about plants, animals and bush medicines.
Willis Walkabouts, T8985 2134 www.bushwalkingholidays.com.au. Good 14-day camping tours departing from Tom Price into the Karijini National Park (it is in 2 sections and participants can choose to do one or both).

✈ Transport

Tom Price *p302*
Air
There are flights from Paraburdoo Airport to **Perth**, and a shuttle runs the 70 km between the airport and Tom Price. Contact the VIC for information.

Car
Car hire is available from Paraburdoo Airport. Car servicing at **Tyrepower**, Bonderoo Rd, T9189 2106, or at **Tom Price Tyres**, Bonderoo Rd, T9189 3370. Petrol can be found at **Shell**, Mine Rd, T9188 1853.

Taxi
For a taxi call T0417 941450.

🛈 Directory

Tom Price *p302*
Banks Westpac ATM, Central Rd.
Internet Access at the Library next to the VIC, or **Nameless Coffee House** (see Eating).
Medical services Chemists: Amcal, same lane as Coles entrance, T9189 1202. Mon-Fri 0830-1730, Sat 0830-1230. **Hospital:** Hospital Dr, T9159 5222. **Police** Court Rd, T9189 1344. **Post** Same lane as Coles entrance.

Contents

Broome & around

★ **Don't miss ...**

1 Pearl Luggers, page 312.
2 Broome Historical Museum, page 312.
3 Cable Beach, page 314.
4 Town Beach Café, page 317.
5 Sun Pictures, page 318.
6 Astronomical tour, page 321.
7 Broome Bird Observatory, page 323.
8 Dampier Peninsula, page 323.

Indian Ocean

Strickland Bay
High Island
One Arm Point Bardi Aboriginal Community
Tallon Island
Cape Leveque
Sunday Island
Mermaid Island
Kooljaman Tourist Complex
One Arm Point
Chile Head
Elephant Point
Lombadina
Cygnet Bay
Lombadina Point
Willie Point
Long Island
Cape Borda
Deep Water Point
Mudnunn
Cunningham Point
Amantangoora Point
Emeriau Point
Pender Bay
Middle Lagoon
North Head
King Sound
Beagle Bay
Sandy Point
Beagle Bay
Beagle Bay Aboriginal Reserve
Derby
Point Coulomb Nature Reserve
8
Dampier Peninsula
Coulomb Point
James Price Point
Mt Clarkson ▲
Quondong Point
Barred Creek
Willie Creek Pearl Farm
Roebuck Roadhouse
Cable Beach 3
Broome 7
1 2 4 5 6
Port Beach
Broome Peninsula
Roebuck Bay

N

20 km
20 miles

The shark's tooth of the Dampier Peninsula marks the start of WA's Kimberley region and the northerly tip of the west coast before it breaks into a maze of inlets and archipelagos. Fringed by intermittent mangrove estuaries and low, deep-red sandstone cliffs, the interior is a plain of low scrub and sparse woodland, usually dry but occasionally soaked by passing cyclones. A sealed highway connects Broome at its southwest corner with Derby in its southeast, and a rough unsealed track heads up through the middle connecting isolated Aboriginal communities. Broome is home to a unique blend of European, Asian and Aboriginal people, with an architecture, culture and history like nowhere else in Australia. Slipping into 'Broometime' can be a seductive experience.

Broome

→ *Colour map 6, B2. Population: 13,700.*

Turquoise water, red cliffs, white sand and green mangroves; Broome is a town full of vivid colour and tropical lushness, with an interesting history and composition quite unlike any other Australian town to boot. Founded because of its proximity to vast beds of the southern ocean's magnificent large oyster, the Pinctada maxima, Broome's past and present is wrapped up in the pearl. In recent years, the refined and expensive resorts at Cable Beach have brought the town much attention and sophistication. Broome's international renown causes a lot of envious mumbling from other towns in the region and many people will tell you that the town has changed beyond recognition in the last decade or so, becoming too crowded and commercial. Although it is probably true that Broome has lost some of its unique character, it remains a fascinating oasis and a very enjoyable place to spend a few days. ⇥ *For listings, see pages 314-322.*

Ins and outs

Getting there
Broome is 610 km from Port Hedland, 1060 km from Kununurra. There are frequent flights from Perth, Alice Springs, Uluru (Ayers Rock) and Darwin, and good bus links too. ⇥ *See Transport, page 321.*

Getting around
Town Bus Service ① *T9193 6585, www.broomebus.com.au*, operates a single winding route between the Vacation Village, the town centre and Cable Beach, and back, daily. Departure times vary depending on season, and day passes are $10, one-way fares $3.50, children $1.50. Multi-rider tickets can also be purchased.

Tourist information
The **VIC** ① *18 Broome Rd, T9192 2222, www.broomevisitorscentre.com.au, Mon-Fri 0800-1700, Sat-Sun 0830-1600*, is also home to a pearl boutique. In the peak winter months avoid visiting the VIC around 1000 when people are trying to find accommodation, as the queue can be very long.

History

Broome was established on the shore of Roebuck Bay in the 1890s as a telegraph cable station and a base for pearl shell merchants and their divers. During the boom years before the First World War, Broome supplied 80% of the world's pearl shell, mostly used for buttons. The first pearl divers were Aboriginal, then later Malaysian, Indonesian, Chinese or Japanese. Consequently the people of Broome are an unusual mix of Aboriginal, Asian and European heritage. When plastic buttons were invented in the 1950s Broome was in trouble, but the pearling industry learnt to produce cultured pearls with the help of the Japanese and has prospered since on the profits of the world's largest and most lustrous pearls, and more recently by tourism.

Sights

Chinatown

Chinatown is the oldest part of town and is still the main focus of Broome. **Carnarvon Street** and **Dampier Terrace** are lined with architecture that is characteristic of the town and its history. Australian corrugated iron and verandas are blended with Chinese flourishes such as red trims and lattice. Except for the architecture, Chinatown bears little resemblance to the days of the late 19th century when it was full of billiard saloons, opium dens, noodle houses and pearl sheds. Carnarvon Street is the main street, lined with tourist shops and cafés, and most of the buildings on this street are original. About halfway down there are monuments to those involved in the pearling industry. The **Cultured Pearling Monument** remembers Kuribayashi, Iwaki and Dureau, men who helped to pioneer the cultured pearl industry after demand for pearl shell fell away. Opposite these three figures, the **Hard Hat Pearl Diver** is a reminder of those who did all

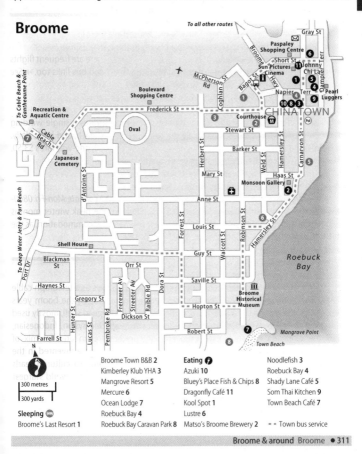

Broome

300 metres
300 yards

Sleeping
Broome's Last Resort **1**
Broome Town B&B **2**
Kimberley Klub YHA **3**
Mangrove Resort **5**
Mercure **6**
Ocean Lodge **7**
Roebuck Bay **4**
Roebuck Bay Caravan Park **8**

Eating
Azuki **10**
Bluey's Place Fish & Chips **8**
Dragonfly Café **11**
Kool Spot **1**
Lustre **6**
Matso's Broome Brewery **2**

Noodlefish **3**
Roebuck Bay **4**
Shady Lane Café **5**
Som Thai Kitchen **9**
Town Beach Café **7**

= = Town bus service

the hard, dangerous work underwater, and a plaque has also been erected by the Aboriginal community in memory of all the Aboriginal pearl divers forced into the job.

Walk through Johnny Chi Lane, lined with historical markers, to Dampier Terrace. At the northern end is the **Streeter Jetty**. This unprepossessing narrow wooden jetty among the mangroves was once the major jetty for pearl luggers. The shell was unloaded here onto rail carts and the luggers would moor in the creek, lying on their bellies in the mud when the tide receded. Modern boats now use the jetty at the Deep Water Port but two luggers survive and can be seen at **Pearl Luggers** ① *T9192 0022, www.pearlluggers. com.au, Mon-Fri 0900-1630, Sat 0900-1500, daily tours (call to check times), $20, children $10, concessions $16.50,* at the other end of Dampier Terrace. This is the best place to learn about the pearling industry of the old days.

Broome town

A succession of roads follow the mangrove coast down towards the town beach. On the way they pass **Matso's** bar and, next door, the **Monsoon Gallery** ① *corner of Hamersley and Carnarvon Sts, T9193 5379, www.monsoongallery.com.au, May-Sep Tue-Sat 1000-1700, Oct-Apr Tue-Sat 1000-1600, free.* The gallery is housed in a fine old pearling master's residence and is worth a visit to see an example of early Broome architecture as well as the fine collection of art and jewellery.

About 1 km south is the **Broome Historical Museum** ① *67 Robinson St, T9192 2075, www.broomemuseum.org.au, Jun-Sep Mon-Fri 1000-1600, Sat-Sun 1000-1300; Oct-May daily 1000-1300, $5, children $1, concessions $3,* which houses a small but well arranged and quite fascinating collection of artefacts, memorabilia and photographs charting the whole history of the European and Asian colonists. All sorts of themes are explored, but most of the displays focus on early colonials, the pearling industry, the Second World War and cyclones.

Not far away is **Town Beach**, a small shallow bay with warm golden sand and Broome's amazing opaque turquoise water, fringed by a low rocky headland on one side and mangroves on the other. A grassy foreshore has a few picnic tables but most people choose to patronize the wonderful café. Swimming is fine here but note the tide times as at low tide the sea retreats into the far distance. Town Beach is the best place to see the phenomenon called **Staircase to the Moon**, when the moonlight shines on pools of water left behind by the tide to create the illusion. Like so much in Broome this is tide-dependent and only happens about once a month between March and October. It also depends on lack of cloud, of course. Pick up a monthly visitor guide from the VIC for 'staircase' dates and tide times.

Heading west from the water, along Guy Street, takes you to the **Shell House** ① *76 Guy St, T9192 1423 (also at 23 Dampier Terr, which is open year-round), May-Sep Mon-Fri 0900-1600, Sat 0900-1300.* Here the owners display their compact collection of 6000 shells from hundreds of mostly local species. The main business of the place is as a shop selling shells and mother-of-pearl jewellery (great for souvenirs and presents), so entry is free.

Via a short maze of roads to the north are the Chinese and Japanese cemeteries. The **Japanese Cemetery** is particularly striking, with its simple rough-hewn headstones. Over 900 Japanese pearl divers are buried here.

Beware of the croc

There are two species of crocodile inhabiting Australia's northern waterways. The **estuarine crocodile**, commonly known as the saltwater croc, or 'saltie', is far and away the most dangerous. Growing up to 6 m long, a big one will think nothing of grabbing a cow or horse given the opportunity and will happily take a human for elevenses. Because of this they were shot on sight for decades by European pastoralists, though their numbers seem to have held up well until someone clicked that both hides and meat could be valuable. Professional hunting started with a vengeance in the 1950s and the population soon crashed. Protected since 1971 it was feared that they would become extinct anyway, but they have recovered well and are now even culled in the Northern Territory. You need to start watching out for them north of Port Hedland and keep watching as far as Maryborough in Queensland. That they are only found in the sea or at the mouths of rivers is a myth, unfortunately propagated by their common name. In fact they will stake territories anywhere suitable upriver, and have been found 600 km inland. They are not fans of cross-country travel, however, and tend to stick to the water. A general rule of thumb for swimming in creeks and pools in the north is to get above a decent-sized waterfall – though this is still no guarantee. If in any doubt whatsoever simply steer well-clear of rivers, riverbanks and waterholes. Absence of a warning sign does not mean absence of a crocodile.

The **freshwater crocodile** is considerably smaller than the saltie and is not territorial. As such it tends to keep away from people and usually only attacks if trod upon or threatened. They are not found as far west as the salties and are found in and east of the Fitzroy River.

It is easy to tell the difference between the two types of crocodile if you look at their snouts. The freshwater crocodile has a very narrow snout, tapering to a point at the end. The saltie has a much wider, chunkier snout.

Broome peninsula

Broome's deep water port lies right at the southern end of the peninsula, on Roebuck Bay. Apart from port facilities there are a couple of reasons to come down here. **The Wharf** restaurant does good fish and chips overlooking the bay, and the jetty is a popular local fishing spot. The beach to the right of the jetty is a good place for a swim at high tide but at low tide it is great fun to fossick among the rocks. Wear shoes and peer around and under rocks to see octopuses, starfish and crustaceans. An unsealed road leads west around the foot of the peninsula to the ocean-facing Gantheaume Point and Cable Beach. It is also possible to reach the area directly from town by following sealed Gantheaume Point Road southwest to the point. **Gantheaume Point** is a jumble of red rock stacks that make a striking contrast to the turquoise sea beyond. It is one of many areas around Broome where dinosaurs left their footprints in the tidal flats. The **dinosaur footprints** are just at the base of the cliff but can only be seen at very low tide. Remember to check the tide times as this only happens once or twice a month (the VIC will be able to advise). There is also a rather uninspiring concrete-lined rock pool at the point, **Anastasia's Pool**, built by a former lighthouse keeper for his arthritic wife to bathe in. All that remains of the lighthouse keeper's house is the brick chimney by the car park. The modern house on the point is a private house. Around the corner, **Reddell Beach** runs along the southern edge of the peninsula. It is known for interesting rock formations and sheer pindan cliffs above the beach. 'Pindan' is an Aboriginal name for the intensely red dirt landscape of the area.

Cable Beach → *Colour map 6, B2.*

Synonymous with holiday luxury in the northwest, Cable, 6 km from the town centre, on the opposite side of the peninsula, is a long, wide, white sand beach that faces west and the setting sun. It was once the point at which the state's telegraph cable headed into the sea on its way to Indonesia and the rest of the world, but the name is now the only reminder of that era. A long grassy foreshore sits atop the ridge at the back of the beach, and there are toilets, picnic tables and a café. It is a relatively safe place to swim and there is usually a lifeguard patrol in winter. If you prefer being on the water rather than in it, then a couple of options present themselves. A small beach shack hires out surf and boogie boards ($3-10 per hour) and is open daily 0830-1630. It also hires out umbrellas and deckchairs. The classic way to watch the sunset at Cable Beach is, unlikely as it may sound, on the back of a camel. There are a couple of operators who offer the experience, see Activities and tours page 320.

The beach was developed by British Lord McAlpine in the late 1980s. He built the **Cable Beach Club** resort and over the last 15 years Cable Beach has become a satellite village of holiday accommodation and facilities. In the centre of this is **Broome Crocodile Park** ① *Cable Beach Rd, T9192 1489, www.malcolmdouglas.com.au, Apr-Nov Mon-Fri 1000-1700, Sat-Sun 1400-1700, daily feeding tour at 1500 plus an extra guided tour Mon-Fri at 1100; Dec-Mar daily feeding tour at 1600, $30, children $20, concessions $25,* the public arm of a large commercial crocodile farming operation. Dozens of pens hold hundreds of crocs and alligators from five species, but mostly the big estuarine (or saltwater) crocodiles of northern Australia. A 5-m-long 'saltie' hungrily grabbing a chicken is a sight well worth seeing. The tours are fascinating and you usually get to see and feel a baby croc. Allow 1½ hours. On Sanctuary Road there is a **Willie Creek** pearl and jewellery shop, open daily.

◉ Broome listings

For Sleeping and Eating price codes and other relevant information, see pages 28-34.

◉ Sleeping

Broome *p310, map p311*
Broome has easily the widest range of accommodation north of Perth. The following is a small selection of what is available. Contact the VIC for other options, and if you're around for a while consider a spell out on the Dampier Peninsula (see page 323). Book well ahead for the peak Apr-Sep season. If coming in Oct-Mar shop around for some excellent deals. In addition to the options listed below, **Broome Bird Observatory**, see page 323, is also a good budget place to stay.

L Broome Town B&B, 15 Stewart St, T9192 2006, www.broometown.com.au. A centrally located boutique B&B designed and built by the owners. The spacious rooms have been tastefully furnished, all with en suite, a/c and TV. The friendly hosts serve up an excellent breakfast. Massage and spa therapies are also available. Recommended.

L-A Mangrove Resort Hotel, 47 Carnarvon St, T9192 1303, www.mangrovehotel.com.au. A large resort-style hotel occupying the best shoreside location in town. The architecture is unremarkable but the food is very good and the luxury suites are quite striking. The **Tides** restaurant serves up excellent meals and the indoor bar offers a range of cocktails and coffees. Wi-Fi available.

L-A Mercure, 1 Weld St, T9195 5900, www.mercure.com.au. Has a number of newly refurbished spa suites and poolside rooms. There is an Irish bar serving a good pint of the black stuff and hearty Irish style meals, or for those wanting a quieter meal there is a also a restaurant serving Modern Australian dishes. Live music most nights in peak season.

A-B Ocean Lodge, 1 Cable Beach Rd, T9193 7700 or T1800 600603, www.ocean lodge.com.au. Reasonably priced motel with friendly staff and good facilities, which include Wi-Fi, a shaded swimming pool and BBQs. All rooms are en suite, a/c and have kitchenettes.

B Broome Oasis B&B, 544 Broome Rd, T9192 2311. Located 5 km out of town, this homely B&B welcomes children and pets. There is one en suite double room or a 2-bedroom self-contained cottage (minimum 2-nights). Breakfasts served on the veranda, Indonesian breakfast and picnic hampers are available on request. Good value in high season as the owners don't hike the prices.

B Roebuck Bay Hotel, Carnarvon St, T9192 1221, www.roey.com.au. Semi self-contained motel rooms with en suite and a/c, some more spacious than others. Mid-range meals are available at **JC's Kitchen** restaurant. There are also several bars.

B-E Kimberley Klub YHA, Frederick St, T9192 3233 and T1800 004 345, www.kimberley klub.com. A superb large hostel, and very much a party destination. Modern, well-maintained and clean, it centres around a large open-plan games, dining and pool area. Facilities include a licensed bar and cheap café, 24-hr internet access (including Wi-Fi), bike and scooter hire, volleyball and badminton courts and well-equipped kitchen. Beds in spacious 6- and 10-bed dorms, plus a few doubles and a fully self-contained room. Beds are pricey, but include breakfast. Cheap but tasty evening meals are also available. Recommended.

D-F Broome's Last Resort, Bagot St, T9193 5000, www.broomeslastresort.com.au.

Tired and slightly grungy hostel favoured by seasonal workers as the cheapest and most convenient to town. Communal facilities are good, however, and include a pool, a licensed bar and a pleasant outdoor area. Most rooms are a/c except for the cheapest dorms.

Caravan parks
D-E Roebuck Bay Caravan Park, 92 Walcott St, Town Beach, T9192 1366, www.roebuckbaycp.com.au. Has foreshore camping sites and a good number of basic a/c on-site vans. It's next to the **Town Beach Café** (see Eating) and a short walk from a small supermarket.

Cable Beach *p314*
LL Cable Beach Club Resort, 26 Cable Beach Rd, T9192 0400 and T1800 199099, www.cablebeachclub.com. Broome's premier holiday accommodation, an exquisitely designed resort hotel with excellent facilities including large swimming pools, tennis courts, day spa, bars and restaurants. Traditional Broome architecture is complemented by polished wooden floors, Asian furniture and antiques, and endless, lush landscaped gardens. One of the country's few large hotels that manages to feel like a small boutique hideaway.

LL-L Bali Hai Resort & Spa, 6 Murray Rd, T9191 3100, www.balihairesort.com. Spacious, self-contained a/c studios in Balinese style with outdoor showers. Located close to Cable Beach with private BBQs and a pool. There is a spa on site but the atmosphere is so relaxing a massage won't be necessary. Low season tariffs are good value.

L The Frangipani, 15 Millington Rd, T9195 5000, www.thefrangipani.com.au. Self-contained a/c apartments set in lush gardens. There are BBQs, day beds and outdoor showers, and the resort boasts 2 pools. Staff are friendly and helpful.

L Cable Beachside Resort, 2 Murray Rd, T9194 2999, www.cablebeachside.com.au. Fully self-contained, well-equipped units grouped around a central saltwater pool area. Free gas BBQs and undercover parking.

A Coconutz B&B, 12 Denham Rd, T9192 5266, www.coconutz.com.au. A short drive out of Broome, this B&B offers a bush setting and views of Cable Beach. Guests sleep in en suite eco tents, with private open-air kitchen and stone bath. Facilities include a swimming pool. Evening meals are available on request. Recommended.

B-E Beaches of Broome, 4 Sanctuary Rd, T9192 6665, www.beachesofbroome.com.au. A modern backpacker resort very near Cable Beach. The facilities include Wi-Fi, a large communal kitchen and a swimming pool. There is a licensed bar and cheap snack meals are available throughout the day. Accommodation is in dorms (8- down to 3-bed) or attractive en suite doubles. Continental breakfast included. Often has special rates so worth enquiring before booking. Recommended.

D-E Cable Beach Backpackers, 12 Sanctuary Rd, T9193 5511, www.cablebeachback packers.com. A resort-style hostel. Facilities are very good, lots of freebies and cheap deals are thrown in, including a free regular town centre and airport shuttle. Rooms are a/c or fan-cooled and include 4- or 8-bed dorms. Volleyball court, internet access, pool table, licensed bar, bike, surfboard and boogie board hire. The tropical courtyard has a pool, deckchairs and hammocks.

Caravan parks and campsites

A-D Cable Beach Caravan Park, Millington Rd, T9192 2066. Even caravan park sites need to be booked well ahead here in peak season. This caravan park has a large number of grassy campsites, a swimming pool, children's playground, campers' kitchen, BBQs as well as a small on-site shop.

B-D Palm Grove Holiday Resort, 1 Murray Rd, T9192 3336, www.palmgrove.com.au. Located close to Cable Beach, this caravan park has a number of powered and unpowered sites as well as park homes. There is also a pool, free gas BBQs, small on-site shop and Wi-Fi access.

🍴 Eating

Broome p310, map p311
Evening bookings advisable at most restaurants between May and Sep.

♥♥♥-♥♥ Azuki, 15 Napier Terr, T9193 7211. Mon-Fri 1130-1430, Mon-Sat 1800-late. A Japanese restaurant serving both classic and contemporary dishes. Bento boxes and excellent sushi and sashimi are available. Dine-in or takeaway. BYO.

♥♥♥-♥♥ Lustre, corner Short and Carnarvon Sts, T9192 1030. Meals from the extensive menu are available Mon-Sat 1200-late, Sun 0900-2200. This stylish, modern bar and restaurant offers steaks, pizzas and seafood. There is also a wide range of cocktails.

♥♥♥-♥♥ Matso's Broome Brewery, corner Hamersley and Carnarvon Sts, T9193 5811, www.matsosbroomebrewery.com.au. Daily 0700-2100. This pub/restaurant has the best setting in town – a classic breezy Broome house with wrap-around verandas overlooking Roebuck Bay. Imaginative Modern Australian cooking, great service and their own range of coolers and beers to taste, including the very refreshing alcoholic ginger and mango beers. A beer on the veranda in the late afternoon is highly recommended. Beer tasters are available and there's live music during peak season. Their famous curries are available Fri-Tue.

♥♥ Som Thai Kitchen, Napier Terr, T9192 6186. Mon-Sat 1100-1400, daily for dinner 1600-2000. A good range of authentic Thai dishes, also takeaway. Licensed and BYO.

♥♥-♥ Noodlefish, Frederick St, T9192 1697. Daily 1800-2100. Simple outdoor setting but the fresh, modern Asian food is excellent. Menu changes frequently to reflect the best of local fish, seafood and local produce. BYO and cash only.

♥♥-♥ Roebuck Bay Hotel, Carnarvon St, T9192 1221. Daily Oct-Apr 1200-1400, 1800-2200 and May-Sep 1200-1000. The restaurant serves mid-range meals, mainly burgers, grills, salads and pasta. There's a roast on Sun. Cheap counter meals are available at the bar.

¶ **Bluey's Place Fish & Chips**, corner Frederick and Hamersley Sts, T9192 1747. Wed-Mon 1100-1400, 1600-2000. Cash only. Serves probably the best and freshest fish 'n' chips in town.

¶ **Land of Pharaohs**, Paspaley Plaza (shopping centre), T9192 6469. Mon-Sat 1000-2100 and Sun for lunch in peak season. This small oriental restaurant offers a good range of authentic Arabic meals including tasty falafel and kebabs. BYO, takeaways available.

¶ **Wharf**, Port Dr, adjacent to the deep water jetty, T9192 5800. Daily 1100-2200. A no-frills licensed restaurant serving fresh and generous fish, seafood, Asian dishes and salads at a price achieved with paper plates and plastic cutlery. Half-price oysters daily 1400-1700. The smart outdoor tables overlook the deep water jetty and Roebuck Bay.

Cafés

¶ **Dragonfly Café**, corner of Carnarvon and Short Sts, T9192 3222. Open 0700-1700. This place serves the best coffee in Broome and also has an excellent veranda for whiling away the time people watching. Open for lunch and dinner the food is good, there's a wide range to choose from and the portions won't disappoint.

¶ **Kool Spot**, 12 Carnarvon St, T9192 5512. Daily 0730-1600. Casual and stylish café with a few outdoor tables and a good range of meals available. A relaxing spot for lunch or breakfast, with a daily specials board. It also does good cakes and tea and coffee. Service can be a bit slow during the lunchtime rush.

¶ **Shady Lane Café**, Johnny Chi Lane, between Carnarvon St and Dampier Terr, T9192 2060. Mon-Fri 0700-1400, Sat 0800-1300. Funky place popular with locals serving breakfast and fresh wraps, rolls and salads, as well as juices and smoothies from its adjacent juice bar. Outdoor tables are quiet and cool under a profusion of palms and the service is very friendly. Recommended.

¶ **Town Beach Café**, Robinson St, T9193 5585. Tue-Sat 0730-1400, Fri-Sat for dinner 1730-late. Another local favourite, this laid-back, unpretentious café is equally at home serving you a pancake and smoothie for breakfast or a superb fish supper. All the tables are out front, covered by sailcloth and overlooking the beach. BYO. Live music on Fri nights during peak season. Recommended.

Cable Beach p314

₮₮₮-₮ **The Old Zoo Café**, 2 Challenor Dr, T9193 6200, www.zoocafe.com.au. Meals 0700-2200 (closed Mon, Oct-Mar). The most intimate of Cable's eateries with an open dining room and small deck overlooking its modest surrounding gardens and ponds. Excellent juices, smoothies, breakfasts and light lunches by day, the expensive evening menu offers inventive takes on traditional Australian themes. Licensed, all the wines are available by the glass.

₮₮₮-₮ **Zanders**, Cable Beach Rd, T9193 5090, www.zanders.com.au. Open 0800-late. This is all about the view, sit in the restaurant or outside the takeaway kiosk and admire the sea. Open for breakfast, lunch and dinner, the food doesn't quite live up to expectation but there's a selection of pizzas and seafood on offer.

₮₮-₮ **Sunset Bar & Café**, at the Cable Beach Resort, T9192 0471, www.cablebeachclub. com. Daily 0630-1000, 1600-late. Offers a range of breakfasts and more expensive evening meals. This is the perfect spot to watch the sun sink into the ocean, but you'll need to arrive early in peak season. The light meals don't embarrass the resort's high standards and are very good value. The resort's other eatery, **Club Restaurant**, T9192 0400, is open daily from 1800.

¶ **Divers Tavern**, 12 Cable Beach Rd, T9193 6066, www.diverstavern.com.au. The pub is open Mon-Sat 1000-2400, Sun to 2200. Large and open plan, this is the best of the town's true Aussie pubs with local cover bands every Fri and Sun, and more frequently during the

peak season. Good hearty meals, including excellent steaks, are served 1200-2130.
Zeebar, 8 Sanctuary Rd, T9193 6511, www.zeebar.com.au. Daily 1200-2400, food 1200-2130. Decorated in sophisticated muted tones, this is the place in Cable Beach to enjoy tapas and live music. If you don't want to spend a sunny afternoon in the shady confines then there are outdoor tables available. The small plates include such dishes as spicy kangaroo and salt and pepper crocodile, but for those with more of an appetite there are large mains and also desserts.

☺ Entertainment

Broome *p310, map p311*
Cinema
Sun Pictures, Carnarvon St, T9192 3738, www.sunpictures.com.au. One of the oldest original picture houses in the world. Built in 1916, the screen is outdoors and most of the deckchair seats are out under the stars. It shows a small selection of current movies on most days ($16.50).

☺ Festivals and events

Broome *p310, map p311*
Apr-Jun The **Broome Arts and Music Festival** presents a variety of exhibitions, live acts and performances.
Aug The **Festival of the Pearl**, known as Shinju Matsuri, is celebrated for a week. This is when you'll see Broome's multicultural community out in force. Events include parades, dragon boat racing and the Shinju Ball. A detailed programme of events can be obtained from the VIC in the weeks preceding the festival.
Aug Opera Under the Stars. One night of opera performed in the amphitheatre near Cable Beach. Book early. A fully licensed bar is available and dinner hampers can be pre-ordered.

O Shopping

Broome *p310, map p311*
Art galleries
There are a number of contemporary and Aboriginal art galleries in Broome. These are interesting for a browse and the majority of the works are for sale.

Books
Kimberley Bookshop, 4 Napier Terr, T9192 1944, www.kimberleybookshop.com.au. Mon-Fri 0900-1700, Sat 1000-1400. Excellent range of new books, especially on Aboriginal culture and Broome history.
Magabala Bookshop, 1 Bagot St, opposite the VIC, T9192 1991, www.magabala.com. Mon-Fri 0900-1630. Australia's oldest independent Aboriginal publishing house, their bookshop offers a wide variety of titles including biography, fiction and children's literature.
Woody's Book Exchange, T9192 8999, Johnny Chi Lane. Mon-Thu 0900-1600, Fri 0900-1630, Sat 0930-1400. A good spot for secondhand or exchange books.

Markets
The **Courthouse Markets** run Sat-Sun 0800-1300, and are a good place to browse for cheaper pearls and souvenirs. Food is available if you've rushed out without breakfast. There is also a **night market** during Staircase to the Moon.

Outdoor
Kimberley Camping Hire, T9192 5282, www.kimberleycampinghire.com. An excellent range of gear. Much essential kit is available for hire, and they make up value hire packs for camping and 4WD expeditions.

Pearls and jewellery
There are half a dozen exclusive pearl boutiques on Dampier Terr. Prices start at $500 and head for the moon.
Deep Sea Moonlight Pearls, corner Johnny Chi Lane and Dampier Terr, T9193 7300. Has some slightly more modern designs.

Linneys, 25 Dampier Terr, T9192 2430, www.linneys.com. Sells fine traditional pearls and the business is owned by a local family.
Paspaley Pearls, 2 Short St, T9192 2203, www.paspaleypearls.com. Very welcoming, professional. An informative video can be played on request.

Shopping centres
Boulevard, Frederick St. This is essentially a **Woolworths** supermarket and a **Target**, with a number of cafés and clothes shops.
Paspaley, Chinatown. **Coles** supermarket (daily 0700-2100), and several other retailers including the chemist and several clothes stores.

▲ Activities and tours

Broome p310, map p311
4WD and bus
Aussie Off Road Tours, T9192 3617, www.aussieoffroadtours.com.au. Brad Bayfield runs 1- to 3-day tours in the Kimberley. All meals are home-made and included.
Chomley Tours, T9192 6195, www.horner.net.au/chomleystours. 1- to 4-day tours in the Dampier Peninsula. Also offers a Peal Farm Trip, which visits the Cygnet Bay Pearl Farm, 200 km north of Broome.
Kimberley Wild, T9193 7778, www.kimberleywild.com. Offers a variety of 2- to 4-day tours within the national park, as well as longer tours further afield. Accommodation and all meals are included. Also run 2½-hr and ½-day Broome tours, exploring its history and heritage.
Pinnacle Tours, T9192 8080, www.pinnacletours.com.au. This outfit heads out on day and night 4WD trips to the Dampier Peninsula, as well as offering 1-day trips for those with less time.

Aerial tours
For flights over the **Kimberley**, see also 'Routes east', page 325. Flights and tours over

and into the Kimberley are usually better value from Derby. A flight over the Kimberley and its offshore islands is visual adventure of the highest order, especially if you can't afford the time or money to take a boat cruise around the coast. Check whether the operator has high-winged aircraft and whether window seats are standard.
Broome Aviation, T9192 1369, www.broomeaviation.com. Flies around the Broome peninsula and Willie Creek (25 mins, $190). Also offers various 4-hr flights and longer, Apr-Nov.
Horizontal Falls Adventure Tours, T9192 2885, www.horizontalfalls.com.au. The a/c seaplane departs daily from Broome to explore Talbot Bay, the Buccaneer Archipelago and Cape Leveque. Whale-watching and customized tours are also available.
King Leopold Air, T9193 7155, www.kingleopoldair.com.au. 25-min flights over Broome's beaches and Roebuck Bay for $140. Also a variety of flights over the western Kimberley and the Bungle Bungles via Windjana Gorge, plus a connection to Cockatoo Island. Also flies from Derby.
Trike Flights, T9193 5697 and T0407 010772. Take budding pilots up in their micro-light trikes for a mini-lesson and aerial sightseeing. A 30-min flight at sunset or sunrise is $185, 1 hr for $245.

Boat/sailing trips
Broome Kayak Adventures, T1300 665888, www.broomeadventure.com.au. 3-hr kayak trips in and around Turtle Bay.
Broome Lugger, T9192 7321, www.broomelugger.com. Runs cruises on a wooden pearling lugger. Trips include champagne breakfast ($105, child $85) or gourmet sunset dinner ($129, child $105), from Apr-Oct.
Spirit of Broome, T9193 5025, www.broomehovercraft.com.au. Historic, scenic and sunset tours by hovercraft. Cost between $105-150.
Willie Pearl Lugger Cruises, T0428 919781, www.williecruises.com.au. Sunset and

afternoon 'boom net' cruises (both $120, children $60). Whale-watching and dolphin cruises in season.

Camel safari

Broome Camel Safaris, T0419 916101, www.broomecamelsafaris.com.au. Offers 1-hr sunset rides for $65, children $45, and 30-min rides at others times for $25. Mon-Sat.
Cable Beach Camel Safaris, T9192 3999. Camel rides from $30-45, children $20-30.
Red Sun Camels, T9193 7423 or T1800 184488. Offers 1-hr sunset rides for $60, children $40, and 30- to 40-min rides at others times for $25-30, children $20-25.
Ships of the Desert, T0419 954022, www.shipsofthedesert.com.au. Morning, sunset and twilight rides, 1 hr, $20-60, children $15-40.

Coastal cruises

A handful of companies offer 1- to 2-week cruises around the Kimberley coast, usually from Broome to Wyndham or the reverse, from Apr-Sep. This coast is a riot of deep red rock headlands and islands, wide tree-lined estuaries, crystal blue waters and beautiful beaches. Cruises usually put a premium on exploring this as much as possible, seeking out the wildlife, including the big 'saltie' crocodiles, looking at ancient Aboriginal rock art and eating freshly caught fish and molluscs. Some have their own on-board helicopters so that passengers get to see some of the Kimberley interior as well. These incredible trips cost about $10,000 or more. There are a couple of shorter duration cruises from Derby from around $1500 for 3 nights. Operators include:
Buccaneer Sea Safaris, T9191 1991, www.buccaneerseasafaris.com.
Kimberley Discovery Cruises, T1800 185960, www.kimberleydiscovery.com.au.
The Great Escape, T9193 5983, www.greatescape.net.au.
Kimberley Cruises, T9527 3630 and T1800 677830, www.kimberleycruises.com, probably has the widest range of tours.

Crab racing

On Sun nights during the winter peak season, head down to the **Beer & Satay Hut** at Town Beach for crab racing. The action starts at 1800, as under the watchful eye of the Crab Master numbers are picked from a hat and lucky punters choose their competing crab.

Diving

The Great Escape Charter Company, 15 Dampier Terr, T9193 5983. Unforgettable 5-, 7- and 10-night dive trips to the Rowley Shoals, from $4120 for 5 nights.
Workline Dive & Tackle, corner Frederick and Hamersley Sts, T9192 2233 and T0415 472 848. Local trips off Gantheaume Point, but only once a fortnight when the tide is very low. Also hires out gear, runs PADI courses and a number of dives around the Rowley Shoals, 3 coral atolls 260 km northwest of Broome that are considered one of the very best, and most pristine diving sites in the world. The season for the shoals is generally May-Oct. Trips out are a minimum 5 nights and cost around $500-800 per day. Can also give advice on fishing.

Fishing

For information on local fishing and any bait or gear, visit **Tackle World**, 33 Carnarvon St, T9192 1669, www.tackleworld.com.au. There are a number of fishing charters running from Broome.
Kimberley Kayak Fishing, T9192 2285, www.kimberleykayakfishing.com.au. Battle a barramundi from a kayak. Fishing trips from $77 for 2 hrs.
Sentosa, T9192 8163, www.sentosa charters.com. Offers full-day fishing trips from $235. Bait, gear, refreshments and lunch provided. Also offers whale-watching tours in season.

Skydiving

Skydive Broome, T0417 011 000, www.skydivebroome.com.au. Offers daily jumps over Cable Beach from sunrise to sunset. Tandem jumps start at $275.

Swimming

Broome Recreation and Aquatic Centre, Cable Beach Rd, T9193 7677. Leisure pool and 25-m saltwater pool.

Tour operators

Astro Tours, T0417 949958, www.astrotours.net. Heads about 10 km out of Broome once or twice an evening up to 4 nights a week (Fri-Sat at 1800, Mon and Wed at 2000) between Apr-Oct. Its guided 2-hr tour of the night sky is both animated and fascinating, one of the country's very best, and 8 telescopes means plenty of viewing time, $75.

Broome Top Deck Tour, T1800 858985, and T0427 850559. Runs 2-hr bus tours around town. Pick-ups from the VIC or can be arranged from accommodation. $50, children $15, concessions $45. Book in advance.

Broome Town Tour, T9192 5041, www.broomesightseeingtours.com. Interesting look at Broome's history and main sights (4 hrs, $90, children $70). Mon-Sat 0800 and 1415.

Broome Trike Tours, T0407 575237, www.broometriketours.com.au. A range of tours, including one that takes people out on a 3-seater Harley Trike for a 1½-hr tour around Broome and the peninsula. There are 6 passenger limo trikes available as well.

Kujurta Buru Aboriginal Cultural Tours, 640 Dora St, T9192 1662, www.kujurta buru.com.au. Broome through Aboriginal eyes – tours can include bush tucker, bush medicines, weapon throwing, learning about hunting techniques and traditional foods. Half-day (3-hr) tours depart Mon-Fri at 0900 and cost $77, children $38.50.

Sun Pictures, Carnarvon St, T9192 3738, www.sunpictures.com.au. The old, outdoor cinema runs 15-min history tours ($5) Mon-Fri 1030 and 1300. See also page 318.

☺ Transport

Broome *p310, map p311*

Air

Qantas has a daily service to **Perth**. Air North flies daily to **Kununurra** and **Darwin**. Skywest, T1300 660 088, flies to **Perth**, as does Virgin Blue.

Bicycle/scooter

Broome Broome, Hamersley St, T9192 2210. Hires out a range of scooters from $35 a day. **Broome Cycles**, 2 Hamersley St, T9192 1871 (also at Cable Beach). Bike hire from $24 day. Mon-Fri 0830-1700, Sat 0830-1400 and during May-Oct Sun 1000-1400.

Topless Rentals, 25 Hunter St, T9193 5017, www.toplessrentals.com.au. Rents scooters, cars and 4WD vehicles.

Bus

Many 4WD tours heading east are one-way trips that will get you to **Kununurra** or **Darwin** but if money or time is tight there is a daily **Greyhound** service to **Derby**, **Kununurra** (14 hrs) and **Darwin** (26 hrs) departing Broome at 1815. The **Perth** service leaves the VIC Tue, Thu and Sat at 0700. Backpacker buses **Easyrider**, T9385 6867, www.easyridertours.com.au, has an 11-day tour from Broome to **Perth**. Western Xposure, T9414 8423, www.westernxposure.com.au, runs several trips, some 4WD, to **Darwin** and **Perth** (via Exmouth or Karijini), and also a tour along the Gibb River Rd and to the Bungle Bungles. See also Activities and tours, above.

Car

Broome Broome, T9192 2210. Has a good range from 3-door hatchbacks to Land Cruisers from $68 to $153 per day. If you're going to do a bit of distance check out **Just Broome**, T9192 6636, www.justbroomecarhire.com.au, which has more free kilometres and cheaper per kilometre excess than most companies (hire costs from $48 a day). **Willie Creek**, T9192 3311, www.williecreekpearls.com.au, is good for small 4WDs.

Car servicing from **Minishull**, Guy St, opposite Shell House, T9192 1168.

Taxi

Call T9192 1133 or **Chinatown Taxis**, T9192 3316, T1800 811772.

⊕ Directory

Broome *p310, map p311*
Banks The major bank branches are in Chinatown, on Canarvon St. **Internet** Broome Community Resource Centre, 40 Dampier Terr, T9193 7153. Mon-Fri 0900-1700, sat 0900-1200. **Galactica DMZ Internet Café**, 2 Hamersley St, behind McDonalds, T9192 5897, cheap internet access and Wi-Fi available for those with laptops. Daily 0800-2000. **Laundry** Broome Laundromat, Paspaley Shopping Centre, daily 0700-2000. **Medical services** Chemists: Chinatown Pharmacy, Paspaley Shopping Centre, Canarvon St, T9192 1399, Mon-Fri 0830-1730, Sat to 1400, Sun 0900-1300. Hospital: Broome District, Robinson St, T9192 9222. **Police** Hamersley St, T9192 0200. **Post** Canarvon St, T9192 1020, Mon-Fri 0900-1700. **Useful contacts** DEC, 111 Herbert St, T9195 5500. Cyclone Information, T1300 659 210. Road Conditions, T138138, www.mainroads.wa.gov.au. Sea Search and Rescue, T9192 8202.

Around Broome

Willie Creek Pearl Farm

① T9192 0000, www.williecreekpearls.com.au, half-day tours $90, children $45, including 37-km transfer from Broome, or $50, children $25, self-drive to Willie Creek (4WD recommended). Special tickets that include entrance to Pearl Luggers on Dampier St are also available.

Strangely for these parts, Willie Creek is actually bigger than it sounds. This wide tidal inlet at the bottom of the Dampier Peninsula is the only Broome pearl farm that receives visitors. In fact it is a demonstration farm. The real business of pearl growing is carried out in a remote coastal spot further north because of security. Unfortunately, thousand dollar pearl oysters can't be left sitting in a public waterway, even if it is crocodile infested. Nevertheless, Willie Creek is a fascinating place to visit as the daily tours explain every aspect of the cultured-pearl industry, including a demonstration of the seeding technique in a fresh oyster. A quick boat trip enables visitors to see how the oysters are suspended in the creek and the tour ends with a look at the finished product in the showroom. They also offer scenic flights over the farm and beaches from $60 per person. The café serves light lunches and cakes.

Broome Bird Observatory

① T9193 5600, www.broomebirdobservatory.com, $5, children free, bookings essential for tours and accommodation.

On the edge of Roebuck Bay, 25 km from Broome, on the highway opposite the Cape Leveque turn-off, this observatory is one of the best places in Australia to see migratory shorebirds. It was established as a research and education facility in 1998 and has counted over 300 bird species in the area since. The sight of thousands of migrating birds departing in April and returning in September and October is magnificent. Regular two-hour tours are held that explore the mangroves or bush and may include seeing the migrations, depending on the time of year ($115 from Broome, self-drive $70). There is also a one-hour introductory walk for $15 and a full-day lake tour ($175 from Broome, self-drive $130, BYO lunch). The Observatory is also a peaceful place to stay. Accommodation includes self-contained chalets (**B**), double, single and bunk rooms (**D-E**) and unpowered bush campsites. Return transfers from Broome for guests staying a minimum of two nights costs around $54 per person return. Twitchers should contact the observatory for details of current workshops and field trips.

Dampier Peninsula → *Colour map 6, B3.*

The Dampier Peninsula forms a large triangle north of Broome, reaching east almost as far as Derby. It is a huge area and most of it is Aboriginal land, home to several Aboriginal communities, of about six different language groups. Access is limited but some communities offer tours and accommodation, an excellent way to spend time with Aboriginal people and see the peninsula. The land is entirely covered in long grass and spindly trees but the coastline continues Broome's spectacular blend of red cliffs, white beaches and chalky blue sea. Just one dirt road traverses the peninsula from Broome to its tip at Cape Leveque (220 km) and it's a shocker. Corrugations, sand, rocks and pools of water make this a road for high-clearance 4WD vehicles only (usually closed in wet season).

The Kimberley

Broome lies at the very western edge of the Kimberley, an area larger than Germany with a population of 30,000. It's a wild and rugged region of gorges and waterfalls, cattle stations and diamond mines, spectacular coastline and ancient Aboriginal art. The Kimberley is part of Australia's tropical north with a summer monsoon that throws a green cloak over the grassy plains and scrub covered ranges, and turns the rivers into powerful torrents. During the dry season the rivers shrink to a series of pools, waterfalls slow to a trickle and heat and humidity drop to a comfortable level. There are only three major roads in the Kimberley and just one of them is sealed, the Great Northern Highway from Broome to Kununurra. Kununurra, on the eastern edge of the state, is surrounded by typically beautiful Kimberley range country and fertile land fed by the Ord River. The Gibb River Road connects the same towns and provides access to some of the region's most beautiful gorges in cattle station country but this is a challenging dirt route. Within the Kimberley are places so remote that you can only see them by boat, plane or 4WD, such as the extraordinary western coast, Mitchell Plateau, Buccaneer Archipelago and beehive domes of the Bungle Bungle range.

The first turn-off, shortly after leaving the sealed road, leads to the **Willie Creek Pearl Farm**, see page 323. The next is the very scenic **Manari Road** (4WD), which follows the coast for about 50 km. This leads to a series of beaches, creeks and cliffs, where you can explore, fish and camp though there are no facilities.

Following the Cape Leveque road for about an hour, the next stop is **Beagle Bay community** ① *call into the office when entering the community, T9192 4913, gold coin donation*. Aboriginal people of the Dampier Peninsula were pursued in the 1860s and 1870s by 'blackbirders' who captured them to work as pearl divers, but by the 1890s Europeans were after their souls. French trappists and German Pallottine monks arrived to found mission settlements and their legacy survives in the unusual church at Beagle Bay. The Sacred Heart Church was built in 1917 and is notable for its altar, walls and floor lined with pearl shell. Fuel is sometimes available, but there's no accommodation.

After leaving Beagle Bay, it is 28 km to the turn-off for **Middle Lagoon** ① *T9192 4002, day visitors $10 per car*, then another 33 km to reach this beautiful and peaceful sandy cove where you can swim and snorkel. Accommodation is available in beach shelters (**D**), self-contained cabins (**A-B**) or campsites. There is no fuel or supplies but ice and drinks are available.

Continuing north for about 50 km, you'll reach the Aboriginal community of **Lombadina** ① *T9192 4936, day visitors $10 car, payable at office or craft shop*. This is also a former mission settlement and many of the 60 people who live here are still Catholic. Visitors can look at the lovely timber church with bark roof and buy local work from the craft shop. The picturesque settlement clusters around neat lawns, mango trees and ghost gums. The Bard people offer the best range of accommodation and tours, including fishing and whale-watching charters (from $220 per person, June-September), tours such as mud crabbing and bush walking ($35-66 per half day) and 4WD day tours departing at 0730 ($99, lunch included). Accommodation is available in four-bed backpacker dorms (**C-D**) and self-contained 2-bedroom units (**A-B**). Fresh bread is baked in an old wood-fired oven three days a week. There are no transfers from Broome, but **Kujurta Buru**, see page 321, runs the Dampier

Peninsula Transfer Service which travels between Broome and the major communities. Refer to their website for a list of destinations, departure days and prices.

Cape Leveque lies at the end of the road, capped by red cliffs, rocky coves and white beaches. **Kooljaman** ① *T9192 4970, www.kooljaman.com.au,* is a popular resort at the cape, owned by the Djarindjin and One Arm Point communities but usually run by non-Aboriginal managers. Accommodation is in beach shelters (**D**), units (**C**), open paperbark cabins (**B**) and safari tents (**A**). Tent sites are also available (with limited power facilities). Although it's very busy here in high season it still feels wild and isolated, helped by the Robinson Crusoe-style huts. Facilities include a kiosk, restaurant (BYO alcohol), scenic flights and boat tours, but most people just come to swim, walk, fish and relax. There is another community, **One Arm Point**, on the eastern side of the peninsula but they do not encourage visitors. Just south of this community is **Mudnunn community** ① *T9192 4121,* who allow unpowered camping and sometimes run mud-crabbing tours in the mangroves ($55), which can be a memorable experience.

Routes east

From Broome the Great Northern Highway heads east across the foot of the Dampier Peninsula and then forks, giving the traveller a choice of two very different routes to the Northern Territory. The northerly fork heads up to Derby and the Gibb River Road, while directly east the Great Northern Highway curls around the bulk of the Kimberley, skirting the deserts to the south.

Derby → *Colour map 6, B3. 220 km from Broome.*

① *T9191 1426, www.derbytourism.com.au,* sits on a narrow spur of land surrounded by tidal mud flats, close to where the mighty Fitzroy River flows into King Sound. Although the town has few attractions for visitors, its position at the start of the Gibb River Road and close to the spectacular Kimberley coast means that tours and cruises from Derby are very good value.

Great Northern Highway

This long run between Derby and Kununurra is split into two very different scenic sections. The first 550 km to Halls Creek are frankly pretty tedious and have little to distract the traveller other than impressive **Geike Gorge** near Fitzroy Crossing, 260 km along the way. After a couple of hours or so spent at the Gorge, **Halls Creek** is a popular stopover and offers a small but broad range of options. The resort-style **Kimberley Hotel** ① *9 Roberta Av, T9168 6101 and T1800 355 228, www.kimberleyhotel.com.au,*(**A-C**), has standard and large motel-style rooms. Facilities include a cocktail bar, à la carte restaurant, swimming pool, laundry and in-house movies. **Halls Creek Motel** ① *main highway, T9168 9600, www.hallscreek.bestwestern.com.au,* (**A-B**), is a Best Western that has similar rooms to the **Kimberley**. Its budget rooms are well-equipped and available as twins or good-value singles. The **caravan park** ① *4 Roberta Av, T9168 6169,* has a few powered and unpowered sites.

The 365 km between Halls Creek and Kununurra has far more striking scenery than that of the Gibb River Road; indeed it is one of the most scenic bits of road in the whole country, and it also gives you a chance to see the magnificent **Purnululu National Park** (the **Bungle Bungles**). Helicopter flights over the Bungles are run by Slingair ① *T9169 1300, www.slingair.com.au, 30 mins, $295.*

Kununurra ① *510 km from Katherine, T9168 1177, www.kununurratourism.com*, is WA's northeastern outpost. Surrounded by range country and the bountiful waters of the Ord River, Kununurra has the most picturesque setting of any town in the Kimberley, and makes an excellent base for the adventurer's playground of the East Kimberley. The **Kununurra Hotel** ① *37 Messmate Way, T9168 0400 and T1800 450 993, www.hotel kununurra.com.au*, (**B**), has various air-conditioned rooms, a pool, laundry facilities, an on-site restaurant and bar. From the town 4WD, flight, canoe and boat tours head out to sights as diverse as the Ord River, Lake Argyle, the Argyle Diamond Mine, The Bungles, El Questro Wilderness Park and Wyndham.

Gibb River Road → *Colour map 6, B4/5.*

This legendary unsealed Kimberley road is both an experience and a challenge. It was created in the 1960s as a way for the cattle stations of this region to get their stock to Derby and Wyndham ports. Although now used more frequently by travellers, the alarming sight of a huge cattle road train barrelling along in clouds of dust is still common. The Gibb River Road traverses about 660 km between Derby and Kununurra (about 250 km shorter than the highway route, but it takes much longer because of the condition of the road) and passes through remote range country and grass plains, threaded with creeks, gorges and waterfalls. Part of the Gibb River Road experience is also staying at the cattle stations along the way, meeting their owners and perhaps taking a tour or scenic flight to explore privately owned landscapes seen by few. There are also good campsites close to several beautiful gorges, where you can go for a walk or swim. Remember this is a rugged road though, and travelling it is less than comfortable. Dusty and bone-jarring conditions means a 4WD is recommended and you should allow at least four days. If you don't have your own vehicle there are plenty of operators offering adventure tours (see Broome, page 319, for a couple of options).

Road conditions vary along the route, during the season and from year to year so it is essential to check current conditions before setting out with **Main Roads WA** ① *T138 138, www.mainroads.wa.gov.au*. Generally the road is only passable in the dry (May-November) and the eastern section is much rougher and more corrugated than the western section. Although you can sometimes travel the road in a 2WD, it is very rough and stony, there are many creek crossings, and many of the stations and gorges off the road are found at the end of even rougher tracks. Finally, the Pentecost River crossing at the eastern end is long and hazardous, and unless the river is dry or extremely low 2WD vehicles will not have the clearance to cross it. Vehicles need to be in excellent condition and you'll need to carry extra fuel, water and spare wheels. For more information see the *Gibb River and Kalumburu Roads Travellers Guide* ($5), produced every year by the Derby Tourist Bureau, which lists current facilities. Available from Derby and Broome VICs, it can also be ordered by phone. If the worst happens, for road rescue from Derby call T9193 1205, or from Kununurra T9169 1556. The website www.exploroz.com has some good information, tips and travellers' comments.

Contents

Background

History

The arrival of man

Meganesia, the then-joined landmass of Australia and New Guinea, was undoubtedly the first landmass to be reached by humans using boats. From their evolution in Africa *Homo erectus*, and then *Homo sapiens*, walked into Asia but the latter's expansion from these strongholds to the 'new worlds' was barred by either water or ice for hundreds of thousands of years. It is true that parts of New Guinea and northwest Australia are tantalizingly close to the islands of southeast Asia, but even during the severest of ice ages there have always been deep channels between them: it has never been possible to walk from Asia to Meganesia.

The Aboriginal ancestors' certain passage by boat is one of three relatively new pieces of key information that have jarred the traditional picture of Aboriginal history. The second is when this happened. There are no dates, not even any folk memories of the first coming of humanity to Meganesia, and that's probably because the time of first migration has been pushed back by slowly accumulating evidence to over 45,000 and possibly as much as 60,000 years ago. Finally it is also now certain that Australian Aboriginals and the original New Guineans are one and the same people, separated by just a few thousand years of cultural divergence, and New Guineans were amongst the earliest and most intensive farmers on the planet.

There is little doubt that the peoples who finally crossed from Asia to Meganesia around 55,000 years ago carried with them one of the most, if not the most, technologically advanced cultures of the time. That they already had a grasp of the potential of agriculture seems likely, as some of those that settled in the northern highlands, later to become isolated as the island of New Guinea, had developed intensive farming systems by as much as 10,000 years ago. Population expansion amongst the early settlers in the new fertile New Guinean lands would have been exponential, and it cannot have been long before groups were heading south in search of new land. It is quite possible that people had reached the very southern tip of WA within a 1000 years of their ancestors reaching the northern coasts.

The early Aborigines carried with them a notable firepower. Stone, bone and wooden weapons honed to perfection during the many generations of island-hopping from Asia. These hunter-gatherers had encountered, for the first time in human history, lands where they were the undisputed top predator. One of their new weapons would have been psychological, a new feeling of unbridled power, a sense of their own dominance. The Australian animals they met would have been woefully ill-prepared for such an encounter.

The few, relatively small mammalian predators could not hope to compete with such a powerful new force, either in direct confrontation or for prey as the human population increased. As for the giant reptiles, the awesome *megalania* (imagine a komodo dragon weighing in at about a tonne) and the giant snake *wonambi* (6 m long with a head the size of a serving tray) were ambush predators, strictly territorial. They would have been a serious hazard to the lone hunter, but in the face of collective competition were as doomed as their mammalian counterparts. The only large Australian predator to survive to the present day is the saltwater crocodile, the feared 'saltie', probably protected by its primarily aquatic habitat. As for the herbivores, the now-vanished giants of the vast Australian plains, there can surely be little doubt that the coming of humanity was the decisive factor in the extinction of so many.

An ecological crisis?

Evidence is also mounting that the coming of humanity had an extraordinarily profound effect on Australian flora. First indirectly and then, in the face of calamity, purposefully. Core samples from around Australia, but particularly in the east, seem to indicate that the now dominant eucalypts were surprisingly rare prior to around 60,000 years ago. These cores also sometimes show high concentrations of carbon – ash – at the point at which the gums began their ascendancy. Could this be another climate-driven coincidence? Again, some researchers think not.

A powerful, and frightening scenario may well have followed the local demise of the large grazers. With very little to eat it the forest undergrowth and plains brush would have proliferated, in wet times an impenetrable green morass, in the dry a huge store of kindling. Forest fires are natural, lightening-ignited phenomena on every continent, and especially common in hot, dry Australia. Massive build-ups of combustible fuel would have resulted in equally massive, and quite catastrophic forest and bushfires, deadly to the native flora and fauna, and humans alike.

In the face of this crisis the early peoples of Australia would have realized they had to keep the brush low artificially. They would have been forced to fight fire with fire, continuously lighting small scale blazes to prevent large-scale conflagrations. Whatever the cause, the adoption of fire for more than just cooking, heating and protection was to have many and widespread consequences.

Most important for the pioneering Australians was the realization that fire could have multiple uses. Not only did it prevent large-scale, life-threatening bushfires, but it was also discovered that controlled blazes had a multiplicity of uses. They could be used for offence or defence against antagonistic neighbours, or to signal distant groups or relations. They could also be used to drive and herd game to favoured trapping areas, and burn-offs encouraged new growth with many of the succulent shoots favoured by many of the Aboriginals' prey. It would also not have been lost on them how much more easily they could navigate, travel and hunt.

A more-or-less constant regime of small-scale bushfires had other less useful consequences. Crucially for the future development of Australian flora, it naturally favoured fire-resistant and fire-promoting species. Foremost amongst these are the eucalypts, the ubiquitous gum trees that once were minor players in the ecology of the continent, but are now almost all-pervading. Dry and wet rainforests have been driven back to relatively tiny refuges around Australia's eastern periphery, while the great gum woodlands have marched on triumphantly.

The Catch-22 of the Aboriginal fire-regime may have helped to lock Australia yet further into another ecological cul-de-sac. The total number of animals a landmass can support, its faunal biomass, depends on a number of factors. Two of these Australia already had a paucity of: water and nutrients. The fire regime would have accelerated erosion, further depleting soil nutrient levels, and would also have significantly lowered the amount of water and nutrients locked up within the plants themselves. Most obviously of all, the potential number of animals is crucially constrained by the sheer biomass of plant material available for feed. With much of this being continually burned off, the amount of prey available to both humans and their competitors would have had a much reduced upper limit.

Partnership with the land

The early pioneers into each part of the continent would have had a relatively easy time of it, but once the honeymoon was over the challenges that faced the first Australians were immense. The extinction of the large herbivores and the bushfire crisis were huge blows to an already very specialized, and hence vulnerable ecology. Without human intervention, massive bushfires could have decreased the viability of many other animal species. As it was, the introduction of the fire regime seems to have stabilized the situation and prevented further degradation of the environment. It was a fix, but a fix that stood the test of time.

As well as coping with a damaged environment and a much reduced quantity of game, most Aboriginal peoples faced challenges rarely faced by humanity. Paramount amongst these was the scarcity and unpredictably of water supply, and the consequent boom-and-bust fluctuations of many of the species of animals hunted for food. Almost against logic this actually seems to have resulted in a better standard of diet than that experienced by many peoples in more stable environments.

That they did so has two chief causes. The relative scarcity of food resulted in the early Australians becoming experts in everything that could possibly have nutritional value, from plant roots to kangaroos, and moths to mussels. In most parts of the continent people could draw on a variety of in-season fruits and animals, more than sufficient to sustain them. In the process they also discovered an extensive natural medicine chest that helped keep them healthy. That this natural larder was not over-stretched is paradoxically because of the boom-and-bust ecology. In many environments the really bad times are rare. Humans, though slow breeders, can build populations that make the most of relatively long periods of prosperity. The ENSO (El Niño Southern Oscillation) driven Australian climate dictated the reverse pattern, with Aboriginal populations kept at the low levels possible in the periods of drought. In times of plenty there was more than enough to go around.

This pegging of population and resultant 'abundance' of food is perhaps one of the reasons why farming was rarely employed by Aboriginal peoples, even though the seeds of agriculture were probably in their cultural baggage. ENSO also makes farming extremely difficult, with attempts at planting crops frequently foiled by drought conditions, but one of the key factors that mitigated against Aboriginal agriculture was the lack of suitable species. It is now becoming accepted that under the experimental conditions of our early ancestors only a handful of plants and animals would have had exactly the right characteristics for domestication. In Australia all the large herbivores that may have been suitable quickly disappeared and to this day only one indigenous crop has been cultivated to any extent by Europeans: the macadamia nut. The unrelated factors of no domesticated animals and continental isolation were to later combine to make the Aboriginals horrifically susceptible to European diseases.

As is now widely appreciated, it is agriculture that has eventually provided any human culture with the excess labour required to build the urban trappings of civilization. Leading a nomadic or semi nomadic, hunter-gatherer lifestyle with little incentive or opportunity for farming, the Australian peoples rarely created permanent settlements. Over most of the continent not even clothes, let alone buildings, were required for warmth. Buildings were also unnecessary for either safety, keeping animals or the storage of foodstuffs. Only in the colder south were some of these trappings adopted. Here some peoples sewed together blankets and clothes from skins and embarked on intensive aquaculture, building sophisticated canals and traps to catch fish and eels.

With strong parallels with the peoples in North America, the Aboriginal peoples came to place a great value on their relationship with the land. Disturbances to their environment, or deviation from the fire regime (sometimes called 'fire-stick farming'), were recognized as threats to survival, and this relationship came to be regarded as a sacred stewardship. Nomadic peoples rarely develop the concept of land ownership, but the peoples of Australia did maintain strict 'territories', each carefully tended and managed by its resident people. Embarking on a journey through another people's land involved careful negotiation, but even so this was not a rare event.

In environments as difficult as most that Australia has to offer, isolation can be lethal. Regional contact was maintained through constant trading, mostly for ochre or precious materials used in the making of jewellery. These were mined in a large number of sites across Australia. There were also great regional meetings, social *corroborees* that usually coincided with an abundant, seasonal food source. Over tens of thousands of years this helped maintain a remarkable consistency of culture across such a vast area.

Given such a prodigious tenure it is hardly surprising that a folk memory of their ancestors' coming to Australia has been lost. Aboriginal history is passed from generation to generation in the form of oral stories, part of the all-pervasive culture of 'dreaming' that also encompasses law, religion, customs and knowledge. These stories talk of a period when powerful ancestors, both human and animal, strode the land, creating natural features, plants, animals and peoples alike. Parts of the dreaming were also immortalized, and illustrated to younger generations through songs and dances, rock art and carvings. It is probable that Australia now has the oldest such art on the planet.

Aboriginal culture is the longest uninterrupted culture the modern world has witnessed. Over tens of thousands of years the first peoples of Australia developed unique strategies to ensure their survival in the face of some of the world's most difficult environments. They built a rich cultural heritage, a phenomenal knowledge of their land and its natural resources, prodigious internal trade routes, a carefully managed environment, and a stable population in harmony with that environment rather than stressing it.

Early European exploration

On the far side of the world, European trading interest in Asia matured in the 15th and 16th centuries, and at last brought Europeans into contact with the only habitable continent they had not yet seen. By the end of the 16th century the published information on the new land was still negligible. Just a few charts that clearly rely more on guesswork than actual knowledge, and a small passage written in 1598 by one Cornelius Wytfliet that begins, "The Australis Terra is the most southern of lands, and is separated from New Guinea by a narrow strait." The situation was, however, about to change. In 1601 the Dutch ship *Duyfken* encountered Cape York Peninsula and, in a nearly aborted voyage of discovery in 1606, the Spaniard Luis de Torres negotiated his way through the strait that now bears his name. That the certain knowledge of the Torres Strait remained, for whatever reason, unavailable to the other sea-faring nations for over 150 years, had a profound effect on how the exploration of Australian shores proceeded.

This is to jump the gun, however, for we need to look at the first really important date of 1584. In that year the overbearing king of Spain, Phillip II, decided to punish the Dutch for their religious heresies by barring their ships to Lisbon, a port that had latterly come into his control. Hitherto the Dutch had done a roaring trade as the hauliers of Europe, picking up the goods the Portuguese brought back from the far east and transporting them all over western seaboard. Phillip, having failed to subjugate them with the sword, was now trying to cut their economic base from under them. The Dutch were nothing if not wilful, however, and instead they set about fetching the goods from the far east themselves. In 1597 the first fleet returned in triumph and in 1611 Hendrik Brouwer discovered that sailing due east from the Cape of Good Hope for 3000 miles, and then turning north, cut about two months off the Holland–Java journey time. Five years later Dirk Hartog, in the trading ship *Eendracht*, overshot the mark and found his namesake island off Shark Bay. This is the first time that we know for certain Europeans stepped onto Western Australian soil. He left an inscribed pewter dinner plate nailed to a post, thus setting something of a trend for plate souveniring among early explorers. A visible landmark really opened the route up, and soon the Dutch were establishing a fair picture of the west coast of what came to be called New Holland, wrecking many of their ships on it in the process, including the infamous *Batavia*.

The next sea captain to purposefully arrive at WA's shores was William de Vlamingh of the Dutch East India Company, in 1697, who removed Hartog's plate and nailed up his own. William Dampier had been the first Englishman on the continent in 1688, landing near Broome, and he visited the northwest again in 1699, naming Shark Bay for its abundance of sharks while exploring in the *Roebuck*. (Despite the name, the sharks in the bay have plenty to eat and a shark attack on humans has never been known in these waters).

In 1772 Francois de St Allouarn landed at Cape Inscription and, ignoring Vlamingh's plate, claimed the land for France (though Cook had landed at Botany Bay two years earlier). More Frenchmen arrived in 1801 and again in 1803 on Baudin's voyages of scientific discovery. The *Geographe* and *Naturaliste* spent 70 days exploring Shark Bay and named most of its geographical features. Captain Hamelin of the *Naturaliste* found time to re-erect Vlamingh's plate, which had slipped into the sand, and added one of his own.

All of these explorers were unimpressed with what seemed to be barren land and had trouble finding fresh water. Their negative reports meant that European settlers stayed away. Of course to the local Aboriginal people the west coast was a cornucopia of seafood and they harvested shellfish, turtles and dugongs as well as the land mammals.

Two of the pewter dinner plates finally found resting places well away from the harsh sun of Shark Bay. Hartog's plate of 1616 lives in the Rikjsmuseum of Amsterdam and Vlamingh's plate of 1697 now belongs to the Maritime Museum in Fremantle. The French government returned it to Australia in 1947. The youngest plate, Hamelin's of 1801, has never been found.

The process of colonization

European designs on Australia only became serious after Captain James Cook was sent by the English government to observe a transit of Venus in Tahiti in 1770. By now the English were very much caught up in the European exploratory spirit and he was instructed, while in the area, to check out New Zealand and, if possible, chart the hitherto unexplored eastern coast of New Holland. In all this he was completely successful, spending six months charting New Zealand and then sailing west as planned. This east coast was sufficiently far from the western coasts that it was entirely possible the two were actually unconnected, and he named the 'new' territory New South Wales. He must have seen the Australian environment at its best and gave glowing descriptions of it in his reports to his government. His positive, though fateful and misinformed opinions were summarized in *The Voyages of Captain Cook*:

"The industry of man has had nothing to do with any part of it, and yet we find all such things as nature hath bestowed upon it in a flourishing state. In this extensive country it can never be doubted but what most sorts of grain, fruit, roots, etc, of every kind, would flourish were they brought hither, planted and cultivated by the hands of industry; and here is provender for more cattle, at all seasons of the year, than can ever be brought into the country."

Two of the most different cultures imaginable were now on an inevitable collision course. No sooner had the British Empire nonchalantly claimed a large new territory than it was ignominiously turfed out of an old one. In 1782 the American colonies successfully gained independence by prosecuting a war against the empire, carving a new future for themselves and creating all sorts of problems for the aghast British government. Not least amongst these issues was what to do with tens of thousands of convicts, who continued to be sentenced to 'transportation', now that the traditional dumping ground was off limits. The other colonies swiftly declined to accept them, and the practice of dropping them off in West Africa was given up on the grounds that this simply meant a nastier death for the transportees than they could have otherwise enjoyed at the end of a noose back home.

Sir Joseph Banks, Cook's wealthy and influential botanist on the *Endeavour*, had suggested New South Wales as early as 1779, but it wasn't until 1786 that Prime Minister William Pitt agreed to the suggestion, then formally put forward by Lord Sydney, the minister responsible for felons. The following year Arthur Phillip's 'first fleet' set out for Botany Bay, less a grand colonial voyage than a handy solution to a pressing problem.

Some 40 years later the British, partly scouting for a penal settlement for re-offenders and partly to counter perceived French ambitions, finally made a small encampment in the western half of the continent, at King William Sound (now Albany) in 1826. In 1828 they dispatched a warship to the Swan River to formally claim western New Holland as a colonial territory, and Captain James Stirling, after much persistent lobbying and government vacillation, was finally sent to found the Swan River Colony in 1829.

As is not unusual in the history of the British invasions of Australia, Stirling discounted the local Aboriginal peoples, offering no treaty and ignoring them entirely in his planning. It took decades for Europeans to even begin to understand the Aboriginals' complex relationship with their land. It is ill understood even today. Most did not care and some, particularly the poor or emancipated, were happy that there were people on a rung lower than theirs. It was assumed that as the Aboriginals did not farm they had no concept or right of ownership; that since they were nomadic they could simply move out of the way; that as their technology was relatively simple so was their culture and indeed so were they as people. From the very beginning there were settlers who considered them sub-human, and right up to the 1960s many Aboriginals believed themselves, not unreasonably, regarded as 'fauna'.

Today it is vigorously debated how much the early authorities were guided by the policy of *terra nullius*, the idea that Australia was an empty land, free for the taking. *Terra nullius* was a legal fiction based on the premise that land ownership was only proved by land cultivation. The colonial authorities did not think that Australia was empty, but that Aboriginal people had no legal claim upon it. At the time it seems likely that whatever angst was occurring in the minds of liberal societies and authorities in England or urban

Australia, the reality on the crucial frontier was promoted by the pioneering settler, over which the authorities had little control. For many that reality was one of conflict. *Terra nullius* was immaterial, there was a future to secure and it was 'either us or them'.

Disease did a lot of the damage, with thousands of Aboriginals undoubtedly dying of smallpox and flu, syphilis and typhoid. The Europeans' long association with domestic animals had fermented a rich brew of the beasties and, like the native Americans before them, the native Australians had little defence. Those that survived were expected to join a Christian mission or work as a farm hand or join the native police; a refusal to do so led to some of the of the most intense confrontations. Some Aboriginals fought back, spearing settlers and attempting to drive them back from whence they had come. The response, both official and not, was often savage. There are known instances of whole groups being rounded up and shot wholesale as retribution for something as trivial as the death of a bullock. On the other hand some groups simply tried to maintain their existence, living off the land as their ancestors had done. Here less brutal, but equally devastating, tactics were sometimes employed by the Europeans, such as the poisoning of their waterholes.

By the late 1860s it was all over bar the shouting. Aboriginal peoples reached some of their lowest populations ever, driven almost entirely from the southwest and with only fragmented peoples clinging to existence on the fringes of European society over much of the rest of the state. Only deep in the northwest deserts and in the Kimberley did their traditional way of life persist relatively untarnished into the 20th century, in parts as late as the 1950s. When in the late 19th century Charles Darwin's theories gained widespread notice, it was widely expected that Aboriginals would become extinct. Their perceived inferiority meant they could not survive in the face of a more 'advanced' people. It was simply a case of the 'survival of the fittest'.

Captain Stirling also committed the usual Australian mistake of grossly exaggerating the excellence of the potential port facilities and the suitability of the local land for agriculture. Partly as a result of these misplaced notions, the early settlements of Fremantle and Perth got off to a very slow start, despite considerable private backing from English speculators. The finding of the relatively fertile Avon Valley in 1830 and the decisive crushing of Aboriginal opposition at the 'battle' of Pinjarra (see page 135) in 1834 did open doors for some settlers, leading to the establishment of a reasonable wool industry, but a generation later in 1850 the entire colony could still only boast a population of 5500 Europeans and the addition of just a couple of other industries including the cutting and export of local sandalwood to China.

Aboriginal people have lived in the southwest, a rich source of vegetation and wildlife, for many thousands of years and a lot of local landscape features are still known by the names given by Nyoongar people. The region was the first of any distance from Perth's Swan River Colony to be prospected by pastoralists and woodsmen, the earliest in the 1830s. In the decades until the turn of the century settlements gradually developed and wool, timber and horses which were all exported from Koombana Bay.'

The convict era

Following strong urging from some of the few thriving Perth businessmen, who appreciated the possibilities cheap labour would present, the colony accepted its first consignment of convicts in 1850 and 10,000 more over the next 18 years. The convicts were considered a most unsavoury addition by many of the settlers, but undoubtedly did help to open up parts of the immense colony at a time when many were to tempted to abandon it in favour of the new eastern goldfields around Ballarat and Bendigo in Victoria. The southwest saw renewed energies with the coming of the convicts, but it was the coastal region between Perth and Shark Bay that was first largely exploited using convict labour. The land known as Greenough Flats proved reasonably fertile, and soon much of this whole stretch of land was being claimed by pastoralists at the expense of the local Aboriginal people. Small ports developed at places like Denison, Geraldton and Gregory, though most swiftly fell into disservice thanks to their relatively poor situations. Mineral prospectors accompanied the pastoralists, and some significant discoveries were made, such as those around Northampton, though gold – the holy grail – eluded them. Later in the 1850s bay islands in the Gascoyne region were mined for guano and the potential of local pearl shell realized. Many pearling settlements sprang up in the north, such as Cossack and Broome, during the 1870s to 1890s. The industry brought many Chinese, Filipinos, Japanese and Malay people and Aboriginal people also worked as pearl divers, although there are reports that some were kidnapped and forced to dive. The pearls were over exploited, however, and the industry crashed during the depression of the 1930s.

The state government encouraged pastoralists to take up land further and further north in the Pilbara and Kimberley regions during the late 1850s and 1860s. Most of the land in the more fertile and temperate regions of the south had been claimed and the government knew that the success of the colony depended on further expansion. Surveyor Francis Gregory was sent to explore the Pilbara region in 1861 and established a base camp at Nickol Bay, near the modern town of Karratha. He believed conditions in the Pilbara were suitable for pastoralists and made enthusiastic reports to the government who quickly offered generous leasing terms. The first pastoralist, Walter Padbury, arrived in 1863 and settled on the De Grey River just north of Port Hedland. The Withnell family arrived the following year at the Tien Tsin harbour (later known as Cossack) and settled by a freshwater pool in the Harding River. A settlement grew around their home and became the first town of the northwest in 1866, when it was named Roebourne after the state Surveyor-General, John Septimus Roe. All over the state pastoralists and settlers found conditions tough, however, and supplemented their income by fishing and harvesting native timber. The pastoral industry struggled, particularly in the north, until an artesian basin was discovered in 1900, ensuring a reliable supply of water for stock.

Of course all of this new land for sheep and wheat was far from empty. Aboriginal people are thought to have continuously inhabited Western Australia for the last 20,000 years at least and, as the British settlers moved in to new areas, their traditional way of life came under unrelenting pressure. Even in the more remote areas waterholes were ruined by stock, sacred sites destroyed and native animals depleted. Violent conflict persisted and many more Aboriginal people were killed in battle or massacred by terrified European settlers, determined to protect themselves and what they perceived to be their legal property. European diseases also continued to devastate many groups and others moved away from their inland country to the new coastal settlements; the combination of a massively disrupted society and the lure of European goods contributing to the decision (or necessity) to move off their land.

The European population of WA slowly increased and as did it so the colony began to prosper, thanks largely to thriving wool and timber industries, and by 1892 there were around 50,000 non-indigenous West Australians thinly spread over the enormous colony. Despite the low population, agricultural progress was matched by important social advances. In 1861 about one in four European Australians were illiterate, a figure reduced to one in 40 by 1892. The unions forced a shorter working day, then a shorter working week, opening up Saturday afternoons for sport and leisure. The outdoor climate, large accessible spaces and large urban populations contrived to ensure that sport itself became almost a religion, and those competing successfully at international level were the new gods. By 1900 Australians were avid followers of home-grown boxers, skullers, horses, cricketers, athletes and footballers. With the rise in sport came a rise in gambling, a habit Australia has never lost. At the same time there was a growing appreciation of indigenous flora and fauna. Bushwalking societies formed and there were moves to declare reserves around outstandingly beautiful natural landmarks. These forerunners of the national parks began to be established in the 1870s and 1880s.

Societies very much at odds with the natural environment were also formed. A nostalgia for 'home' led groups of misguided amateur naturalists to import countless species of plants and animals in the hope that the alien landscape of Australia could be transformed into one huge English garden. Other animals were brought over as pets or for stock, and these too often escaped into the wild. Foxes were introduced, for example, so that people could participate in an authentic hunt. Today dozens of these species have gone feral, each one disturbing the native ecology to a greater or lesser degree.

That much of this progress was at the expense of the traumatized indigenous peoples and the environment they had so carefully managed went largely unnoticed and unremarked. Their cultures were almost fatally fractured and reservoirs of knowledge were disappearing fast. They were rarely actively hunted down any more, though cold-blooded massacres allegedly occurred well into the 1900s, but a decline in aggression did not mean an increase in acceptance. That they would themselves soon disappear entirely still seemed entirely likely to the white population, so there was little need to include them in the colony's future.

Gold and Federation

In 1890 Western Australia finally became self-governing and, as if in celebration (and strangely echoing events in Victoria 40 years before), gold was found near to the modern site of Coolgardie. Other states were experiencing economic chaos, but thanks to the Coolgardie and Kalgoorlie-Boulder gold finds Western Australia finally made the big leap forward in the 1890s that it had witnessed the other colonies make in the 1850s and 1860s. Within months tens of thousands of people had made their way over from the eastern states, and from as far as Britain, China and the United States. One of those from the US was a young Herbert Hoover. They camped in canvas cities, all desperately seeking the big find that would make them their fortune. The gold was there in prodigious quantities and many did indeed become rich. Many more, however, died of disease or accident and a stroll around the cemetery at Coolgardie is a sobering experience – only a handful of the hundreds interred between 1890 and 1920 were over 35.

As well as experiencing gold fever in the 1890s, WA politicians kept a wary eye on the debate over whether Australia should federate or not. Up to about 1890 the six Australian colonies and New Zealand had jealously guarded their independence from each other. Proud of their differences they each operated their own institutions, governments, services and military forces, united only by currency, the environment and a shared heritage. Their military forces were scant, however, and the colonies still relied heavily on the navy of the British Empire for defence. During the late 1800s other nations such as France, Germany, Japan and Russia were becoming powerful, challenging the empire for hegemony over maritime and continental trade routes. In Australia there were very real fears that some of these powers might have designs on Australian territory, and in the late 1880s Britain pointed out that the colonies' military forces were hugely inadequate and would be far more effective if united under a single command structure.

In 1889 the prime minister of New South Wales made a bold step. He suggested that the proposed federation of armed forces be given far greater scope, that it should be widened to a political federation of the colonies. The Commonwealth officially came into existence on 1 January 1901 and it effectively ushered in nationhood. Colonies became states and the relationship with the 'mother country' became more complex. On the one hand ties had never been stronger. Many who held high office were British born, Britain was still Australia's biggest market for most of its exports and British rather than Australian history was still considered more important in schools. On the other hand a British visitor to the new nation had to be careful not to offend local sensibilities. He or she would perhaps be called a 'pommy' (suspected to be a cockney derivative of 'immigrant' from 'pomegranate') instead of the warmer 'new chum' that had been in vogue since the eastern goldrushes of the 1850s. They would also have noticed signs encouraging people to 'buy Australian' and shun imported goods from the empire and elsewhere. This was a clear sign of Australia's growing self-sufficiency and new-found confidence.

Federation also ushered in a raft of legislation that smoothed out policy across the nation. Paramount amongst these was giving women the vote in 1902. Another was the formal introduction of a 'White Australia' policy which, although in line with many nations of the day, seems shocking now and also jars given that the island continent was so manifestly 'Non-White Australia' just 125 years before. Immigration restarted in earnest in the mid-1900s, an integral part of the process being a dictation test in the European language of the immigration official's choice! In the northern regions of Australia where the colonial frontier was still advancing, Aboriginal people were increasingly devastated by violence, disease, starvation and exploitation. The colonial governments had begun to worry that they were witnessing the destruction of Aboriginal people and introduced a raft of legislation to 'protect' them by confining them to certain areas away from Europeans. Additional legislation meant that Aboriginal people could be forced to move to a reserve, were denied citizenship and the vote and were prohibited sexual relations with 'Europeans'.

Between 1890 and 1910 a lot of the remaining land in WA that could be useful to the colonists was utilized, in the south for wheat and wool, in the north for cattle. Pearl shell began to be harvested in massive quantities off the northern coast and a string of small ports was established both for the lugger fleets and to ship cattle. By 1912 WA's population had increased sharply to over 300,000 'whites' plus an uncounted and declining number of Aboriginal people no longer seen as significant.

War and peace

The still very British people of WA rallied to the standard of the empire during the First World War like almost no other former colony. The state provided nearly four times as many soldiers and auxiliary workers as its agreed share and those that went suffered higher casualty rates than any other soldiers in the British Empire. It has been said that because of their extreme courage and resilience they were commonly used as front-line 'shock troops'. Significant monuments in Kings Park, Perth, honour their sacrifice and there is also an avenue of gum trees there, each marked by a plaque commemorating one of the dead.

The Australian Imperial Force (AIF) were all either regular army or volunteers, but had still mustered 300,000 by the end of the First World War. They figured in many theatres of the war, the most celebrated of which has come to be known as Gallipoli. On 25 April 1915 the Anzacs (Australia and New Zealand Army Corps) constituted a large part of a force sent to win control of the banks of the Dardanelles, the narrow channel that connects the Aegean and Marmara seas. The expedition's success would open the allies' supply line through the Mediterranean to the Black Sea and so to Russia.

Though finally forced to retreat, the chief legacy of the campaign was profound for Australians. The Anzacs were seen to display a degree of bravery, mateship and humour not expected in such an untried force. In a seminal moment for the nation, its unbloodied and untested soldiers had faced the fire for the first time and not been found wanting. It is sometimes thought that these expressions of national character were forged on the beaches of Gallipoli, but it is truer to say that it is during the campaign that foreign journalists first saw and publicized these traits that had been slowly maturing for decades. Unseen by the rest of the world, and even by many urban Australians, Australian toughness, independence and cooperation had been won on the pastoral and mining frontiers over the previous century. Of the 300,000 Australians who went to war over 50,000 were killed, a greater number than was lost by America. Many of these were the bravest, most resourceful and most inspiring men of their time. Their loss was profoundly felt, eliciting a huge outpouring of national pride and grief, given substance by literally thousands of memorials erected all over the country.

After the war, returned servicemen and post-war immigrants from Britain and parts of western Europe had to be quickly and efficiently housed and found work. One obvious solution was to grant settlements of bush for clearing and cultivation. In WA's southwest region the timber was largely gone by the end of the First World War and in one scheme the government decided to try to use the region for dairy farming. The Minister for Lands proposed the Group Settlement Scheme in 1921 and 3391 hungry migrants from post-war Britain arrived, keen to have their own piece of earth. Few realized how tough it would be and there are reports of tears when they saw the rough huts and dirt floors they had to live in. They cleared some land, built fences and houses and tried to make a go of it, but by 1924 a third of the 'groupies' had walked off their land with nothing. The depression finished off many of those who stayed on into the 1930s.

There was a significant expansion of the burgeoning 'wheat-belt' throughout the 1920s, though, with new machinery and technology enabling the clearing and farming of huge tracts of land with comparatively few workers. Cattle and sheep farming in the north also boomed with high prices commanded on the world's markets. The good times were not set to last, however, as the global depression of the 1930s certainly did not spare WA. Up to a third of the state's workforce was laid off during the decade, and considerable government assistance was required to stave off actual starvation. The only industry that benefited was Kalgoorlie's gold-mining, which was able to hire labour very cheaply and increase production when every other industry saw output collapse.

The 1930s were also marked by increased misery for many Aboriginal people. Influenced by popular notions of eugenics and racial purity in Europe, Australian state governments thought that 'full bloods' would eventually die out and 'half castes' could be bred out. It was thought that if a woman of both Aboriginal and European descent took a European partner, and her children did the same, then the 'Aboriginal blood' would eventually become so diluted as to be invisible. It was also thought that if children of mixed descent with fairly pale skin could be taken from their Aboriginal mothers at an early age and raised within the white community it would give the child every material advantage and help 'half-castes' to be absorbed into the community. Thus in the Western Australian Aboriginal Act (1936) provisions relating to permission to marry and sexual relations between Aboriginal people and Europeans were strengthened. The state's powers of guardianship were increasingly used to remove children of mixed descent from their mothers and rear them in missions, orphanages or foster homes. This process and some of its consequences are movingly and powerfully portrayed in the film *Rabbit Proof Fence*. In 1937 a conference of the state government Protectors decided 'the destiny of the natives of aboriginal origin, but not of the full blood, lies in their ultimate absorption by the people of the Commonwealth, and it therefore recommends that all efforts be directed to that end.' However, anthropologists working with Aboriginal people in the 1930s did begin to try to educate the rest of society about their culture and various humanitarian groups and Aboriginal protest groups also began to agitate for a change in attitudes.

The advent of world war in 1939 again proved a huge draw to young men of WA, though this time Australia itself was to become geographically involved. Japanese bomber aircraft repeatedly attacked some of the northern towns during 1942-1943, including Broome, and there was widespread belief that an invasion was imminent. This sharp recognition of vulnerability had a deep impression on the Australian psyche and is an aspect of national psychology to this day. The Second World War also marked a reversal in the state's financial fortunes. Wool and wheat prices climbed steadily and continued to do so after 1945. Returning soldiers who moved onto the land in the late 1940s and 1950s had a much better time of it than their predecessors 30 years before.

Post-war prosperity

Prime Minister Ben Chifley's Australia of the late 1940s was a careful nation. Although beaten by the bomb, it was felt that Japan still had considerable potential for aggression and Australia played a leading role in garrisoning the defeated country and prosecuting its war leaders. There was a deep feeling that peace could not last. Russia and China were deemed the major new threats and it was universally felt that a large population would be the best disincentive to invasion, and defence against any such attempt.

The old 'White Australia' policy was energized once more. Chifley's chief minister for immigration, Arthur Calwell, instigated and pursued the most vigorous such programme Australia has ever seen. The nation must 'populate or perish'. It was originally thought that the Brits, still seen as the best 'stock', could make up 90% of the numbers but this proved over-ambitious – they eventually made up around a quarter of the immigrants of the period and some of those were unwittingly expatriated orphans. Calwell had to relax his criteria and was soon fishing in the vast refugee camp that central and southern

Europe had become. The net would be thrown no wider: those of African or Asian origin were definitely not welcome.

Non-British immigrants had to put up with a fair amount of social antagonism. 'Refos' (refugees), 'DPs' (displaced persons) and 'dagos' were taunts frequently slung at the newcomers. The few non-European immigrants and descendants of the earlier Chinese gold-miners fared much worse, suffering at times outright racial vilification. The non-British were, however, to form the foundation of a vibrant and successful urban multi-cultural society.

In 1949 the giant of 20th-century Australian politics, Robert Menzies, strode back into the limelight, leading his new national Liberal party to election victory. A staunch monarchist, he welcomed Queen Elizabeth II to Australia in 1954, the first reigning monarch to make the trip. In 1962 she came to Perth to open the Commonwealth Games, which the city was proudly hosting. The games were a huge success, televised all over the world, and proved a showcase for WA.

Post-war migration helped swell the population of WA to over 700,000 by 1960. The wheat-belt became vast, producing huge quantities of grain for export and an even more valuable amount of wool. Gold production stuttered occasionally but reached its peak in 1961, and the Kimberley and Pilbara cattle runs matured and prospered. Pastoralism struggled with water shortages, disease, cyclones and isolation but remained the major industry in the north until the 1960s. Then minerals other than gold, but almost as valuable, began turning up in the north. Amongst them nickel, iron-ore, bauxite and oil were found in massive quantities, and today they have been joined by the discovery of almost indecent numbers of premium grade diamonds in the eastern Kimberley. The government lifted an embargo on the export of iron ore in 1960 and scientists confirmed that the Pilbara contained massive quantities of high grade ore. Mining companies quickly established new mines, ports, railways and towns to exploit these resources. Dampier, Karratha, Wickham and the inland mining towns of Newman, Tom Price and Paraburdoo were all developed during the 1960-1970s. The Pilbara is now responsible for 40% of Australia's mineral exports, and the Kimberley for 30% of the world's diamonds.

The impact on the culture and environment that existed prior to 1829 cannot be understated. Entire peoples had vanished over much of this subcontinent. Huge tracts of land were cleared of native vegetation to make way for wheat and wool, and much of this has resulted in a rising water table, bringing with it enough salt to ruin huge areas of land for anything, let alone agriculture. Species loss amongst both plant and animal life, particularly in the southwest, will never be accurately known but was certainly substantial. Immediate prosperity also had a radical impact on WA's colonial cultural heritage when much of historic central Perth was bulldozed in the 1960-1970s to make way for modern office blocks.

The life of the remaining Aboriginal people also changed greatly during this period. Since the 1860s many Aboriginal people had lived and worked on pastoral stations, maintaining links with their traditional lands. However pastoralists' exploitation of Aboriginal workers led to resentment and in 1946 Aboriginal pastoral station workers went on strike for equal wages and conditions. They finally got them in 1968 but this meant that station owners simply couldn't or wouldn't employ as many workers. The result was an urban Aboriginal population who had little contact with their own country and the further breakdown of their culture and identity.

Culture shock

Their was, however, a flip-side to post-war optimism. Although the Japanese had failed to establish a modern Asian empire the 'Western' world became convinced that either China or the Soviets might succeed, and many Australians believed that their beloved homeland would be firmly in the sights of any nation with such ambitions.

This fear of communism had two profound effects, which between them later engendered a counter consequence of equal, if not greater importance. Anti-communist hysteria goes a long way to explaining the firm grip that conservative governments were to have on Australian politics for a quarter of a century, with Labor Party members and supporters frequently suspected of being communist sympathizers and even spies. In 1950 Robert Menzies held a national referendum on whether the Communist Party should be banned outright and its members jailed. To the nation's credit the result was a comfortable 'no'. The other major effect of the national mood was an enthusiastic willingness to back up any Asian military efforts against the 'red tide' with practical support. The same year as the referendum saw Australian troops join those from the USA and their other allies in fighting the 'commies' in Korea. A little later, in the year of the Melbourne Olympics (1956), the Soviet Union invaded Hungary and anti-communist fears in Australia were bolstered further by a stream of frightened refugees.

The conservative cauldron simmered on through the height of the Cold War in late 1950s and early 1960s, thus ensuring that Australia, unlike Britain, was ready to send troops in support of another Asian crusade, this time in Vietnam. The Australian commitment was never huge in military terms, committing some 8000 people, but Prime Minister Harold Holt's famous statement, "all the way with LBJ", neatly illustrates the depth of conservative political support. It was also an indication that Australia was shifting from British influence to follow an American lead. Although only a few troops made the journey, some of them were conscripts. This sat uneasily with much of the general public and when conscripts started getting killed unease turned to anger.

The nation became embroiled, for the first time in decades, in serious discussions about the direction and fitness of the national government and its policies. Demonstrations against the war were organized and some marches became violent. Governments frequently clamped down hard, prompting further discussion and protests on the subject of civil liberties. Some people demonstrated simply to express their view that they had a right to demonstrate. A heady brew of general anti-establishment feeling began to ferment, particularly amongst the youth of the day, inspired by their cousins in Europe and the US who were discovering a new independence from their 'elders and betters'.

Aboriginal people were also part of the protest movement and increasingly demanded change. In the early 1960s new legislation appeared in all states that largely removed the paternalistic and restrictive laws relating to Aboriginal people. The federal government enfranchised Aborigines of the Northern Territory (the only region under their control) and WA followed the federal lead. Previously citizenship had only been available to those who applied for it and was subject to certain conditions: in Western Australia that meant not keeping company with any Aboriginal people except the applicant's immediate family for two years before applying and after being granted citizenship.

The granting of rights such as equal wages had to be fought for in some cases, even when the legislation existed, and this could be the catalyst for further activism. When the Gurindji people failed to obtain equal wages from the powerful Lord Vestey of Wave Hill Station in the Northern Territory they walked off the land, led by stockman Vincent

Lingiari, and decided to make a land rights claim for some of Vestey-owned land. As one of his people later said, "We were treated just like dogs. We were lucky to get paid the 50 quid a month we were due, and we lived in tin humpies you had to crawl in and out on your knees. There was no running water. The food was bad – just flour, tea, sugar and bits of beef like the head or feet of a bullock. The Vesteys were hard men. They didn't care about blackfellas." Just 10 years earlier Lingiari and his Gurindji people would probably have been ignominiously, forcefully and quietly evicted, but this was 1966 and sections of society were prepared to listen and help. The ruling conservative Liberal-Country Party rejected the Aboriginals' claim, wary of their own land-owning voters and perhaps of the effects a positive outcome might have on future mineral exploitation. The political wind was, however, changing. The Australian people had soon had enough of the conservatives and were ready for a new broom. In 1972 they finally elected the Labor Party back into power, and with it the charismatic and energetic Gough Whitlam.

Modern Australia

In many ways the brief tenure of Gough Whitlam as national prime minister was the coming of age for Australia. He came to power unencumbered by decades of the politics of fear, and with a zeal to be his own man and make Australia her own nation. Within days the troops were recalled from Vietnam and conscription ended, women were legally granted an equal wage structure, 'White Australia' formally abandoned and a Ministry of Aboriginal Affairs created. Whitlam's policy was "to restore to the Aboriginal people of Australia their lost power of self-determination in economic, social and political affairs". Whitlam spurned the prime ministerial Bentley, ended the old imperial honours system and dumped *God Save the Queen* as the national anthem. He was a political dynamo and exacted an unprecedented work-rate from his colleagues. His policies were not everyone's cup of tea, but no one could argue that his every effort was not aimed at the betterment of Australia and Australians. In 1975 the Gurindji people were given 2000 sq km from the Vestey leases and Whitlam flew to Wave Hill to personally hand over the deeds, symbolically pouring a handful of sand into the palm of Vincent Lingiari as he did so. Even Whitlam's sacking a few months later, a controversial affair involving the governor-general and so the British Crown, had the effect of galvanizing public opinion on the subject of republicanism. Whitlam had permanently altered the mood of the nation and of Australian politics.

In some ways these events were peripheral to matters in WA. The state's residents – known as 'sandgropers' – refer to the rest of Australia as 'the eastern states', sometimes with no little contempt. However, WA soon had a vibrant but highly conservative premier of its own. Liberal Sir Charles Court was Premier of WA from 1974 until 1982 and helped channel the state's undoubted wealth and vitality as no-one had done before. By the end of his tenure over a million people could call themselves Western Australians. The spirit of raw Western Australian entrepreneurship was colourfully personified by Alan Bond, an English immigrant of the late 1950s who was a multi-millionaire by the 1970s. In 1983 Perth famously hosted the world's most famous sailing race, the America's Cup, and Bond decided that the USA's 132-year-old cast-iron hold on the cup needed to be dislodged. As a result of his enthusiasm and determination, his yacht *Australia II* did just that, triumphing to the delight of the whole country.

The 1980s also saw interstate and international tourists start to pay more attention to WA, until then the poor relation of the popular east coast. Mirroring the early European invasion of the state 150 years before, tourists first made for Perth, its hinterland and the southwest Cape-to-Cape region, widely known to travellers as simply 'Margaret River'. Gradually more and more travellers have ventured further and further from the capital: around the south coast, and north to Kalbarri, Shark Bay, Coral Bay and Broome. In the last couple of decades more of the west coast has been 'discovered', as have the whale sharks visiting the Ningaloo Reef and the incredible gorges of Karijini in the Pilbara.

The 1990s was a tumultuous decade for issues involving Aboriginal people. In 1992 the High Court made what was probably the most important decision of the century in the Mabo land rights case. The court ruled that native title (or prior indigenous ownership of land) was not extinguished by the Crown's claim of possession in the Murray Islands of Torres Strait. In other words the legal fiction of *Terra nullias* was overturned and the decision was later enshrined in the Native Title Act (1993). This was a major victory for Aboriginal people, although land owners had to be able to prove a continuous relationship to the land and claims could only be made on Crown land. A land fund was suggested to buy land for the majority of Aboriginal people who were unable to claim land under the Act. Despite the limited nature of native title, conservatives were horrified and lobbied hard against it.

As Australia moved toward a new century, two campaigns aimed at moving the country in a new direction built a considerable head of steam. The first sought to sunder further the ties with Britain and become a republic. The second called for reconciliation and to build better ties between white and black Australians. Reconciliation was seen as important for the future health of the nation. A gesture that would heal the divisions between black and white and allow Australians to move into the future together. The Council for Aboriginal Reconciliation worked on a Declaration of Reconciliation that was presented to the government in 2000. In the same year there were large reconciliation marches all over the country by sections of the community who wanted to say 'sorry' for past injustices, despite the government's refusal to do so. The issue of the republic was to be decided by a 1999 national referendum. The question asked, however, was controversially worded in a way that prevented many republicans assenting to it, and therefore the result was 'no', despite polls showing a majority in favour of a republic.

A new century

The Olympics went to Sydney in 2000, and must be ranked as one of the greatest games ever. The Aboriginal athlete Kathy Freeman won gold in the women's 400-m track sprint, sending the nation into a frenzy of joy. Following the reconciliation movement the victory seemed, to many, serendipitous. However, the huge optimism created by the successful staging of the Olympics seemed to fizzle out with the failure of the republic and the failure to achieve any meaningful reconciliation between indigenous and non-indigenous Australians. Aboriginal people are still coming to terms with the effects of dispossession and the government policies that have affected their lives from 1788 until the present day. By almost every measure of social welfare they are less well off than non-indigenous Australians. For example, the life expectancy of an indigenous person is 17 years less than other Australians, and rectifying this inequality is the great challenge of the future for all Australians.

In the federal election of November 2001 the Liberal-National government under John Howard was returned to power despite the unpopularity of the Goods and Services Tax introduced in 2000, and he was returned again in 2004, shortly thereafter becoming Australia's second-longest serving prime minister. The first campaign was run amid the uncertainty caused by the terrorist attacks of 11 September 2001 and issues of border protection highlighted by the government's handling of the Tampa crisis. Border protection and the detention of asylum seekers had become the hot issues and, as in much of the world, Australian political affairs have continued to be largely dominated by the international threat of terrorism and war rather than local issues. In October 2002 terrorism hit very close to home for Australians, and particularly Western Australians, when two nightclubs were bombed in Bali, killing around 200 people. The proportion of Western Australian holidaymakers killed was high, sending shockwaves through the state's small population. Despite the world climate of fear, the 2004 federal election was fought rather more on domestic issues with the economy seemingly uppermost in the minds of most voters. The WA government has also been stable – though for Labor not Liberal and became more responsive to environmental issues. Logging of old-growth forests was stopped by the state government, as was the potential development of a controversial tourist complex near Coral Bay.

Indeed in 2007 the environment became of increasing importance to all Australians, and it was John Howard's denial of climate change and refusal to sign the Kyoto protocol that played a part in his defeat in the federal election of November 2007. Australians felt it was time for a change and elected a Labor government led by Kevin Rudd, who campaigned on promises to act on climate change, to bring troops home from Iraq and to promote reconciliation between indigenous and non-indigenous Australians. Prime Minister Rudd's first act in government was to sign the Kyoto Protocol in Bali and his second was to formally apologize to indigenous Australians during the first sitting of parliament in February 2008. Saying, "the time has now come for the nation to turn a new page in Australia's history by righting the wrongs of the past and so moving forward with confidence to the future. We apologize for the laws and policies of successive parliaments and governments that have inflicted profound grief, suffering and loss on these our fellow Australians," his words were generally considered to be healing and the apology was welcomed by the Aboriginal community.

The most significant development in Western Australia in recent years has been the incredible growth of the mining sector. Over the last 10 years the state resources industry has grown by an average of 14% each year. Sales of West Australian resources (iron ore, nickel, crude oil, condensate, natural gas, gold, alumina and base metals) were worth $70.9 billion in the 2009-2010 financial year. This is a 42% contribution to the nation's exports. One liquefied natural gas deal with China will earn $1 billion a year for the next 25 years, bringing the kind of prosperity last seen in WA in the 1980s. The WA economy is booming. Well-paid jobs in the mining sector are plentiful, and as many workers are employed on a fly-in (to the northern Pilbara region), fly-out basis, the riches are spread throughout the state.

It's likely that all this money has helped the state take the initiative in water management. Traditionally Perth has relied on its underground aquifer and individual water consumption rates are a third higher here than in Sydney and Melbourne. However, declining rainfall and predictions such as that of environmentalist Tim Flannery, that Perth would become the world's first ghost metropolis due to lack of water, have forced WA to face up to the issue of water. Australia's first large-scale desalination plant was opened in Kwinana, south of Perth, in April 2007 at a cost $387 million. It supplies 130 million litres of drinking water per day; about 17% of Perth's water consumption. A second 45-gigalitre desalination plant is being built in the state's southwest, near Binningup, for completion in 2011. Water experts are also exploring new ways of providing water, including recharging the aquifer with treated waste water.

In 2010 the West Australian Liberal government found itself out of step with the federal Labor government policies. Premier Colin Barnett refused to sign up to a heathcare reform agreement that would make the Commonwealth responsible for 60% of public hospital funding but require the states and territories to surrender about a third of their GST to Canberra. He also wouldn't agree to the terms of a mining tax suggested by Kevin Rudd and modified by Julia Gillard. He continues to fight against WA's diminishing share of GST revenue and promotes Western Australia's 'self-reliance'. As the state governments change over to Liberal (Victoria in late 2010 and NSW likely in 2011) Barnett's strong position as leader of the nation's most productive state will be further bolstered by his political allies.

Politics

Australian politics is of great importance to many Australians, a conversation topic on a par with the weather or sport. This is partly because of the sheer volume of government the country bears, partly because of the colourful characters and events Australian politics seems to throw up, and partly because everyone, by law, has to vote.

Australia's head of state is the reigning monarch of England, a throwback to when that monarch was the head of the British Empire, which the historical Australian colonies were very much part of. The Queen's principle representative in Australia, now usually Australian born, is the governor-general, appointed by the Australian prime minister. His or her role is largely ceremonial though in theory they are invested with considerable powers. In 1975 the serving governor-general, Sir John Kerr, demonstrated some of these by dismissing the government of Gough Whitlam during an unprecedented political crisis.

In practical terms the business of governing the whole country is undertaken by the Federal ('Commonwealth') Parliament based in Canberra. Its 'lower' House of Representatives is constituted by members directly elected from electorates with approximately equally sized populations. The electorates range in size from a small city suburb to that of Kalgoorlie, which encompasses most of WA and is, in fact, the biggest electorate for any MP in the world. The 'upper' house, the Senate, is elected by a form of proportional representation that guarantees each state 12 members, and each territory two. The lower house formulates government policy and the upper house either vetoes or passes it. Both houses are voted for every three years.

There are two major parties, which sit either side of the political fence. The Australian Labor Party (ALP) and the Liberal Party are the two chief protagonists, the ALP being the rough equivalent of the British Labour Party or American Democrats, the Liberals the equivalent of the Conservatives or Republicans. Over the last 70 years the ALP have generally polled slightly higher than the Liberals, but have usually been kept out of office by the latter's alliance with the smaller National Party. The leader of the majority in the lower house forms the country's government and is its prime minister. In late 2007 Kevin Rudd's Labor party finally won government from John Howard's Liberal/National coalition, who had been in power for four terms. Despite coming to power on a wave of popularity, Rudd was the first ever Labor prime minister to be dumped from office during a first term when he was replaced as leader by Julia Gillard in June 2010. However Australia's first female prime minister only just held onto the position after the extraordinary election of August 2010 when Labor and Liberal won 72 and 73 seats respectively. Labor negotiated an alliance with independents and greens to secure the 76 seats needed to able to form a government.

Most of the nation's tax dollar ends up in the Commonwealth coffers. About a third of the federal budget goes in benefit payments, about a fifth on the machinery of government and state institutions, and about a quarter is distributed as payments to individual states. A constant grievance between federal and state governments is the relative proportion of each state's federal income compared to the amount of tax its residents have paid, with bitter (and not untruthful) claims that some states subsidize the others.

In a second tier of government most states also have their own upper and lower houses, and also governors. These too are elected on a three-year cycle, and much the same political parties vie for election. In Western Australia the current government is Liberal and the premier is Colin Barnett.

Culture

Aboriginal art and culture

From the beginning

Aborigine is a Latin word meaning 'from the beginning'; the Romans used it to describe the first inhabitants of Latium and it can be used for any people living in a country from its earliest period. It may seem strange that the first Australians are known by a generic name but its meaning is certainly appropriate for Australian Aboriginal people. Although anthropologists believe that Aboriginal people arrived in Australia 50-60,000 years ago from Southeast Asia, Aboriginal people believe that they have always been here, that they were created here by their spirit ancestors. Before Europeans arrived in Australia Aboriginal people had no collective sense of identity. Their identity was tied to their own part of the country and to their extended family groups. Hence no name existed to describe all of the inhabitants of Australia, in the same way that until relatively recently the inhabitants of Europe would have had no conception of being 'European'.

A continent of many nations

When the First Fleet arrived with its cargo of convicts in 1788 there were somewhere between 300,000 and 750,000 Aboriginal people living in Australia, who belonged to about 500 peoples or groups. It is difficult to make generalizations about Aboriginal people because each group had its own territory, its own language or dialect and its own culture. There were broad cultural similarities between these groups just as different nationalities in Europe had more in common with each other than they had with Chinese or African people for example. Naturally neighbouring groups were more similar to each other; perhaps speaking dialects of the same language and sharing some 'Dreamtime' myths linked to territory borders such as rivers and mountains. However, if a man from Cape York had found himself transported to the Western Desert he would have been unable to communicate with the desert people. He would have found them eating unfamiliar food and using different methods to obtain it. Their art would have been incomprehensible to him and their ceremony meaningless. If he had been able to speak their language he would have found that they had a different explanation of how they came into existence and his own creation ancestors would have been unknown to them. Each group was almost like a small state or nation.

Dreaming

Every traveller in Australia will encounter the concept of 'Dreaming' or the 'Dreamtime'. These words attempt to explain a complex concept that lies at the heart of Aboriginal culture and should not be understood in the English context of something that is not real. Most Aboriginal groups believe that in the beginning the world was featureless. Ancestral beings emerged from the earth and as they moved about the landscape they began to shape it. Some of them created humans by giving birth to them or moulding them from incomplete life forms. Ancestral beings were sometimes human in form but also often animals, rocks, trees or stars, and could transform from one shape to another. Nor were they limited by their form; kangaroos could talk, fish could swim out of water. Wherever these beings went, whatever they did left its mark on the landscape. A mountain might be the fallen body of an ancestor speared to death, a waterhole may be the place a spirit emerged from the earth, a rock bar may show where an ancestor crossed a river, yellow ochre may be the fat of an ancestral kangaroo. In this way the entire continent is mapped with the tracks of the ancestor beings.

Although the time of creation and shaping of the landscape is associated with the temporal notion of 'beginning', it is important to understand that Dreaming is not part of the past. It lies within the present and will determine the future. The ancestral beings have a permanent presence in spiritual or physical form. The ancestors are also still involved in creation. Sexual intercourse is seen as being part of conception but new life can only be created if a conception spirit enters a woman's body. The place where this happens, near a waterhole, spring or sacred site, will determine the child's identification with a particular totem or ancestor. In this way Aboriginal people are directly connected to the ancestral world.

Aboriginal people belonged to a territory because they were descended from the ancestors who formed and shaped that territory. The ancestral beings were sources of life and powerful performers of great deeds but were also capable of being capricious, amoral and dangerous. Yet in their actions they laid down the rules for life. They created ceremony, song and designs to commemorate their deeds or journeys, established marriage and kinship rules and explained how to look after the land. In the simple forms related to outsiders, Dreaming stories often sound like moral fables. Knowledge of the land's creation stories was passed on from generation to generation, increasing in complexity or sacredness as an individual aged. With knowledge came the responsibility to look after sacred creation or resting places. Ceremonies were conducted to ensure the continuation of life forces and fertility. Aboriginal people had no concept of owning the land in the sense that it was a possession that could be traded or given away, but saw themselves as custodians of land in which humans, animals and spirits were inseparable, in fact were one and the same. Consequently Aboriginal people of one group had no interest in possessing the land of another group. Strange country was meaningless to them. To leave your country was to leave your world.

The bonds of kin

In their daily life Aboriginal people usually hunted, gathered and socialized within a small band, perhaps 50 people belonging to one or two families. These bands or clans only came together to form the whole group of several hundred people for ceremonial reasons and at places or times when food was plentiful. Group behaviour and social relations were governed by an intricate kinship system, and guided by the superior knowledge and experience of the elders. This is one of the reasons that the word 'tribe' is not used to describe groups of Aboriginal people, as a tribe by definition is led by a chief and Aboriginal society did not operate in this way. The rules of kinship are far too complicated to explain here, and also varied in different regions, but in essence the kinship system linked the whole group as family. You would call your birth mother 'mother' but you would also call your mother's sisters 'mother' and they would take on the obligations of that role. The same applied for sisters, fathers, uncles and so on. There were specific codes of behaviour for each kin relationship so you would know the appropriate way to behave towards each member of your group. For example, in many Aboriginal societies mothers-in-law and sons-in-law were not allowed to communicate with each other. A neat solution to an age-old problem in human relations!

Kinship also determined whom an individual could marry. In one type of kinship system each person in a group belongs to one of several sections or moieties. The moiety category is inherited from the father and so contains all of an individual's patrilineal relations. That individual can only marry someone from another moiety. Kinship links also exist between people of the same totem or ancestor. People born from the goanna ancestor would be related to all other 'goannas'. Each kinship relationship carried specific responsibilities and rights such as initiating a 'son' or giving food to a 'sister', creating a strong collective society where everyone is tied to each other. By this method food and possessions are distributed equally and because of these kinship obligations it is almost impossible for an individual to accumulate material wealth. This major difference between Aboriginal culture and the dominant ethic in Australian society of Western materialism still creates problems for those trying to live in both worlds. For example a young Aboriginal footballer will often move from his close-knit rural community to Melbourne to play in the AFL and find it very difficult to balance the personal demands of his family against the demands of his team who teach him to pursue personal wealth and glory.

Environment

The laws of the Dreaming provided a broad framework for spiritual and material life but of course Aboriginal culture was not static. Although their society valued continuity above change, parts of their culture were the result of adapting to their environment. Aboriginal people have lived in Australia for so long that they have seen major environmental changes such as climate change, dramatic changes in sea level caused by the last ice age and even volcanic eruptions in southern Australia. The picture that many people have in their minds of an Australian Aboriginal is of a desert-dwelling nomad with few possessions and only a roof of stars over his head at night. Of course some people lived like this but others sewed warm skin cloaks, built bark or stone huts or lived in the same place for several seasons. The ways in which Aboriginal people differed from each other very much depended on the environment that they lived in. Naturally, tools were developed to match the territory; boomerangs were not known to people who lived in areas of dense woodland, nor elaborate fish traps known to inland people. Conversely, Aboriginal people also changed their environment with methods such as 'fire-stick farming'.

Hunting and gathering

Aboriginal people were generally semi-nomadic rather than true nomads but they did not wander about aimlessly. They moved purposefully to specific places within their territory to find food that they knew to be ripening or abundant at certain times of the year. Their long tenure and stable society meant that they knew the qualities of every plant, the behaviour of every animal and the nature of every season intimately. Men hunted large game such as kangaroos with their toolkit of spears, clubs or boomerangs, and women gathered fruit, vegetables, seeds, honey, shellfish and small game such as lizards using their own kit of bags, bowls and digging sticks. Each gender had its own responsibilities and knowledge, including the ceremonies to ensure continuing fertility by commemorating the Dreaming. The need to 'look after country' in this way also determined their movements. Although men were generally more powerful than women, having more authority over family members and ritual, women had their own power base because of their knowledge and the reliability of the food they provided. Although hunting and gathering was labour intensive anthropologists estimate that Aboriginal people only had to spend three to five hours a day working for food, leaving plenty of time for social life and ceremony.

Ceremony and art

Ceremony and art were at the very heart of life for these were the ways in which Aboriginal people maintained their connection with the ancestors. During ceremonies the actions and movements of the ancestors would be recalled in songs and dances that the ancestors themselves had performed and handed down to each clan or group. Not only did the ancestral beings leave a physical record of their travels in the form of the landscape but also in paintings, sacred objects and sculptures that might be shown or used as part of a ceremony. Ceremonies maintained the power and life force of the ancestors thus replenishing the natural environment. Some ceremonies, such as those performed at initiation brought the individual closer to his or her ancestors. Ceremonies performed at death made sure that a person's spirit would re-join the spiritual world. Some were public ceremonies or art forms, others were secret and restricted to those who were responsible for looking after a certain piece of country and the ancestors and stories associated with it.

Function of art

When a person painted and decorated his or her body, they did so with designs and ornaments that the ancestral beings had created. The individual was almost transformed into the ancestor, bringing these beings to life in the present, as do carvings and paintings of spirit beings such as the Rainbow Serpent or an ancestral bandicoot. Art was also a product of the kinship system for one of its obligations was the giving and receiving of goods. The value of the gift was not important in fulfilling this obligation, only the act of giving. As a result Aboriginal people were continually engaged in making material objects such as body ornaments, baskets, tools and weapons, all of which can be considered secular forms of art or craft. Of course these items also needed to be made again as they wore out. One of the features of Aboriginal art was its ephemeral nature; it existed to perform a function rather than be hoarded or kept as a perfect example of the form. Elaborate body paintings that took hours to complete could be smudged by sweat in minutes. They were also sometimes deliberately wiped off to hide or lessen the power of the ancestral image. The same applied to bark paintings that would be discarded or destroyed. Ground sculptures were often temporary, made in sand, or left to decay like the carved and painted pukunami burial poles of the Tiwi people. The most permanent forms were rock engravings and paintings but even these were eroded or painted over in time. Some Aboriginal art was like a blackboard, used to teach and then wiped clean.

A symbolic landscape

The most immediately obvious feature of Aboriginal art is its symbolic nature. Geometric designs such as circles, lines, dots, squares or abstract designs are used in all art forms and often combine to form what seems to be little more than an attractive pattern. Even when figures are used they are also symbolic representations, an emu may be prey or an ancestral being. The symbols do not have a fixed meaning; a circle may represent a waterhole, a camping place or an event. In Aboriginal art symbols are put together to form a map of the landscape. But this is not a literal map where if you could read the 'key' you would see the topography of a piece of countryside, but a mythological map. Features of the landscape are depicted but only in their relation to the creation myth that is the subject of the painting. A wavy line terminating in a circle might represent the journey of the Rainbow Serpent to a waterhole. That landscape may also contain a hill behind the waterhole but if it is not relevant to the serpent's journey it will not be represented, although it may feature in other paintings related to different ancestral beings. Unlike a conventional map, scale is not consistent. The size of a feature is more likely to reflect its importance rather than its actual size or there may be several scales within a painting. Nor is orientation fixed; Aboriginal artists often paint sitting on the ground or at a table and work on the nearest side so there may be no top or bottom to these works.

Artistic licence

As art was a means of expressing identity it follows that only those who belonged to an area of landscape and its Dreaming stories, could paint those stories. No one else would know them. An artist must have the right to paint the image he has in mind and these rights are carefully guarded. This idea is refined further within the clan or group. A father and son of the same clan may know the same story but the father will be able to paint more powerful ancestral beings with more knowledge and detail, because it can take a lifetime to learn all of the knowledge connected to an ancestral being. Rights to paintings can also be established through kinship links, living in an area or taking part in ceremony. To many people Aboriginal art is recognized by its style – dots, X-ray or cross hatching – but what is painted is just as important as how it is painted. Aboriginal people working in traditional forms simply do not paint landscapes, figures or people that they are not spiritually connected to. The idea of painting a landscape simply because it is pretty is utterly foreign to Aboriginal art. Even an artist like Albert Namatjira who painted European landscape watercolours in the 1940s never painted anything but his own Arrernte land in central Australia, although he travelled widely outside it.

Interpretation

How does the viewer understand the meaning of a work of Aboriginal art? Because of the use of symbols and the fact that Dreaming stories are only known to the ancestral descendants, only the painter, and perhaps his close relatives, will be able to fully understand the meaning of a painting. In some areas the whole group may be able to interpret the painting. When you look at Aboriginal art in a gallery it will labelled with the name of the artist, and often his clan or group name, dates and location but the meaning of the painting is not usually revealed. As knowledge of the creation myths illustrated relates to ownership it is not appropriate for the artists to pass on important cultural knowledge to strangers, although sometimes a very simple or limited explanation will be given to buyers. Some artists do interpret their paintings in more detail to anthropologists, land rights lawyers or art experts in order to educate non-indigenous people about Aboriginal culture. Looking at examples of Aboriginal art alongside an interpretation is the best way to comprehend the many layers of meaning possible; these can be found in art books such as the excellent *Aboriginal Art* by Howard Morphy.

Culture in the 21st century

After the British arrived in Australia, many Aboriginal people died from unfamiliar diseases. Those who did not were often moved off their land to missions or reserves, or killed while resisting the strangers attempting to farm or live on their land. The British acted as they did for a variety of reasons; sometimes for their own material gain, sometimes just following orders and sometimes from the genuine desire to help or protect Aboriginal people. Unfortunately the British had no understanding of Aboriginal culture and did not comprehend that separating Aboriginal people from their land was about the most destructive action possible. In unfamiliar country there was no land to look after, no reason to perform ceremony, hand down knowledge or maintain kinship ties. In missions and reserves people had to live with groups who were perhaps recent enemies, who spoke another language, who did not share their religious beliefs. In the missions they were often forbidden to speak their own language and to practise any aspects of ceremonial life that had survived the sundering from their source. It says much for the strength of Aboriginal culture that many aspects of it still exist. Since the paternalism of the Australian government was abandoned in the 1970s and a policy of self-determination implemented, many Aboriginal people from northern and central Australia have moved from government reserves back to their land to live in small remote communities. The production of art for sale in these communities helps them achieve financial independence but also revives their cultural life as the art is used to instruct young people in their Dreaming. Art has always been an integral part of the life of Aboriginal people and all over Australia people continue to express their Aboriginality in a variety of art forms. Aboriginal culture survives but continues to change and adapt as it has for countless thousands of years.

Art forms

When travelling across Australia it is possible to glimpse the regional variation of Aboriginal art. Most of Western Australia's Bradshaw and Wandjina **paintings**, in the Kimberley, can only be found with a guide, however it is possible to find ancient **rock engravings** at easily accessible sites in the Pilbara. The state museum and gallery have superb collections of both traditional and contemporary Aboriginal art and these are excellent places to learn about Aboriginal culture and art. There are also many commercial galleries. The art centres owned and run by Aboriginal communities help build self-sufficiency for Aboriginal people, offer the indigenous perspective and you may be able to see artists at work. Works produced for sale in Australia include bark paintings from Arnhem Land, the dot paintings, batik fabric and wood carvings of the desert regions of Central Australia, baskets and didjeridoos from northern Australia, and wood carvings and screen-printed fabric from the Tiwi Islands. In Western Australia the unique works of artists of the Warmun community in the Kimberley, with their bold forms and textured ochre surface, are highly sought after and there are many talented contemporary Aboriginal artists, such as **Sally Morgan**.

Rock paintings and rock engravings found all over the country constitute Australia's most ancient and enduring art form. Early rock engravings in Koonalda Cave on the Nullabor have been dated to 20,000 years ago but engravings are eroded over time and it is possible that rock engravings were being made 40,000 or even 60,000 years ago. Common forms are circles, lines and animal tracks or animal figures. Many are so ancient that Aboriginal people of the area cannot explain their meaning. Rock painting can also be dated back to many thousands of years ago and was practised until the last few decades. The finest and most extensive rock painting galleries are found in the great rocky escarpment and range country of the north, including the thousands of engravings in the Pilbara.

Painting styles have also changed over the millennia and these help to date paintings too because paintings are generally layered on top of each other. The earliest art forms are stencils, where a mouthful of ochre is spat over the hand, foot or tool to leave a reverse print on the wall. Figures in red ochre (or blood) are also some of the oldest works as red ochre lasts longer than any other colour, seeping into the rock to bond with it permanently.

Dot paintings are the most widely recognized of Aboriginal art forms, highly sought after by international collectors, but also one of the newest forms. Dot paintings are made in the western and central desert regions and relate to an older form used by desert people. In the desert there are few rock surfaces and no trees suitable for stripping off large pieces of bark so the desert people used the ground to commemorate the travels and actions of their ancestral beings. Drawings, or perhaps more correctly sculptures, were created by placing crushed plant matter and feather down on a hard-packed surface. The material would be coloured with ochre or blood. Common designs were spirals or circles and lines. These works were always ceremonial and created by old and knowledgeable men. In the 1970s many desert people were living at Papunya, a community northwest of Alice Springs. An art teacher, Geoff Bardon, encouraged local men to paint a mural on the school wall. A Honey Ant Dreaming painting was created that led to great interest and enthusiasm from men in the community. They began painting their stories on boards, using ochres or poster paints, in the symbolic manner of ground sculptures and ceremonial body painting. Over the next few decades these paintings, increasingly on canvas using acrylic paints, were offered for sale and became incredibly successful, both in Australia and outside it. There is great diversity of colour and style in contemporary desert paintings but the qualities of symbolism and ownership discussed earlier also apply. They are popularly known as dot paintings because the background is completely filled in by areas of dots. These can represent many elements of a landscape; for example clouds, areas of vegetation, the underground chambers of a honey ant's nest, or all three at once. In galleries look out for the incomparable work of **Clifford Possum Tjapaltjarri**, **Kathleen Petyarre**, **Emily Kame Kngwarreye** and **Dorothy Napangardi**.

Aboriginal people all over Australia produced string and fibre from the plants in their region to make functional and ceremonial objects. These **baskets** and other **works of string** have only recently been considered works of art as non-indigenous fibre and textile work has gained in status and as the importance of these objects is increasingly understood. Fibre work is a woman's art, although men sometimes made strong ropes for fishing. Palm leaves, reeds, vines, bark and hair were all used to make string and fibre that was then made into a variety of baskets and bags. These were primarily used to carry food collected during a day's foraging but also held personal possessions. String was also used to made body ornaments such as belts and fringes, armbands and necklaces. Baskets and bags are still made by the women of northern Australia and today's techniques show how new technology is adapted to continue traditional ways. Before the British arrived Aboriginal people had no steel or clay containers and therefore were not able to boil water. Fibre work was coloured by rubbing ochre into the fibre when making it or by painting the finished object with ochre. Now the fibre is dyed in boiling water but the dyes are made by the weavers from natural sources, such as roots and grasses, with great skill and subtlety.

Wooden weapons and **utensils** were often carved with designs that symbolized an ancestor, thus identifying the land of the owner. The beauty of these carvings carries them beyond the purely functional, as does their origin in the Dreaming. Carvings of ancestral figures were also made to be used in ceremonies such as funeral rites. In many communities weapons are no longer made because Aboriginal people now hunt with guns. Shields and clubs are not needed, but nothing has replaced the spear, and people still make clapping sticks or carrying dishes. As well as making the pukumani poles, the Tiwi carve wonderful wooden sculptures of totemic animals and ancestral beings for sale, as do people along the coast and islands of Arnhem Land. People in central Australia also make wooden animal carvings and these are often decorated with pokerwork, a burn from a hot wire. The didjeridoo is still made and used in ceremony in Arnhem Land, where it is called the *yidaki*. The didjeridoo is made from a tree trunk that has been hollowed out by termites so each one is unique and the bumps and knots inside influence the sound it makes.

Contemporary Aboriginal art

The art that is produced in northern and central Australia is contemporary art. Although it has its foundation in an ancient culture, it is also shaped by its present. Contemporary art is also produced by Aboriginal people who live in the urban societies of the south and east. These people may have lost their land, language, religion and families but they still have an Aboriginal identity. The people sometimes called urban Aboriginal artists may have trained in art school and their art possesses the 'Western' quality of reflecting the experience of the individual. They are united in their experience of surviving dispossession, by their personal history and experience of being Aboriginal in a dominant non-indigenous society. Some of the common themes in their work are events of the colonial past, such as massacres, or contemporary issues that affect Aboriginal people such as the fight for land rights or the disproportionately high number of Aboriginal prisoners. Some urban artists have tried to reconnect with their past or, like the late **Lin Onus**, establish links with artists working in more traditional forms and to incorporate clan designs or symbolic elements into their work. To see powerful contemporary Aboriginal art look for the work of **Robert Campbell Jnr, Sally Morgan, Lin Onus, Gordon Bennett, Trevor Nikolls, Fiona Foley** and **Donna Leslie**.

Other Australian art

Australia was colonized during the century of Romanticism in Western Europe when interest in the natural world was at its height. Much of the earliest colonial art came from scientific expeditions and their specimen drawings. Most of these early images look slightly odd as if even the best draughtsman found himself unable to capture the impossibly strange forms of unique Australian species such as the kangaroo. Indeed art from the whole of the first colonial century portrays Australia in a soft northern hemisphere light and in the rich colours of European landscapes. In these finely detailed landscapes the countryside was presented as romantically Gothic or neatly tamed, even bucolic with the addition of cattle or a farmer at work, as seen in the work of **John Glover**, **Louis Buvelot** and **Eugene von Guérard**. In some there would also be quaint representations of a bark hut or black figure belonging to the peaceful 'children of nature'. Given the violence of what was happening to Aboriginal people at the time and the British impression that the new colony was a nasty, brutish place full of convicts, these paintings can be seen as an attempt to portray Australia as peaceful, beautiful and civilized. Things began to change in the 1880s and 1890s, by which time a majority of colonists had been born in Australia.

The Heidelberg School and Australian Impressionism
Increasing pride in being Australian and European Impressionism inspired Australian artists to really look at their environment and cast away conventional techniques, prompting a dramatic change in how the country was portrayed. Truth in light, colour and tone was pursued by artists such as **Arthur Streeton**, **Charles Conder**, **Tom Roberts** and **Frederick McCubbin**, who began painting *en plein air*. In their paintings bright light illuminated the country's real colours; the gold of dried grass, the smoky green of eucalypts and the deep blue of the Australian sky. These artists were known as the Heidelberg School because they painted many of their bush scenes around Heidelberg and Box Hill, just outside Melbourne. Some of Australia's most iconic and popular images were painted at this time. They portrayed the nobility of a hard but independent life in the bush. *Down on his luck* (1889) by Frederick McCubbin is a classic image of a bushman and his swag, staring into his campfire among gum trees. In Tom Roberts' *A break away!* (1891) a heroic lone horsemen tries to control the rush of sheep to a waterhole in drought-stricken country. The same painter's *Shearing the Rams* (1888-1890) again celebrates the noble masculinity of the bush with a shearing-shed scene portraying the industry and camaraderie of the pastoral life. These paintings all represent a golden age that belie the end of the boom times in Victoria, where the economy crashed in the early 1890s, and the reality that most Australians were urban workers rather than bushmen.

Modernism and the Angry Penguins
After Federation in 1901 Australian landscapes became increasingly pretty and idyllic, typified by the languorous beauties enjoying the outdoors in the work of **E Phillips Fox** or **Rupert Bunny**. However, the Great War shocked the sensibilities of those who witnessed it and Australian artists followed the lead of Britain and Europe in embracing Modernism. **Margaret Preston** was influenced by the modernist focus on 'primitive' art to incorporate elements from Aboriginal art into her works, *Aboriginal flowers* (1928) and *Aboriginal Landscape* (1941). **Grace Cossington Smith** looked to Van Gogh for her short brushstrokes of intense colour in interior works such as *The Lacquer Room* (1936).

Hans Heysen worked in the tradition of Streeton and McCubbin, glorifying the south Australian landscape with images of mighty old gum trees and the ancient folds of the Flinders Ranges. Other painters of the 1940s and 1950s were looking at the landscape differently. The outback is presented as a harsh and desolate place in the work of **Russell Drysdale** and **Sidney Nolan**. During the 1940s Nolan produced a famous series of paintings on bushranger Ned Kelly in a whimsical, naïve style in which he expressed a desire to paint the 'stories which take place within the landscape' – an interesting link to Aboriginal art. Nolan belonged to a group of artists called the 'Angry Penguins', along with **Albert Tucker**, **Joy Hester** and **Arthur Boyd**. These artists worked under the patronage of John and Sunday Reed at Heide outside Melbourne, the same area that had inspired the Heidelberg School. Their work reflects the ugliness and uncertainty of the war period. Tucker painted the nightmarish evil that the Second World War had brought to society in paintings like *The Victory Girls* (1943). Boyd worked on moral themes amongst light-sodden landscapes. Other artists were portraying the alienation of urban lives, in stark paintings like **John Brack's** *Collins Street 5 pm* (1955).

Contemporary art

During the 1960s and 1970s Australian artists were influenced by the abstract movement. Artists such as **John Olsen** and **Fred Williams** still produced landscapes but in an intensely personal, emotional and unstructured way. **Brett Whiteley** painted sensuous, colour-drenched Sydney landscapes and disturbing works such as the *Christie Series* (1964) in a surreal or distorted manner reminiscent of Salvador Dali or Francis Bacon. Painting became a less dominant form in this period and the following decades with many artists working in sculpture, installations, video and photography. The 1980s and 1990s were also marked by an intense interest in Aboriginal art, leading to its inclusion within the mainstream venues and discourse of contemporary Australian art.

Literature ▶▶ *See also Books, page 372.*

Australia has a rich literary culture and an admirable body of national literature. Until recently this reflected only the European experience of the country, but increasingly includes Aboriginal voices and those of migrants. Awareness and exploration of the Asia-Pacific cultures of the region is also a new theme. It is not surprising that the main concern for Europeans has been the alien nature of the country they had so recently arrived in; to examine how it was different from their own country and to find both meaning and their own place within it. As in so many cultural fields it has taken a long time for an Australian identity to develop and in literature it has been primarily within the last 50 years. As questions of national identity are resolved Australian writers move towards regional and local identity. One of the features of contemporary Australian literature is the strong sense of place it conveys. The writers and poets discussed below are significant figures of Australian literature who have built up a substantial collection of work but of course there are many more fine writers. See page 372 for more state-based suggestions.

A B 'Banjo' Paterson and Henry Lawson

Paterson and Lawson were both journalists of the 1890s and have done more to define the character of the Australian bushman than any other writers. Both were nationalists, although there were important differences in their work. Paterson wrote the country's most famous bush ballads such as *Waltzing Matilda*, *Clancy of the Overflow* and *The Man from Snowy River*. The latter still outsells all other volumes of Australian poetry. Paterson's was a romantic vision; brave and cheerful men on noble horses worked companionably across this wide land or stood firm against figures of authority. Lawson criticized Paterson in the literary journal, *The Bulletin*, for his idealism saying "the real native outback bushman is narrow minded, densely ignorant, invulnerably thick-headed" and that heat, flies, drought and despair were missing from Paterson's poetry. Lawson was a part of the republican movement of the late 1880s and a prolific writer of poetry and prose based on the people of the bush. His well-crafted short stories present the bush in the clear light of realism and their qualities of understated style, journalistic detail, sympathy for broken characters and ironic humour mean that Lawson's stories are considered among the finest in Australian literature. His best stories are found in the collections *Joe Wilson and His Mates* and *While the Billy Boils*.

Patrick White

Patrick White detested what he saw as the emptiness and materialism at the heart of Australian life yet it inspired his visionary literature with its characters searching for meaning. He wanted to convey a transcendence above human realities, a mystery and poetry that could make an ordinary life bearable. His major novels are *The Tree of Man*, *Voss*, *Riders in the Chariot*, *The Solid Mandala*, *The Vivisector*, *Eye of the Storm* and *Fringe of Leaves*. Never very popular in Australia because of his critical eye and 'difficult' metaphysical style, White won the Nobel Prize for Literature in 1973 for *The Tree of Man* and began to receive more attention at home. His original vision, the dynamism and poetic language of his work are some of the elements that make him a giant of Australian literature.

Thomas Keneally

An energetic and prolific writer with a great store of curiosity, Keneally has ranged all over the world in subject matter yet at the core of his fiction is the individual trying to act with integrity in extreme situations. One of his most important 'Australian' novels is *The Chant of Jimmy Blacksmith*, a fictional representation of the late-19th-century figure, part-Aboriginal Jimmy Governor, who married a white girl and was goaded into murder. Other subjects include Armistice negotiations (*Gossip from the Forest*), Yugoslav partisans in the Second World War (*Season in Purgatory*), the American Civil War (*Confederates*) and Australian immigration policies (*The Tyrant's Novel*) but Keneally's best known novel is *Schindler's Ark*. He won the Booker Prize for this novel, although some complained that the book was hardly fictional, and it was made into the highly successful Spielberg film, *Schindler's List*. Keneally manages to capture historical moments vividly and is that rare kind of writer who is popular yet serious.

Les Murray

Contemporary poet Les Murray can be linked back to the 1890s poets Paterson and Lawson in his central theme of the bush as the source of Australian identity. Respect for pioneers, the laconic and egalitarian bush character, the shaping influence of the land and dislike for the urban life all run through his work. The city verses country theme is informed by Murray's own experience of moving between the two; he grew up on a farming property in NSW, leaving it for university and work, but later managing to buy back part of the family farm in the Bunyah district. The larger-than-life poet is often called the 'Bard of Bunyah'. Murray writes in an accessible and popular style, but is a contemplative and religious thinker of great originality. Murray's reverence for land has led to an interest in Aboriginal culture, expressed in *The Bulahdelah-Taree Holiday Song Cycle*, a series of poems echoing the style and rhythm of an Arnhem Land song cycle. Other major works include the collections *The People's Otherworld* and *Translations from the Natural World*.

Peter Carey

Carey grew up in Victoria, lived for a while in Sydney, but has been based in New York since 1990. Being an expatriate writer has only focussed his view of Australia, a fairly dark vision that wonders what can grow out of dispossession, violence and a penal colony. Carey is a dazzling writer who never repeats himself; each novel is entirely different in genesis, period and character. His earlier novels had magic-realist elements, such as *Bliss* in which advertising man Harry Joy is re-born several times into new realities. Other qualities include surrealism, comedy, the macabre, and a concern for truth and lies. Carey won the Booker Prize in 1988 for *Oscar and Lucinda*, a Victorian novel with echoes of George Eliot and Edmund Gosse, set in 19th-century NSW and centering on the love between two unconventional gamblers. *True History of the Kelly Gang* won Carey the Booker Prize again in 2001 for a feat of language and imagination that is simply breathtaking; Carey puts flesh on the bones of history by getting inside the mind of bushranger Ned Kelly. His other novels are *Illywhacker*, *The Tax Inspector*, *The Unusual Life of Tristan Smith*, *Jack Maggs*, *My Life as a Fake* and the latest, *Theft: A Love Story*.

David Malouf

An elegant and lyrical writer, Malouf is preoccupied by the question of Australian identity. He believes writers need to create mythologies that are the means of a spiritual link between landscape and lives. Places need to be mapped by imagination to acquire meaning or belonging. His own themes are often played out against the background of his own childhood in Brisbane, a richly imagined slow and lush city of the past. In his novels characters are forced by circumstance to find a new way of seeing. *The Great World* follows the lives of Vic and Digger through Second World War prisoner of war camps to examine layers of history and identity. *An Imaginary Life* deals with the Roman poet Ovid in exile from Rome and his relationship with a wolfchild, a poetic novel that explores Australian issues of exile, place and belonging. These themes are continued in *Remembering Babylon*, set in the 1840s when a white boy who has lived with Aborigines for 16 years encounters the first settlers to reach northern Queensland. Malouf also writes poetry and short stories; forms that suit his economic yet powerfully descriptive language.

Tim Winton

Tim Winton is a West Australian author who writes very successfully for both adults and children. His work is marked by a sense of place, particularly the WA coast, and a tight focus on character within an environment. Winton has said of his work "if I can get a grip on the geography, I can get a grip on the people". He certainly does so – his characters are intensely imagined and powerfully 'real', often reinforced by Winton's open endings as if the rest of their lives really are still to be lived. Loneliness and self-doubt are common to his characters as they search for identity and a sense of purpose. *Cloudstreet* is a funny and affectionate tale of two very different families sharing a house in post-war Perth and the dark undercurrents of their ordinary lives. In *The Riders* Fred Scully makes a frantic search across an alien and unfamiliar Europe for his wife. *Dirt Music* is a moving story of loss and loneliness set in the crayfishing towns of the west coast. Luther and Georgie belong to nowhere and nobody and are drawn together, although Luther is determined to be left alone. *The Turning* was a series of lyrical short stories set in Albany where Winton grew up. His latest novel, *Breath*, takes us into the mind of a surfer. No one writes better about the ocean.

Kate Grenville

Grenville's novels are sharply observed, funny and sometimes Gothic explorations of what makes people tick and how they create their own destiny. This writer sees Australian history as a rich source of material; full of stories still to be told, landscape to be described and ways of being 'Australian' to explore. For *Lilian's Story* Grenville was inspired by Sydney eccentric Bea Miles to write the story of an uninhibited woman who makes her own myth at a time when women are supposed to be passive. *Dark Places* is about Lilian's monstrous father and how he distorts truth and reality to justify his actions. *Joan Makes History* re-writes Australian history in the image of women. Joan imagines she is present at all the big moments of Australia's past. *The Idea of Perfection* is about two middle-aged and unattractive people drawn together because they value history and its imperfections. This novel won the Orange Prize for Fiction in 2001. Her triumph though is a trilogy about early Australia: *The Secret River* is about a Thames bargeman transported in 1806 who settles on the Hawkesbury river, to the anger of the local Aboriginal owners; *The Lieutenant* is based on the life of William Dawes, a young naval officer who became friends with an Aboriginal girl and learnt her language; and the third novel is in progress. The first two are among the best ever written about the early encounters between British colonists and the Aboriginal people of Sydney.

Language

When Europeans arrived in Australia there were about 250 Aboriginal languages and many more dialects. These were as different from each other as English and Bengali. Most Aboriginal people spoke three or four languages: including those of neighbouring groups, kin or birth place. Because Aboriginal languages were oral they were easily lost. About 100 languages have disappeared since 1788, another 100 or so are used only by older people and will die out within 10-20 years. Only about 20 languages are commonly spoken today. Many Aboriginal people still speak several languages, of which English may be their second or third language. Aboriginal English is widely spoken; this is a form of English with the structure of Aboriginal languages or English words that do not correspond to the English meaning.

English is the official language of Australia, and it has developed a rich vocabulary all its own in its two centuries of linguistic experimentation. The words and terms listed under Common words and phrases (see page 376) are mostly unique to Australia. American visitors will also find a lot of unfamiliar British terms and slang words in use. Unfortunately many colourful Australian phrases are gradually disappearing under the dominant influence of American television and film.

Music

Popular music

Australian popular music has been heavily influenced by the British and American scenes but has also produced exciting home-grown sounds that are distinctively Australian. The industry suffered from the 'cultural cringe' for some time – the idea that anything Australian is only any good if Britain and America think so. In the last three decades Australians have embraced their own music and there have been many bands that are extremely successful in Australia but unknown outside the country. Australian musicians are limited by their tiny market; if they want to make serious money they must pursue success overseas.

Australian music first came to the notice of the rest of the world in the 1970s, when glam rock outfits **Sherbert** and the **Skyhooks** toured America. **Little River Band** did well in the US with their catchy commercial pop tunes while punk outfit **The Saints** were simultaneously making it big in the UK. However the real success story of the decade was **AC/DC**, one of the greatest heavy-rock bands in the world. Their album *Highway to Hell* was a huge success in 1979 though they lost their lead singer Bon Scott in 1980 to a tragic rock star death.

The 1980s was the decade of the hardworking pub rock band, the sexy funk rock of **INXS**, the stirring political anthems of **Midnight Oil**, and the working class onslaught of **Cold Chisel**. Of these bands INXS had the most success overseas while Midnight Oil and Cold Chisel were huge at home, singing about Australian places, issues and experiences. **Men at Work** had a hit with the quirky *Down Under* and **Crowded House**, led by the master singer-songwriter and New Zealander Neil Finn, seduced the world with tracks like *Don't Dream It's Over*. Singer-songwriters **Richard Clapton** and **Paul Kelly** also came to prominence at this time and both continue to influence the music scene. Paul Kelly's album *Gossip* is a classic – full of finely observed stories about life in Sydney and Melbourne.

Record companies became less willing to take a chance on unproved Australian bands in the 1990s and the decade is marked by developments on the local scene. Strangely, there was a rash of success for ex-soap stars **Kylie Minogue** and **Natalie Imbruglia**, but more so in the UK than at home. Kylie even got serious when she teamed up with ex-**Birthday Party** frontman, **Nick Cave**, on a track for his typically downbeat *Murder Ballads* album. Cave's dark, philosophical stylings have always gone down better in the UK and Europe than Down Under. **The Whitlams**, meanwhile, appealed to sophisticated punters with witty and melodic funk. At the noisier end of the spectrum, **Regurgitator** appeared with an influential and original sound, **Spiderbait** and **Powderfinger** and **Savage Garden** also all made it big. The band that really caught the public imagination though was **Silverchair**, a trio of schoolboys who won a competition to record their grunge classic *Tomorrow*. Aboriginal musicians also had commercial success; bands to look out for include **Yothu Yindi**, **Saltwater** and **Coloured Stone**, and the soulful ballads of **Archie Roach** or energetic pop of Torres Strait Islander **Christine Anu**.

In the 2000s Kylie Minogue just got bigger, and rock had a revival, with **The Vines**, **Wolfmother** and **Jet** all winning international success. **Superjesus**, **Bodyjar**, **Even** and **Killing Heidi** all did well locally and a handful of Australian singer/songwriters had huge debut albums, particularly **Missy Higgins** and **Pete Murray**. Australia loved *Idol*, like the rest of the world and the winners and runners up, such as **Guy Sebastian** and **Shannon Noll**, are still going strong years later. Other Australian singer/songwriters with longevity are **Delta Goodrem**, **Kasey Chambers** and **John Butler**. Names to watch at the end of the decade were **Angus and Julia Stone**, **Tame Impala** and **Sarah Blasko**.

Cinema

First steps

Although Australia produced the world's first feature film in 1906, *The Story of the Kelly Gang*, its budding film industry was soon overwhelmed by a flood of British and American films. It wasn't until the 1970s, when Australia was exploring its cultural identity, that the industry revived. Government funding commonly paid for as much as half of the production costs and Australian themes were encouraged. During this period some classics were made, such as *Picnic at Hanging Rock*. Directed by **Peter Weir**, this is a story of a schoolgirls' picnic that goes horribly wrong when some of the girls disappear into the haunting and mysterious landscape, one of many Australian films to suggest that perhaps the outback has the spiritual power that Aboriginal people believe it does. Weir went on to become a very successful Hollywood director (*Witness*, *Dead Poets Society*, *Truman Show*). *My Brilliant Career* was the beginning of brilliant careers for director **Gillian Armstrong** and actor **Judy Davis**. Davis played an independent young woman of the late 19th century who wanted to escape from the farm and live an intellectual life. The decade was also marked by 'ocker' films made for the home audience portraying the crass, uncouth and exaggerated Australian, like *The Adventures of Barry McKenzie*.

Glamour and heroes

Things changed in the 1980s when the government brought in tax incentives to encourage private investment in the film industry. Direct government funding dropped away to low levels. Naturally under these conditions the emphasis switched to profit rather than artistic merit and many big budget commercial films were made such as *Crocodile Dundee*. In 1981 Peter Weir's *Gallipoli* was a much-loved film about the sacrifices and stupidity of events at Gallipoli, starring a young **Mel Gibson**. In a completely different role Gibson also starred in another successful film that year, *Mad Max II*, shot around Broken Hill in outback NSW. Australian high-country life was romanticised in *The Man from Snowy River*, featuring a lot of handsome, rugged horsemen and spectacular scenery. In 1987 the thriller *Dead Calm* brought **Nicole Kidman** much attention and *Evil Angels* did the same for Uluru in a film about Lindy Chamberlain who claimed that a dingo took her baby from the campsite at the base of the rock in 1980. Even Meryl Streep failed to master an Australian accent to play Chamberlain. Despite these big flashy films, Australian film makers also managed some smaller interesting films looking at relationships, such as *Monkey Grip*, *High Tide*, *My First Wife*, and the extraordinary *Sweetie* in 1989. The first feature film directed by New Zealand born **Jane Campion**, it focuses on the sisters Sweetie and Kay in their dysfunctional suburban family life. Sweetie is perhaps the first of the freaks and misfits that would feature in films of the 1990s.

Money and misfits

The industry changed again in the 1990s when the generous tax concessions of the 1980s were retracted and the country suffered through economic depression in the early years of the decade. Australian film makers had to look overseas for finance and increasingly encourage American producers to use Australian facilities and locations. The new *Fox Studios* in Sydney attracted *The Matrix*, *Star Wars Episode II* and *Mission Impossible II*. The joint finance and production arrangements made it difficult to define an 'Australian' film. Cross-fertilization of talent and general optimism in the industry led Australian film makers to produce some bold and risk-taking films in the 1990s. Issues of identity and gender came to the fore in films that weren't afraid to celebrate the daggy, the misfits or oddballs like *Strictly Ballroom*, *The Adventures of Priscilla, Queen of the Desert* and *Muriel's Wedding*. In less subtle films, like *The Castle* or *Holy Smoke*, Australians were portrayed as well-meaning but hopelessly naïve fools and bumpkins. Other films pursued more serious issues but got less attention outside the country, like *Romper Stomper*, a harrowing look at a gang of racist skinheads in Melbourne starring **Russell Crowe**, or *Dead Heart*, a confronting look at the clash of cultures in central Australia starring **Bryan Brown.**

Beyond 2000

Despite the successes and attention of the 1990s, the Australian film industry still struggles against the behemoth of Hollywood. International financing is still a feature of the industry and it is difficult for distinctively Australian films to get made as they are still perceived as not very marketable outside the country. There is no shortage of superb talent but many of the best Australian actors and directors need work overseas to get the most opportunities. Indeed at present Australian actors are better known than Australian films; Nicole Kidman, Cate Blanchett, Russell Crowe, Eric Bana, Guy Pearce, Toni Collette, Geoffrey Rush, Judy Davis, Hugh Jackman and more are all in huge demand in Britain and America. As is visionary director **Baz Luhrmann** who singlehandedly reinvented the musical film in *Strictly Ballroom*, *Romeo and Juliet* and *Moulin Rouge*. His last film, set in the Kimberley, *Australia*, was greatly hyped and anticipated but many Australians found it disappointing. However it's well worth seeing for the scenery and high-camp drama of it all.

Other films worth looking out for are *Lantana*, a sophisticated tangle of love and betrayal; *Rabbit Proof Fence*, a film bringing alive the trauma of the 'stolen generation' in recreating the true stories of three Aboriginal girls escaping from their mission and walking thousands of miles to find their mother; *Japanese Story*, the moving and visually spectacular tale of an Australian woman's roller-coaster relationship with a Japanese businessman in the Pilbara; and *Yolngu Boy*, an interesting look at contemporary Aboriginal society, following three teenage boys in Arnhem Land as they try to exchange petrol sniffing for something better. *Wolf Creek* was a dark recreation of backpacker murders, not recommended if you are about to hit the road. It is well worth seeking out *Ten Canoes*, a Aboriginal fable set in the paperback forests of Arnhem Land. Inspired by a 1930s photograph, it was filmed entirely in the local language, Yolngu Matha. *Romulus My Father* is one of the best Australian films in years. A moving story of growing up in rural Australia in a troubled immigrant family. *Samson and Delilah* won the Cannes Camera D'Or prize in 2009 but this story of two Aboriginal teenagers living rough in Alice Springs is not at all easy to watch.

Religion

In many areas the ancient Aboriginal belief system has persisted to the present day. The British immigrants, their captives and hangers-on of the 18th and 19th centuries brought with them two forms of Christianity; Protestantism and Catholicism. These are still Australia's two main religions as we enter the 21st century, though in the 1990s Catholics, for the first time, outnumbered the Protestants, who now more usually call themselves Anglicans. Most of these are nominal Christians only, and do not practise or attend church. The constitution of 1901 steered Australian government in a secular, rather than religious direction, though most successive governments throughout the 20th century took Christian beliefs as a major source of inspiration and had significant Christian sympathies.

With the opening up of immigration policy in the 1970s came a broadening of the religious spectrum in Australia. There are now substantial numbers of people following Jewish, Islamic, Hindu and Buddhist and other beliefs.

Land and environment

Geography

There are bits of Western Australia that are staggeringly old. There have been rocks found in the south that date back over four billion years. In fact most of that corner of the continent is made up of something called the Yilgarn Block, a vast chunk of bedrock over two billion years old, and much of Western Australia is nearly as ancient. The coastal areas are younger, and a couple of the deserts are composed of more recent sedimentary rocks, but much of the state is a billion years old or more. The biggest mass of young rock is the great limestone block that is loosely known as the Nullarbor. Much of the western coastal areas are also relatively young, formed while India was pulling away from Western Australia, a process that was complete by about 160 million years ago. As well as being old, the region has also been incredibly stable, with no appreciable seismic activity for hundreds of millions of years.

This ancient provenance goes a long way to explaining why Western Australia, compared with other landmasses, and even the east coast, is so flat. Hundreds of millions of years of weathering have steadily taken their toll, relentlessly grinding down mountain ranges and flattening out the plains. This isn't quite the whole story, however. Australia was once part of the super-continent Gondwana, a huge landmass that broke up between 270 and 40 million years ago to become South America, Antarctica, Africa, India, and the Middle East, as well as the Australasian islands. All this pulling and pushing helped create great vertical movement as well as horizontal. Several eastern and southern parts of the continent sank, creating huge depressions that were periodically inundated. One of these, the Eucla Basin, filled with a sediment that has become the Nullarbor limestone.

Flora and fauna

The isolation, age, and position of Australia have had a tremendous impact on the flora and fauna that have evolved. Until Australia started heading north 40 million years ago, much of it lay within the Antarctic circle and had done so for hundreds of millions of years before that. The Antarctic was not glaciated at this warmer time, but was still very cold with average temperatures of no more than 10°C, and a long dark polar winter. Thus, although animals and plants could in theory migrate from South America to Australia and vice-versa until about 70 million years ago, any such migration would have been extremely slow compared to movements on other landmasses. Hence for many types of plants and animals the effective isolation has been far longer than is immediately apparent.

There have been three particularly decisive factors in the subsequent history of life on the landmass. The first is the relative degradation and leaching of the soils compared with all the other continents. Nutrient rich soils are formed through three primary agents: mountain-building, volcanic activity and glaciation. Western Australia particularly has seen very little of these for hundreds of millions of years. At the same time the constant weathering and extraction of nutrients by plants and animals has steadily leached nutrients from the soils. In short, there is little goodness to go around.

The second major effect on the evolution of Australian life is the long-term climatic stability of the continent. The world has gradually cooled over the last 40 million years. On most continents this has resulted in successive waves of appropriately evolved creatures and plants. Australia, however, has been drifting north toward the equator, more-or-less counterbalancing the cooling. Just one of the results of these first two factors is the diversity of flora in the south of Western Australia. The paucity of nutrients encourages intense specialization, for example some plants settle for more saline soils, others for sandier soils. The long-term climate stability has allowed evolution to experiment to an astounding degree, creating thousands of different species. It may be counter-intuitive to anyone who visits the area, but there is as much diversity of life in southwestern Australia as almost anywhere in the world.

The third major factor is the type of climate the continent experiences. First and foremost it is dry. Even with the monsoonal rains of the far north this is still the world's driest landmass after Antarctica, and has been for millions of years. During the recent ice ages it became dryer still, most of the interior becoming one vast dune-covered desert. To make matters worse the short-term climate dances only weakly to a seasonal tune, and is crucially affected by one of the world's most powerful weather phenomena, ENSO (El Niño Southern Oscillation). This delivers rain and drought to the continent in unpredictable cycles of two to eight years, though the effects are weaker in the west than the east.

Both plants and animals have had to develop unique strategies to cope with this terrible combination of low nutrient levels and sparse, unpredictable rainfall. Paleontologists have found evidence for both placental and marsupial mammals on the early island continent, and indeed a few placental rats and mice have survived down to the present day, but it is tempting to suspect that Australia's unique harsh conditions actually favoured the marsupial way of life. Kangaroos and wallabies have a fascinating approach to procreation. As soon as she has given birth a mother will conceive, but the embryo is not necessarily immediately developed. If drought conditions are in play it will be held in a sort of suspended animation until rains come, and only then will it be born and make its way to the pouch.

When it comes to vertebrate creatures Australian conditions actually seem to have favoured reptiles rather than mammals. This is hardly surprising as reptiles live on around 20% of the food required by mammals of a similar size, and can go without food and water for considerable periods when they have to.

If we could have taken a 4WD trip around Western Australia 60,000 years we would have witnessed a fascinating biota. It is thought that dry rainforests were much more in evidence, covering large areas of the subcontinent, but with undergrowth, and hence the fire risk, kept low by huge herds of herbivores. Some of these were species of kangaroos, but the larger ones were of the now extinct *Zygomaturus* and *Diprotodon* families which weighed up to 2 tonnes and were very distant relatives of the wombats. Larger wombats included pig-sized creatures that dug the largest burrows the world has ever witnessed, as well as titanic tortoises and behemoth birds. Very few attained anywhere near the size of their ecological counterparts on other continents, though the sight of them would still have been impressive.

Mammalian carnivores have long found the Australian conditions difficult, with prey species following boom-and-bust population cycles, but some evolved, mostly from vegetarian ancestors. Most impressive was the 'marsupial lion', *Thylacoleo*, while one of the most extraordinary in terms of evolutionary convergence was the *Thylacine*, commonly known as the Tasmanian Tiger, which survived on that island until at least the 1930s. However, these would probably have fled at the sight of the average human tourist, and certainly at the approach of the real top dog in the Australian hierarchy. That was *Megalania prisca*, an awesome relative of the Komodo dragon that could reach 7 m in length and a tonne in weight. It was probably an ambush predator like its cousin, capable of taking practically anything it wanted, and would have made getting out of our 4WD for a stroll a far more hazardous experience than it is today.

Wildlife

Wildlife is inevitably very much a part of the Western Australian holiday experience. There is no doubt that Australia's rich biodiversity is among the most remarkable and specialist on the planet. Despite the destructive effects that humans have had on the Australian ecosystem for 40,000 years, in particular the last 200 years since the arrival of the Europeans, much of that unique ecology remains.

Provided you remain observant, cautious and have respect, your Australian wildlife experience can be an extremely positive and pleasant one. A visit to a couple of the many wildlife parks and zoos around the state will familiarize you with what exactly is out there, especially Perth Zoo and Aqwa in Perth and Broome Crocodile Park, but the best way of encountering WA's wildlife is to get out into the bush. Try to camp in as many national parks as you can and snorkel wherever the chance arises. This will inevitably result in many unexpected and truly memorable wild encounters. The Department of Environment and Conservation (DEC) is an invaluable source of information and has offices in most major towns and cities (listed in the travelling text). Despite the almost unbearable temptation, do not feed any wild animals, since this merely makes them more dependent on humans and indirectly places them under greater threat.

Marsupials

Marsupials (derived from the Latin word 'marsupium', meaning 'pouch') can essentially be described as mammals that have substituted the uterus for the teat. Their reproductive system is complex: the females have not one, but three vaginas and there is a short gestation and a long lactation. In essence it is a specialist system, almost opportunistic, that has developed to meet harsh environmental demands. At any one time when it comes to kangaroos (as the saying goes), 'there is a bun in the oven, one in the pouch and one young at foot'.

The most famous of the marsupials are of course the **kangaroos** and **wallabies**. There are over 50 species of kangaroos, wallabies and tree kangaroos in Australia. The most well known and commonly seen in WA are the western grey and the red. The red kangaroo, which is the largest, is the one most synonymous with the outback. Joseph Banks, the naturalist on board Captain Cook's ship the *Endeavor*, first described the kangaroo to modern science in 1770. We can only imagine him standing there in front of his peers perhaps having to resort to an impersonation? Your encounters with these, the most famous of Australian creatures, will be frequent and highly entertaining, especially with the greys in the wildlife parks, golf courses and national park campsites. In wildlife parks they are notoriously tame and obsessed with the contents of your pockets, while in the national parks you can sit and have breakfast with them nibbling the grass nearby. Sadly, in the outback your encounters with kangaroos will also commonly be of the dead variety. There are literally thousands of road kills each year involving kangaroos, since they are very inept at avoiding moving vehicles. When travelling in the outback you should avoid dawn and dusk and about an hour either side, since this is the worst time for accidents. Wallabies are generally smaller than their kangaroo cousins, and tend to specialize in exploiting rocky country and thick scrub. Five of 15 species of rock wallabies are found in the northwest and the Karijini and Millstream-Chichester national parks are good places to see them.

Another, very familiar family of marsupials are the **possums**. There are numerous species with the most commonly encountered being the doe-eyed brushtail possum and the smaller western ring-tailed possum. Both are common in urban areas and regularly show up after dusk in campsites. Ironically the brushtail possum is protected in Australia, but after being introduced for the fur trade in New Zealand in the 19th century have reached plague proportions there with an estimated 70 million causing havoc to native species.

Other marsupials include Rottnest's delightful **quokka** (like a miniature wallaby), also found in small numbers around Dwellingup and in the Stirling Ranges; the beautifully striped carnivorous **numbat** (endangered, and also unique to WA) which might be seen, with patience in the Dryandra Woodlands; the rat-like **bandicoot**; and the hugely eared and very rare desert-living **bilby**. Remarkably (although maybe not for Australia), there is also a **marsupial mole** that lives in the desert. **Quolls** are meat-eating marsupials, the largest on the mainland, about the size of a cat with a brownish coat with attractive white spots that may, if you are very lucky, be encountered in the wild.

Monotremes

There are only three living species of monotremes in the world: the **duck-billed platypus** and the **short-beaked echidna**, both of which are endemic to Australia, and the long-beaked echidna that is found only on the islands of New Guinea. They are unique in many ways; the word monotreme means 'one hole'. But, suffice to say, the most remarkable feature is that they are mammals that lay eggs. They have also been around for over 100 million years. The only one now native to WA is the short-beaked echidna. Although it is in no way related to the hedgehog, it looks decidedly like one. Although relatively common they can be quite shy and your best chance of seeing one is probably in the Avon Valley National Park or the Dryandra Woodlands. If approached they adopt the same defence tactics as hedgehogs by curling up, erecting their spines and remarking in gruff 'Echidnaese': 'bugger off'. They are immensely powerful creatures not dissimilar to small spiny tanks, are mainly nocturnal and hunt for insects by emanating electrical signals from the long snout, before catching them with a long sticky tongue.

Eutherians

Although you may be an avid *Star Trek* fan and think you know your Klingons from your Vulcans, you may still not be aware that you yourself are not only a *Homo sapiens*, but also a Eutherian: a placental mammal. Perhaps the most well known placental mammal in Australia is the **dingo**. Although not strictly endemic to Australia, having being introduced (most probably) by Aboriginals over 3000-4000 years ago and derived from an Asian wild dog, they are now seen to be as Australian as Fosters. Found everywhere on the mainland continent, though commonest in the north, they are highly adaptable, opportunist carnivores, which makes them very unpopular with farmers. Interesting features of this sub-species are that they do not, like other dogs, hunt or live in packs and cannot bark or jump, although substantial interbreeding with domestic dogs is blending these traits back in.

The most common native placental mammals, however, are **bats** and **mice**. There are 85 species of bat in Australia, eight of which can be seen in Perth, the most common being the white-striped mastiff whose metallic tik-tik-tiks can be heard at half-second intervals.

Birds

With one of the most impressive bird lists in the world, Australia is a birdwatcher's paradise and even if you are indifferent, you cannot fail to be impressed by their diversity, their colour and their calls. They also enter the 'safe' department, which is something many paranoid folks find profound comfort in. Perhaps the most famous of Australian birds is the **kookaburra**. Although not native to WA it has made its way across here following the advent of colonial migration. Both cheeky and enchanting, they look like huge kingfishers and are indeed the largest of that family. Other than their prevalence, their fearlessness and their extrovert behaviour, it is their laughing call that will remain forever in your psyche. At dawn, when a family group really gets going, it can sound so much fun that you almost feel inclined to rise immediately and share the joke.

Next up is the equally melodic Australian **magpie**. Looking like some smart waiter or wedding groom in their black and white attire they are another common sight, but again it is their fluid carol-like call that remains truly memorable. In the breeding season they are also known to attack people that have the misfortune to stray into their territory by swooping with determination at your head. Just how many bad hair days the dear magpie has caused one can only imagine. If you think one is attacking you, wave your arms about your head as this seems to put them off but the best advice is to move out of their territory which may be as small as one or two trees.

From the cryptic to the colourful, Australia is famous for its psittacines (the **parrot** family), including parakeets, lorikeets, cockatiels, rosellas and budgerigars. There can perhaps be no better demonstration that these species should not be confined to cages, like goldfish are to bowls, than in the vast outback of Australia, their true and natural domain. Out there, against oceanic skies, huge colourful flocks roam in search of food. Largest are the **cockatoos**, which come in sulphur-crested brilliant white, or deepest black, the latter species differentiated by flickers of red, yellow or white in their tails. The smallest are the desert-loving **budgerigars**, shimmering green and yellow in the heat haze. In the far north the **rainbow lorikeet**, looking like some award-winning invention by some manic professor of colour, is a common sight (and sound) while the **northern rosellas** appear like blue and yellow fireworks. **Western rosellas**, seen commonly in the southwest, are the smallest of that family and have very different male and female colours: the former largely vibrant red, the latter mostly green. Other parrots common around the southwest include the yellow-collared green 28s, and the pink and grey **galahs**.

Also in the southwest look out for the metallic blue, iridescent hues of the tiny **fairy wrens** that when first seen simply take your breath away. One of the commonest is the splendid fairy wren, a bird that could hardly be more aptly named.

The largest flighted Australian birds, seen around the far northern lakes and wetlands are the **brolgas** and the black-necked storks, or jabirus. The brolga is a distinctly leggy, grey crane with a dewlap (flap of skin under the chin) and a lovely splash of red confined to its head. The **jabiru** is equally leggy but has a lovely iridescent purple-green neck set off with a daffodil yellow eye and a very impressive rapier-like beak.

Hugely impressive in the beak department (in fact, perhaps possessing the most remarkable of all) is the **pelican**, that large, doleful, webby white character so synonymous with a day at the beach. They are simply wonderful to watch, behaving as if they would love you forever for a mere fish scrap. As well as hanging around wharfs and boat ramps for free handouts they are also regularly seen sleeping on the top of lampposts, seemingly oblivious to the chaotic urbanity beneath. Lakes and harbours in the south are also the favourite haunt of the **black swan**, the faunal emblem of Western Australia. The Australian black swan is the only uniform black swan in the world with the other seven species being predominantly white.

Almost a match when it comes to wingspan is the white-breasted **sea eagle**, which is a glorious sight almost anywhere along the coast, or around inland lakes and waterways. Like any eagle they are consummate predators and in this case are highly adept at catching fish with their incredibly powerful talons. Fairly common in the northern part of the state are the equally huge **wedge-tailed eagles** (or 'wedgies'), Australia's largest raptors with a wingspan of up to 2.5 m. Smug and smirking, they know that for them there is absolutely no need to flee from anyone, or anything. Wedgies are most commonly sighted feeding on road kills, especially kangaroos, which is an ironic twist of our impact on nature, the outback and the Australian environment. Another common raptor in the north is the **whistling kite**, an even more opportunistic feeder on carrion.

The largest Australian bird of all is of course the flightless **emu**, distant cousin to the African ostrich. With long powerful legs they are prevalent all over the state, usually quite shy unless water is scarce, often running off like a group of hairy basketball players on a first time shoplifting spree. Don't try to get too close as they can get very aggressive.

We leave the avian roll-call with a major surprise: the **fairy penguin**, the smallest penguin in the world. Like some interminably cute, chubby little pigeon in a wetsuit, they are found all along the southern coastline of Australia and are easily seen at Penguin Island, off Rockingham. Their scientific name '*Eudyptula*' is Greek for 'good little diver'.

Reptiles

The range of reptile, amphibian and insect species is, not surprisingly, as diverse as any other in Australia and perhaps the group of animals most feared by travellers. For it is here you have the teeth, the fangs and the stingy bits that can potentially cause consummate grief to humans. Many myths and misconceptions exist, but it is true to say that within this group there are some creatures that could bring down a horse, eat it and spit out the empty skin! But let's face it; since they are not out to get us and are merely protecting their ilk and their domain, one cannot fail to be impressed.

First up is the largest and a 'living dinosaur', the crocodile. There are two species in Australia: the **estuarine crocodile** (or 'saltie' as they are known), which is found throughout the Indo-Australian region, and the smaller **freshwater crocodile**, which is endemic. Your best chance of seeing one in the wild is around Broome. Only the saltwater crocodile is partial to meat. The largest was measured at a fearsome 10 m and the largest human 'feeding frenzy' occurred when 1000 Japanese soldiers vanished in a swamp between Burma and Romree Island to escape the British during the Second World War. By morning only 20 were left! Greatly hyped by films and television since the creation of *Tarzan*, it is a sobering thought that a large saltie would eat a lion or tiger for breakfast, could probably handle a grizzly for lunch and even the feared great white shark would think twice about taking one on. Maybe it is their size generally, or their admirable dentition, but either way, there is no doubt they demand our respect. In northern WA warning signs next to rivers and estuaries are a common sight, extolling various recommendations for your due safety, including … 'If out in a boat, DO NOT dangle arms or legs in the water'. Take note that these signs are in deadly earnest.

The enchanting **goanna**, or monitor, is a common sight, especially in campsites. There are actually many species of goanna in Australia (also know as perenties, monitors and bungarras). The biggest, in lizard terms second only to Indonesia's komodo dragons, can reach up to 2 m in length, are carnivores and if threatened run towards anything upright to escape. Of course, this is usually a tree, but not always, so be warned!

There are many other species of lizard that you may encounter on your travels, including the **blue-tongued lizard** (six species, usually referred to as a 'stumpy' or 'bob-tail' in WA), which is about 50 cm in length. If you get too close a blue-tongue will no doubt show you how it got its name. Sitting on a balcony of a late afternoon, you are likely to notice tiny flesh-coloured lizards plastered to the roof or busy catching insects. These are **geckos**, and there are many species in Australia. They manage to cling to smooth surfaces using an incredible adaptation, in the form of tiny hairs on their feet called setae. On a single toe there can be over one million.

When it comes to Australian **snakes** there is no alternative really but to be honest. Australia has 140 species of land snake and about 32 species of sea snake. The bad news? Of these about 100 are venomous with about a dozen able to cause a human fatality. Of the 11 most venomous snakes in the world, Australia has seven of them. These include the rather innocuous looking **taipan**. There are two species, the coastal variety, once considered the most dangerous land snake in the world, and the related western taipan, found later to be worse still. The taipan is particularly dangerous because they are intelligent, have 'a 'nervous' disposition, a 'snap-release' bite and a venom potent enough to reduce a horse to a quivering heap. It gets worse: during an attack they can actually launch themselves off the ground towards their target and until 1955 – wait for it – they enjoyed the unenviable reputation of a 100% kill-rate in human victims. The good news is that, remarkably, you can survive a taipan attack. This is because they can actually recognize that you are human and in doing so be merciful as to bite you, but not release the venom. In fact fatalities are very rare with, at worst, only one or two deaths per year. Hospitals all stock antivenin so there is hope even if you are. For advice on what to do if you do get bitten, see Essentials, page 41.

Other snakes found in WA that you might be better off not seeing include the brown and lightly striped **southern death adder**, the yellow and black **tiger snake**, the small **dugite**, and the uniformly coloured **king brown** (also known as the **mulga**).

Spiders

There are around 2000 species of spiders in Australia, the best known being the diminutive **redback**, a close relative of America's black widow. Common throughout Australia, it is shiny black with a distinctive red mark on its back – a clear warning to keep well clear. They are extremely poisonous but actually quite timid and as long as you desist from sticking your fingers at it or under rocks you would be unlucky to be bitten. The **huntsman** is a very common species seen almost anywhere in Australia, especially indoors. Although not the largest spider on the continent, they can grow to a size that would comfortably cover the palm of your hand. Blessed with the propensity to shock, they are an impressive sight and do bite, but only when provoked, and are not venomous.

Marine mammals and turtles

Although whaling was once practised in Australia to the very point of extinction, it is now thankfully whale watching that is big business. Along the western seaboard of Australia, **humpback whales** are commonly sighted on passage between the tropics and Antarctica between the months of July and October. The **southern right whale** is another species regularly seen in Australian waters, and can be seen off the Cape-to-Cape region between July and December. Several species of dolphin are present including the **bottlenose dolphin**, which is a common sight off almost any beach. There are a number of places along the west coast where you can not only see wild dolphins, but also encounter them personally, notably Monkey Mia in Shark Bay, and Rockingham, Mandurah and Bunbury. Another less well-known sea mammal clinging precariously to a few locales around the coast is the **dugong** or sea cow, which browses exclusively on underwater sea-grass meadows. Shark Bay is the best place to see them, though they can also be seen off Port Hedland. Australia is also a very important breeding ground for **turtles**. It is not unusual to see them on snorkelling trips off the northern coast, but the most memorable way to see these creatures is to quietly visit during the nesting season (October-May). The females haul themselves up at night to lay their eggs, and hatchlings emerge to make a mad dash for the waves. There are nesting beaches near to both Exmouth and Port Hedland. Talk to local tourist or CALM offices before organizing an expedition.

Sharks

There are dozens of sharks inhabiting the seas all around Australia, including the common **grey nurse** and **reef sharks**. Virtually all are completely harmless, but there are a handful of species that definitely aren't, including the large **tiger shark** and, the best known of them all, the **great white shark** of *Jaws* fame. The latter is found in waters all around southern Australia, and is known to occasionally attack humans. Our physical make-up is, however, not to their taste and even those rare attacks only lead to a death about 10% of the time – less than one a year in Australian waters. It is the largest of the carnivorous sharks, growing up to 6 m in length, and surely the most scary to see (this is possible, believe it or not, in South Australia – see www.divedirectory.com.au). If anything could be more jaw-dropping than seeing a great white up close, however, then it has to be eyeballing the incomparable **whale shark**, a huge, gentle filter-feeder. This, the largest fish in the world's oceans, can reach 18 m in length – around the size of a single-decker bus. This prodigious size, coupled with its effortless grace and beautiful colouration make it an intensely exciting creature up close, and this is more than possible (in fact practically guaranteed) if you can get yourself up to Exmouth or Coral Bay between May and July. This is when the sharks come in to feed on the spawn being produced by the corals of the Ningaloo Reef.

Introduced fauna and the future

There is no doubt that your experience of Australian wildlife will be both exciting and memorable. But that experience and its celebration must be replete with the realities of the true state of the Australian environment, which of course also holds true to any other country on earth. It is something we must all bear in mind. A host of introduced animals have combined to have the greatest and most negative impact on the Australian environment since its separation from Gondwanaland 80 million years ago. Species that are currently causing havoc and have done so for some time include the **rabbit**, the **fox** and the **cat**.

There's no doubt that sterling conservation efforts are being made to halt the destruction and that ecotourism plays an important role in conservation generally, but since conservation is a drain on money not a money maker, it inevitably suffers. In WA you can help turn the tide by joining one of DEC's **Landscape** expeditions (see page 47). ▶▶ *See also Responsible travel in Essentials, page 37.*

Vegetation

A visit to the southwest of Western Australia will reveal one of the richest plant communities in the world with an immense variety of plants growing within a wide range of habitats. The southwest botanical province is approximately bordered by a line drawn between Shark Bay and Cape Arid and it is within this region that well in excess of 8000 native plant species are found, many of them growing nowhere else on earth.

The area enjoys a Mediterranean type climate with winter rainfall and warm dry summers. North of Perth the rainfall gradually decreases and summer temperatures are quite high while the southwest corner to the south of Perth has quite a high rainfall and this is reflected in the vegetation.

The term **wildflower** is often misunderstood and only applied to members of the **everlasting** or **paper daisy** family. These are small annuals with papery petals which have an extremely long life when picked and dried, they come in reds, pinks, white and yellow and flower in spring. But wildflower is more widely accepted as the floral display of any native plant, shrub or tree and the range in colour, shape and size of these is enormous and fascinating. A word of warning: it is an offence in WA to pick wildflowers from any roadside, reserve, national park or other public land, so photograph and enjoy but leave them for others to see.

When planning a trip to view the wildflowers remember the species north of Perth flower first, with peak flowering being August and September; while to the south of Perth September and October is the best time to visit. Having made this comment it is also true to say that whenever or wherever you go in Western Australia there will be some wildflowers in bloom and often spectacular displays occur at the most unexpected times.

Some striking flowers to the north include the **Banksias**, more than 70 species of which exist and most of them are endemic. They vary from small prostrate plants to tall trees and the large bottle brush shaped flowers may be red, orange or yellow. The flower spikes on some banksia species grow to 12 cm in diameter and 30 cm long. **Feather flowers** with their brilliant rich colours and soft feathery petals are greatly admired and are among the most beautiful of flowers and are usually small to medium shrubs. The northern inland areas are where the best displays of paper aisies or everlastings are to be found, after a good season they flower profusely and it is common to see hundreds of hectares of them forming solid blocks of colour along the roadsides, a truly captivating spectacle. This is also the habitat of the rare and unusual **wreath lechenaultia**; this little prostrate plant spreads out evenly from its centre to a diameter of 40 cm or so and the red and yellow flowers form only at the ends of the branchlets. Seeing these beautiful little wreaths growing on the bare red soil at the roadside is a sight you will always remember. The **kangaroo paw** is another strange-looking plant, long stems emerge from a clump of long green leaves and the flowers at the top of the stems may be green, yellow or red. A red and green flowering kangaroo paw is the Western Australian floral emblem and is the most attractive of the species. The **West Australian christmas tree** is a sturdy single trunk tree and grows to about 8 m, it is unusual in being a partial parasite, some of its nutrient is obtained by its roots tapping into those of nearby plants and drawing off what it needs. In December masses of large brilliant orange yellow flowers appear and the trees are then a magnificent sight.

South of Perth the **karri** forests are amongst the most beautiful on earth, the tall straight trees with their patchy pale orange to white bark grow to almost 90 m with very few side branches till the crown is reached. They are a significant timber species which yield longer lengths of hardwood than any other hardwood species. The **jarrah** forests are also found in this area, another very important timber tree producing an even more durable timber than the karri. They do not grow as tall and straight as the karri and the bark is dark grey and fibrous and held in longitudinal strips. As a change from looking up at the colossal trees try finding some of the tiny **orchids** on the forest floor, many of them only a few centimetres tall. Over 300 species in all shapes and colours imaginable occur in the southwest. In one of the more bizarre forms the flower imitates the shape of a species of female wasp, the real wasp is fooled and attempts to mate with them so ensuring that pollen is distributed from flower to flower. While at ground level check out the tiny **sun dews**, which trap insects within their dewy tentacles and then digest them for additional nutrient; and around Albany way the **pitcher plant** which traps insects within special pitcher-shaped leaves and metes out a similar fate to its prey. Adding a wealth of blue to the understorey, **blue lechenaultia** is a small shrub which displays clusters of sky-blue flowers in spring time. An unusual plant is the **grass tree** or **balga** (sometimes still referred to as Blackboys), which have a dense fibrous stem of about 30 cm in diameter and up to 3 m long, often branched. From a dense crown of thin green metre-long leaves the white flowers are carried on a stout spike above the foliage. A skirt effect is achieved by the old dry leaves hanging down from the crown. Mention must be made of the **wattles** or **acacia** plants with their masses of beautiful yellow flowers in spring. More than 800 species of them occur in Western Australia varying from small prostrate shrubs to fairly tall trees. Some wattle species were once an important resource for the Aboriginal people, seeds were ground to make a type of flour, the sticky sap was gathered and chewed, bark strips were used for nets and bags and various implements were made from the very hard, dense wood.

Books

Australian history

Diamond, Jared *Guns, Germs and Steel.*
A fascinating explanation of why it is that the
British invaded Australia in 1788, rather than
an Aboriginal fleet that sailed up the Thames,
wide-ranging, a global look at the trends of
human development and history.
Flannery, Tim, editor *The Explorers.*
An amazing insight into the minds of the
early European pioneers is given in these
eyewitness accounts.
Macintyre, Stuart *A Concise History of
Australia.* A general history.
  Books detailing the impact of the British
invasion on the indigenous peoples include:
Boyce, James *Van Diemen's Land.*
A significant new work that suggests white
Tasmanian settlers were 'indigenized' as
much as black Tasmanians were 'colonized'.
Broome, Richard *Aboriginal Australians.* A
good general history of what has happened
to Aboriginal people since 1788 and how
they have responded to their situation.
McGrath, Ann, editor *Contested Ground.* The
Aboriginal voice itself is starting to be heard
in books such as this.
Reynolds, Henry *The Other Side of the
Frontier* or *An Indelible Stain.* Very fine work,
utilizes a lot of compelling primary sources.

Culture

Berndt, Ronald and Catherine *The World of
the First Australians.* The classic work on
Aboriginal culture.
Flood, Josephine *Riches of Ancient Australia.*
A superb look at archaeological and art sites
by region. *Archaeology of the Dreamtime.* An
account of how people first came to Australia
and how they lived. *Rock Art of the
Dreamtime.* For those interested in rock art.
Knightley, Phillip *Australia: A Biography
of a Nation.* Short but snappy, this is in
essence a modern history, but also goes a
long way to getting inside the minds of
today's Australians.

McCulloch, Alan and Susan *The
Encyclopedia of Australian Art.* The major
reference book at a hefty 800 pages.
Morphy, Howard *Aboriginal Art.* An
excellent overview of its subject.
Sayers, Andrew *Australian Art.* A new
history of all Australian art forms from
1788 to the present.
  Penguin Good Australian Wine Guide.
Those intending to drink a lot of Australian
wine may find this annual useful.

Travelogues and memoirs

de Bernières, Louis *Red Dog.* English
novelist who couldn't resist the tales he heard
of an independent kelpie in the Pilbara who
hitched rides with mine workers, and so
turned them into a novella.
Bryson, Bill *Down Under.* Written by an
American, this is probably the best-selling
account of a journey around Australia, and
certainly one of the funniest.
Connolly, Billy *World Tour of Australia.* It
goes without saying that this book is also
very funny.
Davidson, Robyn *Tracks.* A moving and
honest account of the author's solo camel
trip across central and Western Australia.
Jacobson, Howard *In the Land of Oz.* Written
in the 1980s by this Englishman, this is an
amusing, perceptive and thoughtful
account, and still pertinent.
Morgan, Sally *My Place.* The artist's
autobiographical classic account of growing
up in Perth in the 1950s and 1960s and
exploring her Aboriginal heritage.
Winton, Tim *Land's Edge.* A powerfully
evocative account of his love of the Western
Australian coast.

Western Australia in fiction

One of the best ways of getting a flavour of
Western Australian history and culture is to
dive into a great novel. If you only read one
Western Australian novelist it should be the

incomparable Tim Winton. See also Literature, page 357.

Drewe, Robert *The Drowner*. A meditative piece centred on the son of a water diviner working to bring water to the WA goldfields at the turn of the century. *Shark Net*. A gripping memoir about a series of murders in Perth in the 60s.

Jolley, Elizabeth Another well known WA novelist who writes about the lonely and invisible in a darkly comic and unsettling way.

Scott, Kim *Benang*. An award-winning fictional account of a man of Nyoongar and European heritage trying to cope with being bred as his family's 'first white man born'.

Silvey, Craig *Jasper Jones*. This young author from Dwellingup has set the literary scene alight with this funny, heartbreaking tale about a bookish teenager who gets tangled up with the mysterious disappearance of a local girl.

Winton, Tim *Cloudstreet* describes growing up in a ramshackle family house in suburban Perth. *Dirt Music* tells of love between 2 drifters amid a passionate evocation of the West Australian coastline. *Breath* gets inside the mind of a teenager surfer who gets up to life-threatening high jinks to escape the boredom of growing up in small town near Albany.

Ecology, the outdoors and wildlife

Absalom, Jack *Safe Outback Travel*. A trusted manual of driving and camping advice if getting right off the beaten track.

Flannery, Tim *Future Eaters*. A fantastic ecological history of the continent, focusing on its fauna, flora and people, and how they have shaped, and been shaped by the environment.

Hiddin, Les *Bush Tucker Field Guide*. For those worried about getting lost in the bush who may want to brush up on bush tucker.

Low, Tim *Feral Future*. An interesting and alarming study of the current biological invasion of Australia.

Zborowski, Paul *Australia's most dangerous spiders, snakes and marine creatures: Identification and First Aid*. Those who are a little nervous of getting close to Australia's wildlife may be soothed (or terrified) by this useful field guide.

Good generalist wildlife books include:

Menkhorst, Peter *Field Guide to Mammals of Australia*. Another fine field guide et al.

Simpson, Ken *Birds of Australia*. A new and comprehensive guide that is on a par with Slater.

Slater, Peter *Slater Field Guide-Australian Birds*. Tried and trusted guide.

Contents

Footnotes

Common words and phrases

Arvo	Afternoon
B&S Ball	Bachelors' and Spinsters' Ball – young person's excuse to get as drunk as possible and get off with anything that moves
Back of Bourke	Middle of nowhere
Bananabender	Someone from Queensland
Barbie	Barbeque (BBQ)
Bail up	Hold up, forcibly halt
Beauty	('Bewdy') Fantastic, wonderful (also "You beauty")
Billy	Kettle, usually non-electric
Bingo wings	Flabby upper arms
Blowies	Blow flies
Bludger	Layabout, non-worker
Bottleshop	Off-licence
Budgie smugglers	See Speedos
Bull bar/Roo bar	Extra front vehicle bumper
Bush	Generally any non-urban, non-agricultural area
Bushranger	Bush-based outlaw, eg Ned Kelly
Centralian	Someone from central Australia, eg Alice Springs
Chips	Potato crisps
Chook	Chicken
Chunder	Vomit – 'hurl', 'spew' and 'ralph' are also used
Cobber	Friend, friendly term for non-acquaintance ("G'day cobber")
Cocky	Cockatoo, cockroach or farmer
Cray	Crayfish, lobster
Croweater	South Australian
Cyclone	Hurricane
Dag, daggy	Bit of dirty wool around sheep's backside, also uncool or silly
Digger	Goldrush miner, also soldier of the world wars
Dob in	Report on someone to the authorities
Donger	Converted shipping container used for sleeping in
Doona	Duvet
Drongo	Idiot
Dunny	Toilet
Esky	Portable cool box
Fair dinkum	Fair enough, a good show, the truth
Feral	Non-indigenous animal or person who has become 'wild'
Flush	Having plenty of money
Footy	Aussie Rules or Rugby League football
G'day	Hello (corruption of the greeting 'good day')
Give it a burl	Give it a try
Good on us/you	General term of satisfaction, endearment or thanks
Goodo	OK, fine
Grommet	Very young surfer
Hard yakka	Hard physical work

Hot chips	Thick potato chips, french fries
Ice-block	Ice lolly (flavoured ice or ice cream on a stick)
Jackeroo/Jilleroo	Worker (usually young) on a station
Jumbuck	Sheep
Knocker/knock	Person who puts things down, to criticize
Larrikin	Mischievous person
Lay-by	Keep aside (by a shop) until paid for
Lollies	Sweets, candy
Mate	Friend, friendly term for non-acquaintance ("G'day mate")
Mob	Large number of animals or people
Moleskins	Jeans, of brushed cotton
Morning tea	Mid-morning break for cake and tea
Muffin top	Tummy flab that hangs over jeans
Mullet	Popular country hairstyle, short on top, long at back
No worries	Do not worry, no problem
Op-shop	Second-hand clothing shop, proceeds go to charities
Outback	Australia's interior
Park	Parking place
Pokers/pokies	Slot or gambling machines
Property	Often used to denote a large outback farm
Rego	Car registration document
Ripper	Excellent!
Sandgroper	Western Australian
Score	Secure something for free, can also simply mean getting a bargain ("score this for $20")
She'll be right	Everything will turn out ok, honest
Skerrick	A tiny amount
Slab	Case of beer, usually 24 bottles
Smoko	Cigarette break, tea break
Snag	Sausage
Speedos	Brand of swimwear, also used generally to refer to a very brief style of men's swimwear (like underpants)
Station	Often used to denote a large outback farm
Stubbie	Small bottle of beer
Stubbie holder	Keeps small bottles (or cans) of beer cold
Swag	Canvas sleeping bag and mattress, for outdoor use
Sydneysider	Someone from Sydney
TAB	State bookmakers, similar to the UK's Tote
Tassie	Tasmania, or a Tasmanian
Territorian	Someone from the Northern Territory
Thongs	Flip-flops (footwear)
Tinnie	Can of beer
Tucker	Food – bushtucker is gathered or hunted food
Ute	('Yoot') Utility vehicle with a flat-bed rear
Verandah over the toolshed	A man's beer belly or gut
Wet (the)	Northern monsoon season
Willy-willy	Small, harmless swirl of air
Yabby	Edible freshwater crustacean, like a small lobster

Index → *Entries in bold refer to maps*

Notes

Notes

Notes

Notes

Notes

Notes

Acknowledgements

Andrew Swaffer and Katrina O'Brien

Andrew and Katrina would like to thank Sara Chare, Tom Shadwell, Sarah Schimansky and Daniel Casey who hit the long, straight WA roads to update sections of the third and fourth editions. We are very grateful for your hard work and persistence. For previous editions we would like to thank the staff of the many tourist offices and commissions around WA who gave us their time generously to ensure that we made the best of ours. There are too many to mention, but we are particularly grateful to Karen Priest and Sascha Turner from South West WA.

Our thanks too to those we met along the way who helped us out and showed us genuine warmth and hospitality. Again too numerous to list fully, but special mention must be made of: June Anderson, Robbie Atkinson, Chris Ferris, Tony Park, Rob and Julie Saunders, Sandy and Simon Watkin, Corry Westlake, Diving Ventures and everyone at Murchison House Station.

Mention must be made of our contributors. Darroch Donald provided most of the background information on wildlife, and was our original inspiration for researching Australia for the Footprint guides in the first place. Don Bellairs drew on his extensive knowledge of WA flora to provide the section on wildflowers.

Also thanks to the team at Footprint for their commitment, patience and passion. Finally a big thanks to our friends and family: Dennis and Alexandra, whose enthusiastic support helped to make this project possible; Bryan, Mary and Terry, for a constant ear and encouragement; Morag Kerr and Jim and Jo Tippetts for their support, kindness and comfy beds in Perth; and Cliff for his tremendous friendship and bringing Andrew to Oz in the first place. Also thanks to Dr Charlie Easmon who contributed to the health section.

Sara Chare

First and foremost thank you to the mechanic in Dubbo who patched up Betsy the campervan so well she crossed the Nullarbor, tackled the West Coast and made it back to Sydney with no serious problems. I'm also very grateful to Davo in Kalbarri, Sascha Papalia from the tourist board, Jan Brandli, Ningaloo Whaleshark 'n' Dive, and those at Bullara station for their help along the way. Thank you to Andrew and Katrina for the opportunity and for the invaluable itinerary they put together before we set off, but above all thank you to Tom for doing most of the driving and cooking during our months on the road, and for his patience and support, and for agreeing to pay for powered sites so I could charge the laptop. The people we met at campsites and rest stops in Western Australia also deserve a mention for their kindness and hospitality, and for sharing cups of tea, drinking water, useful tips, and their *Camps 5* books.

Credits

Footprint credits
Editor: Nicola Gibbs
Maps: Kevin Feeney
Colour section and cover design: Pepi Bluck

Managing Director: Andy Riddle
Commercial Director: Patrick Dawson
Publisher: Alan Murphy
Publishing Managers: Felicity Laughton, Nicola Gibbs
Digital Editors: Tom Mellors, Jo Williams
Marketing and PR: Liz Harper
Sales: Diane McEntee
Advertising: Renu Sibal
Finance and administration: Elizabeth Taylor

Photography credits
Front cover: Kalbarri National Park, Roland Mayr / photolibrary.com
Back cover: camel ride on Cable Beach Marc Dozier / hemis.fr
Page 1: Sheldon Levis / photolibrary.com
Pages 2-3: Zhou Minyun / Dreamstime.com
Pages 6-7: Jonathan Bird / photolibrary.com
Page 8: Ted Mead / photolibrary.com

Manufactured in India by Nutech Print Services
Pulp from sustainable forests

Footprint feedback
We try as hard as we can to make each guide as up to date as possible but things always change. If you want to let us know about your experiences then go to **footprinttravelguides.com** and send in your comments.

]

Publishing information
Footprint West Coast Australia
4th edition
© Footprint Handbooks Ltd
August 2011

ISBN: 978 1 907263 24 8
CIP DATA: A catalogue record for this book is available from the British Library

® Footprint Handbooks and the Footprint mark are a registered trademark of Footprint Handbooks Ltd

Published by Footprint
6 Riverside Court
Lower Bristol Road
Bath BA2 3DZ, UK
T +44 (0)1225 469141
F +44 (0)1225 469461
footprinttravelguides.com

Distributed in the USA by Globe Pequot Press, Guilford, Connecticut

Map symbols

Administration

- Capital city
- Other city, town
- International border
- Regional border

Roads and travel

- Motorway
- Main road (National highway)
- Minor road
- Track
- Footpath
- Railway
- Railway with station
- Airport
- Bus station
- Metro station
- Cable car
- Funicular
- Ferry

Water features

- River, canal
- Lake, ocean
- Seasonal marshland
- Beach, sandbank
- Waterfall
- Reef

Topographical features

- Contours (approx)
- Mountain, volcano
- Mountain pass
- Escarpment
- Gorge
- Glacier
- Salt flat
- Rocks

Cities and towns

- Main through route
- Main street
- Minor street
- Pedestrianized street

- Tunnel
- Track
- Footpath
- One way-street
- Steps
- Bridge
- Fortified wall
- Park, garden, stadium
- Sleeping
- Eating
- Bars & clubs
- Building
- Sight
- Cathedral, church
- Chinese temple
- Hindu temple
- Meru
- Mosque
- Stupa
- Synagogue
- Tourist office
- Museum
- Post office
- Police
- Bank
- Internet
- Telephone
- Market
- Medical services
- Parking
- Petrol
- Golf
- Detail map
- Related map

Other symbols

- Archaeological site
- National park, wildlife reserve
- Viewing point
- Campsite
- Refuge, lodge
- Castle, fort
- Diving
- Deciduous, coniferous, palm trees
- Hide
- Vineyard, winery
- Distillery
- Shipwreck
- Historic battlefield